Frommer's®

Peru
3rd Edition

by Neil E. Schlecht

D0877836

Here's what the critics say about Frommer's:

"Amazingly easy to use. Very portable, very complete."

—*Booklist*

"Detailed, accurate, and easy-to-read information for all price ranges."
—*Glamour Magazine*

"Hotel information is close to encyclopedic."

—*Des Moines Sunday Register*

"Frommer's Guides have a way of giving you a real feel for a place."
—*Knight Ridder Newspapers*

WILEY
Wiley Publishing, Inc.

About the Author

Neil E. Schlecht first trekked to Machu Picchu in 1983 as a college student spending his year abroad in Quito, Ecuador. The author and co-author of a dozen travel guides (including *Frommer's New York State* and *Spain For Dummies*), he has lived for extensive periods in Brazil and Spain. In addition to travel writing, he has written articles on art and culture, contributed essays to art catalogs, and worked as a photographer. He now resides in New York City.

Published by:

Wiley Publishing, Inc.

111 River St.
Hoboken, NJ 07030-5774

ISBN-13: 978-0-471-78469-2
ISBN-10: 0-471-78469-9

Editor: Jennifer Reilly
Production Editor: Michael Brumitt
Cartographer: Andrew Murphy
Photo Editor: Richard Fox
Production by Wiley Indianapolis Composition Services

Front cover photo: Machu Picchu ruins
Back cover photo: Cuzco: Llama nuzzling woman's cheek

For information on our other products and services or to obtain technical support, please contact our Customer Care Department within the U.S. at 800/762-2974, outside the U.S. at 317/572-3993 or fax 317/572-4002.

Wiley also publishes its books in a variety of electronic formats. Some content that appears in print may not be available in electronic formats.

Contents

List of Maps

An Invitation to the Reader

In researching this book, we discovered many wonderful places—hotels, restaurants, shops, and more. We're sure you'll find others. Please tell us about them, so we can share the information with your fellow travelers in upcoming editions. If you were disappointed with a recommendation, we'd love to know that, too. Please write to:

Frommer's Peru, 3rd Edition
Wiley Publishing, Inc. • 111 River St. • Hoboken, NJ 07030-5774

An Additional Note

Please be advised that travel information is subject to change at any time—and this is especially true of prices. We therefore suggest that you write or call ahead for confirmation when making your travel plans. The authors, editors, and publisher cannot be held responsible for the experiences of readers while traveling. Your safety is important to us, however, so we encourage you to stay alert and be aware of your surroundings. Keep a close eye on cameras, purses, and wallets, all favorite targets of thieves and pickpockets.

Other Great Guides for Your Trip:

Frommer's Argentina
Frommer's Brazil
Frommer's Chile
Frommer's Portable Rio de Janiero
Frommer's South America

Frommer's Star Ratings, Icons & Abbreviations

Every hotel, restaurant, and attraction listing in this guide has been ranked for quality, value, service, amenities, and special features using a **star-rating system.** In country, state, and regional guides, we also rate towns and regions to help you narrow down your choices and budget your time accordingly. Hotels and restaurants are rated on a scale of zero (recommended) to three stars (exceptional). Attractions, shopping, nightlife, towns, and regions are rated according to the following scale: zero stars (recommended), one star (highly recommended), two stars (very highly recommended), and three stars (must-see).

In addition to the star-rating system, we also use **seven feature icons** that point you to the great deals, in-the-know advice, and unique experiences that separate travelers from tourists. Throughout the book, look for:

Finds	Special finds—those places only insiders know about
Fun Fact	Fun facts—details that make travelers more informed and their trips more fun
Kids	Best bets for kids, and advice for the whole family
Moments	Special moments—those experiences that memories are made of
Overrated	Places or experiences not worth your time or money
Tips	Insider tips—great ways to save time and money
Value	Great values—where to get the best deals

The following **abbreviations** are used for credit cards:

AE	American Express	DISC	Discover	V	Visa
DC	Diners Club	MC	MasterCard		

Frommers.com

Now that you have the guidebook to a great trip, visit our website at **www.frommers.com** for travel information on more than 3,000 destinations. With features updated regularly, we give you instant access to the most current trip-planning information available. At Frommers.com, you'll also find the best prices on airfares, accommodations, and car rentals—and you can even book travel online through our travel booking partners. At Frommers.com, you'll also find the following:

- Online updates to our most popular guidebooks
- Vacation sweepstakes and contest giveaways
- Newsletter highlighting the hottest travel trends
- Online travel message boards with featured travel discussions

What's New in Peru

PERU TODAY Former President Alberto Fujimori, who had been living in exile (if international disgrace) in Japan, made an attempt to return to Peru in November 2005, ostensibly to present himself for the presidential election in April 2006, but was arrested upon touching down in Santiago, Chile. Peruvian authorities are seeking to have the ex-president extradited to Peru, where he is wanted on 22 charges, from "hijacking democracy" to "directing death squads."

GETTING AROUND By Plane AeroContinente, formerly Peru's largest airline, was grounded in 2004 after its CEO was first accused by the U.S. government of operating as a drug kingpin, drug smuggling, and laundering drug money. The airline was blacklisted, and Fernando Zevallos was imprisoned (he may be extradited to the U.S. in the future).

By Train The **Ferrocarril Central Andino** (© 01/361-2828; www.ferroviasperu.com.pe), the highest passenger train in the world but notorious for its patchy service record over the past several years, is back up and running again from Lima to Huancayo in the Central Highlands. The scenic passenger train runs once a month between July and September ($38 round-trip), leaving from the Estación de Desamparados in Lima, but its problematic history makes it virtually impossible to plan a trip to Peru around the train trip.

By Bus A long new tract of road from Arequipa to Chivay has been paved, and the final 23km (14 miles) of dirt road should be paved in the near future, making the journey to see the villages and giant Andean condors of Colca Canyon considerably less painful and time-consuming.

A first for South America, a paved highway linking the Pacific and Atlantic Oceans, will connect the southern coast of Peru with Brazil, cutting across the southeastern Amazon of Peru and the Brazilian state of Acre. The construction of the **Inter-Oceanic Highway** entered its final phase in late 2005, with ground broken just north of Puerto Maldonado, and hopes are that the 2,600-km (1,600-mile), $900 million project will be finished by 2010. How this will affect road travel across southern Peru and into the jungle in coming years, though, is still anyone's guess.

LIMA

Where to Stay The long-time favorite hostel of backpackers, **Mochileros** (in Barranco) has closed, though its popular pub, Dirty Nelly's, continues to draw throngs of young people.

Where to Dine Gastón Acurio, Peru's celebrity chef du jour and the driving force behind Lima's best restaurant, **Astrid y Gastón,** is on a roll. Not only has he opened branches of Astrid y Gastón in Bogotá, Quito, and Santiago, but his new restaurant **Cebichería La Mar** (© 01/421-3365), an upscale *cevichería* in Miraflores, is the place Limeños are all lining up to get into. He is also responsible, along with his wife Astrid, for the new **T'anta** (© 01/421-9708), a stylish deli/bar/restaurant with two branches.

One of the fanciest new restaurants in the city was just opening when I was last in Lima, and it's worth checking out if you'd like to dine in a 350-year-old colonial mansion, a veritable house-museum with paintings on loan from the Institute of Culture: **Casa Hacienda Moreyra,** Av. Paz Soldán, San Isidro (© 01/444-4022).

THE CENTRAL COAST & HIGHLANDS

PISCO   Where to Stay   A nice and modestly priced small hotel in an attractive colonial house, adding to the small roster of acceptable accommodations in Pisco, is **Hostal Villa Manuelita,** San Francisco 227 (© 056/535-218).

NASCA   Prices for one-day, round-trip excursions from Lima to Nasca, including overflight to see the famous Nasca Lines, have skyrocketed (to $300–$350 per person) on **AeroCondor** (© 01/614-6014; www.aerocondor.com.pe) and **AeroIca** (© 01/445-0859; www.aeroica.net/ica homeing.html). At present, however, there are still no independent flights from Lima to Nasca or nearby Ica.

Where to Stay   The former Hotel de la Borda, which always had potential but badly needed a makeover, has received one, as well as a name change: **Hotel Majoro,** Ctra. Panamericana Sur Km 452 (© 056/522-750) is now one of the best places in town to stay.

CUSCO

Visitor Information   A new **iPerú office,** Av. El Sol 103, of. 102 (© 084/ 234-498), is open daily from 8:30am to 7:30pm and appears to be more helpful than the larger, central municipal office.

What to See & Do   Cusco's tourist pass, or *boleto turístico,* is still required for visiting 16 of the most important sights in and around Cusco, though the price has doubled; a full ticket now costs S/70 ($20) for adults and S/35 ($10) for students with ID and children. Also,

Cusco's cathedral is no longer included on the *boleto;* admission is separate (S/13 or $3.75 adults, S/4 or $1.15 students and children).

Where to Stay   Casa Andina (© 01/ 446-8848; www.casa-andina.com), the Peruvian hotel chain, now has three hotels in downtown Cusco and will soon be adding one of its new upscale, "Private Collection" hotels in a historic building near Qoricancha. **Niños Hotel** (© 084/ 231-424; www.ninoshotel.com), famous for its good works and great-value rooms, has added a second hotel in Cusco, as well as a bunch more adopted Peruvian street children. Though it's outside the city center, the safe, comfortable and extremely friendly **Torre Dorada** (© 084/241-698; www.torredorada.com.pe) is an excellent family-run inn that provides free transportation back and forth to town and more service than most large luxury hotels. **Casa de la Gringa** (© 084/241-168) has moved to a more convenient location in the San Blas neighborhood, at Pasnapacana 148 (corner of Tandapata).

Where to Dine   Jack's Café Bar, Choquechaca 509 (© 084/806-960) has quickly become one of the most popular gringo hangouts in Cusco, serving very good meals at all hours of the day. The best new upscale restaurant in Cusco is **Cicciolina,** Triunfo 393, 2nd floor (© 084/239-510). A good vegetarian option is **Moni Café Restaurant,** San Agustín 311 (© 084/231-029).

THE SACRED VALLEY OF THE INCAS

Where to Stay   Hoteliers are betting big on the Valle Sagrado; new country-luxury hotels are popping up all over the region. Two of the newest and best are **Casa Andina Private Collection** (© 084/976-550; www.casa-andina.com) and **Libertador Valle Sagrado Lodge** (© 084/251-526; www.vallesagradolodge.com). The old Incaland Hotel has been acquired by the

Libertador chain; now renamed as the **Libertador Tambo del Inka,** Av. Ferrocarril s/n, Urubamba (© **084/201-126**), it is undergoing a massive renovation and will in the next couple of years become one of the valley's largest and most luxurious hotels. Ollantaytambo continues to grow in popularity as a stopover in the Sacred Valley; its newest hotel is **Ollantaytambo Lodge,** Quinta Cruz Esquina s/n (© **084/272-436;** www.ollantatambo lodge.com).

Hiking the Inca Trail   The Camino del Inca, or Inca Trail to Machu Picchu, continues to climb in popularity and price; standard-class treks, the most common and economical service, cost between $280 and $330 per person, including entrance fees. Several international tour operators are now offering alternative treks to Machu Picchu, avoiding the overcrowded Inca Trail (see "Shunning the Masses: Alternatives to the Inca Trail" in chapter 8).

Machu Picchu   Prices continue to rise on the PeruRail trains that are the only way to get to Machu Picchu (other than walking), but none so much as the luxury **Hiram Bingham** train, which now costs $495 round-trip.

PUNO & LAKE TITICACA

Where to Stay   Casa Andina (© **01/ 446-8848;** www.casa-andina.com), the Peruvian hotel chain, now has two hotels in Puno (Puno Plaza and Tikarani) and is adding a third, an installment of their upscale Private Collection series, on the banks of Lake Titicaca. Casa Andina is now also managing the ecolodge on tiny Isla Suasi under its name.

AREQUIPA

What to See & Do   The **Cathedral,** one of the most prominent victims of the 2001 earthquake, has now been fully restored and is open for visits and Mass. **The Museo Santuarios Andinos,** home

to the mummy of Juanita, the Ice Maiden of Ampato, has moved to a new location at La Merced 110 (© **054/200-345**).

Where to Stay   The best new hotel in town—and one of the best small hotels in Peru—is **Casa Arequipa** (© **054/284-219;** www.arequipacasa.com), a small boutique hotel offering real luxury for a bargain price. The old Portal Hotel, which needed quite a bit of TLC to go with its enviable location on the Plaza de Armas, is finally getting it, now that it's part of the **Sonesta Posada del Inca** chain, Portal de Flores 116 (© **054/215-530;** www.sonesta.com). **La Casa de Melgar Hostal,** Melgar 108, Cercado (© **054/222-459;** www.lacasademelgar. com), an excellent small hotel and true bargain, has added a new wing of rooms in a colonial extension.

Where to Dine   My favorite new restaurant in Arequipa is **La Trattoria del Monasterio** (© **054/204-062**), built into the wall of the Santa Catalina monastery; the menu was conceived by the ubiquitous famed chef Gastón Acurio. Restaurant closings include old favorites **Gianni** and **El Pipe.**

Where to Stay   Parador del Colca, Fundo Curiña s/n, on the outskirts of Yanque (© **01/242-3425;** www.orient-expresshotels.com) is finally embarking on an expansion, promised since its acquisition by the luxury hotel chain Orient-Express. The new plan calls for construction of 10 luxury casitas. **Hotel Kuntur Wassi,** La Ladera 360 (© **054/ 832-170;** www.kunturwassi.com) is a great new addition in quiet Cabanaconde, excellent for those looking to spend some time hiking in Colca Canyon.

AMAZONIA

TAMBOPATA & MANU   Formerly called the Tambopata-Candamo Reserve, the Amazon jungle near Puerto Maldonado (and the Madre de Dios and Tambopata rivers) is now officially called the **Tambopata National Reserve.**

Manu Biosphere Reserve Manu remains complicated to get to, especially now that the Peruvian air force has had to take over flights into Boca Manu, the gateway. Manu is primarily for those with plenty of time and money.

Tambopata Recently revamped, **Reserva Amazónica** (© **01/610-0410**; www.inkaterra.com), one of the oldest lodges in the southern Peruvian Amazon, has quickly become its most stylish. Owned by the folks behind Machu Picchu Pueblo Hotel, it has plush African-style bungalows and a swank dining room/lounge, perfect for showing off your safari wear.

NORTHERN PERU

CHICLAYO (Lambayeque) **What to See & Do** The splendid and architecturally stunning **Museo Tumbas Reales Sipán,** Juan Pablo Vizcardo y Guzman s/n (© **074/283-977;** www.tumbasreales.org) is now the repository of one of the most important and fascinating archaeological exhibits in Peru, the Lord of Sipán

(which previously resided at the nearby **Museo Arqueológico Brüning**). Another excellent new archaeological museum, dedicated to finds of the Sicán civilization, is the **Museo Nacional Sicán,** Av. Batán Grande, in Ferreñafe (© **074/286-469;** http://sican.perucultural.org.pe).

Where to Stay The Hotel María Alejandra in Chiclayo has become the **Las Musas Hotel & Casino,** Los Faiques 101 (© **074/273-445**).

CAJAMARCA **Hotel Costa del Sol,** Jr. del Comercio 773 (© **076/822-472;** www.costadelsolperu.com/cajamarca.html), a new upscale but moderately priced hotel in a colonial building right on the Plaza de Armas, adds to Cajamarca's appealing range of accommodations.

After Dark The hangout of choice for gringos and local hipsters is **Casa Luna,** Dos de Mayo 334 (© **076/333-072**).

HUARAZ Phone number prefixes have changed in Huaraz; rather than beginning with a "7," (right after the area code, 043) they now begin with "4." In Carhuaz and Caraz, telephone numbers begin with "3" rather than the old "7."

1

The Best of Peru

Peru is legendary among world travelers looking for exciting new experiences. Stunningly endowed in both natural and man-made attractions, Peru offers much more than most trips can even hope to take in: charming Andean highland towns with colonial architecture, remote jungle lodges in the Amazon basin, soaring snowcapped mountains and volcanoes, a 3,220km (2,000-mile) Pacific coastline, and, of course, Machu Picchu and the stunning legacies of the Incas and other sophisticated pre-Columbian civilizations. Peru is a place of brilliant hand-woven textiles and exuberant celebrations, exotic animals, and fascinating peoples. It is a country bursting with opportunities for memorable travel experiences and outdoor adventure. The following lists describe some of my favorite places and activities, from hotels and restaurants to outdoor experiences and festivals. But the fun of traveling to a fascinatingly diverse country like Peru is compiling your own unforgettable list.

1 The Most Unforgettable Travel Experiences

- **Soaring over the Nasca Lines:** One of South America's great enigmas, these ancient, baffling lines are etched into the desert sands along Peru's southern coast. There are giant trapezoids and triangles, the identifiable shapes of animal and plant figures, and more than 10,000 lines that can only really be seen from the air. Variously thought to be signs from the gods, agricultural and astronomical calendars, or even extraterrestrial airports, the Nasca Lines were constructed between 300 B.C. and A.D. 700. Small-craft overflights dip and glide, and passengers strain their necks against the window to see mysterious figures such as "the Astronaut." See "Nasca" in chapter 6.

- **Gazing at Machu Picchu:** However you get to it—whether you hike the fabled Inca Trail or hop aboard one of the prettiest train rides in South America—Machu Picchu more than lives up to its reputation as one of the most spectacular sites on Earth. The ruins of the legendary "lost city of the Incas" sit majestically among the massive Andes, swathed in clouds. The ceremonial and agricultural center, never discovered or looted by the Spaniards, dates to the mid-1400s but seems even more ancient. Exploring the site is a thrilling experience, especially at sunrise, when dramatic rays of light creep over the mountaintops. See "Machu Picchu & the Inca Trail" in chapter 8.

- **Hiking the Inca Trail:** The legendary trail to Machu Picchu, the Camino del Inca, is one of the world's most rewarding ecoadventures. The arduous 4-day trek leads across astonishing Andean mountain passes and through some of the greatest attractions in Peru, including dozens of Incan ruins, dense cloud forest, and breathtaking mountain scenery. The

The Best of Peru

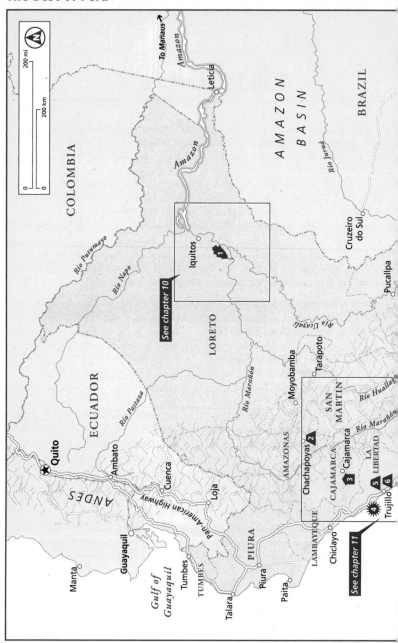

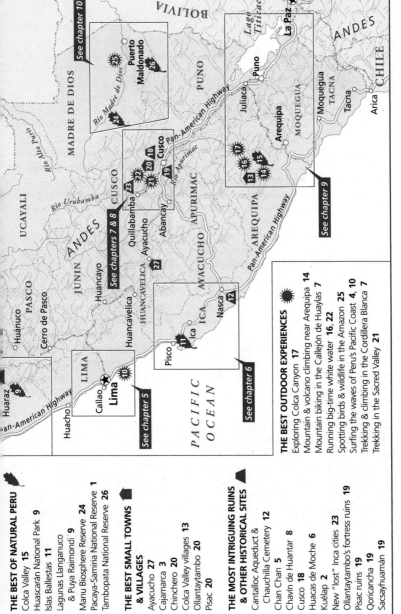

THE BEST OF NATURAL PERU

Colca Valley **15**
Huascarán National Park **9**
Islas Ballestas **11**
Lagunas Llanganuco
  & Puya Raimondi¹ **9**
Manu Biosphere Reserve **24**
Pacaya-Samiria National Reserve **1**
Tambopata National Reserve **26**

THE BEST SMALL TOWNS & VILLAGES

Ayacucho **27**
Cajamarca **3**
Chinchero **20**
Colca Valley villages **13**
Ollantaytambo **20**
Pisac **20**

THE MOST INTRIGUING RUINS & OTHER HISTORICAL SITES

Cantalloc Aqueduct &
  Chauchilla Cemetery **12**
Chan Chan **5**
Chavín de Huantar **8**
Cusco **18**
Huacas de Moche **6**
Kuélap **2**
New "lost" Inca cities **23**
Ollantaytambo's fortress ruins **19**
Pisac ruins **19**
Qoricancha **19**
Sacsayhuamán **19**

THE BEST OUTDOOR EXPERIENCES

Exploring Colca Canyon **17**
Mountain & volcano climbing near Arequipa **14**
Mountain biking in the Callejón de Huaylas **7**
Running big-time white water **16, 22**
Spotting birds & wildlife in the Amazon **25**
Surfing the waves of Peru's Pacific Coast **4, 10**
Trekking & climbing in the Cordillera Blanca **7**
Trekking in the Sacred Valley **21**

trek has a superlative payoff: a sunset arrival at the glorious ruins of Machu Picchu, shrouded in mist at your feet. For those looking for less popular ruins treks, Choquequirao and other alternatives to the Inca Trail await. See "Machu Picchu & the Inca Trail" in chapter 8.

- **Floating on Lake Titicaca:** Lake Titicaca, the world's highest navigable body of water, straddles the border between Peru and Bolivia. To locals, it is a mysterious and sacred place. An hour's boat ride from Puno takes you to the Uros floating islands, where communities dwell upon soft patches of reeds. Visitors have a rare opportunity to experience the ancient cultures of two inhabited natural islands, Amantaní and Taquile, by staying with a local family. The views of the oceanlike lake, at more than 3,600m (12,000 ft.) above sea level, and the star-littered night sky are worth the trip. Even better, for those with an adventuresome spirit and extra time, are kayaking on Titicaca and spending the night on private Suasi Island. See "Puno & Lake Titicaca" in chapter 9.

- **Marveling as Condors Soar over Colca Canyon:** The world's second-deepest canyon (twice as deep as the Grand Canyon), Colca is the best place in South America to see giant Andean condors, majestic birds with wingspans of up to 3.5m (11 ft.). From a stunning lookout point nearly 1,200m (4,000 ft.) above the canyon river, you can watch as the condors appear, slowly circle, and gradually gain altitude with each pass until they soar silently above your head and head off down the river. A truly spine-tingling spectacle, the flight of the big birds might make you feel quite small and insignificant—and certainly less graceful. See "Colca Valley" in chapter 9.

- **Plunging Deep into the Jungle:** However you do it, and in whichever part of the Amazon-basin rainforest you do it, Peru's massive tracts of jungle are not to be missed. The northern jungle is most accessible from Iquitos, and the southern Amazon, which features two phenomenal national reserves, Manu and Tambopata, is approachable from Cusco and Puerto Maldonado. You can take a river cruise, stay at a rustic jungle lodge, or lose yourself with a private guide, making camp and catching dinner along the way. See chapter 10.

2 The Most Intriguing Ruins & Other Historical Sights

- **Cantalloc Aqueduct & Chauchilla Cemetery:** An incredible necropolis dating to around A.D. 1000 and a sophisticated irrigation system in the area around Nasca are two of the south's most interesting archaeological sites. Of the thousands of graves at Chauchilla, 12 underground tombs have been exposed. What they hold is fascinating: the bleached bones of children and adults with dreadlocks, and some of the garments and goodies they were buried with. Close to town, nearly three dozen

aqueducts represent a spectacular engineering feat of the Incas and their predecessors. The canals have air vents forming spirals descending to the water current and are still in use today by local farmers. See "Nasca" in chapter 6.

- **Colonial and Inca Cusco:** Vibrant Cusco, the ancient Incan capital, is a living museum of Peruvian history, with Spanish colonial churches and mansions sitting atop perfectly constructed Incan walls of exquisitely carved granite blocks that fit together without mortar. Streets still have evocative Quechua-language names that date back to Incan times, such as Saqracalle ("Where the demons dwell") and Pumaphaqcha ("Puma's tail"). See "What to See & Do" in chapter 7.

- **Qoricancha–Templo del Sol:** The Incan Temple of the Sun is an exceptional example of the Incas' masterful masonry. Dedicated to sun worship, the greatest temple in the Incan Empire was a gleaming palace of gold before the Spaniards raided it. During the summer solstice, the sun still magically illuminates a niche where the Incan chieftain held court. A sensuously curved wall of stone is one of the greatest remaining examples of Incan stonework. See p. 216.

- **Sacsayhuamán:** On a hill overlooking Cusco, the monumental stonework at Sacsayhuamán forms massive zigzagged defensive walls of three tiers. Built by the Incan emperor Pachacútec in the mid–15th century, some blocks weigh as much as 300 tons, and they fit together seamlessly without mortar. The main pageant of the splendid Inti Raymi festival, one of the greatest expressions of Incan and Quechua culture, is celebrated every June 24 at Sacsayhuamán. See "What to See & Do" in chapter 7.

- **Pisac Ruins:** At the beginning of the Sacred Valley, just 45 minutes from Cusco, are some of the most spectacular Incan ruins in Peru. Equal parts city, religious temple, and military complex—and perhaps a royal estate of the Incan emperor—the ruins enjoy stunning views of the valley. A hike up the hillside to the ruins, beginning at Pisac's main square, is one of the most rewarding climbs you're likely to take. See "Pisac" in chapter 8.

- **Ollantaytambo's Fortress Ruins:** Even though the Incas never finished

this temple for worship and astronomical observation, it is still extraordinary, perhaps the greatest evidence to be found of their unparalleled engineering and craftsmanship. On a rocky outcrop perched above the valley, dozens of rows of incredibly steep stone terraces are carved into the hillside; high above are elegant examples of classic Incan masonry in pink granite. See "Ollantaytambo" in chapter 8.

- **New "Lost" Incan Cities:** Archaeologists keep unearthing fantastic Incan ruins in and around Machu Picchu (which obviously qualifies as the most fascinating ruins of all). Most are still being excavated and documented, but Choquequirao, to which hard-core trekkers put off by the crowds and regulations of the Inca Trail are now hiking, and the recent discoveries Qorihuayrachina, Cota Coca, and Llactapata are all envisioned as new Machu Picchus. See "On the Trail of 'New' Incan Cities: The Discovery Continues" on p. 269.

- **Huacas de Moche:** On the outskirts of Trujillo, this complex of mysterious Moche adobe pyramids, the Temple of the Sun and Temple of the Moon, dates to A.D. 500. The Temple of the Sun (Huaca del Sol), today sadly eroded, is still mammoth—it was once probably the largest man-made structure in the Americas. The smaller Temple of the Moon (Huaca de la Luna) has been excavated; revealed inside are cool polychromatic friezes of a scary figure, the decapitator god. See "Trujillo" in chapter 11.

- **Chan Chan:** A sprawling city of adobe in the Moche Valley, just beyond Trujillo, Chan Chan was the capital of the formidable Chimú empire. Begun around A.D. 1300, it is the largest adobe complex of pre-Columbian America. Among the nine royal palaces, the partially restored Tschudi Palace has unusual friezes and is evocative enough to spur thoughts of the unequalled size and sophistication of this compound of the Chimú kingdom, which reached its apogee in the 15th century before succumbing to the Incas. Chan Chan includes three other sites, all quite spread out, including a modern museum. See "Trujillo" in chapter 11.

- **The Ruins of Kuélap:** The remote site of Kuélap, hidden by thick cloud forest and more than 800 years old, is one of the man-made wonders of Peru waiting to be discovered by visitors. The ruins are still tough and time-consuming to get to, but the fortress complex of 400 round buildings, surrounded by a massive defensive wall, rewards the efforts of adventurous amateur archaeologists. See "The Ruins of Kuélap" on p. 394.

- **Chavín de Huántar:** About 110km (68 miles) from Huaraz and the Cordillera Blanca are the 3,000-year-old ruins of Chavín de Huántar, a fortress-temple with excellent stonework constructed by the Chavín culture from about 1200 to 300 B.C. These are the best-preserved ruins of one of Peru's most sophisticated and influential ancient civilizations. In a subterranean tunnel is the Lanzón, a huge and handsome stone carving and cult object shaped like a dagger. See "Huaraz & the Cordillera Blanca" in chapter 11.

3 The Best Museums

- **Museo Arqueológico Rafael Larco Herrera,** Lima: The world's largest private collection of pre-Columbian art focuses on the Moche dynasty (A.D. 200–700) and its extraordinary ceramics. Packed shelves in this 18th-century colonial building hold an incredible 45,000 pieces. And it wouldn't be a proper presentation of the Moche culture without a Sala Erótica, dedicated to the culture's shockingly explicit ceramic sexual depictions. See p. 138.

- **Museo de la Nación,** Lima: The National Museum traces the art and history of the earliest inhabitants to the Incan Empire. It's sprawling but very well designed, with scale models of major archaeological sites and great carved totems and textiles. See p. 138.

- **Convento y Museo de San Francisco,** Lima: The capital's best colonial-era church, the Convent of St. Francis is a striking 17th-century baroque complex with gorgeous glazed ceramic tiles and carved ceilings. The museum holds excellent examples of religious art and a splendid library, but deep beneath the church are some creepy catacombs, dug in the 16th century to house the remains of tens of thousands of priests and parishioners. See p. 134.

- **Museo Antonini,** Nasca: A private archaeology museum with a mission, this Italian initiative presents artifacts from the sophisticated Nasca culture and details the process of the excavations. In the museum's backyard is the Bisambra aqueduct, an ancient Nasca stone irrigation canal. The museum is in possession of the world's greatest collection of painted textiles, from the huge adobe city of Cahuachi nearby, but as of yet has no place to display them. See p. 172.

- **Convento y Museo de Santa Catalina,** Cusco: This handsome, early-17th-century convent was constructed on top of the Acllawasi, where the Incan emperor sequestered his chosen Virgins of the Sun. The museum's collection of colonial and religious art is terrific, the best place in Peru to study the painters of the famed Escuela Cusqueña, which forged a unique style of Amerindian art by combining indigenous and Spanish styles. See p. 210.

- **Museo de Arte Precolombino,** Cusco: This handsomely designed museum of pre-Columbian art possesses some pristine pieces representing the whole of Peru's history, all taken from Lima's overwhelming Larco Herrera museum. Housed in a colonial mansion on one of Cusco's prettiest squares, the museum is small enough to be engaging rather than exhausting. See p. 215.

- **Monasterio de Santa Catalina,** Arequipa: The Convent of Santa Catalina, founded in 1579, is hands-down the greatest religious monument in Peru. More than a convent, it's an extraordinary architectural complex, with Spanish-style cobblestone streets, passageways, plazas, and cloisters, where more than 200 sequestered nuns once lived (only a handful remain). Spending a sunny afternoon here is like being transported to another world: a small village in Andalucía, Spain. See p. 303.

- **Museo Santuarios Andinos,** Arequipa: The Museum of Andean Sanctuaries focuses on a singular exhibit,

one of the most important recent archaeological finds in Peru: Juanita, the Ice Maiden of Ampato. A 13- or 14-year-old girl sacrificed in the 1500s by Incan priests on a volcano at more than 6,000m (20,000 ft.), "Juanita" was discovered in almost perfect condition in 1995. Her frozen remains, kept inside a high-tech chamber, have been studied by scientific teams from the U.S. and Peru to elicit clues from her DNA. See p. 304.

- **Museo Tumbas Reales Sipán,** Lambayeque: Peru's newest major museum is stunningly modern on the outside, echoing the north's ancient Moche pyramids, and it holds the spectacular tomb of the Lord of Sipán within. One of Peru's most important archaeological discoveries, el Señor de Sipán is a Moche royal figure buried 1,700 years ago with a wealth of ceremonial ornaments and treasures. This museum is perhaps the best expression of Peru's ancient grandeur. See p. 389.

- **Conjunto Monumental de Belén,** Cajamarca: A historic architectural complex of carved volcanic stone, Belén comprises an extraordinary colonial church and two former hospitals housing medical and archaeological exhibits, including textiles and ceramics dating back to 1500 B.C. and interesting ethnographic displays. See p. 399.

4 The Best of Natural Peru

- **Islas Ballestas:** The Ballestas Islands, considered the "Peruvian Galápagos," are home to an amazing roster of protected species, including huge colonies of sea lions, endangered turtles, Humboldt penguins, red boobies, pelicans, turkey vultures, and red-footed cormorants. The islands are so covered with migratory and resident sea birds that they are known for their production of *guano,* or bird droppings. The Ballestas are part of

the Paracas National Reserve, two-thirds of which is ocean. See "Pisco & the Reserva Nacional de Paracas" in chapter 6.

- **Colca Valley:** The Colca Canyon is an awe-inspiring site and the best place in South America to witness giant condors, but the entire area, which Mario Vargas Llosa called the "Valley of Wonders," is extraordinarily scenic. From snowcapped volcanoes to patchwork valleys of green, narrow gorges, and beautiful desert landscapes, Colca has it all. On the way to Colca Canyon, you pass the Salinas and Aguada Blanca Nature Reserve, where you can glimpse vicuñas, llamas, and alpacas from the road. See "Colca Valley" in chapter 9.

- **Tambopata National Reserve:** A huge reserve of rainforest in the *departamento* (province) of Madre de Dios, Tambopata has outstanding biodiversity: more species of birds (nearly 600) and butterflies (1,200) than any place of similar size on Earth, as well as a dozen different types of forest and gorgeous oxbow lakes, and at least 13 endangered animal species. The famous Tambopata macaw clay lick, where thousands of brilliantly colored macaws and parrots gather daily for feedings, ranks as one of the wildlife highlights of Peru. See "The Southern Amazon Jungle" in chapter 10.

- **Manu Biosphere Reserve:** Remote Manu—about as close as you're likely to come to virgin rainforest anywhere—is the second-largest protected area in Peru. Its incredibly varied habitats include Andes highlands, cloud forests, and lowland tropical rainforests. One hectare (2½ acres) of forest in Manu could have 10 times the number of species of trees found in a hectare of temperate forest in Europe or North America, and Manu has the highest bird, mammal, and plant diversity of any park on the planet. The reserve is one of the world's finest for birding (greater even than all of Costa Rica); other wildlife includes giant river otters, cocks-of-the-rock, and perhaps 15,000 animal species, as well as native Amerindian tribes that remain untouched by the modern world. See "The Southern Amazon Jungle" in chapter 10.

- **Pacaya-Samiria National Reserve:** The reserve, nearly 322km (200 miles) south of Iquitos, is the largest protected area in Peru and one of the best conserved in the world. Its dense, pristine rainforest and wetlands comprise 1.5% of Peru's total surface area and contain some of the Amazon's greatest wildlife, including pink dolphins, macaws, black caimans, spider monkeys, and giant river turtles. Found in the reserve (at last count) are 539 species of birds, 101 species of mammals, 256 kinds of fish, and 22 species of orchids. See "Into the Wild: Farther Afield from Iquitos" on p. 362.

- **Huascarán National Park:** For trekkers and climbers, the soaring peaks of the longest tropical mountain range in the world are a South American mecca. It's a visual feast, with 200 alpine lakes, 600 glaciers, and incomparable mountain vistas. The park, a UNESCO Biosphere Reserve and World Heritage Trust site, contains nearly the whole of the 161km (100-mile) Cordillera Blanca. See "Huaraz & the Cordillera Blanca" in chapter 11.

- **Lagunas Llanganuco & Puya Raimondi:** Near Huaraz, the snow-capped peaks of the Cordillera Blanca are the biggest natural draw for trekkers, but the area is replete with all kinds of natural wonders. The Llanganuco lakes are two turquoise, glacier-fed alpine lakes that reflect the snowy summits of several 6,000m (20,000-ft.) mountains. In the valley of Pachacoto, 56km (35 miles) from Huaraz, are the famous Puya Raimondi plants: trippy bromeliad plants that soar up to 12m (39 ft.), flower just once in 100 years, and immediately die. The colorful flowers, against the backdrop of the Cordillera Blanca mountains, make for one of the prettiest pictures in Peru. See "Huaraz & the Cordillera Blanca" in chapter 11.

5 The Best Small Towns & Villages

- **Ayacucho:** A pristine colonial gem of a small city nestled in the Central Highlands, Ayacucho was until the mid-1990s prisoner to a homegrown guerrilla movement that precluded almost all visitors from being able to relish its collection of stunning colonial-era churches. Ayacucho is also ground zero for Peru's best handicrafts, and the best place to pick up treasures direct from artisans. See "A Gem in the Central Highlands: Ayacucho" in chapter 6.

- **Pisac:** The first of the Sacred Valley settlements outside Cusco, Pisac has a greatly colorful and lively artisans' market and some of the most splendid Incan ruins this side of Machu Picchu. A massive fortress complex clings to a cliff high above town, affording sensational views of the valley. See "Pisac" in chapter 8.

- **Chinchero:** Just beyond Cusco, but not technically part of the Sacred Valley, Chinchero is best known for its bustling Sunday artisans' market, one of the best in Peru. But the graceful, traditional Andean town, higher even than Cusco, has mesmerizing views of snowy mountain ranges, a lovely colonial church, and its own Incan ruins. In the pretty main square, you can still see the huge stones and 10 trapezoidal niches of an Incan wall, originally part of a royal palace. See "Urubamba & Environs" in chapter 8.

- **Ollantaytambo:** One of the principal villages of the Sacred Valley of the Incas, "Ollanta" (as the locals call it) is a spectacularly beautiful place along the Urubamba River; the gorge is lined by agricultural terraces, and snowcapped peaks rise in the distance. The ruins of a formidable temple-fortress overlook the old town, a perfect grid of streets built by the Incas, the only such layout remaining in Peru. See "Ollantaytambo" in chapter 8.

- **Colca Valley Villages:** Chivay, on the edge of Colca Canyon, is the valley's main town, but it isn't much more than a laid-back market town with fantastic hot springs on its outskirts. Dotting the Colca Valley and its extraordinary agricultural terracing are 14 charming colonial villages dating to the 16th century, each marked by a centerpiece church. Yanque, Coporaque, Maca, and Lari are among the most attractive towns, but these villages are best appreciated for their adherence to tradition. Natives in the valley are descendants of the pre-Incan ethnic communities Collaguas and Cabanas, and they maintain the vibrant style of traditional dress, highlighted by fantastically embroidered and sequined hats. See "A Typical Guided Tour of Colca Valley" on p. 325.

- **Cajamarca:** A mini-Cusco in the northern highlands, delightful Cajamarca surprisingly doesn't get much tourist traffic—yet. Beautifully framed by the Andes and sumptuous green countryside, with a historic core of colonial buildings where an important Incan city once stood, Cajamarca is elegant and easygoing. It's also very well positioned for day trips into the country and to fascinating archaeological sites; indeed, several of Peru's nicest and most relaxing country hotels are located here. See "Cajamarca" in chapter 11.

6 The Best Outdoor Experiences

- **Trekking in the Sacred Valley:** The most famous trek outside Cusco is, of course, the Inca Trail to Machu Picchu. But if you're not up to 4 strenuous days with a group along a highly structured trail, there are plenty of additional hiking options in the Sacred Valley. Other trails are much less crowded and share some of the same extraordinary scenery. Ollantaytambo and Yucay are the best bases for walks in the pretty countryside of the Urubamba Valley. See chapter 8.

- **Running Big-Time White Water:** Just beyond Cusco in the Urubamba Valley are some excellent river runs, ranging from mild to world-class. Novices can do 1-day trips to get a taste of this thrilling sport, while more experienced rafters can take multiday trips and even hard-core rafting journeys along the Tambopata River in the Amazon jungle. The area around Arequipa and the Colca Canyon in southern Peru is even better for rafting. The easiest and most convenient runs from Arequipa are on the Río Chili. More advanced rafting, ranging up to Class VI, beckons on the Río Majes, Río Colca, and Río Cotahuasi. See "Extreme Sacred Valley: Outdoor Adventure Sports" on p. 240, and "Colca Valley" in chapter 9.

- **Exploring Colca Canyon:** Perhaps second only to the Callejón de Huaylas Valley in northern Peru for quality independent hiking is Colca Canyon. One of the most celebrated hikes is the descent into the canyon itself, from the Cruz del Cóndor lookout. There are others that are even longer and more demanding, but more accessible hikes are also possible; walking from one village to another in the valley should satisfy most peoples' urges to get outdoors. Excursions on horseback throughout the valley and into the canyon are also possible. Hard-core sports enthusiasts might take on remote Cotahuasi Canyon, deeper and more rugged even than Colca. See "Colca Valley" in chapter 9.

- **Mountain & Volcano Climbing Near Arequipa:** For mountaineers (and fit, adventurous travelers), the volcanoes just beyond Arequipa are perfect for some of Peru's best ascents. Several don't demand technical skills. Towering El Misti, which forms part of the Arequipa skyline, is an extremely popular climb, and the city's other major volcano, Chachani, also presents an accessible ascent. Peaks in the Colca Valley are great for serious climbers; these include the Ampato Volcano and Coropuna, which, at more than 6,425m (21,079 ft.) is perhaps the most stunning mountain in the Cotahuasi Valley and is for specialists only. See "Colca Valley" in chapter 9.

- **Spotting Birds & Wildlife in the Peruvian Amazon:** Peru's Amazon rainforest is some of the most biologically diverse on the planet. The southeastern jungle and its two principal protected areas, the Tambopata National Reserve and the Manu Biosphere Reserve, are terrific for viewing wildlife and more than 1,000 species of birds. One of the great birding spectacles is the sight of thousands of macaws and parrots feeding at a clay lick. Keep your eyes peeled for more elusive wildlife, such as caimans, river otters, and even jaguars and tapirs. See "The Southern Amazon Jungle" in chapter 10.

- **Surfing the Waves of Peru's Pacific Coast:** Brazil might be more popularly known as a surfing destination, but wave connoisseurs dig Peru, with 2,000km (1,200 miles) of Pacific coastline and a great variety of left and right reef breaks, point breaks, and big-time waves. Beaches are mostly uncrowded, but the water is cold, and most surfers wear wet suits year-round. More than two dozen beaches attract *surfistas.* Northern Peru, best from October to March, is the top choice of many; surfers hang out in the easygoing fishing village of Huanchaco, but the biggest and best waves in Peru are found at Puerto Chicama (also called Puerto Malabrigo), about 80km (50 miles) up the coast from Trujillo. The best beaches in southern Peru, where surfing is best from April to December (and at its peak in May), are Punta Hermosa, Punta Rocas, Cerro Azul, and Pico Alto. See "Side Trips from Lima" in chapter 5, and "Trujillo" in chapter 11.

- **Trekking & Climbing in the Cordillera Blanca:** The Cordillera Blanca, the highest tropical mountain chain in the world, is almost wholly contained in the protected Huascarán National Park. For walkers and mountaineers, the scenery of snowcapped peaks, glaciers, lakes, and rivers is unrivaled in Peru. Fifty summits soar between 4,800 and 6,662m (15,748–21,857 ft.) high, so naturally, expert mountaineers are drawn to the Cordillera, but trekking and climbing opportunities abound for less experienced outdoor types. The classic trek is the 4- to 5-day Santa Cruz–Llanganuco route, one of the most beautiful in South America. See "Huaraz & the Cordillera Blanca" in chapter 11.

- **Mountain Biking in the Callejón de Huaylas:** Mountain biking is developing some legs in Peru. The top spot is the valley near the Cordillera Blanca, the pristine mountain range in central Peru. Hundreds of mountain and valley horse trails lace lush fields and push past picturesque Andean villages and alpine lakes. Hard-core peddlers can test their lung capacity climbing to 5,000m (16,400-ft.) mountain passes. For cycling camaraderie, check out the Semana del Andinismo in Huaraz, which features a mountain-bike competition. See "Huaraz & the Cordillera Blanca" in chapter 11.

7 The Best Architecture

- **Colonial Lima:** The old center of Lima Centro preserves a wealth of fine colonial-era buildings that have survived fires, earthquakes, and decades of inattention. Churches include San Pedro (the best-preserved example of early colonial religious architecture in the city), La Merced, and San Agustín. Equally interesting are the historic quarter's few remaining *casas coloniales,* such as Casa Riva-Agüero, Casa Aliaga, and Casa de Osambela Oquendo. Though the capital's unruliness makes appreciating its colonial core a bit daunting, it's worth the effort. See "What to See & Do" in chapter 5.

- **Cusco's Incan Masonry:** Everywhere in Cusco's old center are stunning Incan walls, made of giant granite blocks so amazingly carved that they fit together without mortar, like jigsaw puzzle pieces. For the most part, the colonial architecture has not stood up nearly as well as the Incas' bold structures, which are virtually earthquake proof. The best examples are the curved stones at Qoricancha; along Hatunrumiyoc, an alleyway lined with polygonal stones and featuring a 12-angled stone; and another pedestrian-only alleyway, Inca Roca, which has a series of stones that forms the shape of a puma. See "The Magic of Incan Stones: A Walking Tour" on p. 214.

- **Moray:** A peculiar Incan site with a mystical reputation, Moray isn't the Incan version of the Nasca Lines, although it sure looks like it could be. A series of inscrutable ringed terraces sculpted in the earth, the deep-set bowls formed an experimental agricultural center to test new crops and conditions. The different levels produce microclimates, with remarkable differences in temperature from top to bottom. See "Urubamba & Environs" in chapter 8.

- **Ollantaytambo's Old Town:** Though "Ollanta" is best known for its Incan ruins perched on an outcrop, equally spectacular is the grid of perfectly constructed *canchas,* or city blocks, that reveal the Incas as masterful urban planners as well as stonemasons. The 15th-century *canchas,* amazingly preserved, each had a single entrance opening onto a main courtyard. Rippling alongside the lovely stone streets run canals that carry water down from the mountains. See "Ollantaytambo" in chapter 8.

- **Machu Picchu's Temple of the Sun:** Even as ruins, Machu Picchu rises to the stature of great architecture. Brilliant elements of design and stonemasonry can be found around every corner, but perhaps the greatest example of architectural prowess is the Temple of the Sun. A tapered tower, it has the finest stonework in Machu Picchu. A perfectly positioned window allows the sun's rays to come streaming through at dawn on the South American winter solstice in June, illuminating the stone

at the center of the temple. A cave below the temple, carved out of the rock, has a beautifully sculpted altar and series of niches that create mesmerizing morning shadows. See "Machu Picchu & the Inca Trail" in chapter 8.

- **Colonial Arequipa:** The colonial core of Arequipa, Peru's second city, is the most graceful and harmonious in the country. Most of its elegant mansions and churches are carved from *sillar,* or white volcanic stone. The Plaza de Armas is one of the prettiest main squares in Peru, even though the cathedral was recently damaged by a major earthquake. Other colonial churches of note are La Compañía, San Francisco, San Agustín, and the Monasterio de la Recoleta. Arequipa also has some of Peru's finest colonial seigniorial homes, which feature beautiful courtyards, elaborately carved stone facades, and period furnishings. Don't miss Casa del Moral, Casa Ricketts, and Casa Arróspide. See "Arequipa" in chapter 9.

- **Iquitos's Unique Structures:** A humid Amazon river city, Iquitos might not be a place you'd expect to find distinguished architecture, but the rubber barons who made fortunes in the 19th century lined the Malecón Tarapacá riverfront with handsome mansions covered in colorful Portuguese glazed tiles, or *azulejos.* The best are Casa Hernández, Casa Cohen, Casa Morey, and the Logia Unión Amazónica. Also check out the Casa de Fierro, designed by Gustave Eiffel and entirely constructed of iron in Paris and shipped to Peru, or the wild wooden houses on stilts in the often-flooded shantytown district of Belén. See "Iquitos & the Northern Amazon" in chapter 10.

- **Trujillo's Casas Antiguas:** The colorful pastel facades and unique iron window grilles of Trujillo's colonial- and republican-era houses represent one of Peru's finest architectural ensembles. Several have splendid interior courtyards and *mudéjar*-style (Moorish-Christian) details. Fine homes grace the lovely Plaza de Armas and the streets that radiate out from it. Among those outfitted with historic furnishings and open to the public are Palacio Iturregui, Casa Urquiaga (where Simón Bolívar once lived), Casa de la Emancipación, Casa Ganoza Chopitea, and Casa Orbegoso. See "Trujillo" in chapter 11.

- **Cumbe Mayo's Aqueduct:** This weird and wonderful spot near Cajamarca draws visitors for its strange rock formations that mimic a stone forest, but a structure engineered by man, a pre-Incan aqueduct constructed around 1000 B.C., is pure genius. The extraordinary 8km (5-mile) canal is carved from volcanic stone in perfect lines to collect and redirect water on its way to the Pacific Ocean. Right angles slow the flow of water and ease the effects of erosion. The aqueduct is likely the oldest man-made structure in South America. See "Cajamarca" in chapter 11.

8 The Best Festivals & Celebrations

- **Fiesta de la Cruz** (across Peru): The Festival of the Cross isn't as solemnly Catholic as it might sound. Best in Lima, Cusco, and Ica, the festival does feature cross processions (although the decorated crosses are vibrant), but it also displays a surfeit of folk music and dance, the highlight being the daring "scissors dancers," who once performed on top of churches.

- **El Señor de los Milagros** (Lima): The Artist Once Again Known as Prince would love this highly religious procession, with tens of thousands of participants all clad in bright purple. The Lord of Miracles, the largest procession in South America, lasts a full 24 hours. It venerates a miraculous painting of Jesus Christ, which was created by an Angolan slave and survived the devastating 1746 earthquake, even though almost everything around it was felled.

- **Inti Raymi** (Cusco): The Festival of the Sun, one of the greatest pageants in South America, celebrates the winter solstice and honors the Incan sun god with a bounty of colorful Andean parades, music, and dance. It takes over Cusco and transforms the Sacsayhuamán ruins overlooking the city into a majestic stage.

- **Virgen del Carmen** (Paucartambo): The tiny, remote Andean colonial village of Paucartambo is about 4 hours from Cusco, but it hosts one of Peru's wildest festivals. Its 3 days of dance, revelry, drinking, and outlandish, scary costumes pack in thousands who camp all over town (there's almost nowhere to stay) and then wind up at the cemetery.

- **Virgen de la Candelaria** (Puno): Puno, perhaps the epicenter of Peruvian folklore, imbues its festivals with a unique vibrancy. Candlemas (or Virgen de la Candelaria), which is spread over 2 weeks, is one of the greatest folk religious festivals in South America, with an explosion of music, dance, and some of the most fantastic costumes and masks seen anywhere.

- **Puno Week** (Puno): Puno, the fiesta capital of Peru, rises to the occasion for a full week every November to mark its Amerindian roots. A huge procession from Lake Titicaca into town remembers the legend of the first Incan emperor, who emerged from the world's highest navigable lake to establish the Incan Empire.

The procession deviates into dance, music, and oblivion. Day of the Dead, early in the week, is a joyous celebration that prompts picnics at cemeteries.

9 The Best Hotels

- **Miraflores Park Hotel,** Lima (℡ **01/242-3000**): The top business traveler's hotel in Lima, this oasis of refinement and luxury is still small enough to cater to your every whim. The Park Hotel is the height of style, with handsome, spacious rooms, huge bathrooms, and an elegant restaurant and bar. There's a small pool and a gym/sauna on the top floor, overlooking the *malecón,* parks, and the coastline. See p. 118.

- **Country Club Lima Hotel,** Lima (℡ **01/611-9000**): A revived hacienda-style hotel from the 1920s, this grand estate is luxurious and has plenty of character, but it remains a relaxed place that's good for families. Given its high standards, it's not a bad deal, either. At this good retreat from the stress of modern Lima, the country club aspect isn't neglected: Golf and tennis are both available. See p. 123.

- **Libertador Palacio del Inka,** Cusco (℡ **084/231-961**): This distinguished luxury hotel in Cusco is just a couple of blocks from the Plaza de Armas and right across the street from the Incan Temple of the Sun. Elegant and traditional, with excellent service, the Libertador inhabits a colonial house where Francisco Pizarro once lived. Full of art and antiques, the rooms are refined with colonial touches. See p. 193.

- **Hotel Monasterio,** Cusco (℡ **084/ 241-777**): Extraordinarily carved out of a 16th-century monastery, itself built over the foundations of an Incan palace, this Orient-Express

hotel is the most dignified and historic place to stay in Peru. With its own gilded chapel and 18th-century Cusco School art collection, it's an attraction in its own right. Rooms are gracefully decorated with colonial touches, particularly the rooms off the serene first courtyard. See p. 193.

- **Casa Andina Private Collection,** Yanahuara (℡ **084/976-550**): The Sacred Valley is exploding with new upscale accommodations, and this is one of the best, a large, mountain-chalet style hotel. Its lovely setting has great mountain views and is complemented by gardens and a new pool and spa. The best rooms are the two-story suites with private balconies. See p. 244.

- **Machu Picchu Sanctuary Lodge,** Machu Picchu (℡ **084/246-419**): Peru's best-known hotel benefits from one of the world's most enviable locations, perched high on a mountain, just paces from the ruins of Machu Picchu. Remodeled and now charmingly rustic, with a nice restaurant and spectacular gardens boasting jaw-dropping views of the Incan citadel, it is always in high demand, even though it costs a very pretty penny for the privilege of a stay. It's one of those places where if you have to ask the price, you probably should consider alternatives. See p. 276.

- **Machu Picchu Pueblo Hotel,** Aguas Calientes (℡ **084/211-122,** or 084/245-314 for reservations): It's not next to the ruins, but this rustic hotel, a compound of bungalows ensconced in lush tropical gardens and cloud forest, is full of character and by far the nicest place in Aguas Calientes. With loads of nature trails and guided activities, it's a superb retreat for naturalists. And after a day at Machu Picchu, the spring-fed pool is a great alternative to the thermal baths in town. Junior suites, with fireplaces and small terraces, are the most coveted rooms. See p. 277.

- **Casa Andina Private Collection,** Puno (© 051/365-992): A brand-new, upscale hotel perched on the banks of Lake Titicaca, this small but smart hotel has style and excellent service to go along with its stupendous views of the lake. If you can manage it, check out the fabulous luxury suite, with some of the most enviable views anywhere. See p. 296.

- **Sonesta Posada del Inca Lake Titicaca,** Puno (© 051/364-111): Gracing the shores of Lake Titicaca, this hotel is warmly designed, with a roaring fireplace and lots of Peruvian art. Rooms are spacious and comfortable, and many have great views of the lake. Families might be especially interested in the tiny version of a Lake Titicaca floating community. See p. 296.

- **Colca Lodge,** Coporaque (© 054/202-587): A handsome Colca Valley ecolodge that hugs the banks of the river, this rustic hotel is large enough to accommodate groups but sensitively designed enough to ensure privacy and serenity. That's especially true if you find your way to the beautiful stone thermal pools, which no other hotel in the zone can match. See p. 329.

- **Hotel Libertador Trujillo,** Trujillo (© 044/232-741). One of the finest hotels in northern Peru, the Libertador boasts a coveted location overlooking Trujillo's lovely Plaza de Armas. It inhabits a striking colonial mansion and features nice extras, like a courtyard patio, good restaurant, outdoor pool, and both dry and steam saunas. Best of all, it's a very good value. See p. 380.

10 The Best Small Hotels, Inns & Lodges

- **Amazon Yarapa River Lodge,** northern Amazon (© 800/771-3100 or 065/993-1172). A splendid, award-winning conservationist lodge good enough to be partnered with Cornell University and host its faculty and students at its field lab, this place is also perfect for amateur botanists and biologists. Though isolated near the Reserva Nacional Pacaya-Samiria, the largest of Peru's protected areas and one of the top spots for wildlife viewing, the lodge, built by local artisans, is unexpectedly comfortable and attractive, with huge private bungalows, a lounge, and a hammock house overlooking the river.

- **Reserva Amazónica Lodge,** Tambopata (© 800/442-5042 or 01/610-0400). The swankest lodge in the Peruvian Amazon, this is the place for a comfortable jungle experience. You'll still get plenty of jungle, whether spotting birds on a canopy walk, watching for caimans along the river, and stalking monkeys on a small island. But when it comes time to relax, you'll do it in style with cocktails and dinner in the stylish main house before retiring to your plush African-style bungalow. See p. 340.

- **Explorer's Inn,** Tambopata (© 01/447-8888): One of the most renowned and respected ecolodges in the Peruvian Amazon is this 30-year-old pioneer that hosts both eco-tourists and scientists. About 3 hours upriver from Puerto Maldonado, the inn—which features thatched-roof bungalows—is superb for viewing otters, monkeys, and jungle birds. See p. 341.

- **Tahuayo Lodge,** northern Amazon (© **800/262-9669**). The top lodge in Peru's northern Amazon, about 4 hours from Iquitos and associated with the Rainforest Conservation Fund, is the only lodge with access to the terrific Tamshiyacu-Tahuayo Reserve, ideal for wildlife viewing. It's remote and small, but features excellent jungle programs, including zipline canopy ropes for treetop nature viewing. See p. 359.

- **La Posada del Parque Hostal,** Lima (© **01/433-2412**): A gregarious owner runs this great-value small inn, carved out of a 1920s mansion on an exceedingly peaceful street—a rare commodity near the center of Lima. The house bursts with Peruvian popular art, and rooms are spacious and nicely maintained for the bargain price. See p. 118.

- **Niños Hotel,** Cusco (© **084/ 231-424**): Even if this great little inn had no redeeming social and moral value, it would still be one of the best informal places to stay in Peru. The fact that it operates as part of a foundation that dedicates its profits to helping and housing Cusco's street children is a welcome bonus. The small Dutch-owned hotel, located in a restored and nicely if simply decorated colonial house, is charming, immaculate, and a great value. The trick is getting a reservation—try many months in advance of your arrival. See p. 197.

- **Torre Dorada,** Cusco (© **084/ 241-698**): Even though it's outside the city center, this exceptional, extremely friendly, and family-run boutique hotel, in a quiet residential neighborhood 5 minutes from downtown Cusco, more than makes up for the inconvenience with superb service and a warm ambience. The inn isn't luxurious, but you won't find a friendlier place in Peru, and the breakfast buffet is better than most top-flight hotels. See p. 202.

- **Hostal Marani,** Cusco (© **084/249- 462**): Cusco is littered with all kinds of comfortable, good-value *hostales,* but this one, much like the Niños Hotel, wears its heart and commitment to social causes and disadvantaged Peruvian youth on its doorstep. Helping to fund initiatives of a Dutch foundation, the inn, which occupies a lovely colonial house in San Blas, is one of the best bargains in town, with excellent large rooms built around a relaxing Spanish-style courtyard. It's a win-win. See p. 202.

- **Hostal Pisaq,** Pisac (©/fax **084/ 203-062**): On the main square of Pisac, which is overrun on market days, this friendly little inn has neat features for a budget hostel: handpainted murals, a sauna, an attractive courtyard, and a little cafe serving home-cooked meals and great pizza from a wood-burning oven. See p. 239.

- **Libertador Valle Sagrado Lodge,** Yanahuara (© **084/251-526**): A small hotel that looks and feels like a tiny colonial rural village, this is a great spot to absorb the relaxing feel and gorgeous sights of the Sacred Valley. Isolated and serene, with enchanting views and very comfortable rooms and a nice restaurant, it's the kind of place for discriminating individual travelers who'd rather not share a dining room with large groups. See p. 245.

- **El Albergue,** Ollantaytambo (©/fax **084/204-014**): An American-owned hostel right next to the railroad tracks—but much quieter than that would indicate—this comfortable little place has just a few rooms and shared bathrooms. Beds are excellent, and the vibe, with relaxing gardens and Labrador retrievers running around, is great. There's also a cool wood-fired sauna. See p. 253.

- **Casa Arequipa,** Arequipa (☏ **054/ 284-219**): The best new small hotel in Peru is this elite 1950s mansion masquerading as a sophisticated bed and breakfast. It feels like a European boutique hotel, with luxury linens, furnishings, and bathrooms that rival the finest upscale hotels in the country, but for a fraction of the price. Though it's in a residential neighborhood that's a short taxi ride from the beautiful colonial downtown of Arequipa, that minor inconvenience is a very small price to pay. The breakfast buffet and personal attention will make you think you're in a large five-star hotel. See p. 310.

- **La Casa de Melgar Hostal,** Arequipa (☏/fax **054/222-459**): In a pretty colonial house made of *sillar* stone, this small inn exudes style and charm. With thick walls, multiple interior courtyards, and gardens, it's much nicer than most inexpensive hotels. Ground-floor rooms with vaulted brick ceilings look like they're straight out of a movie shoot. See p. 313.

- **Parador del Colca,** Yanque (☏ **01/ 242-3425**): A favorite of sophisticated travelers venturing into the rustic Colca Canyon, the Parador, now owned by Orient-Express, has a unique country charm and elegance. Rooms have loft spaces, and there are private patios with fire pits, an excellent dining room serving fresh country meals, and lots of hiking and horseback-riding opportunities. It enjoys sprawling gardens and views of the canyon. In the midst of an expansion and upgrade, with planned individual luxury casitas, the tiny inn is worth checking out while it's still a true bargain, since it's bound to become one of the swankest rustic inns in the country. See p. 329.

- **Hotel Posada del Puruay,** Cajamarca (☏ **076/828-318,** or 01/336-7869 for reservations): In the gorgeous highland countryside just outside Cajamarca, this country hotel rests in a restored 1830 farmhouse. The grounds, with gardens, horses, and amenities such as a barbecue pit, are sure-fire selling points, but the inn also has huge rooms, friendly personal service, a very good restaurant, and an extensive video library. See p. 403.

- **Hacienda San Vicente,** Cajamarca (☏ **076/822-644**): A small and funky inn in a former hacienda, this unique place probably isn't for everyone. Its oddball rooms are like caves carved into the hillside (rock walls even form a headboard or two). Everything is just a tad "off," but delightfully so. With skylights for moon views and a Gaudí-esque chapel on the premises, this place isn't afraid to be itself. See p. 404.

11 The Best Local Dining Experiences

- **Barbecuing Peruvian-Style:** The Peruvian version of a barbecue get-together is called a *pachamanca;* it's basically cooking meat and veggies over coals or hot stones in a hole in the ground. On weekends in the countryside, mostly in the mountains, you'll see families gathered around smoky subterranean grills, cooking up pork or beef and potatoes and vegetables. (You can also get *pachamanca*-style dishes in some traditional restaurants.)

- **Chugging *Chicha:*** An ancient Andean tradition is the brewing of *chicha,* beer made from fermented maize. You can find it at a few traditional restaurants, but for an authentic Andean experience, the best place to get it is at a simple bar or home that flies the *chicha* flag—a long pole with a red flag or, often, balloon—which is the local way of advertising that there's home-brewed *chicha* available inside. Served warm, in monstrous tumblers for a few pennies, it's not to many foreigners' liking, but it's one of the best ways to go native. *Chicha morada,* a refreshment made from blue corn, is something altogether different: It's sweet and nonalcoholic, and it actually tastes good (especially with ceviche).

- **Going Native with Jungle Cuisine:** Peru's vast Amazon is full of exotic critters and plants, so it's logical that it would produce its own unique cuisine. Some of what restaurateurs deal in is endangered animals, though, so I don't advise satisfying your curiosity to try sea-turtle soup or caiman, even if the locals do it. Local jungle dishes that you don't have to feel bad about trying include *patarashca,* a steamed river fish wrapped in banana leaves; *juanes,* a kind of rice tamale; *timbuche,* a thick soup made with local fish; *paiche,* an Amazon-size local fish; and *chonta,* a hearts of palm salad. If you don't make it to the jungle, another way of going native (in the highlands and along the coast) is to eat *cuy,* or guinea pig. See chapter 9.

- **Relaxing at a *Quinta:*** There are elegant restaurants in Lima, Cusco, Arequipa, and Iquitos, but there's nothing quite like an informal *quinta*—an open-air restaurant specializing in Andean home-cooking. It's an Andean tradition perhaps best explored in the crisp air of Cusco, which has a trio of *quintas* that are especially popular with locals on weekends. Look for informal garden or courtyard settings, large portions of Peruvian cooking, and reasonable prices. Most *quintas* are open only for lunch, so plan on it as your main

meal of the day. Not only will you eat well, but it's also a great way to spend a sunny afternoon. See "Cusco's *Quintas*" on p. 207.

- **Savoring a Pisco Sour:** Peru's national drink is the pisco sour, a delicious concoction made from the white-grape brandy called pisco. Made frothy when mixed with egg whites, lemon juice, sugar, and bitters, it's cold and complex, the closest thing to a Peruvian margarita. Try one with ceviche or a robust Andean meal—or just knock 'em back late at night at a gringo-filled bar.

- **Self-Medicating with *Mate de Coca:*** Coca-leaf tea, a perfectly legal local drink that has been a tradition in the Andes for centuries, is a great way to deal with the high altitude of the mountains, which can make your head spin and your body reel. As soon as you hit Cusco or Puno, head straight for the *mate de coca*—most hotels have it at the ready for their guests. And if that doesn't work, strap on the oxygen tank (many hotels supply that for their guests, too).

- **Slurping Ceviche:** One of the classic dishes of Peruvian coastal cooking is ceviche—raw fish and shellfish marinated in lime or lemon juice and hot chile peppers, and served with raw onion, sweet potato, and toasted corn. It's wonderfully refreshing and spicy. The best place to try one? A seaside *cevichería,* specializing in umpteen varieties of deliciously fresh ceviche.

- **Touring Ica's Bodegas:** Peru, one of the great winemaking countries of the world? Probably not, but the southern desert coast does have a thriving wine industry. The most famous product is pisco, but the many traditional bodegas (wineries) throughout the Ica countryside also make regular table wines. A few bodegas give tours and tastings. Ica hosts a hopping Wine Festival in March, which is a good time to tour the region if you're into wine and general merriment. Harvest time, late February through April, is the other time to visit, when you can see people crushing grapes the old-fashioned way—with their feet. See "Ica" in chapter 6.

12 The Best Restaurants

- **Astrid y Gastón,** Lima (© 01/444-1496): One of the coolest restaurants in the country is this stylish modern place serving a creative brand of creole-Mediterranean fare. Behind a nondescript facade in the Miraflores district, a husband/wife team cooks and runs the colorful colonial dining room and cozy bar, favored by Limeño regulars. See p. 127.

- **Cebichería La Mar,** Lima (© 01/421-3365): A designer and celebrity-chef's take on the neighborhood *cevichería,* this is the hottest restaurant in Lima. It's only open for lunch, though, and doesn't take reservations, so it's a bit of a challenge to get a seat at this stylish hotspot. The focus is on moderately priced, delicious ceviche and traditional Limeño fare served up with hip twists. See p. 129.

- **La Hamaca,** Lima (© 01/242-7978): A mansion stuffed to the rafters with priceless Peruvian art and antiques, and a maze of spectacularly decorated small dining rooms is a cinematic experience. Imagine you're the *dueño* of a sprawling hacienda while you dine on classic Peruvian preparations. Retire upstairs for an elegant evening of dancing on weekends. See p. 128.

- **Restaurant Huaca Pucllana,** Lima (© 01/445-4042): One of the best places for dining in the capital has the most unique location: within the compound of an over 1,500-year-old adobe pyramid. The restaurant is both hip and relaxed, with a covered terrace looking out over the low pyramid and illuminated excavation walkways. The creative Peruvian menu offers new twists on classic *comida criolla* (creole cooking). See p. 128.

- **Manos Morenas,** Lima (© 01/467-0421): The best place for dinner and a show in Lima, this sleek Barranco restaurant serves good *criollo* cooking and features peña and Afro-Peruvian music and dance nightly. It's housed in an elegant early 1900s house, very appealingly converted. The show's not inexpensive, but it's usually a great evening out. See p. 132.

- **Restaurante Illary (Hotel Monasterio),** Cusco (© 084/243-820): Cusco's top fine-dining option is within the exclusive confines of the top hotel in town. Even if the hotel is out of reach, the restaurant makes the perfect splurge date in Cusco. Whether you sit in the glassed-in corridor overlooking the colonial patio or the main dining room that very much looks the part of 16th-century monastery, dining here is a true treat. The Peruvian specialties, like the discreet service, are impeccable. See p. 203.

- **Cicciolina,** Cusco (© 084/239-510): Cusco's restaurant scene is constantly improving, adding more upscale, fine-dining options, and this new restaurant, which serves stylish novo Andino cuisine, is the best example of the trend. You might think you've landed in a chic Tuscan country eatery, but the menu is eclectic, with a soft spot for unusual spices. The hopping bar is a smart haunt for pre-dinner drinks, though the sexy, hushed dining room is the sleekest in Cusco. See p. 204.

- **MAP Café,** Cusco (© 084/242-476): Cusco's most chic and modern restaurant is tucked into the colonial patio of the city's great pre-Columbian art museum. It quietly makes a dramatic statement with its understated, minimalist design: a glass and steel box. The food, nouveau Andean, is every bit as elegant and cleanly presented. With a super wine list and the opportunity to stroll through the museum after dinner, it's a perfect, sophisticated date restaurant. See p. 205.

- **Greens,** Cusco (📞 **084/243-379**): A small and stylish restaurant in the cool San Blas district, Greens has a creative menu and funky decor, including low, comfy sofas and hipster tunes. The excellent, surprising menus of international and Peruvian dishes are reasonably priced. See p. 206.

- **Killa Wasi,** Huicho (Sacred Valley) (📞 **084/201-620**): The restaurant of Hotel Sol y Luna, one of the best places to stay in the Sacred Valley, deters guests from venturing out and draws many from other hotels. The restaurant is elegant but relaxed, and the menu is full of creative *criollo* and nouveau Andean dishes. The pub upstairs is a good spot for a pisco sour late in the day. See "Urubamba & Environs" in chapter 8.

- **Indio Feliz,** Aguas Calientes (📞 **084/211-090**): The town at the bottom of Machu Picchu is a little scrappy, so this Peruvian-French restaurant really stands out. In an attractive and very popular two-level dining room, it offers a great-value three-course menu. If by chance you just completed the 4-day Inca Trail trek, treat yourself to a meal here. See p. 278.

- **Sol de Mayo,** Arequipa (📞 **054/254-148**): This is the best place in town for traditional Arequipeño cooking, which has quite a reputation in Peru. The setting, around a courtyard

garden where strolling musicians play, is delightful. It's a perfect place to sink your teeth into local Peruvian specialties and is a great place to splurge. See p. 316.

- **La Trattoria del Monasterio,** Arequipa (📞 **054/204-062**): A new, stylishly reserved restaurant carved out of the city's most distinguished walls, belonging to the Santa Catalina monastery, this laid-back Italian spot is a real find. With a menu designed by Peru's hottest chef, a nice wine list, a trio of quiet dining rooms, and accessible prices, it's a welcome change from noisier and more solicitous restaurants populating Arequipa's highly trafficked restaurant rows. See p. 316.

- **Zig Zag,** Arequipa (📞 **054/206-020**): This chic and inviting restaurant has a unique specialty: stone-grilled ostrich. Healthier than other meats, ostrich is really good, as is another popular dish served here: alpaca (which is also healthier than red meat). In this two-level space with *sillar* walls and vaulted ceilings, the grilled meat is not the only thing that makes this a memorable dining experience. See p. 317.

- **Montecarlo,** Iquitos (📞 **065/232-246**): The northern Amazon city of Iquitos has a handful of good restaurants serving Peruvian and jungle specialties, but this upscale place—glitzy on the outside but relaxed and elegant on the inside—is the best. Fish dishes are excellent, as is the service. If you want, you can gamble downstairs at the casino. See p. 365.

- **Club Colonial,** Huanchaco (📞 **044/461-015**): An unexpectedly chic and stylish restaurant in the low-key beach resort of Huanchaco, this Belgian-French place has the kind of ambience you'd look to find in Barranco in Lima, not the north coast. The candlelit dining room is like a cool expatriate's house, and the menu is a tantalizing mix of Peruvian and Franco-Belgian items. Whether you order meat or fresh fish, or even a Belgian standard, you're in for a treat. See p. 384.

- **Pueblo Viejo,** Chiclayo (© **074/ 228-863**): Chiclayo might not be the dining capital of Peru, but its best restaurant is very good. An attractive two-story eatery that serves traditional but creative Chiclayano cooking and *comida criolla,* Pueblo Viejo really stands out in the north of Peru. See p. 394.

- **El Querubino,** Cajamarca (© **076/ 830-900**): A brightly decorated restaurant just off the Plaza de Armas, El Querubino is refined and stylish, but relaxed enough to be popular with locals. Dinner often features live but low-key music, and at lunch there's a nice daily list of value specials. See p. 406.

13 The Best Markets & Shopping

- **Miraflores,** Lima: The Peruvian capital has the biggest number of shops and selection of goods from across the country, as might be expected. The Miraflores district has dozens of shops stocked to the rafters with handicrafts from around Peru. For one-stop shopping, there are minimalls of many stalls selling ceramics, textiles, and other souvenirs. The best silver jewelry and antiques shops are also in Miraflores. See "Shopping" in chapter 5.

- **Barrio de San Blas,** Cusco: Galleries around the Plaza de Armas of the old Incan capital are wonderful for all kinds of wool and alpaca fashions and silver jewelry. But especially flavorful is the picturesque and bohemian neighborhood of San Blas, which rises into the hills above Cusco, bursting with the studios and workshops of artists and artisans, as well as art galleries and ceramics shops. You can pop into several studios and see artists at work. See "Shopping" in chapter 7.

- **Pisac's Crafts Market:** Thousands of tourists descend each Sunday morning on Pisac's liveliest handicrafts market, which takes over the central plaza and spills across adjoining streets. Many sellers, decked out in the dress typical of their villages, come from remote populations high in the mountains. Pisac is one of the best spots for colorful Andean textiles, including rugs, alpaca sweaters, and ponchos. See "Pisac" in chapter 8.

- **Pablo Seminario,** Urubamba: Urubamba leaves the Sunday tourist handicrafts markets to other towns in the Sacred Valley, but it's home to one of the coolest ceramics shops in Peru. Pablo Seminario, originally from the north of the country, now operates out of a lovely place that is equal parts home, workshop, storefront, and zoo. His work features funky pre-Columbian motifs. See "Urubamba & Environs" in chapter 8.

- **Chinchero's Handicrafts Market:** It's not as popular as Pisac's market, but in many ways, Chinchero's is more authentic, and the setting is just as spectacular. The big one is on Sunday, when the tourist buses come through, but less-hectic Tuesday and Thursday are probably better for making a deal. The quality of handicrafts is usually quite excellent. Take your camera; the sellers still wear traditional garments. See "Urubamba & Environs" in chapter 8.

- **Isla Taquile,** Lake Titicaca: The Taquile islanders are famous for their dress and exquisite textiles. Travelers can pick up some of the finest woven and embroidered waistbands and wool stocking caps in Peru, including some that are normally reserved for community authorities. Because they're so finely made, Taquile textiles are more expensive than the mass-produced handicrafts you'll find elsewhere in Peru. Islanders operate a co-op on the main plaza and sell from stalls during festivals. See "Puno & Lake Titicaca" in chapter 9.

- **Arequipa:** Alpaca sweaters, ponchos, and hats are classic Peruvian souvenirs, and you can score them across the Andes and in Lima, but Arequipa is the top spot for really excellent export-quality goods. You'll find great designs in baby alpaca, vicuña, and wool. Visit any of the shops near the Plaza de Armas, including the alpaca boutiques that now inhabit the old cloisters of the La Compañía church. Another good spot, for slightly less swank goods, is the general handicrafts market (mercado de artesanía), whose stalls are in what used to be the old town jail. See "Arequipa" in chapter 9.

- **Barrio Belén,** Iquitos: Handicrafts, particularly textiles and other items from the Shipibo tribe in the Amazon, are available at the large artisans' market out by the airport, but shopping of a very different sort is pursued at the popular market in the waterfront Barrio de Belén. The wildly colorful market, which spreads over several long blocks and is a riot of activity, sells everything under the Amazon sun; let your senses be the judge. Look for unusual Amazon fish and fruits, and exotic jungle meats, such as monkey and caiman. When it becomes too much, take a breather at the fresh juice stands. See "Iquitos & the Northern Amazon" in chapter 10.

14 The Best Reasons for Bragging Rights

- **Taking the High Road:** The Ferrocarril Central Andino, called the "Tren Macho," is the highest railway in the world, climbing to more than 4500m (15,000 ft.) on the way from Lima to Huancayo in the Central Highlands. Unfortunately, the passenger railway has experienced all kinds of problems in recent years; even when it's on, it only travels once a month from July to October. If it is running, though, it's a truly thrilling and occasionally vertigo-inducing ride. If you're one of the lucky few to ride it, you've got plenty to brag about. See chapter 5.

- **Surfing Big Sand:** The southern desert of Peru is a strange, unrelenting landscape, but it has the highest sand dunes in South America. An X-sport fast gaining in popularity is surfing the dunes on sand boards and areneros (dune buggies). The biggest are near Nasca, but probably the prettiest spot is the dunes that ring the Huacachina Lagoon outside of Ica. See "Ica" in chapter 6.

- **Gazing at the Stars at Sacsayhuamán:** The Sacsayhuamán ruins are amazing enough by day; imagine those immense, elegantly laid stones at night, high above Cusco. At night, it won't be hard to perceive the Incas' worship of the natural world, in which the moon was a deity. If your visit coincides with a full moon in that gargantuan sky, you'll be talking about it back home for months. A similar experience would be hiking along the Inca Trail and spending that last night before pushing on to Machu Picchu under a full moon. See "What to See & Do" in chapter 7.

- **Lighting It Up at Tres Cruces:** Beyond the remote Andean village of Paucartambo, known for its Virgen de Carmen festival, is Tres Cruces, perched on a mountain ridge on the edge of the Amazon basin. Famous for its almost hallucinogenic, multi-hued sunrise, the spot was held sacred by the Incas, and it's not hard to see why. During the winter months (May–July), the special effects are beyond belief. To enhance your bragging rights, note that Tres Cruces is a royal pain to reach. See "Side Trips from Cusco" in chapter 7.

- **Hopping the Hiram Bingham Train to Machu Picchu:** Once upon a time, you could zip to the most famous Incan ruins by helicopter, but for my money, the new old-world luxury train named for the discoverer of Machu Picchu is even better. With wood-paneled cars, full white-glove meal and cocktail service, on-board Peruvian musicians, and an included tour of the ruins, it's definitely traveling in style. Sure, it costs several times the regular tourist train, but this is Machu Picchu, right? See "Machu Picchu & the Inca Trail" in chapter 8.

- **Scaling Huayna Picchu in Record Time:** Huayna Picchu hovers above Machu Picchu in the classic postcard shot of the ruins. People of all ages and decent physical condition can climb to the summit; to properly boast, you've got to race the steep stone path in close to record time (about 15 min. at last report). Even if you don't beat the record, you can savor the stunning, indescribable view as you wait for your heart rate to return to normal. See "Machu Picchu & the Inca Trail" in chapter 8.

- **Surviving "Dead Woman's Pass":** Hiking the Inca Trail to Machu Picchu is one of the greatest ecoadventures on the planet. Enough said. See "Machu Picchu & the Inca Trail" in chapter 8.

- **Running a Class VI in Colca Canyon:** Extremely technical white-water rafting in the Colca (as well as Cotahuasi) Canyon is the stuff that bragging was made for. Imagine telling your friends that you hurtled down the river at the bottom of a canyon more than twice as deep as the Grand Canyon! This is for hard-core runners only; trips are expensive and lengthy. See "Colca Valley" in chapter 9.

- **Rumbling by Truck to Puerto Maldonado:** If you like tests of sheer perseverance, travel by truck from Cusco to Puerto Maldonado, the gateway to the Tambopata Reserve in the southern Amazon. It'll take between 3 and 10 days on a road that's 95% unpaved, but what's time (and a sore body) to a good story? See "The Southern Amazon Jungle" in chapter 10.

- **Trippin' Amazon-Style:** If spotting wildlife and trekking through primary rainforest isn't stimulating enough, you can do your best to imitate the ancient ways of Amazon tribes and shamans by taking part in an *ayahuasca* ceremony. The natural hallucinogenic potion, made of herbs, roots, and other plants, is supposed to mess with your mind. But for locals, it's a deeply respected ritual. See "Iquitos & the Northern Amazon" in chapter 10.

- **Fishing for Piranha:** If you visit a jungle lodge, you might have the opportunity to head out on the Amazon or its tributaries in a dugout canoe to fish for piranha. Most are surprisingly small, but their famous teeth are very much present. For a special dinner, have the lodge cook fry 'em up for you that night. See "Iquitos & the Northern Amazon" in chapter 10.

- **Bagging 6,000m Peaks in the Cordillera Blanca:** For expert climbers, the Cordillera Blanca is a mountaineering mecca. From May to September, fit climbers can score several 6,000m (20,000-ft.) summits in the Parque Nacional Huascarán in just a couple weeks. Huascarán, at 6,768m (22,205 ft.), is the big one, the highest mountain in the Peruvian Andes and the tallest tropical mountain in the world. See "Huaraz & the Cordillera Blanca" in chapter 11.

15 The Best of Peru Online

- **www.peru.info**: The most comprehensive official Peru site, recently revamped, is the website of PromPerú. It has detailed sections on Peruvian history, festivals, trip-planning, and outdoor "adrenaline rushes," all with extensive pull-down menus, as well as a stock of photo and video images and audio files.

- **www.saexplorers.org**: The website of the rightly famous South American Explorers (based in Ithaca, New York, with clubhouses in Lima, Cusco, and Quito, Ecuador) has vital information such as travel advisories, insurance providers, and links to websites on specific Peruvian destinations. You can also order the club's "Information Packet" of fact sheets and member tips.

- **http://gci275.com/peru**: "Peruvian Graffiti," a website by an American journalist and former resident of Peru, is an engaging compendium of Peruvian history, politics, media, and culture, as well as the latest news, from a very personal perspective. It's an interesting place to start to get a handle on a complicated nation.

- **www.andeantravelweb.com/peru**: The Andean Travel Web, a private website run by gringos in Peru, is a miniguide to the country, with information on all the major destinations and activities, transportation, the latest in Inca Trail regulations, local tour operators, and helpful things such as ecotourism links. It doesn't cover northern Peru, however, sticking to the most well trodden regions.

- **http://gorp.away.com/gorp/location/latamer/peru.htm**: The travel wholesaler GORP features an entire page of personal essays on the great outdoors and adventure sports in Peru, including pieces on running the Amazon and birding, and a Top 20 of adventure activities.

- **www.livinginperu.com**: An English-language site directed toward foreign residents of Peru, this is the best place to get the latest news on Peru, including transportation issues, strikes, political developments, and other practical matters that affect not only residents but visitors. It also contains up-to-date cultural and event information.

- **www.traficoperu.com**: This online travel agent has details on practical matters—domestic airlines, bus transportation, and hotels—plus a few cheap domestic packages, and a good selection of regional and city maps.

2

Planning Your Trip to Peru

Mesmerizing Peru—a land of pre-Columbian ruins and lost cities, Andes Mountains and Amazon jungle—is a destination that many first-time travelers may know little about, beyond the famed Machu Picchu. This chapter details everything you need to know to make planning your trip to Peru less daunting, from the lay of the land and how to get there to money and health concerns. It also covers other critical information for planning your trip, such as tour operators and travel packages, and tips on Peruvian accommodations, dining, and shopping.

1 The Regions in Brief

Peru, which lies just below the equator, is the third-largest country in South America. It is larger than France and Spain combined, covering an area of nearly 1,300,000 sq. km (500,000 sq. miles). Peru shares borders with Ecuador and Colombia to the north, Brazil and Bolivia to the east, and Chile to the south.

Peruvians like to say that their country consists of three distinct geological components: coast, *sierra* (highlands), and *selva* (jungle). The capital, Lima, lies on the coast, but the Amazon rainforest, which makes up nearly two-thirds of Peru, and the bold Andes mountain range dominate the country. Peru's considerable size, natural barriers, and a lack of efficient transportation alternatives make it a somewhat difficult and time-consuming place to get around.

THE CENTRAL COAST & HIGHLANDS The Pacific coastal region is a narrow strip that runs from one end of the country to the other (a distance of some 2,200km/1,400 miles) and is almost entirely desert. Lima lies about halfway down the coast. To the south, in one of the driest areas on Earth, are Pisco, Ica, and Nasca, the cradle of several of Peru's most important ancient civilizations, as well as the famously mysterious Nasca Lines and the Ballestas Islands, promoted locally as "Peru's Galápagos" for their diverse indigenous fauna. Inland and tucked high in the Central Andes, Ayacucho is one of Peru's most fascinating cities, known for its colonial churches and artisanship but less felicitously associated with the Shining Path terrorist group.

CUSCO & THE SACRED VALLEY The dramatic Andes mountains in south-central Peru contain the country's most famous sights, including the former Incan capital of Cusco and scenic highland villages that run the length of the beautiful Sacred Valley. The valley is dotted with singularly impressive Incan ruins, of which Machu Picchu (and the Inca Trail leading to it) is undoubtedly the star. Cusco sits at an elevation of some 3,400m (11,000 ft.). Indigenous culture is particularly strong in the region.

Peru's UNESCO World Heritage Sites

- Cusco city (designated in 1983)
- Machu Picchu Historic Sanctuary (1983)
- Archaeological Site of Chavín (1985)
- Huascarán National Park (1985)
- Manu National Park (1987)
- Chan Chan Archaeological Zone (1988)
- Río Abiseo National Park (1990)
- Historic Center of Lima (1991)
- Nasca Lines (1994)
- Historic Center of Arequipa (2000)

SOUTHERN PERU   Massive Lake Titicaca, shared with Bolivia, is the largest lake in South America and the world's highest navigable body of water (at 3,830m/12,566 ft.). Indigenous peoples inhabit ancient villages on islands (some of them man-made) in the middle of this huge body of water. Puno, at the edge of Lake Titicaca, is a rough-and-tumble town that hosts some of Peru's liveliest festivals. The elegant colonial city of Arequipa is one of Peru's most gorgeously situated, at the base of three snowcapped volcanoes. Nearby is Colca Canyon, twice as deep as the Grand Canyon and site of perhaps the best place in all South America to view the regal condor.

AMAZONIA   Although about 60% of Peru is Amazon rainforest, only about 5% of the country's human inhabitants reside there. One of the world's most dazzling arrays of wildlife—more than 1,700 species of birds (more than the population found in the continental U.S.) and 2,000 species of fish—make it their home. For the visitor, there are two primary jungle destinations. The northern jungle, of which Iquitos is the principal gateway (but accessible only by plane or boat), is the most explored and has the most facilities. Much less trafficked and

more controlled is the Madre de Dios department in the south, which contains Manu Biosphere Reserve, Puerto Maldonado, and Tambopata National Reserve. These can be reached by land or air from Cusco.

NORTHERN PERU   Peru's north is much less visited than the south, even though it possesses some of the country's most outstanding archaeological sights. Trujillo, Chiclayo, and Cajamarca (a lovely small city in the highlands) are the main colonial towns of interest. Near Trujillo and Chiclayo are Chan Chan, Túcume, and Sipán, extraordinary adobe cities, pyramids, and royal tombs and treasures that predate the Incas.

The mountain ranges in the center of Peru, north of Lima, are among the highest in Peru. Within Huascarán National Park, the Cordillera Blanca stretches 200km (124 miles) and contains a dozen peaks more than 5,000m (16,400 ft.) tall; the highest is Huascarán, at 6,768m (22,205 ft.). The region is a favorite of trekkers and outdoor-adventure travelers who come to Peru with white-water rafting, ice climbing, and other sports in mind. The main jumping-off point for these activities is the town of Huaraz. In valleys east of the capital is the important archaeological site Chavín de Huántar.

The Regions in Brief

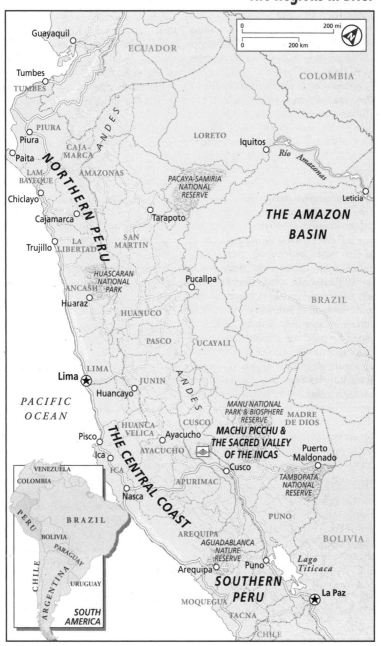

2 Visitor Information

BEFORE YOU GO

Peru doesn't maintain national tourism offices abroad, so your best official source of information before you go is **www.peru.info**, the website of PromPerú (Commission for the Promotion of Peru). Peruvian embassies and consulates usually offer some brochures and other information on traveling to Peru, but it's probably best not to expect too much.

Other helpful trip-planning websites include **www.peruvianembassy.us**, the Peruvian embassy in Washington, D.C.; **www.traficoperu.com/english**, the site for Traficoperu, a travel agency with information about flights, hotels, and special deals; **www.enjoyperu.com**, a similar site with good background information on specific areas; **www.perurail.com**, the official PeruRail website with route and service information; and **www.saexplorers.org**, the South American Explorers website, which is especially good for trekking and adventure travel information. Sites with good information on specific places include **www.huaylas.com** and **www.andeanexplorer.com**, for trekking and other information on Huaraz and the Callejón de Huaylas; and **www.machupicchu.org**, for more information on the celebrated Incan ruins and other sights in the Sacred Valley of the Incas.

IN PERU

Visitor information is not handled by a single, centralized government agency across Peru. PromPerú, the main national organization responsible for tourism promotion and information, works alongside the Ministry of Industry, Tourism & International Business Negotiation (MITINCI) and several private entities. The result is that tourism information is confusingly dispersed among sometimes poorly equipped, small municipal offices and is often limited to regional or, worse, local information. Occasionally, private travel agencies are more adept at dispensing information, although their goal is, of course, to hawk their services.

PromPerú maintains a large bureaucratic office in Lima at Edificio Mitinci, 14th floor, Uno Oeste 50, Urbanización Córpac, San Isidro (© **01/224-9355**); however, it is not convenient for tourists seeking basic information about the country. PromPerú also operates a 24-hour information booth (© **01/574-8000**) in the international terminal of Lima's Jorge Chávez International Airport.

The **Tourist Protection Bureau (Servicio de Protección al Turista),** which handles complaints and questions about consumer rights, operates a 24-hour traveler's assistance line at © **0800/42-579**, or 01/224-7888 in Lima. The Tourist Protection Bureau office is at La Prosa 138, San Borja, Lima (© **01/224-7888**) or toll-free from cities other than Lima (© 0800/42-579). For local branch locations and telephone numbers of the Tourist Protection Bureau, see "Fast Facts" in individual destination chapters.

South American Explorers (www.samexplo.org), with clubhouses in Lima and Cusco, is an excellent source of information, particularly on trekking and mountaineering in Peru. It stocks a good selection of guides, maps, and dossiers on travel and trails, which is available to members. Yearly membership is $40. You can contact the group in the United States at © **800/274-0568** or 607/277-0488; otherwise, visit its Lima office at Piura 135, Miraflores (© **01/445-3306**), or the Cusco office at Choquechaca 188, no. 4 (© **084/245-484**).

For domestic and international **flight information,** call © **01/575-1712** or visit www.lap.com.pe.

3 Entry Requirements & Customs

ENTRY REQUIREMENTS

For information on how to get a passport, go to "Passports" in the "Fast Facts" section of this chapter—the websites listed provide downloadable passport applications as well as the current fees for processing passport applications. For an up-to-date, country-by-country listing of passport requirements around the world, go to the "Foreign Entry Requirement" Web page of the U.S. State Department at **http://travel.state.gov**.

Citizens of the United States, Canada, Great Britain, South Africa, New Zealand, and Australia do not require visas to enter Peru as tourists—only valid passports. Citizens of any of these countries conducting business or enrolled in formal educational programs in Peru do require visas; contact the embassy or consulate in your home country for more information. For information on children's passports and travel, see "Specialized Travel Resources: Family Travel," later in this chapter, and the Fast Facts section of this chapter.

Tourist (or landing) cards, distributed on arriving international flights or at border crossings, are good for stays of up to 90 days. Keep a copy of the tourist card for presentation upon departure from Peru. (If you lose it, you'll have to pay a $4 fine.) A maximum of three extensions of 30 days each, for a total of 180 days, is allowed.

No immunizations are required for entry, although if you plan to travel to jungle regions, read "Health & Safety," later in this chapter.

IN THE U.S.   The Embassy of Peru is located at 1700 Massachusetts Ave. NW, Washington, DC 20036 (© **202/833-9860;** www.peruvianembassy.us). There are Peruvian consulates in New York, Los Angeles, Miami, Boston, Chicago, Denver, Houston, and San Francisco. For their contact information, visit the Peruvian Ministry of Foreign Relations website at www.rree.gob.pe.

IN CANADA   The Embassy of Peru is located at 130 Albert St., Suite 1901, Ottawa, Ontario K1P 5G4 (© **613/238-1777;** emperuca@bellnet.ca). There are Peruvian consulates in Montreal (© **514/844-5123**), Toronto (© **416/963-9696**), and Vancouver (© **604/662-8880**).

IN THE U.K.   The Embassy of Peru is located at 52 Sloane St., London SW1X 9SP (© **020/7235-1917;** www.peru-embassy.co.uk).

IN AUSTRALIA   The Embassy of Peru is located at 43 Culgoa Circuit, O'Malley ACT 2606 (© **02/6286-9507;** www.embaperu.org.au). The Peruvian consulate has an office in Sydney at 30 Clarence St., Level 3, NSW 2000 (© **02/9262-6464**).

IN NEW ZEALAND   The Embassy of Peru is located at Level 8, Cigna House, 40 Mercer St., Wellington (© **04/499-8087;** embassy.peru@xtra.co.nz).

CUSTOMS
WHAT YOU CAN BRING INTO PERU

You are allowed to bring 3 liters of alcohol and 400 cigarettes (20 packs) or 50 cigars into Peru duty-free. New items for personal use, including camera equipment and adventure-sports gear such as mountain bikes and kayaks, are allowed. Travelers may bring in up to $300 in varied gifts, as long as no individual item exceeds $100. To avoid the possibility of having to fill out forms or pay a bond, it's best not to draw attention to expensive, new-looking items that officials might believe you are intent on reselling. (It helps to take them out of their original boxes.)

WHAT YOU CAN TAKE HOME

Exports of protected plant and endangered animal species—live or dead—are strictly prohibited by Peruvian law and should not be purchased. This includes headpieces and necklaces made with macaw feathers, and even common "rain sticks," unless authorized by the Natural Resources Institute (INRENA). Vendors in jungle cities and airports sell live animals and birds, as well as handicrafts made from insects, feathers, or other natural products. Travelers have been detained and arrested by the Ecology Police for carrying such items.

It is also illegal to take pre-Columbian archaeological items, antiques, including ceramics and textiles, and colonial-era art out of Peru. Reproductions of many such items are available, but even their export could cause difficulties at Customs or with overly cautious international courier services if you attempt to send them home. To be safe, look for the word REPRODUCCION or an artist's name stamped on reproduction ceramics, and keep business cards and receipts from shops where you have purchased them. Particularly fine items might require documentation from Peru's National Institute of Culture (INC) verifying that the object is a reproduction and may be exported. You might be able to obtain a certificate of authorization from the INC kiosk at Lima's Jorge Chávez International Airport or the INC office at the National Museum Building, Av. Javier Prado Este 2465, sixth floor, San Borja (© 01/476-9900).

Returning **U.S. citizens** who have been away for at least 48 hours are allowed to bring back, once every 30 days, $800 worth of merchandise duty free. You'll be charged a flat rate of duty on the next $1,000 worth of purchases. Any dollar amount beyond that is dutiable at whatever rates apply. On mailed gifts, the duty-free limit is $200. Be sure to have your receipts or purchases handy to expedite the declaration process. *Note:* If you owe duty, you are required to pay upon your arrival in the United States, either by cash, personal check, government or traveler's check, or money order (and in some locations, Visa or MasterCard).

To avoid paying duty on foreign-made personal items you owned before your trip, bring along a bill of sale, insurance policy, jeweler's appraisal, or receipts of purchase. Or you can register items that can be readily identified by a permanently affixed serial number or marking—think laptop computers and cameras—with Customs before you leave. Take the items to the nearest Customs office or register them with Customs at the airport from which you're departing. You'll receive, at no cost, a Certificate of Registration, which allows duty-free entry for the life of the item.

With some exceptions, you cannot bring fresh fruits and vegetables into the United States. For specifics on what you can bring back, download the invaluable free pamphlet *Know Before You Go!* online at **www.cbp.gov**. (Click on "Travel," and then on "Know Before You Go! Online Brochure.") Or contact the **U.S. Customs and Border Patrol,** 1300 Pennsylvania Ave. NW, Washington, DC 20229 (© **877/287-8667**), and request the pamphlet.

For a clear summary of **Canadian rules,** write for the booklet *I Declare,* issued by the **Canada Border Services Agency** (© **800/461-9999** in Canada, or 204/983-3500; www.cbsa-asfc.gc.ca/E/pub/cp/rc4044). Canada allows its citizens a C$750 exemption, and you're allowed to bring back duty free 1 carton of cigarettes, 1 can of tobacco, 40 imperial ounces of liquor, and 50 cigars. In addition, you're allowed to mail gifts to Canada valued at less than C$60 a day, provided that they're unsolicited and don't contain alcohol or tobacco (write on the package "Unsolicited gift, under $60 value"). All valuables should be declared on the Y-38 form before departure from Canada, including serial numbers of valuables you already own, such as expensive foreign cameras. *Note:* The $750 exemption can be used only once a year and only after an absence of 7 days.

Citizens of the U.K. who are **returning from a non-E.U. country** have a customs allowance of 200 cigarettes; 50 cigars; 250 grams of smoking tobacco; 2 liters of still table wine; 1 liter of spirits or strong liqueurs (over 22% volume); 2 liters of fortified wine, sparkling wine, or other liqueurs; 60cc (ml) perfume; 250cc (ml) of toilet water; and £145 worth of all other goods, including gifts and souvenirs. People under 17 cannot have the tobacco or alcohol allowance. For more information, contact HM Customs & Excise at © **0845/010-9000** (from outside the U.K., 020/8929-0152), or consult its website at www.hmce.gov.uk.

The duty-free allowance in **Australia** is A$400, or, for those under 18, A$200. Citizens can bring in 250 cigarettes or 250 grams of loose tobacco, and 1,125 milliliters of alcohol. If you're returning with valuables you already own, such as foreign-made cameras, you should file form B263. A helpful brochure available from Australian consulates or Customs offices is *Know Before You Go.* For more information, call the **Australian Customs Service** at © **1300/363-263,** or log on to www.customs.gov.au.

The duty-free allowance for **New Zealand** is NZ$700. Citizens over 17 can bring in 200 cigarettes, 50 cigars, or 250 grams of tobacco (or a mixture of all three if their combined weight doesn't exceed 250g), plus 4.5 liters of wine and beer, or 1.125 liters of liquor. New Zealand currency does not carry import or export restrictions. Fill out a certificate of export, listing the valuables you are taking out of the country; that way, you can bring them back without paying duty. Most questions are answered in a free pamphlet available at New Zealand consulates and Customs offices: *New Zealand Customs Guide for Travellers, Notice no. 4.* For more information, contact **New Zealand Customs,** The Customhouse, 17–21 Whitmore St., Box 2218, Wellington (© **04/473-6099** or 0800/428-786; www.customs.govt.nz).

4 Money

On the whole, Peru is inexpensive by North American and European standards, although it is slightly more expensive than its Andean neighbors, Ecuador and Bolivia. Peruvians tend to haggle over prices and accept that others haggle also, except in major stores and restaurants. In the bigger cities, prices for virtually everything are higher, especially in Lima; in addition, prices can rise in the high season, such as the Independence Day holidays (late July), Easter week (Mar or Apr), or Christmas, due to heavy demand, especially for hotel rooms and bus and plane tickets.

CURRENCY

Peru's official currency is the **nuevo sol (S/),** divided into 100 *centavos.* Coins are issued in denominations of 5, 10, 20, and 50 centavos, and banknotes in denominations of 10, 20, 50, 100, and 200 soles. At press time, the rate of exchange was creeping back up to approximately S/3.50 to $1 (rates are pretty consistent across the country). The U.S. dollar is the second currency; many hotels post their rates in dollars, and plenty of shops, taxi drivers, restaurants, and hotels across Peru accept U.S. dollars for payment. *Note:* Since all but the least expensive Peruvian hotels charge prices solely in dollars, only U.S. dollar rates are often listed for hotels in this book.

It is often difficult to pay with large banknotes (in either soles or dollars). Try to carry denominations of 50 and lower in both.

You'll avoid lines at airport ATMs (automated teller machines) by exchanging at least some money—just enough to cover airport incidentals and transportation to your hotel—before you leave home (though don't expect the exchange rate to be ideal). You can exchange money at your local American Express or Thomas Cook office or at your bank. American Express also dispenses traveler's checks and foreign currency via www.americanexpress.com or Ⓒ **800/807-6233,** but they'll charge a $15 order fee and additional shipping costs.

EXCHANGING MONEY

Peru is still very much a cash society. In villages and small towns, it could be impossible to cash traveler's checks or use credit cards. Make sure that you have cash (in both soles and U.S. dollars) on hand. If you pay in dollars, you will likely receive change in soles, so be aware of the correct exchange rate. U.S. dollars are by far the easiest foreign currency to exchange. Currencies other than U.S. dollars receive very poor exchange rates.

Banks are no longer the place of choice in Peru for exchanging money: Lines are too long, the task is too time-consuming, and rates are often lower than at *casas de cambio* (exchange houses) or by using credit- or debit-card ATMs or money-changers, which are legal in Peru. If you can't avoid banks, all cities and towns have branches of major international and local banks; see "Fast Facts" in individual destination chapters for locations. Money-changers, often wearing colored smocks with "$" insignias, can be found on the street. They offer current rates of exchange, but count your money carefully (you can simplify this by exchanging

easily calculable amounts, such as $10 or $100), and make sure you have not received any counterfeit bills.

Counterfeit banknotes and even coins are common, and merchants and consumers across Peru vigorously check the authenticity of money before accepting payment or change. (The simplest way: Hold the banknote up to the light to see the watermark.) Many people also refuse to accept banknotes that are not in good condition (including those with small tears, that have been written on, and even that are simply well worn), and visitors are wise to do the same when receiving change, to avoid problems with other payments. Do not accept bills with tears (no matter how small) or taped bills.

Making change in Peru is often a problem. You should carry small bills and even then be prepared to wait for change. At one bar in Iquitos, I tried to pay with a S/20 note (less than $6) and the waiter said, "Hold on, I'm going to get change"—and he hopped on a bicycle and took off, not reappearing with correct change for nearly a half-hour.

ATMs

Automatic teller machines (ATMs) are the best way of getting cash in Peru; they're found in most towns and cities, although not on every street corner. ATMs allow customers to withdraw money in either Peruvian soles or U.S. dollars. Screen instructions are in English as well as Spanish. Some bank ATMs dispense money only to those who hold accounts there. Most ATMs in Peru accept only one type of credit/debit card and international money network, either **Cirrus** (Ⓒ **800/424-7787;** www.mastercard.com) or **PLUS** (Ⓒ **800/843-7587;** www.visa.com). Visa and MasterCard ATM cards are the most widely accepted; Visa/PLUS is the most common.

Be sure you know your personal identification number (PIN) and daily withdrawal limit before you depart. At some

The Peruvian Sol

For American Readers At this writing, US$1 equals approximately S/3.50. This was the rate of exchange used to calculate the dollar equivalents given throughout this edition.

For Canadian Readers At this writing, C$1 equals approximately S/2.85. This was the rate of exchange used to calculate the Canadian dollar values in the table below.

For British Readers At this writing, £1 equals approximately S/5.7. This was the rate of exchange used to calculate the pound values in the table below.

For European (E.U.) Readers At this writing, 1€ equals approximately S/3.9. This was the rate of exchange used to calculate the euro values in the table below.

Nuevo Sol	U.S. $	CAN $	U.K. £	E.U. €
10	2.80	3.50	1.75	2.50
20	5.70	7.00	3.50	5.10
30	8.60	10.50	5.25	7.70
40	11.40	14.00	7.00	10.25
50	14.30	17.50	8.75	13.00
100	29.00	35.00	18.00	255.00
200	57.00	70.00	35.00	51.00
300	86.00	105.00	53.00	77.00
400	115.00	140.00	70.00	103.00
500	143.00	175.00	88.00	128.00
1,000	286.00	350.00	175.00	256.00

ATMs, your personal identification number (PIN) must contain four digits. *Note:* Remember that many banks impose a fee every time you use a card at another bank's ATM, and that fee can be higher for international transactions (up to $5 or more) than for domestic ones (where they're rarely more than $2). In addition, the bank from which you withdraw cash may charge its own fee. For international withdrawal fees, ask your bank.

TRAVELER'S CHECKS

You can buy traveler's checks at most banks. They are offered in denominations of $20, $50, $100, $500, and sometimes $1000. Generally, you'll pay a service charge ranging from 1% to 4%.

The most popular traveler's checks are offered by **American Express** (© 800/807-6233 or 800/221-7282 for card holders—this number accepts collect calls, offers service in several foreign languages, and exempts Amex gold and platinum cardholders from the 1% fee); **Visa** (© 800/732-1322)—AAA members can obtain Visa checks for a $9.95 fee (for checks up to $1,500) at most AAA offices or by calling © 866/339-3378; and **MasterCard** (© 800/223-9920).

American Express, Thomas Cook, Visa, and **MasterCard** offer **foreign currency traveler's checks,** which are useful if you're traveling to one country, or to the Euro zone; they're accepted at locations where dollar checks may not be.

If you carry traveler's checks, keep a record of their serial numbers separate from your checks in the event that they are stolen or lost. You'll get a refund faster if you know the numbers.

CREDIT CARDS

Credit cards are another safe way to carry money. They also provide a convenient record of all your expenses, and they generally offer relatively good exchange rates. You can withdraw cash advances from your credit cards at banks or ATMs, provided you know your PIN. Keep in mind that you'll pay interest from the moment of your withdrawal, even if you pay your monthly bills on time. Also, note that many banks now assess a 1% to 3% "transaction fee" on **all** charges you incur abroad (whether you're using the local currency or your native currency).

For tips and telephone numbers to call if your wallet is stolen or lost, go to "Lost & Found" in the "Fast Facts" section of this chapter.

5 When to Go

PEAK SEASON

Peak travel season for foreigners is in great part determined by weather. Peru experiences two very distinct seasons, wet and dry—terms that are much more relevant than "summer" and "winter." Peru's high season for travel coincides with the driest months: May through October, with by far the greatest number of visitors in July and August. May and September are particularly fine months to visit much of the country. Airlines and hotels also consider the period from mid-December through mid-January as peak season.

From June to September (winter in the Southern Hemisphere) in the highlands, days are clear and often spectacularly sunny, with chilly or downright cold nights, especially at high elevations. For trekking in the mountains, including the Inca Trail, these are by far the best months. This is also the best time of the year to visit the Amazon basin: Mosquitoes are fewer, and many fauna stay close to the rivers (although some people prefer to travel in the jungle during the wet season, when higher water levels allow more river penetration). Note that Peruvians travel in huge numbers around July 28, the national holiday, and finding accommodations in popular destinations around this time can be difficult.

CLIMATE

Generally, May through October is the dry season; November through April is the rainy season, and the wettest months are January through April. In mountain areas, roads and trek paths can become impassable. Peru's climate, though, is markedly different among its three regions. The coast is predominantly arid and mild, the Andean region is temperate to cold, and the eastern lowlands are tropically warm and humid.

On the desert **coast,** summer (Dec–Apr) is hot and dry, with temperatures reaching 77°F to 95°F (25°C–35°C) or more along the north coast. In winter (May–Oct), temperatures are much milder, though with high humidity. Much of the coast, including Lima, is shrouded in a gray mist called *garúa*. Only extreme northern beaches are warm enough for swimming.

In the **highlands** from May to October, rain is scarce. Daytime temperatures reach a warm 68°F to 77°F (20°C–25°C), and nights are often quite cold (near freezing), especially in June and July. Rainfall is very abundant from December to March, when temperatures are slightly milder—64°F to 68°F (18°C–20°C) dropping only to 59°F (15°C) at night. The wettest months are January and

Lima's Average Temperatures & Precipitation

	Jan	Feb	Mar	Apr	May	June	July	Aug	Sept	Oct	Nov	Dec
Avg. High (°F)	77	79	79	75	70	66	63	63	63	66	68	73
Avg. High (°C)	25	26	26	24	21	19	17	17	17	19	20	23
Avg. Low (°F)	66	68	66	65	61	59	57	56	56	57	61	63
Avg. Low (°C)	19	20	19	18	16	15	14	13	13	14	16	17
Wet Days	1	0	0	0	1	1	1	2	1	0	0	0

Cusco's Average Temperatures & Precipitation

	Jan	Feb	Mar	Apr	May	June	July	Aug	Sept	Oct	Nov	Dec
Avg. High (°F)	66	66	67	68	68	67	67	68	68	70	69	68
Avg. High (°C)	19	19	19	20	20	19	19	20	20	21	21	20
Avg. Low (°F)	44	44	44	41	37	34	34	34	39	42	43	43
Avg. Low (°C)	7	7	7	5	3	1	1	1	4	6	6	6
Wet Days	12	11	10	6	4	3	4	3	2	2	1	5

February. Most mornings are dry, but clouds move in during the afternoon and produce heavy downpours.

Although the Amazon **jungle** is consistently humid and tropical, with significant rainfall year-round, it, too, experiences two clearly different seasons. During the dry season (May–Oct), temperatures reach 86°F to 100°F (30°C–38°C) during the day. From November to April, there are frequent rain showers (which last only a few hours at a time), causing the rivers to swell; temperatures are similarly steamy.

PUBLIC HOLIDAYS

National public holidays in Peru include New Year's Day (Jan 1), Three Kings Day (Jan 6), Maundy Thursday and Good Friday (Easter week, Mar or Apr), Labor Day (May 1), Fiestas Patrias (July 28–29), Battle of Angamos (Oct 8), All Saints' Day (Nov 1), Feast of the Immaculate Conception (Dec 8), and Christmas (Dec 24–25).

For additional information about regional festivals, see individual destination chapters.

PERU CALENDAR OF EVENTS

January

Entrega de Varas, Cusco. Community elders *(yayas)* designate the highest authorities of their villages in this pre-Columbian festival, which is celebrated with *chicha* (fermented maize beer) and *llonque* (sugar-cane alcohol); the mayor accepts the scepter symbolizing his power. This custom has been glossed over with Occidental formalities. January 1.

Fiesta de la Santa Tierra, Lake Titicaca. The main festival on Isla Amantaní sees the population split in two—half at the Temple of Pachamama and the other half at the Temple of Pachatata, symbolizing the islanders' ancient dualistic belief system. Third Thursday in January.

Marinera Dance Festival, Trujillo. One of the stateliest dances in Peru, the flirtatious marinera involves a couple, each partner with a handkerchief in his or her right hand. The man wears a wide-brimmed hat and poncho, and the woman wears a lace Moche dress. For 10 days, the festival, which draws couples from all over the country, is held in the Gran Chimú soccer stadium. There are also float processions throughout the city and dancing in the Plaza de Armas. January 20 to 30.

February

Virgen de la Candelaria (Candlemas), Puno. Puno lives up to its billing as Folk Capital of the Americas with this festival, which gathers more than 200 musicians and dance troupes. On the festival's main day, February 2, the Virgen is led through the city in a colorful procession of priests and pagans carefully maintaining the hierarchy. Especially thrilling is the dance of the demons, or *la diablada.* Dancers in wild costumes and masks blow panpipes and make offerings to the earth goddess Pachamama. February 1 to 14.

Carnaval. Lively pre-Lenten festivities. (Look out for balloons filled with water—or worse.) Cajamarca is reputed to have the best and wildest parties; Puno and Cusco are also good. The weekend before Ash Wednesday.

March

Festival Internacional de la Vendimia (Wine Festival), Ica. A celebration of the grape harvest and the region's wine and pisco brandy, with fairs, beauty contests, floats, and musical festivals, including Afro-Peruvian dance. Second week of March.

Las Cruces de Porcón, Porcón. Near Cajamarca, a dawn procession of massive decorated wooden crosses through the valley of Porcón re-creates the entry of Christ into Jerusalem. The main day of the festival, Palm Sunday, presents four separate ceremonies. Ultimately, the crosses are decorated with mirrors (symbolizing the souls of the dead), and locals hang metal bells to announce the arrival of the crosses to the community. Mid-March to first week of April.

Semana Santa. Handsome and spectacularly reverent processions mark Easter Week. The finest are in Cusco and Ayacucho. Late March/early April.

Lord of the Earthquakes, Cusco. Representing a 17th-century painting of Christ on the cross that is said to have saved the city from a devastating earthquake, the image of the Lord of Earthquakes (*El Señor de los Temblores*) is carried through the streets of Cusco in a reverential procession, much like the Incas once paraded the mummies of their chieftains and high priests. Easter Monday, late March/early April.

April

Peruvian Paso Horse Festival, Pachacámac. The Peruvian Paso horse, one of the world's most beautiful breeds, is celebrated with the most important annual national competition at the Mamacona stables near Pachacámac, 30km (19 miles) south of Lima. April 15 to 20.

May

Fiesta de la Cruz. The Festival of the Cross features folk music and dance, including "scissors dancers," and processions in which communities decorate crosses and prepare them for the procession to neighboring churches. The *danzantes de tijeras* (scissors dancers) re-create old times, when they performed on top of church bell towers. Today the objective is still to outdo one another with daring feats. Celebrations are especially lively in Lima, Cusco, and Ica. May 2 and 3.

Qoyllur Rit'i, Quispicanchis, near Cusco. A massive indigenous pilgrimage marks this ritual, which is tied to the fertility of the land and the worship of Apus, the spirits of the mountains. It forms part of the greatest festival of native Indian nations in the hemisphere: Qoyllur Rit'i. The main ceremony is held at the foot of Mount Ausangate, with 10,000 pilgrims climbing to the snowline along with dancers in full costume representing mythical characters. Others head to the summit, in search of the Snow Star, and take huge blocks of ice back down on their backs—holy water for irrigation purposes. First week in May.

Fiesta de Mayo, Huaraz. Also known as *El Señor de la Soledad,* this festival is celebrated with traditional dances, ski races, and a lantern procession. May 2 to 10.

June

Corpus Christi, Cusco. A procession of saints and virgins arrives at the Catedral to "greet" the body of Christ. Members of nearby churches also take their patron saints in a procession. An overnight vigil is followed by a new procession around the Plaza de Armas, with images of five virgins clad in embroidered tunics and the images of four saints: Sebastian, Blas, Joseph, and the Apostle Santiago (St. James). Early June.

Virgen del Carmen, Paucartambo. In a remote highland village 4 hours from Cusco, thousands come to honor the Virgen del Carmen, or Mamacha Carmen, patron saint of the mestizo population, with 4 days of splendidly festive music and dance, as well as some of the wildest costumes in Peru. Dancers even perform daring moves on rooftops. The festival ends in the cemetery in a show of respect for the souls of the dead. Pisac also celebrates the Virgen del Carmen festival, almost as colorfully. June 15 to 18.

Semana del Andinismo, Huaraz and Callejón de Huaylas. For outdoors fanatics, this celebration of outdoor adventure includes opportunities to partake in trekking, skiing, mountain biking, rafting, rock climbing, and hang gliding—and plenty of parties to accompany them. Mid- to late June.

Inti Raymi, Cusco. The Incan Festival of the Sun—the mother of all pre-Columbian festivals—celebrates the winter solstice and honors the sun god with traditional pageantry, parades, and dances. One of the most vibrant and exciting of all Andean festivals, it draws thousands of visitors who fill Cusco's hotels. The principal event takes place at the Sacsayhuamán ruins and includes the sacrifice of a pair of llamas. General celebrations last several days. June 24.

San Juan, Cusco and Iquitos. The feast day of St. John the Baptist, a symbol of fertility and sensuality, is the most important date on the festival calendar in the entire Peruvian jungle. John the Baptist has taken on a major symbolic significance because of the importance of water as a vital element in the entire Amazon region. Events include fiestas with lots of music and regional cuisine. In Iquitos, don't miss the aphrodisiac potions with suggestive names. June 24 in Cusco, June 25 in Iquitos.

San Pedro/San Pablo, near fishing villages in Lima and Chiclayo. The patron saints of fishermen and farmers, Saint Peter and Saint Paul, are honored; figures of the saints are carried with incense, prayers, and hymns down to the sea and are taken by launch around the bay to bless the waters. June 29.

July

Fiesta de Santiago, Isla Taquile. A festive and very traditional pageant of color, with exuberant dances and women in layered, multicolored skirts. July 25 and August 1 and 2.

Fiestas Patrias. A series of patriotic parties mark Peru's independence from

Spain in 1821. Official parades and functions are augmented by cockfighting, bullfighting, and Peruvian Paso horse exhibitions in other towns. The best celebrations are in Cusco, Puno, Isla Taquile, and Lima. July 28 and 29.

August
Santa Rosa de Lima, Lima. Major devotional processions honor the patron saint of Lima. August 30.

September
International Spring Festival, Trujillo. Trujillo celebrates the festival of spring with marinera dance, decorated streets and houses, floats, and schoolchildren dancing in the streets—led, of course, by the pageant beauty queen. Last week in September.

October
El Señor de los Milagros, Lima. The Lord of Miracles is the largest procession in South America, and it dates from colonial times. Lasting nearly 24 hours and involving tens of thousands of purple-clad participants, it celebrates a Christ image (painted by an Angolan slave) that survived the 1746 earthquake and has since become the most venerated image in the capital. October 18.

November
Todos Santos and **Día de los Muertos.** Peruvians salute the dead by visiting cemeteries with flowers and food. Families hold candlelight vigils in the cemetery until dawn. The holiday is most vibrantly celebrated in the highlands. November 1 and 2.

Puno Week, Puno. A major procession from the shores of the lake to the town stadium celebrates Manco Cápac, who, according to legend, rose from the waters of Lake Titicaca to establish the Incan Empire. Dances and music take over Puno, with events often taking a turn for the inebriated. Spectacular "Day of the Dead" celebrations coincide with Puno Week. First week of November.

December
Santuranticuy Fair, Cusco. One of the largest arts-and-crafts fairs in Peru—literally, "saints for sale"—is held in the Plaza de Armas. Artisans lay out blankets around the square, as in traditional Andean markets, and sell figurines and Nativity scenes as well as ceramics, carvings, pottery, and *retablos* (altars). Vendors sell hot rum punch called *ponche.* December 24.

6 Travel Insurance

The cost of travel insurance varies widely, depending on the cost and length of your trip, your age and health, and the type of trip you're taking, but expect to pay between 5% and 8% of the vacation itself. You can get estimates from various providers through **http://InsureMyTrip. com.** Enter your trip cost and dates, your age, and other information, for prices from more than a dozen companies.

TRIP-CANCELLATION INSUR-ANCE Trip-cancellation insurance will help retrieve your money if you have to back out of a trip or depart early, or if your travel supplier goes bankrupt.

Permissible reasons for trip cancellation can range from sickness to natural disasters to the State Department declaring a destination unsafe for travel.

For more information, contact one of the following recommended insurers: **Access America** (© 866/807-3982; www.accessamerica.com); **Travel Guard International** (© 800/826-4919; www. travelguard.com); **Travel Insured International** (© 800/243-3174; www. travelinsured.com); and **Travelex Insurance Services** (© 888/457-4602; www. travelex-insurance.com).

⌜Tips⌝ Medical Insurance Warning

Under U.S. law, insurance companies are not required to cover any medical expenses incurred in countries on the U.S. State Department's Travel Advisory List, even if their policies indicate that they will cover out-of-country medical expenses. Some supplemental carriers (such as the ones listed in this chapter) will sell travelers coverage for these areas. You can view the Travel Advisory List on the State Department's website at **http://travel.state.gov**. Peru (or specific regions in the country) has appeared on this list in the recent past.

MEDICAL INSURANCE For travel overseas, most U.S. health plans (including Medicare and Medicaid) do not provide coverage, and the ones that do often require you to pay for services upfront and reimburse you only after you return home. As a safety net, you may want to buy travel medical insurance, particularly if you're traveling to a remote or high-risk area where emergency evacuation might be necessary. If you require additional medical insurance, try **MEDEX Assistance** (✆ 410/453-6300; www.medexassist.com) or **Travel Assistance International** (✆ 800/821-2828; www.travelassistance.com; for general information on services, call the company's Worldwide Assistance Services, Inc., at ✆ **800/777-8710**).

LOST-LUGGAGE INSURANCE On flights within the U.S., checked baggage is covered up to $2,500 per ticketed passenger. On international flights (including U.S. portions of international trips), baggage coverage is limited to approximately $9.07 per pound, up to approximately $635 per checked bag. If you plan to check items more valuable than what's covered by the standard liability, see if your homeowner's policy covers your valuables, get baggage insurance as part of your comprehensive travel-insurance package, or buy Travel Guard's "BagTrak" product.

If your luggage is lost, immediately file a lost-luggage claim at the airport, detailing the luggage contents. Most airlines require that you report delayed, damaged, or lost baggage within 4 hours of arrival. The airlines are required to deliver luggage, once found, directly to your house or destination free of charge.

7 Health & Safety

STAYING HEALTHY

Contact the **International Association for Medical Assistance to Travelers (IAMAT;** ✆ **716/754-4883** or, in Canada, 416/652-0137; www.iamat.org) for tips on travel and health concerns, and for lists of local, English-speaking doctors. The United States **Centers for Disease Control and Prevention** (✆ **800/311-3435;** www.cdc.gov) provides up-to-date information on health hazards by region or country and offers tips on food safety. The website **www.tripprep.com**, sponsored by a consortium of travel medicine practitioners, may also offer helpful advice on traveling abroad. You can find listings of reliable clinics overseas at the **International Society of Travel Medicine** (www.istm.org).

No vaccinations are officially required of travelers to Peru, but you are wise to take certain precautions, especially if you are planning to travel to jungle regions.

A yellow-fever vaccine is strongly recommended for trips to the Amazon.

Peruvian authorities confirmed an outbreak of yellow fever in the northeastern Department of Amazona in December 2005. The Pan American Health Organization reported an outbreak and 52 total cases of yellow fever in Peru during the first 6 months of 2004, with slightly more than half of those resulting in death. (However, just two of those occurred in areas covered in this chapter, Loreto and Madre de Dios.)

The **Centers for Disease Control and Prevention** (© **800/311-3435;** www.cdc.gov) warn that there is a risk of malaria and yellow fever in all areas except Arequipa, Moquegua, Puno, and Tacna, although Lima and the highland tourist areas (Cusco, Machu Picchu, and Lake Titicaca) are not at risk.

In the airport at Puerto Maldonado, in the southern jungle, public nurses are usually on hand to administer yellow-fever shots to travelers who have not received the vaccination. Carry your vaccination records with you if you are traveling to the jungle. The Centers for Disease Control and Prevention also recommend taking antimalarial drugs at least 1 week before arriving in the jungle, during your stay there, and for at least 4 weeks afterward.

The CDC also recommends vaccines for hepatitis A and B and typhoid, as well as booster doses for tetanus, diphtheria, and measles, although you might want to weigh your potential exposure before getting all these shots. For additional information on travel to tropical South America, including World Health Organization news of disease outbreaks in particular areas, see the CDC website at www.cdc.gov/travel/tropsam.htm. Also of interest is the WHO's informational page on Peru, www.who.int/countries/per/en.

MEDICAL ATTENTION

Prescriptions can be filled at *farmacias* and *boticas;* it's best to know the generic name of your drug. For most health matters that are not serious, a pharmacist will be able to help and prescribe something. In the case of more serious health issues, contact your hotel, the tourist information office, or, in the most extreme case, your consulate or embassy for a doctor referral. Hospitals with English-speaking doctors are listed in individual destination chapters.

It's wise to get all vaccinations and obtain malarial pills before arriving in Peru, but if you decide at the last minute to go to the jungle and need to get a vaccine in the country, you can go to the following **Oficinas de Vacunación** in Lima: Av. del Ejército 1756, San Isidro (© **01/264-6889**); Jorge Chávez International Airport, second floor; and the International Vaccination Center, Dos de Mayo National Hospital, Av. Grau, block 13.

COMMON AILMENTS

As a tropical South American country, Peru presents certain health risks and concerns, but major concerns are limited to those traveling outside urban areas and to the Amazon jungle. The most common ailments for visitors to Peru are common traveler's diarrhea and altitude sickness, or **acute mountain sickness (AMS),** called *soroche* locally.

ALTITUDE SICKNESS   Cusco sits at an elevation of about 3,400m (11,000 ft.), and Lake Titicaca sits at 3,830m (12,566 ft.). At these altitudes, shortness of breath and heart pounding are normal, given the paucity of oxygen. Some people experience intense headaches, loss of appetite, extreme fatigue, and nausea. Most symptoms develop the first day at high altitude, although occasionally travelers have delayed reactions. The best advice is to rest on your first day in the highlands. Drink plenty of liquids, including the local remedy *mate de coca,* or coca-leaf tea. (Coca, as opposed to cocaine, is a mild sedative, and it's perfectly legal to consume coca tea or chew coca leaves in Peru, though it's not legal to bring back coca leaves.) Avoid alcohol and heavy food intake. Give yourself at least a day or two to acclimatize before launching into strenuous activities. Many hotels in Cusco offer oxygen for those severely affected with headaches and shortness of breath. If symptoms persist or become more severe, seek medical attention. People with heart or lung problems and persons with the sickle cell trait could develop serious health complications at high altitudes, or even die from medical conditions exacerbated by high altitude.

SUN EXPOSURE   Limit your exposure to the sun, especially during the first few days of your trip and at high altitudes, from 11am to 2pm. Even though it can be chilly or cold in the Andes, the sun is a killer (the higher the altitude and thinner the air, the more dangerous the sun's harmful rays are). Along Peru's desert coast, the sun is also extremely potent and likely to burn visitors who don't take adequate precautions. Wear a hat and use a sunscreen with a high protection factor (SPF 30 or higher), and apply it liberally. Remember that children require more protection than do adults. Heat exhaustion and heat stroke are serious maladies and are not difficult to get if you don't take proper precautions in Peru.

DIETARY DISTRESS   Visitors should drink only bottled water, which is widely available. Do not drink tap water, even in major hotels, and try to avoid drinks with ice. If you're trekking in the mountains or visiting remote rural areas where bottled water is not available, boil water to purify it or use water-purification tablets. Carry bottled water with you at all times (especially on long bus or train rides); the heat of the desert and the high altitudes of the Andes will dehydrate you very quickly.

You're safer eating fruits that you can peel or salads and fruits washed with purified water, as well as foods that have been thoroughly cooked. Shellfish should be avoided by most; although ceviche is one of Peru's classic dishes, travelers should at least know that the fish and shellfish in it are not cooked, but marinated. That said, many, if not most, travelers eat it with few or no problems. (Your best bet is to eat ceviche only at clean, upscale places.) Vegetarian restaurants can be found in most cities (look for branches of the chain Govinda in the largest cities). If no vegetarian restaurant is available, most others will be able to accommodate you with salads, fruits, and vegetables such as *papas* (potatoes) and *palta* (avocado), although *palta rellena* is usually stuffed with chicken or tuna.

WHAT TO DO IF YOU GET SICK AWAY FROM HOME

Any foreign consulate can provide a list of area doctors who speak English. If you get sick, consider asking your hotel concierge to recommend a local doctor—even his or her own. You can also try the emergency room at a local hospital. Many hospitals also have walk-in clinics for emergency cases that are not life-threatening; you may not get immediate attention, but you won't pay the high price of an emergency room visit. Hospitals and emergency numbers are listed under "Fast Facts: Peru," p. 73.

If you suffer from a chronic illness, consult your doctor before your departure. Pack **prescription medications** in your carry-on luggage, and carry prescription medications in their original containers, with pharmacy labels—otherwise they won't make it through airport security. Also carry copies of your prescriptions in case you lose your pills or run out. Don't forget an extra pair of contact lenses or prescription glasses. Carry the generic name of prescription medicines, in case a local pharmacist is unfamiliar with the brand name.

For travel abroad, you may have to pay all medical costs upfront and be reimbursed later. See "Medical Insurance," under "Travel Insurance," above.

STAYING SAFE

Peru has not earned a great reputation for safety among travelers, although the situation is no longer as dangerous as during the violent crime wave and terrorist threats of the late 1980s and early 1990s. Personal safety is an issue to be taken extremely seriously in most large Peruvian cities, especially Lima, Cusco, Arequipa, and Huaraz. Simple theft and pickpocketing are fairly common; most thieves look for moments when travelers, laden with bags and struggling with maps, are distracted. Assaults and robbery are rarer, but have been reported in many cities. In most heavily touristed places in Peru, a heightened police presence is noticeable, however.

Although most visitors travel freely throughout Peru without incident, warnings must be heeded seriously. In downtown Lima and the city's residential and hotel areas, the risk of street crime, including theft and muggings, remains high. Carjackings, assaults, and armed robberies are not unheard of in Lima. Occasional armed attacks at automatic teller machines occur. Be especially vigilant at Lima's international airport, where a number of robberies and attacks have been reported. Street crime is prevalent in Cusco, Arequipa, and Puno, and pickpockets are known to patrol public markets. In Cusco, "strangle" muggings (in which victims are choked unconscious and then relieved of all belongings) were reported in recent years, particularly on the streets leading off the Plaza de Armas, in the San Blas neighborhood, and near the train station. You should still not walk alone late at night on deserted streets. There were at least three reports of rape in Cusco in 2005, one by a gang. In rural areas outside Cusco, trekkers should travel in groups. A group of hikers along the Inca Trail was attacked and robbed as recently as November 2005.

In major cities, taxis hailed on the street can lead to assaults—I highly recommend using telephone-dispatched radio taxis, especially at night. Ask your hotel or restaurant to call a cab, or call one yourself from the list of recommended taxi companies in the individual city chapters.

Travelers should exercise extreme caution on public city transportation, where pickpockets are rife, and on long-distance buses and trains (especially at night), where thieves employ any number of strategies to relieve passengers of their bags. You need to be supremely vigilant, even to the extreme of locking your backpack and suitcases to luggage racks. Be extremely careful in all train and bus stations. Several provincial and inter-city buses and *combis* traveling from cities to villages have also been attacked and passengers robbed.

In general, do not wear expensive jewelry, keep expensive camera equipment out of view as much as possible, and use

---

Tips Discrimination in Peru

In Peru's larger cities, including Lima and Arequipa, Afro-Peruvians and Amerindian populations occupy the bottom rung of the economic ladder, and they are frequently blamed by the white population for much of the cities' crime. That perception can be consciously or subconsciously directed at travelers of color, who might experience some discrimination, most often expressed in less-than-welcoming receptions at hotels or restaurants. A number of nightclubs in Lima maintain unofficial discriminatory admissions policies.

a money belt inside your pants or shirt to safeguard cash, credit cards, and passport. Wear your daypack on your chest rather than your back when walking in crowded areas. The time to be most careful is when you have most of your belongings on your person—for example, when going from airport or train or bus station to your hotel. At airports, it's best to spend a little more for official airport taxis; if in doubt, request the driver's official ID. Don't venture beyond airport grounds for a street taxi. Have your hotel call a taxi for your trip to the airport or bus station.

Report any criminal activity to the nearest police station or tourism police office; contact information is listed in the "Fast Facts" section in individual destination chapters.

In addition to safety and health concerns, travelers planning a trip to Peru should keep a close watch on current events. Although the large-scale terrorist activities of the local groups Sendero Luminoso and MRTA were largely stamped out in the early 1990s, the U.S. State Department reported a resurfacing of the long-dormant Maoist terrorist network Sendero Luminoso in remote parts of the central highlands in late 2001. In March 2002, a radical offshoot of the Sendero Luminoso was blamed for a car bomb attack that killed 10 near the U.S. embassy in Lima. Two more isolated attacks in 2003 were attributed to Sendero Luminoso. Neither group, however, is currently considered to be active in any of the areas covered in this book. Peru's political situation remains a bit tenuous, especially after strikes by farmers and teachers in the last couple of years and possible instability related to the 2006 presidential election. However, at present, stability concerns should not deter anyone from traveling to the country. Before you depart, check for travel advisories for your home country.

ECOTOURISM

The **International Ecotourism Society (TIES)** defines ecotourism as "responsible travel to natural areas that conserves the environment and improves the well-being of local people." You can find eco-friendly travel tips, statistics, and touring companies and associations—listed by destination under "Travel Choice"—at the TIES website, www.ecotourism.org. **Ecotravel.com** is part online magazine and part ecodirectory that lets you search for touring companies in several categories (water-based, land-based, spiritually oriented, and so on). Also check out **Conservation International** (www.conservation.org)—which, with *National Geographic Traveler*, annually presents **World Legacy Awards** (www.wlaward.org) to those travel tour operators, businesses, organizations, and places that have made a significant contribution to sustainable tourism.

Peru is an ecotourism paradise, and many of the companies organizing good, sustainable travel initiatives can be found in chapter 4, "The Active Vacation Planner."

8 Specialized Travel Resources

TRAVELERS WITH DISABILITIES

Most disabilities shouldn't stop anyone from traveling. However, Peru is considerably less equipped for accessible travel than are most parts of North America and Europe. Comparatively few hotels are outfitted for travelers with disabilities, and only a smattering of restaurants, museums, and means of public transportation makes special accommodations for such patrons. There are few ramps, very few wheelchair-accessible bathrooms, and almost no telephones for the hearing impaired. Representatives of Peru's National Tourism Ministry were present at a recent Society for Accessible Travel and Hospitality conference; Peru was the only country in South America that attended, indicating its willingness to make its travel offerings more attractive to travelers with disabilities.

Request a copy of "Tourism for the People with Disabilities: The First Evaluation of Accessibility to Peru's Tourist Infrastructure," from the Peruvian embassy in your home country, before your visit to Peru. The 99-page report features evaluations of hotels, restaurants, museums, attractions, airports, and other services in Lima, Cusco, Aguas Calientes, Iquitos, and Trujillo. For additional information on Peru's access for travelers with disabilities, see **www.disability world.org/Aug-Sept2000/International/ peru.htm**.

One Peruvian hotel chain, **Posadas del Inca** (www.sonesta.com), stands out in a country where few places are equipped for accessible travel. With properties in Lima, Cusco, Yucay, and Puno, it maintains rooms that are accessible for travelers with disabilities in every hotel. See individual destination chapters for full reviews.

Many travel agencies offer customized tours and itineraries for travelers with disabilities. **Apumayo Expediciones** (℃ **054/246-018**; www.apumayo.com) is way out in front in Peru, offering tours specifically designed for travelers with physical disabilities. **Accessible Journeys** (℃ **800/846-4537** or 610/521-0339; www.disabilitytravel.com) caters specifically to slow walkers and wheelchair travelers and their families and friends; th organization offers a 10-day "Peru Explorer" trip to Lima, Paracas, Cusco, the Sacred Valley, and Machu Picchu. **InkaNatura Travel** (www.inkanatura. com) is also particularly well equipped to deal with travelers with disabilities: Beyond the website's specifics on Peru, it is an excellent resource with all kinds of general information and answers to frequently asked questions about traveling with disabilities.

A helpful website for accessible travel in Peru is **Access-Able Travel Source** (www.access-able.com), which offers detailed destination articles on accessible travel in Peru and a wealth of specific information about Aguas Calientes, Chiclayo, Cusco, Huanchaco, Iquitos, Lima, the Chicama and Moche valleys, Pisac, Trujillo, and Yucay. Within individual reviews, you'll find information on ramps, door sizes, room sizes, bathrooms, and wheelchair availability.

Avis Rent a Car has an "Avis Access" program that offers such services as a dedicated 24-hour toll-free number (℃ **888/879-4273**) for customers with special travel needs; special car features such as swivel seats, spinner knobs, and hand controls; and accessible bus service.

Organizations that offer assistance to travelers with disabilities include **Moss-Rehab** (www.mossresourcenet.org); the **American Foundation for the Blind** (AFB; ℃ **800/232-5463**; www.afb.org); and **SATH** (Society for Accessible Travel & Hospitality; ℃ **212/447-7284;** www. sath.org). **AirAmbulanceCard.com** is now partnered with SATH and allows you to preselect top-notch hospitals in case of an emergency.

The community website **iCan** (www. icanonline.net/channels/travel) has destination guides and several regular columns on accessible travel. Also check out the quarterly magazine *Emerging Horizons* (www.emerginghorizons.com), and *Open World* magazine, published by SATH.

GAY & LESBIAN TRAVELERS

Although the Incan nation flag looks remarkably similar to the gay rainbow flag, Peru, a predominantly Catholic and socially conservative country, could not be considered among the world's most progressive in terms of societal freedoms for gays and lesbians. It is still a male-dominated, macho society where homosexuality is considered deviant. Across

Peru, there is still considerable prejudice exhibited toward gays and lesbians who are out, or men—be they straight or gay—who are thought to be effeminate. *Maricón* (fag) is a commonly used derogatory term.

In the larger cities, especially Lima and Cusco, there are a number of establishments—bars, discos, inns, and restaurants—that are either gay-friendly or predominantly gay. Outside those areas, and in the small towns and villages of rural Peru, openly gay behavior is unlikely to be tolerated by the general population.

There are a number of helpful websites for gay and lesbian travelers to Peru. **Gay Peru** (www.gayperu.com) includes gay-oriented package tours, news items, and nightclubs and hotels (with versions in both English and Spanish). **Purple Roofs** (www.purpleroofs.com) has a decent listing of gay and lesbian lodgings, restaurants, and nightclubs throughout Peru. **Gay Lima** (http://gaylimape.tripod.com) covers Lima and other parts of Peru, with English-language information on nightclubs and gay-friendly establishments and activities. There's a version of the website in English. **deCajon.com** (www.decajon.com), which lists events, restaurants, and bars, has a special category of gay establishments. If you can read Spanish, **deambiente.com** (www.deambiente.com) also has a detailed listings and articles about gay life in Peru. **GlobalGayz** (www.globalgayz.com) includes a very interesting article on gay life in Peru. Among other things, it details the former Fujimori government's dismissal of homosexual diplomats and other public servants.

Gay.com Travel (© 800/929-2268 or 415/644-8044; www.gay.com/travel or www.outandabout.com), is an excellent online successor to the popular *Out & About* print magazine. It provides regularly updated information about gay-owned, gay-oriented, and gay-friendly lodging, dining, sightseeing, nightlife, and shopping establishments.

SENIOR TRAVEL

Peru as a nation greatly respects the contributions and wisdom of society's elders, but that consideration doesn't necessarily translate into automatic deferential treatment of senior tourists. Discounts for seniors are not automatic across Peru. Still, you should mention the fact that you're a senior when you first make your travel reservations; although almost all airlines have cancelled their senior discount and coupon book programs, many hotels still offer lower rates for seniors.

Members of **AARP** (formerly known as the American Association of Retired Persons), 601 E St. NW, Washington, DC 20049 (© 888/687-2277; www.aarp.org), get discounts on hotels, airfares, and car rentals. AARP offers members a wide range of benefits, including *AARP: The Magazine* and a monthly newsletter. Anyone over 50 can join.

Many reliable agencies and organizations target the 50-plus market. **Elderhostel** (© 877/426-8056; www.elderhostel.org) arranges study programs for people 55 and over (and a spouse or companion of any age) in more than 80 countries, including Peru. Most courses last 2 to 4 weeks, and many include airfare, accommodations in university dormitories or modest inns, meals, and tuition. **ElderTreks** (© 800/741-7956; www.eldertreks.com) offers small-group tours to off-the-beaten-path or adventure-travel locations, restricted to travelers 50 and older; it currently offers a 19-day trip to Peru and Bolivia.

Recommended publications offering travel resources and discounts for seniors include the quarterly magazine *Travel 50 & Beyond* (www.travel50andbeyond.com); *Travel Unlimited: Uncommon Adventures for the Mature Traveler*

(Avalon); and *101 Tips for Mature Travelers,* available from Grand Circle Travel (© **800/221-2610** or 617/350-7500; www.gct.com).

FAMILY TRAVEL

If you have enough trouble getting your kids out of the house in the morning, dragging them thousands of miles away might seem like an insurmountable challenge. But family travel can be immensely rewarding, giving you new ways of seeing the world through smaller pairs of eyes.

Peruvians are extremely family-oriented, and children arouse friendly interest in locals. Although there aren't many established conventions, accommodations, or discounts for families traveling with children, Peru can be an excellent country in which to travel, as long as families remain flexible and are able to surmount difficulties in transportation, food, and accommodations.

Few hotels automatically offer discounts for children or allow children to stay free with their parents. Negotiation with hotels is required. On buses, children have to pay full fare if they occupy a seat (which is why you'll see most kids sitting on their parent's or sibling's lap). Many museums and other attractions offer discounts for children under 6. Children's meals are rarely found at restaurants in Peru, but sometimes it's possible to specially order smaller portions. Peruvian food might be very foreign to many children—how many kids, or adults, for that matter, will be keen on tasting roasted guinea pig?—but familiar foods, such as fried chicken, pizza, and spaghetti, are easy to find in almost all Peruvian towns. Throughout this guide, look for the icons designating kid-friendly attractions, hotels, and restaurants.

Familyhostel (© **800/733-9753**; www.learn.unh.edu/familyhostel) takes the whole family, including kids 8 to 15, on moderately priced domestic and international learning vacations. Lectures, field trips, and sightseeing are guided by a team of academics.

Recommended family travel websites include **Family Travel Forum** (www.familytravelforum.com); **Family Travel Network** (www.familytravelnetwork.com); **Traveling Internationally with Your Kids** (www.travelwithyourkids.com); and **Family Travel Files** (www.the familytravelfiles.com).

WOMEN TRAVELERS

Peru continues to be a very macho, male-dominated society. Although women are a growing part of the professional workforce and a relatively recent feminist movement is evident in urban areas, women do not yet occupy the (still unequal) position they do in many Western societies. Still, women should not encounter any insurmountable difficulties traveling in Peru.

However, women should not be surprised to encounter perhaps unwelcome attention from men, especially if traveling alone. Many Peruvian men consider *gringas*—essentially, any foreign women—to be more sexually open than Peruvian women; thus, foreigners are frequently the targets of their advances. Blonde women are frequently singled out. *Piropos,* come-ons that are usually meant as innocuous compliments rather than as crude assessments of a woman's physical attractiveness or sexuality, are common in Latin America. However, comments can occasionally be crude and demeaning, and groping is not unheard of in public places (such as on crowded buses). Sexual assaults are rare, but the threat felt by some women, especially if they do not comprehend the Spanish slang employed in come-ons, is understandable.

Many men, as well as Peruvian women, might be curious about why a woman isn't married or traveling with a boyfriend. A woman traveling alone could elicit comments of sympathy or even pity. Wearing a ring on your wedding finger and deflecting comments and advances with a story about your husband working in Lima and meeting you in 2 days (or something to that effect) could be a useful tactic. In general, the problem is much more pronounced in large cities than in small towns and the countryside. Amerindian populations are conservative and even shy in dealing with foreigners, including women.

Women on the receiving end of cat-calls and aggressive come-ons should do what Peruvian women do: Ignore them. If that doesn't succeed, contact the tourist police (offices are listed in the "Fast Facts" section of individual destination chapters). Although some Peruvian men might be innocently interested in meeting a foreign woman, it is not a good idea to accept an invitation to go anywhere alone with a man.

Women traveling in a group with other females, or especially with a man, are less likely to attract unwanted attention from men. Although I would hesitate to tell a woman friend that she should not travel alone in Peru, traveling with even one other woman might feel like a safer situation for many women, at least psychologically. If you are traveling alone, never walk alone at night anywhere—always call for a registered taxi. It's also a good idea to have a whistle handy; a piercing sound blast will deter almost any aggressor.

Check out the award-winning website **Journeywoman** (www.journeywoman. com), a "real life" women's travel-information network where you can sign up for a free e-mail newsletter and get advice on everything from etiquette and dress to safety; or the travel guide *Safety and Security for Women Who Travel* by Sheila Swan and Peter Laufer (Travelers' Tales, Inc.), offering common-sense tips on safe travel.

STUDENT TRAVEL

If you're traveling internationally, you'd be wise to arm yourself with an **International Student Identity Card (ISIC)**, which offers substantial savings on rail passes, plane tickets, and entrance fees. It also provides you with basic health and life insurance and a 24-hour help line. The card is available from **STA Travel** (© **800/781-4040** in North America; www.sta.com or www.statravel. com; or www.statravel.co.uk in the U.K.), the biggest student travel agency in the world. If you're no longer a student but are still under 26, you can get an **International Youth Travel Card (IYTC)** from the same people, which entitles you to some discounts (but not on museum admissions). **Travel CUTS** (© **800/667-2887** or 416/614-2887; www.travelcuts.com) offers similar services for both Canadians and U.S. residents. Irish students may prefer to turn to **USIT** (© **01/602-1600;** www. usitnow.ie), an Ireland-based specialist in student, youth, and independent travel.

SINGLE TRAVELERS

Many reputable tour companies offer singles-only trips. **Singles Travel International** (© **877/765-6874;** www.singles travelintl.com) offers singles-only trips to places like London, Fiji, and the Greek Islands. **Backroads** (© **800/462-2848;** www.backroads.com) offers more than 160 active-travel trips to 30 destinations worldwide, including Bali, Morocco, and Costa Rica.

For more information, check out Eleanor Berman's latest edition of *Traveling Solo: Advice and Ideas for More Than 250 Great Vacations* (Globe Pequot), a guide with advice on traveling alone, either solo or as part of a group tour. (It has been updated for 2005.)

9 Planning Your Trip Online

SURFING FOR AIRFARES

The most popular online travel agencies are **Travelocity** (**www.travelocity.com**, or www.travelocity.co.uk); **Expedia** (**www.expedia.com**, www.expedia.co.uk, or www.expedia.ca); and **Orbitz** (www.orbitz.com).

In addition, most airlines now offer online-only fares that even their phone agents know nothing about. For the websites of airlines that fly to and from your destination, go to "Getting There," p. 52.

Other helpful websites for booking airline tickets online include:

- www.biddingfortravel.com
- www.cheapflights.com
- www.hotwire.com
- www.kayak.com
- www.lastminutetravel.com
- www.opodo.co.uk
- www.priceline.com
- www.sidestep.com
- www.site59.com
- www.smartertravel.com

SURFING FOR HOTELS

In addition to **Travelocity, Expedia, Orbitz, Priceline,** and **Hotwire** (see above), the following websites will help you with booking hotel rooms online:

- www.hotels.com
- www.quickbook.com
- www.travelaxe.net
- www.travelweb.com
- www.tripadvisor.com

It's a good idea to **get a confirmation number** and **make a printout** of any online booking transaction. Remember to check individual **hotel websites** for deals, as well as **Peru-based brokers and discounters** such as www.peruhotel.com, www.perudiscover.com, www.hotelsperu.com, www.enjoyperu.com, and www.peru-hotels.com.

SURFING FOR RENTAL CARS

For booking rental cars online, the best deals are usually found at rental-car company websites, although all the major online travel agencies also offer rental-car reservations services. Priceline and Hotwire work well for rental cars, too; the only "mystery" is which major rental company you get; for most travelers, the difference among Hertz, Avis, and Budget is negligible.

TRAVEL BLOGS & TRAVELOGUES

More and more travelers are using travel web logs, or **blogs,** to chronicle their journeys online. Search for blogs about Peru at **www.travelblog.com** or post your own travelogue at **www.travelblog.org**. For blogs that cover general travel news and highlight various destinations, try **www.writtenroad.com** or Gawker Media's snarky **www.gridskipper.com**. For more literary travel essays, try Salon.com's travel section (**www.salon.com/wanderlust**), and **www.worldhum.com**, which also has an extensive list of other travel-related journals, blogs, online communities, newspaper coverage, and bookstores.

10 The 21st-Century Traveler

INTERNET ACCESS AWAY FROM HOME

WITHOUT YOUR OWN COMPUTER

In Peru, by far the easiest way to check your e-mail and surf the Web is to drop in at the Internet *cabinas* (booths) that can be found in virtually every city and even small town. Connections are usually fast, and the service is as little as 20¢ per hour. Many Internet cabinas are starting to feature software programs such as Net2Phone, which allows you to call abroad through the Internet for ridiculously low prices.

Online Traveler's Toolbox

Veteran travelers usually carry some essential items to make their trips easier. Following is a selection of online tools to bookmark and use:

- **Airplane Seating** and **Food.** Find out which seats to reserve and which to avoid (and more) on all major domestic airlines at www.seatguru.com. And check out the type of meal (with photos) you'll likely be served on airlines around the world at www.airlinemeals.net.
- **Foreign Languages for Travelers** (www.travlang.com). Learn basic terms in more than 70 languages, and click on any underlined phrase to hear what it sounds like.
- **Intellicast** (www.intellicast.com) and **Weather.com** (www.weather.com). Get weather forecasts for all 50 states and for cities around the world.
- **Travel Warnings** (http://travel.state.gov, www.fco.gov.uk/travel, www.voyage.gc.ca, www.dfat.gov.au/consular/advice). These sites report on places where health concerns or unrest might threaten American, British, Canadian, and Australian travelers. Generally, U.S. warnings are the most paranoid; Australian warnings are the most relaxed.
- **Universal Currency Converter** (www.xe.com/ucc). See what your dollar or pound is worth in more than 100 other countries.
- **Visa ATM Locator** (www.visa.com) for locations of PLUS ATMs worldwide, or **MasterCard ATM Locator** (www.mastercard.com) for locations of Cirrus ATMs worldwide.

(Connections, however, aren't always perfect.) Although there's no definitive directory for cybercafes, two places to start looking are **www.cybercaptive.com** and **www.cybercafe.com**. I've also included specific recommendations in the "Fast Facts" section of every destination.

Aside from formal cybercafes, most **youth hostels** nowadays have at least one computer with Internet access. In Peru, many **nightclubs** and **bars** offer Web hookups. Avoid **hotel business centers,** unless you're willing to pay exorbitant rates.

Most major airports now have **Internet kiosks** scattered throughout their gates. These kiosks, which you'll also see in shopping malls, hotel lobbies, and tourist information offices around the world, give you basic Web access for a per-minute fee that's usually higher than cybercafe prices. The kiosks' clunkiness

and high price means they should be avoided whenever possible.

WITH YOUR OWN COMPUTER

For dial-up access, most business-class hotels throughout Peru offer dataports for laptop modems. You can bring your own cables and adapters, but most hotels rent them for around $10. **Call your hotel in advance** to see what your options are.

In addition, major Internet Service Providers (ISPs) have **local access numbers** around the world, allowing you to go online by placing a local call. Check your ISP's website or call its toll-free number and ask how you can use your current account away from home, and how much it will cost.

The **iPass** network also has dial-up numbers around the world. You'll have to sign up with an iPass provider, who will then tell you how to set up your computer for your destination(s). For a list of iPass providers, go to www.ipass.com and click on "Individuals Buy Now." One solid provider is **i2roam** (www.i2roam.com; ℰ **866/811-6209** or 920/235-0475).

USING A CELLPHONE

The three letters that define much of the world's wireless capabilities are GSM (Global System for Mobiles), a big, seamless network that makes for easy cross-border cellphone use throughout Europe and dozens of other countries worldwide. In the U.S., T-Mobile, AT&T Wireless, and Cingular use this quasi-universal system; in Canada, Microcell and some Rogers customers are GSM, and all Europeans and most Australians use GSM. If your cellphone is on a GSM system, and you have a world-capable multiband phone such as many Sony Ericsson, Motorola, or Samsung models, you can make and receive calls across civilized areas around much of the globe. Just call your wireless operator and ask for "international roaming" to be activated on your account. Unfortunately, per-minute charges can be high—usually $1 to $1.50 in Western Europe and up to $5 in places like Russia and Indonesia.

For many, **renting** a phone is a good idea. (Even worldphone owners will have to rent new phones if they're traveling to non-GSM regions, such as Japan or Korea.) While you can rent a phone from any number of overseas sites, including

kiosks at airports and at car-rental agencies, we suggest renting the phone before you leave home. North Americans can rent one before leaving home from **InTouch USA** (ℰ 800/872-7626; www.intouch global.com) or **RoadPost** (ℰ 888/290-1606 or 905/272-5665; www.roadpost. com). InTouch will also, for free, advise you on whether your existing phone will work overseas; simply call ℰ **703/222-7161** between 9am and 4pm EST, or go to **http://intouchglobal.com/travel.htm**.

Buying a phone can be economically attractive, as many nations have cheap prepaid phone systems. Once you arrive at your destination, stop by a local cellphone shop and get the cheapest package; you'll probably pay less than $100 for a phone and a starter calling card. Local calls may be as low as 10¢ per minute, and in many countries incoming calls are free.

Wilderness adventurers, or those heading to less-developed countries, might consider renting a **satellite phone ("satphone")**. It's different from a cellphone in that it connects to satellites and works where there's no cellular signal or ground-based tower. You can rent satellite phones from RoadPost (see above). InTouch USA (see above) offers a wider range of satphones but at higher rates. Per-minute call charges can be even cheaper than roaming charges with a regular cellphone, but the phone itself is more expensive. As of this writing, satphones were outrageously expensive to buy, so don't even think about it.

11 Getting There

BY BUS

You can travel overland to Peru through Ecuador, Bolivia, or Chile. Although the journey isn't short, Lima can be reached from major neighboring cities. If traveling from Quito or Guayaquil, you'll pass through the major northern coastal cities on the way to Lima. From Bolivia, there

is frequent service from La Paz and Copacabana to Puno and then on to Cusco. From Chile, most buses travel from Arica to Tacna, making connections to either Arequipa or Lima.

BY PLANE

All overseas flights from North America and Europe arrive at Lima's **Jorge Chávez**

International Airport (✆ 01/517-3502; www.lap.com.pe). International flights to Iquitos in the northern Amazon region might be resumed at some point in the near future, perhaps from Miami, but it is only a possibility at this point.

In Peru, it is very important to reconfirm airline tickets in advance. For local flights, reconfirm 48 hours in advance; for international flights, reconfirm 72 hours before traveling. The airport tax on domestic flights is $5.04, and $28.24 on international flights. The tax must be paid—in cash only—before boarding.

FROM NORTH AMERICA From the United States, there are direct flights to Lima from Miami, the main hub for Latin America, as well as New York, Newark, Houston, Dallas, and Atlanta. The major carriers are **American** (through Dallas or Miami, with infrequent nonstops from New York; ✆ 800/433-7300; www.aa.com), **Delta** (Atlanta; ✆ 800/241-4141; www.delta.com), **Continental** (Houston and Newark; ✆ 800/231-0856; www.continental.com), and **LAN,** with direct overnight flights from New York and Miami (LanChile/LanPeru; ✆ **866/435-9526;** www.lan.com).

Continental has probably the most comprehensive service to Lima, with daily nonstops from Newark and Houston. Often the lowest fares from the United States are with **LAN. American** also occasionally features very good deals on airfares to Lima from the United States.

From Canada, American, Continental, and Delta all fly to Peru, making stops at their hubs in the United States first. **Air Canada** (✆ **888/247-2262;** www.air-canada.ca) makes connections with other carriers at U.S. stops, usually Miami. **LAN** (✆ **866/435-9526**) uses other carriers to the United States, making stops in New York, Miami, or Los Angeles on the way to Lima. (For example, you can purchase a LAN ticket from Canada to Peru, with a layover in the U.S., but you will fly a partner airline to the U.S. and then change to a LAN airliner for travel on to Peru.)

FROM THE U.K. There are no direct flights to Lima from London or any other part of the United Kingdom or Ireland; getting to Peru involves a layover in either another part of Europe or the United States. **American** (✆ 207/365-0777 in London, or 0845/778-9789), **Continental** (✆ 0845/607-6760), and **Delta** (✆ 845/600-0950) fly through their U.S. hubs on the way to Lima. European carriers make stops in continental Europe: Contact **Iberia** (through Madrid; ✆ 870/609-0500; www.iberia.com), **KLM** (Amsterdam; ✆ 08705/074-074; www.klm.com), or **Lufthansa** (✆ 0845/773-7747; www.lufthansa.com).

FROM AUSTRALIA & NEW ZEALAND From Australia and New Zealand, you can either fly to Buenos Aires on **Aerolíneas Argentinas** (✆ 02/9234-9000 in Australia or ✆09/379-3675 in New Zealand; www.aerolineas.com.au) and then connect to Lima, or go through Los Angeles (or Buenos Aires), with **Qantas** (✆ 13-13-13 in Australia or 800/808-767 in New Zealand; www.qantas.com) or **Air New Zealand** (✆ 0800/737-000; www.airnz.co.nz). **LAN** (✆ 300/361-400 in Australia and 9/977-2233 in New Zealand) also makes stops in Los Angeles on the way to Lima.

GETTING THROUGH THE AIRPORT

With the federalization of airport security, security procedures at U.S. airports are more stable and consistent than ever. Generally, you'll be fine if you arrive at the airport **1 hour** before a domestic flight and **2 hours** before an international flight; if you show up late, tell an airline employee and she'll probably whisk you to the front of the line.

Bring a **current, government-issued photo ID** such as a driver's license or passport. Keep your ID ready to show at check-in, the security checkpoint, and sometimes even the gate. (Children under 18 do not need photo IDs for domestic flights, but they do for international flights to most countries.)

In 2003, the TSA phased out **gate check-in** at all U.S. airports. Passengers with e-tickets, which have made paper tickets nearly obsolete, can beat the ticket-counter lines by using airport **electronic kiosks** or even **online check-in** from their home computers. Online check-in involves logging on to your airlines' website, accessing your reservation, and printing out your boarding pass—and the airline may even offer you bonus miles to do so! If you're using a kiosk at the airport, bring the credit card you used to book the ticket or your frequent-flier card. Print out your boarding pass from the kiosk and simply proceed to the security checkpoint with your pass and a photo ID. If you're checking bags or looking to snag an exit-row seat, you will be able to do so using most airline kiosks. Even the smaller airlines are employing the kiosk system, but always call your airline to make sure these alternatives are available. **Curbside check-in** is also a good way to avoid lines, although a few airlines still don't allow it; call for your airline's policy before you go.

Security checkpoint lines are getting shorter than they were during 2001 and 2002, but an orange alert, suspicious passenger, or high passenger volume can still make for a long wait. If you have trouble standing for long periods of time, tell an airline employee; the airline will provide a wheelchair. Speed up security by **not wearing metal objects** such as big belt buckles. If you've got metallic body parts, a note from your doctor can prevent a long chat with the security screeners. Keep in mind that only **ticketed passengers** are allowed past security, except for people escorting passengers with disabilities or children.

Federalization has stabilized **what you can carry on** and **what you can't.** The general rule is that sharp things are out, nail clippers are okay, and food and beverages must be passed through the X-ray machine—but that security screeners can't make you drink from your coffee cup. Bring food in your carry-on rather than checking it; explosive-detection machines used on checked luggage have been known to mistake food (especially chocolate, for some reason) for bombs. Travelers in the U.S. are allowed one carry-on bag, plus a "personal item" such as a purse, briefcase, or laptop bag. Carry-on hoarders can stuff all sorts of things into a laptop bag; as long as it has a laptop in it, it's still considered a personal item. The TSA has issued a list of restricted items; check the website (www.tsa.gov) for details.

Airport screeners might decide that your checked luggage needs to be searched by hand. You can now purchase luggage locks that allow screeners to open and relock a checked bag if hand-searching is necessary. Look for Travel Sentry certified locks at luggage or travel shops and Brookstone stores (you can buy them online at www.brookstone.com). These locks, approved by the TSA, can be opened by luggage inspectors with a special code or key. For more information on the locks, visit www.travelsentry.org. If you use something other than TSA-approved locks, your lock will be cut off your suitcase if a TSA agent needs to hand-search your luggage.

FLYING FOR LESS: TIPS FOR GETTING THE BEST AIRFARE

Passengers sharing the same airplane cabin rarely pay the same fare. Travelers who need to purchase tickets at the last minute, change their itinerary at a moment's notice, or fly one-way often get stuck paying the premium rate. Here are some ways to keep your airfare costs down:

- Passengers who can book their ticket **long in advance,** who can **stay over Saturday night,** or who **fly midweek** or **at less-trafficked hours** will pay a fraction of the full fare. If your schedule is flexible, say so, and ask if you can secure a cheaper fare by changing your flight plans.

- You can also save on airfares by keeping an eye out in local newspapers for **promotional specials** or **fare wars,** when airlines lower prices on their most popular routes. You rarely see fare wars offered for peak travel times, but if you can travel in the off-months, you might snag a bargain.

- Search **the Internet** for cheap fares (see "Planning Your Trip Online," earlier in this chapter).

- Try to book a ticket **in its country of origin.** For instance, if you're planning a one-way flight from Wellington to Cusco, a New Zealand–based travel agent will probably have the lowest fares. For multileg trips, book in the country of the first leg; for example, book London–New York–Miami–Lima in the U.K.

- **Consolidators,** also known as bucket shops, are great sources for international tickets, although they usually can't beat the Internet on fares within North America. Start by looking in Sunday newspaper travel sections; U.S. travelers should focus on the *New York Times, Los Angeles Times,* and *Miami Herald.* For less developed destinations, small travel agents who cater to immigrant communities in large cities often have the best deals. *Beware:*

Bucket shop tickets are usually nonrefundable or rigged with stiff cancellation penalties, often as high as 50% to 75% of the ticket price, and some put you on charter airlines with questionable safety records.

- Several reliable consolidators are worldwide and available on the Net. **STA Travel** is now the world's leader in student travel, thanks to its purchase of Council Travel. It also offers good fares for travelers of all ages. **ELTExpress** (aka Flights.com; © **800/TRAV-800;** www.eltexpress. com) started in Europe and has excellent fares worldwide, but particularly to that continent. It also has "local" websites in 12 countries. **FlyCheap** (© **800/FLY-CHEAP;** www.1800 flycheap.com) is owned by package-holiday megalith MyTravel and so has especially good access to fares for sunny destinations. **Air Tickets Direct** (© **800/778-3447;** www.air ticketsdirect.com) is based in Montreal and leverages the currently weak Canadian dollar for low fares; it'll also book trips to places that U.S. travel agents won't touch, such as Cuba.

- Join **frequent-flier clubs.** Accrue enough miles, and you'll be rewarded with free flights and elite status. It's free, and you'll get the best choice of seats, faster response to phone inquiries, and prompter service if your luggage is stolen, your flight is canceled or delayed, or you want to change your seat. You don't need to fly to build frequent-flier miles—**frequent-flier credit cards** can provide thousands of miles for doing your everyday shopping.

12 Packages for the Independent Traveler

Package tours are simply a way to buy the airfare, accommodations, and other elements of your trip (such as car rentals, airport transfers, and sometimes even

activities) at the same time and often at discounted prices.

One good source of package deals is the airlines themselves. Most major airlines offer air/land packages, including **American Airlines Vacations** (© 800/321-2121; www.aavacations.com), **Delta Vacations** (© 800/221-6666; www.deltavacations.com), **Continental Airlines Vacations** (© 800/301-3800; www.covacations.com), and **United Vacations** (© 888/854-3899; www.unitedvacations.com). Several big **online travel agencies**—Expedia, Travelocity, Orbitz, Site59, and Lastminute.com—also do a brisk business in packages.

Miami is usually the jumping-off point for package deals to Peru. The following are just a few among the longtime packagers to Peru and other destinations in Central and South America. **Analie Tours** (© **800/811-6027;** www.analie tours.com) offers a variety of Peru packages, such as one that includes airfare from Miami, travel to Lima, Cusco, to the Sacred Valley and Machu Picchu, and all transfers within Peru ($1170). You can fly out of a number of other U.S. gateways for a couple hundred dollars more, and Lake Titicaca, Amazon, and other extensions are possible. **Marnella Tours** (© **866/993-0033;** www.marnellatours.com) offers a 6-day Machu Picchu Adventure package, including airfare and meals, starting at $1085, as well as plenty of other multi-day and city packages

throughout Peru. **Tara Tours** (© **800/327-0080** or 305/278-4464; www.tara tours.com) is also worth a look; it usually offers several air/land packages to Peru, as well as tours such as the 9-day "Tara's Inka Journey" (Cusco, Machu Picchu, Lima, and the Amazon), starting at $2,581 per person.

Fly Latin America, based in Costa Rica (© **888/246-1431;** www.flylatin america.net/peru) has good airfares to Peru from North America and all over, as well as air/hotel and tour packages.

Travel packages are also listed in the travel section of your local Sunday newspaper. Or check ads in the national travel magazines such as *Arthur Frommer's Budget Travel Magazine, Travel + Leisure, National Geographic Traveler,* and *Condé Nast Traveler.*

Before you invest in a package tour, ask about the **accommodations choices** and prices for each. Then look up the hotels' reviews in a Frommer's guide and check their rates online for your specific dates of travel. You'll also want to find out what **type of room** you get. If you need a certain type of room, ask for it; don't take whatever is thrown your way.

Finally, look for **hidden expenses.** Ask whether airport departure fees and taxes, for example, are included in the total cost.

13 Escorted General-Interest Tours

Escorted tours are structured group tours, with a group leader. The price usually includes everything from airfare to hotels, meals, tours, admission costs, and local transportation.

RECOMMENDED ESCORTED TOUR OPERATORS
NORTH AMERICA– AND EUROPE-BASED COMPANIES
- **Abercrombie & Kent** ✿✿ (© **800/554-7016;** www.abercrombiekent.com) calls itself the "original luxury travel company." It recently introduced

South America into its extensive lineup of luxury trips, which are well managed and pampered, with stays in many of the finest hotels available. The tours aren't cheap, but if you want to go in style, A&K is the way to go. Group size is generally limited to 16 people. Several Peru itineraries are available (such as the 9-day "Wonders of Peru," a family adventure, and combo trips with Bolivia and the Galápagos); check the website for occasional discounts on selected tours and dates.

- **Adventure Life Journeys** 𝒜𝒜 (℡ **800/344-6118** or 406/541-2677; www.adventure-life.com), based in Missoula, Montana, is an Andean specialist with a roster of interesting Peru trips that focus mainly on eco-tours and adventure trips, including some to off-the-beaten-path destinations.

- **Adventures Abroad** (℡ **800/665-3998;** www.adventures-abroad.com), with offices in Washington state as well as the U.K., Canada, Australia, and New Zealand, has a massive database of trips. The tour operator prides itself on small group travel, from 4 to 21 participants. Peruvian offerings are highlights tours, ranging from 7 to 21 days, but longer trips include features such as hiking the Inca Trail. Several trips combine either Ecuador or Bolivia with Peruvian attractions.

- **Butterfield & Robinson** 𝒜 (℡ **866/551-9090** or 800/6781-1477 in Europe; www.butterfield. com) is a top upscale tour company that promotes biking and walking trips. You'll stay at some of the country's finest hotels and will get full van support for any light adventure trips. To Peru, it offers an 8-day "Machu Picchu Found" tour that includes the Inca Trail. Trips are top-of-the-line (with commensurate pricing, about $5,000 per person).

- **Exito Latin American Travel** (℡ **800/655-4053;** www.exito-travel.com) has a limited number of Peru packages, including the Inca Trail to Machu Picchu and jungle lodge tours. It's also a very good source for finding discounted airfares to Peru and elsewhere in Latin America, as well as language programs.

- **GAP Adventures** (℡ **800/708-7761** or 0870/999-0144 in the U.K.; www.gapadventures.com), the "Great Adventure People," focuses on adventure-oriented "independent travel

with the security of a group" in Central and South America. It offers a huge number and variety of Peru trips. Some trips are more comfortable; others are a bit edgier. Most trips have a maximum size of 12 travelers.

- **Kon-Tiki Tours** has offices in New York (℡ **877/566-8454** or 212/206-3710; www.kontiki.org) and Lima. These South American travel specialists offer a huge variety of Peru trips, including rainforest expeditions, spiritual sojourns, trekking and adventure-sports tours, and targeted cultural programs.

- **Ladatco Tours** (℡ **800/327-6162;** www.ladatco.com) has specialized in tours to Central and South America for 3 decades. Its Explorer Tours are locally hosted and include hotel, sightseeing with an English-speaking guide, and all land, cruise, and air transportation. Tours are grouped by theme, such as "Mystic" and "Inca." There are also "Pampered Adventure" programs and custom-designed tours—in all, more than two dozen trips to Peru throughout high season. Tours are a bit pricey but are well designed, and prices include airfare from Miami.

- **Latin America Escapes, Inc.** (℡ **800/510-5999** or 530/879-9292; www.latinamericanescapes. com), is a California-based company that offers fully escorted adventure trips, cultural tours, and natural history programs in Peru, as well as customized trips with your own private guide and driver and fully hosted independent tours with all major details (transportation, hotels, and tours) included. Check the website for current specials.

- **Nature Expeditions International** (℡ **800/869-0639;** www.naturexp. com) has a good reputation for package tours and has been in business since 1973. It offers a good 10-day highlights trip to Lima, Cusco, the Sacred Valley, and Arequipa, as well as a 7-day trip to Lima, Cusco, and Machu Picchu.

- **Overseas Adventure Travel** ⚜ (℃ **800/493-6824;** www.oattravel. com) is an English outfit with economical small-group (10–16 people) tours, such as its "Real Affordable Peru" trip (11 days, $1,495). Another tour combines Machu Picchu and the Galápagos Islands.

- **Peru for Less** ⚜ (℃ **877/269-0309** or 203/002-0571 in the U.K.; www.peruforless.com), a Texas-based company, lives up to its plainspoken name, guaranteeing "the lowest prices outside Peru." It has at least a half-dozen affordable Peru tour packages, such as "Historical Peru," which visits Lima, Paracas, Nasca, Arequipa, Cusco, and Machu Picchu. Tours include guides, hotels, all visits and transfers, plus daily breakfast.

- **Peru Horizons Travel & Tours** (℃ **800/333-9361;** www.peru-travel. com) offers economical vacation packages to most parts of Peru, including Machu Picchu, Cusco, Lima, the Nasca Lines, the Amazon, the Inca Trail, Trujillo, Lake Titicaca, Puno, Arequipa, Ica, and Urubamba.

- **Southwind Adventures** ⚜ (℃ **800/377-9463** or 303/972-0701; www. southwindadventures.com) plans distinctive and high-end adventure trips with a cultural emphasis in South America. Among them are 16 Peruvian trips, from mountain biking to specialty tours such as the Kuélap ruins, and cool offerings such as "Inca Visions," a photography workshop tour. Custom trips include a 21-day Grand Andean Traverse trekking expedition, with possibilities for bird-watching, rafting, and family adventure.

- **Tambo Tours** ⚜ (℃ **888/2-GO-PERU** or 001/281-528-9448; www. tambotours.com), based in Houston, is a Peru specialist and one of the best spots to shop for a package deal to Peru. It offers a wide array of great-value trips to most parts of the country, as well as customized tours and discounted airfares.

- **Tico Travel** (℃ **800/493-8426;** www.ticotravel.com), an established expert on Costa Rica and Central America, with an office in Ft. Lauderdale, Florida, now offers packages to Peru and discounted airfares. Its good-value 4- to 9-day packages cover Cusco, Lima, and Lake Titicaca.

PERU-BASED COMPANIES

- **Chaska Tours** ⚜ (℃ **084/240-424;** www.chaskatours.com) is a professional, multi-purpose Cusco-based company offering a large menu of travel itineraries both in groups and tailored for individuals (you can go right on the website and fill out a custom request form). It has everything from day tours in Cusco and jungle tours to off-the-beaten path trekking and mountain biking excursions and jam-packed 11-day trips that take in Cusco, the Sacred Valley, Titicaca, and the Amazon.

- **Class Adventure Travel** ⚜ (℃ **01/444-2220;** www.cat-travel.com) is a very professional and dependable Dutch-owned and -operated firm with offices in Lima and Cusco, as well as Argentina, Bolivia, and Brazil. It offers adventure (rafting and trekking) and jungle tours, long trips (a 17-day "Ancient Cultures of Peru" trip), short trips (a 7-day Cusco and Puno trip), and design-your-own tours. If you arrive in Peru and then decide to book a tour, CAT is one of the best general agencies to contact.

- **Fiesta Tours International** (© 01/ 225-1336; www.fiestatoursperu.com) has a multitude of trips within Peru, such as its 6-day "Discover Peru" tour. It also deals in airfares from Miami or Los Angeles.
- **Peru Gateway** (© 888/671-2852 or 01/444-3027; www.peru-explorer. com) also has an extensive roster of Peru tours and a good selection of hotels.

Despite the fact that escorted tours require big deposits and predetermine hotels, restaurants, and itineraries, many people derive security and peace of mind from the structure they offer. Escorted tours—whether they're navigated by bus, motor coach, train, or boat—let travelers sit back and enjoy the trip without having to drive or worry about details. They take you to the maximum number of sights in the minimum amount of time with the least amount of hassle. They're particularly convenient for people with limited mobility and they can be a great way to make new friends.

On the downside, you'll have little opportunity for serendipitous interactions with locals. The tours can be jam-packed with activities, leaving little room for individual sightseeing, whim, or adventure—plus they also often focus on the heavily touristed sites, so you miss out on many a lesser-known gem.

Before you invest in an escorted tour, request a complete **schedule** of the trip to find out how much sightseeing is planned and whether you'll have enough time to relax or have an adventure of your own. Also ask about the **cancellation policy:** Is

a deposit required? Can they cancel the trip if enough people don't sign up? Do you get a refund if they cancel? If *you* cancel? How late can you cancel if you are unable to go? When must you pay in full? If you choose an escorted tour, think strongly about purchasing trip-cancellation insurance, especially if the tour operator asks you to pay in advance. See the section on "Travel Insurance," p. 42. If you plan to travel alone, find out if they'll charge a **single supplement** or whether they can pair you with a roommate.

The **size** of the group is also important to know up front. Generally, the smaller the group, the more flexible the itinerary, and the less time you'll spend waiting for people to get on and off the bus. Find out the **demographics** of the group as well. What is the age range? What is the gender breakdown? Is this mostly a trip for couples or singles?

Discuss what is included in the **price.** You may have to pay for transportation to and from the airport. A box lunch may be included in an excursion, but drinks might cost extra. Tips may not be included. Find out if you will be charged if you decide to opt out of certain activities or meals.

Before you invest in a package tour, get some answers. Ask about the **accommodations choices** and prices for each. Then look up the hotels' reviews in a Frommer's guide and check their rates online for your specific dates of travel. You'll also want to find out what **type of room** you get. If you need a certain type of room, ask for it; don't take whatever is thrown your way.

14 Getting Around

Because of its size and natural barriers, including difficult mountain terrain, long stretches of desert coast, and extensive rainforest, Peru is complicated to navigate. Train service is very limited,

covering only a few principal tourist routes, and many trips take several days by land. Visitors with limited time tend to fly everywhere they can. Travel overland, though very inexpensive, can be extremely time-consuming and uncomfortable. However, for certain routes, intercity buses are your only real option.

BY PLANE

Flying to major destinations within Peru is the only practical way around the country if you want to see several places in a couple weeks or less. Peru is a deceptively large country, and natural barriers make getting around rather difficult. Most major Peruvian cities can be reached by air, although not always directly. Some places in the jungle, such as Iquitos, can be reached only by airplane (or a very long and arduous boat ride). Flying to major destinations, such as Lima, Cusco, Arequipa, Puerto Maldonado, and Iquitos, is simple and relatively inexpensive. One-way flights to most destinations are between $69 and $119 (prices, in U.S. dollars, fluctuate according to season). Puno (and Lake Titicaca), however, require passengers to fly first to Juliaca before continuing by land the rest of the way (45km/28 miles)—a reality that prompts many to take a direct train or bus from Cusco to Puno.

Peru's carriers, some of which are small airlines with limited flight schedules, include **AeroCondor** (🕿 **305/531-1407** in North America, or 01/614-6000; www.aerocondor.com.pe), **LAN** (Lan-Peru) (🕿 **866/435-9526** in the U.S., or 305/670-9999; 01/213-8200 in Lima; www.lan.com), **LC Busre** (01/619-1300; www.lcbusre.com.pe), **StarPerú** (🕿 **01/ 705-9000;** www.starperu.com) **Taca Peru** (🕿 **800/400-TACA** in the U.S., or 01/511-8222; www.taca.com), and **TANS Perú** (🕿 **01/611-5555;** www.tans peru.com.pe).

All airlines fly in and out of Lima. LAN is the only domestic airline that flies to most major destinations in Peru. Aero-Condor flies to Arequipa, Ayacucho, Cusco, Puerto Maldonado, Cajamarca, and Iquitos. LC Busre flies to Cajamarca and Ayacucho, while StarPerú goes to Trujillo, Chiclayo, Iquitos, and Cusco. Taca flies to Arequipa and Cusco. TANS Perú's destinations are Arequipa, Cusco, Iquitos, and Puerto Maldonado.

Connections through Lima are often necessary, although many destinations are accessible directly from Arequipa and Cusco, and some routes might be limited to only several days a week. Both flight schedules and fares are apt to change frequently and without notice. One-way fares are generally half the round-trip fare. Flights should be booked several days in advance, especially in high season, and you should also make sure that you get to the airport at least 45 minutes in advance to avoid being bumped from a flight.

LAN has an air pass program for those who fly to Peru on its airline. Passengers may buy a minimum of three flight coupons for $89 each (purchase must be made prior to landing in Peru). Depending on your flight schedule, however, this program may not save you much money over purchasing flights once in Peru.

BY TRAIN

The four tourist or passenger train routes operated by PeruRail (a private company owned by Orient-Express) are all very popular and scenic journeys. Because luggage theft has long been a problem on Peruvian trains, you should (if possible) purchase a premium-class ticket that limits access to ticketed passengers.

By far the most popular train routes in Peru connect Cusco, the Sacred Valley, and Machu Picchu. The **Sacred Valley Railway** goes from Urubamba to Ollantaytambo and on to Machu Picchu and back ($71.50 round-trip; $43 one-way). All trains traveling to Machu Picchu from Cusco stop first at Ollantaytambo. The Backpacker shuttle ($53 round-trip, April–Oct only) originates in Ollantaytambo, and the Vistadome originates in either Urubamba or Cusco and makes stops in Ollantaytambo on the way to Machu Picchu.

Most visitors head directly to Machu Picchu from Cusco, a truly spectacular journey. There are three tourist trains from Cusco to Machu Picchu, taking just under 4 hours: the **Backpacker,** the slowest and least expensive ($68 round-trip; $44 one-way); the **Vistadome,** the faster first-class service ($105 round-trip; $62 one-way); and the top-of-the-line luxury line **Hiram Bingham,** named after the discoverer of Machu Picchu ($495 round-trip only, including two meals, cocktails, and a guided tour at the ruins).

The **Titicaca Route** journey from Cusco to Puno is one of the most scenic and popular in Peru, although it is rather slow. Andean Explorer (first class, which includes breakfast and lunch) costs $119 one-way; Backpacker (tourist) class costs $17. All trains stop in Juliaca en route.

Train service from Arequipa to Puno is now available by charter only, although it could be revived sometime in the near future (see www.perurail.com for updates).

There are no PeruRail train passes. For additional information, visit the **Peru-Rail** website at www.perurail.com or call ✆ **01/444-5020** in Lima, 084/238-722 in Cusco, 051/351-041 in Puno.

The **Ferrocarril Central Andino,** the spectacular high-altitude journey from Lima to Huancayo in the Central Highlands—the world's highest passenger line—is again in service for passenger travel after being shut down until a few years ago, though its notoriously problematic history makes it very difficult to plan a trip around riding the train. You should definitely check in advance to see if it is running and what the schedule is. It runs just once a month from April to October ($38 round-trip). For more information, including packages and schedules, call ✆ **01/361-2828** or visit www.ferroviasperu.com.pe.

BY BUS

Buses are the cheapest and most popular form of transportation in Peru—for many Peruvians, they are the only means of getting around—and they have by far the greatest reach. A complex network of private bus companies crisscrosses Peru, with many competing lines covering the most popular routes. Many companies operate their own bus stations, and their locations, dispersed across many cities, can be endlessly frustrating to travelers. Luggage theft is an issue on many buses; passengers should keep a watchful eye on carry-on items and pay close attention when bags are unloaded. Only a few long-distance companies have luxury buses comparable in comforts to European models (bathrooms, reclining seats, and movies). These premium-class ("Royal" or "Imperial" class) buses cost up to twice as much as regular-service buses, although for many travelers, the additional comfort and services are worth the difference in cost (which remains inexpensive).

For many short distances (such as Cusco to Pisac), colectivos (smaller buses without assigned seats) are the fastest and cheapest option.

Ormeño (✆ **01/472-5000;** www.grupo-ormeno.com), **Cruz del Sur** (✆ **01/424-6158;** www.cruzdelsur.com.pe), **Oltursa (01/225-4499;** www.oltursa.com.pe), and **Civa** (✆ **01/332-5236;** www.civa.com.pe) are among the bus companies with the best reputations for long-distance treks. Given the extremely confusing nature of bus companies, terminals, and destinations—which makes it impossible to even begin to list every possible option here—it is best to approach a local tourism information office or travel agency (most of which sell long-distance bus tickets) with a destination in mind and let the office direct you to the terminal for the best service (and, if possible, book the ticket for you).

Combi or Carro? Getting Around in and out of Town

Getting around Peru demands a mastery of terms that designate varied modes of transportation and a bewildering array of vehicles that aren't always easy to distinguish.

Within cities, travelers have several options. The most convenient and expensive are **taxis,** which function, for the most part, like taxis elsewhere in the world. However, taxis in Peru are wholly unregulated; in addition to registered, licensed taxis, you'll find "taxi" drivers who are merely folks with access to a two-bit car—usually rented for the purpose—and a taxi sticker to plunk inside the windshield. In Lima, this is overwhelmingly the case, and unregistered taxi drivers can be difficult to negotiate with for a fair price. There are no meters, meaning that you have to negotiate a price before (not after) accepting a ride. In other cities, such as Cusco, taxis conform to standard pricing (S/2 or 55¢, within town), so taking cabs outside of Lima is a considerably less daunting proposition for most travelers.

Combis are vans that function as private bus services. They often race from one end of town to another, with fare collectors hanging out the door barking the name of the route. Combis also cover routes between towns. *Colectivos* are essentially indistinguishable from combis—they are vans that cover regular routes (such as between Cusco and Pisac), and they usually depart when they're full. Routes are often so popular, though, that colectivos leave regularly, as often as every 15 minutes, throughout the day. For intercity transport, there is a similar slate of options. *Micros* are small buses, often old and quite colorful, that travel between cities. Both colectivos and micros are quite crowded, have a reputation for pickpockets, and can be hailed at any place along the street without regard for bus stops. You pay a *cobrador* (money collector), who usually hangs out at the door barking destinations at would-be travelers rather than the driver.

Autobuses (also called *buses* or *ómnibuses*) are large coaches for long-distance travel on scheduled intercity routes. Classes of buses are distinguished by price and comfort: *Económico* is a bare-bones bus with little more than a driver and an assigned seat; classes designated *especial* (or sometimes "Inka") have reclining seats, videos, refreshments, and bathrooms.

As if that complex web of terms weren't enough to get a handle on, there's an additional warning to heed: It's not uncommon to hear locals refer—loosely and confusingly—to buses as *carros* (which normally just means "car") and to colectivos as *taxis.*

BY CAR

Getting around Peru by means of a rental car isn't the easiest or best option for the great majority of travelers. It is also far from the cheapest. Distances are long, the terrain is either difficult or unrelentingly boring for long stretches along the desert coast, roads are often not in very good condition, Peruvian drivers are aggressive, and accident rates are very high. The U.S. State Department warns against driving in Peru, particularly at night or alone on rural roads at any time of day. A four-wheel-drive vehicle is the best option in many places, but trucks and Jeeps are exceedingly expensive for most travelers.

However, if you want maximum flexibility and independence for travels in a particular region (say, to get around the Sacred Valley outside of Cusco, or to visit Colca Canyon beyond Arequipa) and you have several people to share the cost with you, a rental car could be a decent option. By no means should you plan to rent a car in Lima and head off for the major sights across the country; you'll spend all your time in the car. It is much more feasible to fly or take a bus to a given destination and rent a car there. The major international rental agencies are found in Lima, and a handful of international and local companies operate in other cities, such as Cusco and Arequipa. Costs average about $30 to $50 a day, plus 18% insurance, for an economy-size vehicle.

To rent a car, you need to be at least 25 years old and have a valid driver's license and passport. Deposit by credit card is usually required. Driving under the influence of alcohol or drugs is a criminal offense.

Major rental companies in Peru include **Avis** (𝒞 01/575-0912, ext. 4155; www.avis.com), **Budget** (𝒞 01/575-1674; www.budget.com), **Dollar** (𝒞 01/444-3050), **Hertz** (𝒞 01/575-1390; www.hertz.com); **InterService Rent a Car** (𝒞 01/442-2256), **National Car Rental** (𝒞 01/433-3750; www.nationalcar.com), and **Paz Rent a Car** (𝒞 01/436-3941).

For mechanical assistance, contact the **Touring Automóvil Club del Perú (Touring Club of Peru)** in Lima at 𝒞 **01/221-3225,** or in Cusco at 084/224-561.

15 Tips on Accommodations

THE HOTEL SCENE

A wide range of accommodations—including world-class luxury hotels in modern high-rise buildings and 16th-century monasteries, affordable small hotels in colonial houses, rustic rainforest lodges, and inexpensive budget inns—can be found in Peru. Midrange options have expanded in recent years, but the large majority of accommodations still court budget travelers and backpackers (outside Lima's hosting of international business travelers). During high season (June–Oct), and especially at times of national holidays and important festivals (Christmas, New Year's, Carnaval and Easter week, the week leading up to Inti Raymi, and Fiestas Patrias), advance reservations are recommended. This is especially true of hotels in the moderate and expensive categories in places such as Cusco and Machu Picchu.

Accommodations go by many names in Peru. *Hotel* generally refers only to comfortable hotels with a range of services, but *hostal* (or *hostales,* plural) is used for a wide variety of smaller hotels, inns, and pensions. (Note that *hostal* is distinct from the English-language term "hostel.") At the lower end are mostly *hospedajes, pensiones,* and *residenciales.* However, these terms are often poor indicators—if they are indicators at all—of an establishment's quality or services. Required signs outside reflect these categories: H (hotel), HS *(hostal),* HR *(hotel residencial),* and P *(pensión).* As in most countries, the government's hotel-rating system means that establishments are awarded stars for the presence of certain criteria—a pool, restaurant, elevator, and so on—more than for standards of luxury. Thus, it is not always true that the hotel with the most stars is necessarily the most comfortable or elegant. Luxury hotels are rare outside Lima and Cusco; budget accommodations are plentiful across the country, and many of them are quite good for the price. Some represent amazing values at less than $30 a night for a double—with a dose of local character and breakfast, to boot.

In-room air-conditioning isn't as common, especially in lower-priced and moderately priced inns and hotels, as it is in many countries. In highland towns, such as Cusco and Puno, that's not usually a problem, as even in warmer months it gets pretty cool at night. In coastal and jungle towns (and at jungle lodges), it gets considerably warmer, though most hotels that don't offer A/C units have ceiling or other fans. If you're concerned about having A/C in your room in a warmer destination, it may be necessary to bump up to a more expensive hotel.

Advance reservations are strongly recommended during high season (June–Oct) and during national holidays and important festivals. This is especially true of hotels in the middle and upper categories in popular places such as Cusco and Machu Picchu. Many hotels quote their rates in U.S. dollars. If you pay in cash, the price will be converted into soles at the going rate. Note that at most budget and many midrange hotels, credit cards are not accepted. Most published rates can be negotiated and travelers can often get greatly reduced rates outside of peak season simply by asking. This is especially true of jungle lodges, where published international prices differ greatly from the rate one might obtain on-site. Hotel taxes and service charges are an issue that has caused some confusion in recent years. Most upper-level hotels add a 19% general sales tax (IGV) and a 10% service charge to the bill. However, foreigners who can demonstrate they live outside of Peru are not charged the 19% tax (though they are responsible for the 10% service charge). In practice, hotels sometimes either mistakenly or purposely include the IGV on everyone's bill; presentation of a passport is sufficient to have the tax deducted from your tab. Many hotels—usually those at the midlevel and lower ranges—simplify matters by including the tax in their rates; at these establishments, you cannot expect to have the tax removed from your charges. At high-end hotels, be sure to review your bill and ask for an explanation of additional taxes and charges. Prices in this book do not include taxes and service charges unless otherwise noted.

Safety is an issue at many hotels, especially at the lower end, and extreme care should be taken with regard to personal belongings left in the hotel. Leaving valuables lying around is asking for trouble. Except for hotels at the lowest levels, all have safety deposit boxes. (Only luxury hotels have room safes.) Place your belongings in a carefully sealed envelope. If you arrive in a town without previously arranged accommodations, you should be at least minimally wary of taxi drivers and others who insist on showing you to a hotel. Occasionally, these will provide excellent tips, but, in general, they will merely be taking you to a place where they are confident they can earn a commission. A final precaution worth mentioning is the electric heater found on many showerheads. These can be dangerous, and touching them while functioning can prompt an unwelcome electric jolt.

The great majority of hotels in Peru are small and midsize independent inns; few international hotel chains operate in Peru. You'll find a Holiday Inn here and a Marriott, Best Western, or Orient-Express hotel there, but, by and large, the chains you'll come into contact with are Peruvian chains. The most prominent, although they have only a handful of hotels each, are Casa Andina, Sonesta, and Libertador. Casa Andina and Sonesta hotels are comfortable, decorated similarly, and generally good values. Casa

Andina also has an upscale line of Private Collection hotels in a few choice spots. The Libertador hotels are elegant four- and five-star establishments, largely in historic buildings.

SAVING ON YOUR HOTEL ROOM

The **rack rate** is the maximum rate that a hotel charges for a room. Hardly anybody pays this price, however. To lower the cost of your room:

- **Ask about special rates or other discounts.** Always ask whether a room less expensive than the first one quoted is available, or whether any special rates apply to you. You might qualify for corporate, student, military, senior, or other discounts. Find out the hotel policy on children—do kids stay free in the room, or is there a special rate?
- **Dial direct.** When booking a room in a chain hotel, you'll often get a better deal by calling the individual hotel's reservation desk than the chain's main number.
- **Book online.** Many hotels offer Internet-only discounts or supply rooms to Priceline, Hotwire, or Expedia at rates much lower than the ones you can get through the hotel itself.
- **Remember the law of supply and demand.** Resort hotels are most crowded and, therefore, most expensive on weekends, so discounts are usually available for midweek stays. Business hotels in downtown locations are busiest during the week, so you can expect big discounts over the weekend. Many hotels have high-season and low-season prices, and booking the day after high season ends can mean big discounts.
- **Look into group or long-stay discounts.** If you come as part of a large group, you should be able to negotiate a bargain rate because the hotel can then guarantee occupancy in a number of rooms. Likewise, if you're planning a long stay (at least 5 days), you might qualify for a discount. As a general rule, expect 1 night free after a 7-night stay.
- **Avoid excess charges and hidden costs.** When you book a room, ask whether the hotel charges for parking. Use your own cellphone, pay phones, or prepaid phone cards instead of dialing direct from hotel phones, which usually have exorbitant rates. And don't be tempted by the room's mini-bar offerings: Most hotels charge through the nose for water, soda, and snacks. Finally, ask about local taxes and service charges, which can increase the cost of a room by 15% or more.
- **Book an efficiency.** A room with a kitchenette allows you to shop for groceries and cook your own meals. This is a big money saver, especially for families on long stays.

LANDING THE BEST ROOM

Somebody has to get the best room in the house. It might as well be you. You can start by joining the hotel's frequent-guest program, which may make you eligible for upgrades. A hotel-branded credit card usually gives its owner "silver" or "gold" status in frequent-guest programs for free. Always ask about a corner room. They're often larger and quieter, with more windows and light, and they often cost the same as standard rooms. When you make your reservation, ask if the hotel is renovating; if it is, request a room away from the construction. Ask about nonsmoking rooms, rooms with views, and rooms with twin, queen-, or king-size beds. If you're a light sleeper, request a quiet room away from vending machines, elevators, restaurants, bars, and discos. Ask for a room that has been most recently renovated or redecorated.

If you aren't happy with your room when you arrive, ask for another one. Most lodgings will be willing to accommodate you.

16 Tips on Dining

Peruvian cuisine is incredibly varied and accomplished, for many travelers an exciting and delicious surprise. It is among the best and most diverse cuisines found in Latin America and is one of the most important contributors to the wave of pan-Latino restaurants gaining popularity in many parts of the world. Peruvian cooking differs significantly by region, and subcategories mirror exactly the country's geographical variety: coastal, highlands, and tropical. The common denominator among them is a blend of indigenous and Spanish (or broader European) influences, which has evolved over the past 4 centuries. Traditional Peruvian coastal cooking is often referred to as *comida criolla,* and it's found across Peru.

Coastal preparations concentrate on seafood and shellfish, as might be expected. The star dish, and the most exported example of Peruvian cuisine, is ceviche, a classic preparation of raw fish and shellfish marinated (not cooked) in lime or lemon juice and hot chile peppers, served with raw onion, sweet potato, and toasted corn. Ceviche has been around since the time of some of Peru's earliest civilizations, although a traditional Andean argument over whether Peruvians or Ecuadorians should be credited with creating it persists. *Cevicherías* usually serve several types of ceviche as well as a good roster of other seafood. Other coastal favorites include *escabeche* (a tasty fish concoction served with peppers, eggs, olives, onions, and prawns), *conchitas* (scallops), and *corvina* (sea bass). Land-based favorites are *cabrito* (roast kid) and *ají de gallina* (a tangy creamed chicken and chile dish).

Highlanders favor a more substantial style of cooking. Corn and potatoes were staples of the Incas and other mountain civilizations before them. Meat, served with rice and potatoes, is a mainstay of the diet, as is trout *(trucha). Lomo saltado,* strips of beef mixed with onions, tomatoes, peppers, and french-fried potatoes and served with rice, seems to be on every menu. *Rocoto relleno,* a hot bell pepper stuffed with vegetables and meat, and *papa rellena,* a potato stuffed with veggies and then fried, are just as common (but are occasionally extremely spicy). Soups are excellent. In the countryside, you might see people in the fields digging small cooking holes in the ground. They are preparing *pachamanca,* a roast cooked over stones. It's the Peruvian version of a picnic; on weekends, you'll often see families outside Cusco and other places stirring smoking fires in the ground while the kids play soccer nearby. *Cuy* (guinea pig) is considered a delicacy in many parts of Peru, including the sierra, but its elevated status was never much apparent to me. It comes roasted or fried, with head and feet upturned on the plate.

In the Amazon jungle regions, most people fish for their food, and their diets consist almost entirely of fish such as river trout and *paiche* (a huge river fish). Restaurants feature both of these, with accompaniments including yuca (a root), *palmitos* (palm hearts) and *chonta* (palm-heart salad), bananas and plantains, and rice tamales known as *juanes.* Common menu items such as chicken and game are complemented by exotic fare such as caiman, wild boar, turtle, monkey, and piranha fish.

In addition to Peruvian cooking, visitors will find plenty of international restaurants, including a particularly Peruvian variation, *chifas* (restaurants serving Peruvian-influenced Chinese food, developed by the large immigrant Chinese population), a mainstay among many non-Chinese Peruvians. *Chifas* are nearly as common as restaurants serving *pollo a la brasa* (spit-roasted chicken), which are everywhere in Peru.

Drinking is less of an event in Peru. Peruvian wines and beers are improving, but still can't really compare with superior examples found elsewhere on the continent (Chile and Argentina, predominantly). Most wines in better restaurants come from those three countries. Yet one indigenous drink stands out: *pisco,* a powerful white-grape brandy. The pisco sour (a cocktail mixed with pisco, egg whites, lemon juice, sugar, and bitters) is effectively Peru's margarita: tasty, refreshing, and ubiquitous. Pisco is also taken straight. Peruvians everywhere drink *chicha,* a tangy, fermented brew made from maize and inherited from the Incas. Often served warm in huge glasses, it is unlikely to please the palates of most foreign visitors, although it's certainly worth a try if you come upon a small, informal place with the *chicha* flag flying in a rural village (literally—it means something akin to "fresh *chicha* available inside"). *Chicha morada,* on the other hand, is nothing to be afraid of. It is a delicious nonalcoholic beverage, deep purple in color, prepared with blue corn and served chilled. *Masato* is a beer made from yuca, typical of the Amazon region.

Among the more interesting dining customs—beyond the eating of guinea pig—is the lovely habit of offering a sip of beer or *chicha* before the meal to Pachamama, or Mother Earth. Many Peruvians still ritualistically thank the earth for its bounty, and they show their appreciation by spilling just a bit before raising the drink to their own mouths.

Restaurants range from the rustic and incredibly inexpensive to polished places with impeccable service and international menus. Set three-course meals are referred to by a variety of terms: *menú del día, menú económico, menú ejecutivo, menú de la casa,* and *menú turístico.* They are all essentially the same thing and can sometimes be had for as little as $3. In general, you should ask about the preparation of many Peruvian dishes because many are quite spicy. Informal eateries serving Peruvian cooking are frequently called *picanterías* and *chicherías.*

Fixed-price lunch deals are referred to as menús del día (or simply menú). The majority of restaurants include taxes and services in their prices, and your bill will reflect the menu prices. Others (including some upscale restaurants), however, separate taxes and services, and the bill can get pretty byzantine, especially when it comes to imported wine. You might see a subtotal, followed by a 10% service charge, a 20% "selectivo" wine tax, and an 18% IGV (general sales tax). It's crazy. Fortunately, the restaurants that do this are rare.

Note: Some upscale restaurants will place a couple of small plates of cheese, sausage, olives, or other tidbits on your table to nibble on as you wait for your meal. In almost all cases, you will be charged for these items, called a *cubierto,* or cover. Usually, it'll add S/5 to S/15 ($1.40–$4.30) to your bill. If you don't touch the stuff, in theory you shouldn't have to pay for it because you didn't order it, but many restaurants automatically tack on the charge—and few are the customers who don't consider the *cubierto* part of the cost of eating out.

⌐Tips **Peruvian Cuisine Online**

For more information on Peruvian cooking, check out **www.cocinaperuana.com**, which features a history of Peruvian cuisine, a glossary, recipes, and a guide to restaurants in Peru.

Dining hours are not much different from typical mealtimes in cities in North America or Great Britain, except that dinner *(cena)* is generally eaten after 8pm in restaurants. Peruvians do not eat nearly as late as Spaniards. Although lunch *(almuerzo)* is the main meal of the day, for most visitors, it generally is not the grand midday affair it is in Spain, unless you are dining at an outdoor *quinta*, where most locals linger over lunch for a couple hours.

17 Tips on Shopping

Peru is one of the top shopping destinations in Latin America, with some of the finest and best-priced crafts anywhere. Its long traditions of textile weaving and colorful markets bursting with tourists have produced a dazzling display of alpaca-wool sweaters, blankets, ponchos, shawls, scarves, typical Peruvian hats, and other woven items. Peru's ancient indigenous civilizations were some of the world's greatest potters, and reproductions of Moche, Nasca, Paracas, and other ceramics are available. (Until recently, it was surprisingly easy to get your hands on the real thing, but that's no longer the case.) In some cities—especially Lima, Cusco, and Arequipa—antique textiles and ceramics are still available. Some dealers handle pieces that are 1,000 years old or more (and others simply claim their pieces are that old). However, exporting such pre-Columbian artifacts from Peru is illegal.

Lima and Cusco have the lion's share of tourist-oriented shops and markets—particularly in Lima, you can find items produced all over the country—but other places might be just as good for shopping. Locals in Puno and Taquile Island on Lake Titicaca produce spectacular textiles, and Arequipa is perhaps the best place in Peru to purchase very fine, extremely soft baby-alpaca items. Handcrafted *retablos* (altars) from Ayacucho, depicting weddings and other domestic scenes, are famous throughout Peru and are available across the country. The Shipibo tribe of the northern Amazon produces excellent hand-painted textiles and decorative pottery. You'll also see items in the jungle made from endangered species—alligator skins, turtle shells, and the like. Purchasing these items is illegal, and it only encourages locals to further harm the natural environment and its inhabitants.

Baby alpaca and very rare vicuña are the finest woolens and are amazingly soft. Although many merchants are happy to claim that every woven wool item in their possession is alpaca or baby alpaca, much of what is sold in many tourist centers is anything but. Most, if not all, of the very cheap (S/15–S/50 or $4.30–$14) sweaters, shawls, hats, and gloves are made of acrylic or acrylic blends, and some even are blends of natural fibers and fiberglass. If your new "alpaca" sweater stinks when it gets wet, it's llama wool. If you want the real thing—which is not as cheap but still much less expensive than what you'd pay for alpaca of such fine quality in other countries—visit one of the established chain stores in large cities (most have "alpaca" in the name). Arequipa is one of the finest centers for alpaca goods, though Cusco and Lima are also excellent places to shop for alpaca.

The *artesanía* (popular arts) center par excellence of Peru is the highlands city of Ayacucho. The distinctive ceramic churches and *retablos* that are mainstays of handicrafts shops across Peru all come from Ayacucho (and a couple of small towns nearby), although a number of artisans have relocated to larger cities to more effectively market their wares.

In Lima, Cusco, and most tourist centers, there are scores of general, look-alike *artesanía* shops, and prices might not be any higher than what you'd find at street markets. At stores and in open markets, bargaining—gentle, good-natured haggling over prices—is accepted and even expected. However, when it gets down to ridiculously small amounts of money, it's best to recognize that you are already getting a great deal on probably handmade goods and you should relinquish the fight over a few *soles.*

18 Recommended Books & Films

NONFICTION

The classic work on Incan history and the Spanish conquistadors is *The Conquest of the Incas* (Harvest Books, 2003), by John Hemming, a very readable narrative of the fall of a short-lived but uniquely accomplished empire. *Lost City of the Incas* (Phoenix Press, 2003), is the travelogue and still-amazing story of Hiram Bingham, the Yale academic who brought the "lost city" to the world's attention in 1911. Bingham's book, in a new paperback edition, makes for a very interesting read, especially after so many years of speculation and theory about the site. Also available by Bingham is *Inca Land: Explorations in the Highlands of Peru* (National Geographic, 2003), detailing four expeditions into the Peruvian Andes, originally published in 1922.

The Incas and their Ancestors (Thames and Hudson, 2001), by Michael Moseley, is a good account of the Incan Empire and, importantly, its lesser-known predecessors. For most readers, it serves as a good introduction to Peru's archaeology and the sites they will visit, although some people find that it reads too much like a textbook. Illustrations include black-and-white photographs of Incan drawings and a few color photos. A terrific story of a recent archaeological find is *Discovering the Ice Maiden: My Adventures on Ampato* (National Geographic Society, 1998), by Johan Reinhard. The account of Reinhard's discovery of a mummified Incan princess sacrificed 500 years ago on a volcano summit in southern Peru details the team's search and its race to save what is considered one of the most important archaeological discoveries in recent decades. The book contains excellent color photographs of the maiden who can now be viewed in Arequipa. Reinhard's *The Ice Maiden: Inca Mummies, Mountain Gods, and Sacred Sites in the Andes* (National Geographic, 2005) is a memoir of archaeological adventures and the impact of his discovery of Juanita (both on him personally and the interpretation of Peruvian history).

The Peru Reader: History, Culture, Politics (Duke University Press, 1995), edited by Orin Starn, is one of the finest primers on Peru's recent history and political culture. It includes essays by several distinguished voices, including Mario Vargas Llosa.

The Madness of Things Peruvian, Democracy Under Siege, by Alvaro Vargas Llosa (Transaction Publishers, 1994) isn't easy to find, and it only chronicles up to the mid-'90s, but it is a well-rendered analysis of the failings of Peruvian democracy. Robin Kirk's *The Monkey's Paw: New Chronicles from Peru* (University of Massachusetts Press, 1997) is a story of the impact of social and economic upheaval in Peru on marginalized peoples, with the homegrown guerrilla movements taking center stage.

Naturalists and birders might want to pick up *A Field Guide to the Birds of Peru* (Ibis Pub Co., 2001), by James F. Clements, although it is perhaps not the comprehensive field guide that a country as biologically diverse as Peru deserves. Many serious birders prefer *A Guide to the Birds of Colombia* (Princeton University Press, 1986), by Steven Hilty and William Brown, probably the definitive regional guide (and covering many of the birds also found in Peru). Also of interest is *A Parrot Without a Name: The Search for the Last Unknown Birds on Earth* (University of Texas Press, 1991), by Don Stap, an account of John O'Neill and LSU scientists documenting new species in the jungles of Peru.

Peru: The Ecotravellers' Wildlife Guide (Academic Press, 2000), by biologists David Pearson and Les Beletsky, is a 500-page handbook survey of Peruvian flora and fauna, including information about conservation, habitats, national parks, and reserves. It's a good introduction for readers ready to explore the Peruvian outdoors, from the Andes to the Amazon and other repositories of Peru's magnificent animal and plant life. The book is nicely illustrated and useful for identification purposes.

Peter Frost's *Exploring Cusco* (Nuevas Imágenes, 1999) is one of the best-detailed local guides, with excellent historical information and frank commentary by the author, a longtime Cusco resident, on the ancient Incan capital, the Sacred Valley, and, of course, Machu Picchu. *Peru & Bolivia: Backpacking and Trekking* (Bradt Publications, 1999), by Hilary Bradt, is a trusty guide, now in its third decade, of classic treks in Peru and Bolivia. Although it's in its seventh edition, with several new walks and treks added, some readers find it outdated. Still, it's a good all-around guide for trekkers and walkers.

The Cloud Forest: A Chronicle of the South American Wilderness (Ingram, 1996) is a travelogue by Peter Matthiessen, who trekked some 10,000 miles through South America, including the Amazon and Machu Picchu. Matthiessen found larger-than-life characters and ancient trails deep in the jungle, experiences that led to the author's fictional novel *At Play in the Fields of the Lord* (Vintage Books, 1991). Set in the unnamed Peruvian jungle, it's a thriller about the travails of the missionary Martin Quarrier and an outsider, Lewis Moon, a mercenary who takes a much different tack while immersing himself in a foreign culture. Both are displaced outsiders whose lives have an irreversible impact on native Amerindian communities deep in the Amazon. The book was later made into an occasionally pretty but silly movie starring John Lithgow, Daryl Hannah, and Tom Beringer with a bowl-cut and face paint.

FICTION

The towering figure in contemporary Peruvian fiction is Mario Vargas Llosa, Peru's most famous novelist and a perennial candidate for the Nobel Prize, who was nearly elected the country's president back in 1990. It's difficult to choose from among his oeuvre of thoroughly praised works; *Aunt Julia and the Scriptwriter* (Penguin, 1995) is one of his most popular works, but it's without the heft of others, such as *The Real Life of Alejandro Mayta* (Noonday Press, 1998), a dense meditation on Peruvian and South American revolutionary politics that blurs the lines between truth and fiction, or *Death in the Andes* (Penguin, 1997), a deep penetration into the contemporary psyche and politics of Peru. Another side of the author is evident in the small erotic gem *In Praise of the Stepmother* (Penguin, 1991), a surprising and beautifully illustrated book. His powerful book *The Feast of the Goat* (Farrar Straus & Giroux, 2001), about the Dominican dictator Rafael Trujillo, made the year-end best lists of many critics in 2001. Vargas Llosa might be a difficult and "heavy" writer, but he is an unusually engaging one.

César Vallejo, born in Peru in 1892, is one of the great poets of Latin America and the Spanish language. *Complete Posthumous Poetry* (University of California Press, 1980), in translation, and *Trilce* (Wesleyan University Press, 2000), a bilingual publication, are the best places to start with this great poet. Vallejo wrote some of the poems in *Trilce,* a wildly creative and innovative avant-garde work that today is considered a masterpiece of modernism, while in prison. Vallejo later fled to Europe and immersed himself in the Spanish Civil War.

FILMS

Peru's indigenous film industry trails far behind those of its neighbors Argentina and Brazil. The best-known films about or featuring Peru are foreign. Two recent documentaries try to untangle the lasting impact of disgraced former president Alberto Fujimori. *The Fall of Fujimori: When Democracy and Terrorism Collide* (Stardust Productions, 2006) is a portrait of the eccentric ex-President and his controversial war against guerrilla movements in Peru. *State of Fear* (Skylight Pictures, 2006), based on the findings of the Peruvian Truth Commission, chronicles the two-decade-long reign of terror by Shining Path. It doesn't shy away from documenting the abuses of the government in fighting terrorism.

Touching the Void (IFC Films 2004), now available on DVD, is the harrowing dramatic reenactment (based on the book by Joe Simpson) of a climber's disastrous and near-fatal accident climbing in the Andes mountains near Huaraz. It is gripping, but may derail any mountaineering plans you had.

The Dancer Upstairs (Fox Searchlight 2003), a drama directed by John Malkovich and starring Javier Bardem, is a political thriller loosely based on the hunt for Abimael Guzman, the Shining Path leader, and the complicated story of the American Lori Benson, implicated and imprisoned as a terrorist collaborator in Peru (though the movie is set in an unnamed South American nation). *The Motorcycle Diaries* (MCA Home Video, 2005), an excellent 2004 film by Walter Salles about the young Che Guevara, is in large part a travelogue of Argentina, Chile, Colombia, and Venezuela, but Machu Picchu plays a scene-stealing role.

FAST FACTS: Peru

American Express There's an office in Lima at Jr. de la Unión 630 (© 01/ 428-9779); it's open Monday through Friday from 9am to 5pm. There are other offices at Av. Larco 747-753, Miraflores, Lima (©01/444-4239); and Av. Paseo de la Republica 3220, San Isidro, Lima (© 01/441-2769). Both offices are housed with Viajes Falabella travel agencies. They will replace stolen or lost traveler's checks and sell American Express checks with an Amex card, but they do not cash their own checks.

Addresses "Jr." doesn't mean "junior"; it is a designation meaning "Jirón," or street, just as "Av." (sometimes "Avda.") is an abbreviation for "Avenida," or avenue. "Ctra." is the abbreviation for *carretera,* or highway; cdra. means *cuadra,* or block; and "of." is used to designate office *(oficina)* number. Perhaps the most confusing element in Peruvian street addresses is "s/n," which frequently appears in place of a number after the name of the street. "S/n" means "sin número," or no number. The house or building with such an address simply is unnumbered.

Area Codes Note that even though many area codes across Peru were changed back in 2003, many published telephone numbers still contain old area codes.

Lima, 01; Ica, Nasca, and Pisco, 056; Cusco and the Sacred Valley, 084; Puerto Maldonado, 082; Puno/Lake Titicaca, 051; Arequipa, 054; Huaraz, 043; Trujillo, 044; Cajamarca, 076; Chiclayo, 074; and Iquitos, 065.

ATM Networks See "Money," earlier in this chapter.

Business Hours Most stores are open from 9 or 10am to 12:30pm, and from 3 to 5 or 8pm. Banks are generally open Monday through Friday from 9:30am to 4pm, although some stay open until 6pm. In major cities, most banks are also open Saturday from 9:30am to 12:30pm. Offices are open from 8:30am to 12:30pm and 3 to 6pm, although many operate continuously from 9am to 5pm. Government offices are open Monday through Friday from 9:30am to 12:30pm and 3 to 5pm.

Car Rentals See "Getting Around," earlier in this chapter.

Currency See "Money," earlier in this chapter.

Doctors & Hospitals Medical care is of a generally high standard in Lima, Cusco, and Arequipa, and is adequate in other major cities, where you are likely to find English-speaking doctors. However, medical care is of a lesser standard in rural areas and small villages, where it is much less common to find an English-speaking physician. Many physicians and hospitals require immediate cash payment for health services, and they do not accept U.S. medical insurance (even if your policy applies overseas). You should check with your insurance company to see if your policy provides for overseas medical evacuation.

It's best to get vaccinations and obtain malaria pills before arriving in Peru, but if you decide at the last minute to go to the jungle and need to get a vaccine in the country, you may go to the following Oficinas de Vacunación in Lima: Av. del Ejército 1756, San Isidro (© **01/264-6889**); Jorge Chávez International Airport, Second Floor; International Vaccination Center, Dos de Mayo National Hospital, Avenida Grau, block 13 (© **01/517-1845**). You can also get a yellow fever shot at the airport in Puerto Maldonado before traveling to the Amazon jungle.

Driving Rules See "Getting Around," earlier in this chapter.

Drug Laws Until recently, Peru was the world's largest producer of coca leaves, the base product that is mostly shipped to Colombia for processing into cocaine. Cocaine and other illegal substances are perhaps not as ubiquitous in Peru as one might think, although in Lima and Cusco, they are commonly offered to foreigners. (This is especially dangerous; many would-be dealers also operate as police informants, and some are said to be undercover narcotics officers themselves.) Penalties for the possession and use of or trafficking in illegal drugs in Peru are strict; convicted offenders can expect long jail sentences and substantial fines. Peruvian police routinely detain drug smugglers at Lima's international airport and land-border crossings. Since 1995, more than 40 U.S. citizens have been convicted of narcotics trafficking in Peru. If you are arrested on drug charges, you will face protracted pretrial detention in poor prison conditions.

Coca leaves, either chewed or brewed for tea, are not illegal in Peru, where they're not considered a narcotic. The use of coca leaves is an ancient tradition dating back to pre-Columbian civilizations in Peru. You might very well find that *mate de coca* (coca-leaf tea) is very helpful in battling altitude sickness. However, if you attempt to take coca leaves back to your home country from Peru, you should expect them to be confiscated, and you could even find yourself prosecuted.

Drugstores For locations, consult a phone book's Yellow Pages under "Farmacias" and "Boticas." In Lima, large multiservice pharmacies that are open 24 hours include **Farmacia Deza,** Av. Conquistadores 1140, San Isidro (© **01/440-3798**), and branches of the chain **Superfarma** (one is at Av. Benavides 2849; © **01/222-1575**).

Electricity All outlets are 220 volts, 60 cycles AC (except in Arequipa, which operates on 50 cycles), with two-prong outlets that accept both flat and round prongs. Some large hotels also have 110-volt outlets.

Embassies & Consulates The following are all in Lima: **U.S.,** Av. La Encalada, block 17, Monterrico (© 01/434-3000); **Australia,** Víctor A. Belaúnde 147/Vía Principal 155, building 3, office no. 1301, San Isidro (© 01/222-8281); **Canada,** Libertad 130, Miraflores (© 01/444-4015); **U.K.** and **New Zealand,** Torre Parque Mar, 22nd floor, Av. Jose Larco 1301, Miraflores (© 01/617-3000); **South Africa,** Vía Principal 155, office no. 801, San Isidro (© 01/440-9996); and **Ireland,** Angamos Oeste 340, Miraflores (© 01/446-3878). The **United States** maintains a consulate in Cusco, at the Binational Center (Instituto Cultural Peruano–Norte Americano, or ICPNA), Av. Tullumayo 125–127 (© 084/962-1369); the **United Kingdom** also has an honorary consulate in Cusco at Urbanizacion Magisterial, G-5 Segunda Etapa (© 084/226-671).

Emergencies In case of an emergency, call the 24-hour **traveler's hot line** at © **01/574-8000,** or the **tourist police,** or POLTUR (© **01/460-1060** in Lima, or 01/460-0965; see "Fast Facts" in individual destination chapters for branch information). The general police emergency number is © **105.** The **Tourist Protection Service** can also assist in contacting police to report a crime; call © **01/224-7888** in Lima, or 0800/4-2579 toll-free from any private phone (the toll-free number cannot be dialed from a public pay phone).

Etiquette & Customs See "Etiquette & Customs" in appendix A.

Guides Officially licensed guides are available on-site at many archaeological sites and other places of interest to foreigners. They can be contracted directly, although you should verify their ability to speak English if you do not comprehend Spanish well. Establish a price beforehand. Many cities are battling a scourge of unlicensed and unscrupulous guides who provide inferior services or, worse, cheat visitors. As a general rule, do not accept unsolicited offers to arrange excursions, transportation, and hotel accommodations. For a full day's guide, tip S/19 to S/40 ($5–$10).

Holidays See "When to Go," earlier in this chapter.

Information See "Visitor Information," earlier in this chapter.

Internet Access Public Internet booths, or cabinas, have proliferated throughout Peru, especially in major cities such as Lima, Cusco, and Arequipa. Most cities have several, if not dozens, to choose from, but few are of the cybercafe variety. Most are simple cubicles with terminals; occasionally, printers are available.

Look for "speedy" connections, which means high-speed DSL lines. The average cost for 1 hour is very inexpensive, usually less than $1. Many cabinas now feature software to make very inexpensive international phone calls via the Internet. Only the best hotels have modem lines in the rooms. Note that Internet locations open and close all the time. A partial but current list of sites (mostly in Lima) can be found at http://cybercaptive.com.

Language Spanish is the official language of Peru. The Amerindian languages Quechua (recently given official status) and Aymara are spoken primarily in the highlands. (Aymara is mostly limited to the area around Lake Titicaca.) English is not widely spoken but is understood by those affiliated with the tourist industry in major cities and tourist destinations. Most people you meet on the street will have only a very rudimentary understanding of English, if that. Learning a few key phrases of Spanish will help immensely. Check the glossary at the back of this book, and consider picking up a copy of the *Berlitz Latin American Spanish Language* dictionary.

Legal Aid If you need legal assistance, your best bets are your embassy (which, depending on the situation, might not be able to help you much) and the **Tourist Protection Service** (© **0800/4-2579** toll-free, or 01/574-8000 24-hr.), which might be able to direct you to an English-speaking attorney or legal assistance organization.

Note that bribing a police officer or public official is illegal in Peru, even if it is a relatively constant feature of traffic stops and the like.

If a police officer claims to be an undercover cop, do not automatically assume that he is telling the truth. Do not get in any vehicle with such a person. Demand the assistance of your embassy or consulate, or of the Tourist Protection Service.

Liquor Laws A legal drinking age is not strictly enforced in Peru. Anyone over the age of 16 is unlikely to have any problems ordering liquor in any bar or other establishment. Wine, beer, and alcohol are widely available—sold daily at grocery stores, liquor stores, and in all cafes, bars, and restaurants—and consumed widely, especially in public during festivals. There appears to be very little taboo associated with public inebriation at festivals. Bars are open until midnight or later, while nightclubs and discos are often open until dawn.

Lost & Found Be sure to tell all of your credit card companies the minute you discover your wallet has been lost or stolen and file a report at the nearest police precinct. Your credit-card company or insurer may require a police report number or record of the loss. Most credit card companies have an emergency toll-free number to call if your card is lost or stolen; they may be able to wire you a cash advance immediately or deliver an emergency credit card in a day or two. **Visa's** U.S. emergency number is © **800/847-2911** or 410/581-9994. **American Express** cardholders and traveler's check holders should call © **800/ 221-7282**. **MasterCard** holders should call © **800/307-7309** or 636/722-7111. For other credit cards, call the toll-free number directory at © **800/555-1212**.

To report lost or stolen credit cards in Peru, call **Visa** (collect) at © **410/ 581-9994**; **MasterCard** at © **800/622-7747**; **American Express** at © **0800/51-531** or collect at 801/945-9450; and **Diners Club** at © **01/221-2050**.

If you need emergency cash over the weekend when all banks and American Express offices are closed, you can have money wired to you via **Western Union** (© **800/325-6000**; www.westernunion.com).

Identity theft and fraud are potential complications of losing your wallet, especially if you've lost your driver's license along with your cash and credit cards. Notify the major credit-reporting bureaus immediately; placing a fraud alert on your records may protect you against liability for criminal activity. The three major U.S. credit-reporting agencies are **Equifax** (© **800/766-0008**; www. equifax.com), **Experian** (© **888/397-3742**; www.experian.com), and **TransUnion** (© **800/680-7289**; www.transunion.com). Finally, if you've lost all forms of photo ID, call your airline and explain the situation; they might allow you to board the plane if you have a copy of your passport or birth certificate and a copy of the police report you've filed.

Mail Peru's postal service is reasonably efficient, especially now that it is managed by a private company **(Serpost S.A.).** Post offices are open Monday through Saturday from 8am to 8pm; some are also open Sunday from 9am to 1pm. Major cities have a main post office and often several smaller branch offices. Letters and postcards to North America take between 10 days and 2 weeks, and cost S/5.50 ($1.60); to Europe, S/6 ($1.70). If you are purchasing large quantities of textiles and other handicrafts, you can send packages home from post offices, but it is not inexpensive—more than $100 for 10 kilograms (22 lb.), similar to what it costs to use DHL, where you're likely to have an easier time communicating. UPS is found in several cities, but for inexplicable reasons, its courier services cost nearly three times as much as those of DHL.

Maps Good topographical maps are available from the **Instituto Geográfico Nacional (IGN),** located at Av. Aramburú 1190, San Isidro, Lima (© **01/475-9960** or 01/475-3030). Hiking maps are available from the **South American Explorers Club,** Piura 135, Miraflores, Lima (© **01/445-3306**), and Choquechaca 188, Apto. 4, Cusco (© **084/245-484**).

Newspapers & Magazines In Lima, you will find copies (although rarely same-day publications) of the *International Herald Tribune,* the *Miami Herald,* and the odd European newspaper, as well as *Time, Newsweek,* and other special-interest publications. All might be at least several days old. Top-flight hotels sometimes offer free daily fax summations of the *New York Times* to their guests. Otherwise, your best source for timely news is likely to be checking in with news outlet websites. Outside Lima, international newspapers and magazines are hard to come by. Among local publications, look for *Rumbos,* a glossy Peruvian travel magazine in English and Spanish with excellent photography. If you read Spanish, *El Comercio* and *La República* are two of the best daily newspapers.

Passports **For Residents of the United States:** Whether you're applying in person or by mail, you can download passport applications from the U.S. State Department website at **http://travel.state.gov**. To find your regional passport office, either check the U.S. State Department website or call the **National Passport Information Center** toll-free number (© **877/487-2778**) for automated information.

For Residents of Canada: Passport applications are available at travel agencies throughout Canada or from the central **Passport Office,** Department of Foreign Affairs and International Trade, Ottawa, ON K1A 0G3 (© **800/567-6868;** www.ppt.gc.ca).

For Residents of the United Kingdom: To pick up an application for a standard 10-year passport (5-yr. passport for children under 16), visit your nearest passport office, major post office, or travel agency, or contact the **United Kingdom Passport Service** at © 0870/521-0410 or search its website at www.ukpa. gov.uk.

For Residents of Ireland: You can apply for a 10-year passport at the **Passport Office,** Setanta Centre, Molesworth Street, Dublin 2 (© **01/671-1633;** www.irl gov.ie/iveagh). Those under age 18 and over 65 must apply for a €12 3-year passport. You can also apply at 1A South Mall, Cork (© **021/272-525**) or at most main post offices.

For Residents of Australia: You can pick up an application from your local post office or any branch of Passports Australia, but you must schedule an interview at the passport office to present your application materials. Call the **Australian Passport Information Service** at © **131-232,** or visit the government website at www.passports.gov.au.

For Residents of New Zealand: You can pick up a passport application at any New Zealand Passports Office or download it from their website. Contact the **Passports Office** at © **0800/225-050** in New Zealand or 04/474-8100, or log on to www.passports.govt.nz.

Police Peru has special tourist police forces (Policía Nacional de Turismo) with offices and personnel in all major tourist destinations, including Lima, Cusco, Arequipa, and Puno, as well as a dozen other cities. You are more likely to get a satisfactory response, not to mention someone who speaks at least some English, from the tourist police rather than from the regular national police (PNP). The number for the tourist police in Lima is © **01/225-8698** or 01/225-8699. For other cities, see "Emergencies" above and "Fast Facts" in individual destination chapters. Tourist police officers are distinguished by their white shirts.

Restrooms Public lavatories are rarely available except in railway stations, restaurants, and theaters. Many Peruvian men choose to urinate in public, against a wall in full view, especially late at night; it's not recommended that you emulate them. Use the bathroom of a bar, cafe, or restaurant; if it feels uncomfortable to dart in and out, have a coffee at the bar. Public restrooms are labeled WC (water closet), DAMAS (Ladies), and CABALLEROS or HOMBRES (Men). Toilet paper is not always provided, and when it is, most establishments request that patrons throw it in the wastebasket rather than the toilet, to avoid clogging.

Safety See "Health & Safety," earlier in this chapter.

Smoking Smoking is common in Peru, and it is rare to find a hotel, restaurant, or bar with nonsmoking rooms. However, there are now a few hotels (usually high-end) and restaurants with nonsmoking rooms, and the trend is growing, albeit slowly. There are nonsmoking cars on trains, and most long-distance buses are also nonsmoking.

Taxes A general sales tax (IGV) is added automatically to most consumer bills (19%). In some upmarket hotels or restaurants, service charges of 10% are often added. At all airports, passengers must pay a departure tax: $28.24 for international flights, and $5.04 for domestic flights, payable in cash only.

Telephones Peru's telephone system has been much improved since it was privatized and acquired by Spain's Telefónica in the mid-1990s. (There are now several additional players in the market, including Bell South.) It is relatively simple to make local and long-distance domestic and international calls from pay phones, which accept coins and phone cards *(tarjetas telefónicas)*. Most phone booths display country and city codes, and contain instructions in English and Spanish.

Peru's country code is **51**. *Note:* Many area codes across Peru were changed in 2003, and many published telephone numbers still contain old area codes.

To call Peru: If you're calling Peru from the United States:

1. Dial the international access code: 011.
2. Dial the country code 51.
3. Dial the city code (1, 84, 54, etc.) and then the number. The whole number you'd dial (for Cusco) would be 011-51-84-000-0000.

To make international calls: To make international calls from Peru, first dial 00 and then the country code (U.S. or Canada 1, U.K. 44, Ireland 353, Australia 61, New Zealand 64). Next you dial the area code and number. For example, if you wanted to call the British Embassy in Washington, D.C., you would dial 00-1-202-588-7800.

The easiest way to make a long-distance call is to purchase a phone card (maximum S/30 or $8.50). Many of these cards, purchased at newspaper kiosks and street vendors who sell nothing else, are called **Tarjeta 147**. To use such a card, first rub off the secret number. Dial the numbers 1-4-7 and then dial the 12-digit number on your card. A voice recording will tell you (in Spanish only) the value remaining on the card and instruct you to dial the desired telephone number. It will then tell you how many minutes you can expect to talk with the amount remaining. You can also make international calls from Telefónica offices and hotels, although surcharges levied at the latter can be extraordinarily expensive. A new and very inexpensive way to make international calls is through Internet software such as Net2Phone, which more Internet booths in Peru are featuring. Rates are as low as 20¢ per minute to the United States. Some cabinas even have private booths from which to talk. Reception, however, can be spotty.

For **directory and operator assistance,** see the "Telephone Tips" in the inside front cover of this book.

Toll-free numbers: Numbers beginning with 0800 within Peru are toll-free when called from a private phone (not from a public pay phone), but calling an 800 number in the States from Peru is not toll-free. In fact, it costs the same as an overseas call.

For local calls: You do not need to dial the area code (01 for Lima, three digits for all other cities); dial only the number. To make a long-distance call within Peru, dial the city code (including the zero) + telephone number. For international calls, dial 00 + country code + city code + telephone number.

Time Zone Peru is 5 hours behind GMT (Greenwich mean time). Peru does not observe daylight saving time.

Tipping Most people leave about a 10% tip for the waitstaff in restaurants. In nicer restaurants that add a 10% service charge, many patrons tip an additional 5% or 10% (because little, if any, of that service charge will ever make it to the waiter's pocket). Taxi drivers are not usually tipped unless they provide additional service. Bilingual tour guides should be tipped ($1–$2 per person for a short visit, and $5 or more per person for a full day). If you have a private guide, tip about $10.

Water Visitors should drink only bottled water, which is widely available. Do not drink tap water, even in major hotels. Try to avoid drinks with ice. *Agua con gas* is carbonated; *agua sin gas* is still.

3

Suggested Peru Itineraries

Unless you have at least 3 weeks or a month to spend in Peru, you probably won't get to see as much of the country as you'd like. Peru is large, and there are considerable geographic and transportation barriers that make zipping around the country very difficult. A real danger is trying to do too much in too short a period. Even on relatively short trips of 2 weeks or less, you have to take into account those hefty distances and complicated transportation routes, not to mention natural factors—such as jet lag and acclimatization to high altitude—that require most visitors to slow down.

1 The Best of Peru in 1 Week: Cusco, Machu Picchu & the Sacred Valley

Though Peru boasts astounding variety, most people don't have time to experience the range of its offerings (that's what return trips are for!). For first-timers, there's one place they've absolutely got to see: Machu Picchu. I've got no problem with that: It's where I was determined to go before I'd ever stepped foot on the South American continent. In a single week, there's just enough time to see the best of Incan Peru (and it won't involve crazed travel from one place to the next all over Peru). This itinerary will give you an idea of how to best experience the ancient Incan capital, the empire's alluring, once-thought-lost imperial city, and the Urubamba Valley that the Incas held sacred.

Day ❶: Arrive in Lima; transfer to Cusco

All international flights arrive in Lima, but try to arrange it so that an overnight flight gets you there very early in the morning, with time enough to get an 8am or 9am flight to Cusco. With only a week in Peru, there's little need to linger in Lima if you can avoid it.

Take it easy in Cusco on your first day. Drink a lot of water (and perhaps some coca-leaf tea) and get a good night's rest. The altitude (more than 3,400m/11,000 ft.) combined with an overnight international flight will prove very taxing. Have lunch at **Jack's Café Bar** (p. 209), a popular gringo hangout. Limit yourself to taking a stroll around the delightful **Plaza**

de Armas (p. 210), popping into the tourist information office to pick up your *boleto turístico* (tourist ticket for the main sights in Cusco and the Sacred Valley) and choosing a spot for dinner. I'd suggest **Cicciolina** or **A Mi Manera** (p. 206), or for views of the Plaza de Armas, **La Retama** (p. 205).

Day ❷: Colonial Cusco

Sticking to the area near the Plaza de Armas, visit the **Cathedral** (p. 212) and the **Santa Catalina Convent** (p. 210) in the morning. After lunch, see the superb **Qoricancha (Temple of the Sun;** p. 216) to get an idea of the Incas' incredible masonry and the clash of native and Spanish culture. Take a walk along the

The Best of Peru in 1 Week

- **1** Lima
- **2** Cusco
- **3** Pisac
- **4** Ollantaytambo
- **5** Machu Picchu
- **6** Cusco
- **7** Lima

Calles Loreto and **Hatunrumiyoc** to see some more Incan stonework. In Plaza Nazarenas, check out the beautifully designed **Precolombian Art Museum** (p. 215) and some of the upscale alpaca goods shops on the square. Have a pisco sour at one of the lively cafes or bars near the Plaza de Armas and make your way up bustling **Calle Procuradores,** Cusco's gringo alley and restaurant row. If you're dining on a budget, pick a restaurant; if you're looking for something more refined, try **MAP Café** (p. 205) or **Illary** (p. 203), the restaurant at Hotel Monasterio.

Day **3**: Sacred Valley: Pisac

With luck your third day in Peru will be a Tuesday, Wednesday, or (better yet) Sunday—those are market days in the Urubamba Valley (the **Valle Sagrado de los Incas**). Take a combi or taxi to Pisac and check out the popular and lively **artisans' market.** Have lunch at **Ulrike's Café** (p. 239) right on the main square. After lunch either hike up to or grab a taxi to the **Incan ruins** (p. 238) looming above town. Pisac's ruins will give you a taste of what you're about to see in Ollantaytambo and Machu Picchu. Head a little farther along in the valley (again by taxi or combi) to a rustic country hotel near **Urubamba** or **Yucay,** where you'll have dinner and spend the night.

Day **4**: Sacred Valley: Ollantaytambo

Wake early and take a taxi to **Ollantaytambo** (p. 249), where you'll want to arrive as close to opening as possible to explore the **Fortress Ruins** (p. 251) before the busloads arrive. Then take a walk around Ollanta's **Old Town** (p. 252) and grab lunch. If you have the energy and can manage a few hours after lunch, go for a hike in the Valley, perhaps to **Salineras de Maras** (p. 247), the ancient salt mines near Urubamba.

If you don't mind moving around, you could transfer to a hotel in Ollanta to enjoy it at night when there are few tourists (and be there for the train the next morning to Machu Picchu). Otherwise head back to your hotel near Urubamba.

Day ⑤: What You Came For: Machu Picchu

Catch the early morning train from Ollantaytambo to **Aguas Calientes** (p. 256), the rough-edged town that sits below **Machu Picchu** (p. 260). Catch the bus up to the ruins and spend the day exploring them (hiking up to the **Huayna Picchu peak** for panoramic views if you're in shape; see p. 264). Have lunch at the Machu Picchu Sanctuary Lodge next to the ruins and stay until late in the afternoon, after the large tour groups have left. Spend the night either next to the ruins (if you've got deep pockets) or back down in Aguas Calientes (which is actually more fun). Hit the bars along the railroad tracks to share stories with some of the grungy folks who've survived the Inca Trail.

Day ⑥: Back to Cusco

Now that you've acclimatized to the Andes and seen some of the greatest legacies of the Incas, head back by train to the old Incan capital, Cusco. In the afternoon, stroll around the hilly **San Blas** (p. 215) neighborhood, site of dozens of cool shops and art galleries. Do some shopping for handicrafts, souvenirs, and art. If Machu Picchu and Ollantaytambo have intensified your interest in Incan architecture, catch a cab (or walk up to) the fantastic ruins, **Sacsayhuamán** (p. 219), overlooking the city. Have a celebratory dinner at **Greens** (p. 206) in San Blas and get a taste of Cusco's hopping nightlife at one of the pubs or nightclubs.

Day ⑦: Back to Lima and Back Home

Do some final shopping in Cusco before catching a flight to Lima. You'll probably have an evening flight back home, so you may have enough time for a ceviche lunch in Lima and, if you're ambitious, a short tour of colonial **Lima Centro** (p. 112) in the late afternoon.

2 The Best of Peru in 2 Weeks

This itinerary will allow you to experience the greatest of southern Peru, from its historic colonial cities to its natural wonders. First on everyone's list, of course, are the lively ancient Incan capital Cusco and that empire's legendary lost city, Machu Picchu. But in a relatively short amount of time you can also delve into dense Amazonian jungle; Lake Titicaca, the world's highest navigable body of water; and one of the world's deepest canyons, Colca. Plenty of people linger, particularly in Cusco and the Sacred Valley of the Incas (especially if they want to hike the Inca Trail to Machu Picchu), or don't have a full 2 weeks for travel in Peru. In that case, it's probably best to concentrate on a particular region so that you don't lose too much time traveling. Of course, if your primary interest is wildlife viewing in the great Amazon, you'll want to plan everything around a 4- to 7-day jungle expedition deep into Tambopata National Reserve, Manu Biosphere Reserve, or the jungle around Iquitos in northern Peru.

Day ❶: Arrive in Lima

All international flights go into the rather chaotic capital, Lima, and even though most people are headed elsewhere, you may find yourself obligated to spend at least a day in Lima. Make the most of it by touring the colonial quarter, or perhaps visiting one of the country's great museums, such as the **Museo Arqueológico Rafael Larco Herrera** or **Museo de la Nación,** and hitting either a great *cevichería* or a cutting-edge *novo andino* restaurant. See chapter 5.

Then get out of Lima and on your way to Peru's greatest attractions. (If you're able to get an overnight flight that puts you into Lima early in the morning, you may want to consider flying immediately to Cusco to save time and avoid the hassles of Lima.)

Days ❷–❸: On to Cusco, Old Incan Capital

Although you may want to hit Cusco running, the city's altitude, more than 3,400m/11,000 feet, is daunting to most travelers. Spend a couple of days seeing the old Incan capital at a relaxed pace, making sure to hang out around the **Plaza de Armas** and visit the **Cathedral, Santa Catalina Convent,** and **Qoricancha** (Temple of the Sun). Cusco is one of the best places in Peru to shop, eat, and party, so make sure to squeeze those vital activities in with sightseeing. See chapter 7.

Day ❹: The Stuff of Legend: Machu Picchu

Though I think Machu Picchu deserves an overnight stay (and even 2 days exploring the ruins), if you're trying to see the best of Peru in 2 weeks, you can't afford the time. So take the morning train from Cusco to Machu Picchu (**Aguas Calientes**), South America's number one attraction. Spend the middle part of the day exploring the ruins here (p. 260) and then head back to Cusco on the train.

Day ❺: Cusco

If you weren't able to catch an archaeology museum in Lima, or even if you did, check out the beautifully designed **Museo de Arte Precolombino** (p. 215). Enjoy some of the lively cafes, bars, and restaurants of Cusco; you'll find plenty while strolling around the **Barrio de San Blas** (p. 215). If you have time and plenty of energy, catch a cab (or walk up to) the fantastic ruins, **Sacsayhuamán,** (p. 219) overlooking the city.

Days ❻–❽: Into the Jungle

Take an early morning, half-hour flight from Cusco to **Puerto Maldonado,** the gateway to the southern Peruvian Amazon jungle of **Tambopata National Reserve** (p. 338). Board a boat for a 2-day, 1-night trip to one of the jungle lodges along the Río Madre de Dios. A 3-day, 2-night adventure, either within 1 hour of Puerto Maldonado or 4 to 5 hours away along the Río Tambopata, is even better, if you have the time. On the third day, head back to Puerto and then catch a flight to Cusco. Spend the night in Cusco.

Day ❾: South to Lake Titicaca

From Cusco, take the extraordinarily scenic train to **Puno** and **Lake Titicaca** (or if you want to visit some of the Incan ruins en route, take one of the premium tour bus services that makes a day of the journey). Spend the night in Puno and rest up (and get accustomed to the even higher altitude) for the next day's boat trip out on the lake. See chapter 9.

Day ❿: Lake Titicaca and Isla Taquile

While an overnight trip that allows you to spend a night with a family either on Isla Taquile or Amantaní is the best way to experience the people and customs of Titicaca, you can also do a 1-day trip that allows you to visit the **Uros floating islands** and the fascinating culture of **Isla Taquile.** See chapter 9.

The Best of Peru in 2 Weeks

1 Lima
2 Cusco
3 Machu Picchu
4 Puerto Maldonado
5 Tambopata
National Reserve
6 Puno
7 Lake Titicaca
8 Arequipa
9 Colca Valley
10 Lima

Day **11**: Arequipa

Catch an early morning flight from Juliaca (the nearest airport, an hour from Puno) to Arequipa, the elegant southern city known as "La Ciudad Blanca" for its beautiful colonial buildings made of *sillar*, or white volcanic stone. Stay close to the gorgeous **Plaza de Armas** and spend the afternoon at the wondrous **Monasterio de Santa Catalina,** one of the finest examples of colonial religious architecture in the Americas. See chapter 9.

Days **12–13**: Colca Valley

From Arequipa, set off on a 2-day, 1-night exploration of **Colca Canyon,** the best spot in South America to observe giant Andean condors, which soar overhead at **Cruz del Condor.** Explore some of the villages of the valley, as well as the thermal baths, on the first day and spend the night at a rustic hotel in Colca before marveling at the condors the next morning. For those with less time, it's possible, though brutal, to "do" Colca on a 1-day adventure, leaving very early in the morning (practically the middle of the night) to get there in time for the condors' lift-off at 9am. See chapter 9.

Day **14**: Morning in Arequipa, then back to Lima

Spend the morning shopping for alpaca goods before flying to **Lima,** where you'll catch your flight back home.

3 Ten Days with the Kids in Peru

Traveling to Peru with small children will be a challenge; though Peruvians are very family-oriented, transportation difficulties and the rugged appeal of many of Peru's primary attractions may test parents' resourcefulness and patience, as well as that of the children. Slightly older and adventurous children, however, should revel in the archaeological grandeur of Machu Picchu, the indigenous peoples of Lake Titicaca, and the phenomenal flora and fauna of the Amazon jungle. A trip with children may not differ much with respect to the places one chooses to visit, though there are some specific things to do and ways to do them in those places that may appeal more to kids. Families should approach Peru as an excellent learning experience about South American history, ecology, and Peruvian culture.

Days ❶–❷: The Sacred Valley of the Incas

Families will probably want to stick to the tried-and-true highlights of Peru, beginning with Cusco and Machu Picchu. Instead of beginning in the old Incan capital, however, it might make more sense to head straight to the **Sacred Valley of the Incas,** where the altitude is lower (requiring less acclimatization) and there is more open space. Stay at one of the area's rustic country hotels, where kids can go horseback riding and teenagers can go whitewater rafting or mountain biking in the Valley. Athletic kids should like climbing the Incan ruins of **Ollantaytambo** and **Pisac,** where they can admire not only Incan ingenuity but also the stunning mountain views. See chapter 8.

Day ❸: Machu Picchu

Children will greatly enjoy the **scenic train** to Machu Picchu. It's a good idea to consider spending the night in Aguas Calientes, as seeing the ruins of Machu Picchu involves a lot of climbing and you'll require stamina to see it thoroughly. Very athletic children will eat up the hike to **Huayna Picchu** (p. 264), which provides some of the most dramatic panoramic views you're likely to stumble across. Nearly as good, and less challenging, are routes from the **Intipunku** (the Sun Gate, where hikers come upon the site from the Inca Trail; see p. 266). After a visit to the ruins, check out the **thermal baths** in town. The Machu Picchu Pueblo Hotel, though expensive, has great grounds, birding walks, and a swimming pool.

Days ❹–❻: From Cusco to the Jungle

A short flight from Cusco to Puerto Maldonado and a drive to the pier is all it takes to plunge into the Amazon jungle. Two good lodges that don't require too much river travel time are **Reserva Amazonica** (for families that may enjoy a bit of pampering) and **Sandoval Lake Lodge** (for those who prefer to rough it a bit); see p. 340 and 340. The first has a private treetop canopy walk, which kids should love, and a small island that is a private refuge for several types of monkeys; boats take guests out at night to look for caimans on the river. A 3-day, 2-night stay is a good option.

Days ❼: A Breather in Cusco

Fly back to Cusco and spend the day getting to know the city. Kids should appreciate the blocks of **Incan masonry** that fit together like a giant jigsaw puzzle; have them try to locate the puma stone on Calle Inca Roca and the 12-angled stone on Calle Hatunrumiyoc. There are always Quechua families with dressed-up llamas wandering the streets. At the ruins of **Sacsayhuamán** (p. 219), on a hill overlooking Cusco, are huge rocks with slick grooves— kids of all ages use them as slides. Cusco is

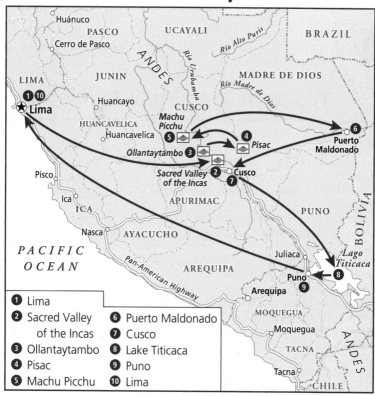

full of fun and funky restaurants, such as **Chez Maggy** (p. 208), that will appeal to kids.

Days 8–10: Lake Titicaca

The long but terrifically **scenic train** ride from Cusco to Lake Titicaca is one of the best in South America. Stay in a hotel perched on the edge of the lake, and head out on a **boat tour** of Titicaca (either day-long or with an overnight stay). Kids should marvel at the natives who live on the floating islands, and older kids who like to rough it will enjoy visiting the communities on **Isla Taquile** (p. 290) and staying overnight with a family on **Isla Amantaní** (p. 292). The next day fly from Puno (Juliaca, actually) to Lima for your flight home. If you have extra time in Lima, which isn't exactly a family-friendly city, take older kids to the **Museo Arqueológico Rafael Larco Herrera** (p. 138) to survey the sometimes eye-popping ceramics of ancient Peruvian civilizations.

4

The Active Vacation Planner

The word "Peru" is derived from a word in Quechua signifying "land of abundance." There is little question that, in its distinct *costa, sierra,* and *selva* (coast, highlands, and jungle) regions, Peru is indeed blessed with an enormous variety of wilderness and some of the world's greatest and most diverse plant and animal species. It has been reported that Peru contains 84 of the known 104 biosystems in the world; more than 400 species of mammals and 300 species of reptiles; 50,000 plant species (among them the world's highest count of orchids, more than 3,000 kinds); and nearly 2,000 bird species, about 10% of the world's total. With desert sands, dense Amazon rainforest canopy, amazing Andean peaks, and the world's deepest canyons, Peru is a country that definitely inspires travelers to get active and get outdoors.

Peru is perhaps the most diverse and best-equipped outdoors destination in South America. It is now rare to see visitors from abroad come to Peru with the intention of staying clean and dry in pressed slacks and loafers. Almost every gringo who sets foot beyond Lima is more properly outfitted in Gore-Tex water-repellent gear, fleece pullovers, hiking boots, and daypacks. In the minds of many nonspecialists, getting outdoors in Peru is still limited to easily reached jungle treks and lodges, day hikes in the valleys, and—if you're really adventurous—treks along ancient Incan trails. Whether that's your speed or you want to go hard-core, plunging deep into the jungle or mountains, it isn't hard to come up with a plan to experience the best of natural Peru.

Amazingly, given its natural abundance, Peru is still relatively new to the ecotourism game. Its infrastructure to receive large groups of ecotourists is not quite as developed as that of some other countries, such as Costa Rica. But Peru is quickly catching up, and tour operators, guides, and agencies, both local and international, are increasingly specializing in outdoor and active travel. The oldest jungle lodges in the Peruvian Amazon have been around for more than 30 years. Lodges, climbing and rafting expeditions, and birding and hiking trips all cater to environmentally aware travelers with deep interests in nature and seeing "the real Peru."

Whether you want to make active travel the sole focus of your trip or treat it as just an add-on, there are many different ways to approach it. This chapter lays out your options, from tour operators who run multi-activity package tours (and frequently include stays at ecolodges) to the best spots in Peru to get outdoors (with listings of tour operators, guides, and outfitters that specialize in each), and it provides an overview of the country's national parks and nature reserves. You'll also find a handful of tips on health and safety in the wilderness, what to bring, and educational and volunteer travel options for those with the time and desire to work toward the maintenance and preservation of Peru's natural wonders and gain a more in-depth understanding of Peru's culture and people.

1 Organized Adventure Trips

Because most travelers have limited time and resources, organized ecotourism or adventure travel packages, arranged by tour operators abroad or in Peru, are popular ways of combining cultural and outdoor activities. Bird-watching, horseback riding, rafting, and hiking can be teamed with visits to destinations such as Cusco, the Sacred (Urubamba) Valley and Machu Picchu, or Arequipa and Lake Titicaca.

Traveling with a group has several advantages over traveling independently. Your accommodations and transportation are arranged, and most (if not all) of your meals are included in the cost of a package. If your tour operator has a reasonable amount of experience and a decent track record, you should proceed to each of your destinations quickly without the snags and long delays that you might face if you're traveling on your own. You'll also have the opportunity to meet like-minded travelers who are interested in nature and active sports. Some group trekking trips include *porteros* or *arrieros* (porters or muleteers) who carry extra equipment. On some luxury treks of the Inca Trail, porters will even carry your backpack, so all you have to do is hike your lazy self up and over the mountain passes.

In the best cases of organized outdoors travel, group size is kept small (10–15 people), and tours are escorted by knowledgeable guides who are either naturalists or biologists. Be sure to inquire about difficulty levels when you're choosing a tour. While most companies offer "soft adventure" packages that those in decent but not overly athletic shape can handle, others focus on more hard-core activities geared toward very fit and seasoned adventure travelers.

See also the escorted tour operators listed in "Escorted General-Interest Tours" in chapter 2. Several operators offer adventure and outdoors components to their more standard Peru packages.

U.S. & INTERNATIONAL ADVENTURE TOUR OPERATORS

These agencies and operators specialize in well-organized and coordinated tours that cover your entire stay. Many travelers prefer to have everything arranged and confirmed before arriving in Peru—a good idea for first-timers and during high season (especially for travel to Cusco and its immediate environs, including the Inca Trail). Many of these operators are not cheap; 10-day tours generally cost upwards of $2,000 or more per person, and most do not include airfare to Peru.

Adventure Life ★★ (② 800/344-6118; www.adventure-life.com), based in Missoula, Montana, and specializing in Central and South America, has an interesting roster of rugged Peru trips, frequently with a community focus, including a 12-day multi-sport tour (mountain biking, hiking, rafting, jungle tour, and Machu Picchu), rainforest ecolodge tours, and a 10-day "Cachiccata Trek: The Inca Trail Less Traveled," as well as plenty of tour extensions. One Peru trip is specifically designed to raise

---

Tips Inca Trail Regulations

Trekkers could once do the Inca Trail on their own, but new regulations imposed by the Peruvian government to limit environmental degradation and damage to the trail itself now require all trekkers to go with officially sanctioned groups. See the "Inca Trail Regulations" box and "Inca Trail Tour Agencies," both in chapter 8, for more information.

money (40% of trip cost) for the organization's nonprofit fund (which aims to give back to local communities).

Adventure Specialists ✦ (© 719/630-7195; www.adventurespecialists.org) travels only to the Copper Canyon (Mexico), Colorado, and Peru. In Peru, it specializes in treks, horse trips, and archaeology expeditions, as well as wildlife and birding adventures by dugout canoe in the Manu Biosphere Reserve. The founder is one of the archaeologists credited with the November 2003 rediscovery of Llactapata, a "lost" Incan city.

Amazonia Expeditions (© 800/262-9669 or 813/907-8475; www.perujungle. com or www.peruandes.com) offers good-value, personalized, and flexible ecotourism trips to the Peruvian jungle and the Andes. Trips of up to 7 days are all-inclusive (even laundry and tips are included). Jungle trips are to the Tahuayo Lodge (4 hr. from Iquitos) and the Tamshiyacu-Tahuayo Reserve (they are the only licensed tour operator to the latter). The two websites focus on the group's jungle adventures and Incan ruins/Andes treks respectively.

Andean Treks ✦ (© 800/683-8148 or 617/924-1974; www.andeantreks.com) is a Latin American adventure-tour operator that focuses on trekking in the Andes and exploring the jungle throughout Peru. Its roster of reasonably priced trips for all levels includes cloud-forest treks, llama trekking, trips to Manu and Tambopata, and highlands treks that combine white-water rafting or Amazon lodge stays. Trips range from easy to hard-core.

Condor Journeys and Adventures (© 01700/741-318; www.condorjourneys-adventures.com) is one of the top U.K. agencies organizing package tours to Latin America. Condor offers a huge number of varied trips to Peru, including archaeology tours and lots of soft- and hard-core adventure and outdoor travel: hiking programs along Incan roads, horseback treks to Machu Picchu, rainforest and white-water rafting in canyons and along the Apurímac and Urubamba, mountain-biking expeditions, and special, unusual programs such as "Mystical Peru" and hikes to Salcantay and Vilcabamba by llama.

GorpTravel (© 877/440-GORP; http://gorp.away.com), a self-styled "Guide to Outdoor Travel," is a wholesaler with a vast range of options for adventure and more general travel throughout Peru and the world. It recently offered more than 60 outdoor-oriented vacations to Peru (including a "Peru Top 20" list). A few are basic highlights trips, while others are cultural and language vacations or specialist adventures for very active and adventurous sorts. "Adventure Plus" membership ($59) gets you a 5% rebate on many trips, as well as other discounts.

International Expeditions (© 800/633-4734 or 205/428-1700; www.international expeditions.com) features Amazon cruises and jungle-lodge tours (including the most luxurious river cruises, run by Jungle Expeditions). The main tours to Peru are an Amazon Explorer "Jungles of Peru" and a 9-day Amazon Voyage. Visitors help with reforestation projects and participate in conservation programs and tree planting with local naturalists. Extensions to Cusco, Machu Picchu, Lima, and the Nasca Lines are available.

Journeys International ✦ (© 800/255-8735 or 734/665-4407; www.journeys-intl.com), based in Ann Arbor, Michigan, offers small-group (4–12 people) natural history tours guided by naturalists. Trips include the 11-day "Inca Trail Trek & Amazon," featuring Peru highlights along with a rainforest expedition to the Tambopata National Reserve; an 8-day "Amazon Wildlife Odyssey"; the 9-day "Amazon & Andes

Odyssey," which includes the Tambopata National Reserve along with Cusco, Machu Picchu, and the Sacred Valley; an 8-day river cruise on the Amazon; a kayaking adventure on Lake Titicaca; and special Amazon and Incan trips for families.

Mountain Travel-Sobek ⚐⚐⚐ (✆ **888/687-6235** or 510/594-600, or 01494/448-901 in the U.K.; www.mtsobek.com) offers seven itineraries to Peru, including the 8-day "Andean Explorer," with day hikes and rafting. Options for mountaineers and committed trekkers include 13 days of strenuous trekking in Cordillera Blanca (mostly camping); a shorter 5-day (but still hard-core) trekking option in the same area; and a challenging 15-day rafting trip along the River Tambopata (half camping, half inns). A new, unique trip is the off-the-beaten path "Other Inca Trail." Trips are helpfully rated for difficulty.

Overseas Adventure Travel ⚐ (✆ **800/493-6824**; www.oattravel.com) offers natural history and "soft adventure" itineraries, with optional add-on excursions. Tours are limited to 16 people and are guided by naturalists. All accommodations are in small hotels, lodges, or tent camps. The 11-day "Real Affordable Peru" includes rafting on the Urubamba and a *curandero* healing ceremony. The 19-day "Machu Picchu & Galápagos" tour features a good bit of walking. There are also Amazon River cruises and rainforest trips.

Southwind Adventures ⚐ (✆ **800/377-9463** or 303/972-0701; www.southwind adventures.com), based in Littleton, Colorado, does unique high-end, tailored trips that include mountain biking in the Sacred Valley, a hard-core 16-day Vilcabamba trekking expedition, an Urubamba weaver's route, rainforest trips and Amazon cruises, and a Cordillera Blanca climbing expedition. Trips often include both camping and stays at rustic inns.

Tropical Nature Travel ⚐⚐⚐ (✆ **877/827-8350**; www.tropicalnaturetravel.com) is known as one of the most sophisticated conservation groups organizing travel to jungle wildlife lodges in Manu and Tambopata. In tandem with its local conservation partner, InkaNatura, it operates four lodges, including Manu Wildlife Center, Cock of the Rock Lodge, Sandoval Lake Lodge, and the new Heath River Wildlife Center; and its Amazon jungle trips can't be beat. The outfit has expanded its itineraries to include trekking, rafting, and archaeology culture trips to places such as Chachapoyas and Colca Canyon.

Wilderness Travel ⚐⚐⚐ (✆ **800/368-2794** or 510/558-2488; www.wilderness travel.com) is a Berkeley-based outfitter specializing in cultural, wildlife, and hiking group tours that are arranged with tiered pricing (the cost of the trip varies according to group size). There are seven tours to Peru, including a 20-day Cordillera Huayhuash trek, and a unique Salcantay "hidden" trail to Machu Picchu. The rather pricey trips are graded according to difficulty and are described with suggested reading lists.

Wildland Adventures ⚐⚐⚐ (✆ **800/345-4453** or 206/365-0686; www.wildland. com), based in Seattle, is one of the top international outdoor-tour companies with operations in Peru. It offers excellent special-interest trekking and rainforest expedition programs, with customizing options. There are lodge-based programs, primarily in the jungle; trekking expeditions, such as the 9-day Cordillera Blanca trek; and special adventures focusing on photographing Peru. Wildland's programs are well designed, guides are very professional, and the organization is focused on authentic travel experiences.

In addition to these companies, many environmental organizations regularly offer organized trips to Peru. The **Nature Conservancy** (© 800/628-6860 or 703/841-4250; www.nature.org/aboutus/travel/travel) offers "conservation journeys" with members; the trips change from year to year, but past trips to Peru have included a riverboat Amazon voyage that visits the Nature Conservancy project in the Pacaya-Samiria National Reserve. The **Smithsonian Institute** (© 202/357-4700; www.si.edu) offers study tours for members, which have included a river cruise of the northern Amazon and a long (and expensive) trip down the Amazon from Belém, Brazil, to Pevas, Peru. The **National Audubon Society** (© 800/967-7425 or 212/979-3066; www.audubon.org) also offers trips, which focus on birding and natural history. A good resource for information on ecotravel is **Sacred Earth** (www.sacredearth.com), a loose consortium of "ethnobotanists" and ecotravelers that publishes an e-zine and has links to a half-dozen featured trips and workshops to Peru, including Manu camping journeys and shamanistic "listening to the plants" tours of the northern Amazon.

PERUVIAN TOUR AGENCIES

Many tour companies based in the United States and elsewhere subcontract portions of their tours to established Peruvian companies. In some cases, independent travelers can benefit by organizing their tours directly with local companies. Prices on the ground can be much cheaper than contracting a tour from abroad, but there are risks of not getting what you want when you want it. Also, the world of subcontracting can be byzantine, and even Peruvian travel agencies hire out adventure and outdoor specialists.

Local agencies offering adventure options abound, especially in Cusco, Arequipa, Huaraz, and Iquitos. These agencies can arrange everything from white-water rafting to day treks to horseback riding. Some tours might be held only when there are enough interested people or on fixed dates, so it's worthwhile to contact a few of the companies before you leave for Peru to find out what they might be doing when you arrive.

Class Adventure Travel ⋆ (© 01/444-2220; www.cat-travel.com) is a fine all-purpose agency with offices in Lima and Cusco (it has also recently expanded, with offices in Bolivia, Chile, and Argentina). In addition to professionally organizing virtually any kind of travel detail in Peru, its adventure offerings include rafting, trekking, and jungle tours.

Explorandes ⋆⋆ (© 01/445-0532 in Lima; www.explorandes.com) has been doing trekking and river expeditions in Peru for 25 years. One of the top high-end agencies for treks and mountaineering in Peru, it's reasonably priced and especially good for forming very small private groups. It offers a number of soft adventure trips (with stays in hotels and full- and half-day river trips) and an even more impressive lineup of real adventure, including cool, unique trips such as llama trekking to Chavín, a festival trek, rafting on the Apurímac River, treks on southern peaks around Cusco, and hard-core trekking in the Cordillera Blanca and Huayhuash. Amazon extensions are available.

Peru Expeditions Overland ⋆ (© 01/447-2057; www.peru-expeditions.com) is a Lima-based company run by Rafael Belmonte, an amiable fellow and dedicated cyclist. His company runs all kinds of cool trips across Peru, including treks, four-wheel-drive vehicle tours, and mountain biking, as well as more standard tours to destinations such as Arequipa, Cusco, and Colca Canyon.

SAS Travel Peru ⚘ (© 084/225-205; www.sastravelperu.com) is one of the most popular agencies organizing outdoor travel for backpackers and budget-minded travelers in Cusco. Its roster includes a number of short treks in the Cusco area and a couple of longer, more challenging mountain treks lasting up to a week. Jungle treks are to Manu and Tambopata. SAS also offers white-water rafting, paragliding, climbing, mountain biking, and horseback riding.

2 Activities A to Z

The listings in this section describe the best places to practice particular sports and activities and include the top tour operators and outfitters. If you want to focus on only one active sport during your trip to Peru, these companies are your best bets for quality equipment and knowledgeable service—but almost all of them will allow you to combine one activity with another or engage in general cultural sightseeing.

BALLOONING & HANG GLIDING

In the mid-1970s, two foreigners constructed a balloon out of cotton and reed in an effort to prove that ancient cultures could have used balloons to design the mysterious Nasca Line drawings in the southern desert sands. Too bad that didn't spark a wild interest in ballooning and hang gliding in Peru. So many parts of the country would be absolutely glorious to fly silently over: the Sacred Valley, the Nasca Lines, the valleys of the Callejón de Huaylas, the magnificent pre-Columbian ruins, and the great canyons near Arequipa. Alas, the only outfitter operating balloon flights in Peru is a U.S.-owned company, **Globos de los Andes,** Av. de la Cultura 220, ste. 36, Cusco (© 084/232-352; www.globosperu.com), and even it offers flights on an inconsistent basis, mainly in the Urubamba Valley. If you're interested, contact the company before your trip to Peru (and have other backup plans). Flights are generally May through August only.

BIRD-WATCHING

Peru is one of the greatest countries on earth for birders. The bird population in Peru is, incredibly, about 10% of the world's total. With nearly 2,000 species of resident and migrant birds identified throughout Peru, great bird-watching sites abound.

Manu Biosphere Reserve, believed to have the highest concentration of bird life on the planet, is legendary among birders. It boasts more than 1,000 species of birds. Cocks-of-the-rock, quetzals, toucanets, tanagers, and seven species of colorful macaws await patient birders. Some visitors have spotted as many as 500 species in relatively short visits to Manu. For specialists, the **Manu Wildlife Center** has the best reputation among birders, although **Pantiacolla Lodge** is also highly recommended.

The **Tambopata National Reserve** is also extraordinary for birding and more accessible than Manu. The reserve, about a third the size of Costa Rica, claims more species of birds (around 600) and butterflies (more than 1,200) than any place of similar size. Both Tambopata and Manu are famous for their *collpas,* or salt licks, where hundreds of macaws, parrots, and other birds appear daily to feed. Nearer to Puerto Maldonado, good birding areas include the Sandoval and Valencia lakes, but they cannot compare to either of the major reserves. **Explorer's Inn** is renowned as one of the top birding lodges in South America.

In the northern Amazon, the **Pacaya-Samiria National Reserve** is home to more than 500 species of birds. The northern Amazon doesn't have quite the reputation that

Outdoor Adventures in Peru

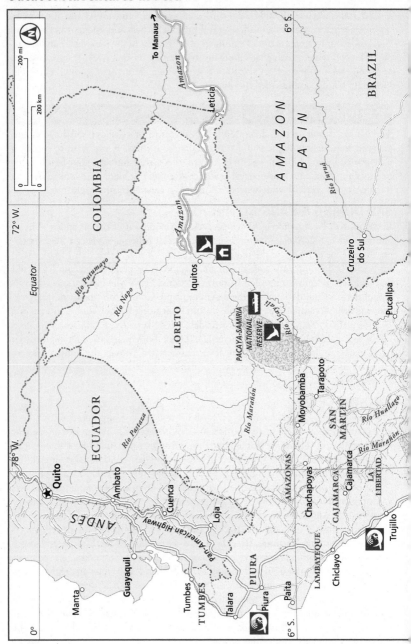

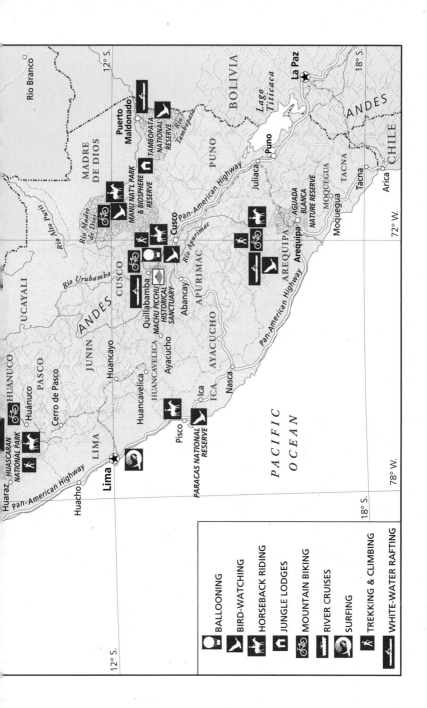

BALLOONING

BIRD-WATCHING

HORSEBACK RIDING

JUNGLE LODGES

MOUNTAIN BIKING

RIVER CRUISES

SURFING

TREKKING & CLIMBING

WHITE-WATER RAFTING

(*Fun Fact* **Butterflies**

Peru has become famous among bird-watchers, but naturalists who are fans of butterflies are in for an equal treat. Peru has the greatest diversity of butterflies in the world and the largest number of species: 3,700 (more than those found in all of subequatorial Africa).

---

the varied cloud forests leading to Manu and the rest of the southeastern jungle do, although there is excellent birding in and around the protected Machu Picchu Sanctuary. **Machu Picchu Pueblo Hotel** organizes birding tours and has more than 100 species of birds on its property in Aguas Calientes.

A handful of jungle lodges and river-cruise operators offer specialized birding options, but none is as complete as the trips offered by the specialist tour operators below. Sites worth visiting for birders are **Ornifolks,** a network of birding enthusiasts (www.ornifolks.org), and **WorldTwitch** (www.worldtwitch.com), which have links to birding lodges, tour operators, and organizations throughout Peru, as well as the Americas and the Caribbean. A portal with good information on birding in Peru is **www.birding-peru.com**; it features birding forums, information about specialized tour operators, and birding news items.

Although Peru is one of the top birding destinations in the world, specialists complain about the lack of an essential field guide. See "Recommended Books & Films" in chapter 2 for a discussion on books about birding in Peru.

TOUR OPERATORS

Birding Peru (www.birdingperu.org) is a Peru-based tour operator that links to birding trips offered by major outfitters to all regions of the country, including the highlands, coasts, and rainforest.

Field Guides ℱ (✆ **800/728-4953** or 512/263-7295; www.fieldguides.com) is a specialty bird-watching travel operator with trips worldwide. It features six birding trips to Peru, including the Manu Biosphere Reserve, Tambopata, Machu Picchu and the eastern slope of the Andes, the Amazon, and a 24-day tour of the endemic-rich region of northern Peru. Group size is limited to 14 participants.

Kolibri Expeditions ℱ (✆ **01/476-5016;** www.kolibriexpeditions.com), based in Lima, offers birding tours across Peru and South America. Most are no-frills, budget camping trips, but the outfit now also offers a few pampered, high-end trips (such as the "Marvelous Spatuletail Tours").

Tanager Tours ℱ (✆ **054/426-210;** www.tanagertours.com) is a Dutch-owned specialist bird-watching tour operator based in Arequipa. It organizes birding trips to Manu, Puerto Maldonado, and many other spots in Peru.

Wings ℱ (✆ **888/293-6443** or 520/320-9868; www.wingsbirds.com) is a specialty bird-watching travel operator with nearly 30 years of experience in the field. It promotes three trips to Peru, including an 18-day trip to Machu Picchu and the Manu Biosphere Reserve and one to the north and Andes in search of the long-whiskered owlet. Group size is usually between 6 and 18 people.

HORSEBACK RIDING

Lovers of horseback riding will find several areas in Peru to pursue their interest, as well as hotels and operators that can arrange everything from a couple hours in a saddle to

2-week trips on horseback. The best areas for treks on horseback are the Colca Canyon, near Arequipa, and the Callejón de Huaylas, the valley near the peaks of the Cordillera Blanca; a couple of local and international tour operators offer horse trekking in those areas. Otherwise, your options are mostly limited to a few country hotels in Cajamarca, the Sacred Valley, and Colca Valley.

In the area around Pisco, horseback riding is available at **Ocucaje Sun & Wine Resort,** and in Ica, at **Hotel Las Dunas.** On the outskirts of Cusco, the **Incatambo Hacienda Hotel** has horses, and beasts are available for walking between the ruins (Sacsayhuamán, Q'enko, Puca Pucara, and Tambomachay) just beyond Cusco. In the Sacred Valley, check out **Hotel Royal Inka Pisac, Sonesta Posada del Inca,** and **Hotel Sol y Luna;** in Ollantaytambo, you can usually arrange horseback riding along valley trails by asking around the main square. The **Parador de Colca** has horses for treks in the Colca Valley and Canyon; local agencies in Arequipa that arrange horseback treks through the Colca Canyon include **Colca Trek** (① 054/202-461; www.colcatrek.com) and **Peru Trekking** (① 054/223-404). In Huaraz, try **Andino Club Hotel** (p. 415) or **Monttrek** (see below), which arranges good horseback mountain and valley treks. A number of country hotels just outside Cajamarca have horses for riding, including **Hotel Laguna Seca, Hotel Posada del Puruay, Hacienda San Vicente,** and **Hostal Portada del Sol Hacienda.** Finally, most people go to the jungle for bird-watching or canoe trips, but **Manu Expeditions** (① 084/226-671; www.manuexpeditions.com) organizes horseback riding from the Manu Wildlife Center.

TOUR OPERATORS

Adventure Specialists (① 719/630-7195; www.adventurespecialists.org) organizes horse-supported Machu Picchu treks, including the unique 8-day "Machu Picchu Pony Express."

Monttrek (① 043/421-121), based in Huaraz, offers horseback riding and other adventure sports in the area around the Cordillera Blanca.

Perol Chico (① 084/213-386 or 084/624-475; www.perolchico.com), in Urubamba, operates a ranch and is one of the top horseback-riding agencies in Peru, offering full riding vacations with Peruvian Paso horses and stays at the ranch, as well as 1- and 2-day day rides.

Southwind Adventures (① 800/377-9463 or 303/972-0701; www.southwind adventures.com) offers horse-packing among its roster of adventure trips in Peru.

Viento-Sur (① 084/201-620; www.aventurasvientosur.com), affiliated with Hotel Sol y Luna in Urubamba, organizes horseback-riding programs that range from a half-day trip to 14-day trips in the Sacred Valley on Peruvian Paso horses.

JUNGLE LODGES & TOURS

Nearly two-thirds of Peru is rainforest, and options for exploring it are myriad, from jungle lodges to independently guided treks, to river cruises. The most important issue is choosing which major jungle destination fits best with your interest, time, and budget. Nearly all the international and Peruvian tour operators and wholesalers that do outdoor and adventure travel—for that matter, almost all agencies that handle travel to Peru—have some sort of jungle packages available. Some, of course, are more immersion-oriented than others. You can do a jungle add-on to a trip to Cusco or a full-scale jungle trek and cruise lasting 2 weeks or more. See the earlier tour operators listed in "Organized Adventure Trips," the packagers listed in "Escorted General-Interest Tours" (in chapter 2), and, of course, the individual lodges and companies in chapter 10.

Which Jungle? Comparing Piranhas and Monkeys

Choosing where to go in the Peruvian jungle is complicated. To begin, you need to define how much time and money you can spend, how you want to get there, and how much immersion—expeditions range from light to hard-core—you're interested in once there.

Cusco is the best base for excursions to the southern jungle, while ecolodges and cruise trips in the northern jungle are accessible from Iquitos, to which most visitors fly. For many, the relative proximity of the southern Amazon basin to Cusco and the Sacred Valley makes a jungle experience in that part of the country all the more appealing.

Of the major jungle regions, the Manu Biosphere Reserve is the least touched by man. It is the most inaccessible zone and, therefore, also the most expensive for expeditions. Most visits require close to a week. But Manu also provides perhaps the best opportunities for viewing Amazon wildlife (especially birds). The Tambopata National Reserve also offers excellent jungle experiences and wildlife, including easy access to the splendid macaw clay lick, with less expenditure of time and money.

Peru's northeastern jungle near Iquitos has suffered the most penetration by man and tour operators, having been accessible to travelers for much longer than other parts of the Peruvian jungle. For travelers, though, the region is more convenient, with many more expeditions and lodges operating there, and prices are generally more affordable. Note, however, that the chances of phenomenal large mammal sightings—which are remote anywhere—are even slimmer in the northern Amazon. Travelers with limited time and budgets often fly to Iquitos (by far the most interesting jungle city in Peru) and hop on an inexpensive jungle lodge tour from there, although similarly reasonably priced tours are available from Puerto Maldonado in the south.

MOUNTAIN BIKING

Mountain biking is still in its infancy in Peru, although fat-tire options are growing fast. **Colca Valley** and **Canyon, Huaraz** and the **Callejón de Huaylas,** and the **Sacred Valley** are the major areas for off-road cycling. The **Manu jungle** is also good for hard-core biking. Several tour companies in those places rent bikes, and the quality of the equipment is continually being upgraded. If you plan to do a lot of biking and are very attached to your rig, bring your own. See individual destination chapters for rental listings.

My favorite mountain-biking spots are horse and mountain trails in the spectacular Callejón de Huaylas, which provide the kind of amazing climbing found in the Rockies of the western United States and mountain views that are second to none. Mountain bikers, along with other adventure sports fans, descend on Huaraz and the valley every June for its celebrated Semana del Andinismo. The Colca Valley is also an outstanding region for hardcore mountain biking, though there are fewer tour outfitters targeting the area. For gentler but also incredibly scenic trail riding, you can't beat the Sacred Valley.

TOUR OPERATORS & OUTFITTERS

In Huaraz and the Callejón de Huaylas, the top two agencies for mountain biking are **Mountain Bike Adventures** ⋒ (© **043/424-259;** www.chakinaniperu.com), run by Julio Olaza, and **Pony Expeditions** ⋒ (© **043/391-642;** www.ponyexpeditions.com), run by Alberto Cafferata.

Peru Bike ⋒ (© **01/449-5234;** www.perubike.com), based in Lima, has a great schedule of Andes mountain-biking trips across Peru, including Huascarán and Lake Titicaca loops, and cool day trips, on GT bikes. **Monttrek** (© **043/421-121**) also offers organized mountain-biking tours. **Peru Expeditions Overland** (© **01/447-2057;** www.peru-expeditions.com) is run by a former top cyclist and offers mountain-biking trips in the Sacred Valley to Machu Picchu.

In Cusco, **Peru Discovery,** Triunfo (Sunturwasi) 392, of. 113 (© **054/247-007;** www.perudiscovery.com) is the top specialist, with a half-dozen bike trips that include hard-core excursions. The local outfitters **Amazonas Explorer** (© **084/236-826;** www.amazonas-explorer.com), **Apumayo Expediciones** (© **084/246-018;** www.apumayo.com), **Eric Adventures** (© **866/978-4630** or **084/228-475;** www.ericadventures.com), and **Instinct Travel** (© **084/233-451;** www.instinct-travel.com) offer 1- to 5-day organized mountain-biking excursions for novices and experienced single-trackers. **Manu Ecological Adventures** (© **084/261-640;** www.cbc.org.pe/manu) and **Manu Nature Tours** (© **084/252-721;** www.manuperu.com) offer mountain-biking add-ons to lodge stays and jungle treks. In Arequipa, **Colca Trek** (© **054/202-461;** www.colcatrek.com) and **Peru Trekking** (© **054/223-404**) offer mountain biking in the Colca Canyon. See individual destination chapters for more information.

Pedal Peru ⋒ (© **800/708-8604;** www.pedalperu.com), based in Colorado, organizes mountain-biking tours from abroad. Most trips are in the Cordillera Blanca, but they also cover Cusco and northern Peru (including two unique trips: road cycling from Cusco to La Paz, and a combo mountain bike/boat trip from Cusco to Manu Biosphere Reserve), all on full-suspension Specialized Rockhoppers.

RIVER CRUISES

River cruises along the Amazon and its tributaries are one of the best ways to experience the Peruvian jungle. Cruises give travelers the option of floating luxury and good meals, as well as the ability to stop in and see several different environments and river and jungle communities. The huge and remote **Pacaya-Samiria National Reserve** is one of the best and most up-and-coming zones for cruises into pristine jungle and wetlands; see chapter 10 for details. Iquitos-based **Jungle Expeditions** (© **065/261-583** or 01/241-3232 for reservations, 800/633-4734 in the U.S. and Canada; www.junglex.com) and **Amazon Tours and Cruises** (© **065/231-611,** or 800/423-2791 in the U.S. and Canada; www.amazontours.net) offer a variety of river cruises in the northern Amazon. **International Expeditions** (© **800/633-4734** or 205/428-1700; www.internationalexpeditions.com) is one of the most experienced tour operators organizing luxurious river cruises from the United States.

SURFING

Peru has quietly become one of the world's top surfing destinations. It has 2,000km (1,200 miles) of Pacific coastline and huge possibilities for left and right reef breaks, point breaks, and monster waves, and boarders can hit the surf year-round. Northern beaches, especially Puerto Chicama north of Trujillo, and Cabo Blanco, even farther

---

Fun Fact Whose Board Came First?

Surfing is generally thought to have its origins in Polynesia or the South Sea Islands, but several historians claim that men first hopped aboard things not so dissimilar to modern surfboards in ancient Peru some 2,000 years ago. Textiles and pottery of pre-Columbian, north-coast civilizations depict men cruising waves on totora-reed rafts (although they were more likely fishermen in search of dinner than rad dudes out looking for point breaks).

---

north, draw surfers to some of the best waves in South America. There are also good surfing beaches south of Lima. The north is best from October to March, while the surfing in the south is good April through December and tops in May. The best surfing site, with Web cams and reports on water conditions and the best beaches up and down Peru, is **www.peruazul.com**. Check out **www.wannasurf.com/spot/South_America/Peru** for basic surfing information and maps, as well as **Wave Hunters** (see below) for good information and surf tours to Peru. For more details, see "Outdoor Activities & Spectator Sports" and "Side Trips from Lima," in chapter 5, and "Trujillo," in chapter 11.

TOUR OPERATORS

Wave Hunters (℗ 888/899-8823; www.wavehunters.com/peru/peru.asp), offers a surfeit of good information on Peru's coastline and celebrated waves, as well as different, inexpensive small-group surfing tours in central and northern Peru, including stays at Pico Alto International Surf Camp in Punta Hermosa.

Pure Vacations (℗ 44/01-227/264-264; www.purevacations.com/surf/peru) based in the U.K., has organized surf travel since 1999 and combines northern Peru with Ecuador for 14-day surf trips.

TREKKING & MOUNTAIN CLIMBING

Peru is one of the world's great trekking and mountain-climbing destinations, and its mountains and gorgeous valleys, ideal for everything from hard-core climbs to 6,000m (19,700-ft.) peaks to gentle walks through green valleys, are one of the country's calling cards. Experienced mountaineers, ice climbers, trekkers, and regular old athletic types and hikers beeline to Peru to experience the grandeur of the great Cordillera Blanca, the volcanoes and canyons around Arequipa, and, of course, the Andes mountains in and around Cusco. The most celebrated trek, of course, is the Inca Trail to Machu Picchu—truly one of the world's most rewarding treks, provided that the crowds don't get you down in high season. Many agencies in Cusco offer guided treks to Machu Picchu; so do larger international operators, some of whom are now offering newer alternatives to the Inca Trail. See chapter 8 for additional information on recommended tour operators.

Trekking circuits of varying degrees of difficulty lace the valleys and mountain ridges of Peru's *sierra*. Yet only a few have become popular, commercial trekking routes. Independent trekkers who like to blaze their own trail (metaphorically speaking—you should always stick to existing trails) have a surfeit of options in Peru for uncrowded treks.

For adventure tourism, trekking and climbing rank with expeditions into the Amazon jungle as the biggest outdoor draws in Peru. Scores of outfitters, both international and local, organize a full run of mountain-climbing and trekking package tours.

If you do outdoor travel in Peru, you should include soft trekking, at a minimum, and many agencies specialize in trekking and climbing. Independent travelers can hook up with local agencies for tailored experiences. And travelers of all stripes can set out on easy treks in any of the areas above. There are details on accessible trekking in the destination chapters; see especially chapters 8, 9, and 11.

The best months for climbing are during the dry season, between May and September (June–Aug is perhaps best). In Huaraz, the Semana de Andinismo, held annually in June, attracts mountain climbers from around the world.

One of the best independent resources for hiking and climbing information in Peru is the **South American Explorers** clubhouses in Lima and Cusco (© **01/445-3306** in Lima, or 084/245-484 in Cusco; www.samexplo.org). You have to become a member first ($50 per year) for full access to their trail reports and other information, but if you're serious about trails and climbs in Peru, it's money well spent. You can join via the website or on the spot at a clubhouse.

TOUR OPERATORS

For trekking, there are numerous candidates to organize trekking tours of Peru from abroad. See "Organized Adventure Trips," earlier in this chapter, for complete listings. Among the best are **Adventure Specialists, Andean Treks, Mountain Travel-Sobek, Southwind Adventures, Wildland Adventures,** and **Wilderness Travel.** All have plenty of options, good guides, and high levels of professionalism. One of the top Peruvian operators with a national reach is **Explorandes;** it and all the agencies authorized to lead Inca Trail treks offer many options in Cusco and across Peru.

The local agencies listed in chapters 8, 9, and 11 are the best places to turn if you want to organize some trekking or climbing once on the ground in Peru. There are also excellent local agencies specializing in experienced mountain-climbing expeditions in Arequipa, Huaraz, and Caraz. The best groups arrange a large number of area climbs and have equipment rental. Several have a 24-hour mountain-rescue service.

WHITE-WATER RAFTING

Peru, home to the origin of the mighty Amazon and great canyon rivers, has some stunning opportunities for white-water rafting. Whether you're a total novice or a world-class river runner, Peru has fantastic white water suited to your abilities. The rivers flowing through the **Colca** and **Cotahuasi canyons,** other rivers nearer to Arequipa, and the Andean rivers of the **Urubamba Valley** stand out. A good adventurous experience is rafting in the Amazon jungle on the **Tambopata River.** There's also good white water on the **Río Santa** in the Callejón de Huaylas.

If you're just experimenting with river rafting, stick to Class II and III rivers. If you already know your way around a raft and a paddle, there are plenty of Class IV and V sections to run. Hard-core runners come to Peru for some fantastic, multiday rafting trips to Class V and even Class VI rivers in remote canyons. The best months for rafting are May through September, when water levels are low. (During the rainy season, canyon rivers can be extremely dangerous.)

TOUR OPERATORS

A half-dozen agencies in Arequipa, Cusco, and the Sacred Valley organize a range of local white-water opportunities. See chapters 8 and 9 for more information. Specialists include **Amazonas Explorer** ☆ (© **800/882-7238** in the U.S.; www.amazonas-explorer.com; in the U.S., booked through River Travel Center at annien@rivers.com), which offers white-water rafting tours that can be combined with Inca Trail treks. Trips, which feature small groups, can be booked from abroad. Among its Peru trips are rafting on the Río Apurímac, inflatable canoeing on the source of the Amazon (combined with trekking the Inca Trail), rainforest rafting, and extreme Class IV to VI in Cotahuasi, the world's deepest canyon.

SwissRaft Peru, Plateros 369 (© **084/264-414;** www.swissraft-peru.com), based in Cusco, organizes 1-day rafting trips year-round on the Apurímac, Cusipata, and Chuquicahuana, as well as 4-day trips on the Apurímac.

3 Peru's National Parks & Nature Reserves

Peru's extraordinary natural environment features a wealth of protected areas, wildlife reserves, and archaeological zones. Dozens of national parks and nature preserves make up a bit more than 10% of Peru. The majority of these national parks and nature reserves are undeveloped tropical forests, with few services or facilities available for tourism. Others, however, offer easier access to their wealth of natural wonders. The discussion below is not a complete listing of all of Peru's national parks and protected areas. Rather, it details the ones that are the most accessible and most rewarding for visitors, including several of the largest and most biodiverse on the planet.

Many of them require visitor's permits, for a small fee. If you go with an organized tour, the tour operators almost always take care of the bureaucratic details and include the fees in their package price. See the listings of specialty tour operators in "Organized Adventure Trips," earlier in this chapter.

Peru's protected natural areas go by several names in Spanish, according to distinct legal statutes and protections: *parques nacionales* (national parks), *reserves nacionales* (national reserves), *sanctuarios nacionales/históricos* (national or historic sanctuaries), and *zonas reservadas* (reserve zones), among others.

MANU NATIONAL PARK & BIOSPHERE RESERVE ✦✦✦

Manu is probably the most famous national park in Peru. Covering nearly a million hectares, Manu National Park & Biosphere Reserve is the second-largest protected area in the country and one of the largest in South America. It is also thought to be the most biodiverse zone on Earth. Created in 1973, the park reserve is on the eastern slopes of the Andes within the Amazon basin and comprises an extraordinary variety of habitats, including tropical lowland forest, mountain forest, and grasslands. The reserve zone contains the lower Manu River, the Río Alto Madre de Dios, and a number of beautiful oxbow lakes. About 1,000 bird species—about a quarter of all birds known in South America and 10% of all species in the world—and more than 200 species of mammals have been identified. Also found in the park are at least 13 endangered wildlife species, including black caimans, giant river otters, and ocelots. Botanists have claimed that Manu has a greater number of plant species than any other protected area on Earth.

Manu is superb for observing wildlife, but trips to Manu are lengthy and costly. Most trips bus travelers in and fly them out by light aircraft. There are very few lodges within the designated reserve and cultural zones, and access to the reserve zone is by organized tour. Independent visits are possible in the cultural zone only.

TAMBOPATA NATIONAL RESERVE ✦✦✦

The Tambopata Reserve is more accessible and less restrictive than Manu. The park is made up principally of lowland forest along the Tambopata River. There are a number of lodges in and around the reserve, accessible from Puerto Maldonado. The

---

Fun Fact **Giant Otters**

One of the most fascinating creatures visitors have a chance of spotting in the southeastern Amazon basin in Peru is the giant otter *(Pteronura brasiliensis),* the largest of the 13 otter species in the world. Hunted for its pelt, it has landed on the World Conservation Union ignominious Red List of Endangered Species and has probably been eliminated in Argentina and Uruguay. It has recovered in Peru, but less than a couple hundred probably exist.

Giant otters today are primarily "hunted" by tourists and photographers. The large and very active animals are found in lakes and rivers of tropical lowlands, where they can rather easily be observed. Conservationists are concerned that otters in Manu and Tambopata, among other places, have suffered from human interference in the form of tourist canoes, which leads to long-term changes in behavior and decreases in reproduction. Less invasive observation towers and viewing platforms have been constructed in Cochas Otorongo and Salvador in the Manu Biosphere Reserve. The Giant Otter Project of the Frankfurt Zoological Society (www.giantotters.com/rainforest) is overseeing monitoring and protection of the species in the Pacaya-Samiria National Reserve and the Manu and Bahuaja-Sonene national parks in southeastern Peru.

---

lodges offer shorter stays but usually include naturalist-led expeditions to remote areas. Independent travel with a guide can also be arranged in Puerto Maldonado. Although Manu is more celebrated and probably more pristine, with greater species diversity, the flora and fauna that can be observed by most visitors at Tambopata are remarkably similar.

HUASCARÁN NATIONAL PARK ✦✦✦

Home to a chain of snowcapped mountains that comprise the longest tropical range in the world, the 161km (100-mile) Cordillera Blanca in the central Andes, Huascarán is a mecca for climbers and a host of outdoor and adventure travelers. Its scenery and offerings—mountain climbing, trekking, horseback riding, white-water rafting, fishing, and mountain biking, among others—are perhaps unequaled in the Americas. With 200 alpine lakes, 600 glaciers, spectacular mountain vistas, and nearby ancient pre-Columbian ruins, though, Huascarán is also a magnet for travelers who want to appreciate the scenery with just their eyes, not necessarily their legs and lungs.

Named for the highest peak in Peru, the park's altitude ranges from 2,500 to 6,768m (8,202–22,205 ft.) and includes more than two dozen snowcapped peaks above 6,000m (19,700 ft.). Huascarán is the second-highest park in the South American Andes. Climbing and trekking opportunities range from expert to moderate, with the latter easily managed by anyone in good shape. Arrangements for manageable 2-day walks and 2-week camping hikes crisscrossing the formidable passes of the Cordillera can be easily arranged in Huaraz and Caraz.

For independent treks in the park, a permit must be obtained from the park office in Huaraz. Some locals and foreign visitors have recently complained that the national park is not being managed as well as it might be, and that trash has accumulated along the major trails.

MACHU PICCHU HISTORICAL SANCTUARY 🐾🐾

Machu Picchu is much more than the famous Incan ruins carved into a mountainside. The Machu Picchu Historical Sanctuary, named a UNESCO natural and cultural World Heritage Site in 1983, is a designated archaeological zone and 33,000-hectare (81,545-acre) preserve. International concern over environmental damage to Machu Picchu and the Inca Trail led the Peruvian government to introduce more stringent measures to protect the zone's natural heritage, including limits on the number of people allowed on the trail. Proposals that would severely compromise the natural environment, such as the building of cable cars to the ruins, have been defeated, at least for now.

International environmental and conservation groups, such as World Parks Endowment, have been lobbying the Peruvian government to create a large Incan National Park and expand the protected area around Machu Picchu into the neighboring Vilcanota and Vilcabamba mountains, which would establish a major protected area.

PACAYA-SAMIRIA NATIONAL RESERVE 🐾🐾

The largest natural reserve in Peru, Pacaya-Samiria is one of the Amazon's (and the world's) richest wildlife habitats. Covering more than 2 million hectares (4.94 million acres) of pristine rainforest and wetlands in the north-central Amazon region (about 322km/200 miles south of Iquitos), the reserve is difficult to penetrate during the rainy season (Dec–Mar). The reserve is full of rivers and lakes, and it boasts some of the Amazon's most abundant species of flora and fauna.

Pacaya-Samiria is considerably less accessible than the jungle farther north and is much less visited than Manu or Tambopata. Several tour operators now organize river cruises, canoe trips, and camping expeditions, and a couple of native communities are now promoting camping trips and immersion experiences. A permit from INRENA, the Peruvian parks authority, is required to enter the preserve.

PARACAS NATIONAL RESERVE 🐾

South of Lima, in the department of Ica on the southern coast, this peninsula is blessed with an abundance of marine wildlife and seabirds. About two-thirds of the 335,000-hectare (827,800-acre) reserve is ocean; the desert landscape is barren and rather absent of most plant life. The Ballestas Islands, contained within the nature preserve, are rich in bird and sea lion life, and present excellent and very accessible opportunities for viewing wildlife up close.

---

4 Tips on Health, Safety & Etiquette in the Peruvian Wilderness

Although many outdoor travel itineraries in Peru require no special medications or vaccinations, there are special considerations for jungle travel. Additionally, acclimatization to the high altitude of the Andes is essential for anyone seeking to do trekking or climbing in the mountains.

For tropical travel in Peru, the Centers for Disease Control and Prevention recommends vaccinations against yellow fever, hepatitis A or immunoglobulin (IG), hepatitis B, typhoid, and booster doses for tetanus-diphtheria and measles, as well as pills for malaria. For more detailed information, see "Health & Safety," in chapter 2.

Most tours and activities are extremely safe, but there are risks involved in any adventure activity. The risks involved in mountain climbing, ice climbing, and whitewater rafting are considerable. Know and respect your own physical limits and skills (or lack thereof) before undertaking any high-risk activity.

Be prepared for extremes in temperature and rainfall, and wide fluctuations in weather. A sunny morning hike can quickly become a cold and wet ordeal, so it's a good idea to carry some form of rain gear when hiking in the rainforest, bring sufficient protection against the cold at high altitudes, and have a dry change of clothing waiting at the end of the trail. Be sure to bring plenty of sunscreen, no matter where you travel. See "What to Bring," below, for more suggestions.

If you do any trekking or camping, exercise caution with the native species that live in natural habitats. Don't go poking under rocks or fallen branches: Snakebites are very rare, but don't do anything to increase the odds. If you do encounter a snake, stay calm, don't make any sudden movements, and *do not* try to handle it. The chance of getting bitten by a venomous snake is small; however, if you're bitten, wash out the bite and surrounding area very thoroughly (don't go Hollywood and try to suck out the venom). Because the bite might cause swelling, remove your jewelry. If symptoms persist, seek medical attention; the best way to demonstrate to a doctor what kind of snake bit you, of course, is to hand over the dead snake—certainly not always possible. Also beware of centipedes, scorpions, and spiders, including tarantulas, brown recluses, and black widows. If you are bitten by a dog or another creature, such as a bat, there is a risk of rabies. Wash out the wound thoroughly with soap and water, and seek medical attention. For a detailed "disease risk analysis" and other precautions, take a look at **Travel Medicine**'s website at **www.travmed.com**.

Avoid swimming in jungle rivers unless a guide or local operator can vouch for their safety. Although white-water sections and stretches in mountainous areas are generally pretty safe, many rivers in the Amazon basin are home to contingents of crocodile and caiman populations.

Bugs and bug bites (and blisters) will probably be your greatest health concern in the Peruvian wilderness. For the most part, bugs are merely an inconvenience, although mosquitoes can carry malaria or dengue (see "Health & Safety" in chapter 2 for more information). Strong repellent and proper clothing will minimize both the danger and the inconvenience. On beaches, you might be bitten by sand fleas. These nearly invisible insects leave an irritating welt. Try not to scratch because this can lead to open sores and infections.

However, in all probability, Peru's bounteous nature needs to be protected from visitors more than visitors need to be protected from it. A fundamental component of enjoying nature is leaving the natural environment undisturbed. The responsible outdoor traveler's maxim is: Take nothing but memories (and photos); leave nothing but footprints. Do not cut or uproot plants or flowers. Pack out everything you pack in, and *never* litter. Leave places the way you found them. If you see garbage lying around in protected areas, pack it out, along with your own trash. Don't scratch your name or any other graffiti on trees or ancient monuments. On trails, bury your excrement as far as possible from the trail. Over the years, too many insensitive trekkers along the Inca Trail, among other spots, did not follow this common-sense advice and did so much damage that international organizations such as UNESCO worried about the trail's survival.

To support local communities and appreciate what you have the rare opportunity to experience, it's a great idea to use (and adequately tip or pay) local guides and porters, and support locally owned businesses and artisans.

5 What to Bring

Outdoor and adventure travel in Peru requires some special gear, and it's a good idea to come prepared; you're more likely to find a better selection of equipment, apparel, and other outdoor gear at home than you are in Peru. You can rent some equipment, such as crampons for ice climbing, but you'd be wise to bring most nontechnical items with you.

The most basic items for travelers to Peru who are doing any sort of light adventure, such as trekking or jungle lodge stays, are (already broken-in) **hiking boots** (it's not a bad idea to take them in a carry-on or wear them on the plane, to avoid their loss), outdoor apparel such as **fleece pullovers,** and a **daypack.**

Essential gear for almost all travelers to Peru includes:

- a sun hat
- sunscreen
- cold-weather and water-repellent clothing
- light trekking shoes or boots
- several pairs of thick socks

Additional items for light adventure include:

- good backpacking or climbing boots
- a base layer (thermal underwear or wicking-quality shirt)
- malarial pills (if traveling to jungle regions)
- insect repellent
- a pocketknife
- toilet paper
- a flashlight or headlamp
- a mosquito net
- a sleeping bag
- diarrhea medicine
- energy bars or other trail snack foods
- sports sandals or comfortable slides for post-climbing and trekking, or for river and wet-weather wear
- a water bottle or other portable hydration system
- a good internal-frame backpack

More stuff for hard-core adventure travel includes:

- food supplies and cooking equipment
- a filter and/or water-purification tablets
- a first-aid kit
- a compass and whistle
- a tent, camping stove, and cookware
- adequate fuel
- topographical maps of trails

6 Volunteer & Study Programs

Study and volunteer programs, including Spanish-language programs, are often a great way to travel in and experience a country with greater depth than most independent and package travel allows. Cultural immersion and integration with locals are the aims of many such programs, leading to a richer and more unique experience for many travelers.

Volunteering, in particular, often leads to greater culture sensitivity and cross-cultural learning experiences. Especially in a mostly poor country such as Peru, volunteers see up-close the realities of the lack of running water and electricity, the relative absence of luxuries, and simple, home-cooked foods—not to mention local customs and traditions. These aspects of Peruvian life might be considerably more difficult to apprehend if staying in nice hotels and dining at upscale restaurants.

Most volunteer organizations are not-for-profit entities that charge participants to go abroad (to cover administrative and other costs), so volunteering isn't usually a way to get a free vacation. If you're concerned, though, ask about the cost breakdown for costs and field expenses. Any established, reputable volunteer organization should be willing to do this. Then you could always compare those costs to what traveling on your own would amount to.

Below are several institutions and organizations that work on humanitarian and sustainable development projects in Peru. Some international relief organizations, such as **Doctors Without Borders** (www.doctorswithoutborders.org) and **CARE** (www.care.org), accept volunteers to work crises and relief efforts. The devastating earthquake in southern Peru in 2001 was one such episode that brought hundreds of volunteers to Peru.

VOLUNTEER PROGRAMS

Cross-Cultural Solutions ✺✺ (✆ **800/380-4777** or 914/632-0022; www.crossculturalsolutions.org), with offices in New Rochelle, New York, and Brighton, U.K., offers week-long volunteer programs in Peru (in Lima, Ayacucho, and Trujillo). The "Volunteer Abroad" section lists a number of opportunities for volunteering in Peru, including CARE, volunteer teaching, and environmental research. **Projects Abroad** ✺✺ (✆ **888/839-3535**; www.projects-abroad.org), with headquarters in New York and a local field office in Urubamba (in the Sacred Valley), organizes several unique volunteer opportunities in Peru, including Incan restoration projects (such as the magnificent Sacsayhuamán ruins on the outskirts of Cusco), rainforest conservation, teaching and nursing. **Habitat for Humanity** ✺✺✺ (✆ **800/422-4828** or 229/924-6935; www.habitat.org), with a base in Arequipa (Comité Nacional Hábitat para la Humanidad Perú; ✆ 054/422-724), and **Volunteers for Peace** (✆ **802/259-2759**; www.vfp.org) also offer opportunities in Peru.

RESEARCH OPPORTUNITIES

Earthwatch Institute (✆ **800/776-0188** or 978/461-0081; www.earthwatch.org) has a unique mission: It sends travelers out to work in the field alongside scientists involved in archaeology and environmental conservation. There are three Peru research and education trips: You can join a 13-day excavation of a pre-Incan site, assist with research of Peruvian macaws, or document the biology of Andean rivers. But the trips are not all work; they're a way to see a fascinating slice of the country from an insider's—academic or conservationist—perspective.

SPANISH-LANGUAGE PROGRAMS

Local language schools, primarily located in Cusco and offering both short- and long-term study programs, often with home stays, are listed in chapter 7. **Study Abroad International** (www.studyabroadinternational.com) lists a number of Spanish-study programs in Cusco. **GorpTravel** (✆ **877/440-GORP**; http://gorptravel.com) occasionally lists Spanish-study programs of short duration in Peru and other South American countries; follow the "Education/Learning" link on the website for options.

5

Lima

Lima once ranked as the richest and most important city in the Americas and was considered to be the most beautiful colonial settlement in the region. Founded in 1535 by the conquistador Francisco Pizarro, the Spanish Crown's "City of Kings" quickly became the center of power and trade for the entire American viceregency that stretched from Quito to Santiago. Lima was home to some of the Americas' finest baroque and Renaissance churches, palaces, and mansions, as well as the continent's first university, founded in 1551. For 2 centuries, the capital also served as the headquarters of the Spanish Inquisition.

When Spain created a rival vice regency in Río de la Plata, which subsequently grew rich from silver mines, Lima quickly fell into decline. An earthquake decimated the city in 1746, leaving more than 4,000 dead and few buildings standing. Today the capital of Peru is a sprawling, chaotic, and mostly unlovely metropolis, and many visitors dart through it as fast as possible—or they bypass it altogether. Peru's blistering poverty is more apparent here than perhaps anywhere else: Depressing shantytowns called *pueblos jóvenes* lacerate the outer rings of the city. The despair of a large segment of the capital's largely migrant and *mestizo* population contrasts uncomfortably with the ritzy apartment and office buildings in the residential suburbs. And as if that weren't enough, for most of the year, an unrelenting gray cloud called the *garúa* hangs heavily

overhead, obscuring the coastline and dulling the city's appearance. Although it virtually never rains in Lima, the sun comes out only from December to April; the rest of the time, Lima makes London look like Lisbon.

Lima has calmed down a bit since the chaotic 1980s and 1990s, when the city was the scene of carjackings, kidnappings, embassy takeovers, and strong-arm political maneuvers. But the city still feels schizophrenic; outer suburbs such as Barranco are relatively gentle oases, worlds apart from the congestion and grime of the rest of the city. Although middle-class Limeños from residential *barrios* are again venturing downtown along with foreign visitors, there are still plenty of locals who consider central Lima off-limits.

For many visitors, Lima demands too much effort to sift beneath the soot and uncover the city's rewards, especially when such extraordinary treasures hover over the horizon in the Andes mountains and in the Amazon jungle. So why come to Lima except to beeline it to Cusco or elsewhere? If you skip Lima altogether, you'll miss a vital part of what Peru is today. With a population of eight million—about one-third Peru's population—and as the seat of the national government and the headquarters of most industry, Lima thoroughly dominates Peru's political and commercial life. The country's best museums are here, and so are its finest restaurants and nightlife (a gastronomic tour of Peru should definitely begin in Lima). Many of the classic colonial buildings in

Lima at a Glance

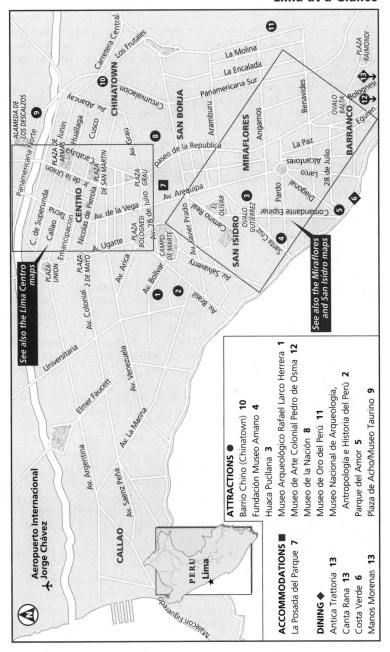

ATTRACTIONS ●

Barrio Chino (Chinatown) 10
Fundación Museo Amano 4
Huaca Pucllana 3
Museo Arqueológico Rafael Larco Herrera 1
Museo de Arte Colonial Pedro de Osma 12
Museo de la Nación 8
Museo de Oro del Perú 11
Museo Nacional de Arqueología,
  Antropología e Historia del Perú 2
Parque del Amor 5
Plaza de Acho/Museo Taurino 9

ACCOMMODATIONS ■

La Posada del Parque 7

DINING ◆

Antica Trattoria 13
Canta Rana 13
Costa Verde 6
Manos Morenas 13

the old *centro* are being refurbished and are newly welcoming to visitors.

Even if you have only a day or two for Lima, the city's art and archaeology museums serve as perfect introductions to the rich history and culture you'll encounter elsewhere in the country. Not to be missed are the Museo de la Nación, which traces the history of Peru's ancient civilizations, and the Rafael Larco Herrera Museum, the world's largest private collection of pre-Columbian art. If you also squeeze in a tour of colonial Lima, dine at a great *criollo* (creole) restaurant or *cevichería*, soak up some energetic nightlife, and browse the country's best shops; you might just come away from Lima pleasantly surprised, if not exactly enamored of the city.

1 Orientation

ARRIVING

Lima is the gateway for most international arrivals to Peru; see "Getting There" in chapter 2 for more detailed information.

BY PLANE

All flights from North America and Europe arrive at Lima's **Aeropuerto Internacional Jorge Chávez** (✆ 01/511-6055), located 16km (10 miles) west of the city center. Lima is connected by air with all major cities in Peru; there are regular flights to Ayacucho, Cusco, Puerto Maldonado, Juliaca, Arequipa, Tacna, Cajamarca, Chiclayo, Trujillo, Pucallpa, Iquitos, Tarapoto, and Piura. The major domestic airlines are **AeroCondor** (✆ 305/531-1407 in the U.S., or 01/614-6000; www.aerocondor.com.pe), **LanPeru** (✆ 212/582-3250 in the U.S., or 01/213-8200; www.lan.com), **LC Busre** (✆ 01/619-1300; www.lcbusre.com.pe), **StarPerú** (✆ 01/705-9000; www.starperu.com), **Taca Peru** (✆ 01/213-7000; www.grupotaca.com), and **TANS** (✆ 01/611-5555; www.tansperu.com.pe).

The airport has a tourist information booth (in the international terminal only), two 24-hour currency-exchange windows, three banks, ATMs, a post office, and car-rental desks, including **Avis** (✆ 01/575-1637, ext. 4155; www.avis.com), **Budget** (✆ 01/575-1674; www.budget.com), and **Hertz** (✆ 01/575-1390; www.hertz.com). The tourist information booth can help with hotel reservations. The arrival and departure terminals can be very congested, especially when long lines form to pay departure taxes, when a number of flights arrive at once, and early in the morning when many flights depart Lima for Cusco. Be very mindful of your luggage and other belongings at all times. To get through large groups of travelers and relatives all hovering about, you might need to forget about being polite and simply push your way through the crowd.

Domestic departures require payment of a $5.04 exit tax; for international departures, the tax is $28.24. You must take your boarding pass to one of the booths in either terminal and stand in line to pay and receive a stamp indicating payment (in cash only) before proceeding to the departures area. Remember to reconfirm your flight at least 48 hours in advance and arrive at the airport with ample time before your flight. *Flights are frequently overbooked,* and passengers who have not reconfirmed their flights or who arrive later than (usually) 45 minutes before scheduled departure risk being bumped from the flight. Flights to Cusco are especially popular; make your reservations as far in advance as possible. Also check to be sure that you will have enough time to make your connecting flight if coming from overseas, and that you haven't been sold a charter flight inadvertently (American Airlines did this to me, and I was forced to stay over a day in Lima until I could get a regular flight the next day).

To get from the airport to Lima—either downtown or to suburbs such as Miraflores, San Isidro, and Barranco (the sites of most tourist hotels)—you can take a taxi or private bus. When you exit with your luggage, you will immediately be besieged with taxi offers; the ones nearest the door are invariably the most expensive. **Taxis** inside the security area at the international arrivals terminal charge around $20 to Miraflores and $15 to downtown Lima (Lima Centro). You can try bargaining or go just beyond the security area, where prices drop to about $10 to Miraflores and $8 to Lima Centro. The **Urbanito Airport shuttle service** (© 01/814-6932 or 99/573-238) delivers passengers to the doors of their hotels. Stop by the desk in the international terminal; buses to downtown S/21 ($6) and Miraflores and San Isidro S/28 ($8) leave every half-hour or so. The shuttle stops at the hotel of each passenger; at peak hours, if there are many passengers, this might not be the fastest way from the airport. Unless you're alone, it's also probably not the cheapest. Call a day ahead to arrange a pickup for your return to the airport. Private **limousine taxis** (*taxis ejecutivos,* or *remises*) also have desks in the airport; their fares range from S/105 ($30) to S/175 ($50) round-trip. One to try is **MitsuTaxi** (© **01/349-7722**).

BY BUS

Lima is connected by bus to neighboring countries and all major cities in Peru. No central bus terminal exists, however; the multitude of bus companies serving various regions of the country all have terminals in Lima, making bus arrivals and departures exceedingly confusing for most travelers. Many terminals are located downtown, although several companies have their bases in the suburbs. Most bus terminals have nasty reputations for thievery and general unpleasantness; your best bet is to grab your things and hop into a cab pronto.

Of the dozens of bus companies servicing the capital and points around the country, the largest with frequent service in and out of Lima are **Ormeño,** Av. Javier Prado Este 1059, San Isidro (© 01/426-7595), Av. Carlos Zavala 177 (© 01/427-5679), and reservations (© 01/472-5000; www.grupo-ormeno.com); **Cruz del Sur,** Av. Javier Prado Este 1101, La Victoria (© 01/424-6158), and Jr. Quilca (© 01/424-1005; www.cruzdelsur.com.pe); **Civa,** Av. Paseo de la República 575 (© 01/332-5236; www.civa.com.pe); and **Oltursa,** Av. Aramburú 1160, San Isidro (© 01/225-4499; www.oltursa.com.pe).

BY TRAIN

Lima is the starting point of the **Ferrocarril Central Andino Railroad** (© **01/ 361-2828;** www.ferroviasperu.com.pe), the highest railway in the world (up to 4,781m/15,686 ft). However, the line has a problematic history (enough to discourage any reasonable traveler from planning his trip to Peru around it): the so-called "Tren Macho" was shut down for most of the 1980s and 1990s, and in recent years the passenger train to and from Huancayo has departed only once a month—when it has departed at all—from July to October. The 12- to 15-hour journey costs $38 round-trip. When running, it leaves downtown Lima at the **Estación Central de Desamparados,** Jr. Ancash 201 (© **01/361-2828,** ext. 222), just behind the Government Palace. Check in advance of your trip with tourism authorities to verify that the train is indeed running (there are plans to convert the train to natural gas and reduce travel time to 4 hours, but don't hold your breath waiting for this to happen).

A taxi from the station to your downtown hotel costs S/4 ($1.15); to Miraflores, it costs S/10 ($2.85).

VISITOR INFORMATION

A 24-hour tourist information booth, **iPerú** (📞 **01/574-8000**), operates in the international terminal at the Jorge Chávez International Airport. The most helpful **iPerú** office is in Miraflores, at the **Larcomar** shopping mall, Módulo 14, Av. Malecón de la Reserva 610 (📞 **01/445-9400**), open daily from noon to 8pm. Another office is in San Isidro at Jorge Basadre 610 (📞 **01/421-1627**), open Monday through Friday from 8:30am to 6:30pm. The **Oficina de Información Turística** in Lima Centro is located at Pasaje Los Escribanos 145, just off the Plaza de Armas, in Lima Centro (📞 **01/427-6080**); it's open Monday through Saturday from 9am to 6pm.

One of the best private agencies for arrangements and city tours, as well as general information, is **Fertur Perú,** Jr. Junín 211 and Azángaro 105, within the Hotel España (📞 **01/427-1958**). Another excellent spot for information and advice, particularly on outdoor and adventure travel in Peru, such as trekking, mountaineering, and rafting, is the **South American Explorers,** Piura 135, Miraflores (📞 **01/445-3306; www.samexplo.org**). The organization is legendary among veteran South American travelers, and it's not a bad idea to become a member ($50) before traveling so that you can take advantage of its resources (you can also join on the spot). The clubhouse in Lima maintains a great library of maps, books, trail information, trip reports, and storage facilities. The Lima clubhouse is open Monday through Friday from 9:30am to 5pm (Wed until 8pm), and Saturday from 9:30am to 1pm. There are also clubhouses in Cusco and Quito, Ecuador.

CITY LAYOUT

Lima is an exceedingly diffuse city, complicated to get around. The city center, known as Lima Centro, abuts the Río Rímac and the Rímac district across the river. The city beyond central Lima is a warren of ill-defined neighborhoods; most visitors are likely to set foot in only San Isidro, Miraflores, and Barranco, which hug the coast and the circuit of urban beaches leading to the so-called "Costa Verde." Major thoroughfares leading from the city center to outer neighborhoods are Avenida Benavides (to Callao); Avenida Brasil (to Pueblo Libre); Avenida Arequipa, Avenida Tacna, and Avenida Garcilaso de la Vega (to San Isidro and Miraflores); Paseo de la República (also known as Vía Expresa) and Avenida Panamá (to Miraflores and Barranco); and Avenida Panamericana Sur (to San Borja and south of Lima).

THE NEIGHBORHOODS IN BRIEF

Lima Centro Lima Centro is the historic heart of the city, where the Spaniards built the country's capital in colonial fashion. It has repeatedly suffered from earthquakes, fires, and neglect, so although it was once the continent's most important colonial city, stunning examples of the original town are less prevalent than one might expect. Much of Lima Centro is dirty, unsafe, crowded, and chaotic, although city officials are finally getting to much-needed restoration of the remaining historic buildings and have drastically upgraded police presence in the city center (making it just about as safe as anywhere in the city during the day). The great majority of visitors stay in outer suburbs rather than Lima Centro; most hotels are small *hostales* (inns) aimed at budget travelers and backpackers. The absolute heart of the Lima Centro is the Plaza de Armas, site of La Catedral (Cathedral) and government palaces, and nearly all the colonial mansions and churches of interest are within walking distance of the square. Several of Lima's top museums are in **Pueblo Libre,** a couple kilometers southwest of Lima Centro, while **San Borja,** a couple kilometers directly south of Lima Centro, holds two of the finest collections in all of Peru.

Miraflores & San Isidro San Isidro and Miraflores, the most exclusive residential and commercial neighborhoods where most tourist hotels are located, are farther south (5–8km/3–5 miles) toward the coast. These districts are now the commercial heart of the city, having usurped that title from Lima Centro some years ago. San Isidro holds many of the city's top luxury hotels and a slew of offices and shopping malls. Miraflores is the focus of most travelers' visits to Lima; it contains the greatest number and variety of hotels, bars, and restaurants, as well as shopping outlets. A number of the city's finest hotels are along the *malecón* (boulevard) in Miraflores. Although San Isidro and Miraflores are middle-class neighborhoods, both are congested and not entirely free of crime.

Barranco Barranco, several kilometers farther out along the ocean, is a tranquil former seaside village that is the city's coolest and most relaxed district, now known primarily for its nightlife. It is where you'll find several of Lima's best restaurants, bars, and live-music spots, frequented by Limeños and visitors alike. The next district along the beach is **Chorrillos,** a residential neighborhood known primarily for its *Pantanos de Villa,* or swamps that are rich with flora and fauna.

2 Getting Around

Navigating Lima is a complicated and time-consuming task, made difficult by the city's sprawling character (many of the best hotels and restaurants are far from downtown, spread among three or more residential neighborhoods), heavy traffic and pollution, and a chaotic network of confusing and crowded *colectivos* and unregulated taxis.

BY TAXI

Taxis hailed on the street are a reasonable and relatively quick way to get around in Lima. However, taxis are wholly unregulated by the government: All anyone has to do to become a taxi driver is get his hands on a vehicle—of any size and condition, although most are tiny Daewoo "Ticos"—and plunk a cheap TAXI sticker inside the windshield. Then he is free to charge whatever he thinks he can get—with no meters, no laws, and nobody to answer to except the free market. One has to counsel visitors to be a bit wary taking taxis in Lima, even though I personally have never had problems greater than a dispute over a fare. (If you're not fluent in Spanish, and even if you are but you have an obviously non-Peruvian appearance, be prepared to negotiate fares.) Limeños tell enough stories of theft and even the occasional violent crime in unregistered cabs to make hailing one on the street inadvisable for older visitors or for those with little command of Spanish or experience traveling in Latin America. If you hail a taxi on the street, taxi drivers themselves have told me, try to pick out older drivers; many contend that young punks are almost wholly responsible for taxi crime. If the issue of getting into quasi-official cabs makes you nervous, by all means call a

Lima Taxis: The Runaround

Besides the issue of safety, there's another cause for concern when getting in a taxi in Lima: The drivers very often don't know where the heck they're going. They are notoriously ignorant of the city they drive in. I tried to get one in Miraflores to take me to Barranco, the next neighborhood along the coast (5 miles away) and the most popular nightlife destination in Lima. The driver looked at me blankly. "You've never heard of Barranco?" I asked, incredulous. "Perhaps you can lead me?" he asked. Yeah, and perhaps you can pay me. Time and time again in Lima, I, a resident of New York, have had to give directions. The reason for such unfamiliarity is that many taxi drivers are newly arrived immigrants from mountain villages and other cities across Peru. They come to Lima, rent someone's vehicle and a TAXI sticker, and become taxi drivers without so much as a glance at a map. That's another reason to call an official cab.

registered company from your hotel or restaurant—especially at night (even though the fare can be twice as much).

Registered, reputable taxi companies—the safest option—include **Taxi Amigo** (© **01/349-0177**), **Taxi Móvil** (© **01/422-6890**), **Taxi Line** (© **01/330-2795**), and **Taxi Seguro** (© **01/275-2020**). Whether you call or hail a taxi, you'll need to establish a price beforehand—be prepared to bargain. Most fares range from $2 to $5. From Miraflores to downtown, expect to pay S/8 to S/10 ($2.30–$2.85); from Miraflores to San Isidro, about S/5 ($1.40); from San Isidro to downtown, S/5 to S/7 ($1.40–$2); from Miraflores to Museo de Oro, S/8 to S/10 ($2.30–$2.85); and from Miraflores to Barranco, S/7 ($2). Note that when you hail a taxi on the street, the fare requested will surely be a bit higher; it makes sense to try to haggle.

BY BUS

Micros and *combis* are very inexpensive means of transportation in the city (see "Combi or Carro?" box in chapter 2 for more info). Routes are more or less identified by signs with street names placed in the windshield, making many trips confusing for those unfamiliar with Lima. Some do nothing more than race up and down long avenues (for example, TODO AREQUIPA means it travels the length of Av. Arequipa). For assistance, ask a local for help; most Limeños know the incredibly complex bus system surprisingly well. Although they sometimes seem to hurtle down the street, because they make so many stops, trips from the outer suburbs to downtown can be quite slow. Most micros and combis cost S/1.5 or S/2 (40¢–55¢), and slightly more after midnight and on Sunday and holidays. When you want to get off, shout *baja* (getting off) or *esquina* (at the corner).

From Lima Centro to Miraflores, look for buses with signs in the windows indicating LARCO–SCHELL–MIRAFLORES (or some combination thereof). From Miraflores to downtown Lima, you should hop on a bus headed along WILSON/TACNA. Buses to Barranco have signs that read CHORILLOS/HUAYLAS.

BY FOOT

Lima can be navigated by foot only a neighborhood at a time (and even then, congestion and pollution strongly discourage much walking). Lima Centro and Barranco are best seen by foot, and, although large, Miraflores is also walkable. Between neighborhoods, however, a taxi is essential.

FAST FACTS: Lima

Airport See "Arriving," earlier in this chapter.

American Express There's an office in Lima at Jr. de la Unión 630 (✆ **01/428-9779**). There are other offices at Av. Larco 747–753, Miraflores, Lima (✆ **01/444-4239**); and Av. Paseo de la Republica 3220, San Isidro, Lima (✆ **01/441-2769**). Both offices are housed with Viajes Falabella travel agencies. They will replace stolen or lost traveler's checks and sell American Express checks with an Amex card, but they do not cash their own checks. All three offices are open Monday through Friday from 9am to 5pm

Babysitters Your best bet is to inquire at your hotel for babysitting services. Many of the higher-quality hotels offer babysitting; if yours doesn't, the concierge might be able to recommend a service.

Banks/Currency Exchange Peruvian and international banks with currency-exchange bureaus and ATMs are plentiful throughout Lima Centro, especially in the outer neighborhoods such as Miraflores, San Isidro, and Barranco, which are full of shopping centers, hotels, and restaurants. Money-changers, usually wearing colored smocks (sometimes with obvious "$" insignias), patrol the main streets off Parque Central in Miraflores and central Lima with calculators and dollars in hand.

Principal banks include **Banco Central,** Jr. Antonio Miró Quesada 441 (✆ 01/427-6250); **Banco Continental,** Av. Los Paracas s/n (✆ 01/436-1469); **Banco de Comercio,** Jr. Lampa 560 (✆ 01/428-9400); **Banco Wiese,** Jr. Cusco 245 (✆ 01/428-6000); and **Citibank,** Miguel Dasso 121, San Isidro (✆ 01/442-5146).

Car Rentals See "Arriving," earlier in this chapter.

Dentists & Doctors The U.S. and British embassies (see "Embassies & Consulates," below) provide lists of English-speaking doctors, dentists, and other healthcare personnel in Lima. For dentists, you might also try contacting the **International Academy of Integrated Dentistry,** Calle Centauro 177, Urbanización Los Granados, Monterrico, Surco (✆ **01/435-2153**). Additionally, see "Hospitals," below.

Drugstores Two huge, multiservice pharmacies open 24 hours a day are **Farmacia Deza,** Av. Conquistadores 1140, San Isidro (✆ **01/440-3798**); and **Pharmax,** Av. Salaverry 3100, San Isidro, in the Centro Comercio El Polo (✆ **01/264-2282**). A chain with a number of storefronts across Lima is **Superfarma,** at Av. Benavides 2849 (✆ **01/222-1575**) and Avenida Armendariz, Miraflores (✆ **01/446-3333**). These and other pharmacies have 24-hour delivery service. For additional locations, consult the Yellow Pages under "Farmacias" and "Boticas."

Embassies & Consulates U.S., Av. La Encalada, block 17, Monterrico (✆ **01/434-3000**); **Australia,** Víctor A. Belaúnde 147/Vía Principal 155, office 1301, San Isidro (✆ **01/222-8281**); **Canada,** Libertad 130, Miraflores (✆ **01/444-4015**); **U.K.** and **New Zealand,** Torre Parque Mar, 22nd floor, Av. Jose Larco 1301, Miraflores (✆ **01/617-3000**).

Emergencies In case of an emergency, call the 24-hour **traveler's hot line** (✆ **01/574-8000**) or the **tourist police,** or POLTUR (✆ **01/460-1060** in Lima, or

01/460-0965). The **INDECOPI** 24-hour hot line can also assist in contacting police to report a crime (© **01/224-7888** in Lima, 01/224-8600, or toll free 0800/42579 from any private phone).The general **police** emergency number is © **105**; for **fire,** dial © **116.**

Hospitals English-speaking medical personnel and 24-hour emergency services are available at the following hospitals and clinics: **Clínica Anglo-Americana,** Alfredo Salazar, block 3, San Isidro (© 01/221-3656); **Clínica San Borja,** Guardia Civil 337, San Borja (© 01/475-4000); **Maison de Sante,** Calle Miguel Adgouin 208–222, near the Palacio de Justicia (© 01/428-3000, emergency 01/427-2941); and **Clínica Ricardo Palma,** Av. Javier Prado Este 1066, San Isidro (© 01/224-2224). For an ambulance, call **Alerta Médica,** at © 01/470-5000, or **San Cristóbal,** at © 01/440-0200.

Internet Access Internet *cabinas* (booths) are everywhere in Lima. Rates are about S/1.5 to S/2 (40¢–55¢) per hour, and most are open daily from 9am to 10pm or later. Try **Telnet,** Jr. Camaná 315; **Internet Pardo,** Av. José Pardo 620; **Cybersandeg,** Jr. de la Unión 853, office 112; **Wamnet,** corner of Diez Canseco and Alcanfores, mezzanine, Miraflores; or **C@bin@s de Internet,** Diez Canseco 380, Miraflores.

Maps Tourist-information booths give out free maps, but in a sprawling, confusing city such as Lima, they are inadequate for more than basic indications. Probably the best street map available is the "Lima 2000" map sold at bookstores and kiosks. Good topographical maps are available from the **Instituto Geográfico Nacional (IGN),** located at Av. Aramburú 1190, San Isidro (© **01/475-9960**). Hiking maps are available from the **South American Explorers,** Piura 135, Miraflores (© **01/445-3306**).

Newspapers & Magazines In Lima, you will find copies (although rarely same-day publications) of the *International Herald Tribune* and the *Miami Herald,* as well as *Time, Newsweek,* and other special-interest publications. Top-flight hotels sometimes offer free daily fax summations of the *New York Times* to their guests. Among local publications, look for *Rumbos,* a glossy Peruvian travel magazine in English and Spanish with excellent photography. If you read Spanish, *El Comercio* and *La República* are two of the best daily newspapers.

Police The **Policía Nacional de Turismo (National Tourism Police)** has staff members that speak English and are specifically trained to handle the needs of foreign visitors. The main office in Lima is at Av. Javier Prado Este 2465, fifth floor, San Borja (next to the Museo de la Nación); the 24-hour tourist police line is © **01/574-8000.** Also see "Emergencies" above.

Post Office/Mail Lima's main post office *(Central de Correos)* is located on the Plaza de Armas at Camaná 195 (© **01/427-0370**) in central Lima. The Miraflores branch is at Petit Thouars 5201 (© **01/445-0697**); the San Isidro branch is at Calle Las Palmeras 205 (© **01/422-0981**). A **DHL/Western Union** office is located at Nicolás de Piérola 808 (© **01/424-5820**).

Restrooms The only public restrooms you're likely to find will be in airport and bus terminals, bars and restaurants, museums, and hotels. Sometimes it's easier to duck into a large hotel than into a restaurant.

Safety In downtown Lima and the city's residential and hotel areas, the risk of street crime remains high. Although carjackings, assaults, and armed robberies are not routine, they're not unheard of either. Armed attacks at ATMs have also occurred. Use ATMs during the day, with other people present. Most thefts occur on public transportation, such as buses and combis. There have been several reports of thieves who've boarded buses in and out of Lima to cities both north and south of the capital, relieving passengers at gunpoint of their valuables. Be very careful with your belongings; leave your passport and other valuables in the hotel safe and use a money belt. Public street markets are also frequented by thieves, as are parks (especially at night) and the beaches in and around Lima.

Although the large-scale terrorist activities of the local groups Sendero Luminoso and MRTA were largely stamped out in the early 1990s, there have been reports of a possible resurgence. Neither group, however, is currently active in any of the areas covered in this book.

Also see "Getting Around" above.

Taxis See "Getting Around," above.

Telephone Lima's area code is 01. It need not be dialed when making local calls within Lima, but it must be dialed when calling Lima from another city. Telephone booths are found throughout the city; the principal Telefónica del Perú office, where you can make long-distance and international calls, is on Plaza San Martín (Carabaya 937) in Lima Centro (℃ **01/224-9355**). It's open Monday through Saturday from 8am to 6pm and Sunday 8am to 1pm.

3 Where to Stay

Lima Centro has its share of hotels and budget inns, but most people head out to the residential neighborhoods of Miraflores, San Isidro, and, to a lesser extent, Barranco. These barrios have little in the way of sights, but they are more convenient for nightlife and shopping, and probably safer, if not necessarily much quieter.

Hotel rates in Lima are the highest in the country, especially at the top end. There are plenty of midrange and budget choices, although few have the charm of affordable *hostales* in other cities. Particularly at the top echelon, hotels tack on taxes and service charges to quoted rates, whereas most moderate and less-expensive inns quote rates that already include all taxes and service charges. Be on the lookout for any hotel that tries to charge you the 18% IGV (sales tax) on the basic room rate in addition to a 10% service charge. Foreigners and non-residents with the passport to prove it should be exempt from the IGV (but not the service charge). Unless otherwise noted, prices do not include taxes, service charges, or breakfast. Most *hostales* in Lima—unlike in Cusco, Arequipa, and a few other highland towns—do feature 24-hour hot water.

LIMA CENTRO
INEXPENSIVE
Hostal de las Artes 𝕂 𝓥𝓪𝓵𝓾𝓮   Well located on the southern fringes of Lima Centro, a block from Plaza Bolognesi, this small Dutch-owned *hostal* is very friendly and well run—and one of the best budget bargains in town. It occupies an attractive, restored

19th-century colonial-style house and has a pretty patio. It's safe, clean, and understandably very popular with backpackers and other value-conscious travelers. Some rooms could afford to be spruced up a bit, so if several are available, ask to see a couple on different floors. The *hostal* is also very gay-friendly, and it features solar heating. In case this one's full, the owners also operate a second, more basic *hostal* around the corner.

Jr. Chota 1460, Lima. © **01/433-0031.** Fax 01/428-5546. http://arteswelcome.tripod.com. 18 units. $18–$20 double with private bathroom; $5 per person dormitory style. Rates include airport transfer (by prior arrangement). No credit cards. *In room:* No phone.

Hotel España *Value*   Near the Convento de San Francisco and just 4 blocks from the Plaza de Armas, this extremely popular budget *hostal* has a funky flair and communal atmosphere. If you're looking to hook up with backpackers from around the globe and set off to explore Peru, you can't do better than Hotel España. It occupies a rambling colonial building chock-full of paintings, ceramics, faux Roman busts, plants, and even the occasional mummy and skull. A maze of rooms, most with shared bathrooms and some with odd numbers such as D3 and G2, are located up a winding staircase. The rooms themselves are simple, with concrete floors but brightly colored walls; they're well kept, but with cheesy bedspreads. The leafy rooftop garden terrace, with views of San Francisco, is a good place to hang out and trade travel tales. Security is said to be a little lax, so store your stuff in the lockers. Hot water goes to the early bird. The place can be noisy and even a little nuts, but that's part of its charm.

Azángaro 105, Lima. ©/fax **01/428-5546.** www.hotelespanaperu.com/ingles. 30 units. $9 double without bathroom; $12 double with bathroom. No credit cards. **Amenities:** Cafe; travel agency; laundry service. *In room:* No phone.

Hotel La Casona   This is a decent budget option for those who want to be in the thick of Lima Centro's colonial quarter, within close range of churches and mansions, and about a 10-minute walk from the Plaza de Armas. La Casona is pleasant and friendly, built around an airy central courtyard. Rooms are basic, with high ceilings; a few are rather dismal and can be uncomfortably humid, so ask to see several. Many rooms come equipped with curious 1950s and 1960s furniture and grandma-style big box TVs. In an attempt to compete with the more popular España and Europa hotels, it has converted a few rooms into "Backpacker's," dorm-style accommodations containing bathrooms.

Jr. Moquegua 289, Lima. ©/fax **01/426-6552.** 40 units. S/30 ($8.55) double; S/12 ($3.40) per person in dorm rooms. Rates include taxes. No credit cards. Covered parking. **Amenities:** Restaurant; room service. *In room:* No phone.

La Posada del Parque Hostal ★★ *Value*   Monica Moreno runs this fantastic-value, safe and delightful guesthouse, which occupies a lovely 1920s *casona* on what has to be one of the most peaceful streets near the center of Lima—it's a long cul-de-sac lined with gardens and other stately homes. Her house, in the Santa Beatriz district, is full of Peruvian popular art and offers unusual amenities at such an economical rate, such as Internet access, satellite TV, and homemade pizzas and beer upon request. Monica is more than willing to help travelers with all their needs. The rooms are spacious and impeccable, with excellent bathrooms and hot water. The owner also has a one-bedroom suite (Suite del Parque) nearby, which is perfect for longer stays.

Parque Hernán Velarde 60, Santa Beatriz, Lima. © **01/433-2412.** Fax 01/332-6927. www.incacountry.com. 9 units. $33 double. Rate includes taxes. *In room:* TV, no phone.

My, what an inefficient way to fish.

Ring toss, good. Horseshoes, bad.

Faster! Faster! Faster!

We take care of the fiddly bits, from providing over 43,000 customer reviews of hotels, to helping you find our best fares, to giving you 24/7 customer service. So you can focus on the only thing that matters. Goofing off.

travelocity
You'll never roam alone

travelocity.com   1-888-TRAVELOCITY   AOL Keyword: Travel

Where to Stay & Dine in Lima Centro

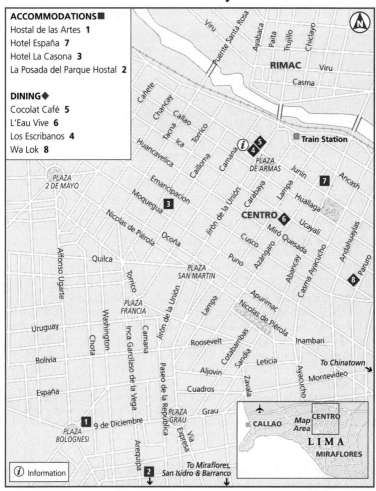

ACCOMMODATIONS■
Hostal de las Artes **1**
Hotel España **7**
Hotel La Casona **3**
La Posada del Parque Hostal **2**

DINING◆
Cocolat Café **5**
L'Eau Vive **6**
Los Escribanos **4**
Wa Lok **8**

RIMAC

■ Train Station

PLAZA
2 DE MAYO

PLAZA
DE ARMAS

CENTRO

PLAZA
SAN MARTIN

PLAZA
FRANCIA

To Chinatown

PLAZA
GRAU

PLAZA
BOLOGNESI

9 de Diciembre

To Miraflores,
San Isidro & Barranco

(i) Information

CALLAO   Map
Area

CENTRO

LIMA

MIRAFLORES

MIRAFLORES
VERY EXPENSIVE
Miraflores Park Hotel ✸✸✸   Lima's most elegant hotel, the Park Hotel bathes business executives and upscale tourists in unsurpassed luxury. It hugs the *malecón*, the park-lined avenue that traces the Lima coastline. From the cozy, library-like lobby and handsome restaurant to the tastefully appointed, plush rooms (including marble and granite bathrooms most New Yorkers would give their left arms to live in), the hotel is a distinguished address from head to foot. All rooms are suites with comfortable king-size beds and sitting areas equipped with large televisions and VCRs, fax machines, two phone lines, and dataports. Many rooms have ocean views—at least for the few days of the year when you can see the coast in Lima. Special promotional rates are often available online.

Av. Malecón de la Reserva 1035, Miraflores, Lima. ℂ **01/242-3000.** Fax 01/242-3393. www.mira-park.com. 81 units. $350–$365 deluxe double; from $405 suite. AE, DC, MC, V. **Amenities:** Restaurant; bar; cafe; small outdoor rooftop pool; squash court; exercise room; sauna; concierge; extensive business center; salon; 24-hr. room service; laundry service. *In room:* A/C, TV/VCR, fax, dataport, minibar, hair dryer.

EXPENSIVE

JW Marriott Hotel & Casino 🏛🏛   This upscale business traveler's hotel isn't as luxurious as the exclusive Park Plaza or Swissôtel, but it's more affordable, making it a very good value given the overall quality and dependability of the Marriott chain. It's a gleaming, ultramodern high-rise building hugging the coast and parks along the *malecón*, replete with glitzy ground-floor shops and a much-frequented casino. It seems to serve mostly short- and long-term business travelers from North and South America, but it's perfectly fine for leisure travelers and families. Children can be easily entertained at the outdoor pool or on the tennis court. Rooms are very well equipped and comfortable, with nice bathrooms, if without a whole lot of individual character. Inexpensive weekend rates are frequently available, making the Marriott one of the best values in Lima.

Av. Malecón de la Reserva 615, Miraflores, Lima. ℂ **01/217-7000.** Fax 01/217-7100. http://marriott.com/property/ propertypage/LIMDT. 300 units. $200–$295 double; $395–$415 suite. AE, DC, MC, V. Valet parking. **Amenities:** 2 restaurants; cafe; outdoor pool; health club; sauna; concierge; extensive business center; salon; 24-hr. room service; laundry service. *In room:* A/C, TV, dataport, minibar, hair dryer, safe.

Sonesta Posada del Inca Miraflores 🏛 *Value*   The Miraflores branch of a chain with a handful of hotels across Peru, this small modern hotel has an excellent location and is efficient and professionally run. Centrally located just 2 blocks from Parque Central (Parque Kennedy), it's within easy walking distance of Miraflores' many nightclubs, restaurants, and shops. The well-appointed rooms aren't huge, but they come with very comfortable beds, good-size bathrooms, and an ocher-and-deep-green color scheme with plaid bedspreads.

Alcanfores 329, Miraflores, Lima. ℂ **800/SONESTA,** or 01/241-7688. Fax 01/447-1164. www.sonesta.com/ peru_miraflores. 28 units. $95 double; $118 suite. Rates include taxes, service charge, and breakfast buffet. AE, DC, MC, V. Free parking. **Amenities:** 24-hr. cafe and bar; fitness center (½ block from hotel); concierge; business center; room service; babysitting; laundry service; nonsmoking rooms. *In room:* A/C, TV, minibar, hair dryer on request, safe.

MODERATE

Casa Andina Miraflores Hotel 🏛 *Value*   Well located, and well executed, like all Casa Andina properties, this midsize hotel—surprisingly enough, the only one the Peruvian chain has in the capital—has ample bedrooms that are cheerfully decorated, with brightly striped bedspreads and sunburnt yellow walls. Marble bathrooms are large, and the breakfast buffet is a winner. Casa Andina is perfect for the traveler who seeks comfort, good value, and no unpleasant surprises.

Av. 28 de Julio 1088, Miraflores, Lima. ℂ **01/241-4050.** Fax 01/241-4051. www.casa-andina.com. 49 units. $75–$85 double. Rates include breakfast buffet. AE, DC, MC, V. **Amenities:** Concierge; business center; room service; babysitting; laundry service; nonsmoking rooms. *In room:* A/C, TV, minibar, hair dryer on request, safe.

Hotel Antigua Miraflores 🏛 *Finds*   This charming early-20th-century mansion, full of authentic Peruvian touches and color, calls itself "a hidden treasure in the heart of Miraflores." As many return visitors know, that's not just hype. The hotel is owned and operated by a North American who's a long-time Lima resident. The house is

Where to Stay & Dine in Miraflores

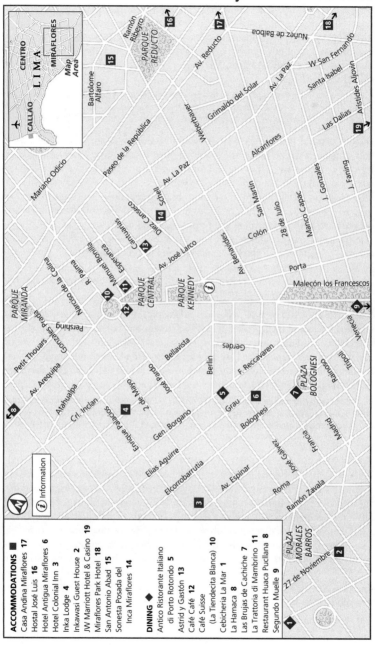

ACCOMMODATIONS ■

Casa Andina Miraflores **17**
Hostal José Luis **16**
Hotel Antigua Miraflores **6**
Hotel Colonial Inn **3**
Inka Lodge **4**
Inkawasi Guest House **2**
JW Marriott Hotel & Casino **19**
Miraflores Park Hotel **18**
San Antonio Abad **15**
Sonesta Posada del
  Inca Miraflores **14**

DINING ◆

Antico Ristorante Italiano
  di Porto Rotondo **5**
Astrid y Gastón **13**
Café Café **12**
Café Suisse
  (La Tiendecita Blanca) **10**
Cebichería La Mar **1**
La Hamaca **8**
Las Brujas de Cachiche **7**
La Trattoria di Mambrino **11**
Restaurant Huaca Pucllana **8**
Segundo Muelle **9**

ⓘ Information

elegant and tasteful, lined with colonial Peruvian art and built around a leafy courtyard. The staff is exceptionally helpful and friendly. Rooms range from huge suites with large Jacuzzis and kitchenettes to comfortable double rooms with handcrafted furniture and good-quality beds. Most bathrooms are quite luxurious, with colonial tiles, brass fixtures, and bathtubs. The public rooms look more like an art gallery than a hotel lobby (the paintings are for sale).

Av. Grau 350, Miraflores, Lima. (C) 01/241-6116. Fax 01/241-6115. http://peru-hotels-inns.com. 35 units. $74–$89 double; $104 suite. Rates include taxes and a nice selection of breakfasts. AE, DC, MC, V. Free parking. **Amenities:** Restaurant; bar; small gym; Jacuzzi; tour desk; room service; laundry service. *In room:* A/C, TV, minibar, hair dryer.

Hotel Colonial Inn   On a busy avenue in Miraflores, flush with fast-food restaurants and stores galore, this oddly charming small hotel, a large yellow colonial building on a corner, is a surprising retreat for a modest price. Popular and often full, it has lots of colonial flavor, from the masculine staircases and grand Spanish-style chairs and fireplace in the public rooms, to the wood-beamed restaurant with copper pots hanging above the arches and armor on the walls. Carpeted rooms have interesting touches, such as their own arches above the beds, dark-wood ceilings, and lanternlike lamps. The tile bathrooms are a good size, with bathtubs; the suites have large Jacuzzis. The attached restaurant, La Tasca, has good-value fixed-price lunches.

Comandante Espinar 310, Miraflores, Lima. (C) **01/241-7471.** Fax 01/445-7587. www.hotelcolonialinn.com. 37 units. $60 double. Rate includes taxes and breakfast buffet. AE, DC, MC, V. Limited street parking. **Amenities:** Restaurant; bar; room service; laundry service. *In room:* TV, minibar, safe.

San Antonio Abad *&* *Value*   Named for a saint, this clean and very friendly neighborhood hotel aims high. Its goal is to be welcoming and comfortable, and it succeeds. The colonial building, near the commercial center of Miraflores and several parks, has a garden terrace, fireplace, and sitting room. The rooms, which are simply decorated but ample, have private bathrooms with hot water around the clock. Because of street noise (ever present in Lima), you might ask for a room with an interior courtyard view.

Av. Ramón Ribeyro 301, Miraflores, Lima. (C) 01/447-6766. Fax 01/446-4208. www.hotelsanantonioabad.com. 24 units. $55 double; $120 suite. Rates include taxes, breakfast buffet, and airport pickup. AE, DC, MC, V. Free parking. **Amenities:** Restaurant; bar; room service; laundry service. *In room:* A/C, TV, minibar; hair dryer on request.

INEXPENSIVE

Hostal José Luis   With only overgrown vegetation creeping over a high wall and no sign out front, this private youth-hostel-like B&B has operated on word of mouth for nearly 20 years. Deceptively large, with a capacity for nearly 60 guests, it's one of the cheapest places in Miraflores. It's secluded in a quiet residential part of the district, a 10-minute walk from Parque Central and its hubbub of nightlife and shops. As the name would indicate, there's a family feeling here, with cooking and laundry facilities. The common rooms are busy with furnishings and patterned wallpaper, but many rooms have bunk beds, dorm-room style. All have private bathrooms and 24-hour hot water.

Francisco de Paula Ugarriza 727, Miraflores, Lima. (C) **01/444-1015.** Fax 01/446-7177. www.hoteljoseluis.com. 20 units. $10 per person. Rate includes taxes and breakfast. Limited street parking. *In room:* No phone.

Inka Lodge *&* *Value*   The best new budget inn in Lima is this modern, spotless and well-run small *hostal* with very good facilities, such as a roof terrace, computers with Internet access, kitchen use, and storage lockers. Rooms aren't large, but they're tastefully decorated for the price, and the location, on a quiet street just 5 blocks from

Parque Kennedy in the heart of Miraflores, is safe and convenient. Choose from doubles with shared baths or rooms for three or more, or dorm rooms with bunk beds. Bathrooms are very well maintained. Though the inn's web site claims it has a "homely atmosphere," I think what they mean is that, for a budget inn, it actually has character, and quite a bit at that. Thoughtful touches like free bottled water and coffee around the clock are uncommon among budget *hostales*.

Elias Aguirre 278, Miraflores, Lima. © 01/242-6989. www.inkalodge.com. 7 units. $25 double with shared bath; $10–$12 per person in shared dorm rooms. Rates include taxes and continental breakfast. Limited street parking. **Amenities:** Laundry service; high-speed Internet; storage lockers; kitchen use. *In room:* A/C, TV, no phone.

Inkawasi Guest House *(Value (Kids*   Designed to appeal to backpackers, this pleasant bed-and-breakfast is a step up from most Peruvian *hostales*. It features an airy and comfortable homey atmosphere in a secure part of Miraflores, just a few blocks from shops, restaurants, banks, and cinemas. There are two fully equipped kitchens available to guests, an interior patio and garden, and a roof garden and barbecue area. All rooms have private bathrooms, and suites have a queen-size bed, a desk, a kitchenette with a microwave, a minibar, and cable TV. The inn is especially family-friendly; kids can enjoy a play area with toys and children's videos.

Alfredo Salazar 345, Miraflores, Lima. ©/fax 01/422-7724. 10 units. $10 per person, or $25–$35 double; $45 suite. Rates include taxes and continental breakfast. Use of kitchen $2 a day; extra bed $5; children's bed $2. Limited street parking. **Amenities:** Laundry service. *In room:* TV, minibar, and kitchenette in suites, no phone.

SAN ISIDRO
VERY EXPENSIVE
Country Club Lima Hotel *(Kids*   This incredibly grand, lovely, and sprawling hacienda-style hotel, built in 1927 and wholly refurbished in 1998, is a swank and character-filled place to rest your head in Lima. Although it appears large, the hotel is actually very cozy, friendly, and low-key. Rooms—all of which are suites, with separate work areas—are large and very luxurious, with tons of antiques and old-world appeal (although they don't skimp on modern conveniences). Many of the huge marble bathrooms have large Jacuzzis and separate showers. A member of the Leading Hotels of the World, it is ideal for just about anyone, including families, but it is especially perfect for stressed-out business travelers who've seen one too many blandly elegant hotels. Public rooms are very refined and inviting, with chandeliers and very high wood-beam ceilings, a close approximation of a local nobleman's estate. It's not surprising that the hotel hosts frequent social functions. There's live music Friday and Saturday evenings in the elegant restaurant, and afternoon tea is served to the accompaniment of live piano music. Appropriately enough, the Country Club Hotel sits next to a golf course and tennis club (guest privileges included). The hotel is pretty fairly priced for this kind of luxury and service; it also offers very good corporate rates, and packages and special offers are often available (check the website).

Los Eucaliptos 590, San Isidro, Lima. © 800/745-8883 in the U.S. and Canada, or 01/611-9000. Fax 01/611-9002. www.hotelcountry.com. 75 units. $250–$305 double; $375–$1,000 suite. AE, DC, MC, V. Valet parking. **Amenities:** 3 restaurants; bar; outdoor pool; access to nearby Lima Golf Club; sauna; fitness center; concierge; business center; salon; 24-hr. room service; laundry service; nonsmoking rooms. *In room:* A/C, TV, dataport, minibar, safe.

Swissôtel Lima *(Kids*   One of Lima's most exclusive and sophisticated properties is this sparkling high-rise hotel. Formerly the Peruvian-owned Oro Verde, it takes its pedigree as part of the international Swissôtel chain very seriously: The hotel is very Continental classy. The lobby is awash in fine carpets, corridors are curiously lined with giant neoclassical columns, restaurants serve Swiss and Italian as well as Peruvian fare, and service is, of course, eminently efficient. Rooms are spacious and well appointed. Executive rooms include a work desk, two telephone lines, a coffee machine, a private executive lounge/board room, and cocktails (!). For business facilities, this property rivals the Marriott and Miraflores Park Hotel, although I find the latter the most distinguished of the three. Value rates and packages are often available.

Vía Central 150 (Centro Empresarial Real), San Isidro, Lima. ✆ 01/421-4400. Fax 01/4214422. http://lima.swissotel. com. 244 units. $215–$240 double; $290–$1,200 suite. Rates include taxes and service charge. AE, DC, MC, V. Valet parking. **Amenities:** 3 restaurants; cafeteria; bar/lounge; small heated outdoor pool; fitness center; spa; sauna; concierge; tour desk; business center and secretarial services; salon; 24-hr. room service; laundry service; nonsmoking rooms. *In room:* A/C, TV, safe.

EXPENSIVE

Libertador San Isidro Golf ✦ *Value*   Smack in the middle of the San Isidro financial district, the Libertador—which overlooks the private Lima Golf Club—is relatively unassuming and tranquil, especially considering the more imposing and flashier hotels nearby. Still, that's its charm. It doesn't try too hard, but it gets the job done for guests who are both business travelers and tourists. Part of a five-member very well-run Peruvian chain of upscale hotels, this midsize offering is handsomely decorated with modern art, some Kilim rugs, and bold colors, eschewing the typical blandness of business hotels. This hotel also has a nice top-floor restaurant and bar with good views. It's quite a good value, especially if you can get an upgrade to a junior suite.

Los Eucaliptos 550, San Isidro, Lima. ✆ 01/421-6666. Fax 01/442-3011. www.libertador.com.pe. 43 units. $120 double; $150–$305 suite. AE, DC, MC, V. Valet parking. **Amenities:** Restaurant; bar; gym; Jacuzzi; sauna; concierge; laundry service. *In room:* A/C, TV, minibar.

Sonesta Lima Hotel El Olívar ✦✦ *Value*   The Sonesta chain's top-of-the-line property, aimed squarely at visiting business travelers, is named for the historic Olive Grove Park, which it faces. This seven-story hotel is well located for its clientele, in a peaceful section of the San Isidro business district of the city. The rooms, a step up from the more rustic decor in the chain's Posada del Inca, are quite large, with boldly colored fabrics and beige marble bathrooms. Service is friendly and efficient, and the amenities outdo those of most hotels in the city. The recently revamped restaurant is winning accolades in the Peruvian press, and is an excellent spot for lunch or dinner. Business travelers on a tighter budget who nonetheless wish to stay in San Isidro should also check out the Sonesta Posada del Inca, an easygoing sister property whose guests are allowed to use the pool and excellent gym at El Olívar. It's located just a few blocks away at Av. Conquistadores 490 (✆ 01/222-4373; $105 double including taxes).

Pancho Fierro 194, San Isidro, Lima. ✆ 800/SONESTA, or 01/712-6000. Fax 01/712-6099. www.sonesta.com/ peru_lima. 134 units. $195–$230 double; $290–$400 suite. Rates include breakfast buffet. Children under 8 stay free in parent's room. Weekend deals $99 per night. AE, DC, MC, V. Free parking. **Amenities:** 2 restaurants; cafe; cocktail lounge; bar; fitness center w/rooftop outdoor pool; Jacuzzi; sauna; concierge; business and conference center; salon; massage; babysitting; 24-hr. room service; laundry service; nonsmoking rooms. *In room:* A/C, TV/VCR w/pay movies, minibar, hair dryer, safe.

Where to Stay & Dine in San Isidro

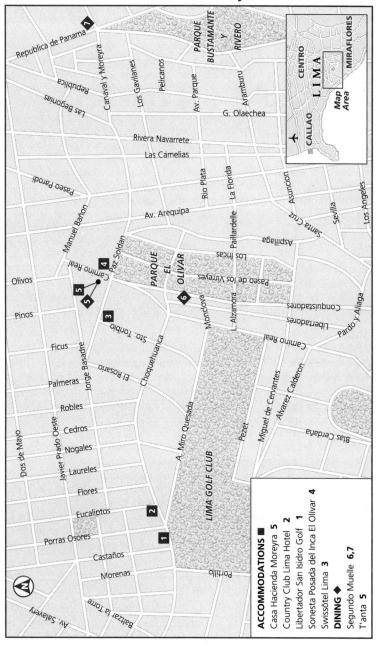

ACCOMMODATIONS ■
Casa Hacienda Moreyra **5**
Country Club Lima Hotel **2**
Libertador San Isidro Golf **1**
Sonesta Posada del Inca El Olivar **4**
SwissÔtel Lima **3**
DINING ◆
Segundo Muelle **6,7**
T'anta **5**

4 Where to Dine

As one might expect, Lima presents the most cosmopolitan dining city in all of Peru, with restaurants of all budgets and a wide range of cuisines—from upscale seafood restaurants and *comida criolla* (coastal Peruvian cooking), to Chinese and plenty of Italian, French, and other international restaurants. Lima is the top spot in the country to sample the dish Peru is perhaps best known for: *ceviche*. Sometimes entire streets and neighborhoods specialize in a single type of food. In Lima Centro, you can visit the *chifas* of Chinatown, and in Miraflores, a pedestrian street off Parque Central (Boulevard San Remo) is referred to as "Little Italy" for its scores of look-alike pizzerias and Italian restaurants. Don't mind the restaurant menu hawkers; it's touristy but also lively and fun.

Restaurants are, predictably, most crowded in the early evening, especially Thursday through Saturday. In the business districts of Miraflores and San Isidro, lunch can also get quite busy—at least in the nicer restaurants that are popular with local and international businessmen. One of the fanciest new restaurants in the city was just opening when I was last in Lima, and it's worth checking out if you'd like to dine in a 350-year-old colonial mansion, a veritable house-museum with paintings on loan from the Institute of Culture: **Casa Hacienda Moreyra,** Av. Paz Soldán, San Isidro (*©* **01/444-4022**).

To locate restaurants in Lima Centro, Miraflores, and San Isidro, see the maps "Where to Stay & Dine in Lima Centro" (p. 119), "Where to Stay & Dine in Miraflores" (p. 121), and "Where to Stay & Dine in San Isidro" (p. 125).

LIMA CENTRO
MODERATE
L'Eau Vive FRENCH/PERUVIAN   If you're feeling obscenely rich in this impoverished country, you'll do a tiny bit of good and feel better by eating here. The restaurant, run by a French order of nuns, donates its proceeds to charity. In a colonial palace 2 blocks from the Plaza de Armas and across the street from one of Lima's most important mansions, Torre Tagle, it features several large dining rooms with high ceilings. If you come for the cheap lunch *menú,* though, you'll have to sit in the simpler front rooms. The "a la carte" dining rooms are considerably more elegant. The lunch menú is a deal, and at night you get a pious show free with dinner: The nuns sing "Ave Maria" promptly at 9:30pm. The French menu includes items such as prawn bisque, trout baked in cognac, and grilled meats; it also incorporates some international dishes from around the globe—chiefly, the many countries from which the order's nuns come. The restaurant's heyday was clearly a few years ago, and some travelers have complained that the food and service weren't up to snuff, but this is still an old favorite you can feel good about patronizing, even if it's not the finest meal you can have in Lima.

Ucayali 370. *©* **01/427-5612.** Reservations recommended on weekend nights. Main courses S/9–S/43 ($2.55–$12); menú del día S/8–S/12 ($2.30–$3.40). AE, MC, V. Mon–Sat 12:30–3pm and 7:30–9:30pm.

Los Escribanos PERUVIAN   On one of Lima Centro's more appealing streets, a tiny pedestrian passageway near the Plaza de Armas, this unassumingly elegant two-story eatery has an attractive terrace with outdoor tables. Popular with local businessmen and travelers who trickle out of the tourism information office next door, it offers particularly good deals at lunch (with bargain *platos únicos* and a fixed-price menu that's served until 9pm). The evening menu lists plenty of *criollo* and seafood plates from the Peruvian coast, including gourmet dishes with pre-Columbian influences. At lunch, though, most people sit down to more standard fare, such as grilled trout and fettuccine Alfredo, served with a salad and beverage.

Pasaje Nicolás de Ribera El Viejo (Los Escribanos) 137–141. (ⓒ 01/427-9102. Reservations recommended on weekend nights. Main courses S/10–S/28 ($2.85–$8); menú del día S/25 ($7.15). MC, V. Mon–Thurs 9am–9pm; Fri–Sat 9am–midnight.

INEXPENSIVE

Cocolat Café BISTRO   A good and quick spot for lunch or dinner is this simple little bistro on the popular pedestrian passageway, near the Plaza de Armas, that's lined with restaurants. It serves sandwiches, salads, and sides such as empanadas; the midday menú is a good deal: just $4 for an appetizer and main course, or under $6 for a full "chef's menu." Top it off with a great selection of homemade chocolates and good coffee, and you might just want to linger for a while on the sidewalk terrace. It's also a good spot for breakfast.

Pasaje Nicolás de Ribera El Viejo (Los Escribanos) 121. (ⓒ 01/427-4471. Reservations not accepted. Main courses S/7–S/10 ($2–$2.85); menú del día S/14–S/20 ($4–$5.70). No credit cards. Mon–Sat 8am–6:30pm.

MIRAFLORES & SAN ISIDRO
VERY EXPENSIVE

Astrid y Gastón ✮✮✮ PERUVIAN/INTERNATIONAL   Hidden discreetly behind a nonchalant facade (though one of an antique colonial house), on a busy side street leading to Parque Central, is this warm and chic modern colonial dining room and cozy bar. It continues to be my favorite restaurant in Peru. Gastón Acurio is the celebrity chef of the moment, with a burgeoning empire of fine-dining restaurants not only in Lima but a handful of other cities on the continent (and coming soon to the U.S.) and a cooking show on TV. His signature restaurant in the capital is warm and elegant, with high, white peaked ceilings and orange walls decorated with colorful modern art. In back is an open kitchen, where Gastón can be seen cooking with his staff, and a secluded wine-salon dining room. The place is sophisticated and hip but low-key, a description that could fit most of its clients, who all seem to be regulars. The menu might be called *criollo*-Mediterranean: Peruvian with a light touch. Try spicy roasted kid or the excellent fish called *noble robado,* served in miso sauce with crunchy oysters. The list of desserts—the work of Astrid, the other half of the husband–wife team—is nearly as long as the main course menu, and they are spectacular.

Tips Peruvian *Chifas*

Chinatown (Barrio Chino), southeast of the Plaza de Armas and next to the Mercado Central (beyond the Chinese arch on Jr. Ucayali), is a good place to sample the Peruvian take on Chinese food. These *chifas,* inexpensive restaurants with similar menus, are everywhere in the small but dense neighborhood. Among those worth visiting (generally open daily 9am–10pm or later) are **Wa Lok,** Jr. Paruro 864 (ⓒ **01/427-2750**), probably the best known in the neighborhood; and **Salón China,** Jr. Ucayali 727 (ⓒ **01/428-8350**), which serves a good lunch buffet for S/30 ($8.55).

Cantuarias 175, Miraflores. ✆ 01/444-1496. Reservations recommended. Main courses S/39–S/79 ($11–$23). AE, DC, MC, V. Mon–Sat 12:30–3:30pm and 7:30pm–midnight.

La Hamaca ✿✿✿ *Finds* PERUVIAN/INTERNATIONAL   Sometimes the setting is so splendid that the food hardly enters into the equation. That's not exactly the case here—the solid but expensive *criollo* preparations are certainly satisfying—but the interior of this art- and antiques-filled three-story mansion, with a warren of sumptuously decorated small dining rooms, would outclass just about any kitchen. One of Lima's most seductive restaurants, it is a splurge but well worth it for an extraordinary experience. The house looks like a cinematically art-directed Mexican hacienda, and some pieces of the owner's private collection on display are extremely valuable. The restaurant plays host to its share of bigwigs, who enjoy simple, traditional Peruvian specialties such as *ají de gallina* (chile cream chicken) and *tacu tacu* (Peru's standard, slightly spicy rice and beans), as well as nicely prepared dishes such as sole in a langoustine and garlic salsa. On Friday and Saturday evenings, there is dancing on the top floor (dining at the restaurant is not required), which draws a sophisticated, mature crowd.

Av. Arequipa 4698, Miraflores. ✆ 01/242-7978. Reservations recommended. Main courses S/28–S/65 ($8–$19). AE, DC, MC, V. Mon–Sat 12:30–4pm and 7:30–11pm.

Las Brujas de Cachiche ✿✿ PERUVIAN *(CRIOLLO)*   The "Witches of Cachiche" celebrates 2,000 years of local culture with a menu that's a tour of the "magical" cuisines of pre-Columbian Peru. The chef even uses ancient recipes and ingredients. The extensive menu includes classic Peruvian dishes, such as *ají de gallina,* but concentrates on fresh fish and shellfish and fine cuts of meat with interesting twists and unusual accompaniments. Brujas de Cachiche sole is prepared with Asian and *criollo* spices, and served with peas and bell peppers sautéed in soybean sauce. A steak in pisco-butter sauce is served with braised mushrooms. Among the excellent desserts, several continue the indigenous theme, such as *mazamorra morada* (purple corn pudding and dried fruit). The restaurant, in a sprawling old house with several warmly decorated dining rooms, is popular both night and day with well-heeled Limeños, expat businessmen and foreign government officials, and tourists; it's exclusive and it's expensive, but it's worth the splurge. A lunch buffet is served Tuesday through Friday and Sunday from 11am to 4pm, and gastronomic festivals are frequent.

Jr. Bolognesi 460, Miraflores. ✆ 01/447-1883. Reservations recommended. Main courses S/30–S/62 ($8.50–$18); lunch buffet S/70($20), including 2 glasses of wine. AE, DC, MC, V. Mon–Sat 1pm–midnight; Sun noon–5pm.

Restaurant Huaca Pucllana ✿✿✿ NOUVEAU PERUVIAN   Located in an unparalleled setting—within the compound of a 1,500-year-old adobe pyramid built by the original inhabitants of Lima—is one of the city's greatest dining surprises. A beautiful and serene upscale restaurant with knockout views of the pyramid, secluded in the midst of Lima's chaotic jumble, makes for a remarkable night out. The low hump of adobe bricks and excavation walkways are illuminated at night, and diners can take a tour of the construction and digs after dinner. The restaurant is handsomely designed in a rustic colonial style; you can dine indoors or out, but the best spot is surely the covered terrace. The menu is creative Peruvian, with fusion touches spicing up classic *criollo* cooking. Excellent appetizers include *humitas verdes* (tamales) and *causitas pucllana* (balls of mashed potatoes with shrimp and avocado). Main courses are focused on meats, such as rack of lamb, but I had an excellent marinated grouper with an interesting Asian twist. Desserts are worth saving room for; the napoleon, with chocolate mousse and passion-fruit sorbet between chocolate cookies, is heavenly.

General Borgoño, Block 8 (Huaca Pucllana), Miraflores. (*C*) **01/445-4042.** Reservations recommended. Main courses S/34–S/79 ($9.70–$23). AE, DC, MC, V. Mon–Sat 12:30pm–midnight; Sun, 12:30–4pm.

EXPENSIVE

La Trattoria di Mambrino *Kids* ITALIAN   One of Lima's most popular and enduring Italian eateries is this attractive bistro, owned by an Italian gentleman who makes the rounds on most evenings. Decorated in warm Roman tones, the restaurant is often packed with families and young couples. La Trattoria bakes its own delicious rustic bread—with a bit of olive oil, it's an appetizer in itself. Among the many excellent homemade pastas are several stuffed versions, such as the agnolotti with three meats: rabbit, pork, and beef. There are daily specials, such as ragout of rabbit over pappardelle, and stuffed peppers with prawns. Pizzas from the wood-burning oven and large fresh salads round out the menu.

Manuel Bonilla 106, Miraflores. (*C*) **01/446-7002.** Reservations recommended. Main courses S/20–S/55 ($5.70–$16). AE, DC, MC, V. Daily 1–3:15pm and 8–11:15pm.

MODERATE

Antico Ristorante Italiano di Porto Rotondo ITALIAN   A pretty yellow colonial house with an inviting library-like club bar off to one side, Porto Rotondo is a sophisticated retreat in the midst of Miraflores' hustle and bustle. Inside you'll find deep red walls, black-and-white tile floors, and large mirrors. The menu focuses on classic and well-prepared Italian dishes: ravioli, risotto, gnocchi, and osso buco, as well as fresh fish. Some nights, there are many more people sitting at the bar than around the dining tables in the next room.

Recavarren 265, Miraflores. (*C*) **01/447-9575.** Reservations recommended. Main courses S/25–S/36 ($7.15–$10). MC, V. Daily noon–4pm and 8pm–midnight.

Café Suisse (La Tiendecita Blanca) *Kids* SWISS/INTERNATIONAL   This classic old-style cafe, a Lima institution since 1937, is decorated with cool enamel doors and staffed by waitresses in folkloric red-and-white dresses. It's best known for its exquisite pastries, cakes, breads, and gourmet food shop, but "the little white store" is also a good little restaurant, perfect for lunch and even breakfast. Choose from fresh-baked quiches, *empanadas* (turnover pastries served stuffed or empty), and sandwiches, or go Swiss with a fondue for two. There's a daily four-course lunch menú de la casa for $12. Of course, if you spot that long counter bursting with homemade desserts, you might be unable to resist spoiling your meal.

Av. Larco 111, Miraflores. (*C*) **01/445-9797.** Reservations not accepted. Main courses S/25–S/39 ($7.15–$11). AE, DC, MC, V. Daily 7am–midnight.

Cebichería La Mar *CEVICHERIA*/SEAFOOD   The restaurant everyone in Lima seems to be lining up for to get in—no reservations are accepted, so get there early or sneak in late in the afternoon—is this upscale *cevichería,* courtesy of hot chef Gastón Acurio. Fashionable, stylishly designed, and moderately priced, it represents the best of traditional Limeño cooking, but with an edge. Some ceviche purists will tell you that you don't need to go to a hip, expensive spot for ceviche, and while it's true the most authentic ceviche spots are no-frills neighborhood joints, there's nothing wrong with jazzing up the formula in my book. The airy, plant-filled space has a chic, modern touch, with an angular, poured concrete facade, bamboo roof, turquoise chairs, and cement floors. The fish—choose from a couple dozen types of ceviche, as well as rice-based seafood dishes and whole fish—is always fresh and carefully prepared. Although La Mar is only open for lunch, it features a cool cocktail bar with great pisco-based drinks, like the "Cholopolitan," that would surely be a hit late into the night were it to stay open. But owing to *cevichería* tradition, it's strictly a daytime affair. For now.

Av. La Mar 770, Miraflores. ✆ 01/421-3365. Reservations not accepted. Main courses S/12–S/29 ($3.40–$8.30). AE, DC, MC, V. Mon–Fri, noon–5pm; Sat–Sun 11:30am–5:30pm.

Segundo Muelle *CEVICHERIA*/SEAFOOD   At the top of most people's lists of favorite Peruvian dishes is ceviche, and you won't have trouble finding a *cevichería* any-where along the coast. Often you have to choose between either very upscale or down-and-dirty versions. This informal lunch-only place in Miraflores, across from the cheesy Parque del Amor and oceanfront *malecón,* is one of the most reasonable options in Lima for excellent fresh fish and ceviche plates without any fuss. Choose between a sim-ple, almost cafeteria-style interior and an upstairs outdoor deck with sea views. If you're new to ceviche, you can't go wrong with the *mixto* (white fish, octopus, prawns, snails, scallops, and squid). There is a long list of other fish dishes, including sole, salmon, seafood pastas, and various rice and seafood plates. Top off your meal with *chicha morada,* a purple corn beverage made with pineapple and lemon—it's sweet and deli-cious. Kids' plates are available for S/12 ($3.40). There are other branches in San Isidro at Av. Conquistadores 490 and Av. Carnaval y Moreyra 605.

Malecón Cisneros 156, Miraflores. ✆ 01/241-5040. www.segundomuelle.com. Reservations not accepted. Main courses S/18–S/35 ($5.15–$10). MC, V. Daily noon–5pm.

T'anta ✆ PERUVIAN/DELI/CAFE   Like a Peruvian Dean & Deluca (an upscale deli/market in New York City), T'anta (which means "bread" in Quechua) serves deli-cious, casual eats in its cafe or prepared foods to go. From fresh salads and panini to Peruvian sandwiches called *sánguches* and home-made pastas and terrific desserts, this stylish but informal place, the brainchild of Astrid (the dessert wizard of Astrid y Gastón fame) hits the spot no matter what you're in the mood for, or when. It's very chic and modern, with poured concrete and an angled glass wall. You may come for a coffee or a cocktail, but I guarantee that you'll end up at least having dessert. One dessert that had me coming back for more was the *tartita de maracuyá* (passion-fruit tart).

Pancho Fierro 117, San Isidro. ✆ 01/421-9708. Reservations not accepted. Main courses S/19–S/29 ($5.40–$8.30). AE, DC, MC, V. Daily 8am–midnight.

INEXPENSIVE

Café Café SANDWICHES/COFFEE   A tried-and-true people-watching spot with a menu of 100-plus drinks and dozens of gourmet coffees, this agreeable two-story cafe, located just off the main park in Miraflores, is also ideal for a quick lunch or sim-ple dinner. The predominantly young crowd drops by not only to meet up with friends and hang out at the outdoor tables, but also to sample inexpensive pizzas, sal-ads, or one of the 26 sandwiches. For folks in need of a real meal, there are also larger plates, including a fish of the day. It's also a good spot to have a quick and inexpen-sive breakfast. This spot is just one of several branches in town.

Mártir Olaya 250, Miraflores. ✆ 01/445-1165. Main courses S/8–S/34 ($2.30–$9.70). AE, DC, MC, V. Daily 8:30am–1:30am.

Cevicherías

You can't really go to Peru—especially Lima—without sitting down for an irresistibly fresh plate of ceviche, the tantalizing plate of raw fish and shell-fish that's marinated in lime or lemon juice and chile peppers and served with toasted corn, sweet potato, and raw onion. The citrus juices "cook" the fish, so it's not really raw the way sushi is. Plenty of restaurants of all stripes—from lowly neighborhood joints to snooty fine-dining spots popular with government bureaucrats and visiting businessmen—offer ceviche, but you really have to go to an authentic *cevichería* (also written "cebichería") for the true experience. In addition to **Segundo Muelle** (p. 130) and **Canta Rana** (p. 132), others worth checking out are **Punta Sal,** Malecón Cisneros, block 3, at the corner of Trípoli in Miraflores (© 01/242-4524), one of a small chain of informal *cevicherías* pretty similar to Segundo Muelle; and **El-Kapallaq,** 4844 Av. Petit Thouars, Miraflores (© 01/444-4149), an upscale seafood and ceviche restaurant that, in the opinion of some locals, has no equal in the city. A hip new take on the *cevichería* is Gastón Acurio's **Cebichería La Mar** (p. 129). Peruvians view ceviche as a daytime dish, and most *cevicherías* aren't open for dinner; for the full experience, go at lunchtime and order a classic pisco sour to start, followed by *chicha morada* (or, if you're feeling kinky, a bottle of curiously neon-yellow Inka Cola).

BARRANCO

To locate the following restaurants, see the "Lima at a Glance" map on p. 109.

VERY EXPENSIVE

Costa Verde ⋆ *Overrated* SEAFOOD   Any time a restaurant in Peru lists all prices in dollars, you know it's not going to be cheap. Costa Verde, perched on a promontory jutting out into the ocean along the "green coast" south of Miraflores, is probably as expensive a meal as you'll have in Peru, but it's also good enough to draw a decent number of Limeños celebrating special occasions. It draws a bigger share of foreigners, as evidenced by the touristy little national flags the hostess places on everyone's table. (I suggest telling her you're from Iceland or Zimbabwe, just to see how well stocked they are in miniature flags.) The restaurant is attractive enough, but it's the big-time seafood buffet that makes everyone's eyes bulge. There's a daily lunch buffet and also a huge gourmet dinner buffet ($60 a head—in Peru!), which the restaurant claims is registered in the *Guinness World Records.* The regular menu seems not to have changed in more than 3 decades of business, but you can't really argue with sea bass with wild mushrooms and morel sauce with scallop mousse, or basil and ricotta gnocchi with river shrimp in saffron sauce. Not in the mood for fish? Try the pork loin in beer-and-honey sauce. Sit in the glass-enclosed atrium—although it's rather devoid of character, you'll get to hear the sound of waves crashing against the shore. Then again, that could be the sound of your bank account crashing and burning.

Circuito de Playas (Playa Barranquito), Barranco. © 01/227-1244. Reservations recommended. Main courses $13–$29. AE, DC, MC, V. Daily noon–midnight.

EXPENSIVE

Manos Morenas 𝒦𝒦 𝓚𝓲𝓭𝓼 PERUVIAN *(CRIOLLO)*   In a beautiful early 1900s house on a quiet, leafy street in Barranco, this is one of the coolest restaurants in Lima. The name makes reference to the country's small but culturally potent Afro-Peruvian population and its traditions, influences crucial to both the menu and the lively, costumed music-and-dance shows that the restaurant has become famous for. The main dining room, in what was the house's interior patio, is very appealing, with handsome wood chairs and tables, and art for sale on the elegant yellow walls. A nice bar greets you at the entrance, in case you have to wait for a table. The kitchen, staffed by women dressed like the restaurant's logo of a black woman in a head wrap, creates excellent versions of Peruvian standards such as *lomo saltado, ají de gallina, tamalitos verdes* (green tamales), and *papa rellena* (stuffed potatoes). *Corvina Manos Morenas* is sea bass served with mashed potatoes, spinach, prawns, and a béchamel sauce. The restaurant charges a substantial cover (S/40 or $11) for the live shows, which are featured Tuesday through Thursday from 9pm to 1am, and Friday and Saturday from 10:30pm to 1am.

Av. Pedro de Osma 409, Barranco. ℭ **01/467-0421.** Reservations recommended. Main courses S/17–S/48 ($4.85–$14); menú turístico $13–$16. AE, DC, MC, V. Mon–Sat 12:30–4pm and 7pm–1am.

MODERATE

Antica Trattoria 𝒦 𝓥𝓪𝓵𝓾𝓮 𝓚𝓲𝓭𝓼 ITALIAN   This charming and laid-back Italian restaurant perfectly suits the surrounding neighborhood, which has large doses of both qualities. It has a number of small, separate dining rooms decorated with a rustic and minimalist masculinity: stucco walls, dark wood-beamed ceilings, country-style wood tables, and simple, solid chairs. The house specialty is gourmet pizza from the wood-fired ovens, but the menu has several tempting ideas to lure you away from pizza, such as homemade pastas and osso buco, or delicious *lomo fino a la tagliata* (beef buried under a mound of arugula). The relaxed environment makes this a great date place, as well as the perfect spot for dinner before stepping out to one of Barranco's live music or dance clubs.

San Martín 201, Barranco. ℭ **01/247-5752.** Reservations recommended. Main courses S/19–S/35 ($5.40–$10). AE, DC, MC, V. Daily noon–midnight.

Canta Rana 𝒦𝒦 𝓕𝓲𝓷𝓭𝓼 *CEVICHERIA*/SEAFOOD   A relaxed and informal place that looks almost like the interior of a garage and is immensely popular with locals, "the Singing Frog" is one of the best spots in town for ceviche and fresh seafood in classic Peruvian coastal preparations. The menu lists 15 types of sea bass, including one stuffed with langoustines, as well as infinite varieties of ceviche. The traditional ceviche is served on a flat plate with heaps of purple onions, some *choclo* (maize), and a wedge of *camote* (sweet potato). The best way to wash it down is with a chilled pitcher of *chicha morada*. The shacklike interior is decorated with simple wood tables, and the walls are festooned with *fútbol* paraphernalia. For a high dose of local color and excellent seafood, Canta Rana's a perfect lunch spot.

Génova 101, Barranco. ℭ **01/477-8934.** Reservations recommended. Main courses S/17–S/30 ($4.85–$8.55). AE, MC, V. Sun–Thurs 7:30am–4pm; Fri–Sat 7:30am–11pm.

5 What to See & Do

Many visitors to Lima are merely on their way to other places in Peru; few people spend more than a couple of days in the capital. But because nearly all transport goes through Lima, most people take advantage of layovers to see what distinguishes the

What to See & Do in Lima Centro

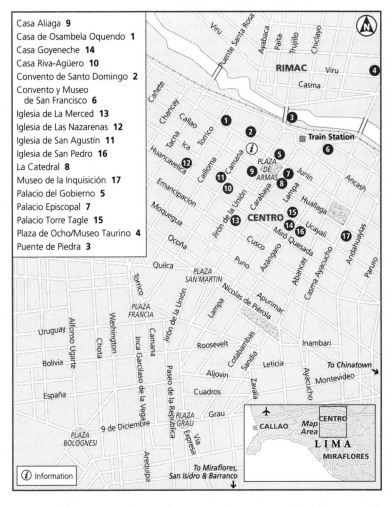

Casa Aliaga **9**
Casa de Osambela Oquendo **1**
Casa Goyeneche **14**
Casa Riva-Agüero **10**
Convento de Santo Domingo **2**
Convento y Museo
  de San Francisco **6**
Iglesia de La Merced **13**
Iglesia de Las Nazarenas **12**
Iglesia de San Agustín **11**
Iglesia de San Pedro **16**
La Catedral **8**
Museo de la Inquisición **17**
Palacio del Gobierno **5**
Palacio Episcopal **7**
Palacio Torre Tagle **15**
Plaza de Ocho/Museo Taurino **4**
Puente de Piedra **3**

city: its colonial old quarter—once the finest in the Americas—and several of the finest museums in Peru, all of which serve as magnificent introductions to Peruvian history and culture.

Much of the historic center has suffered from sad neglect; the municipal government is committed to restoring the aesthetic value, but, with limited funds, it faces a daunting task. Today central Lima has a noticeable police presence and is considerably safer than it was just a few years ago. A full day in Lima Centro should suffice; depending on your interests, you could spend anywhere from a day to a week traipsing through Lima's many museum collections, many of which are dispersed in otherwise unremarkable neighborhoods.

LIMA CENTRO: COLONIAL LIMA

Lima's grand **Plaza de Armas** (also called the **Plaza Mayor,** or **Main Square**), the original center of the city and the site where Francisco Pizarro founded the city in 1535, is essentially a modern reconstruction. The disastrous 1746 earthquake that initiated the city's decline leveled most of the 16th- and 17th-century buildings in the old center. The plaza has witnessed everything from bullfights to Inquisition-related executions. The oldest surviving element of the square is the central bronze fountain, which dates from 1651. Today the square, although perhaps not the most beautiful or languid in South America, is still rather distinguished beneath a surface level of grime and bustle (and it has been named a UNESCO World Heritage Site). The major palaces and cathedral are mostly harmonious in architectural style and color. (The facades are a mix of natural stone and a once-bold yellow color now dulled by smog and mist.) On the north side of the square is the early-20th-century **Palacio del Gobierno (Presidential Palace),** where a changing of the guard takes place daily at noon; free guided visits of the palace are offered Monday through Friday from 10am to 12:30pm. The **Municipalidad de Lima (City Hall)** is on the west side of the plaza. Across the square is **La Catedral (Cathedral),** rebuilt after the earthquake, making it by far the oldest building on the square, and, next to the cathedral, the **Palacio Episcopal (Archbishop's Palace),** distinguished by an extraordinary wooden balcony.

A block north of the Plaza de Armas, behind the Presidential Palace, is the Río Rímac and a 17th-century Roman-style bridge, the **Puente de Piedra** (literally, "stone bridge"). It leads to the once-fashionable **Rímac** district, today considerably less chic—some would say downright dangerous—although it is the location of a few of Lima's best *peñas,* or live *criollo* music clubs. The **Plaza de Acho bullring,** once the largest in the world, and the decent **Museo Taurino (Bullfighting Museum)** are near the river at Hualgayoc 332 (© **01/482-3360**). The museum is open Monday through Friday from 9am to 3pm, and Saturday from 9am to 2pm, and admission is S/6 ($1.70). The ring is in full swing during the Fiestas Patrias (national holidays) at the end of July; the regular season runs October through December.

Five blocks southwest of Plaza de Armas is Lima Centro's other grand square, **Plaza San Martín.** Inaugurated in 1921, this stately square with handsome gardens was recently renovated. At its center is a large monument to the South American liberator, José de San Martín.

Lima's **Barrio Chino,** the largest Chinese community in South America (200,000 plus), is the best place to get a taste of the Peruvian twist on traditional Chinese cooking in the neighborhood's *chifas.* For recommendations, see the "Peruvian *Chifas*" box on p. 127. The official boundary of Chinatown is the large gate on Jr. Ucayali.

THE TOP ATTRACTIONS

Convento y Museo de San Francisco 🌟🌟   Probably the most spectacular of Lima's colonial-era churches, the Convent of Saint Francis is a strikingly restored, yellow-and-white 17th-century complex that survived the massive earthquake in 1746. The facade is a favorite of thousands of pigeons, who rest on rows of ridges that rise up the towers—so much so that, from a distance, it looks like black spots add an unexpectedly funky flavor to the baroque church. Cloisters and interiors are lined with beautiful *azulejos* (glazed ceramic tiles) from Seville; carved *mudéjar* (Moorish-style) ceilings are overhead. The mandatory guided tour takes visitors past the cloisters to a fine museum of religious art, with beautifully carved saints and a series of portraits of the apostles by the studio of Francisco Zurbarán, the famed Spanish painter. For many, though, the most fascinating component of the visit is the descent into the catacombs, which were dug beginning in 1546 as a burial ground for priests and others. (As many as 75,000 bodies were interred here before the main cemetery was built.) File past loads of bones—it's unknown how many levels down they go—and see a round well lined with perfectly laid skulls and femurs. Also of great interest are the church, outfitted with an impressive neoclassical altar, and a fantastic 17th-century library with 20,000 books, many of which date to the first years after Lima's foundation. A breathtaking carved Moorish ceiling over a staircase is a reconstruction of the original from 1625. Allow 1½ hours to see it all, including waiting time for an English-language tour.

Ancash s/n (Plaza de San Francisco). © 01/426-7377. Admission S/5 ($1.40) adults, S/2.50 (70¢) students. Guides available in English and Spanish. Daily 9am–6pm.

La Catedral ✺   Lima's baroque cathedral, an enlargement of an earlier one from 1555, was completed in 1625. It suffered damages in earthquakes in 1687 and was decimated by the big one in 1746. The present building, again damaged by tremors in 1940, is an 18th-century reconstruction of the early plans. Twin yellow towers sandwich an elaborate stone facade. Inside are several notable churrigueresque (Spanish baroque) altars and carved wooden choir stalls, but the cathedral is best known for the chapel where Francisco Pizarro lies and a small **Museo de Arte Religioso (Museum of Religious Art)** housed in the rear of the church.

Immediately to the right after you enter the church is a chapel decorated in magnificent Venetian mosaics and marble. In case you don't know whose earthly remains are inside the tomb, letters in mosaic tiles over the arch of the chapel spell out FRANCISCO PIZARRO. The founder of Lima and killer of the Incas' emperor was himself assassinated in the Plaza de Armas in 1541, but his remains weren't brought to the cathedral until 1985. (They were discovered in a crypt in 1977.) Look closely at the mosaic on the far wall, which depicts his coat of arms, Atahualpa reaching into his coffer to cough up a ransom in the hopes of attaining his release, and other symbols of Pizarro's life. The museum has a few fabulous painted-glass mirrors from Cusco, a collection of unsigned paintings, and a seated sculpture of Jesus, with his chin resting pensively on his hand; it's as bloody a figure of Christ as you're likely to see. Allow about an hour for a visit.

Plaza de Armas. © 01/427-5980. Admission to cathedral and museum S/10 ($2.85) adults, S/5 ($1.40) students. Guides available in English and Spanish (voluntary tip). Mon–Sat 10am–5pm.

Museo de la Inquisición _(Finds_   This magnificent mansion across the street from the House of Congress once belonged to the family considered the founders of Lima, but it became the tribunal for the notorious Spanish Inquisition. Today it is a museum that soberly addresses religious intolerance from the Middle Ages through colonial times. The handsomely restored house itself is worth a visit because it's a fine peek at the elegant rooms of a prominent 16th-century colonial home (including the intricately carved ceiling of the Tribunal room). But its unfortunate history is plainly evident in the catacombs, which served as prison cells; on view are several instruments of torture. At least 32 Peruvians died here during the Inquisition, which persisted until 1820. The guided tour lasts about an hour.

Plaza Bolívar (Junín 548). © 01/427-5980. Free admission. Guided tours in English, Spanish, French, and Portuguese. Daily 10am–6pm.

COLONIAL CHURCH ROUNDUP 🎨🎨

Lima Centro has a number of fine colonial-era churches worth visiting. Most are open Monday through Saturday for visits, and most have free admission.

Directly south of La Catedral on Azángaro at Ucayali, **San Pedro** (📞 01/428-3017), a Jesuit church that dates to 1638, is perhaps the best-preserved example of early colonial religious architecture in the city. The exterior is simple and rather austere, but the interior is rich with gilded altars and balconies. The bold main altar, with columns and balconies and sculpted figures, is particularly impressive. There are also some beautiful 17th- and 18th-century baroque *retablos* (altars) of carved wood and gold leaf. A small museum of colonial art is to the right of the entrance of the church, which is open Monday through Saturday from 7am to noon and 5 to 8pm; admission is free.

Iglesia de La Merced, Jr. de la Unión at Miró Quesada (📞 01/427-8199), 2 blocks southwest of the Plaza de Armas, was erected on the site of Lima's first Mass in 1534. The 18th-century church has a striking carved baroque colonial facade. Inside, the sacristy, embellished with Moorish tiles, and the main altar are excellent examples of the period. The church also possesses a nice collection of colonial art. Yet it is perhaps most notable for the devoted followers of Padre Urraca, a 17th-century priest; they come daily in droves to pay their respects, praying and touching the large silver cross dedicated to him in the nave on the right, and leaving many mementos of their veneration. The church is open Monday through Saturday from 8am to noon and 4 to 8pm.

Practically destroyed during an 1895 revolution, **San Agustín,** located at the corner of Jr. Ica and Jr. Camaná (📞 01/427-7548), is distinguished by a spectacular churrigueresque facade, one of the best of its kind in Peru, dating to the early 18th century. San Agustín's official hours are Monday through Sunday from 8 to 11am and 4:30 to 7pm, but, in practice, it's frequently closed. The **Convento de Santo Domingo,** located at the corner of Conde de Superunda and Camaná, toward the River Rímac (📞 01/427-6793), draws many Peruvians to visit the tombs of Santa Rosa de Lima and San Martín de Porras. It is perhaps of less interest to foreign visitors, although it does have a very nice main cloister. It's open Monday through Saturday from 9am to 12:30pm and 3 to 6pm; admission costs S/3 (85¢).

Las Nazarenas, at the corner of Huancavelica and Avenida Tacna on the northwest edge of the colonial center (📞 01/423-5718), has a remarkable history. It was constructed in the 18th century around a locally famous painting of Christ by an Angolan slave. Known as "El Señor de los Milagros," the image, painted on the wall of a simple abode (many slaves lived in this area on the fringes of the city), survived the massive 1655 earthquake, even though everything around it crumbled. People began to flock to the painting, and soon the Catholic Church constructed a house of worship for it. Behind the altar, on the still-standing wall, is an oil replica, which is paraded through the streets on a 1-ton silver litter during the El Señor de los Milagros festival, which is one of Lima's largest and is held on October 18, 19, and 28 and November 1. Everyone wears purple during the procession. Las Nazarenas is open Monday through Saturday from 6:30am to noon and 5 to 8:30pm.

COLONIAL PALACE ROUNDUP 🎨

The historic quarter of Lima, the old administrative capital of Spain's South American colonies, once boasted many of the finest mansions in the hemisphere. Repeated devastation by earthquakes and more recent public and private inability to maintain

Tips **Me Ama, No Me Ama, Me Ama . . .**

A curious park along the ocean at the edge of Miraflores, much beloved by Limeños looking to score, is the **Parque del Amor** (literally, "Love Park"), a cut-rate imitation of Antonio Gaudí's Parque Guell in Barcelona, Spain. It features good views of the sea (when it's not shrouded in heavy fog), benches swathed in broken-tile mosaics, and, most amusingly, a giant, grotesque statue of a couple making out—which is pretty much what everyone does nearby. Benches are inscribed with thickly sentimental murmurs of love, such as *vuelve mi palomita*. If it's Valentines Day, stand back.

many of the superb surviving *casas coloniales,* however, has left Lima with only a handful of houses open to the public.

Casa Riva-Agüero, Camaná 459 (© **01/427-9275**), is an impressive 18th-century mansion with a beautiful green-and-red courtyard that now belongs to the Catholic University of Peru. It has a small folk-art museum in the restored and furnished interior. The house is open Tuesday through Saturday from 10am to 1pm and 2 to 7:30pm; admission costs S/2 (55¢). **Casa Aliaga,** Jr. de la Unión 224 (© **01/427-6624**), is the oldest surviving house in Lima, dating from 1535. It is also one of Lima's finest mansions, with an extraordinary inner patio and elegant salons, and it continues to be owned and lived in by descendants of the original family. The house can be visited only as part of a city tour ($25) conducted exclusively by **Lima Tours** (© **01/424-5110**). A worthy alternative if you don't want to spring for a guided tour is **Casa de Osambela Oquendo,** Conde de Superunda 298 (© **01/428-7919**). The tallest house in colonial Lima, today it belongs to the Ministry of Education. Although it's still not officially open for visits, the caretaker, Lizardo Retes Bustamante, will show visitors around, including up four levels to the baby-blue cupola-mirador for views over the city. (The original owner built the house so he could see all the way to the port.) Next door is a 1770 house in a lamentable state; squatters inhabit it. The Osambela house has a spectacular patio, 40 bedrooms, and 8 wooden balconies to the street, a sure sign of the owner's great wealth. It's open daily from 9am to 5pm; admission is free, but tips are accepted.

A couple blocks east of the Plaza de Armas at Ucayali 363 is **Palacio Torre Tagle,** the most famous palace in Lima and one of the most handsome in Peru. Today the early-18th-century palace, built by a marquis who was treasurer of the Royal Spanish fleet, belongs to the Peruvian Foreign Ministry and, sadly, can no longer be visited by the public. Its exterior, with a gorgeous baroque stone doorway and carved dark-wood balconies, is very much worth a look (and you might get a peek inside the courtyard if a group of dark suits enters or leaves when you're passing by). Across the street from Torre Tagle, **Casa Goyeneche** (also called **Casa de Rada**) is another impressive 18th-century mansion, with distinct French influences; it's also not open to the public (although you might be able to manage a peek at the patio). Those with a specific interest in colonial architecture might also want to have a look at the facades of **Casa Negreiros,** Jr. Azángaro 532; **Casa de las Trece Monedas,** Jr. Ancash 536; **Casa Barbieri,** Jr. Callao at Rufino Torrico; **Casa de Pilatos,** Jr. Ancash 390; and **Casa la Riva,** Jr. Ica 426.

THE TOP MUSEUMS

To locate the following museums, see the "Lima at a Glance" map on p. 109.

Museo Arqueológico Rafael Larco Herrera 🏛🏛 Founded in 1926, this museum has the largest private collection of pre-Columbian art in the world. It concentrates on the Moche Dynasty, especially on its refined ceramics, with an estimated 45,000 pieces—including incredibly fine textiles, jewelry, and stonework from several other ancient cultures—all housed in an 18th-century colonial building. Rafael Larco Hoyle is considered the founder of Peruvian archaeology (he named the museum after his father); he wrote the seminal study *Los Mochicas* in 1938, although he succeeded in publishing only six chapters. (The rest has now been posthumously published.)

The Moche (A.D. 200–700), who lived along the northern coast in the large area near present-day Trujillo and Cajamarca, are credited with achieving one of the greatest artistic expressions of ancient Peru. The collection might be overwhelming to visitors who know little about the Moche, but one soon learns that the pottery gives clues to all elements of their society: diseases, curing practices, architecture, transportation, dance, agriculture, music, and religion. The Moche are also celebrated in the modern world for their erotic ceramics. The Sala Erótica is removed from the general collection, like the porn section in a video store. It's outdoors, downstairs, and across the garden. The Moche depicted sex in realistic, humorous, moralistic, religious, and—above all—explicit terms; the most common and even a few deviant practices are represented. If you're traveling with kids, expect giggles or questions about the ancient Peruvians' mighty phalluses. Plan on spending 2 hours to see it all.

Av. Bolívar 1515, Pueblo Libre. ☎ 01/461-1312. http://museolarco.perucultural.org.pe. Admission S/25 ($7.15) adults, S/12 ($3.40) students. Private guides available in English and Spanish (tip basis, minimum S/10 or $2.85). Daily 9am–6pm. Take a taxi or the "Todo Brasil" colectivo to Av. Brasil, and then another to Av. Bolívar. If you're coming from the Museo Nacional de Arqueología, Antropología e Historia del Perú (below), walk along the blue path.

Museo de la Nación 🏛🏛🏛 *Kids* Peru's ancient history is exceedingly complicated—not to mention new territory for most visitors to the country. Indeed, Peru's pre-Columbian civilizations were among the most sophisticated of their times; when Egypt was building pyramids, people in Peru were constructing great cities. Lima's National Museum, the city's biggest and one of the most important in Peru, guides visitors through the highlights of overlapping and conquering cultures and their achievements, seen not only in architecture (including scale models of most major ruins in Peru), but also in highly advanced ceramics and textiles. The exhibits, spread over three rambling floors, are ordered chronologically—very helpful for getting a grip on these many cultures dispersed across Peru. They trace the art and history of the earliest inhabitants to the Incan Empire, the last before colonization by the Spaniards. In case you aren't able to make it to the archaeology-rich north of Peru, pay special attention to the facsimile of the Lord of Sipán discovery, one of the most important in the world in recent years. For the most part, explanations accompanying the exhibits are in both Spanish and English. Allow 2 to 3 hours for your visit.

Av. Javier Prado Este 2465, San Borja. ☎ 01/476-9878. Admission S/6 ($1.70) adults, S/3 (85¢) seniors, S/1 (30¢) students. Tues–Sun 9am–6pm. Guides in several languages can be contracted. You can get here by colectivo along Av. Prado from Av. Arequipa, but it is much simpler to take a taxi from Lima Centro or Miraflores/San Isidro.

Museo Nacional de Arqueología, Antropología e Historia del Perú With such a mouthful of an official name, you might expect the National Museum of Archaeology, Anthropology, and History to be the Peruvian equivalent of the Met. It's not (especially because much of the museum's huge collection remains in storage), but

---

Overrated All That Glitters Isn't Necessarily Gold

The privately held **Museo de Oro del Perú (Gold Museum),** for decades the most visited museum in Peru, was part of a must-see museum triumvirate in Lima only a few years ago. But that was before the National Institute of Culture and the Tourism Protection Bureau declared just about everything in the museum—some 7,000 or more pieces—to be fake. The massive collection, mainly consisting of supposed pre-Columbian gold, was assembled by one man, Miguel Mujica Gallo—who, curiously enough, died just days before the investigation into his collection was launched. Although the museum was expensive and poorly organized, all that glittering gold—augmented by hundreds, if not thousands, of ceremonial objects, hundreds of tapestries, masks, ancient weapons, clothing, several mummies, and military weaponry and uniforms from medieval Europe to ancient Japan—certainly caught many a visitor's eye over the years. It's pretty difficult to recommend visiting such a fraudulent collection today, however. The museum is located at Av. Alonso de Molina 1100, Monterrico (© **01/345-1292;** daily 11:30am–7pm; admission S/30 or $8.50 for adults, S/15 or $4.30 for students). A taxi is the most direct way here; coming by colectivo involves taking at least two buses along Arequipa to Avenida Angamos, changing to one marked UNIVERSIDAD DE LIMA, and asking the driver to let you off at the Museo de Oro.

---

it's a worthwhile and enjoyable museum that covers Peruvian civilization from prehistoric times to the colonial and republican periods. There are ceramics, carved stone figures and obelisks, metalwork and jewelry, and lovely textiles. On view are early ceramics from 2800 B.C. in the central Andes, the great granite Tello Obelisk from the Chavín period, burial tombs, and mummies in the fetal position wrapped in burial blankets. There's also a selection of erotic ceramics from the Moche culture, but it's not nearly as extensive as that of the Museo Arqueológico Rafael Larco Herrera (p. 138). Individual rooms are dedicated to the Nasca, Paracas, Moche, and Chimú cultures. Toward the end of the exhibit, which wanders around the central courtyard of the handsome 19th-century Quinta de los Libertadores mansion (once lived in by South American independence heroes San Martín and Bolívar), is a large-scale model of Machu Picchu with buttons that allows visitors to identify key sectors of the complex. Basic descriptions throughout the museum are mostly in Spanish, although some are also in English. Allow about an hour for your visit.

From the museum, you can follow a walking path along a painted blue line to the Rafael Larco Herrera Museum. It's about a mile away, or 20 minutes straight into traffic on Antonio de Sucre (make sure you turn at the Metro supermarket on Leguía Melendes).

Plaza Bolívar s/n, Pueblo Libre. © 01/463-5070. Admission S/10 ($2.85) adults, S/3 (85¢) students. Private guides available in English and Spanish (tip basis, minimum S/10/$2.85). Tues–Sat 9am–5pm; Sun 10am–4pm. Take a taxi here, or take the "Todo Brasil" colectivo to Av. Vivanco and then take a 15-min. walk.

OTHER MUSEUMS

To locate Fundación Museo Amano and Museo de Arte Colonial Pedro de Osma, see the "Lima at a Glance" map on p. 109.

Tips **Bonito Barranco**

Although it's a residential neighborhood and not immediately thought of as a tourist sight, apart from the small Museo de Arte Colonial Pedro de Osma (below), the charming seaside district of Barranco is one of the highlights of Lima. Its serenity and laid-back artiness is a contrast to the untidy and seedy character of rest of the city. A stroll around the tranquil side streets of brightly colored bungalows is the best way to restore your sanity. It's little wonder that artists and writers have long been drawn to Barranco. Beneath the poetically named wooden footbridge Puente de los Suspiros (Bridge of Sighs) is a gentle passageway, La Bajada de Baños, which leads to a sea lookout and is lined with lovely, squat single-family houses, spindly trees, and stout cacti. During the day-time, the barrio is decidedly tropical, but at night the area is transformed into Lima's hot spot, with locals and visitors flocking to discos and watering holes—much to the dismay of local residents who don't own a bar or restaurant.

Fundación Museo Amano ✦ *Finds*   This very nicely designed museum features a collection of artifacts belonging to a single collector, representing some of Peru's most important civilizations, including the Chimú and the Nasca. The textiles and ceram-ics are among the best displayed in Lima, and the collection really shows the strength of Chancay weaving (a culture from the northern coast), which you might not see a whole lot of elsewhere. You really have to want to see the collection, though (and qual-ify, as restrictive as that sounds); it's open for limited hours and only by previous appointment to small groups. Allow about an hour or more.

Calle Retiro 160, Miraflores. ✆ 01/441-2909. Free admission (donations accepted). Mon–Fri 3–5pm by appoint-ment and guided tour in Spanish. Take a taxi to the 11th block of Av. Angamos Oeste/Av. Santa Cruz.

Museo de Arte Colonial Pedro de Osma ✦   This private museum, located in a historic Barranco mansion (Palacio de Osma), focuses on colonial Peruvian art from areas that were among the most distinguished cultural centers of the day, including Cusco, Arequipa, and Ayacucho. As with the Amano Museum, you'll need to call for an appointment, although you can also drop by and hope to get a guide with a sym-pathetic ear. Plan on spending an hour here.

Pedro de Osma 421, Barranco. ✆ 01/467-0141. Admission S/10 ($2.85) adults, S/5 ($1.40) students. Tues–Sun 10am–1:30pm and 2:30–6pm. By colectivo from Av. Tacna to Barranco.

6 Organized Tours

Lima is a large, sprawling, and confusing city, so if you want to make quick work of a visit, an organized tour of the major sights might be the best option. Standard city tours are offered by innumerable agencies. Among the most dependable is **Lima Tours,** Belén 1040 (✆ **01/424-5110;** www.limatours.com.pe), which is the only organized tour with access to the Casa Aliaga, one of the most historic colonial man-sions in Lima. A standard half-day tour of Lima Centro costs $25. Lima Tours also offers visits to Pachacámac as part of its "Lima Arqueológica" tours, as well as high-lights packages across Peru.

   Lima Visión, Jr. Chiclayo 444, Miraflores (✆ **01/447-7710;** www.peruvision.com), offers day-long sightseeing tours of Lima, including a choice of excursions for $70, as

Archaeological Sites in Lima

Lima is hardly the epicenter of pre-Columbian Peru, and few visitors have more than the museums featuring ancient Peruvian cultures on their minds when they hit the capital. Surprisingly, there are a handful of *huacas*—adobe pyramids—that date to around A.D. 500 and earlier interspersed among the modern constructions of the city. The archaeological sites are junior examples of those found in northern Peru, near Chiclayo and Trujillo. If you're not headed north, Lima's *huacas,* which have small museums attached, are worth a visit.

In San Isidro is **Huaca Huallamarca** (also called Pan de Azúcar, or "Sugar Loaf"), located at the corner of Avenida Nicolás de Rivera and Avenida El Rosario. The perhaps overzealously restored adobe temple of the Maranga Lima culture has several platforms and is frequently illuminated for special presentations. It's open Tuesday through Sunday from 9am to 5pm; admission is S/5 ($1.40) for adults and S/3 (85¢) for students. Also in San Isidro is the **Huaca Juliana,** a pre-Incan mound dating to A.D. 400. It's at Calle Belén at Pezet and keeps the same hours as Huallamarca; admission is free. **Huaca Pucllana** is a sacred pyramid, built during the 4th century and still undergoing excavation, in Miraflores at the corner of calles General Borgoño (Block 8) and Tarapacá, near Avenida Arequipa (✆ **01/445-8695**). It has a small park, a restaurant, and an *artesanía* gallery. From the pyramid's top, you can see the roofs of this busy residential and business district. It's open Wednesday through Monday from 9am to 5pm; admission is S/5 ($1.40) and S/3 (85¢) for students.

Unfortunately, these sites occasionally do not keep consistent hours, so you might find yourself staring through a chain-link fence if there's no one on hand to let you in.

well as 2-hour tours for $20. **Contacto Lima** (✆ **01/224-3854;** contactolima@tsi.com.pe) offers half-day city tours of "colonial and modern Lima" ($20), full-day tours ($70), museum tours ($25), and trail riding on Peruvian pacing horses, as well as tours to Nasca and Paracas, south of Lima. **Fertur Perú,** Jr. Junín 211 (✆ **01/427-1958;** http://ferturperu.tripod.com), with an office in the Hotel España (and a new branch opening in 2004 in Miraflores), is a highly professional outfit with reasonably priced city tours and 4-day packages to sights across Peru. **Class Adventure Travel,** Grimaldo del Solar 463 Miraflores (✆ **01/444-2220;** www.cat-travel.com), is an excellent all-purpose agency run by a knowledgeable and friendly Dutch couple; it offers a 3-day city tour and travel arrangements around Peru.

Free short **walking tours** of Lima are frequently offered by the Municipalidad de Lima (Town Hall). For the latest schedule, call ✆ **01/427-4848** or 01/427-6080, ext. 222.

Finally, although it sounds a bit uncomfortably close to those stag or bachelorette bus parties where everyone drinks their way across town dead set on making fools of their guest of honor, **El Bus Parrandero,** Av. Benavides 330, of. 101, Miraflores (✆ **01/445-4755;** www.busparrandero.com), is a colorful party bus promoting gregarious evening tours of Lima, with unlimited drinks, snacks, and live music. Tours are given Monday through Saturday from 8 to 11pm and 9pm to midnight; the ride costs $20. If you've got your heart set on reliving (or continuing) your college days while you're in Lima, *¡adelante!*

7 Outdoor Activities & Spectator Sports

BEACHES   Although Lima is perched on the Pacific coast, Rio de Janeiro it's not. Still, several beaches in Miraflores and Barranco are frequented by locals, especially surfers, in the summer months. The beaches are unfit for swimming, however: The waters are heavily polluted and plagued by very strong currents. Worse, they're stalking grounds for thieves. Although the beaches aren't that appealing in and of themselves, they might serve those with an interest in people-watching: The sands are very much frequented by Limeños in the summer (Dec–Mar). Much nicer and cleaner beaches are located immediately south of Lima (see "Side Trips from Lima," later).

BICYCLING & JOGGING   Given Lima's chaotic traffic, jogging is best confined to parks. Probably the best area is the bicycling and jogging paths along the *malecón* in Miraflores, near the Marriott and Miraflores Park hotels. Contact the **Club de Bicicleta de Montaña (Mountain Bike Club),** Calle César Ortega s/n (✆ **01/872-4021**), which has information about routes near Lima and places to rent mountain bikes.

BULLFIGHTING   Bullfighting in Peru, less of a national craze than in Spain or Mexico, is held in July and in the main season from October to December at the 18th-century **Plaza de Acho,** Jr. Hualgayoc 332, in Rímac (✆ **01/315-5000** or 01/481-1467), the third-oldest ring in the world. Events are held Sunday afternoon. The *fiestas taurinas* bring matadors from Spain and take place at the same time as the Señor de los Milagros in October. Tickets, which range from about $20 to nearly $100 for a single event (depending on whether seats are in the shade), can be obtained at the box office at the bullring. They can also be purchased at **Farmacia Deza,** Av. Conquistadores 1140, San Isidro (✆ **01/440-3798**), or by phone from **Teleticket** (✆ **01/242-2823**). Inquire about advance tickets by sending an e-mail to plazadeacho@peru.com.

GOLF   Golf courses in Lima aren't open to nonmembers. Your best bet for golf is to stay at one of the exclusive hotels with golf privileges at the Lima Golf Club in San Isidro: **Country Club Lima Hotel** (p. 123) and **Sonesta Posada del Inca El Olívar** (p. 124).

PERUVIAN PACING HORSES   Peruvian Paso horses *(caballos de paso),* which have a unique four-beat lateral gait, are considered by many to be the world's smoothest riding horse and also one of the showiest of all horse breeds. If you're already a fan of the breed, or just a fan of horses in general, seeing them on their home turf could be exciting. There are *concursos* (show events) scheduled at different times of the year; there's a big one in April (free admission). Information about exhibitions is available from the **Asociación Nacional de Caballos Peruanos de Paso,** Bellavista 549, Miraflores (✆ **01/444-6920** or 01/447-6331).

SOCCER   Important league and national *fútbol* (soccer) matches are held at the venerable 50-year-old **Estadio Nacional,** Paseo de la República, blocks 7–9, located just 5 minutes from the city center. Popular teams include Alianza Lima, Alianza Atlético, Universitario (known as "La U"), and Sporting Cristal. Tickets ($3–$25) for most matches can be purchased the same day at the stadium or from **Teleticket** (✆ **01/242-2823**).

SURFING   Although several beaches in Miraflores and Barranco are popular with surfers in summer and are fine for beginners, the best beaches in southern Peru—Punta Hermosa, Punta Rocas (highly recommended), Cerro Azul, and Pico Alto (which is supposed to have the biggest waves)—are beyond Lima. Surfing in southern Peru is best April through December (and at its peak in May); surfers who hit the waves year-round usually do it in wet suits. Check out **www.wannasurf.com/spot/ South_America/Peru/Lima** for specialist information, including a chart of southern beaches that specifies skill level and breaks. Information, equipment, boards (for sale only), and accessories are available at **O'Neills,** Av. Santa Cruz 851, Miraflores (✆ **01/242-4486**) and Focus, Leonardo DaVinci 208, San Borja (✆ **01/475-8459**).

8 Shopping

The capital has the greatest variety of shopping in Peru, from tony boutiques to artisan and antiques shops. Shopping at markets in *sierra* villages and buying direct from artisans on Lake Titicaca are better experiences, certainly, but don't discount the fact that, unless you ship the loot home, you'll most likely have to bring it back to Lima anyway. In Lima, you can find traditional handicrafts from across Peru; prices are not usually much higher, and the selection might be even better than in the regions where the items are made. One exception is alpaca goods, which are better purchased in the areas around Cusco, Puno, and Arequipa, in terms of both price and selection.

Miraflores is where most shoppers congregate, although there are also several outlets in Lima Centro and elsewhere in the city. Most shops are open from 9:30am to 12:30pm and 3 to 8pm. Most prices include an 18% sales tax, which, unfortunately, is refundable only on purchases made at the international departure lounge of Jorge Chávez International Airport.

ANTIQUES & JEWELRY

Look for silver jewelry and antiques along Avenida La Paz in Miraflores. *Platerías* and *joyerías* (silver and jewelry shops) worth a visit are **Ilaria** ✪, Av. Larco 1325 (✆ 01/ 444-2347), and **El Tupo,** La Paz 553 (✆ 01/444-1511). In downtown Lima, **Joyería Gold/Gems Perú,** Pasaje Santa Rosa 119 (✆ 01/426-7267), stocks Colombian emeralds and fashionable, inexpensive Italian steel jewelry. Miraflores antiques shops include **El Almacén de Arte,** Francia 339 (✆ 01/445-6264), and **Porta 735,** Porta 735 (✆ 01/447-6158). A shop I particularly like is **La Casa Azul** ✪, Alfonso Ugarte 150 (✆ 01/446-6380), which specializes in colonial furniture, religious art, and other fantastic decorative pieces. The friendly owners can help arrange shipping and assist with getting INC export approval for especially valuable pieces.

HANDICRAFTS & TEXTILES

Miraflores houses the lion's share of Lima's well-stocked shops, which overflow with handicrafts from around Peru, including weavings, ceramics, and silver. A terrific shop with carefully chosen, unique items of artisanship is **Killari** ✪✪, Alcanfores 699 (✆ 01/447-8684). Several dozen large souvenir and handicrafts shops are clustered on and around Avenida Ricardo Palma (a good one is **Artesanías Miraflores,** no. 205) and Avenida Petit Thouars (try **Artesanía Expo Inti,** no. 5495).

Handicrafts shops elsewhere in Miraflores include **Agua y Tierra,** Diez Canseco 298 (✆ 01/445-6980), and **Silvania Prints,** Diez Canseco 378 (✆ 01/242-0667). Alpaca sweaters and other items can be had at **Alpaca 111,** Av. Larco 671 (Larcomar shopping center; (© 01/447-1623); **Alpaca Peru,** Diez Canseco 315 (© 01/241-4175); **Mon Repos,** Centro Comercial Camino Real (© 01/221-5331); and **All Alpaca,** Av. Schell 375 (© 01/427-4704). One of the largest shops, which stocks a huge range of Peruvian handicrafts from all over the country, is **Peru Artcrafts** ⚔, in the Larcomar shopping mall, Malecón de la Reserva 610 (© 01/446-5429). Although it's considerably more expensive than other shops (all prices are in dollars), it's perhaps the best for last-minute and one-stop shopping.

Another great spot for handicrafts from around Peru in Lima Centro is the **Santo Domingo** *artesanía* **arcades** across the street from the Santo Domingo convent on Conde de Superunda and Camaná. In Miraflores, a giant *artesanía* market with dozens of stalls is the **Mercado Indio,** 5245 Av. Petit Thouars (at General Vidal). In fact, almost all of Av. Petit Thouars, from Ricardo Palma to Vidal, is lined with well-stocked handicrafts shops. For fine *retablos* and artisanship typical of Ayacucho (which produces some of Peru's most notable pieces), visit the **Museo-Galería Popular de Ayacucho,** Av. Pedro de Osma 116, Barranco (© **01/247-0599**).

MARKETS & MALLS

Lima Centro's crowded **Mercado Central (Central Market)** is south of the Plaza Mayor, at the edge of Chinatown; you'll find just about everything there, but you should take your wits and leave your valuables at home. The **Feria Artesanal (Artisans' Market,** also called the Mercado Indio, or Indian Market, but not to be confused with the Mercado Indio in Miraflores) has a wide variety of handicrafts of varying quality, but at lower prices than most tourist-oriented shops in Lima Centro or Miraflores (quality might also be a bit lower than at those shops). Haggling is a good idea. The market is located at Avenida de la Marina (blocks 6–10) in Pueblo Libre; it's open daily from noon to 8pm.

There are small handicrafts markets, open late to catch bar and post-dinner crowds, in the main squares in both Miraflores and Barranco. The **Jockey Plaza Shopping Center** (© **01/437-4100**) is a modern American-style shopping mall—the newest, biggest, and best in Lima—with department stores, restaurants, movie theaters, a supermarket, and some 200 exclusive shops. It's located next to the Jockey Club of Peru at Hipódromo de Monterrico, at the intersection of Javier Prado and Avenida Panamericana Sur in Surco. It's open daily from 11am to 9pm. **Centro Comercial Larcomar** (© **01/445-7776**) in Miraflores along the *malecón* and Parque Salazar (near the Marriott hotel), is one of the swankest malls in Lima, with a slew of restaurants, movie theaters, and upscale shops overlooking the ocean.

9 Lima After Dark

As the largest city in the country, with a population of immigrants from around the country and the most international flavor, Lima certainly has Peru's most varied nightlife scene. Whether you're into jazz, *criollo,* Latin, or rock music, you'll find it in Lima. The best after-dark scenes are in Miraflores and particularly Barranco, which is transformed from a sleepy artists' and writers' community during the day to party central at night. Although it has a number of high-octane clubs and discos, it also has some of the city's best peñas and bars, especially those with ocean views just past the Puente de los Suspiros, or "Bridge of Sighs."

Bars open at about 8pm, but discos and live-music clubs don't generally get started until 10pm or later. Many are open very late, until 3 or 4am or even later.

THE PERFORMING ARTS

Lima's stunning **Teatro Municipal,** the pride of the local performing-arts scene and the primary locale for theater, ballet, opera, and symphony performances, burned to the ground in 1998. Since then, the National Symphony Orchestra and the National Ballet Company have performed at the **Museo de la Nación,** Av. Javier Prado (℡ 01/ 476-9875). The 1940s-era **Teatro Segura,** Huancavelica 265 (℡ 01/426-7206) has picked up some of the slack for opera and concerts. Frequent cultural events, including films and music recitals, are held every week at the **Centro Cultural Ricardo Palma,** Larco Herrera 770, Miraflores (℡ 01/446-3959), and the **British Council,** Calle Alberto Lynch 110, San Isidro (℡ 01/221-7552). The **Instituto Cultural Peruano Norteamericano,** located at the corner of Angamos and Arequipa in Miraflores (℡ 01/446-0381), hosts theater, jazz, classical, and folk music. See the daily newspaper *El Comercio* (www.elcomercioperu.com.pe) or **www.decajon.com** for updated lists of live performing-arts events in Lima (in Spanish only).

Lima has a good theater scene, although, as one might expect, nearly all plays are in Spanish. If you speak Spanish or are willing to give a Spanish play a try, two of Lima's best theaters are **Teatro Canout,** Av. Petit Thouars 4550, Miraflores (℡ 01/422-5373), and **Teatro Auditorio Miraflores,** Av. Larco 1036, Miraflores (℡ 01/447-9378). Tickets are available at the box offices.

BARS, LIVE MUSIC & CLUBS

BARS & PUBS

MIRAFLORES   **Freiheit,** Lima 471, in front of Parque Kennedy (℡ **01/247-4630**), is a warmly decorated bar, in the style of a German tavern. The dance floor is separate from the bar area. There's a drink minimum on weekends. **O´Murphy's Irish Pub,** Shell 627 (℡ **01/242-1212**), is a longtime favorite drinking hole with a small menu of pub grub. Of course, expect a pool table, darts, Guinness on tap, and Brits and Irishmen hoisting it. They also host live music on Thursday. **Son de Cuba,** Bulevar San Ramón 277 (℡ **01/445-1444**), is on the pedestrian street called "Little Italy" by locals, but the club focuses on Caribbean rhythms and drinks Tuesday through Sunday.

BARRANCO   The area past the Puente de los Suspiros in Barranco has some of the coolest watering holes in Lima. Check out **La Posada del Mirador** ⨯, Pasaje La Ermita 104 (℡ **01/477-1120**) and **Nuevo Acantilado de Barranco,** Pasaje La Ermita 102 (℡ **01/247-2145**). Both occupy old houses overlooking the ocean and have spectacular verdant settings with indoor and outdoor garden seating. A trendy bar drawing a younger crowd is **Amnesia,** Bulevar Sánchez Carrión 153, just off the municipal square (℡ **01/477-9577**). It's open only Thursday through Saturday. **Posada del Angel,** Av. Pedro de Osma 164 (and 222; ℡ **01/247-0341**), is a baroque cafe-bar with two locations on the same street and occasional live jazz and folk music. **Dirty Nelly's,** Av. Pedro de Osma 135, Barranco (℡ **01/477-4506**), the bar at the now-defunct hostel Mochileros, is a cool pub that hops with young people who spill out into the courtyard.

LIMA CENTRO   There are two excellent pubs downtown owned by the same folks. One is **Rincón Cervecero,** a German-style bierhall, at Jr. de la Unión 1045 (℡ **01/ 428-1422**). The other, **Estadio Fútbol Club,** Av. Nicolás de Piérola 926 (℡ **01/428-8866**), is strictly for *fútbol* fans: It's a three-level bar (and disco on weekends) that amounts to a museum of the sport, and with dozens of big-screen TVs, it can get pretty rowdy when a big Peruvian or international game is on.

LIVE MUSIC

BARRANCO   My vote for best live-music club in Lima is **La Noche** 𝕬𝕬, Bolognesi 307 (© **01/477-5829**). Despite its prosaic name, this sprawling multilevel club feels like a swank tree house, with a great stage and sound system and good bands every night that run the gamut of styles (although it's frequently jazz), plus a hip mixed Limeño and international crowd. Monday night jam sessions (no cover charge) are particularly good; otherwise, cover charges range from S/5 to S/15 ($1.50–$4.30). There's also a La Noche outpost in Central Lima, at the corner of Jr. Camaná and Jr. Quilca. Artsy **El Ekeko,** Av. Grau 266 (© **01/247-3148**), is a two-level place with live music Wednesday through Saturday. Most acts fall within the Latin category—often Cuban. Cover charges range from S/10 to S/20 ($2.85–$5.70). **La Estación de Barranco** 𝕬, Pedro de Osma 112 (© **01/247-0344**), is another nice place, housed in an old train station, with live music Tuesday through Saturday and a slightly more mature crowd (both locals and tourists); the music on tap is often *música criolla*. The classic upstairs bar **La Taberna de Barranco** 𝕬, Av. Grau 268 (no phone), schedules both live rock and pop for the youngsters (often early shows beginning at 9pm), and occasional peña and Afro-Peruvian shows late on weekends for a more sophisticated crowd. Either way, the bar is one of the coolest in town, even if it's gone much more commercial in the last few years.

MIRAFLORES   Satchmo, Av. La Paz 538 (© **01/444-4957**), is a classy joint with a variable roster of live bands, including jazz combos—as the name would indicate. It's a good date spot. Cover charges range from S/20 to S/45 ($5.70–$13). Another great spot for live jazz (as well as bossa nova and Afro-Peruvian evenings) is **Jazz Zone,** Av. La Paz 656, Pasaje El Suche (© **01/241-8139**). **Crocodilo Verde,** Francisca de Paula 226 (© **01/442-8425**), has jazz on Wednesday and a variable program of live music on weekends.

PEÑAS

You should check out at least one peña, a performance at a *criollo* music club that quite often inspires rousing vocal and dance participation, during your stay in Lima. Cover charges range from $1 (30¢) to $10 ($2.90), depending on the act.

MIRAFLORES   Caballero de Fina Estampa 𝕬, Av. del Ejército 800 (© **01/441-0552**), named for one of the most famous Peruvian songs of all time, is one of the chicest peñas, with a large colonial salon and balconies. The cover charge is a little hefty for Lima: S/45 ($13). **Sachún,** Av. del Ejército 657 (© **01/441-4465**), is favored by tourists and middle-class Limeños who aren't shy about participating with their feet and vocal cords. The cover charge ranges from S/25 to S/45 ($7.15–$13).

BARRANCO   De Rompe y Raja 𝕬, Manuel Segura 127 (© **01/247-3271**), is a favorite of locals. Look for the popular Matices Negros, an Afro-Peruvian dance trio. The cover is usually around S/25 ($7.14). **Las Guitarras,** Manuel Segura 295 (© **01/479-1874**), is where locals go to play an active part in their peña. A cool spot, it's open Friday and Saturday only, with no cover charge and no credit cards accepted. The excellent restaurant **Manos Morenas** 𝕬, Pedro de Osma 409 (© **01/467-0421**), is a sophisticated peña with a $12 cover charge. Shows are given Tuesday through Thursday from 9pm onward, and Friday and Saturday from 10:30pm until 2am or so. **La Candelaria,** Bolognesi 292 (© **01/247-1314**), is a comfortable club celebrating Peruvian folklore. It's open Friday and Saturday from 9pm onward; the cover is S/25 ($7.15).

For a unique experience, check out the totally informal and impromptu shows at **Songoro Cosongo,** Ayacucho 281 at the edge of Puente de Suspiros (© **01/ 247-4730**). The owner gets together with local and invited musicians and jams at this airy old house with a distinctly Cuban feel; you'll hear Peruvian classics, Afro-Peruvian numbers, and Cuban *son,* depending on their mood. The home-cooked food is inexpensive and delicious. **Del Carajo,** Av. Jorge Chávez 403 (© **01/247-7023**), on the road to Las Palmas, is another top peña with good live music, percussion, and dance shows Tuesday through Saturday starting at 10pm.

LIMA CENTRO   Brisas del Titicaca ☆☆, Jr. Walkulski 168, the first block of Av. Brasil, near Plaza Bolognesi, (© **01/332-1901**), is a cultural institution with *noches folklóricas* and some of the best shows in Lima. It's open Wednesday and Thursday from 8pm, and Friday and Saturday from 10pm.

DANCE CLUBS

Many of Lima's discos are predominantly young and wild affairs. The main drags in Barranco, Av. Grau and Pasaje Sánchez Carrión (a pedestrian alley off the main square), are lined with raucous clubs that go late into the evening and annoy Barranco residents. Check out **Deja-Vu,** Av. Grau 294 (© **01/247-6989**); the decor is based on TV commercials, and "waitress shows" tease horny patrons. It's a dancefest from Monday to Saturday; the music trips from techno to trance. **Kitsch,** Bolognesi 743, Barranco (no phone), is one of Lima's hottest bars—literally, sometimes it turns into a sweatbox—with over-the-top decor and recorded tunes that range from 1970s and 1980s pop to Latin and techno. **Tequila Rock,** Diez Canseco 146, Miraflores (© **01/444-3661**), continues to be one of Lima's most popular discos, although it's a bit of a meat (or hooker's) market and doesn't usually get going after 2am.

GAY & LESBIAN NIGHTLIFE

Although Peru as a whole remains fervently Catholic and many gay and lesbian Peruvians feel constricted in the expression of their lifestyle, Lima is the most progressive city in the country, with the most facilities and resources for gays and lesbians, including a significant number of nightclubs. Among the most popular are **Gitano 2,050,** Berlín 231, Miraflores (no phone), probably the best-known gay disco in the city, with two cruising balconies overlooking the dance floor; **Downtown Vale Todo,** Pasaje los Pinos 160, Miraflores (© **01/444-6433**), currently the most popular club with go-go boys, with occasional shows and strippers; **Café Bar Kitsch,** Bolognesi 743, Barranco (no phone), a funky and highly original bar/disco that's also very popular with straights; and **Perseo Palace,** Av. Aviación 2514, San Borja (© **01/224-3731**), a lively disco with an eclectic soundtrack and large dance floor. All are open Wednesday through Saturday (Gitano 2,050 is open Sun as well); cover charges range from S/7 to S/25 ($2–$7.15). A gay-oriented combination sauna/gym/bar/video lounge is **Sauna Tivoli,** Av. Petit Thouars s/n, San Isidro (© **01/222-1705**). It's open daily from 2 to 10pm; the cover charge is S/25 ($7.15). There's more information on gay Lima and gay Peru on **http://gaylimape.tripod.com**.

CINEMA

Most foreign movies in Lima are shown in their original language with subtitles. Art and classic films are shown at the **Filmoteca de Lima** in the Lima Museo de Arte, Paseo Colón 125, Lima Cercado (© **01/423-4732**), and **El Cinematógrafo,** Pérez Roca 196, Barranco (© **01/477-1961**). Commercial movie houses worth checking out include **Multicines Starvisión El Pacífico,** Av. José Pardo 121, near the round-about at Parque Central, Miraflores (✆ **01/445-6990**); **Cinemark Perú Jockey Plaza,** Av. Javier Prado 4200 (✆ **01/435-9262**); and **Multicines Larcomar,** Malecón de la Reserva 610, Miraflores (✆ **01/446-7336**). Most theaters in the suburbs cost more than the ones in Lima Centro (S/10–S/15 or $2.85–$4.30, as opposed to S/4–S/8 or $1.15–$2.30), but they're more modern and better equipped. Several have special matinee prices and discounts on Tuesday. For a list of films *subtituladas* (with subtitles), consult the Friday edition of *El Comercio.* The term *doblada* means "dubbed."

CASINOS

Peruvians are big on casinos, and many of the larger upscale hotels favored by business travelers have casinos attached. Some of the better ones are the Stellaris Casino at the **JW Marriott Hotel** (p. 120); **Grand Hotel Miraflores,** Av. 28 de Julio 151, Miraflores (✆ **01/447-9641**); **Country Club Lima Hotel** (p. 123); and **Sheraton Hotel & Casino,** Paseo de la República 170, Centro (✆ **01/433-3320**). Most casinos are open Monday through Thursday from 5pm to 2am, and Friday through Saturday from 5pm to 5am.

10 Side Trips from Lima

Most visitors to Lima, having seen the highlights of the colonial center and a few museums, head out on long-distance buses and planes to Cusco and Machu Picchu, Nasca, Arequipa, and north to the jungle. However, if you have time for an excursion or two closer to the Peruvian capital, consider the pre-Columbian ruins at Pachacámac or the attractive beaches south of Lima.

THE SOUTHERN BEACHES
30–70km (19–43 miles) S of Lima

The best beaches easily accessible from Lima line the coast south of the city. Popular spots along the shadeless, arid desert landscape are El Silencio, Punta Hermosa (a good place for ceviche and fresh fish in any number of rustic seafood restaurants), Punta Negra, Santa María, and Pucusana. Probably the best bet is Pucusana, a small fishing village, although it's the farthest beach from Lima. The attractive beaches are very popular with Limeños during the summer months; on weekends, the southern coast is a long line of caravans of sun-seekers.

Note: Even though you can swim in the ocean at this distance from the capital, the currents are very strong, and great caution should be exercised. You should also be careful with your possessions because thieves frequent these beaches. Finally, be forewarned that the beaches are only moderately attractive—certainly few people's idea of a tropical beach paradise.

GETTING THERE   Unless you have wheels, the best way to tour the beaches south of Lima is to hop on a combi, like Limeños do. Those marked "San Bartolo" (another one of the beaches) leave from Angamos and Panamericana Sur in Lima; others at Jirón Montevideo and Jirón Ayacucho in Lima Centro will also get you to the beaches. You'll have to tell the driver at which beach you want to get off (or hop off wherever a number of fellow bus travelers do), and then walk a mile or less down to the beach.

The ride costs S/3 to S/5 (85¢–$1.40) and takes anywhere from 45 minutes to 2 hours. The beaches and their markers are as follows: El Silencio, Km 42; Punta Hermosa, Km 44; Punta Rocas, Km 45; Punta Negra, Km 46; San Bartolo, Km 52; Santa María, Km 55; and Pucusana, Km 65.

PACHACAMAC

31km (19 miles) S of Lima

The finest ruins within easy reach of Lima, **Pachacámac,** in the Lurín Valley, was inhabited by several pre-Columbian cultures before the Incas. The extensive site, a sacred city and holy place of pilgrimage, includes plazas, adobe-brick palaces, and pyramidal temples, some of which have been rebuilt by the Peruvian government. It makes for an interesting visit, especially if you're not planning on heading north to the archaeological sites near Chiclayo and Trujillo.

The principal ceremonial center of the Peruvian coast, the earliest constructions date to the first century, although the site reached its apex during the Huari (or Wari) culture (10th c.). Pilgrims came to pay homage to the feared oracle and creator-god, Pachacámac, who was believed to be responsible for earthquakes and matters of state such as war. The Incas conquered the site in the 15th century, and it was one of the most important shrines in the Americas during their rule, although its ceremonial importance began to wane soon afterward. However, two of the most important structures on-site, the Temple of the Sun and the Acllahuasi (or Mamacuña) palace (where "chosen maidens" served the Inca), both date to the Incan occupation. Hernán Pizarro and his gold-hungry troops arrived in 1533 but were disappointed to find a paucity of riches. On the premises is a small museum of pre-Columbian artifacts, including textiles and the dual-personage carved wooden idol of Pachacámac, god of fire and son of the sun god.

The site (© **01/430-0168**), which occupies a low hill, is large; allow at least a couple of hours to visit by foot (the visit from Lima can be completed in a half-day). English-speaking guides are usually available for hire at the entrance if you do not arrive with a guide-led group. The site is open daily from 9am to 4pm. Admission is S/5.50 ($1.60) for adults, S/2 (55¢) for students, and S/1 (30¢) for children.

GETTING THERE   Pachacámac is about 45 minutes from Lima by car or bus. Combis (with signs reading PACHACAMAC/LURIN) leave from Avenida Abancay and the corner of Ayacucho and Montevideo in Lima Centro. The most convenient way to visit—cheaper than hiring a taxi, unless there are several of you—is by a half-day organized tour, offered by Lima Vision, Lima Tours, and other companies; see "Organized Tours," earlier in this chapter. Most tours cost between $25 and $35 per person, including transportation and guide.

6

The Central Coast & Highlands

South of Lima along the coast, the hot and extraordinarily dry desert province of Ica—one of the most arid places on Earth—contains one of Peru's most exotic, inscrutable sights: The Nasca Lines, huge pre-Columbian desert drawings, have raised many questions and given rise to wild theories about Peru's ancient past. The region forms part of the oldest geological strata in the country; fossils date back as far as the Tertiary or Quaternary eras. The Paracas and Nasca cultures that took root here (roughly 1300 B.C.–A.D. 700) were two of Peru's most advanced. Little was known about the two cultures until the 20th century, but they are acclaimed today for their exquisite textile weavings and ceramics, among the finest produced by pre-Columbian Peru.

Nasca is a small and unassuming town, rocked a few years ago by a major earthquake that nearly leveled it. Indeed, the town might go entirely unnoticed by visitors to Peru were it not for the mysterious and mind-boggling Nasca Lines nearby. In addition, there are several additional sites in and around Nasca that are intimately tied to the ancient cultures that once settled and irrigated these desert lands, including remarkable stone aqueducts—evidence of advanced engineering—and an evocative burial ground. Although the Nasca Lines reign as the undisputed highlight of the region, this stretch of arid coast and pampas south of Lima has other things to offer the visitor who's not in too much of a rush to roar on to Cusco, Arequipa, or Lake Titicaca.

Within easy reach of Nasca are the towns Ica and Pisco, and the nearby Reserva Nacional de Paracas (Paracas National Reserve), known for the Ballestas Islands, which locals liken to Ecuador's Galápagos Islands. That claim might be a slight exaggeration, but the maritime sanctuary, encompassing the Paracas Peninsula and a lovely bay with curious rock formations, swells with unusual flora and fauna, including thousands of sea lions, flamingos, and endangered Humboldt penguins. Pisco is a dusty, unremarkable town that will sound familiar to anyone who's had a drink in a Peruvian bar or restaurant: The country's famous cocktail, the pisco sour, is made with the white-grape brandy that shares its name with the town. The region's wineries (actually nearer to Ica) make Peru's best wines and, of course, pisco. Ica, the capital of the department, is a small, enjoyable town with stifling heat and a collection of attractive churches, notable colonial mansions, and one of the better small museums in the country. The nearby Huacachina Lagoon is a beautiful green-and-blue oasis in the midst of the monochrome desert.

Ayacucho, a lovely colonial town in the Central Highlands, is newly welcoming to outsiders after years spent in the grips of Peru's homegrown guerrilla movement, the Shining Path. Ayacucho has the country's finest collection of colonial-era churches, and it's also the epicenter of Peru's most celebrated artisans, whose work is shown across the country.

Paracas, Ica, and Nasca are all within striking distance of Lima, but for those with limited time, a visit to the region could complicate moving on to other places in Peru. The only flights available from Lima are 1-day Nasca Lines overflights. Otherwise, you'll need to travel overland along the desert coast to get to the department of Ica, and by land again if you're headed to any of the other major destinations in Peru—in all likelihood, adding a couple of days to your trip. (For many travelers, that will mean returning to the capital and catching a flight.) The vast Carretera Panamericana (Pan-American Hwy.), a two-lane strip of asphalt that extends the length of Peru from the Ecuadorian border all the way down to Chile, slices through this section of the desert lowlands, and bus travel is direct, if not always visually stimulating. Many visitors move on by bus from Nasca to Arequipa or Lake Titicaca. Although Ayacucho is a long and winding Andean bus ride from Lima or Ica, you can now fly there from the capital (but not yet from Cusco or other cities).

1 Pisco & the Reserva Nacional de Paracas ★

260km (162 miles) S of Lima; 75km (47 miles) NW of Ica; 205km (127 miles) NW of Nasca

The first town of any size to the south of Lima, Pisco is also the first settlement beyond the beaches outside the capital that draws the attention of travelers. Yet that interest has little to do with the (rather lacking) attributes of the town and almost everything to do with the natural attractions in abundance at the nearby Ballestas Islands and Paracas National Reserve, just 22km (14 miles) from the center of Pisco. A few kilometers west of the Pan-American Highway, Pisco is a small port and fishing village of very modest interest (beyond the Moorish-inspired Municipal Palace) that sometimes serves as a base for those wanting to visit Paracas Peninsula and Bay without paying the higher prices commanded by the resort.

ESSENTIALS
GETTING THERE
There are frequent buses up and down the coast from Lima to Arequipa, with stops in between. From Lima, frequent buses normally take between 3 and 4 hours to reach Pisco. However, because the town is not directly on the Carretera Panamericana, not all coastal buses stop there. Be sure to confirm that the bus won't merely leave you on the side of the road en route to Ica (which would result in the hassle of getting a *combi* to town).

Ormeño travels from Lima to Pisco and to Ica, Nasca, and Arequipa. In Lima, the office is located at Av. Carlos Zavala 177 (© 01/426-7595); the Pisco office is at San Francisco 259, 1 block from the Plaza de Armas (© 056/522-058). Soyuz-Peru connects Pisco with Lima and Ica; you'll find an office in Lima at Av. Carlos Zavala 221 (© 01/428-6252), and in Pisco at Av. Ernesto R. Diez Canseco 41 (© 056/224-138). Bus terminals are located right in the center of town, on or just off the Plaza de Armas. Frequent *colectivos* travel to Ica from Pisco.

VISITOR INFORMATION
The **Municipality of Pisco office** at the Plaza de Armas (© 056/532-525) might be able to provide some rudimentary tourist information; a better bet is one of the travel agencies offering tours to Paracas and other places in the region. See "By Organized Tour" in "Getting Around," below.

FAST FACTS   Banco de Crédito, Pérez Figuerola 162 (© 056/532-954), has a Visa-compatible ATM. You'll also find *cambistas,* or money exchangers, hovering around the Plaza de Armas.

Fun Fact El Libertador

General José de San Martín—immersed in the continent-wide campaign for independence from Spain and already having liberated Chile and Argentina—made landfall with an army of 4,500 men at Paracas in 1819 and established his headquarters in Pisco. Here began his legendary battle for Peru's independence, which he declared in Huacho in 1821. San Martín was subsequently named the "Protector of Peru" and went about constructing its new republican government.

ACCOMMODATIONS ■
Hostal Posada Hispana **1**
Hostal Villa Manuelita **2**

DINING ◆
Don Manuel **4**
Hostal Posada Hispana **1**
Restaurant El Catamaran **3**

If you need medical attention, go to **Hospital Antonio Skrabonja Antoncich (ESSALUD),** San Francisco 322 (✆ Emergencia **056/532-784**) or **San Juan de Dios,** Av. San Juan de Dios 350 (✆ **056/532-332**). In an emergency, you can reach the **police** at the Plaza de Armas (Calle San Francisco; ✆ **056/532-165**).

The **post office** at Av. Federico Uranga 211, Independencia (✆ **056/220-208**) is open Monday through Saturday from 8am to 6pm. There's a **Telefónica del Perú** office at Bolognesi 298; it's open daily from 9am to 6pm.

GETTING AROUND

The best way to get around Pisco itself is on foot because anything of interest—hotels, restaurants, the cathedral—is only minutes from the Plaza de Armas. Taxis are readily available and cheap for any trip within the city (S/3–S/4 or about $1). For transport to the Paracas National Reserve and other areas of interest, you can hire a taxi (less than S/17 or $4.85) or travel by bus. The most efficient way to see the highlights of the area is with a tour company, especially because there is no public transportation on the peninsula or within the reserve.

BY BUS Combis to the Ballestas Islands and Paracas National Reserve (marked EL CHACO–PARACAS) depart from the Pisco market on Fermín Tangus.

Paracas Culture

Paracas might be best known for its great natural coastal beauty and wildlife, but the region is no less recognized (especially among archaeologists and historians) as the home of several advanced cultures that thrived in Peru before the Incas. The so-called *hombre de Santo Domingo* (Santo Domingo man), whose remains date to 7000 B.C., was found on the west shore of the Bay of Paracas.

Little was known about the Paracas culture, an ancient Amerindian civilization founded along the south-central coast more than 3,000 years ago, until 1925, when the Peruvian archaeologist Julio C. Tello discovered extraordinary burial sites, now referred to as the Paracas Necropolis, concealed by the desert sand dunes on the isthmus of the Península de Paracas. The arid climate and layers of sand had done wonders to protect extraordinary embroidered textiles—largely found within burial sites—that today are recognized as the finest representatives of pre-Columbian Peruvian woven art. The Paracas culture produced textiles of unrivaled color, technique, and design. The most exquisite examples of funereal textiles are found at Lima's Museo de la Nación (p. 138), but there are also fine pieces in Ica at the Museo Regional (p. 162) and at the Museo de Sitio Julio C. Tello within the Paracas National Reserve (p. 155).

Also found at the sites were skulls that reveal fascinating information about the Paracas social structure and notions of physical beauty. The Paracas employed methods to alter the shape of the skull, elongating it with weights and boards, to connote social status. Many of the skulls found in the Paracas Necropolis have stretched and sloped craniums. The Paracas people also practiced a crude form of brain surgery called trepanation. Like medieval physicians, who believed bloodletting aimed at the forehead was a cure-all, Paracas doctors surgically drilled holes in the skull to treat both physical trauma and, it seems, psychological disorders. The formation of scar tissue indicates that many of the patients actually survived the operations, although, of course, it's impossible to say how their physical or behavioral problems were affected.

The Paracas culture flourished from roughly 1300 B.C. to A.D. 200, but scholars are most knowledgeable about the late period of development, from 300 B.C. to A.D. 200. At the Paracas Necropolis, researchers discovered more than 400 funerary bundles, each consisting of a mummified priest or nobleman swathed in brilliantly woven and embroidered funeral tapestries. The large and exceptionally detailed, colorful weavings feature repetitive motifs of birds, fish, and other animals, revealing a keen sense of textile design and artistry.

Little is known about the disappearance of the Paracas culture around A.D. 200. Farther south along the coast, the Nasca culture reigned for about 5 centuries, itself eventually succeeded by the Huari and then Ica cultures, the last of which succumbed to the expanding Incan Empire by the 15th century.

BY BOAT   Boat tours of the Paracas Bay and Ballestas Islands are available right on the El Chaco waterfront (S/35 or $10 per person) or by arranging an organized tour.

BY ORGANIZED TOUR   The following companies all offer packages to the Ballestas Islands and Paracas National Reserve (as well as tours to Tambo Colorado and Nasca): **Zarcillo Connections,** Callao 137 (© **056/536-543;** www.ballestasisland. com); **Ballestas Travel Service,** San Francisco 249 (© **056/533-095**); and, near Ica, **Huacachina Tours,** Av. La Angostura 355, L-47, in front of the Hotel Las Dunas (© **056/256-582;** huacachinatours@cterra.com.pe).

WHAT TO SEE & DO
RESERVA NACIONAL DE PARACAS *
The Paracas Bay and Peninsula, along with the small Ballestas Islands, compose the Paracas National Reserve, a place of gorgeous unpopulated beaches, strange desert vistas, and spectacular wildlife. Established in 1975, Paracas is the primary marine conservation center in Peru. The 14,504-sq.-km (5,600-sq.-mile) reserve, which can be visited year-round, is about two-thirds ocean, so don't come expecting to see a zoolike array of plants and animals at every turn—except on the Ballestas, where several thousand sea lions, in addition to many other species, lie about in plain view.

Exploring Paracas
What is not water in the Paracas National Reserve is hot and dry land, with no transportation to speak of except for independently hired taxis. For this reason, most tourists tend to visit the reserve as part of an organized tour. However, adventurous travelers with plenty of water, sunscreen, and stamina can get to know the peninsula and its rich marine birdlife on their own, camping far from other humans. Safety has become a concern in recent years, though, so camping alone is not a good idea.

Dirt roads crisscross the Paracas Peninsula, and a paved road goes around it, out toward Punta Pejerrey, near the Candelabro (see "Islas Ballestas," below). The dirt roads are the most interesting, reaching minuscule fishing villages such as attractive **Lagunillas** and a clifftop lookout point, **Mirador de los Lobos,** with views of the ocean and lots of sea lions. Across the isthmus from the Bahía de Paracas (and opposite Lagunillas) is a curious cave formation known as the **Cathedral,** a rocky outcrop that, with the assistance of wind and sea erosion, has taken on the appearance of a church tower. Sea otters populate the cave floor.

To hike around the peninsula, it's about 21km (13 miles) round-trip to the lookout point (5km/3 miles from the Tello Museum to Lagunillas). Begin at a turnoff left of the paved road beyond the museum. There are few facilities of any kind on the peninsula. You are allowed to camp on the beautiful beaches (where you might see no other humans, just pelicans and other birds), and there are a couple of seafood restaurants in Lagunillas—Tía Fela's is the best place around for fresh fish.

Museo de Sitio Julio C. Tello   Named for the Peruvian archaeologist credited with uncovering many of the mysteries of the ancient Paracas culture, the Julio Tello Site Museum is located just past the entrance to the Paracas National Reserve, 5km (3 miles) from Paracas beach. It contains a small but instructive exhibit of ceramics and textiles that depict the evolution of the Paracas culture. The Paracas were experts at mummifying their dead; in the mummies, you can see the peculiar practices of cranial deformation and cranial trepanation, or brain surgery. The Paracas also admired trophy heads, and warriors often attached the heads of defeated foes to their armor to instill fear into their opponents.

Paracas National Preserve

0		5 mi
0		5 km

Islas Ballestas ❶

Boat Tours

↑ To Pisco

Playa Talpo ❷

Punta Pejerrey

○Puerto San Martín

To Santa Cruz →

Cerro Talpo

El Chaco ❸ ❹ Park Boundary

Isla San Gallán

Playa Los Viejos

Bahía de Paracas

❺

Playa Culebras

Cerro Los Colorados

Paracas

PACIFIC OCEAN

Península de Paracas

❻

ⓘ ❼

Punta Lagarto

Cerro Lechuza

Cerro Colorado

PERU

★ Lima

Punta Lechuza

Cerro Arquillo

ⓘ Lagunillas

PARACAS NATIONAL RESERVE

❽ Punta Arquillo

❾

Pampa Las Salinas

ATTRACTIONS ●
Candelabro **2**
Cathedral (La Catedral) **9**
Islas Ballestas **1**
Mirador de los Lobos **8**
Museo de Sitio Julio C. Tello **7**
Paracas Necropolis **6**

ACCOMMODATIONS ■
Hotel El Mirador **4**
Hotel Paracas **5**

ⓘ Information
⋯⋯ Highway
‑ ‑ Road (unpaved)

Isla Zárate

Salinas de Otuma

DINING ◆
El Chaco **3**

Near the museum is the Paracas Necropolis (100 B.C.–A.D. 300), comprising the archaeological sites of Cabezas Largas and Cerro Colorado. First explored in the 1920s, it is the oldest discovered site in the region. Tello uncovered Paracas burial sites containing superb funerary cloths, skulls, and other artifacts—all key elements in his groundbreaking studies of the Paracas culture. However, there is very little to see today at the sites. About 270m (886 ft.) toward the bay is a viewing tower, constructed to allow viewings of the dozens (or hundreds) of pink flamingos often gathered on the beach (usually July–Nov only).

Carretera Pisco, Puerto San Martín Km 27, Paracas. ℂ **056/620-436.** Admission S/6 ($1.70) adults, S/3 (85¢) students and seniors, S/1 (30¢) children under 10. Daily 9am–5pm.

Islas Ballestas 🐾🐾

The primary focus of a visit to the reserve is a boat tour of the Ballestas (pronounced "Bah-*yehs*-tahs") Islands. Although the islands can't possibly live up to locals' touting of them as the "Peruvian Galápagos," the Ballestas do afford tantalizing close-up views (without allowing visitors on the islands) of the habitat's rich roster of protected species, including huge colonies of barking sea lions, endangered turtles and Humboldt penguins, red boobies, pelicans, turkey vultures, and red-footed cormorants. During the summer months (Jan–Mar), baby sea lions are born, and the community becomes even more populous and noisy. The wall-like, cantilevered islands are literally covered with birds; 110 migratory and resident sea birds have been documented, and the bay is a stopover point in the Alaska–Patagonia migration route. Packs of dolphins are occasionally seen slicing through the water, and, less frequently, humpbacked whales and soaring Andean condors can also be glimpsed.

The islands are often referred to by locals as *las islas guaneras* because they are covered in bird droppings. (*Guano* is the Quechua word for excrement.) The nitrogen-rich guano is harvested every 10 years and made into fertilizer. (A factory can be seen on the first island.) No humans other than the guano collectors—no doubt a contender for worst job title in the world—are allowed on the islands, and all the species in the reserve are protected by law. In practice, however, there are no specially assigned police officers or boats available to enforce protection.

En route to the islands, boats pass the famous **Candelabro,** a giant candelabra-like drawing etched into a cliff overlooking the bay. The huge etching, 126m long and 72m wide (413 ft. by 236 ft.), looks as though it could be a cousin to the Nasca Lines, and it is similarly shrouded in mystery. Some believe that it's a ritualistic symbol of the Paracas or Nasca cultures, while others contend that it dates only to the 18th or 19th century, when it served as a protective symbol and navigational guide for fishermen and sailors.

Most organized tours take visitors from the San Andrés port to the El Balneario resort, a beach playground for upscale residents of Lima, and then on to Playa El Chaco, where boats leave for 1-hour tours of the Ballestas. You can also independently contract an island boat tour here from one of the 13 operators on the main street. Tours run about S/35 ($10) per person, and each boat has an English- or French-speaking guide on board. Most start early in the morning, between 7 and 8am. Visitors are not allowed to set foot on the islands, although boats get close enough for good viewing. Sweaters and windbreakers, hats, and sunscreen are essential.

TAMBO COLORADO

An Incan fortress and probably the best-preserved ancient architectural complex on the central coast, this outpost is thought to have been an administration checkpoint for Andean coastal migration. It was probably also where the Incan chieftain and his minions stayed for periods as he traveled back and forth between the Incan capital, Cusco, and coastal settlements. Unlike other archaeological sites, where the characteristic vibrant colors have long faded, here at least some of the original red, white, and yellow walls are still preserved. (The name of the complex, *colorado,* refers to the red color of the walls.) Also unique in the Incan canon, the structures here were constructed not of neatly cut stone, but of materials that could be used for long-term construction, given the lack of rain on the desert coast.

The complex contains a central plaza, storehouses, living quarters, and military installations. If you're headed to Cusco, you can be assured of seeing more impressive Incan sites, but Tambo Colorado is rewarding for archaeology fans and Incan completists.

Tips **Organized Tours**

Most people visit the Paracas National Reserve and Ballestas Islands as part of organized tours. Guides, transportation, and entrance fees are all included in the price. Those who prefer to visit the reserve on their own must pay an entrance fee upon entering the reserve (S/5 or $1.40 for adults and students 14 and older; free for children under 14). You can enter the reserve without a guide, but it's highly recommended that you contract one in order to get the most out of a visit. Much that is unique about the area—its climate and conditions, and its migratory wildlife—is not always immediately obvious.

The site is quite removed from Pisco—about 45km (28 miles) northeast of town. It lies about 5km (3 miles) outside the town of Humay, to which you can take a bus, but service is erratic. If you are intent on seeing Tambo Colorado, it's advisable to either go with an organized guided tour or hire a taxi, which will take you out to the site, wait for you, and return you to Pisco for about S/105 ($30). The site is open daily from 9am to 5pm; admission is S/5 ($1.50).

WHERE TO STAY
EXPENSIVE
Hotel Paracas ★ *Kids*   The only hotel that lives up to the official billing of Paracas as a resort within the nature reserve, this is a large Mediterranean-style hotel on the bay and one of the best places to stay in the region. Airy and beachy, it has great views of the water. Rooms, furnished with bamboo appointments, have either bay or garden views, and all have small terraces. With features including a children's playground, water-skiing, and paddleboats, it's an especially good option for families. The hotel organizes its own Ballestas Islands visits, slightly more expensive than those down at El Chaco waterfront in Paracas, and it can arrange trips to the Nasca Lines as well. The hotel serves good lunch buffets, open to nonguests.

Av. Paracas 173, Paracas National Reserve, Pisco. © **056/545-100** or 01/445-9376 for reservations. Fax 01/446-5079 in Lima. www.hotelparacas.com. 105 units. $72–$105 double; $119–$319 bungalows and suites. Rates include taxes. MC, V. **Amenities:** Restaurant; bar; 3 outdoor pools; miniature golf; 2 tennis courts; children's playground. *In room:* A/C, TV.

MODERATE
Hotel El Mirador   El Mirador is well situated near the sand dunes at the entrance to the nature reserve, about 16km (10 miles) south of Pisco. It has ample grounds and a nice terrace with sea views, as well as an appealing swimming pool. The well-furnished rooms are pretty nice, with carpeted floors and wood-beamed ceilings.

Carretera Paracas Km 20, Paracas National Reserve, Pisco. ©/fax **564/545-086**, or ©/fax 01/423-8618 for reservations. www.elmiradorhotel.com. 35 units. $38–$41 double. Rate includes taxes and breakfast. MC, V. **Amenities:** Restaurant; bar; outdoor pool; children's game room.

INEXPENSIVE
Hostal Posada Hispana ★ *Finds*   This small, charming, colonial-style hotel is managed by a Spaniard and his Peruvian wife. The popular and good-value inn is clean and quite nicely decorated for the price; it's also only 1½ blocks from the Plaza de Armas. The rooms have loft spaces and bathrooms, and the hotel has a backyard garden. The *hostal* also operates a restaurant that serves paella, pizzas, and Peruvian dishes.

Bolognesi 236, Pisco. ℂ/fax **056/536-363**. www.posadahispana.com. 24 units. $30 double. Rate includes taxes. No credit cards. **Amenities:** Restaurant; laundry service. *In room:* TV.

Hostal Villa Manuelita ℛ *Value*   One of the most recent additions to the lackluster Pisco hotel scene is this charming, centrally located colonial house, which is colorfully and nicely restored. It's just a half-block from the main square and offers spacious, handsomely decorated rooms that are a very good value. The house features a large living room and a Spanish-style central courtyard with a fountain—definitely a step up from most inexpensive accommodations.

San Francisco 227, Pisco. ℂ/fax **056/535-218**. 16 units. $28 double. Rate includes taxes. No credit cards. **Amenities:** Restaurant/pizzeria. *In room:* TV, minibar.

WHERE TO DINE

Pisco offers nothing special in terms of restaurants, although the informal seafood eateries at the **El Chaco** waterfront in Paracas, where launches for the Islas Ballestas depart, are popular with travelers. The best bet there is **El Chorito,** El Chaco s/n (ℂ 056/545-054) which is part of a *hostal.* In Pisco, there are several inexpensive cafes and pizzerias on or near the Plaza de Armas, and a number of restaurants along the pedestrian boulevard (Comercio) with tourist *menús* (inexpensive set meals). **Hostal Posada Hispana** ℛ (see "Where to Stay," above) has a good-value bistro-style restaurant serving pizzas, pastas, and paella, and is easily as good as anything you'll find in town. **Hotel El Mirador** (see "Where to Stay," above) also has a pretty decent restaurant. For inexpensive mussels and ceviche, try the *cevichería* **Los Choritos Mágicos,** 28 de Julio 116 (ℂ **056/534-158**). **Restaurant El Catamarán,** Jr. Comercio 166 (ℂ **056/680-327**), serves the town's best pizzas and has a very cheap menú. The most upmarket of the restaurants along the walkway, **Don Manuel,** Jr. Comercio 179 (ℂ **056/532-035**), serves a variety of inexpensive full meals, including *churrasco* (grilled meats) and good fresh fish.

2 Ica

300km (186 miles) S of Lima; 75km (47 miles) SE of Pisco; 130km (81 miles) NW of Nasca

Capital of the department and surrounded by sand dunes, Ica is a surprisingly large and bustling colonial town, given the scorching desert sun its inhabitants have to contend with. Like Pisco, most of the principal attractions are located beyond the city. Ica is known primarily for its bodegas, wineries that produce a range of wines and pisco, the white-grape brandy that is the essential ingredient in the national drink, the ubiquitous pisco sour (served as a welcome drink at bars, hotels, and restaurants throughout Peru). Also welcome to travelers in the unrelentingly dry, sandy pampas of the department is the Huacachina Lagoon, a pretty and unexpected oasis amid palm trees and dunes on the outskirts of Ica. In Ica proper is a small collection of interesting colonial mansions and churches, as well as the surprisingly excellent Museo Regional, with some splendid exhibits on the area's rich archaeological finds.

Ica was first settled as early as 10,000 years ago and then inhabited by a succession of advanced cultures, including the Paracas, Nasca, Wari, and Ica civilizations. The Inca Pachacútec incorporated the Ica, Nasca, and Chincha valley territories in the 15th century, but by the mid–16th century, the Spaniards had arrived, and Jerónimo Luis de Cabrera founded the *Villa de Valverde del Valle de Ica,* which grew in importance as a commercial center focusing on wine and cotton production.

ESSENTIALS
GETTING THERE
There are frequent buses from Lima to Ica (4 hr.), which drop passengers in the center of town. Frequent service also connects Ica to Nasca (2 hr.) and Pisco (45 min.). **Cruz del Sur,** Avenida Paseo de la República, Lima (© **01/424-6158**), and **Ormeño,** Av. Carlos Zavala 177, Lima (© **01/426-7595**), travel between Lima, Pisco, Nasca, and Arequipa. **Soyuz-Peru,** Av. Carlos Zavala 221, Lima (© **01/428-6252**), connects Ica with Lima and Pisco, and is the fastest and best service (with the most frequent departures) from either city. Bus terminals in Ica are located in the center of town on or just off Lambayeque, a couple of blocks west of the Plaza de Armas.

VISITOR INFORMATION
The **tourist information office** is located at Grau 150 (© **056/227-287**), and the **tourism police** can be found on the Plaza de Armas (© **056/227-673**).

FAST FACTS   Banco de Crédito, Av. Grau 109 at the corner of Callao (© **056/ 233-711**), has an ATM. You'll also find money exchangers on the Plaza de Armas.

For medical attention, go to **Hospital Félix Torrealva Gutiérrez,** Bolívar 1065 (© **056/234-798**), or **Hospital de Apoyo,** Camino a Huacachina s/n (© **056/235-231,** or 056/235-101 for emergencies). If you need the **police,** its headquarters are located at Lambayeque, block 1 (© **056/224-553**).

You'll find a **post office** at San Martín 156 (© **056/234-549**); it's open Monday through Saturday from 8am to 6pm. There's a **Telefónica del Perú** office at Jr. Huanuco 289 (© **056/217-247**); it's open daily.

GETTING AROUND
Ica is quite spread out, and getting around town will most likely involve taking inexpensive taxis, which flood the streets. (Most trips in town cost less than S/7 or $2.) Taxis are especially useful in visiting the wineries located outside of town. There are also *ciclotaxis,* or bicycle rickshaws, which are cheaper still but less secure. Some visitors enjoy taking them out to Huacachina.

You can arrange Nasca Lines overflights from Ica, although it's considerably more common (not to mention cheaper) to organize them in Nasca. If you want to do it from Ica, contact **AeroCondor,** in the Hotel Las Dunas at Av. La Angostura 400 (© **056/256-820** or 01/442-5112). For other organized tours, contact **Huacachina**

Tips **No Wine Until It's Time**

Ica celebrates a wine-harvest festival *(Festival Internacional de la Vendimia)* during early March. The second Friday of the month is a major holiday throughout the Ica department. Many activities take place in the vineyards, although around town there are concerts, handicraft fairs, Peruvian *caballos de paso* (step horses) shows, beauty pageants, and cockfighting. (Don't these last two always go together?) It's a great time to get your fill of pisco. The lovely maiden chosen as the Queen of the Festival gets to doff her shoes and squish grapes in a huge wine vat, to the titillation of all.

Another date to remember: July 25 is the **Día Internacional del Pisco** across Peru, and everybody gets drunk on a national scale.

Ica

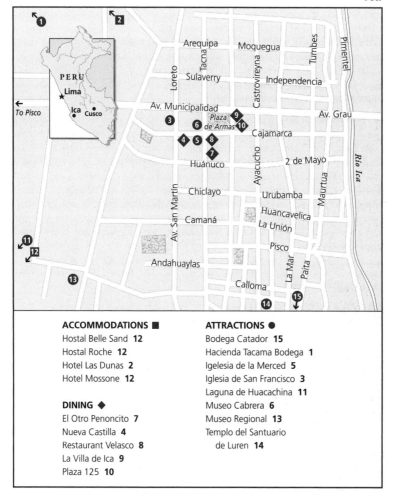

ACCOMMODATIONS ■
Hostal Belle Sand **12**
Hostal Roche **12**
Hotel Las Dunas **2**
Hotel Mossone **12**

DINING ◆
El Otro Penoncito **7**
Nueva Castilla **4**
Restaurant Velasco **8**
La Villa de Ica **9**
Plaza 125 **10**

ATTRACTIONS ●
Bodega Catador **15**
Hacienda Tacama Bodega **1**
Igelesia de la Merced **5**
Iglesia de San Francisco **3**
Laguna de Huacachina **11**
Museo Cabrera **6**
Museo Regional **13**
Templo del Santuario
    de Luren **14**

Tours, Av. La Angostura 355, L-47, in front of the Hotel Las Dunas (© **056/ 256-582**), or **Pelican Travel & Service,** Independencia 156 and Lima 121 (© **056/ 225-211**). For additional flight information, call the Aeródromo de Ica, Carretera Panamericana Sur Km 299 (© **056/256-230**).

WHAT TO SEE & DO
MUSEUMS
Museo Cabrera *(Finds* An oddly idiosyncratic museum that specializes in purportedly ancient stones, this private unmarked collection is worth a visit if you prize the "art" of highly personal collecting. With more than 10,000 stones, including a series of fancifully engraved stones with depictions of primitive life (including dinosaurs), the collection makes an entertaining, if almost assuredly fraudulent, case for the nature of pre-Incan Peruvian civilizations. Dr. Javier Cabrera, a descendant of one of

Ica's founders, claimed that his stones proved the validity of his unique theories that an unprecedented advanced Stone Age culture flourished in Peru long before the reign of the Incan Empire. Regardless of the truth, the stones were engraved by talented artisans, many of whom are still living today. A visit to this museum will be brief—in 15 or 20 minutes, you will have seen all you need to see.

Bolívar 170 (Plaza de Armas). (℃) **056/231-933.** Admission only by guided tour, S/17.5 ($5). Mon–Sat 9am–1pm and 4–8pm (although hours are not always maintained).

Museo Regional de Ica *Finds* Ica's Regional Museum, founded in 1946 and frequently hailed as one of the best small museums in the country, houses a very good collection of intricate Paracas textiles, Nasca ceramics, mummies, fossils, deformed skulls, and trophy heads, as well as colonial and republican art. The well-organized collection also includes important pieces from the Huari, Ica, Chincha, and Incan civilizations, giving visitors an excellent primer on the region's rich history and archaeology. You'll find *quipus,* knotted strings used by the Incas, who, in lieu of a writing system, made and maintained calculations, records, and historical notes with them; and a large-scale model (⅕₀₀) of the Nasca Lines behind the museum. Allow about 45 minutes for a visit.

Jr. Ayabaca, Block 8 s/n. (℃) **056/234-383.** Admission S/5 ($1.40) for adults, S/2 (55¢) for students. Mon–Sat 8am–7pm; Sun 9am–1pm. The museum is about a mile, or a 20-min. walk, from Ica's Plaza de Armas; you can also take bus no. 17 from the plaza to reach it.

BODEGAS (WINERIES)

Dispersed throughout the Ica countryside are some 85 traditional artisanal wineries that produce pisco and regular table wines. Several of the larger bodegas welcome visits; these can be interesting because pisco is such a unique Peruvian product, but they're unlikely to be the most fascinating winery tours you'll experience in your lifetime. They don't usually draw big crowds, so visits can be a little homespun and even haphazard. If you don't have your own transportation, the best way to visit the following bodegas is to either take a taxi or check with one of the travel agencies in town (see "Getting Around," above) about organized tours. Tours given on the premises of the wineries are frequently in Spanish only. For 3-day/2-night package tours from Lima to Ica, which include transportation, bodega visits, meals, city tours, and accommodations, call **Fly Peru/La Ruta del Pisco** at (℃) **01/445-3900;** the cost is $69 to $99 per person, depending on the hotels.

Harvest time, from late February to April, is by far the best time to visit. At other times, the bodegas can be very quiet; it might be difficult finding someone to give a tour, but you might also have the chance to sit down for a drink with the owner.

Bodega Catador Located in the Subtanjalla district 7km (4⅓ miles) from Ica, this interesting and ancient bodega, resuscitated in 1970, offers free tours and tastings. It has a small wine museum, and a restaurant and tavern that often have live music. (The winery curiously calls this a "discotheque.") A small Centro Turístico displays photographs and videos of the production process.

Fondo Tres Esquinas 102 (Carretera Panamericana Sur Km 296), Subtanjalla, Ica. (℃) **056/403-295** or 056/403-427. Free admission. Daily 8am–6pm.

Bodega Ocucaje *Finds* About 35km (22 miles) south of Ica, on the grounds of a colonial hacienda, this remote traditional winery, which dates to the 16th century, is where the locally famous Vino Fond de Cave was born. The winery also operates a country

> ### *Fun Fact* **Pisco Sour**
>
> The pisco sours that groups of tourists get served as welcome drinks at restaurants and hotels across the country are often light and frothy—pale imitations of more potent and tart pisco sours that are the real thing. Here's the recipe for an authentic pisco sour:
>
> 2 oz. pisco
> 1 oz. lime juice
> 1/4 oz. simple syrup
> 1/2 egg white
> 1 dash Angostura bitters
> Shake with ice and strain into glass; garnish with bitters on the creamy top.

inn, the handsome Ocucaje Sun & Wine Resort (p. 165), with all-inclusive packages, sports, and winery tours.

Av. Principal s/n. ✆ **056/408-001** or 056/837-049. www.ocucaje.com. S/10 ($2.85) per person. Mon–Fri 9am–noon and 2–5pm; Sat 9am–noon.

Bodegas Vista Alegre   Just 3km (1¾ miles) north of the center of Ica in the La Tinguiña district, this winery is one of the oldest and largest in Peru. It was a Jesuit hacienda until the late 18th century; in 1857, the winery was established by the Picasso brothers, and it's now well known for its pisco production. To get there on foot, walk on Avenida Grau from the Plaza de Armas, cross over the Ica River, and turn left; the gate entrance to the colonial hacienda is impossible to miss.

Camino a La Tinguiña Km 2, Ica. ✆ **056/232-919**. www.vistaalegre.com.pe. Mon–Fri 9am–2pm.

Hacienda Tacama Bodega ✿   About 10km (6¼ miles) northeast of Ica, housed in a 16th-century colonial hacienda, this winery, one of the largest producers in the region, is known internationally and exports its pisco and wines to a number of countries. The Olaechea family has owned the winery since 1889. Despite the farm building's age—it's one of the oldest in the valley—the bodega uses modern technology. The vineyard is still irrigated, incredibly, by the amazing Achirana irrigation canal built by the Incas.

Camino a La Tinguiña s/n, Ica. ✆ **056/228-395**. Daily 9am–3pm.

COLONIAL CHURCHES & MANSIONS

Ica has several colonial churches and mansions of note, even though many have been felled by earthquakes over the years. The most important church to worshippers is the neoclassical **Templo del Santuario de Luren,** Calle Ayacucho at Piura, where the venerated image of the patron saint of the city, El Señor de Luren, is kept; during Holy Week and the third week of October, it is paraded around the city in well-attended processions. **Iglesia de La Merced** (also called **La Catedral**), on the southwest corner of the Plaza de Armas, is a late-19th-century colonial church with a handsomely carved altar. **Iglesia de San Jerónimo,** Cajamarca 262, is primarily of interest for its altar mural. **Iglesia de San Francisco,** though constructed in 1950, is notable for its stained glass; it's at Avenida Municipalidad at Avenida San Martín.

Among the most attractive of Ica's *casonas,* or colonial mansions, are the **Casona del Marqués de Torre** (today the Banco Continental), on the first block of Calle Libertad;

Casa Mendiola, on Calle Bolívar; **Casona Alvarado,** a Greco-Roman imitation at Cajamarca 178; and **Casona Colonial El Portón,** Calle Loreto 223.

OUTDOOR FUN

LAGUNA DE HUACACHINA 🏖🏖 If you stumble upon this gentle, beautiful oasis in the middle of the desert, surrounded by massive sand dunes and palm trees, you might think it's a mirage. Only 5km (3 miles) southwest of the center of Ica, Huacachina (pronounced "Wah-kah-*chee*-nah") Lagoon is a great place to relax and swim (although the water can be pretty murky) if you're suffering from the heat, and there's a small resort village with a few hotels and restaurants. A boardwalk rings the lagoon. Locals contend that the sulfur-rich waters of the lagoon have curative medicinal properties. Kids can go sand boarding on the dunes (one of the restaurants and the Hostal Rocha rent out boards) or paddleboat across the lagoon. Regular buses to Huacachina depart from the Plaza de Armas in Ica; better yet, you can take an inexpensive and quick taxi.

SAND BOARDING In the sand dune–laden desert landscapes in southern Peru, surfing the dunes on sand boards and rumbling across the sands in *areneros* (dune buggies) are popular sports. The largest sand dunes in South America, reaching a height of 2,000m (6,560 ft.), are just 8km (5 miles) from Nasca, and there are also really high dunes around the Huacachina Lagoon outside of Ica.

Sand boarding, a cross between downhill skiing and snowboarding on grainy stuff rather than white powder, is fairly easy to do (or that's what they tell me). You can really build up some speed, and accomplished boarders can maneuver almost like they would on the slopes. It can be very hot, though, and tough going, because there aren't any lifts to transport you back up the dune. After a few spills, you'll be covered in sand. Accidents can occur, so it's best to get some instruction from a local or the outfit renting the boards.

Adrenaline-fueled adventure trips in buggies are available through local tours (information is available at the **Hotel Paracas;** see p. 158) or at the 210m (690-ft.) dunes around the Huacachina Lagoon outside of Ica, where a restaurant and the Hostal Rocha rent sand boards (about S/3 or 85¢ an hour; see p. 165). For more information on the sport and competitions in Peru, see www.peruboarding.com/Sandboarding/sandboarding.html.

WHERE TO STAY

Most of the best hotel options lie beyond the center of Ica; the majority of those in town are rather unappealing budget choices that have inconsistent hot water.

EXPENSIVE

Hotel Las Dunas 🏖 *Kids* On the outskirts of Ica is this sprawling complex of white Mediterranean-style villas with pretty landscaped grounds, three swimming pools, and good sports opportunities, including horseback riding, golf, tennis, *frontón* (something like a cross between paddle tennis and jai alai), sand boarding, and volleyball. In terms of services and amenities, if not necessarily character, it's a step up from the other top hotel in the area, the Mossone (see below). Rooms are surprisingly large and nicely furnished, and most have garden views. A terrific bonus is the planetarium that provides a good introduction to the Nasca Lines (admission S/17.5 or $5).

Av. La Angostura 400, Ica. ⓒ/fax **056/256-224,** or 01/241-8000 for reservations. www.lasdunashotel.com. 106 units. Sun–Thurs $76 double; weekends $93 double. Rates include taxes. AE, DC, MC, V. **Amenities:** Restaurant; cafeteria; bar; 2 outdoor pools; small gym; sauna; 24-hr room service. *In room:* A/C, TV, minibar, safe, Jacuzzis (suites only).

MODERATE

Hotel Mossone 🏨🏨 *Kids*   At the Huacachina Lagoon is a fancy, colonial-style hotel in a century-old mansion that was a famous luxury resort hotel back in the 1920s. Though it slipped into neglect for a few decades, it has been given new life because of a restoration over the past few years. It features a pleasant outdoor pool, an interior garden patio, beautiful grounds, and a restaurant veranda overlooking the lagoon. Rooms are elegantly furnished and have parquet floors. Its restaurant, featuring a relaxing deck overlooking the oasis waters, is the best on the lagoon. Although Las Dunas and Ocucaje have more amenities and activities, the Mossone has quite a bit more character and ambience, and the hotel's location on Huacachina Lagoon is an attraction in itself.

Balneario de Huacachina, Ica. ℂ **056/236-136,** or 01/261-0240 for reservations. Fax 056/236-137. reservas@derramajae.org.pe. 43 units. $71 double; $85 suite. Rates include taxes. AE, DC, MC, V. **Amenities:** Restaurant; bar; outdoor pool; room service. In room: TV.

Ocucaje Sun & Wine Resort 🏨 *Kids*   A lovely, homey destination resort in the countryside about a half-hour's drive from Ica, Ocucaje is primarily a winery, but its hotel is popular as a country retreat among Limeños and other well-heeled guests with time to relax. Rooms are ample and comfortably furnished. Sports options include tennis, volleyball, swimming, horseback riding, biking, and dune-buggy excursions. The hotel offers packages that include all meals, wines, and a tourist *criollo* (creole) music show (2 nights, $100–$130 per person).

Carretera Panamericana Sur Km 336, Ica. ℂ **056/837-049,** or 01/444-4059 for reservations. Fax 056/836-103. 55 units. $64–$77 double. Rates include taxes and breakfast. Several meal plans and packages available. AE, DC, MC, V. **Amenities:** Restaurant; outdoor pool; tennis courts; Jacuzzi; sauna; game room. In room: A/C, TV.

INEXPENSIVE

Hostal Belle Sand   Located a few kilometers north of Ica, this *hostal* features an outdoor pool with a sun terrace and sand boards for rent. The *hostal* is best suited for backpackers and laid-back sand boarders.

Av. Casuarinas B1-3, Residencial La Angostura. ℂ **056/256-039.** Fax 056/256-814. ecotourica@terra.com.pe. 21 units. $20 double. No credit cards. **Amenities:** Cafeteria; bar.

Hostal Rocha *Value*   This small family-run inn is in a nice but somewhat rundown old house with large rooms and terraces with lagoon views. Rooms are adequate for the very low prices; some rooms have balconies. Popular with backpackers, the *hostal* has bikes and sand boards for rent.

Balneario de Huacachina, Ica. ℂ **056/222-256.** 10 units. S/10 ($2.85) per person w/shared bathroom; S/30 ($8.55) double w/private bathroom. No credit cards. **Amenities:** Outdoor pool.

WHERE TO DINE

Despite its size, Ica doesn't offer much in the way of fine dining. Most locals and visitors tend to gravitate toward the Plaza de Armas and the handful of sandwich shops, rotisserie-chicken places, and informal restaurants there.

Grab some snacks, breakfast, or a tourist set lunch, along with some local wines, at **La Villa de Ica,** Lima 139 at the Plaza de Armas (ℂ **056/213-108**). **Plaza 125,** Lima 125 at the Plaza de Armas (ℂ **056/211-816**), serves grilled meats, rotisserie chicken, and barbecue, as well as regional specialties, to a mixed crowd of families and young people. **El Otro Peñoncito,** Bolívar 422 (ℂ **056/233-920**), is the nicest restaurant in the city center, with a hugely varied menu of *criollo* (creole) specialties and basic chicken, meat, and fish dishes, including some vegetarian plates. Sometimes there's live music in the evenings. **Nueva Castilla,** Libertad 252 (© **056/213-140**), is a pretty nice restaurant serving Peruvian fare; there's a small patio. After dinner on weekends, the music is pumped up and the restaurant becomes a disco of sorts. **Restaurant Velasco,** Libertad 137 (© **056/218-182**), is a popular cafeteria-style restaurant and bakery serving both Peruvian and international dishes at very afford-able prices, as well as a selection of baked goods and other desserts and coffee.

3 Nasca ⭑

443km (275 miles) S of Lima

Nasca (also spelled Nazca) would just be a dusty little desert town of little interest were it not for the strange presence of massive, mysterious drawings—the famous Nasca Lines—etched into the sands of the pampas more than a millennium ago. Ancient peoples created a vast tapestry of "geoglyphs"—trapezoids and triangles, 70-odd ani-mal and plant figures, and more than 10,000 lines—that have baffled observers for decades. They are so large, with some figures reaching dimensions of 300m (1,000 ft.), that they can be appreciated only from the air. Over the years, theorists have posited that they were signs from the gods, agricultural and astronomical calendars, or even extraterrestrial airports. Some believe that the drawers of the lines must themselves have had the ability to fly, perhaps in hot-air balloons, over the designs below. The wildest theories, today discredited by all but fringe-dwelling true believers, prompted the old book and movie *The Chariots of the Gods.*

The town and the drawings are named for the Nasca culture (300 B.C.–A.D. 700), which succeeded the Paracas civilization along the southern desert coast. Little was known about the Nasca until the beginning of the 20th century. Today the Nasca are renowned for their exquisitely stylized pottery, among the finest of pre-Columbian Peru. The small town of Nasca was devastated by a monstrous earthquake in 1996 and is just getting back on its feet. Most constructions in town were adobe, which crum-bled and were replaced by hastily built concrete houses. The new construction adds to the dusty frontier feel of the town.

The surrounding desert is a strangely impressive place. Flying over the Nasca Lines, you see an unending expanse of craggy, dusty, origami-like folds in the sands, like deep wrinkles in a wizened face. Certainly, nothing in the region equals the impact of a flight over the lines, but the town does have a couple of good museums and two archaeological sites that evoke the Nasca culture that flourished in the area.

ESSENTIALS

GETTING THERE

From Lima, **Cruz del Sur** buses (© **01/424-6158**) pass through Nasca on the way to Arequipa; the trip to Nasca takes 6 to 7 hours. **Ormeño** (© **01/472-5000**) makes the trip from Lima as well as Cusco (24-plus hr.) and Arequipa (10 hr.), and, like Cruz

---

⟮ *Fun Fact* **Say What?**

The Nasca people were evidently deeply rooted in the hot and painfully arid southern desert landscape that they inhabited in spite of numerous earth-quakes and that they fought valiantly to farm. The word "Nasca" comes from the Quechua *nanasca,* which means pain and suffering.

Nasca

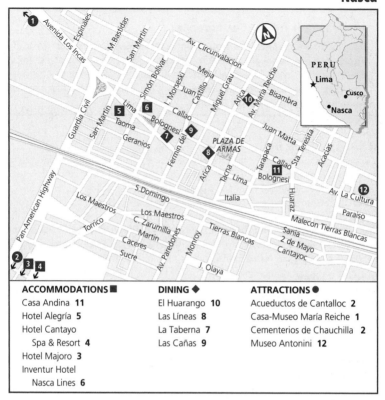

ACCOMMODATIONS ■
Casa Andina **11**
Hotel Alegría **5**
Hotel Cantayo
  Spa & Resort **4**
Hotel Majoro **3**
Inventur Hotel
  Nasca Lines **6**

DINING ◆
El Huarango **10**
Las Líneas **8**
La Taberna **7**
Las Cañas **9**

ATTRACTIONS ●
Acueductos de Cantalloc **2**
Casa-Museo María Reiche **1**
Cementerios de Chauchilla **2**
Museo Antonini **12**

del Sur, returns to Lima. **Expreso Wari** (© **01/423-6640**) also makes the long journey between Cusco and Nasca (20–22 hr.).

VISITOR INFORMATION
The **tourist information office** (© **056/522-418**), Callao 783 (Plaza de Armas) in the Municipal building, offers maps, hotel and tourism packages, and guide information. It's open Monday to Friday from 9am to 3pm. Tourist information can also be obtained from one of the travel agencies in town, such as Alegría Tours, although they are understandably interested in selling tour packages.

FAST FACTS **Banco de Crédito** (© **056/522-445**), at avenidas Grau and Lima, has an ATM with the Visa logo, as does **Banco de la Nación** (no phone), Lima 431. For medical attention, go to **EsSalud,** María Reiche 308 (© **056/522-438**), or **Hospital de Apoyo,** Callao s/n (at Morsesky; © **056/522-586**). The **police** (© **056/ 522-442**) are located on Los Incas, next to the roundabout on Lima and Panamericana, near the Ormeño station.

The **post office** is located at Fermín de Castillo 379, between Callao and Bolognesi; it's open Monday through Friday from 9am to 5pm. The **Telefónica del Perú** office (© **056/523-045**) is at Lima 545; it's open daily from 8am to 10pm.

(*Tips* **Take It from a Cartographer**

Frommer's cartographer Nick Trotter highly recommends picking up the Instituto Geográfico Nacional's extremely detailed topographical map of the Nasca Lines, available from IGN (www.ignperu.gob.pe) or from the South American Explorers (www.saexplorers.org). Nick says it's a must-have for any traveler who's serious about exploring the lines.

WHAT TO SEE & DO

Visitors who want to see more than the Nasca Lines would probably benefit from arranging a group tour with one of the Nasca travel agencies because the major archaeological sites are scattered about the valley and complicated to get to. For flights over the lines, it's sometimes best to simply go to the airport and purchase tickets directly from one of the charter airlines there. The following agencies all offer city and regional packages and information on the area: **Alegría Tours,** Jr. Lima 168 (© 056/522-444; www.alegriatours peru.com); **Nanasca Tours,** Lima 160 (© 034/522-917); **Nasca Travel,** Lima 438 (© 056/522-085); and **Nasca Trails,** Jr. Bolognesi 299 (© 056/522-858).

NASCA LINES 👌👌

The unique Nasca Lines remain one of the great enigmas of the South American continent. The San José desert, bisected by the great Pan-American Highway that runs the length of Peru, is spectacularly marked by 70 giant plant and animal figures, as well as a warren of mysterious geometric lines, carved into the barren surface. Throughout the Nasca Valley, an area of nearly 1,000 sq. km (390 sq. miles), there are at least 10,000 lines and 300 different figures. Most are found alongside a 48km (30-mile) stretch of the Pan-American Highway. Some of the biggest and best-known figures are about 21km (13 miles) north of Nasca. Most experts believe they were constructed by the Nasca (pre-Incan) culture between 300 B.C. and A.D. 700, although predecessor and successor cultures—the Paracas and Huari—might have also contributed to the desert canvas. The lines were discovered in the 1920s when commercial airlines began flights over the Peruvian desert. From the sky, they appeared to be some sort of primitive landing strips.

As enigmatic as they are, the Nasca Lines are not some sort of desert-sands Rorschach inkblot; the figures are real and easily identifiable from the air. With the naked eye from the window of an airplane, you'll spot the outlines of a parrot, hummingbird, spider, condor, dog, whale, monkey with a tail wound like a top, giant spirals, huge trapezoids, and, perhaps oddest of all, a cartoonish anthropomorphic figure with its hand raised to the sky that has come to be known as the "Astronaut." Some figures are as much as 300m (1,000 ft.) long, while some lines are 30m (100 ft.) wide and stretch more than 9.5km (6 miles).

Questions have long confounded observers. Who constructed these huge figures and lines? And, of course, why? Apparently, over many generations, the Nasca people removed hard stones turned dark by the sun to "draw" the lines in the fine, lighter-colored sand. The incredibly dry desert conditions—it rains only about 50 centimeters a year, on average—preserved the lines and figures for more than 1,000 years. Why the lines were constructed is more difficult to answer, especially considering that the authors were unable to see their work in its entirety without any sort of aerial perspective. The scientist who dedicated her life to study of the lines was a German mathematician, María

The Nasca Lines

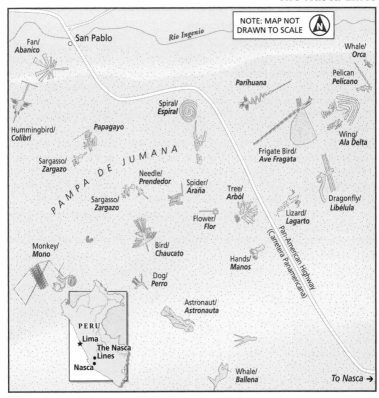

NOTE: MAP NOT DRAWN TO SCALE

San Pablo

Río Ingenio

Fan/ *Abanico*

Whale/ *Orca*

Pelican *Pelícano*

Parihuana

Spiral/ *Espiral*

Hummingbird/ *Colibrí*

Papagayo

P A M P A   D E   J U M A N A

Sargasso/ *Zargazo*

Needle/ *Prendedor*

Spider/ *Araña*

Tree/ *Arból*

Frigate Bird/ *Ave Fragata*

Wing/ *Ala Delta*

Sargasso/ *Zargazo*

Flower/ *Flor*

Lizard/ *Lagarto*

Dragonfly/ *Libélula*

Monkey/ *Mono*

Bird/ *Chaucato*

Hands/ *Manos*

Dog/ *Perro*

(Carretera Panamericana)

Pan-American Highway

Astronaut/ *Astronauta*

PERU

Lima

The Nasca Lines

Nasca

Whale/ *Ballena*

To Nasca →

Reiche. For 5 decades, she lived austerely in the Peruvian desert and walked alone among the lines, taking painstaking measurements and making drawings of the site. She concluded that the lines formed a giant astronomical calendar, crucial to calculating planting and harvest times. According to this theory, the Nasca were able to predict the arrival of rains, a valuable commodity in such a barren territory. Other theories abound, though. Nasca is a seismic zone, with 300 fault lines beneath the surface and hundreds of subterranean canals; an American scientist, David Johnson, proposed that the trapezoids held clues to subterranean water sources. Some suggest that the lines not only led to water sources, but that they were pilgrimage routes, part of the Nasca's ritual worship of water. Notions of extraterrestrials and the Nasca's ability themselves to fly over the lines have been dismissed by most serious observers.

An observation tower *(mirador)* stands beside the Pan-American Highway (about 19km/12 miles north of Nasca), but it allows only a vague and partial view of three figures: the hands, lizard, and tree. The view from the tower (S/3 or 85¢ for adults, S/2 or 55¢ for students) is vastly inferior to the multiple bird's-eye views one gets on the overflight, but it's the best you'll be able to do if you can't take the stomach-turning dips and dives of the light-craft flights. (Only 10 min. into one recent flight, the four French travelers onboard with me were all tossing their *petits déjeuners* into the white plastic bags that had been thoughtfully provided.)

Tips Cahuachi & El Estaquería

Cahuachi, an ancient adobe complex west of the Nasca Lines—said by some to be twice as large as Chan Chan, the massive city of the Chimú along the north coast—was the most important ceremonial and administrative center belonging to the Nasca culture. The ruins, in poor condition and, in large part, buried under sand, are still undergoing excavation. Because of ongoing work, only a handful of temples and pyramids may be visited, and only by guided tour. (The major agencies in Nasca usually offer the site as part of a group tour for around $10 per person.) Also on the premises is **El Estaquería,** a construction of rows of *huarango* trees that probably marked important grave sites. The ruins are 30km (19 miles) from Nasca. The director of the Antonini Museum in Nasca has unearthed a spectacular collection of painted textiles, made with seven different dyes, at Cahuachi that he hopes to eventually exhibit in a new museum in Nasca. Many of the finest examples of Nasca ceramics in existence were also discovered at Cahuachi.

The small aircraft seat between three and five passengers. A half-dozen small charter airlines offered flights over the lines from the small airport in Nasca. Flights cost $50 to $79 (those originating in Ica run about $130–$150) and last 35 to 45 minutes. Pilots give very basic descriptions of the figures as they fly overhead. If you're interested in seeing the lines only and you don't have time for the town of Nasca or the surrounding area, by far the most convenient—although certainly not the cheapest—way is as part of a 1-day round-trip package from Lima. Unfortunately, there are no independent flights from Lima to Nasca (or from any other city to Nasca). Aero-Condor does the roundtrip tour from Lima for $348 per person, minimum two people. AeroIca offers a similar package for $299 per person, while Aeroparacas offers a Lima-Nasca package for $199 per person, and one that includes Paracas for $209. Aeroparacas also offers a package deal that includes a night's accommodations in Nasca, overflight, and tour of Chauchilla for $68 per person.

For best visibility, try to go in the morning or late afternoon, but be prepared for conditions that frequently delay flights and occasionally make taking off impossible.

Nasca Lines overflights from Nasca's Aeródromo de Nasca (© **056/523-665**), Carretera Panamericana Sur Km 447 include **AeroCondor,** Hostal El Nido del Cóndor (© **056/522-402,** or 01/614-6014 in Lima); **Alas Peruanas,** Alegría Tours, Jr. Lima 168 (© **056/522-444**); and **Aeroparacas,** Jr. Lima 185 (© **056/521-027** or 01/271-6941 in Lima). Also worth a look for those with an interest in the Nasca Lines is the small **planetarium** at the Invertur Hotel Nazca Lines (p. 172).

OTHER NOTABLE SIGHTS NEAR NASCA

Acueductos de Cantalloc   About 4km (2½ miles) southwest of Nasca are very well-preserved stone aqueducts, part of a sophisticated subterranean system constructed by the Nasca to irrigate the fields in the pampas. There are 35 beautifully built Incan or pre-Incan aqueducts, or *puquios,* with surface air vents that form spirals descending to the water current. The canals, many **S**-shaped to slow the flow of water, still function and are used by local farmers. Nearby, Los Paredones, the ruins of an Incan trade center, is in poor shape, requiring a fertile imagination to conjure the activity that once reigned here.

Carretera Puquio–Cusco. Admission $3. Daily 8am–5pm. To get here, you must come by taxi (S/15–S/20 or $4.30–$5.70 round-trip, including waiting time) or tour group (S/35 or $10 per person).

Casa-Museo María Reiche   The German mathematician María Reiche was the foremost expert on the Nasca Lines, earning her the nickname "Dame of the Desert." She dedicated most of her adult life to studying them, debunking the loonier theories about their purposes, and doing more than even the Peruvian government to publicize the lines' existence. Reiche died in 1998 at the age of 95. Today the simple room where she worked and lived, which her tomb has been placed next to, has been converted into a small museum paying tribute to Reiche's life and the Lines, complete with maps, models, plans, and photos. The Casa-Museo (also variously referred to as Museo de Sitio María Reiche Newman and Museo Regional María Reiche) is located in the district called San Pablo, between Ica and Nasca. Allow a half-hour to tour the museum.

Caserío la Pascana, Carretera Panamericana Sur Km 420 (27km/17 miles from Nasca), San Pablo. (C) **056/234-383** or 056/522-428. Admission S/3 (85¢). Mon–Fri 9am–7pm; Sat 8:30am–6:30 pm; Sun 9am–1pm.

Cementerios de Chauchilla ☞   About 30km (19 miles) south of Nasca is an extensive valley of tombs from the Inca-Chincha period (A.D. 1000–1400). It is a necropolis rather than a mere cemetery: Thousands of graves have been uncovered in the area. Only 12 underground tombs are exposed for visitors, although they present a rich picture of the ancient culture of the desert valley. One tomb holds only children, and others are populated with the remains of adults with thick, Rasta-like dreadlocks. The cemetery has been open to the public since only 1997, and only in the past year were the tombs covered with thatch roofs—which is why many skulls appear whitewashed from the blazing desert sun. The desert's very dry conditions helped preserve the mummies over the centuries. Fragments of textiles, feathers, and even bone are scattered about the site, clues to the cemetery's discovery by *huaqueros* (grave robbers) and how underfunded this project remains. Allow about 3 to 4 hours for travel time and viewing the necropolis.

Admission S/4 ($1.15). Daily 8am–5pm. Getting to Chauchilla is complicated, since there is no public transportation to the site; taxi (S/60 or $17 round-trip, including waiting time) and tour group (S/35 or $10 per person) are the only options.

Fun Fact **Nasca Culture**

The Nasca civilization is best known for its artistry on a grand scale: those massive and monstrously baffling line drawings on the desert floor of the coastal pampas. But among scholars, the culture is acclaimed for producing the most sophisticated ceramists of pre-Columbian Peru and ingenious engineers who irrigated their desert fields with hydraulic systems and aqueducts that carried underground water.

The Nasca succeeded the Paracas in the desert region south of present-day Lima. Whereas the Paracas were extraordinary weavers and designers of textiles, the Nasca culture distinguished itself with highly artistic pottery. Its glazed ceramics featured vivid but earthy colors and symbolic motifs, and mineral-based pigments ensured lasting colors. Many of the stylized figures and lines on Nasca pottery closely echo the Nasca Lines, reinforcing theories about the latter's authorship.

Museo Antonini ⭐ *Kids*   This excellent private archaeology museum, a labor of love inaugurated by an Italian foundation in 1999, addresses local Nasca culture with excellent exhibits that detail the process as well as the results of archaeological excavations in the area. On view are fine ceramics, trophy heads worn by warriors after beheadings to inspire fear among enemies, musical instruments, and a few well-preserved mummies. In the gardens out back are the Bisambra aqueduct, an ancient Nasca stone irrigation canal, reproductions of tombs, and scale models of the Nasca Lines. The director hopes one day soon to be able to open a new museum in Nasca to show off the world's greatest collection of painted textiles—made with seven different types of vegetable dyes—all uncovered from the huge adobe city of Cahuachi nearby. Plan to spend about an hour here.

Av. de la Cultura 600 (Bisambra), a 10-min. walk from the Plaza de Armas. ℰ **056/523-444**. Admission S/10 ($2.85). Daily 9am–7pm.

WHERE TO STAY

There are plenty of low-end accommodations in Nasca and a handful of slightly more comfortable, if unspectacular, options in town and out by the airport.

EXPENSIVE

Hotel Cantayo Spa & Resort ⭐⭐ *Finds*   Located next to the Cantalloc Aqueduct, this grand, mission-style hacienda has been converted into a sprawling spa hotel. Rustic and peaceful, it features sweeping panoramic mountain views, large rooms adorned with Balinese and Tibetan touches, a huge swimming pool, extensive gardens, and a jogging track. The Italian owners have positioned it as a relaxing refuge, which takes its cues from the region's more spiritual and mystical attractions, offering a menu of exoticism: tai chi, yoga, Japanese meditation, and not only massages and facials but Watsu treatments. If you consider yourself more grounded than that, you can indulge in horseback riding and long walks around the property. The hotel's restaurant is the finest in Nasca and worth a visit even if you aren't staying here.

Carretera Puquio–Cusco, Nasca. ℰ **056/522-345**. Fax 056/522-283. www.hotelcantayo.com. 40 units. $160–$200 double. Rates include taxes and breakfast. AE, DC, MC, V. **Amenities:** Restaurant; 2 outdoor pools; room service; spa; Jacuzzi; laundry service. *In room:* A/C, TV.

Invertur Hotel Nazca Lines *Kids*   For many years the most upscale hotel in town, the Hotel Nazca Lines has been surpassed by the new hotels and remodels, but is still pretty popular for its amenities: It has a pretty courtyard with a good-size clean pool and tennis courts. The nice rooms have air-conditioning, dated furnishings, and tile and iron accents. The Lines' fabled caretaker, María Reiche, lived here for many years in room no. 130. On the premises are a restaurant and a planetarium named for Reiche, with Nasca Lines presentations.

Jr. Bolognesi s/n, Nasca. ℰ **056/522-293**. Fax 056/522-112. nazca@invertur.com.pe. 34 units. $85 double. Rate includes taxes. DC, MC, V. **Amenities:** Restaurant; outdoor pool; 2 tennis courts. *In room:* A/C, TV.

MODERATE

Casa Andina ⭐ *Kids*   Though there are no other chains in Nasca, Casa Andina, a small group of Peruvian hotels, is making sure it's got all the top tourist spots in the country covered. This 2-year-old hotel follows the company's midsize, midrange, and always consistent formula. Located downtown, 1 block from the main square and about 5 minutes from the airfield where flights depart for the Nasca Lines, it is the largest hotel in Nasca. Rooms are ample, with colorful interiors and nice, clean bathrooms, and are built along a sunny, open-air interior corridor. The outdoor pool isn't large, but it has a large terrace and is appreciated by families and more upscale travelers (for whom there are few good options in Nasca).

Jr. Bolognesi 367, Nasca. © 056/523-563. Fax 056/52-1067. www.casa-andina.com. 60 units. $75 double. Rates include taxes and breakfast buffet. AE, DC, MC, V. **Amenities:** Restaurant; small outdoor pool; business center. *In room:* A/C, TV, hair dryer upon request.

Hotel Majoro ★★ (Finds)   This rustic old hacienda—the old Hotel de la Borda—features simple rooms around courtyards and tranquil, extensive gardens full of bougainvillea. Its new owners have pumped much-needed investment and life into the place, though it retains the feel of an elegant country house. The common areas have been completely transformed and are now warm and inviting. Accommodations are spacious, clean, and charming where they were once dumpy. It's set in Majoro, a few kilometers along a dusty road beyond the airport.

Carretera Panamericana Sur Km 452, (Majoro) Nasca. ©/fax **056/522-750.** www.hotelmajoro.com. 39 units. $70 double. Rate includes taxes and breakfast. MC, V. **Amenities:** Restaurant; bar; outdoor pool; game room. *In room:* TV.

INEXPENSIVE
Hotel Alegría ★ (Value)   The down-to-earth and traveler-friendly Alegría is the most popular inexpensive hotel in town, a good place to meet up with others exploring this region of Peru. It operates a good travel agency and has loads of facilities and services, including free Internet access for guests, bus-station pickup, and luggage storage. Some of the new chalet-style rooms have air-conditioning. It also has a nice garden.

Lima 168, Nasca. ©/fax **056/522-444.** www.nazcaperu.com. 43 units. $30–$35 double. Rate includes taxes, continental breakfast, and prearranged pickup from bus stop. DC, MC, V. **Amenities:** Restaurant; bar; outdoor pool; laundry service. *In room:* A/C in some units, TV.

WHERE TO DINE
Your dining choices are rather limited in Nasca, as they are throughout the region. Most people come just to view the Nasca Lines, they don't stay many nights, and they tend to eat at their hotels. Hotels with decent restaurants include the Alegría and El Nido del Cóndor. The restaurants at Hotel Invertur Nazca Lines and Hotel Cantayo Spa & Resort are a cut above (see "Where to Stay," above, for reviews of all four hotels).

   Las Líneas, Jr. Arica 299-A (© **056/522-066**), serves Peruvian fare such as ceviche and garlic chicken, even though it looks like a Chinese restaurant. **El Huarango,** Jr. Arica 602 (© **056/521-287**), is one of the better restaurants in Nasca, offering good-value meals and a rooftop garden. **La Taberna** ★, Jr. Lima 321 (© **056/806-783**), is a good restaurant—probably the best in town—with a varied international menu, live music on weekends, and the graffiti scrawlings of hundreds of international travelers who came before you. **Las Cañas,** Bolognesi 279 (© **056/806-891**), serves a large menu of Peruvian and international dishes, including ceviche, pastas, salads, and hamburgers; it's quite a hangout on weekend nights.

4 A Gem in the Central Highlands: Ayacucho ★★
585km (364 miles) SE of Lima; 337km (209 miles) NE of Pisco; 590km (367 miles) W of Cusco

Located high in the Central Andes—and hijacked in the 1980s by Shining Path terrorists who claimed the city as their base and cut it off from Peru and the rest of the world for much of the past 2 decades—dignified Ayacucho has at last escaped bloody conflict and is begging to be discovered. A colonial gem, with more of its Spanish architecture intact than almost any other city in Peru, the city claims the crown as the epicenter of Peruvian *artesanía* (popular art). The renowned *retablos* (see box on *retablos* below), ceramic churches, and whimsical red-clay figurines one sees all over Peru (and in Latin American shops from Austin to Amsterdam) are all produced locally.

Locals are fond of saying that the critical developments in Peruvian history are tied to Ayacucho. As the site of the earliest-known human presence in Peru, in nearby Pikimachay, and the one-time capital of the powerful Huari culture (200–100 B.C.), Ayacucho—originally called Huamanga, a name many locals insist on still using today—is best known as a place where crucial battles for the soul of Peru have taken place. The Chanca people bravely resisted the aggressively expanding Incan Empire, and the bloody Battle of Ayacucho against Spanish forces in 1824 launched the country's independence.

Given its history, it's not surprising that Ayacucho means "City of Blood" or "City of the Dead." Yet Ayacucho has much more to offer than its notoriety: Visitors will find it a welcoming and spectacularly serene city seemingly cleansed of its violent legacy. It's so easygoing and unassuming that it's almost inconceivable that it could have been held hostage for so long by terrorists intent on rending Peruvian society.

Still, this graceful colonial town can't escape its tumultuous past, and that's one of the best reasons to pay a visit before it becomes better known. As it looks to distance itself from the guerrilla violence of the 1980s and early 1990s, Ayacucho is keen to attract travelers on a large scale. Nestled into the Andes Mountains it boasts an overflowing collection of colonial churches within blocks of the Plaza Mayor—as well as a spectacular Easter week festival and carnival celebrations.

ESSENTIALS
GETTING THERE
BY PLANE   By far the best way to get to Ayacucho is to fly from Lima on **AeroCondor** (© **01/614-6000**), which flies there four times a week, or **LC Busre** (© **01/619-1300**), which flies daily; the flight is 1 hour and costs about $60. The **Alfredo Mendivil Duarte** airport (© **066/812-418**) is east of downtown on Av. del Ejército 950. Taxis, which charge S/4 to S/5 ($1.15–$1.40) to downtown, await arriving flights.

BY BUS   Executive service buses from Lima via Pisco or Ica take about 9 hours on a very demanding road through the mountains; contact **Ormeño** (© **01/472-5000**) or **Cruz del Sur** (© **01/424-6158**). Executive buses are infinitely preferable to regular service; note that they travel at night only on the direct return to Lima. There is no central bus terminal in Ayacucho; **Cruz del Sur** is located on Av. Mariscal Cáceres 1264 (© **066/812-813**), and **Ormeño** is at Jr. Libertad 257 (© **066/812-495**).

VISITOR INFORMATION
A small **iPerú** tourist counter greets arriving planes at the airport every morning from 6:30 to 8:30am. The **iPerú** office at Portal Municipal 48 (Plaza Mayor; © **066/818-305**) is extremely helpful and is open Monday through Saturday from 8:30am to 7:30pm, and Sunday from 8:30am to 2:30pm.

FAST FACTS   **Banco de Crédito,** (© **056/522-445**) Portal Unión 27 (Plaza Mayor), has a Visa-compatible ATM. You'll also find money-changers hanging around the Plaza Mayor. Several pharmacies line Jr. 28 de Julio, including **Farmacia del Pino,** Jr. 28 de Julio 123 (© **066/812-080**). For emergencies, contact the **National Tourism Police** at Jr. 2 de Mayo 100 (at Jr. Arequipa; © **066/812-055**). The 24-hour **National**

Ayacucho

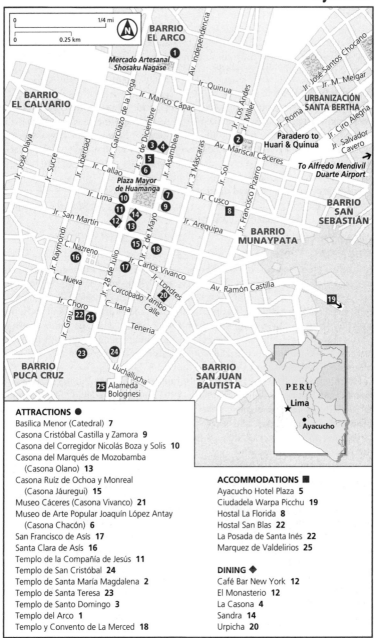

ATTRACTIONS ●
Basílica Menor (Catedral) **7**
Casona Cristóbal Castilla y Zamora **9**
Casona del Corregidor Nicolás Boza y Solis **10**
Casona del Marqués de Mozobamba
  (Casona Olano) **13**
Casona Ruíz de Ochoa y Monreal
  (Casona Jáuregui) **15**
Museo Cáceres (Casona Vivanco) **21**
Museo de Arte Popular Joaquín López Antay
  (Casona Chacón) **6**
San Francisco de Asís **17**
Santa Clara de Asís **16**
Templo de la Compañía de Jesús **11**
Templo de San Cristóbal **24**
Templo de Santa María Magdalena **2**
Templo de Santa Teresa **23**
Templo de Santo Domingo **3**
Templo del Arco **1**
Templo y Convento de La Merced **18**

ACCOMMODATIONS ■
Ayacucho Hotel Plaza **5**
Ciudadela Warpa Picchu **19**
Hostal La Florida **8**
Hostal San Blas **22**
La Posada de Santa Inés **22**
Marquez de Valdelirios **25**

DINING ◆
Café Bar New York **12**
El Monasterio **12**
La Casona **4**
Sandra **14**
Urpicha **20**

Police office is at Jr. 28 de Julio 325 (© 066/812-332). The main hospital is **Hospital Regional de Ayacucho,** Av. Independencia 355 (© 066/312-180). The **post office** at Jr. Asamblea 295 (© 066/812-224) is open Monday through Saturday from 8am to 8pm. For guided tours and transportation in the area, contact **Wari Tours,** Portal Independencia 70 (© 066/811-415).

GETTING AROUND

The best way to get around Ayacucho itself is on foot because most places of interest—hotels, restaurants, the cathedral—are only minutes from the Plaza Mayor. Taxis and mototaxis are readily available and cheap for any trip within the city; taxis charge S/3 to S/4 (about $1), and mototaxis charge S/1 to S/2 (about 30¢–55¢). A taxi to the Barrio de Santa Ana is a good idea, but if you want the driver to wait while you explore the *artesanía* galleries, negotiate a price beforehand.

For transport to Quinua and other outlying attractions, colectivos depart from the *paradero* at the corner of Jr. Salvador Cavero and Jr. Ciro Alegría in the eastern part of Ayacucho (Urbanización Santa Bertha).

WHAT TO SEE & DO
MUSEUMS & COLONIAL HOUSES

Ayacucho's pretty and placid **Plaza Mayor** 🏵🏵 (also called the **Plaza de Armas**), lined by grand 16th- to 18th-century homes with stone arches and colonial red-tile roofs, is the heart of the city. It is one of the best surviving examples of colonial architecture in Peru. Eight walkways radiate out from the center in the form of a star, and you'll probably find yourself crisscrossing the square several times a day. The plaza's lovely gardens and soaring views of the cathedral and surrounding mountains make it a perfect place to occupy an iron bench and watch locals get their pictures made around the Monument to Antonio José de Sucre in the center.

On the south side of the plaza (Portal Municipal 49) is the Basílica Menor, or **La Catedral** 🏵, ordered built by King Philip in 1612 and completed in 1672. Beyond an ornate stone facade and two bell towers are three naves, an elaborately carved pulpit, silver and gold-leaf altars, and a collection of colonial-era religious paintings. The cathedral is open to visitors Monday through Saturday from 5 to 7pm, and Sunday from 9am to 5pm; admission is free.

In a handsome colonial building on the east side of the Plaza Mayor (Portal Unión 28) is the **Museo de Arte Popular Joaquín López Antay** 🏵 (no phone). The museum, which is the best place to get an overview of the highly prized artisanry and crafts that Ayacucho and surrounding villages are so renowned for, occupies several rooms around the central courtyard (the BCP bank inside the courtyard could be one of the best-looking banks you've seen). You'll find an excellent selection of colorful and tactile hand-woven rugs, filigreed silver, and ubiquitous ceramic churches and red-clay figures of musicians. On display are several works of Peru's most famous *retablista* (altar artist), for whom the museum is named. López Antay, who had a number of international exhibits and was awarded the National Culture Prize in 1975, considered himself a sculptor rather than an artisan. Don't miss the second floor, which has some of the finest examples of popular art, many of them valuable antiques. The museum is open Tuesday through Friday from 10:15am to 5:30pm, and Saturday from 9:45am to 12:15pm; admission is free.

The **Museo Cáceres** (also known as Casona Vivanco), Jr. 28 de Julio 508 (© **056/ 620-436**), is a good example of a historic colonial-era casona, or mansion. Inside is a

Ayacucho's Renowned *Retablos*

Ayacucho has a long tradition of finely crafted *artesanía,* and the city and environs are said to produce 40 different specialized crafts. Perhaps most famous and emblematic of Ayacucho are the *retablos,* wooden boxes that open to show off two or three levels of busy scenes populated by dozens of laboriously hand-carved and -painted figures. A tradition brought by Spaniards and first produced in Peru during early colonial times in the 16th century, they were then known as Cajones de San Marcos or San Antonio, and they served as portable altars that devotees of St. Mark or St. Anthony carried with them on their travels through the Andes. The *retablos* were often used in efforts to convert indigenous peoples to Catholicism. Although the scenes depicted were once strictly religious, today they represent quotidian scenes of life in the *sierra,* from weddings to harvest scenes and popular festivals (although nativity scenes remain very popular).

The doors and exterior usually feature brightly painted flowers, and the *retablos* range from miniature versions with tiny figurines to others that are 1.8m (6 ft.) tall and hold 100 or more figures inside. *Retablos* are so identifiable with Ayacucho that there are enormous ones in the airport (more than 3m/10 ft. tall) at the luggage turnstile, and newspaper kiosks around the Plaza Mayor are decorated like oversize *retablos.*

Other handicrafts that are indigenous to the region are red-clay ceramics, including humorous depictions of groups of musicians and small bulls, and model churches; tightly woven and brightly colored *tejidos,* or textiles; carved alabaster, or *piedra de Huamanga;* figures of saints; crucifixes; chess sets; and art naïf *tablas de Sarhua.*

collection of original Escuela Cusqueña art, carved baroque furniture, colonial ceramics, and leather Spanish trunks. The original inhabitant of the house, Mariscal Cáceres, was a hero of Peru's War of the Pacific with Chile. The museum is open daily from 9am to 1pm and from 2 to 6pm; admission is S/2 (60¢).

The Plaza Mayor is lined with other notable colonial houses, which belonged to the most powerful citizens of Ayacucho, including **Casona Cristóbal Castilla y Zamora,** Portal Municipal 50 (© 066/812-230; Mon–Fri 8:15am–3:45pm); and **Casona del Corregidor Nicolás Boza y Solís,** Portal Constitución 15 (© 066/812-229; Mon–Fri 8am–noon and 2–6pm). **Casona del Marqués de Mozobamba** (also known as **Casona Olano**), Jr. 28 de Julio 175, is one of the most distinguished examples of 16th-century colonial architecture in the city. **Casona Ruíz de Ochoa y Monreal** (better known as **Casona Jáuregui**), Jr. 2 de Mayo 210 (© 066/814-299; Mon–Fri 8am–5pm), facing Templo de La Merced, is a handsomely restored, bright yellow 18th-century house with stone arches and blue doors, balconies, and shutters.

COLONIAL CHURCHES

Anyone with an interest in colonial churches will be in heaven in Ayacucho, which overflows with nearly three dozen examples, dating back as far as 1540, in a relatively small downtown area. In fact, Ayacucho is one of the few Peruvian cities that retains a significant colonial architectural core. Most churches can be visited only during Mass hours on Sunday (except where noted below).

North of the Plaza Mayor, and perhaps the most visually striking of the collection, is the finely sculpted **Templo de Santo Domingo** (1548), Jr. 9 de Diciembre at Jr. Bellido. The city's second convent, its unique facade is marked by rustic earth-colored bricks, two towers framing a row of spikes, and three Romanesque arches at the ground level.

The majority of churches are south and west of the Plaza Mayor. Little except for an exterior wall and an original squat bell tower remains of **Templo de San Cristóbal,** Jr. 28 de Julio at Jr. 2 de Mayo, the first church in Ayacucho, constructed in 1540 and one of the oldest churches in South America. Built of brick and adobe, it was quite evidently a simple and rustic design. **Templo de la Compañía de Jesús** (1605), Jr. 28 de Julio between Jr. Lima and Jr. San Martín, founded as a Jesuit school and church, is an imposing baroque brick structure a half block west of the Plaza Mayor. Its massive towers were added in the 18th century. **Templo y Convento de La Merced** (1540), Jr. 2 de Mayo at Jr. San Martín, the second church and first convent in Ayacucho, is well worth a visit. It was begun the year of the Spanish founding of the city.

Templo de Santa Teresa (1703), Jr. 28 de Julio s/n, faces a pretty, serene plaza across from San Cristóbal. You must first enter the convent, to the right of the church, and ask permission to visit the church (it remains a convent of 20 cloistered Carmelite nuns), which is entered around the corner from the plaza. The main altar is a fabulously chunky example of gold-leaf carving. **Santa Clara de Asís** (1568), Jr. Grau at

---

Moments Ayacucho's Celebrated Festivals

Ayacucho plays host to some of the most spectacular popular festivals in Peru. The weeklong Easter celebration, **Semana Santa** *АӐА*, features nightly candlelit processions and daily fairs. It culminates in a stunning and emotional procession on Easter Sunday that makes its way around the Plaza Mayor. The procession is marked by the annual appearance of a massive (15 by 8m/49 by 26 ft. high) throne made entirely of white wax and carried by 200 people. Note that all hotels and *hostales* in Ayacucho are booked months in advance for Easter week, although you might find additional lodging offered in private homes.

Carnaval Ayacuchano is an authentic Quechua carnival celebration, one of the most colorful in the country. For 3 days in February or March, dancing and festivities take over the streets of Ayacucho, including the official proclamation of the *Ño Carnavalon,* or giant papier-mâché figure of the Rey Momo. The celebration also includes the unveiling of political songs, elaborate masks, and the Festival del Puchero, a typical Carnaval Ayacuchano dish served on Tuesday of Holy Week. In rural areas, carnival celebrations are starkly traditional, marked by manifestations such as ancient fertility rites.

The **Bajada de los Reyes Magos (the arrival of the Three Kings)** on January 6 and **La Virgen de la Candelaria** on February 2 are two other notable festivals, though they're not nearly as popular as Carnaval and Semana Santa. For more information on festivals in Ayacucho, contact **iPerú** (© 066/818-305; www. promperu.gob.pe) or visit the city calendar at www.ayacuchoperu.com/turismo/calendario.php.

Nazareno, the first monastery in Ayacucho and the second in Peru, has the largest tower in the city. Inside are good examples of *mudéjar* (Moorish-style) woodcarving and an interesting sculpture of the Immaculate Conception on the main altar.

Other colonial churches of interest to completists are **San Francisco de Asís** (1552), Jr. 28 de Julio at Jr. Vivanco, the only church besides the cathedral to have three naves; the baroque **Templo de Santa María Magdalena** (1588), Jr. Sol at Avenida Mariscal Cáceres, founded by the Dominican order but a three-time victim of fire; and the small and sweet snow-white **Templo del Arco** (1822), Plazoleta María Parado de Bellido, near the Mercado Artesanal in the El Arco district (north of the Plaza Mayor). In any direction you walk, however, there are lasting examples of religious architecture marking Ayacucho's colonial importance.

WHERE TO STAY

Given its years in the hinterlands of the tourism circuit, it's not surprising that Ayacucho isn't exactly overflowing with good hotel choices. Still, there's a large, if uninspiring, hotel that caters mostly to business travelers and a small selection of easygoing, family-run *hostales*. In addition to the accommodations listed below, options include **Hostal San Blas,** Jr. Chorro 161 (© **066/814-185;** hostalsanblas@hotmail.com; S/20 or $5.70 double), and **La Posada de Santa Inés,** Jr. Chorro 139 (© **066/814-185;** posada_staines@hotmail.com; S/15 or $4.30 double), both for budget backpackers only. A more interesting option, if you don't mind staying outside of town, is **Ciudadela Warpa Picchu,** Km 5 Carretera a Cusco (© **066/819-462;** $50 double), a Belgian-owned, modern country-style hotel with a full gym, a restaurant, an outdoor pool, and some spa services.

MODERATE

Ayacucho Hotel Plaza   A deceptively splendid facade hides a rather disappointingly plain hotel that is far more functional than luxurious. As the largest hotel in town, and one that offers a full complement of services and amenities—and a location only 2 blocks from the Plaza Mayor—the Ayacucho Hotel Plaza is the choice of business travelers to Ayacucho. Besides the exterior, about all that can be said for the hotel is that it's built around a central courtyard and that the rooms have high ceilings. Rooms are plain, if not dumpy, and not as good as a couple of *hostales* that charge one-third the price. It's a shame because, with an upgrade that lent as much care to the rooms and service as to the attention-getting outside, it could be a nice place to stay. But I wouldn't hold my breath waiting for that development.

Jr. 9 de Diciembre 184 (at Jr. Lima), Ayacucho. © **066/812-202.** Fax 01/460-652779 in Lima. hplaza@derramajae.org.pe. 80 units. $51 double; $76 suite. Rates include taxes. AE, DISC, MC, V. **Amenities:** Restaurant; bar. *In room:* A/C, TV.

INEXPENSIVE

Hostal La Florida *Value*   A relaxed and friendly, family-run small *hostal* just 3 blocks from the main square, this is one of the better spots in town. It's secure, quiet, and clean, and rooms on the top floor across the small, leafy courtyard have excellent views of the surrounding rooftops and mountains. En-suite bathrooms are small but very clean, and—a rarity at this price—rooms have cable TV. There's a cute little cafe next door, a good spot for breakfast and other informal meals.

Jr. Cusco 310, Ayacucho. © **066/812-565.** 12 units. S/50 ($14) double. Rate includes taxes. No credit cards. **Amenities:** Cafe. *In room:* TV.

Marquez de Valdelirios 🌟 *(finds)* My top choice in Ayacucho isn't luxurious, but this *hostal,* housed in a handsome colonial house, is a real find. On the outside, it looks almost high design, with artfully placed blue flowerpots against the stark white stucco walls and deep wood exterior. On a very peaceful, well-manicured boulevard just a few blocks north of the busy downtown (a 10-min. walk from the Plaza Mayor), it feels like a retreat. Rooms, which are all on the interior, are comfortably outfitted, if not overly large. They might not live up to the promise of the exterior, but for the bargain price, they're more than comfortable. Breakfast is served on the sunny terrace.

Alameda Bolognesi 720–724, Ayacucho. ℂ **066/818-944** or 066/814-014. 14 units. S/60 ($17) double. Rate includes taxes and breakfast. No credit cards. **Amenities:** Bar. *In room:* TV.

WHERE TO DINE

Down-to-earth Ayacucho is a great place to sample traditional Quechua specialties. It's also known for its artisanal wheat bread. In addition to the restaurants below, a great spot for breakfast or a simple lunch is **Sandra,** Jr. 28 de Julio 183 (no phone), a cute little cafe and *juguería* (juice bar). It serves a huge cafe con leche, massive *jarras* of fresh juices, and tamales, salads, and sandwiches on herb-crusted pita bread. Within the courtyard of the Centro Cultural, Jr. 28 de Julio 178, there are a couple of good cafes for light meals, snacks, coffee, dessert, and breakfast; check out **Café Bar New York** (ℂ **066/813-079**), which has seats outdoors overlooking the patio.

INEXPENSIVE

El Monasterio *(Value)* PERUVIAN Occupying a corner of the Centro Cultural courtyard, with outdoor tables, this restaurant is essentially a *pollería*—a simple restaurant serving roasted chicken—in a slightly upscale location. There are other things on the menu, but I never once saw anyone order anything but the chicken. And with good reason: It's flavorful and plentiful, and it's a steal. For just a couple of bucks, you can get a quarter of a roasted chicken, french fries, and salad. The other items on the menu are the usual Andean suspects: *lomo saltado* and pastas.

Jr. 28 de Julio 178 (in Centro Cultural). ℂ **066/813-905.** Reservations not accepted. Main courses S/5–S/14 ($1.40–$4). No credit cards. Daily 11am–11pm.

La Casona 🌟 PERUVIAN Though brightly lit, this comfortable restaurant, as popular with locals as it is with visitors to Ayacucho, is a nice spot to sample a varied and good-value menu of Andean *criollo* cooking. Built around a pleasant, plant-filled courtyard, the restaurant features grilled meats, roast chicken, trout, and a host of *platos tradicionales,* or regional specialties, such as *chancho al horno con qapchi* (oven-baked pork). A nice appetizer is the huge avocado stuffed with chicken—a meal in itself. Most dishes come with either golden potatoes or salad.

Jr. Bellido 463. ℂ **066/812-733.** Reservations recommended on weekends. Main courses S/8–S/20 ($2.30–$5.70). AE, MC, V. Daily 7am–10pm.

Urpicha 🌟 *(finds)* PERUVIAN Tucked down a small alley off Jr. Londres, the winding street populated by dozens of hair salons, this laid-back restaurant inhabits the gorgeous interior of a colonial house decorated with Peruvian popular art and overlooking an abundant and sunny garden of cacti, ivy, and flowering plants. On a lazy afternoon, it's the perfect spot to linger on the lovely covered terrace and enjoy local *criollo sierra* specialties such as *adobo asado* (juicy roast pork), fried trout, and *ají de gallina.* More unusual dishes, such as *puca picante con chicharrón* (potatoes in red sauce with peanuts, rice, and pork), are available for the more adventurous diner. A good sampler plate mixes a half-dozen Andean specialties. The chilled pitchers of blue-corn *chicha morada* are the perfect accompaniment.

Jr. Londres 272. ⓒ **066/813-905.** Reservations recommended on weekends. Main courses S/7–S/20 ($2–$5.70). No credit cards. Daily 11am–4pm and 7–10pm.

SHOPPING

The best spot in town to shop for the famous *retablos,* ceramic churches, and other typical *artesanía* of the Ayacucho region is the **Mercado Artesanal Shosaku Nagase,** Plazoleta María Parado de Bellido (5 blocks north of the Plaza Mayor). At this sprawling facility, the government operates training programs for those wanting to work in the production of handicrafts, and there are two buildings full of stalls selling local works. Its selection is good, though perhaps similar to what you might find in Lima.

   Barrio Santa Ana 𝒢, some 10 blocks southwest of the Plaza Mayor, is the heart of Quechua culture and *artesanía.* Around the main square, Plazuela de Santa Ana, are several family-run galleries. At several, you can watch textiles and rugs being created. Some rugs are highly valued and have been exhibited internationally. Visit Alejandro Gallardo's **Galería Latina,** Plazuela de Santa Ana 105 (ⓒ 066/528-315); **Alfonso Sulca Chávez,** Plazuela de Santa Ana 83 (ⓒ 066/812-990); and **Galería Arte Popular de Fortunato Fernández,** Plazuela de Santa Ana 63–64 (ⓒ 066/813-192). **Galería Wari,** Mariscal Cáceres 302 (ⓒ 066/812-529), is the studio and home of Gregorio Sulca, a highly celebrated textile and plastic artist who has exhibited his sophisticated rugs, paintings, and other pieces based on deep research into the Quechua culture in Germany and the U.S. If he's around and you speak Spanish, it's worth engaging him in conversation for an explanation of some fundamental Quechua philosophy and the historical and theoretical underpinnings of his (very expensive) work.

   The finest handicrafts shopping, however, is found at the source of most of the typical regional *artesanía.* The tiny pueblo Quinua is where most of the ceramic churches and *retablos* are made by local artisans, and it is a fascinating Quechua village. Prices are cheaper than in Ayacucho and much cheaper than in Lima or Cusco; the selection also is much better. See "A Trip to Quinua, Handicrafts Capital of Peru," below.

A TRIP TO QUINUA, HANDICRAFTS CAPITAL OF PERU 𝒢𝒢

Although Ayacucho is well known throughout the country as the popular arts capital of Peru, most of the famous *artesanía* originate from Quinua, a lovely and gentle sierra town located 37km (23 miles) northeast of Ayacucho. If you'd prefer to buy at the source, preferably from the artisan who crafted the work rather than from a mere salesperson, Quinua is tops in Peru. The red-tile roof of nearly every house in town is topped with a ceramic church of the kind foreigners are more likely to buy and display on a table or bookshelf. The churches serve as roofbound protectors against evil spirits.

   A beautiful stone passageway leads up to the main cobblestone plaza, populated by whitewashed buildings and the village church. Even though local artisans export their ceramic churches and figures of musicians around the world, Quinua is still the kind of place where little girls whisper and point at visiting gringos.

   Local Quechua artisans have become very adept at commercializing and marketing their artisanry. Traditionally, all the ceramic pieces were unpainted or in earth tones. Increasingly, artisans have introduced pastels and bright colors, and the two traditional church towers have gradually begun to bend outward fancifully. But classic pieces are still produced. A few of the best-known local ceramists, including Mamerto

Sánchez, have now moved their studios to more profitable environs such as Lima, cutting out the middle man. There are touristy stalls near the main road and a couple of shops, but for the best shopping, you'll need to venture up the stairs to the heart of the village. The peaceful back streets behind the Plazuela de Armas, especially Jirón Sucre and Jirón San Martín, are where to find the best popular art galleries, and its not unusual to find pottery firing and hand painting taking place.

Galería Familia Sánchez, Jr. San Martín 151 (© **066/810-212**), is the studio and gallery of Mamerto Sánchez's son. Walter follows in his father's footsteps, and his studio produces some of the best ceramic pieces and churches in Quinua. Across the street is **Galería Ayllu,** which also has a little outdoor bar. A number of galleries, including **Artesanía Anclla** and **Artesanía El Quinuino,** are clustered on Jirón San Martín. A medium-size church costs between S/20 and S/40 ($5.70–$11). Antique *retablos* and churches are difficult to find; your best bet is with antiques dealers in Lima or Cusco.

A few restaurants and *hostales* can accommodate you if you want to linger or spend the night in peaceful Quinua. You won't have much to do besides visit *artesanía* galleries, but you'd be hard-pressed to find a simpler, prettier, and more authentic *sierra* town. The small **Hostal Las Américas,** Jr. San Martín s/n, above Artesanía Anclla (© **066/965-7721;** S/20 or $5.70 double), has comfortable rooms in the house of one of the best-known local artisans.

To get to Quinua, take a colectivo at the corner of Jirón Salvador Cavero and Jr. Ciro Alegría in the east part of Ayacucho (Urbanización Santa Bertha). The trip (S/3 or 85¢) takes about an hour, and vans return hourly.

On the way to Quinua, 22km (14 miles) north of Ayacucho, is the **Huari** (also spelled **Wari**) **archaeological complex** ⭐, one of the oldest urban walled centers in the Americas, dating to around A.D. 600. The Huari culture, perhaps the first centrally governed "nation" in the Andes, was one of the most important in early Peru; its empire stretched north to Cajamarca and south to Cusco. The ruins, though badly deteriorated, are of thick, 10m-high (33-ft.) stone walls, houses, tunnels, and flat ceremonial areas, which are well worth a visit for anyone with an interest in pre-Incan archaeology. Archaeologists have theorized that Huari urban planning and their system of religious, political, and military organization served as a model for the Incas. The city, which contained three levels of underground burial chambers, once had as many as 50,000 inhabitants; it was abandoned around A.D. 800. On-site are a visitor center and small museum (Museo de Sitio Wari) exhibiting photographs, dioramas, and artifacts discovered at the complex. The ruins are open Tuesday through Sunday from 10am to 5pm; admission is S/3 (85¢).

Cusco

The storied capital of the Incan Empire and gateway to the imperial city of Machu Picchu, **Cusco** (also spelled Cuzco) ★★★ is one of the undisputed highlights of South America. Stately and historic, with stone streets and building foundations laid by the Incas more than 5 centuries ago, the town is much more than a mere history lesson; it is also surprisingly dynamic, enlivened by throngs of travelers who have transformed the historic center around the Plaza de Armas into a mecca of sorts for South American adventurers. Yet for all its popularity, Cusco is one of those rare places—perhaps like Bali, Katmandu, or Prague—that seems able to preserve its unique character and enduring appeal despite its prominence on the international tourism radar.

Cusco looks and feels like the very definition of an Andean capital. It's a fascinating blend of pre-Columbian and colonial history and contemporary mestizo culture. The Incas made *Q'osqo* (meaning "navel of the world" in Quechua) the political, military, and cultural center of their empire, which stretched up and down the Andes, from Ecuador through Bolivia and all the way to Chile. Cusco was the empire's holy city, and it was also the epicenter of the legendary Incan network of roads connecting all points in the empire.

The Spanish conquistadors understood that it was essential to topple the capital city to take control of the region, a feat they ultimately accomplished after an epic battle at Sacsayhuamán. The Spaniards razed most Incan buildings and monuments, but, in many cases, they found the structures so well engineered that they built upon the very foundations of Incan Cusco. Many perfectly constructed Incan stone walls, examples of unrivaled stonemasonry, still stand. After a devastating earthquake in 1650, Cusco became a largely baroque city.

The result is a city that showcases plainly evident layers of history. Cusco's highlights include both Incan ruins—such as Sacsayhuamán, a seemingly impregnable fortress on a hill overlooking the city, and Qoricancha, the Temple of the Sun—and colonial-era baroque and Renaissance churches and mansions. The heart of the historic center has suffered relatively few modern intrusions, and despite the staggering number of souvenir shops, travel agencies, hotels, and restaurants overflowing with visitors, it doesn't take an impossibly fertile imagination to conjure the magnificent capital of the 16th century.

Today Cusco thrives as one of the most vibrant expressions of Amerindian and mestizo culture anywhere in the Americas. Every June, the city is packed during Inti Raymi, the celebration of the winter solstice and the sun god, a deeply religious festival that is also a magical display of pre-Columbian music and dance. Thousands trek out to Paucartambo for the riveting Virgen del Carmen festival in mid-July. Other traditional arts also flourish. Cusco is the handicrafts center of Peru, and its streets and markets teem with merchants and their extraordinary textiles, many hand-woven using the exact techniques of their ancestors.

Cusco

Spectacularly cradled by the bold southeastern Andes Mountains that were so fundamental to the Incan belief system, Cusco sits at a daunting altitude of 3,400m (11,000 ft.). The air is noticeably thinner here than in almost any city in South America, and the city, best explored on foot, demands arduous hiking up precipitous stone steps, leaving even the fittest of travelers gasping for breath and saddled with headaches and nausea. It usually takes a couple of days to get acclimatized before moving on from Cusco to explore the mountain villages of the Urubamba Valley (also known as the Sacred Valley), the Amazon basin, and, of course, Machu Picchu, but many visitors find Cusco so seductive that they either delay their plans to explore the surrounding region or add a few days to their trip to allow more time in the city. Increasingly, travelers are basing themselves in one of the lower-altitude villages of the Sacred Valley, but there is so much to see and do in Cusco that an overnight stay is pretty much required of anyone who hasn't previously spent time in the area.

Cusco's beautiful natural setting, colorful festivals, sheer number of sights—unparalleled in Peru—and facilities and services organized for travelers make it the top destination in Peru and one of the most exciting places in South America. It is loaded with good and, in many cases, embarrassingly cheap restaurants, *hostales* (inns), and lively bars that cater to enthusiastic crowds of young and old gringos outfitted with the latest in fleece wear, backpacks, and hiking boots. For the burgeoning crowd that comes to Peru to do justice to all that high-tech adventure gear, superb trekking, river-rafting, and mountain-biking opportunities abound throughout the Sacred Valley. Yet for some it's a challenge to leave Cusco; its charms become quickly addictive, and many travelers linger in the old Incan capital, even forsaking other travel plans in Peru.

As well as Cusco seems to handle the burden of its popularity—which seems to increase steadily year by year—for some travelers, the incessant hawking of postcards, cigarettes, restaurants and travel agencies, and hordes of gringos who look just like they do can be a bit overwhelming. Those looking for a more peaceful introduction to the Andes might choose to spend more time in the Sacred Valley (see chapter 8). As much as I love Cusco, every time I visit, I find the city just a little bit more overwhelmed by its tourist industry. Although resilient Cusco is not yet Marrakech in terms of hassles and sensory overload, it might be headed there.

The positive side of the equation, of course, is the vital role that tourism plays in propping up the local economy. Cusco is one of the only provinces in Peru that is not mired in economic crisis. Cusqueños are understandably pleased to receive international visitors and are remarkably forgiving of their excesses, but many locals quietly voice concerns about being pushed out of the city while they watch every last colonial house give way to yet another hotel, cafe, or discothèque.

1 Orientation

ARRIVING

BY PLANE

Most visitors arrive by plane from Lima (a 1-hr. trip). In high season, flights arrive by the dozens from Lima as well as Arequipa, Puerto Maldonado, and La Paz, Bolivia, at **Aeropuerto Internacional Velasco Astete** (© 084/222-611), located 5km (3 miles) southeast of the historic center of Cusco. All major Peruvian airlines fly into Cusco, including **AeroCondor** (© 01/514-6000; www.aerocondor.com.pe), **LanPeru** (© 01/213-8200; www.lan.com), **Taca Peru** (© 01/511-8222; www.taca.com), **Aviandina** (© 01/447-8080; www.aerolineasperuanas.com/aviandina.htm), and **TANS Perú** (© 01/611-5555; www.tansperu.com.pe). A number of tour operators have booths in the arrivals terminal, and there is also a tourist information booth, an ATM, and a currency exchange.

Transportation from the airport to downtown Cusco, about 20 minutes away, is by taxi or private hotel car. (A less convenient *combi,* or small bus, passes outside the airport car park and goes to Plaza San Francisco; unless you have almost no baggage and your hotel is right on that square, it's not worth the few soles you'll save to take a combi.) Most hotels, even less expensive *hostales,* are happy to arrange airport pickup. If you take a taxi, note that the fare is likely to drop precipitously if you merely refuse the first offer you get (likely to be S/15–S/20 or $4.30–$5.70). Taxi fare to Cusco is officially S/10 ($2.85) from the airport to the center, although you can often get one for as little as S/5 ($1.40).

When you exit with your luggage, you will be besieged with offers from taxi and tour-company representatives, many of whom will pretend to have your name on their "arrivals list," just to take you into town and try to score a commission from one of hundreds of tour operators. If you have arranged for your hotel to pick you up, be certain that you are dealing with someone authorized by the hotel and who possesses your exact arrival information.

Tips **Making the Connection to Cusco**

Flights to Cusco are massively popular, so make your reservations as early as possible if you are arriving from another Peruvian city. Flights are occasionally delayed by poor weather, and sometimes from Lima it is necessary to go through Arequipa if direct flights to Cusco are sold out. Although it is now possible to arrive from North America on an overnight flight that theoretically will put you into Lima in time for an early morning flight to Cusco, the window is often quite tight, and a fair number of travelers miss their connecting flights. Also, be sure that your travel agent or airline hasn't inadvertently booked you on a charter, rather than regular, flight to Cusco.

The airport departure tax is S/14.52 ($4.15) for domestic flights and S/40.38 ($11.54) for international flights.

BY BUS

Buses to Cusco arrive from Lima, Arequipa, Puno/Juliaca, and Puerto Maldonado in the Amazon basin. The journey from Lima to Cusco takes 26 hours by land; from Puno, 9 to 10 hours; and from Arequipa, 12 hours. There is no single, central bus terminal in Cusco. Buses arrive either at a terminal on Avenida Pachacútec or (more commonly) at the newer **Terminal Terrestre,** Av. Vellejos Santoni, cdra. 2, Santiago (© 084/224-471), (several kilometers from the city center on the way to the airport). Buses to and from the Sacred Valley (Urubamba buses, which go through either Pisac or Chinchero) use small, makeshift terminals on Calle Puputi s/n, cdra. 2 and Av, Grau s/n, cdra. 1. For service from Lima, contact the major companies, including **Ormeño** (© 01/426-7595), **Cruz del Sur** (© 01/424-1005), **Oltursa** (© 01/475-5679), and **Civa** (© 01/332-5236). From Puno, the following offer daily service to Cusco: **First Class** (© 051/365-192), **Cruz del Sur** (© 051/622-626), and **Inka Express** (© 051/365-654; www.inka express.com). From Arequipa, your best bests are **Civa** (© 054/426-563) and **Cruz del Sur** (© 054/221-909).

BY TRAIN

Cusco has two main PeruRail train stations. Trains from Puno and Arequipa arrive at **Estación de Huanchaq** (also spelled Wanchaq), Av. Pachacútec s/n (© 084/238-722 or 084/221-992; www.perurail.com), at the southeast end of Avenida El Sol. Trains from Ollantaytambo, Machu Picchu, and the Amazon jungle arrive at **Estación de San Pedro,** Calle Cascaparo s/n (© 084/221-352 or 084/221-313), southwest of the Plaza de Armas. Thieves operate in and around both stations, but visitors should be particularly cautious at San Pedro station, which is near the crowded Mercado Central.

VISITOR INFORMATION

As the top tourist destination in Peru, Cusco is well equipped with information outlets. There's a branch of the **Oficina de Información Turística** (© 084/380-145) at the Velasco Astete Airport in the arrivals terminal; it's open daily from 6:30am to 12:30pm. The principal **Oficina de Información Turística** is located on Mantas 117-A, a block from the Plaza de Armas (© 084/222-032). It's open Monday through Saturday from 7am to 7pm and Sunday from 7am to noon. It's very helpful and efficient, and it sells the essential *boleto turístico* (tourist ticket; see "Cusco's *Boleto Turístico"* on

p. 212). However, the new **iPerú office,** Av. El Sol, 103, of. 102 (© **084/234-498**) has been better stocked with information and been more helpful on recent visits; it's open daily from 8:30am to 7:30pm. Another information office is located in the **Terminal Terrestre de Huanchaq** train station, Av. Pachacútec s/n (© **084/238-722**); it's open Monday through Saturday from 8am to 6:30pm.

South American Explorers has an office and club in Cusco at Choquechaca 188, no. 4 (© **084/245-484;** www.samexplo.org). The office stores luggage, maintains lists of trail reports for members, and has a library of useful information for trekking and mountaineering. If you're traveling extensively, and independently, through Peru, it's worth becoming a member of this helpful group.

CITY LAYOUT

The Incas designed their capital in the shape of a puma, with the head at the north end, at Sacsayhuamán (whose zigzagged walls are said to have represented the animal's teeth). This is pretty difficult to appreciate today; even though much of the original layout of the city remains, it has been engulfed by growth. Still, most of Cusco can be seen easily on foot, certainly the best way to take in this historic mountain city that is equal parts Incan capital, post-Conquest colonial city, and modern tourist magnet.

The old center of the city is organized around the stunning and busy Plaza de Armas, the focal point of life in Cusco. The streets that radiate out from the square— Plateros, Mantas, Loreto, Triunfo, Procuradores, and others—are loaded with travel agencies, shops, restaurants, bars, and hotels. The major avenue leading from the plaza southeast to the modern section of the city is Avenida El Sol, where most banks are located. The district of San Blas is perhaps Cusco's most picturesque barrio; the labyrinthlike neighborhood spills on cobblestone streets off Cuesta San Blas, which leads to crooked alleys and streets and viewing points high above the city.

Much of what interests most visitors is within easy walking distance of the Plaza de Armas. The major Incan ruins are within walking distance for energetic sorts who enjoy a good uphill hike.

Tips Altitude Acclimatization

You'll need to take it easy for the first few hours or even couple of days in Cusco—which sits at an altitude of just over 11,000 feet—to adjust to the elevation. Pounding headaches and shortness of breath are the most common ailments, though some travelers are afflicted with nausea. Drink lots of water, avoid heavy meals, and do as the locals do: Drink *mate de coca,* or coca-leaf tea. (Don't worry, you won't get high or arrested, but you will adjust a little more smoothly to the thin air.) If that doesn't cure you, ask whether your hotel has an oxygen tank you can use for a few moments of assisted breathing. If you're really suffering, look for an over-the-counter medication in the pharmacy called "Sorojchi Pills." And if that doesn't do the trick, it may be time to seek medical assistance; see "Fast Facts," below. Those who think they may have an especially hard time with the altitude might consider staying the first couple of nights in the slightly lower Sacred Valley (near Urubamba, Yanahuara, or Ollantaytambo); see chapter 8.

Tips **Cusco = Cuzco = Q'osqo**

Spanish and English spellings derived from the Quechua language are a little haphazard in Cusco, especially because there has been a linguistic movement to try to recuperate and value indigenous culture. Thus, you might see Inca written as Inka; Cusco as Cuzco, Qosqo, or Q'osqo; Qoricancha as Coricancha or Koricancha; Huanchaq as Huanchac or Wanchac; Sacsayhuamán as Sacsaywaman; and Q'enko as Qenko, Kenko, or Qenqo. You're likely to stumble across others, with similar alphabetical prestidigitation, all used interchangeably.

---

2 Getting Around

Getting around Cusco is straightforward and relatively simple, especially because so many of the city sights are in walking distance of the Plaza de Armas in the historic center. You will mostly depend on leg power and omnipresent, inexpensive taxis to make your way around town.

BY FOOT

Most of Cusco is best navigated by foot, although because of the city's 11,000-foot elevation and steep climbs, walking is demanding. Allow extra time to get around, and carry a bottle of water. You can walk to the major ruins just beyond the city—Sacsayhuamán and Q'enko—but you should be rather fit to do so. It's also best to undertake those walks in a small group and not alone.

BY TAXI

Unlike in Lima, taxis are regulated in Cusco and charge standard rates (although they do not have meters). Taxis are inexpensive (S/2–S/3 or 60–85¢ for any trip within the historic core during the day, S/3–S/5 or 85¢–$1.40 at night) and are a good way to get around, especially at night. Hailing a cab in Cusco is considerably less daunting than in Lima, but you still should call a registered taxi when traveling from your hotel to train or bus stations or the airport, and when returning to your hotel late at night (there have been reports of muggings and even rapes tied to rogue taxis). Licensed taxi companies include **Okarina** (② 084/247-080) and **Aló Cusco** (② 084/222-222). Taxis can be hired for return trips to nearby ruins or for half or full days. To the airport, taxis charge S/10 ($2.85) from the city center; to the distant Terminal Terrestre (bus station), they charge S/7 ($2).

BY TRANVIA

A *tranvía* is a vehicle designed to look like the old mule-pulled streetcars that once traversed Cusco; they cart visitors around the city on sightseeing tours for a modest sum. Catch the **Tranvía de Cusco** on the Plaza de Armas, departing at 10 and 11:30am and 2pm, 3:30, and 5pm. Tours last 85 minutes and cost S/7 ($2) for adults and S/5 ($1.40) for students. For more information, call ② **084/962-732.**

BY BUS

Most buses—called variously *colectivos, micros,* and combis—cost S/1.5 (40¢), slightly more after midnight, on Sunday, and on holidays. You aren't likely to need buses often, or ever, within the city, though the colectivos that run up and down Avenida El Sol are also a useful option for some hotels, travel agencies, and shopping markets (taxis are much easier and not much more expensive). A bus departs from Plaza San Francisco to the airport, but it isn't very convenient. Buses and combis are most frequently used to travel from Cusco to towns in the Sacred Valley, such as Pisac, Calca, and Urubamba. Those buses depart from small terminals on Calle Puputi s/n cdra. 2 (via Pisac) and Av. Grau s/n cdra. 1 (via Chinchero).

BY TRAIN
The most popular means to visit Machu Picchu and the Sacred Valley sights is by train. Trains to Ollantaytambo and Machu Picchu Pueblo (also called Aguas Calientes) leave from **Estación de San Pedro,** Calle Cascaparo s/n (✆ **084/221-352** or 084/221-313), southwest of the Plaza de Armas. Reservations for these trains, especially in high season (May–Sept), should be made at least a day in advance. Make reservations online at www.perurail.com or by calling PeruRail at **Estación Huanchaq,** Av. Pachacútec s/n (✆ **084/238-722**).

BY CAR
Renting a car in the Cusco region—more than likely to visit the beautiful Sacred Valley mountain villages—is a more practical idea than in most parts of Peru. Rental agencies include **Avis,** Av. El Sol 808 (✆ **084/248-800**), and **Localiza,** Av. Industrial J-3, Urbanización Huancaro (✆ **084/233-131**). Rates range from S/140 ($40) per day for a standard four-door to S/227.50 ($65) per day for a Jeep Cherokee four-wheel-drive. Check also with **4x4 Cusco,** Urb. San Borja, Huanchaq (✆ **084/227-730;** www.4x4 cusco.com), which has pickups and even Toyota Land Cruisers.

For information on driving around the Cusco department, and in case of emergencies, contact the **Touring Automóvil Club del Perú,** Av. El Sol 349, second floor (✆ **084/224-561**). The office is open Monday through Friday from 9am to 1pm and 3:30 to 7:30pm, and Saturday from 9am to 1pm.

Tips A Safety Note
Over the years, Cusco, which on the surface seems to be an easygoing, if increasingly congested, Andean city, has earned a reputation for being somewhat unsafe for foreign visitors, especially at night, when violent muggings (some using the "chokehold" method) have been known to occur on empty streets. There have also been reports of rapes, attempted rapes, and other sexual assaults in the past couple of years. While I have never had a problem in the city in more than 20 years, it's advisable to take some precautions and remain vigilant at all times. Do not walk alone late at night (young women should travel in groups larger than two); have restaurants and bars call registered taxis to transfer you to your hotel. Be wary of unlicensed, rogue taxis in the city and surrounding environs. Young people staying in inexpensive hostels should be particularly cautious of hotel visitors and belongings. Robberies and attacks have occurred at the ruins at Sacsayhuamán on the outskirts of the city and even along the Inca Trail. Please refer to "Safety" in "Fast Facts: Cusco" for more details.

FAST FACTS: Cusco

Airport See "Arriving" in "Orientation," earlier in this chapter.

Banks/Currency Exchange Most Peruvian and international banks with currency-exchange bureaus and ATMs are located along Avenida El Sol. Moneychangers, usually wearing colored smocks, patrol the main streets off the Plaza de Armas and Avenida El Sol. Banks include **Banco Santander Central Hispano,** Av. El Sol 459; **Banco de Crédito,** Av. El Sol 189; and **Banco Continental,** Av. El Sol 366. The external ATMs nearest the Plaza de Armas are at **Banco de Crédito,** Av. El Sol 189; **Banco del Sur,** Av. El Sol 457; and **Banco Latino,** Av. El Sol 395. There are also a couple located at the entrances to stores and restaurants on the Plaza de Armas and at the Huanchaq train station. Several small *casas de cambio,* with similar rates to banks, operate out of travel agencies and shops on Plaza de Armas and Avenida El Sol.

Car Rentals See "Getting Around," above.

Consulates U.S., in the Binational Center (Instituto Cultural Peruana Norte Americano; ICPNA), Av. Tullumayo 125 (© **084/245-102,** or cell, **084/962-1369;** consagentcuzco@terra.com.pe); U.K., at Manu Expeditions, Urbanización Magisterial, G-5 Segunda Etap (© **084/239-974;** bwalker@terra.com.pe). Both are open daily from 9am to noon and 3 to 5pm.

Dentists/Doctors In an emergency, contact the **Tourist Medical Assistance (TMA),** Heladeros 157 (© **084/260-101**). It offers 24-hour emergency medical services, health information, and legal assistance.

Drugstores For locations, consult a phone book Yellow Pages under "Farmacias" and "Boticas."

Emergency For general emergencies and the **police,** call © 105. For the **tourist police,** call © 084/249-654. To report a **fire,** call © 103. In a medical emergency, go to **Hospital EsSalud,** Av. Anselmo Alvarez s/n (© 084/223-030), or contact **Tourist Medical Assistance** (© 084/260-101).

Hospitals English-speaking medical personnel are available at the following hospitals and clinics: **Hospital EsSalud,** Av. Anselmo Alvarez s/n (© 084/237-341); **Clínica Pardo,** Av. de la Cultura 710 (© 084/624-186); **Hospital Antonio Loren,** Plazoleta Belén s/n (© 084/226-511); **Hospital Regional,** Av. de la Cultura s/n (© 084/223-691); and **Clínica Paredes,** Lechugal 405 (© 084/225-265).

For **yellow-fever** vaccinations, try Hospital Antonio Loren on Tuesday or Hospital Regional on Saturday from 9am to 1pm.

Internet Access Internet *cabinas* are everywhere in the old section of Cusco, and many permit cheap oversees Internet-based (Web2Phone) calls for as little as S/1 (30¢) per minute. Rates are generally S/1.50 (40¢) per hour. Most keep very late hours, opening at 9am and staying open until 11pm or midnight. A few of the many cabinas around town include **Explora,** Arequipa 251; **Speed X,** Procuradores 50 and Tecsecocha 400; **@Internet,** Portal de Panes 123; and **Cyber-Planet,** Almagro 200. Several nightspots, including **Ukuku's** and **Mama Africa** (see "Cusco After Dark," later in this chapter) also have computers and Internet access, which is convenient if you got an e-mail address rather than a phone number from a cute guy or girl at the bar.

Language Schools For intensive Spanish courses, try **Escuela Amauta,** Suecia 480 (© 084/241-422; www.amautaspanish.com), or **Academia Latinoamericana de Español,** Av. El Sol 580 (© 084/243-364). Both schools are very popular with short- and long-term visitors to Cusco.

Laundry Three to try: **Lavandería Louis,** Choquechaca 264 (© 084/243-485); **Easy Wash,** Ruinas 457 (© 084/238-124); and **Totem Wash,** Saphy 726 (© 084/145-367).

Maps The main tourist information office gives out free maps, and, for most visitors, these should be sufficient. (Cusco is easy to manage and a joy to wander around and even get lost in.) More detailed maps, and maps of the Inca Trail and other hiking trails in the Cusco region, are available at bookstores.

Massage There are several spots in town, but one of the best massages I've had in Peru was at **Cusco Massage Center,** Portal de Carnes 260, 3rd floor (© 084/963-2592), where a 1-hour full-body massage will set you back S/87.5 ($25).

Police The **Policía Nacional de Turismo (National Tourism Police)** has an English-speaking staff that is specifically trained to handle the needs of foreign visitors. The office is at Saphy 510 (© 084/249-654). You can also contact **iPerú/INDECOPI** (Servicio de Protección al Turista, or Tourist Protection Bureau), Portal Carrizos 250, Plaza de Armas (© 084/252-974); the staff is available daily from 8am to 8pm.

Post Office/Mail Cusco's main post office, Av. El Sol 800 (© 084/224-212), is open Monday through Saturday from 7:30am to 7:30pm and Sunday from 7:30am to 2pm.

A **DHL/Western Union** office is located at Av. El Sol 627-A (© 084/244-167). It's open Monday through Friday from 8:30am to 1pm and 3 to 7pm.

Restrooms You'll find public restrooms in the airport and at bus terminals, bars, restaurants, museums, and hotels. As many bars and restaurants as there are in Cusco, finding a bathroom shouldn't be a problem.

Safety Over the years, Cusco has earned a reputation for being rather unsafe for foreign visitors, especially at night, when violent muggings and attacks have been known to occur on empty streets. Most alarming are rapes, sexual assaults, and so-called "strangle muggings," in which thieves attack unsuspecting victims (usually on deserted streets), applying pressure to the neck and leaving the victim momentarily unconscious—giving themselves time enough to relieve the victims of their belongings. Women should avoid isolated areas, especially at night. Cusco might appear laid-back and good-natured, but it's a good idea to be at your most vigilant, especially in the neighborhoods of San Blas, in the side streets leading off the Plaza de Armas, near the Central Market, and at bus and train hubs. Incidents of drink-spiking have been reported; be aware of your drinking companions in bars and don't allow strangers to buy you drinks. Try always to travel in groups (never walk alone late at night), and call a taxi to transfer you to your hotel from restaurants and bus and rail stations.

Taxis See "Getting Around," above.

Telephone Cusco's area code is 084. The principal **Telefónica del Perú** office, for long-distance and international calls, is at Av. El Sol 382-6 (© 084/241-114). It's open Monday through Saturday from 8am to 10pm.

Tour Operators & Travel Agencies Cusco is swimming in travel agencies—several hundred of all sizes, many apparently offering the exact same packages, compete for your attention. Only a few dozen have solid reputations, however, and many should be flat-out avoided. Do not contract any would-be travel agent on the street, and do not hand over money for a trip or package without visiting the outfit in its office. If you have any questions about an agency, particularly one not listed by name and recommended in this chapter, do not hesitate to inquire about its reputation in the Tourist Information Office.

For travel arrangements around Peru, as well as city tours and Sacred Valley, Machu Picchu, Inca Trail, and Amazon jungle trips, see the relevant sections below and in chapters 8 and 10.

3 Where to Stay

Cusco, as the top tourist destination in Peru, where virtually every visitor seems to pass and stay a few days, has developed a remarkable cornucopia of lodgings, with hundreds of hotels, inns, and *hostales* of all stripes and prices. More continue to sprout, and few seem to close. Although the sheer number of offerings, particularly at the midrange and budget levels, means that you can pretty confidently land in Cusco without a reservation (outside of popular festivals like Inti Raymi and Fiestas Patrias at the end of June and July) and find a decent place to stay, many of the better and more popular hotels at all levels fill up throughout high season and even in shoulder months. In my opinion, it's better to firm up a reservation as soon as you know your dates of stay in Cusco.

Most of the city's most desirable accommodations are very central, within walking distance of the Plaza de Armas. The San Blas neighborhood is also within walking distance, although many hotels and *hostales* in that district involve very steep climbs up the hillside. (The upside is that guests are rewarded with some of the finest views in the city.) Some visitors will want to avoid hotels and inns too close to the Plaza de Armas; that zone's crowded bars and discos, many open until sunrise, tend to produce throngs of rambunctious and usually inebriated young people who stumble downstairs and howl at the moon or bellow at the people who just rejected them inside.

Hot water is an issue at many hotels, even those that swear they offer 24-hour hot showers. Many hotels and inns will arrange free airport transfers if you communicate your arrival information to them in advance.

Cusco possesses only a couple of truly excellent high-end hotels, and few good hotels at the next tier. In Cusco, an eternal backpackers' delight, there remains a glut of accommodations at the moderate and budget levels. However, several *hostales* have more atmosphere and are likely to provide a better overall experience than more expensive—and more institutional—hotels. Prices listed below are rack rates for travel in high season; unless otherwise noted, rates do not include taxes or service charges. During the low season (Nov–Apr), prices often drop precipitously, even at midrange inns and backpacker hostels—sometimes as much as 50%—as the glut of hotels fights for a much-reduced number of visitors.

Several of the *hostales* reviewed below are cozy, family-run places, but travelers looking for even greater contact with a Peruvian family might want to check out the very inexpensive inns belonging to the **Asociación de Casas Familiares (Family Home**

Tips **No Sleeping In**

Most Cusco hotels have annoyingly early checkout times—often 9 or 9:30am—due to the deluge of early morning flight arrivals to the city. At least in high season, hotels are very serious about your need to rise and shine, but you can always store your bags until later.

Association), which operates a website (www.cusco.net/familyhouse) with listings of guesthouses with one or more rooms available for short- or long-term stays.

NEAR THE PLAZA DE ARMAS
VERY EXPENSIVE

Hotel Monasterio ✿✿✿   Peru's most extraordinary place to stay, this beautiful hotel occupies the San Antonio Abad monastery, constructed in 1592 on the foundations of an Incan palace. An Orient-Express and Leading Small Hotels of the World property, the Hotel Monasterio—converted into a hotel in 1995—exudes grace and luxury. As much a museum as a hotel, it has its own opulent gilded chapel and 18th-century Escuela Cusqueña art collection.

Located on quiet Las Nazarenas square between the bohemian San Blas district and the main square, the hotel makes fine use of several courtyards with stone arches; one is set up for lunch outdoors, about as beautiful a setting as is to be found in Cusco. Rooms are impeccably decorated in both colonial and modern styles, with large Cusqueña School paintings; the accommodations off the first courtyard are more traditionally designed and feel more authentic. For a special treat, consider one of the two-story junior suites. One restaurant, Tupay, is housed in the original vaulted refectory of the monastery; early risers, many on their way to Machu Picchu, enjoy a terrific breakfast buffet serenaded by Gregorian chants. The elegant dinner restaurant Illary is the finest in Cusco. As a special bonus, the hotel is the first in the world to offer oxygen piped directly into rooms through the ventilation ($30 per day). It sounded gimmicky to me, but my wife, who was suffering from a bout of *soroche* (altitude sickness), says she slept wonderfully and woke up without the pounding headaches.

Palacios 136 (Plazoleta Nazarenas), Cusco. ✆ **084/241-777.** Fax 084/246-983. http://monasterio.orient-express. com. 122 units. $435 deluxe double; $520–$1150 Rates include breakfast buffet. AE, DC, MC, V. **Amenities:** 2 restaurants; cafe; bar; concierge; executive services and meeting rooms; 24-hr. room service; laundry service. *In room:* A/C, TV/VCR, minibar, hair dryer, safe.

Libertador Palacio del Inka ✿✿   One of Cusco's top two hotels, the Libertador could just as easily be called the Conquistador. Directly across from the Incan Temple of the Sun and built on the foundations of the "Aclla Huyasi," where the Incan chieftain kept maidens, this elegant traditional hotel occupies a historic house once inhabited by none other than Francisco Pizarro. The handsome art- and antiques-filled hotel, just 4 blocks from the Plaza de Armas, is built around a dramatic colonial courtyard marked by perfect arches, terra-cotta tiles, and a Spanish-style fountain. The swank lobby has a massive pyramidal skylight and exposed Incan walls. Guest rooms are spacious and refined; furnishings have rustic colonial touches, and the marble bathrooms are large and well equipped. Many rooms have small terraces. But the Libertador perhaps most distinguishes itself with extremely attentive and professional service. The fine but pricey restaurant, Inti Raymi, is built around the edges of the courtyard and features a nightly dance and music show.

San Agustín 400 (Plazoleta Santo Domingo 259), Cusco. ✆ **084/231-961**. Fax 01/233-152. www.summithotels.com. 254 units. $185 deluxe double; $215–$350 suite. Rates include taxes. AE, DC, MC, V. **Amenities:** Restaurant; coffee shop; fitness center; sauna; concierge; business center and executive services; salon; 24-hr. room service; laundry service. *In room:* A/C, TV/VCR, fax and dataport in some units, minibar, hair dryer, safe.

EXPENSIVE

Novotel Cusco ⋐   One of Cusco's newest upmarket hotels, a member of the French Novotel chain, is built around the guts of a lovely 16th-century colonial building with a spectacular central courtyard. Most of the rooms, however, are in newly built additions. Opened in 2001, the hotel is modern and dependable, with good services and amenities, although, in most regards, it's a notch below the city's two top-flight luxury hotels. The modern rooms are well equipped and brightly colored, but are otherwise standard accommodations. At this level, it's worth spending the extra money to get one of the superior rooms in the converted colonial section of the hotel; they are larger and much more atmospheric. The hotel, a short distance from the Plaza de Armas, features a nice gardenside restaurant serving French fare, and a warm bar with a fireplace. Deals might be available online or by asking for better rates.

San Agustín 239 (corner of Pasaje Santa Mónica), Cusco. ✆ **084/881-030**. Fax 084/228-855. www.novotel.com. 99 units. $118–$186 double. Rates include taxes and breakfast. AE, DC, MC, V. **Amenities:** Restaurant; bar; sauna; concierge; business facilities; salon; 24-hr room service; babysitting; laundry service. *In room:* AC, TV, minibar, hair dryer.

Picoaga Hotel ⋐   A very nice, more reasonably priced alternative to Cusco's top two luxury hotels, Picoaga also occupies a historic building—in this case a 17th-century mansion that once belonged to a Spanish nobleman, the marquis of Picoaga. Just minutes from the Plaza de Armas, the hotel is set around a lovely arcaded courtyard— or, at least, one portion of it is. A newer wing is in a dated and much less appealing modern section at the rear of the hotel. Ask for a room in the front section overlooking the patio. Rooms there, about a third of the total, are larger, have high ceilings, and are decorated with colonial-style furniture and floral prints. Rooms are nice but certainly not over-the-top elegant. (**Another tip:** Request a room on the back side of the courtyard rather than one facing the street because traffic and street noise on Santa Teresa fires up, oh, right about 5:39am.) Picoaga has more colonial character than the Novotel Cusco, although the latter offers better service.

Santa Teresa 344, Cusco. ✆ **084/252-330**. Fax 084/221-246. www.picoagahotel.com. 70 units. $140 double; $170 suites. Rates include breakfast buffet. AE, DC, MC, V. **Amenities:** 2 restaurants; fireplace bar; game room; concierge; 24-hr. room service; laundry service. *In room:* A/C, TV, minibar, hair dryer, safe.

MODERATE

Casa Andina Cusco Koricancha ⋐ ⓥₐₗᵤₑ   Similar in concept to the Sonesta Posadas del Inca, this very professionally run, midprice hotel is one of three—soon to be four—belonging to this upstart Peruvian hotel chain. Visitors to Casa Andina know what to expect: excellent service and clean, ample rooms that are colorfully decorated. The hotel on San Agustín, 3 blocks from the main square, is built around a restful colonial courtyard and is in a somewhat quieter neighborhood, while the other two, smaller locations, are virtually on top of the Plaza de Armas. All have the same prices and same features (though the Cusco Catedral hotel has an Incan wall within the hotel). Look for the new, upscale "Private Collection" Casa Andina in a historic house near Qoricancha sometime in late 2006.

San Agustín 371, Cusco. ✆ **084/252-633**. Reservations in Lima, ✆ 01/446-8848. Fax 084/222-908. www.casa-andina.com. 57 units. $88 double. Rate includes taxes and breakfast buffet. AE, DC, MC, V. **Amenities:** Concierge; business facilities; babysitting; laundry service. *In room:* TV, minibar, safe, hair dryer on request.

Where to Stay in Central Cusco

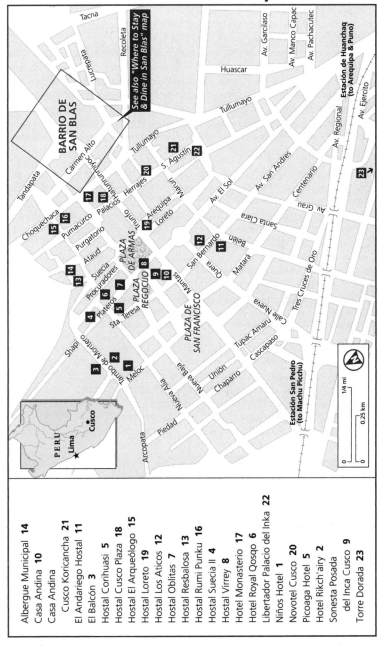

Albergue Municipal **14**
Casa Andina **10**
Casa Andina
  Cusco Koricancha **21**
El Andariego Hostal **11**
El Balcón **3**
Hostal Corihuasi **5**
Hostal Cusco Plaza **18**
Hostal El Arqueólogo **15**
Hostal Loreto **19**
Hostal Los Aticos **12**
Hostal Oblitas **7**
Hostal Resbalosa **13**
Hostal Rumi Punku **16**
Hostal Suecia II **4**
Hostal Virrey **8**
Hotel Monasterio **17**
Hotel Royal Qosqo **6**
Libertador Palacio del Inka **22**
Niños Hotel **1**
Novotel Cusco **20**
Picoaga Hotel **5**
Hotel Rikch'airy **2**
Sonesta Posada
  del Inca Cusco **9**
Torre Dorada **23**

El Andariego Hostal *(Finds)* This family-owned, cozy, and centrally located, though well hidden, *hostal* is a quiet, genial place that retains a great deal of the flavor of a 19th-century Cusco colonial house. Set back from a busy street across an interior patio, it has just 8 rooms, a few of which are great values. Rooms 101 (which fronts a small garden) and 103, both of which have functioning wood-burning fireplaces and exposed stone walls, are my favorite. They're large and comfortable, with hardwood floors and a smattering of antiques as well as clean tile bathrooms. Other rooms are also nice, if not quite as unique. The owners will prepare dinners on request.

San Andrés 270, Cusco. *(C)*/fax **084/225-593**. www.andariegocusco.com. 8 units. $40 double. Rate includes taxes and continental breakfast. MC, V. **Amenities:** Restaurant/bar; 24-hour room service; dataport. *In room:* Satellite TV.

Hostal Cusco Plaza I & II *(Finds)* One of two locations, this mini-chain *hostal* offers decent value in a midprice package. The original hotel has the superior location, sharing the same great square with Hotel Monasterio and the Museo de Arte Precolombino. It's a small, simple affair featuring a great central courtyard (with tables for breakfast) and straightforward decor, including nice parquet floors. A few of the rooms have spectacular views; no. 304 is by far the best, with huge windows and an arched ceiling. The newer location doesn't have as distinguished an address, although it occupies a lovely, if rather dark, 18th-century building with a glassed-in central patio. Rooms are sparsely decorated, with modest, functional bathrooms. Ask for one of the high-ceilinged rooms.

Cusco Plaza I: Plaza Nazarenas 181, Cusco. *(C)* **084/246-161.** Fax 084/263-842. www.cuscoplazahotels.com. 33 units. $65 double. Cusco Plaza II: Saphy 486, Cusco. *(C)* **084/263-000.** Fax 084/262-001. 24 units. $75 double. Rates at both *hostales* include taxes and breakfast. AE, DC, MC, V. **Amenities:** Room service; laundry service. *In room:* TV.

Hostal El Arqueólogo *(Finds) (Kids)* It takes a little effort to uncover this *hostal,* named for the profession responsible for discovering so much of Peru's pre-Columbian past and owned by a Frenchman who's a longtime resident of Cusco. Located down a stone alleyway and tucked behind the unprepossessing facade of a late-19th-century house just 5 minutes from the Plaza de Armas, it certainly doesn't jump out at you. Once inside, though, you'll find a lovely sunny garden—with ample space for kids to play— and rooms that run along a corridor overlooking the patio. Rooms are simply furnished but comfortable and cozy. The large Inka suite has a garden as well as panoramic city views for not much more money. The French restaurant, La Vie en Rose, is fairly upscale and surprisingly good for an inn of this size. Also on-site is a large, efficient travel agency.

Pumacurco 408, Cusco. *(C)* **084/232-569.** Fax 084/235-126. www.hotelarqueologo.com. 20 units. $59–$69 double; $79–$89 suite. Rates include taxes and breakfast buffet. MC, V. **Amenities:** Restaurant; travel agency; small business center with Internet; room service; laundry service. *In room:* TV, hair dryer, no phone.

Hostal Rumi Punku *(⋆) (Finds)* A glance at the name or address of this idiosyncratic family-owned hostel will give you an indication of its strong connection to Cusco's Incan roots. The massive portal to the street is a fascinating original Incan construction of perfectly cut stones, once part of a sacred Incan temple. (The door is one of only three belonging to private houses in Cusco, and elderly residents of the city used to do the sign of the cross upon passing it.) There's more to the *hostal* than might appear from the street. Inside is a charming, flower-filled colonial courtyard with a cute little chapel and gardens along a large Incan wall. The clean bedrooms are ample, with hardwood floors and Norwegian thermal blankets. The top-floor dining room, where breakfast is served, has excellent panoramic views of Cusco's rooftops. The hostel is on the way up to Sacsayhuamán, but only a short walk from the Plaza de Armas. Rumi Punku, by the way, means "door of stone" in Quechua. For 2006, the inn is adding a sauna and Jacuzzi.

Choquechaca 339, Cusco. ℭ **084/221-102.** Fax 084/242-741. www.rumipunku.com. 30 units. $40–$50 per person. Rates include taxes and continental breakfast buffet. MC, V. **Amenities:** Restaurant; laundry service.

Sonesta Posada del Inca ℱ   Like the rest of the hotels belonging to this small and very well-run Peruvian group, the Posada del Inca is cozy, cheery, and a good value. It's sandwiched between the Plaza de Armas and Plaza Regocijo—about as centrally located as you can be in Cusco, without too much of the additional all-night noise of being right on the plaza. Rooms aren't large, but they are comfortable, and the homey lounge has a fireplace. Deals are often available, including one with the possibility of staying 1 night at this hotel and another night at the chain's lovely place in the Urubamba valley (in Yucay) for a slightly discounted rate.

Portal Espinar 108, Cusco. ℭ **800/SONESTA** for reservations, or 01/222-4777 or 084/227-061. Fax 084/248-484. www.sonesta.com. 23 units. $100–$125 double. Rate includes taxes and breakfast buffet. AE, DC, MC, V. **Amenities:** Cafe/restaurant; concierge; business center; room service; babysitting; laundry service. *In room:* TV, minibar, hair dryer.

INEXPENSIVE

Albergue Municipal *Value*   On the way to the Sacsayhuamán ruins, with enviable views over the top of Cusco, this youth hostel has a nice location away from the fray and none of the nasty institutional feel you find at most hostels. It also has extremely clean dorm rooms with bunk beds, great sitting areas, a TV room, and a nice cafeteria.

Kiskapata 240, San Cristóbal, Cusco. ℭ **084/252-506.** Fax 084/226-701. albergue@municusco.gob.pe. 11 units (64 beds). $6 per person, dorm room; $9 per person, double with shared bath. No credit cards. **Amenities:** Cafeteria; laundry service. *In room:* No phone.

Hostal Resbalosa *Finds*   A longtime favorite of backpackers, this inn is named for the steep cobblestoned street it's on (which makes access a little tricky) rather than any innate shady quality. (*Resbalosa* means "slippery.") The good-size rooms have hardwood floors, large windows, and immaculate bathrooms with pretty dependable hot-water showers. Try to get one with a view. There's a large rooftop terrace, perfect for sunning and just hanging out, enjoying the 180-degree views. The steep, pedestrian-only cobblestone street means you'll have to haul your pack up, but it's good training for the Inca Trail.

Resbalosa 394, Cusco. ℭ **084/224-839.** 20 units. S/32 ($9.15) double with shared bath; S/60 ($17) double with private bath. No credit cards. **Amenities:** Laundry facilities. *In room:* No phone.

Niños Hotel ℱℱℱ *Value* *Kids*   The Dutch owner of the charming "Children's Hotel" says she has a story to tell, and it's an inspirational one. Jolanda van den Berg, in just 7 years in Peru, has mounted a small empire of goodwill through the Foundation Niños Unidos Peruanos: She adopted 12 Peruvian street children; constructed an extremely warm and inviting (not to mention great-value) hotel in the old section of Cusco that puts all its profits toward care for needy children; constructed a learning center and restaurant for 125 such kids; and created a second center with athletic facilities and additional medical attention for another 125 disadvantaged youth of Cusco.

The good news for travelers is that, if you are lucky enough to get a room here (reservations generally must be made about 6 months in advance), you won't have to suffer for your financial contribution to such an important cause. The main hotel, in a restored colonial house just 10 minutes from the Plaza de Armas, is one of the finest,

Kids   Family-Friendly Hotels

Hostal El Arqueólogo (p. 196)   This quiet inn has a sunny garden where the kids can play and parents can relax and read. There's a very good French restaurant and a travel agency on the premises, so you won't have to troop all over town if you don't want to.

Hostal Los Áticos (p. 200)   The very inexpensive apartments have separate bedrooms and living rooms with sofa beds, plus kitchenettes. It's perfect for a family of four on a budget.

Hostal Rumi Punku (p. 196)   This family-owned *hostal* has a pretty, flower-filled colonial courtyard, gardens, and a historic Incan wall. There's plenty of room for the kids to run about behind the massive Incan portal.

Niños Hotel (p. 197)   The very definition of a family-friendly hotel, this one was built to allow Cusco street kids to become part of a family. Profits go to care for another 125 needy children. The restored colonial house is one of the most charming and best-maintained small inns around. Reserve well in advance. Families should inquire about the newest addition and excellent-value apartments, at another location, for longer stays.

cleanest, and most comfortable inexpensive inns in Peru. The large rooms—named for the couple's adopted children—are very nearly minimalist chic, with hardwood floors and quality beds, and they ring a lovely sunny courtyard, where breakfast is served. The ambitious Niños project has now added a second hotel, also in a historic building, and, incredibly, has taken in two more families (totaling 15 girls and another 2 boys). On the same street as the second hotel are four terrific apartments for longer stays, ideal for small families, in the first of the children's learning and day-care facilities.

Meloq 442, Cusco. (C) 084/231-424. www.ninoshotel.com. 20 units. $34 double w/bathroom; $28 double w/shared bathroom. Apartments $10 per person per day; monthly rates available. Rates include taxes and continental breakfast. No credit cards. **Amenities:** Restaurant/cafe; laundry service. *In room:* No phone.

SAN BLAS
MODERATE
Casa de Campo Hostal *Finds*   Lodged in the hills of the traditional neighborhood San Blas, Casa de Campo means "country house," and the air up here, high above Cusco, has the freshness of country air. An organic complex, its chalet-style rooms appear to have sprouted one from the other. A friendly and comfortable place, it's nonetheless not for everyone, especially not those who are tired of climbing the steps of Incan ruins. The climb up to the hotel is taxing enough, but once inside the gate, guests must use their remaining reserves to amble up several more flights of stone steps.

Once there, though, you're rewarded with nice gardens and several terraces with unparalleled sweeping views of the city and surrounding mountains, as well as a cozy lounge with a large fireplace. Rooms are rather small, but they have good, firm beds and are rustically decorated, with exposed wood beams and thick wool blankets. (It's generally considerably cooler up here than just 15 min. down in Cusco.) One special room has a fireplace (for the same price as a regular room); another is like a cottage towering above the city. All rooms have 24-hour hot water. The staff will build a fire

Where to Stay & Dine in San Blas

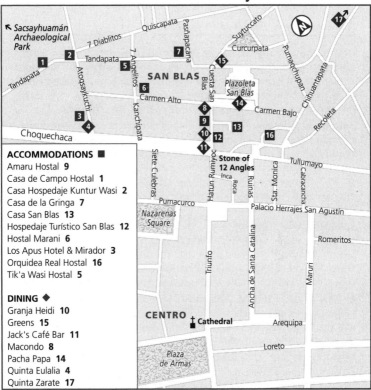

ACCOMMODATIONS ■
Amaru Hostal **9**
Casa de Campo Hostal **1**
Casa Hospedaje Kuntur Wasi **2**
Casa de la Gringa **7**
Casa San Blas **13**
Hospedaje Turístico San Blas **12**
Hostal Marani **6**
Los Apus Hotel & Mirador **3**
Orquidea Real Hostal **16**
Tik'a Wasi Hostal **5**

DINING ◆
Granja Heidi **10**
Greens **15**
Jack's Café Bar **11**
Macondo **8**
Pacha Papa **14**
Quinta Eulalia **4**
Quinta Zarate **17**

in the bar on request and arrange a free city tour in Cusco. The owners also operate the Amauta Spanish-language school and Tertulia travel agency, as well as a new, rustic hotel in Urubamba in the Sacred Valley.

Tandapata 296, San Blas, Cusco. ✆ **084/243-069**. Fax 084/244-404. www.hotelcasadecampo.com. 25 units. $45–$55 double. Rates include taxes, continental breakfast, and airport pickup. AE, MC, V. **Amenities:** Restaurant; laundry service. *In room:* No phone in some units.

Casa San Blas *(Finds* A modern boutique hotel tucked down a small, dead-end alleyway off pedestrian-only Cuesta San Blas, and approaching the artsy neighborhood of the same name, this new establishment has a lot going for it. Excellent location and good services are principal among its advantages. If I were going to stay here, it would be in one of the two-level suites with kitchenettes and spectacular views of Cusco from upstairs. Other rooms are comfortable, but plain and not nearly as inviting (all doubles are interior with no views). The hotel's panoramic-view terrace is an excellent spot to relax, write postcards, and check out the city creeping up into the hills.

Tocuyeros 566, San Blas, Cusco. ✆ **888/569-1769** in U.S. and Canada or 084/251-563. Fax 084/237-900. www.casasanblas.com. 18 units. $87 double; $110–$120 suite. Rate includes taxes and breakfast. AE, DC, MC, V. **Amenities:** Restaurant; piano bar; 24-hr. room service; Internet access; laundry service; massage room. *In room:* TV, safe.

Los Apus Hotel & Mirador ☞ Swiss-managed, with a bit of a chalet feel, this small hotel on a quiet, hilly street in San Blas is a nice, homey find. It has a gorgeous, airy

More Hotels & *Hostales* in Cusco

Despite the amazing number of accommodations strewn across the city, Cusco can get very crowded in high season; particularly if you're in town during the Inti Raymi festival (late June), July, and August, finding a place to rest your head can be headache inducing. Here are a few more recommended places to try (although a couple of them are often full).

Casa de la Gringa ✦ *(Finds)*   In a new and much more convenient location, this tranquil and friendly South African–owned house is a real find and is a favorite of those who come to Cusco on spiritual and mystical journeys. Its rooms are nicely decorated, with a touch of bohemian flair and lively, colorful art. It features a lounge and an annexed cottage, with a patio with glass-enclosed roof for star-gazing. Pasnapacana 148 (corner Tandapata), San Blas, Cusco. ℂ/fax **084/241-168.** $9 per person.

Casa Hospedaje Kuntur Wasi   This tiny, family-run inn is popular with Europeans, tucked up in the San Blas district. The small terrace has amazing views of Cusco. Rooms are plain, but they have pretty good beds, and there's laundry service. Tandapata 352, San Blas, Cusco. ℂ/fax **084/227-570.** $16 double with shared bathroom; $18 double with private bathroom.

El Balcón *(Finds)*   This handsome early-17th-century colonial building has long balconies and excellent views of the city. The rooms are comfortable, and there's an inviting atmosphere throughout. Tambo de Montero 222, Cusco. ℂ **084/236-738.** Fax 084/225-352. $45–$55 double (breakfast included).

Hostal Corihuasi   On a street leading up above Cusco, this small, cozy and rustic *hostal* has a great living room/breakfast area with a fireplace and superlative panoramic views; those same views come with a handful of rooms (nos. 1, 20, 6, 8, and 10). Suecia 561, Cusco. ℂ/fax **084/232-233.** $45 double.

Hostal Loreto   This *hostal* is popular with many travelers for the original Incan stone walls featured in some rooms. The rooms can be very cold and dark, despite electric heaters. Still, it's just a few paces from Qoricancha and the Plaza de Armas, and all rooms have private baths with hot water. Loreto 115, Cusco. ℂ **084/226-352.** $40 double.

Hostal Los Áticos ✦ *(Kids)*   A great option for families, these cozy rooms and apartments have a separate bedroom with a double bed, a living room with a sofa bed, a kitchenette, and a desk. It's excellent for long stays. Quera 253, Cusco. ℂ **084/231-710.** Fax 084/231-388. www.losaticos.com. $45 apartment (up to 4 people); $30 double.

lobby atrium, tranquil reading areas, and an attractive rooftop terrace with excellent views of Cusco. Accommodations pale a bit in comparison with the hotel's public amenities, but on the whole they are a good value. The first-floor rooms have higher ceilings, but those on the third and fourth floors—many of which have private balconies—have the best views.

Hostal Oblitas Just up the street from the Plaza de Armas, this small family-run hotel is homey and an excellent value. Breakfast is served in a dining room that will make you feel like you're staying at a Peruvian friend's house. Plateros 358A, Cusco. ⓒ/fax 084/223-871. $33 double.

Hostal Rikch'ariy Popular with backpackers, this small place has nice basic rooms, laundry service, and a pretty garden with good views, as well as helpful English-speaking owners. Tambo de Montero 219, Cusco. ⓒ 084/236-606. $12 per person.

Hostal San Isidro Labrador *(Finds* This is a pleasant, safe, and comfortable midrange choice, with just 14 rooms set back from busy Calle Saphy in colonial digs set around a long courtyard. Rooms are rather small but clean; several second-floor rooms have high ceilings, wood beams, and skylights. Saphy 440, Cusco. ⓒ 084/226-241. labrador@qnet.com.pe. $45 double.

Hostal Suecia II At the top of Procuradores, this friendly and consistently popular backpackers' inn is a notch above most others. It has comfortable rooms, an enclosed and covered courtyard, hot water, and nice beds. It's usually a great place to form Inca Trail groups. Tecsecocha 465, Cusco. ⓒ 084/239-757. $10 double with shared bathroom; $15 double with private bathroom.

Hostal Virrey If you're dying to be right on the Plaza de Armas, you can't do much better than this small inn. Two rooms have stunning views of classic Cusco. Portal Comercio 165, Cusco. ⓒ 084/221-771. Fax 084/235-349. $50 double.

Hotel Royal Qosqo This popular little inn has a good vibe and a good location near the top of Procuradores. If you want to hang where the action is, this is one of your best low-rent bets. There's hot water from 6 to 10am only. Tecsecocha 2, Cusco. ⓒ/fax 084/226-221. S/70 ($20) double with private bathroom; S/40 ($11) double with shared bathroom.

Pensión Alemana This small, German-run San Blas hotel aims to be a large B&B and is a good value. It is very clean, if a little spartan and functional-feeling, with a nice garden area and terrace with views of Cusco below. Room no. 1, which is large and light, has great views and is your best bet. Tandapata 260, San Blas, Cusco. ⓒ 084/226-861. www.cuzco-stay.de. $37–$45 double.

Tik'a Wasi Hostal A San Blas *hostal* with vehicular access—a rarity in this neighborhood—this attractive inn has a cafeteria, comfortable carpeted rooms, a TV lounge, 24-hour room service (another rarity among small *hostales*), and laundry service. Tandapata 491, San Blas, Cusco. ⓒ/fax 084/231-609. $45 double.

Atocsaycuchi 515 (corner of Choquechaca), San Blas, Cusco. ⓒ 084/264-243. Fax 084/264-211. www.losapushotel.com. 20 units. $109 double. Rate includes taxes and breakfast. AE, DC, MC, V. **Amenities:** Restaurant; 24-hr. room service; laundry service. *In room:* TV, safe.

Orquídea Real Hostal *⭐ (Finds* Hidden away along a narrow street wedged into the hill to San Blas, this tiny, unassuming inn has several surprises inside, beginning with some of the greatest views in Cusco and continuing to the rarity of a working fireplace in each room (a true benefit at this chilly elevation). The colonial building has origi-nal Incan walls and exposed wood beams, and the rustic accommodations are simply decorated in a cozy mountain lodge aesthetic. All rooms are oriented toward Cusco below, offering panoramic views; no. 20 is a suite with a little sitting room, available for the same price. There's hot water 24 hours a day. The company that owns the inn also offers a wide variety of all-inclusive package deals and tours in Cusco and across Peru (see its website).

Alabado 520, San Blas, Cusco. ©/fax **084/221-662;** for reservations, © 877/260-2423 toll-free in the U.S. or 01/444-3032. Fax 877/260-2209 toll-free in the U.S. or 01/242-1273. www.orquidea.net. 11 units. $39–$44 double. Rates include taxes, continental breakfast, and airport pickup. AE, MC, V. **Amenities:** Cafeteria; laundry service. *In room:* TV, safe.

INEXPENSIVE

Amaru Hostal 🏵 *(Value*   Popular with legions of backpackers, this hostel, in a pretty colonial-republican house in the midst of the San Blas artist studios and shops, has a lovely balconied patio, with a very nice garden area that tends to attract sunbathers and with good views of Cusco. Rooms are very comfortable, attractively decorated, and a good value (although some are quite small). Several have colonial-style furnish-ings and lots of natural light. (Ask to see several rooms, if you can.) It's a very friendly and relaxed place, as is its nearby sister property, Amaru Hostal II, on Chihmpata 642 (© 084/223-521).

Cuesta San Blas 541, San Blas, Cusco. ©/fax **084/225-933.** http://cusco.net/amaru. 16 units. $25 double with pri-vate bath; $16 double with shared bath. Rates include taxes, continental breakfast, and airport pickup. No credit cards. **Amenities:** Coffee shop; laundry service. *In room:* No phone.

Hospedaje Turístico San Blas *(Value*   About halfway up the principal artery that wends its way up (and up) the artsy San Blas district is one of its most attractive inex-pensive inns. Rooms are pretty spacious and warmly decorated. The airy colonial house has a glassed-in courtyard and a sun terrace with good views (and 24-hr. hot water). This inn is a nice step up from run-of-the-mill budget options in Cusco, and it's a good place to meet up with fellow travelers.

Cuesta San Blas 526, San Blas, Cusco. ©/fax **084/225-781.** 20 units. $20 double with private bath; $14 double with shared bath. Rates include taxes, continental breakfast, and airport pickup. No credit cards. **Amenities:** Coffee shop. *In room:* No phone.

Hostal Marani 🏵🏵 *(Finds*   Similar in commitment and heritage to the better-known and slightly nicer Niños Hotel—both are Dutch-owned and very active in social pro-grams to benefit disadvantaged Peruvian children—this handsome *hostal* is very well designed and maintained. It occupies a nice colonial-era house in San Blas and features spacious, light, and impeccable rooms with spotless tiled bathrooms. The rooms are located around a traditional Spanish-style courtyard, where guests often take their break-fasts and read in the afternoon. Ask about off-season discounts. The *hostal* has a close affiliation with the HoPe Foundation, a Dutch nonprofit that has funded dozens of schools, hospitals, and other development programs in Cusco and rural Andean villages.

Carmen Alto 194, San Blas, Cusco. ©/fax **084/249-462.** www.hostalmarani.com. 17 units. $36 double. Rate includes taxes and breakfast. No credit cards. **Amenities:** Cafe; laundry service. *In room:* No phone.

OUTSKIRTS OF CUSCO

Torre Dorada 🏵🏵 *(Finds*   In general, I don't recommend many hotels outside city centers, since convenience is of the utmost importance to me and most travelers.

However, this personalized boutique hotel in a quiet residential neighborhood (just 5 minutes from downtown, and the hotel generously ferries its guests back and forth for free) is so exceptional that I can't overlook it. While not luxurious, the four-story, modern construction offers services and attention to detail that are nearly the equal of five-star hotels (but it's much friendlier doing it). It's a particularly good place to stay if you are concerned about safety, undisturbed about not being able to walk to and from the city, and perhaps uncertain about a trip to Cusco or lacking in Spanish skills. The staff goes out of its way to look out for guests and make their trips enjoyable and easygoing; I've never encountered anyone like Peggy and her family. Rooms are simple but very well outfitted and impeccable. The breakfast buffet, served in a top-floor dining room with great views, outclasses most luxury hotels.

Calle los Cipreses, Residencial Huancaro, Cusco. ⓒ **084/241-698.** Fax 084/224-255. www.torredorada.com.pe. 18 units. $80 double. Rate includes taxes and buffet breakfast. AE, DC, MC, V. **Amenities:** TV lounge; dataport; safe; laundry service; airport pickup and free taxi service.

4 Where to Dine

Visitors to Cusco have a huge array of restaurants and cafes at their disposal; eateries have sprouted up even faster than *hostales* and bars, and most are clustered around the main drags leading from Plaza de Armas. Many of the city's most popular restaurants are large tourist joints with Andean music shows, while many more are economical, informal places favored by backpackers and adventure travelers—some offer midday three-course meals *(menús del día)* for as little as S/6 or S/7 (about $2). However, Cusco is also blessed with a growing number of upscale dining options, which tend to be good values, and the dining scene has improved every year as it expands to accommodate new, and more sophisticated, visitors to the city. Though you can still eat very inexpensively, Cusco is now also a place to reward yourself with a good meal if you've been in the jungle or been trekking in the mountains.

Traditional cheap eateries line the narrow length of Calle Procuradores, which leads off the Plaza de Armas across from the Compañía de Jesús church and is sometimes referred to as "Gringo Alley." Many are pizzerias, and Cusco has become known for its wood-fired, crispy-crust pizzas. Lurking about the Plaza de Armas are hawkers armed with menus, hoping to lure you inside restaurants. Most represent decent, upstanding restaurants, but if you know where you want to dine, a polite "no, gracias" is usually all it takes to get them off your trail. Several bars, such as Los Perros and The Muse also double as (often quite good) restaurants, primarily for their young and hip clients who'd prefer to get their food the same place as their cocktails.

Not all restaurants in Cusco accept credit cards; many of those that do, especially the cheaper places, will levy a 10% surcharge to use plastic, so you're better off carrying cash (either soles or dollars). Top-flight restaurants often charge both a 10% service charge and 18% sales tax, neither of which is included in the prices listed below.

For restaurants in San Blas, see the "Where to Stay & Dine in San Blas" map on p. 199.

VERY EXPENSIVE

Restaurante Illary (Hotel Monasterio) ✦✦✦ PERUVIAN/INTERNATIONAL
Cusco has a surfeit of fun, informal, and inexpensive Andean restaurants, but only a couple truly qualify as fine dining. It's probably not surprising that the Hotel Monasterio contains Cusco's most uncommonly refined restaurant. It's also the most expensive in

town (tellingly, prices are in dollars), but it is well worth the splurge even if you can't afford the pricey rooms. A glassed-in corridor overlooks the handsome colonial patio of the former monastery, while the main dining room is a series of intimate rooms sumptuously decorated with Cusqueña School artwork, stone arches, and wood-beamed ceilings. Peruvian specialties include alpaca tenderloin with corn, sweet pepper chile, and mint sauce; and duck-and-rice stew with coriander. Nicely prepared international fish and meat dishes dominate the menu, including poached kingfish rolls with shrimp mousse, and rack of lamb with black-pepper crust and tomato marmalade. Service is consistently impeccable, and desserts and the wine list are beyond tempting. If you can swing it for one special evening, dinner either here or at MAP Café (see below) is highly recommended.

Plaza Nazarenas. ✆ **084/243-820.** Reservations recommended. Main courses $13–$21. AE, DC, MC, V. Daily 11am–4pm and 7–11pm.

EXPENSIVE

Cicciolina ★★ *Finds* NOVO ANDINO Upstairs in the same courtyard as the restaurant A Mi Manera (see below) is this new and delightfully chic restaurant, which looks ripped from the Tuscan countryside. Enter through a long, appealing, and country-elegant bar, decorated with bunches of garlic, peppers, and fresh-cut flowers. The bar is a great spot for a pre-dinner drink, or dinner itself, if you don't mind the garrulous bar patrons. The dining room at the back, one of the few places in Cusco for true fine dining, is refined, with high-backed chairs, deep red walls, and large antique mirrors. It features a high ceiling and exposed beams. The menu focuses on unusual spices and accents, with a number of adventurous dishes. You might start with escalibada (sweet peppers, onions, eggplant, and tomatoes, roasted with herbs) or spicy barbecued calamari, prawns, and scallops, which is served with a minty rice noodle salad. Main courses include superb, large salads (including a yummy combination of roast beef and vegetables) and very good homemade pastas and exotic dishes like alpaca filet and a Moroccan tagine.

Triunfo 393, 2nd floor. ✆ **084/239-510.** Reservations recommended. Main courses S/22–S/36 ($6.30–$10). AE, DC, MC, V. Daily 11am–midnight.

El Truco ★ PERUVIAN In a 17th-century *casona* that operated as a mint for the Spanish viceregency and later as a gambling house, El Truco combines good Peruvian cooking and *platos típicos* with a loud and lively *peña* (*criollo* music) show every night (8:30–10:30pm). The restaurant, virtually an institution now that it has been around for over 40 years, has an attractive colonial interior and offers a daily lunch buffet of Peruvian specialties. At night, it's a la carte only. Dishes include pork tamales, roast pork, roast lamb, and stuffed rocoto peppers. The lively music-and-dance shows, along with consistently good food, make El Truco very popular with upscale tour groups.

Plaza Regocijo 261. ✆ **084/232-441.** Reservations recommended. Main courses S/16–S/38 ($4.55–$11); daily lunch buffet S/35 ($10). AE, DC, MC, V. Mon–Sat noon–11pm.

Inka Grill ★ PERUVIAN/NOVO ANDINO A large and attractive modern two-level place right on the Plaza de Armas, popular with both young and old, the distinguished but pricey Inka Grill serves what might be called *novo andino* fare and is one of Cusco's better dining experiences. Start with a bowl of yummy *camote* (sweet potato) chips and green salsa. The best dishes are Peruvian standards such as sautéed alpaca tenderloin served over *quinoa* (a grain) and *ají de gallina* (shredded chicken with nuts, cheese, and chile peppers), and desserts such as a coca-leaf crème brûlée.

Where to Dine in Central Cusco

See also "Where to Stay & Dine in San Blas" map

BARRIO DE SAN BLAS

PERU
Lima
Cusco

Al Grano **12**
A Mi Manera **9**
Chez Maggy **3**
Cicciolina **10**
El Cuate **5**
El Truco **1**
Inka Grill **7**
Kusikuy **6**
La Retama **8**
La Tertulia **3**
Map Cafe **9**
Moni Cafe
   Restaurante **13**
Pucara **2**
Restaurante Illary **11**

The extensive menu also includes a wide range of international dishes such as pizza, pasta, and risotto. If you like Inka Grill, check out MAP Café, its more upscale and sophisticated cousin within the Museo de Arte Precolombino.

Portal de Panes 115. ✆ 084/262-992. Reservations recommended. S/23–S/55 ($6.55–$16). AE, DC, MC, V. Mon–Sat 8am–midnight.

La Retama ✸ ⓚ PERUVIAN/INTERNATIONAL   Overlooking the Plaza de Armas from a huge second-floor space, La Retama is one of Cusco's most enduring favorites. The views and nightly folklore shows bring in the tour groups, of course, but the food is good enough to warrant a visit even by those who fear long tables with group leaders and interpreters. The menu focuses on classic Peruvian dishes, such as pink trout and king fish from Lake Titicaca, *seco de cordero* (lamb), *anticucho de lomo* (beef bro-chette), *cuy* (guinea pig), and trout ceviche. International dishes include chicken curry and trout Florentine. The restaurant's walls are lined with the art and handicrafts of Peru, and there's also a gift shop (see comment above about tour groups).

Portal de Panes 123, 2nd floor. ✆ 084/226-372. Reservations required. Main courses S/18–S/39 ($5.15–$11). AE, DC, MC, V. Tues–Sat noon–midnight; Mon 6:30pm–midnight.

MAP Café ✸✸✸ NOVO ANDINO/INTERNATIONAL   Though the name might seem a bit misleading, causing one to conjure a globetrotter's bohemian hangout, this is in fact one of Cusco's most stylish and elegant restaurants Housed in a modern, minimalist glass and steel box with few adornments other than views of the handsome colonial patio it sits in the middle of—Casa Cabera, now the beautifully designed Museo de Arte Precolombino—it places its focus squarely on the food, which is elegantly prepared and presented. Standouts include the sesame-crusted tuna and penne rigate in pisco cream sauce. For diners in the mood for a taste of creative Andean cuisine, the guinea pig confit with rocoto peppers is a daring dish. The wine list is one of the city's finest. As a bonus, the museum is open until 10pm, making it possible to make a dinner and pre-Columbian date of the evening.

Casa Cabrera (in Museo de Arte Precolombino), Plaza Nazarenas 231. © 084/242-476. Reservations required. Main courses S/21–S/50 ($6–$14). AE, DC, MC, V. Daily noon–3pm and 6pm–midnight.

MODERATE

A Mi Manera ⍟ (Finds NOVA ANDINO   A handsome and friendly little upstairs restaurant—entered through the colonial courtyard—on an overlooked little square 1 block from Plaza Nazarenas, this is one of the most relaxed spots in town. It serves excellent, creative Andean dishes with plenty of vegetarian options. Traditionalists should check out the *rocoto relleno* (stuffed peppers with meat, peanuts, and raisins), *adobo* (chicken made with chichi and yuca), or the *orgía de papas* (an "orgy" of spicy and cheesy potatoes). The house specialty is the traditional oven-baked *cuy* (guinea pig) with stuffed pepper and potatoes (which requires a reservation 3 hr. in advance). There are also homemade pastas, including several with twists, such as the Andean quinoa gnocchi. The wine list is pretty good, but for Andean dishes, the best accompaniment is *chicha morada,* the chilled nonalcoholic beverage brewed from purple corn. Breakfast is also served.

Triunfo 393, 2nd floor. © 084/243-629. Reservations recommended. Main courses S/18–S/35 ($5.15–$10). AE, DC, MC, V. Daily 8am–11pm.

Greens ⍟⍟ (Value INTERNATIONAL/NOVO ANDINO   In the heart of San Blas, on an atmospheric street just off the *plazoleta,* Greens is one of Cusco's most stylish and romantic restaurants. The intimate and often crowded space has deep-green walls with modern art, an open kitchen, and a handful of candlelit tables mixed with hipster sofas near the fireplace for more informal dining. The soundtrack of laid-back dance beats, the creative and funky menu, and the reasonable prices appeal to a cool young crowd. The decor, presentation, and quality of the food are unusual in most parts of Peru; in fact, Tanya Miller, the restaurant's owner, previously worked in several London restaurants. On the menu, you'll find steak, chicken, and curries, all excellent. Try the beef tenderloin in red-wine-and-onion sauce, served with raisin rice, or the tropical chicken curry with bananas, peaches, and strawberries. On Sunday, the restaurant features a roast of chicken, potatoes, veggies, and homemade apple pie that has become locally famous; it's by advanced reservation only. Happy hour (two-for-one) is every evening from 6:30 to 8pm.

Tandapata 700, San Blas. © 084/243-379. Reservations recommended. Main courses S/22–S/30 ($6.30–$8.60). No credit cards. Daily noon–3pm and 6pm–midnight.

Kusikuy ⍟ (Finds ANDEAN/INTERNATIONAL   If you've resisted trying the Andean specialty that makes most foreigners recoil or at least raise an eyebrow, this could be the place to get adventurous. The restaurant's name in Quechua means "happy little guinea pig," so *cuy al horno* is, of course, the house dish. The rest of the menu focuses on other typical Peruvian dishes and adds stuff for gringos, such as pastas and basic chicken and meat dishes. It also serves a good-value lunch menú (which one day featured soup, chicken in red wine with rice, and pudding, plus juice). The cozy and good-looking loft-like space, in a new location on a hilly street above the Plaza de Armas, is warmly decorated with hardwood tables, and a mix of antiques and musical instruments from the Amazon. With pillows and couches, it is also a cool, relaxed spot for a drink. Suecia 339. (C) **084/262-870.** Reservations not accepted. Main courses S/12–S/38 ($3.40–$11). MC, V. Mon–Sat 8am–midnight.

Macondo (Value) LATIN AMERICAN/INTERNATIONAL   This hip cafe/bar puts its claim to insider coolness on the door—the name is a reference to the town that is the setting for García Márquez's *One Hundred Years of Solitude.* Macondo looks more

---

Cusco's *Quintas*

When the day warms up under a huge blue sky in Cusco, you'll want to be outside. Cusco doesn't have many sidewalk cafes, but it does have a trio of *quintas,* traditional open-air restaurants that are most popular with locals on weekends. These are places to get large portions of good-quality Peruvian cooking at pretty reasonable prices. Among the dishes they all offer are tamales, *cuy chactado* (fried guinea pig with potatoes), *chicharrón* (deep-fried pork, usually served with mint, onions, and corn), alpaca steak, *lechón* (suckling pig), and *costillas* (ribs). You can also get classics such as *rocoto relleno* (stuffed hot peppers) and *papa rellena* (potatoes stuffed with meat or vegetables). Vegetarian options include *sopa de quinoa* (grain soup), fried yuca, and *torta de papa* (potato omelets). *Quintas* are open only for lunch (noon–5 or 6pm), and most people make a visit their main meal of the day. Main courses cost between S/15 and S/45 ($4.30–$13).

Pachapapa   Across from the small church in San Blas, this popular *quinta* serves a full menu of authentic Andean dishes. Its delightful setting, in a relaxing and attractive courtyard with potted plants and white-washed walls, also makes it an excellent place to take a breather while traipsing around hilly San Blas, to enjoy light items like soups and salads, as well as a full bar menu. From the wood-fired oven comes one of the house specialties, *cuy* (guinea pig served with Huacatay mint), as do the trout and even a spicy ham and cheese calzone. Plazoleta San Blas 120. (C) **084/241-318.**

Quinta Eulalia (Kids) (Kids)   Eulalia has been around since 1941, making it Cusco's oldest *quinta.* From a lovely colonial courtyard (only a 5-min. walk from the Plaza de Armas), there are views of the San Cristóbal district to the surrounding hills from the upper eating area. It's a great place to dine on a sunny day, and the Andean specialties are reasonably priced. Choquechaca 384. (C) **084/224-951.**

Quinta Zárate (Finds) (Finds)   Located at the eastern end of town, this place has a lovely, spacious garden area with great views of the Cusco valley. Portions are very large, and the trout is a standout; try the *ceviche de trucha* (trout marinated in lime and spices). This *quinta* is pretty difficult to find; a taxi is recommended. Totora Paccha 763, at the end of Calle Tandapata. (C) **084/245-114.**

like an artsy coffeehouse than a restaurant, and the soundtrack is generally trendy tropical rhythms. The cooking is nearly as funky and imaginative as the decor. Dishes, such as the alpaca mignon with bacon in mushroom and white-wine sauce, are very well presented and served in generous portions. Much of the menu echoes the laid-back tropical theme. *Juanes* are chicken, rice, and salsa wrapped in a Bijao leaf, and chicken kabobs are accompanied by peanut sauce, like a satay. Well suited for the bohemian neighborhood of San Blas, this friendly cafe serves a variety of splashy cocktails (with two daily happy hours) and is gay-friendly. Its owners operate the kitschy bar-restaurant Fallen Angel on Plaza Nazarenas.

Cuesta San Blas 571, San Blas. ℂ **084/229-415**. Reservations not accepted. Main courses S/19–S/25 ($5.40–$7.15). MC, V. Mon–Sat 8:30am–10pm; Sun 3–10pm.

Pucara *Value* PERUVIAN/INTERNATIONAL   Just off the Plaza de Armas, this intimate, dimly lit restaurant has small wood tables, exposed wood beams, and cloth lamps hanging low over the tables. As one of the first restaurants tourists stumble onto right off the main square, and as one of the better values in the historic center, it's generally packed. It has a few odd touches: On the walls are framed picture cutouts of the dishes, and the waitstaff is a group of local women in yellow jackets and hairnet caps. But don't let that turn you off; it has a nice selection of traditional Peruvian and international dishes, including a tasty lomo saltado and *ají de gallina,* several different soups, and a variety of whitefish preparations.

Plateros 309. ℂ **084/222-027**. Reservations not accepted. Main courses S/12–S/32 ($3.40–$9.15). No credit cards. Mon–Sat 12:30–10pm.

INEXPENSIVE

Al Grano ASIAN   A quiet corner cafe, with lots of natural light and decorated with Andean textiles and featuring exposed Incan stonework, this little place doesn't specialize in standard *criollo* (creole) fare, as you might expect. On the menu are items from Indonesia, India, Pakistan, and Sri Lanka, including chutneys, vegetarian curries, and lamb in spices and yogurt. Most dishes are pretty mild. There's a very cheap daily menú, served until 3pm, as well as daily specials. Al Grano also has a range of great baked goods for dessert (try the brownie or spice cake) and good coffee and tea.

Santa Catalina Ancha 398 (at San Agustín). ℂ **084/228-032**. Reservations not accepted. Main courses S/6–S/22 ($1.70–$6.30); menú del día S/7.50 ($2.15). No credit cards. Mon–Sat 10am–9pm.

Chez Maggy *Value* *Kids* PIZZERIA/PERUVIAN   This bustling little joint, which has been around for over 25 years and spawned several branches in Cusco and other parts of Peru, has a bit of everything, from trout and alpaca to homemade pastas to Mexican food, but most people jam their way in for the freshly baked pizzas made in a traditional wood-burning brick oven. They're some of the best in Cusco (even though every other restaurant in Cusco seems to be a pizzeria). Chez Maggy is usually packed in the evenings, and there's often live Andina music when roaming street musicians pop in to entertain diners. The restaurant is a long corridor with shared bench tables full of gringos—a good way to meet other travelers because you'll be jockeying for elbow space with them. Incredibly, three other locations are along Procuradores, better known as Gringo Alley. If you want a pizza on the terrace of your *hostal,* Chez Maggy will deliver for free.

Plateros 348. ℂ **084/234-861**. Reservations not accepted. Main courses S/12–S/30 ($3.40–$8.60). MC, V. Daily 6–11pm.

El Cuate *Kids* MEXICAN   I'm usually wary about trying out Mexican restaurants while traveling in countries other than Mexico because they almost always serve a crummy imitation of Tex-Mex under a cheesy sombrero on the wall. But this animated hole-in-the-wall on "Gringo Alley" dishes out good-value, pretty authentic Mexican food for scores of backpacker types. El Cuate was Cusco's first Mexican restaurant, and its success has spawned several imitators who've felt compelled to add Mexican dishes to their Peruvian and Italian menus. But if you're sure you want Mexican, this is still the place to come. It has a number of bargain menús offering six courses for S/25 ($7.15) or S/15 ($4.30), or five items for just S/10 ($2.85), offered at lunch and dinner; and dishes such as *enchiladas suizas* (cheese enchiladas), Mexican soup, tacos, and burritos. With long bench tables, often shared, it's a jovial place.

Procuradores 386. ⓒ **084/227-003.** Reservations not accepted. Main courses S/10–S/25 ($2.85–$7.15). MC. Daily 11am–midnight.

Granja Heidi *Finds* HEALTH FOOD/VEGETARIAN   Although easily overlooked, given its second-floor interior location in San Blas, this easygoing eatery with an emphasis on healthy, good-value meals (especially outstanding breakfasts) is worth tracking down. With a high ceiling and the airy, sun-filled look of an art studio, it's perfect for the neighborhood. Run by a German woman who has a farm of the same name outside Cusco, the restaurant features fresh ingredients and products, such as yogurt, cheese, and quiches, that taste like they came straight from the farm. You might expect only stuff that's strictly good for you, but the menu also offers surprising meat dishes, including ostrich steak, and typical Peruvian dishes. The daily menú (served until 9:30pm) offers vegetarian and nonvegetarian choices and might start with pumpkin soup, followed by lamb or a veggie stir-fry, fruit salad, and tea. Don't pass on dessert, or you'll miss excellent home-baked cakes, such as the cheesecake or the irresistible Nelson Mandela chocolate cake.

Cuesta San Blas 525, San Blas. ⓒ **084/238-383.** Reservations not accepted. Main courses S/10–S/18 ($2.85–$5.15); menú del día S/7.50 ($2.15). No credit cards. Daily 8am–9:30pm.

Jack's Café Bar *Value* CAFE/INTERNATIONAL   One of the most popular gringo hangouts in Cusco, owned by the guy who runs the one thriving Irish pub in town, Jack's isn't just a spot to have a drink and check out some American and British magazines; it serves very fresh, very good meals throughout the day, and features enough variety that you wouldn't be the first to eat here several times during your stay. For breakfast, try the scrumptious fluffy pancakes. At lunch, order one of the towering salads or creative gourmet sandwiches. Finish with a dinner of "really hot green chicken curry" or a red wine, beef, and mushroom casserole. There are plenty of items for vegetarians, smoothies, wine and beer, as well as great coffee drinks and hot chocolate (for those cool Andean nights). And it's a friendly place to linger and meet folks, to boot.

Choquechaca 509 (corner of Cuesta San Blas). ⓒ **084/806-960.** Reservations not accepted. Main courses S/8–S/19 ($2.30–$5.40). No credit cards. Daily 7am–10pm.

La Tertulia *Value Kids* BREAKFAST/CAFE FARE   A classic Cusco spot for breakfast or other light meals, this little restaurant, up a tight spiral staircase from a travel agency, is a gringo hangout par excellence. The name means "discussion," which is fitting because people gather here to read newspapers and foreign magazines, and to exchange books and advice on hiking the Inca Trail and other far-flung adventures across South America. Many come to fuel up as early as 6:30am before setting out on one of those trips, and the superb breakfast buffet does the trick. You'll get all-you-can-eat eggs, fruit salads, yogurt, granola, amazing homemade whole-meal bread, French toast, tamales, fresh juices, and coffee—truly the breakfast of champions and an excellent value. The breakfast menu also features 16 types of crepes. There's a set-lunch deal and a nice salad bar, as well as pizzas, sandwiches, and fondues. If you feel bad about stuffing yourself at breakfast, you can feel good about the fact that La Tertulia donates S/1 (30¢) of each buffet to a Peruvian orphanage. You can also take salsa dance classes, but I wouldn't recommend trying it after breakfast.

Procuradores 44, 2nd floor. © **084/241-422.** Reservations not accepted. Main courses S/8–S/20 ($2.30–$5.70); breakfast buffet S/12 ($3.40). MC. V. Daily 7am–3pm and 5–11pm.

Moni Café Restaurant *finds* HEALTH FOOD/VEGETARIAN   This tiny cafe, a couple of blocks off the Plaza de Armas, is an unpretentious gringo hangout and a good spot for freshly prepared vegetarian fare. Its offers appetizers like Nepalese tomato soup and main courses like eggplant curry and spinach and ricotta lasagna, accompanied by juices, beers, and smoothies. Everything is made to order.

San Agustín 311. © **084/231-029.** Reservations not accepted. Main courses S/19–S/26 ($5.40–$7.40). No credit cards. Mon–Sat 9am–3pm and 6–9pm.

5 What to See & Do

The stately and lively **Plaza de Armas** *ƙƙ*, lined by arcades and carved wooden balconies, and framed by the Andes, is the focal point of Cusco. After Machu Picchu, it is one of the most familiar sights in Peru. You will cross it, relax on the benches in its center, and pass under the porticoes that line the square with shops, restaurants, travel agencies, and bars innumerable times during your stay in Cusco. The plaza—which was twice its present size in Incan days—has two of Cusco's foremost churches and the remains of original Incan walls on the northwest side of the square, thought to be the foundation of the Inca Pachacútec's palace.

Many principal sights within the historic quarter of Cusco and beyond the city are included in the *boleto turístico* (see below), but a few very worthwhile places of interest, such as the Templo del Qoricancha (Temple of the Sun) and Museo de Arte Precolombino (MAP), are not included.

AROUND THE PLAZA DE ARMAS

Convento y Museo de Santa Catalina *ƙƙ*   A small convent a couple of blocks west of the Plaza de Armas, Santa Catalina was built between 1601 and 1610 on top of the Acllawasi, where the Incan emperor sequestered his chosen Virgins of the Sun. The convent contains a museum of colonial and religious art. The collection includes an excellent selection of Escuela Cusqueña paintings, featuring some of the greatest works of Amerindian art—a combination of indigenous and typically Spanish styles—in Cusco. The collection includes four paintings of the Lord of the Earthquakes (El Señor de los Temblores) painted by Amerindians. The interior of the monastery is quite beautiful, with painted arches and an interesting chapel with baroque frescoes of Incan vegetation. Other items of interest include very macabre statues of Jesus and an extraordinary trunk that, when opened, displays the life of Christ in 3-D figurines. (It was employed by the Catholic Church's "traveling salesmen," who were used to convert the natives in far-flung regions of Peru.) The main altar of the convent church is tucked behind steel bars.

Santa Catalina Angosta s/n. © **084/226-032.** Admission included in *boleto turístico*. Daily 8:30am–5:30pm.

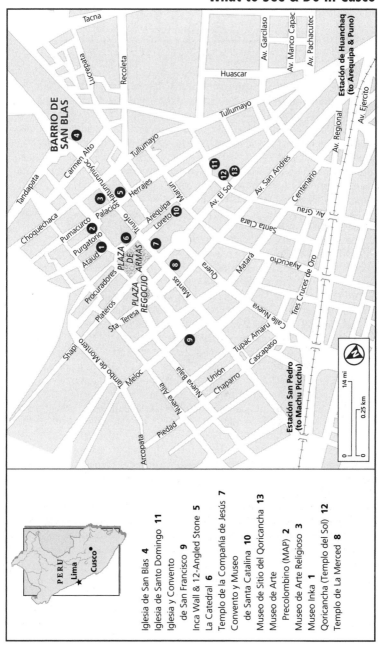

Iglesia de San Blas **4**
Iglesia de Santo Domingo **11**
Iglesia y Convento
de San Francisco **9**
Inca Wall & 12-Angled Stone **5**
La Catedral **6**
Templo de la Compañía de Jesús **7**
Convento y Museo
de Santa Catalina **10**
Museo de Sitio del Qoricancha **13**
Museo de Arte
Precolombino (MAP) **2**
Museo de Arte Religioso **3**
Museo Inka **1**
Qoricancha (Templo del Sol) **12**
Templo de La Merced **8**

Value   Cusco's *Boleto Turístico*

Cusco's municipal tourism (Calle Mantas 117-A) office sells a tourist pass, or *boleto turístico,* that is virtually essential for visiting the city and surrounding areas. It is your admission to 16 of the most important places of interest in and around Cusco, including some of the major draws in the Sacred Valley. Though it has doubled in price in the last few years, the *boleto* is still a good value, and you cannot get into some churches and museums without it. The full ticket costs S/70 ($20) for adults and S/35 ($10) for students with ID and children, is valid for 10 days, and is available at the tourism office at Mantas 117-A ((© **084/263-176**), open Monday through Friday from 8am to 6:30pm and Saturday from 8am to 2pm.

In addition to the main Tourist Office, the *boleto* can be purchased at: OFEC, Av. El Sol 103, office 106 (Galerías Turísticas; © **084/227-037**), from 8am–6pm Monday through Saturday, and Casa Garcilaso, at the corner of Garcilaso y Helaceros s/n (© **084/226-919**).

The *boleto* allows admission to the following sights: Convento y Museo de Santa Catalina, Museo Municipal de Arte Contemporáneo, Museo Histórico Regional, Museo de Sitio Qoricancha, Museo de Arte Popular, Centro Qosqo de Arte Nativo de Danzas Folklóricas, Monumento Pachacuteq, Museo Palacio Municipal, and the Incan ruins of Sacsayhuamán, Q'enko, Pukapukara, Tambomachay, Pikillacta, and Tipón, and the Valle Sagrado attractions of Pisac, Ollantaytambo, and Chinchero.

La Catedral, the imposing cathedral on the Plaza de Armas, was formerly included in the *boleto* but now you must pay a separate admission fee. Other principal attractions not covered by the *boleto* include the Templo del Qoricancha (Temple of the Sun), Museo Inca, and Iglesia de San Blas.

Not all of these attractions are indispensable, and you probably won't end up checking off absolutely everything on your color photo–coded *boleto,* but it remains the best admission ticket in Cusco. (You can also buy a partial ticket for S/40, or $11, but it only covers attractions in the city.) Make sure you carry the ticket with you when you're planning to make visits (especially on daytrips outside the city), as guards will demand to see it so that they can punch a hole alongside the corresponding picture. Students must also carry their International Student Identification Card (ISIC), as guards often demand to see that ID to prove that they didn't fraudulently obtain a student *boleto* and thus cheat the city out of 10 bucks.

La Catedral 𝒶𝒶   Built on the site of the palace of the Inca Viracocha, Cusco's cathedral, which dominates the Plaza de Armas, is a beautiful religious and artistic monument. Two years ago, it completed a massive restoration ahead of schedule. Completed in 1669 in the Renaissance style, the cathedral possesses some 400 canvasses of the distinguished Escuela Cusqueña that were painted from the 16th to 18th centuries. There are also amazing woodcarvings, including the spectacular cedar choir stalls. The main altar—which weighs more than 401 kilograms (884 lb.) and is fashioned from silver mined in Potosí, Bolivia—features the patron saint of Cusco. To the right of the altar is a particularly Peruvian painting of the Last Supper, with the apostles drinking *chicha* (fermented maize beer) and eating *cuy* (guinea pig). The **Capilla del Triunfo** (the first Christian church in Cusco) is next door, to the right of the main church. It holds a painting by Alonso Cortés de Monroy of the devastating earthquake of 1650. To the right of the entrance to the Capilla (the right nave, next to the choir stalls) is an altar adorned by the locally famous "El Negrito" (also known as "El Señor de los Temblores," or Lord of the Earthquakes), a brown-skinned figure of Christ on the cross known as the protector of Cusco. The figure was paraded around the city by frightened residents during the 1650 earthquake (which, miracle or not, ceased shortly thereafter). So strong is continued faith in El Negrito that locals deliver dozens of fresh flowers in his honor on a daily basis. The figure's crown was stolen a couple of years ago and not recovered; the one now adorning his head is gold, a gift of a parishioner.

The entrance to the cathedral and ticket office, where you can purchase the *boleto turístico,* is actually at the entrance to the **Capilla de la Sagrada Familia,** to the left of the main door and steps.

Plaza de Armas (north side). No phone. S/13 ($3.70) adults, S/4 ($1.15) students and children. Mon–Sat 10–6pm; Sun 2–6pm.

Templo de la Compañía de Jesús ✰   Cater-cornered to the cathedral is this Jesuit church, which rivals the former in grandeur and prominence on the square (an intentional move by the Jesuits, and one that had Church diplomats running back and forth to the Vatican). Begun in the late 16th century, it was almost entirely demolished by the quake of 1650, rebuilt, and finally finished 18 years later. Like the cathedral, it was also built on the site of an important palace, that of the Inca Huayna

The Cusco School of Art

The colonial-era **Escuela Cusqueña,** or Cusco School of Art, that originated in the ancient Incan capital was a synthesis of traditional Spanish painting with local, mestizo elements—not surprising, perhaps, because its practitioners were themselves of mixed blood. Popular in the 17th and 18th centuries, the style spread from Cusco as far as Ecuador and Argentina. The most famous members of the school were Diego Quispe Tito, Juan Espinosa de los Monteros, and Antonio Sinchi Roca, even though the authors of a large majority of works associated with the school are anonymous. Most paintings were devotional in nature, with richly decorative surfaces. Artists incorporated recognizable Andean elements into their oil paintings, such as local flora and fauna, customs, and traditions—one depiction of the Last Supper has the apostles feasting on guinea pig and drinking *chicha*—and representations of Jesus looking downward, like the Indians who were forbidden to look Spaniards in the eye. Original Escuela Cusqueña works are found in La Catedral, the Convent of Santa Catalina, the Museum of Religious Art, and a handful of other churches in Cusco. Reproductions of original paintings, ranging from excellent in quality to laughable, are available across Cusco, particularly in the galleries and shops of the San Blas district.

✫✫ The Magic of Incan Stones: A Walking Tour

Dominating the ancient streets of Cusco are dramatic **Incan walls** ✫✫✫, constructed of mammoth granite blocks so exquisitely carved that they fit together without mortar, like jigsaw-puzzle pieces. The Spaniards razed many Incan constructions but built others right on top of the original foundations. (Even hell-bent on destruction, they recognized the value of good engineering.) In many cases, colonial architecture has not stood up nearly as well as the Incas' bold structures, which were designed to withstand the immensity of seismic shifts common in this part of Peru.

Apart from the main attractions detailed in this section, a brief walking tour will take you past some of the finest Incan constructions that remain in the city. East of the Plaza de Armas, **Calle Loreto** is one of the best-known Incan thoroughfares. The massive wall on the left side, composed of meticulously cut rectangular stones, was once part of the Acllahuasi, or the "House of the Chosen Maidens," the Incan emperor's Virgins of the Sun. This is the oldest surviving Incan wall in Cusco and one of the most distinguished. Northeast of the Plaza de Armas, off Calle Palacio, is **Hatunrumiyoc**, a cobblestone street lined with impressive walls of polygonal stones. Past the Archbishop's Palace on the right side is the famed **12-angled stone** (now appropriated as the symbol of Cuzqueña beer), which is magnificently fitted into the wall. Originally, this wall belonged to the palace of the Inca Roca. This large stone is impressively cut; the Incas almost routinely fitted many-cornered stones (with as many as 32, as seen at Machu Picchu, or even 44 angles) into structures. From Hatunrumiyoc, make your first right down another pedestrian alleyway, Inca Roca; about halfway down on the right side is a series of stones said to form the shape of a **puma,** including the head, large paws, and tail. It's not all that obvious, so if you see someone else studying the wall, ask him to point out the figure. **Siete Culebras (Seven Snakes),** the alleyway connecting Plaza Nazarenas to Choquechaca, contains Incan stones that form the foundation of the chapel within the Hotel Monasterio. Other streets with notable Incan foundations are **Herrajes, Pasaje Arequipa,** and **Santa Catalina Angosta.** Only a couple genuine Incan **portals** remain. One is at Choquechaca 339 (the doorway to a recommended *hostal,* Rumi Punku), and another is at Romeritos 402, near Qoricancha.

Not every impressive stone wall in Cusco is Incan in origin, however. Many are transitional period (post-Conquest) constructions, built by local masons in the service of Spanish bosses. Peter Frost's *Exploring Cusco* (available in local bookstores) has a good explanation of what to look for to distinguish an original from what amounts to a copy.

Cápac (said to be the most beautiful of all the Incan rulers' palaces). Inside, it's rather gloomy, but the gilded altar is stunning, especially when illuminated. The church possesses several important works of art, including a picture of Saint Ignatius de Loyola, by the local painter Marcos Zapata, and the Cristo de Burgos crucifixion by the main altar. Also of note are the paintings to either side of the entrance, which depict the marriages of Saint Ignatius's nephews; one is the very symbol of Peru's mestizo character, as the granddaughter of Manco Inca weds the man who captured the last Inca, Tupac Amaru, the leader of an Indian uprising.

Plaza de Armas (southeast side). Free admission. Mass Mon–Sat 7am, noon, and 6pm; Sun 7:30, 11:30am, 6, and 7pm. Variable opening hours for visits; enter whenever open between Masses (usually possible Mon–Sat 11am–noon and 3–4pm).

Museo Inka ✹ (Kids)   Housed in the impressive Admirals Palace, this museum contains artifacts designed to trace Peruvian history from pre-Incan civilizations and Incan culture, including the impact of the Conquest and colonial times on the native cultures. On view are ceramics, textiles, jewelry, mummies, architectural models, and an interesting collection—reputed to be the world's largest—of Incan drinking vessels (*qeros*) carved out of wood, many meticulously painted. The museum is a good introduction to Incan culture, and there are explanations in English. The palace itself is one of Cusco's finest colonial mansions, with a superbly ornate portal indicating the importance of its owner; the house was built on top of yet another Incan palace at the beginning of the 17th century. In the courtyard is a studio of women weaving traditional textiles. Allow 1½ to 2 hours to see the entire collection.

Cuesta del Almirante 103 (corner of Ataúd and Tucumán). ✆ 084/237-380. Admission not included in *boleto turístico;* S/10 ($2.85) adults, S/5 ($1.40) students. Mon–Fri 8am–6pm; Sat and holidays, 9am–4pm.

SOUTH & EAST OF THE PLAZA DE ARMAS

Barrio de San Blas ✹✹   Cusco's most atmospheric and picturesque neighborhood, San Blas, a short but increasingly steep walk from the Plaza de Armas, is lined with artists' studios and artisans' workshops, and stuffed with tourist haunts—many of the best bars and restaurants and a surfeit of hostels. It's a great area to wander around—many streets are pedestrian-only—though you should exercise caution with your belongings, especially at night. The neighborhood also affords some of the most spectacular panoramic vistas in the city. In the small plaza at the top and to the right of Cuesta San Blas is the little white **Iglesia de San Blas** ✹, said to be the oldest parish church in Cusco (admission apart from *boleto turístico;* S/6, or $1.70). Although it's a simple adobe structure, it contains a marvelously carved churrigueresque cedar pulpit. Some have gone as far as proclaiming it the finest example of woodcarving in the world; carved from a single tree trunk, it is certainly great. The pulpit comes with an odd story, and it's difficult to determine whether it's fact or folklore: It is said that the carpenter who created it was rewarded by having his skull placed within his masterwork (at the top, beneath the feet of St. Paul) upon his death. Also worth a look is the baroque gold-leaf main altar.

Museo de Arte Precolombino (MAP) ✹✹   A new sumptuously designed, 3-year-old addition to the Cusco cultural landscape, this archaeological museum features part of the vast collection of pre-Columbian works belonging to the Rafael Larco Herrera Museum in Lima. Housed in an erstwhile Incan ceremonial court, Santa Clara convent, and later colonial mansion (Casa Cabrera) of the Conquistador Alonso Díaz are 450 pieces—about 1% of the pieces in storage at the museum in Lima—dating from 1250 B.C. to A.D. 1532. Beautifully illuminated halls carefully exhibit gold and silver handicrafts, jewelry, ceramics, and other artifacts depicting the rich traditions from the Nasca, Moche, Huari, Chimú, Chancay, and Incan cultures. Although the number of pieces isn't overwhelming, they are all beautifully lighted and displayed. Scattered about are comments about "primitive" art by major Western artists such as Paul

Klee, and deviating from the museum's main thrust is a room of Cusqueña School religious painting. The museum—which is open late and in the courtyard boasts one of the city's finest restaurants, in a contemporary glass box—is especially worthwhile for anyone unable to visit the major museums in Lima or any of the premier sites in northern Peru. Allow 1 or 2 hours for your visit. Within the courtyard, housed in a minimalist glass box, is MAP Café (p. 205), one of Cusco's finest restaurants.

Casa Cabrera, Plaza de las Nazarenas s/n. ✆ 084/237-380. Admission S/16 ($4.55) adults, S/8 ($2.30) students. Daily 9am–11pm.

Museo de Arte Religioso (Palacio Arzobispal)   On the corner of one of Cusco's most extraordinary streets, Hatunrumiyoc, a pedestrian alleyway lined with magnificent Incan stonemasonry (see "The Magic of Incan Stones: A Walking Tour" on p. 214), the Museum of Religious Art is housed in a handsome colonial palace that previously belonged to the Archbishop of Cusco (before that, it was the site of the palace of Inca Roca and then the home of a Spanish marquis). Inside is a nice collection of colonial religious paintings, notable for the historical detail they convey, but the extravagant old house—with its impressive portal and Moorish-style doors, balcony, carved-cedar ceilings, stunning stained-glass windows, and small chapel—is pretty nearly the main draw. Plan to spend about 1 to 2 hours here.

Corner of Hatunrumiyoc and Palacio. ✆ 084/225-211. Admission included in *boleto turístico*. 8am–12:30pm and 3–6pm.

Museo de Sitio de Qoricancha   In three small rooms, this underground museum, located across the garden from the vastly more interesting Temple of the Sun and Church of Santo Domingo, presents a decent collection of ceramics, metalwork, and textile weavings of Incan and pre-Incan civilizations, as well as a host of other archaeological finds. The museum pales in comparison to the Museo de Arte Precolombino and Museo Inka, however. Allow about a half-hour for your visit, tops.

Av. El Sol s/n (across the esplanade from Qoricancha). Admission by *boleto turístico*. Mon–Sat 9:30am–5:30pm.

Qoricancha (Templo del Sol) & Santo Domingo 🏛🏛🏛   Qoricancha and Santo Domingo together form perhaps the most vivid illustration in Cusco of Andean culture's collision with Western Europe. Like the Great Mosque in Córdoba, Spain— where Christians dared to build a massive church within the perfect Muslim shrine—the temple of one culture sits atop and encloses the other. The extraordinarily crafted Temple of the Sun was the most sumptuous temple in the Incan Empire and the apogee of the Incas' naturalistic belief system. Some 4,000 of the highest-ranking priests and their attendants were housed here. Dedicated to worship of the sun, it was apparently a glittering palace straight out of El Dorado legend: *Qoricancha* means "golden courtyard" in Quechua, and in addition to hundreds of gold panels lining its walls, there were life-size gold figures, solid-gold altars, and a huge golden sun disc. The sun disc reflected the sun and bathed the temple in light. During the summer solstice, the sun still shines directly into a niche where only the Incan chieftain was permitted to sit. Other temples and shrines existed for the worship of lesser natural gods: the moon, Venus, thunder, lightning, and rainbows. Qoricancha was the main astronomical observatory for the Incas.

After the Spaniards ransacked the temple and emptied it of gold (which they melted down, of course), the exquisite polished stone walls were employed as the foundations of the Convent of Santo Domingo, constructed in the 17th century. The baroque church pales next to the fine stonemasonry of the Incas—and that's to say nothing

⌢ Fun Fact Hang a Right at Donkey Lips

Cusco is littered with difficult-to-pronounce, wildly spelled street names that date to Incan times. In the bohemian neighborhood of San Blas, though, they're particularly colorful. Here's a primer of atmospheric street names and their literal meanings:

Atoqsayk'uchi   Where the fox got tired
Tandapata   Place of taking turns
Asnoqchutun   Donkey lips
Siete Diablitos   Seven Little Devils
Siete Angelitos   Seven Little Angels
Usphacalle   Place of sterility/place of ashes
Saqracalle   Where the demons dwell
Pumaphaqcha   Puma's tail
Cajonpata   Place shaped like a box
Rayanpata   Place of myrtle flowers
One to seek out: **P'asñapakana**   Where the young women are hidden
And, finally, one to avoid: **P'aqlachapata**   Place of bald men

---

about the original glory of the Sun Temple. Today all that remains is Incan stonework. Thankfully, a large section of the cloister has been removed, revealing four original chambers of the temple, all smoothly tapered examples of Incan trapezoidal architecture. Stand on the small platform in the first chamber and see the perfect symmetry of openings in the stone chambers. A series of Incan stones displayed reveals the fascinating concept of male and female blocks, and how they fit together. The 6m (20-ft.) curved wall beneath the west end of the church, visible from the street, remains undamaged by repeated earthquakes and is perhaps the greatest extant example of Incan stonework. The curvature and fit of the massive dark stones is astounding.

After the Spaniards took Cusco, Francisco Pizarro's brother Juan was given the eviscerated Temple of the Sun. He died soon afterward, though, at the battle at Sacsayhuamán, and he left the temple to the Dominicans, in whose hands it remains.

Plazoleta Santo Domingo. ✆ 084/222-071. Not included in *boleto turístico;* Admission S/6 ($1.70) adults, S/3 (85¢) students. Mon–Sat 8am–5pm; Sun 2–5pm.

SOUTHWEST OF THE PLAZA DE ARMAS

Templo de La Merced ⌁   Erected in 1536 and rebuilt after the great earthquake in the 17th century, La Merced ranks just below the cathedral and the La Compañía church in importance. It has a beautiful facade and lovely cloisters with a mural depicting the life of the Merced Order's founder. The sacristy contains a small museum of religious art, including a fantastic solid-gold monstrance swathed in precious stones. In the vaults of the church are the remains of two famous conquistadors, Diego de Almagro and Gonzalo Pizarro.

Calle Mantas s/n. ✆ 084/231-831. S/5 ($1.70) adults. Mon–Sat 8:30am–noon and 2–5pm.

Iglesia y Convento de San Francisco   This large and austere 17th-century convent church, thoughtfully restored, extends the length of the square of the same name. It is best known for its collection of colonial art works, including paintings by Marcos Zapata and Diego Quispe Tito, both of considerable local renown. A monumental canvas

Cusco Festivals

Cusco explodes with joyous celebration of both its Amerindian roots and Christian influences during festivals, which are crowded but splendid times to be in the city if you can find accommodations. It's worth planning your trip around one of the following fiestas, if possible.

Inti Raymi, the fiesta of the winter solstice (June 24, but lasting for days before and afterward), is certainly the star attraction. It's an eruption of Incan folk dances, exuberant costumes, and grand pageants and parades, including a massive one that takes over the stately Sacsayhuamán ruins overlooking the city. Inti Raymi is one of the finest expressions of local popular culture on the continent, a faithful re-enactment of the traditional Incan Festival of the Sun. It culminates in high priests sacrificing two llamas, one black and one white, to predict the fortunes of the coming year. Cusco's **Carnaval week,** with lots of music, dance, and processions of its own, is part of the buildup for Inti Raymi.

Semana Santa, or Easter week (late Mar or Apr), is an exciting traditional expression of religious faith, with stately processions through the streets of Cusco, including a great procession led by El Señor de los Temblores (Lord of the Earthquakes) on Easter Monday. On Good Friday, booths selling traditional Easter dishes are set up on the streets.

In early May, the **Fiesta de las Cruces (Festival of the Crosses),** a celebration popular throughout the highlands, is marked by communities decorating large crosses that are then delivered to churches. Crucifix vigils are held on all hilltops that are crowned by crosses. Festivities, as always accompanied by lively dancing, give thanks for bountiful harvests. Early June's **Corpus Christi** festival is another momentous occasion, with colorful religious parades featuring 15 effigies of saints through the city and events at the Plaza de Armas and the cathedral (where the effigies are displayed for a week).

On December 24, Cusco celebrates the **Santuranticuy Festival,** one of the largest arts-and-crafts fairs in Peru. Hundreds of artisans lay out blankets in the Plaza de Armas and sell carved Nativity figures and saints' images, in addition to ceramics and *retablos* (altars). The tradition was begun by the Bethlehemite Order and Franciscan Friars.

A hugely popular Andean festival that attracts droves from Cusco and the entire region is the **Virgen del Carmen,** celebrated principally in Paucartambo (see "Side Trips from Cusco," later in this chapter) and with only a slightly lesser degree of exuberance in Pisac and smaller highland villages.

(12 by 9m/39 by 30 ft.) that details the genealogy of the Franciscan family (almost 700 individuals) is by Juan Espinoza de los Monteros. The Franciscans also decorated the convent with ceiling frescoes and a number of morbid displays of skulls and bones. The church is worth a visit mainly for those with extra time in Cusco.

Plaza de San Francisco s/n. (C) **084/221-361.** Admission S/3 (85¢) adults, S/2 (60¢) students. Mon–Sat 9am–4pm.

INCAN RUINS NEAR CUSCO ★★★

The best way to see the following set of Incan ruins just outside Cusco is as part of a half-day tour. The hardy might want to approach it as an athletic archaeological expedition: If you've got 15km (9⅓ miles) of walking and climbing at high altitude in you, it's a beautiful trek. Otherwise, you can walk to Sacsayhuamán and nearby Q'enko (the climb from the Plaza de Armas is strenuous and takes 30–45 min.), and take a colectivo or taxi to the other sites. Alternatively, you can take a Pisac/Urubamba minibus (leaving from the bus station at Calle Intiqhawarina, off Av. Tullumayo, or Huáscar 128) and tell the driver you want to get off at Tambomachay, the ruins farthest from Cusco, and work your way back on foot. Some even make the rounds by horseback. You can easily and cheaply contract a horse at Sacsayhuamán, but don't expect a chance to ride freely in the countryside—you'll walk rather slowly to all the sites alongside a guide.

Visitors with less time in Cusco or less interest in taxing themselves might want to join a guided tour, probably the most popular and easiest way of seeing the sites. Virtually any of the scads of travel agencies and tour operators in the old center of Cusco offer them. Some well-rated traditional agencies with a variety of programs include **Milla Turismo,** Portal Comercio 195, Plaza de Armas (✆ **084/234-181;** www.milla turismo.com); **SAS Travel,** Portal Panes 167, Plaza de Armas (✆ **084/255-205;** www.sastravelperu.com); and **Top Vacations,** Portal Confiturías 265, Plaza de Armas (✆ **084/263-278**).

Admission to the following sites is by *boleto turístico,* and they are all open daily from 7am to 6pm. Guides, official and unofficial, hover around the ruins; negotiate a price or decide upon a proper tip. There are a handful of other Incan ruins on the outskirts of Cusco, but the ones discussed below are the most interesting.

These sites are generally safe, but at certain times of day—usually dawn and dusk before and after tour groups' visits—several ruins are said to be favored by thieves. It's best to be alert and, if possible, go accompanied.

SACSAYHUAMÁN ★★★

The greatest and nearest to Cusco of the ruins, Sacsayhuamán reveals some of the Incas' most extraordinary architecture and monumental stonework. Usually referred to as a garrison or fortress—because it was constructed with forbidding, castlelike walls—it was more likely a religious temple, although most experts believe it also had military significance. The Incan emperor Pachacútec began the site's construction in the mid–15th century, although it took nearly 100 years and many thousands of men to complete it. Massive blocks of limestone and other types of stone were brought from as far as 32km (20 miles) away.

The ruins, a steep 30-minute (or longer) walk from the center, cover a huge area, but they constitute perhaps one-quarter of the original complex, which could easily

---

Fun Fact **Those Fabulously "Sexy" Ruins**

The pronunciation of Sacsayhuamán, like many Quechua words, proves difficult for most foreigners to wrap their tongues around, so locals and tour guides have several jokes that point to its similarity to the words "sexy woman" in English. You haven't really experienced Cusco until you've heard the joke with that punch line a dozen times—from old men, guides, and even little kids.

Incan Ruins near Cusco

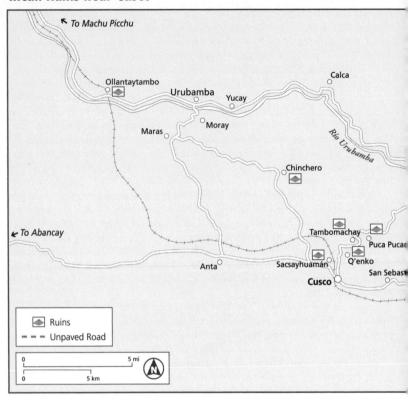

house more than 10,000 men. Today, what survive are the astounding outer walls, constructed in a zigzag formation of three tiers. (In the puma-shaped layout of the Incan capital, Sacsayhuamán was said to form the animal's head, and the zigzag of the defense walls forms the teeth.) Many of the base stones employed are almost unimaginably massive; some are 3.5m (11 ft.) tall, and one is said to weigh 300 tons. Like all Incan constructions, the stones fit together perfectly without aid of mortar. It's easy to see how hard it would have been to attack these ramparts with 22 distinct zigzags; the design would automatically expose the flanks of an opponent.

Above the walls are the circular foundations of three towers that once stood here; they were used for storage of provisions and water. The complex suffered such extensive destruction that little is known about the actual purposes Sacsayhuamán served. What is known is that it was the site of one of the bloodiest battles between the Spaniards and native Cusqueños. More than 2 years after the Spaniards had initially marched on Cusco and installed a puppet government, the anointed Inca (Manco Inca) led a seditious campaign that took back Sacsayhuamán and nearly defeated the Spaniards in a siege of the Incan capital. Juan Pizarro and his vastly outnumbered but superior armed forces stormed Sacsayhuamán in a horrific battle in 1536 that left thousands dead. Legend speaks of their remains as carrion for giant condors in the open fields here. After the defeat of the Incan troops and the definitive Spanish occupation

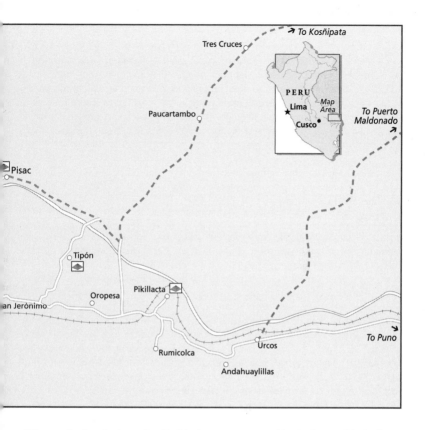

of Cusco, the Spaniards made off with the more manageably sized stone blocks from Sacsayhuamán to build houses and other structures in the city below.

The Inti Raymi festival is celebrated here annually, and it is truly a great spectacle—one of the finest in Peru (see "Cusco Festivals" on p. 218). A flat, grassy esplanade (where the main ceremony of the festival is celebrated) separates the defense walls from a small hill where you'll find the "Inca's Throne" and large rocks with well-worn grooves, used by children and often adults as slides. Nearby is a series of claustrophobia-inducing tunnels—pass through them if you dare.

Night visits to the ruins are permitted from 8 to 10pm. Under a full moon in the huge starlit Andean sky, Sacsayhuamán is so breathtaking that you'll instantly grasp the Incas' worship of the natural world, in which both the sun and the moon were considered deities. If you go at night, take a flashlight and a few friends; security is a little lax, and assaults on foreigners have occurred.

Walking directions: There are a couple of paths up to the ruins from downtown Cusco. You can take Almirante, Suecia, or Plateros. Head northwest from the Plaza de Armas. Take Palacio (behind the cathedral) until you reach stairs and signs to the ruins; or at the end of Suecia, climb either Huaynapata or Resbalosa (the name means "slippery") until you come to a curve and the old Incan road. Past the San Cristóbal church at the top, beyond a plaza with fruit-juice stands, is the main entrance to the

---

> ## Fun Fact Can't Leave Well Enough Alone
>
> The Peruvian authorities are notorious for messing with ancient Incan ruins, try-ing to rebuild them rather than let them be what they are: ruins. You'll notice at Sacsayhuamán and other Incan sites that unnecessary and misleading restoration has been undertaken. The grotesque result is that small gaps where original stones are missing have been filled in with obviously new and misplaced garden rocks—a disgrace to the perfection pursued and achieved by Incan stonemasons.

---

ruins. Plan to spend about an hour here for a brief run-through, and up to 3 hours if you're really interested or a photography buff or if you have kids who want to play on the slides and in the tunnels.

Q'ENKO ⚔

The road from Sacsayhuamán leads past fields where, on weekends, Cusqueños play soc-cer and have cookouts, to the temple and amphitheater of Q'enko (*Kehn*-koh), a distance of about a kilometer (½ mile). The ruins are due east of the giant white statue of Christ crowning the hill next to Sacsayhuamán; follow the main road, and you'll see signs for Q'enko, which appears on the right. A great limestone outcrop was hollowed out by the Incas, and, in the void, they constructed a cavelike altar. (Some have claimed that the smooth stone table inside was used for animal sacrifices.) Visitors can duck down into the caves and tunnels beneath the rock. You can also climb on the rock and see the many channels cut into the rock, where it is thought that either *chicha* or, more salaciously, sac-rificial blood coursed during ceremonies. Q'enko might very well have been a site of rit-ual ceremonies performed in fertility rites and solstice and equinox celebrations. Allow a half-hour to tour the site, plus the time it takes you to get there.

PUCA PUCARA

A small fortress (the name means "red fort") just off the main Cusco–Pisac road, this might have been some sort of storage facility or lodge, or perhaps a guard post on the road from Cusco to the villages of the Sacred Valley. It is probably the least impressive of the sites, although it has nice views of the surrounding countryside. From Q'enko, Puca Pucara is a 90-minute to 2-hour walk along the main road; allow a half-hour for your visit.

TAMBOMACHAY

On the road to Pisac (and a short, signposted walk off the main road), this site is also known as Los Baños del Inca (Incan Baths). Located near a spring just a short walk beyond Puca Pucara, the ruins consist of three tiers of stone platforms. Water still flows across a sophisticated system of aqueducts and canals in the small complex of terraces and a pool, but these were not baths as we know them (although ritualistic bathing might have taken place here). Most likely this was a place of water ceremonies and worship. The exquisite stonework indicates that the baños were used by high priests and nobility only. Plan on spending an hour here.

6 Especially for Kids

Cusco is a blast to walk around, so entertaining the kids and finding suitable restau-rants and things to do shouldn't be a problem for most families. Kids old enough to appreciate a bit of history might enjoy the exceptionally laid-out **Museo de Arte Pre-colombino (MAP),** as well as the **Museo Inka,** both of which will give them a good grounding in pre-Columbian civilizations and Incan culture. Beside ceramics and textiles, the Museo Inka displays cool mummies and tiny hand-painted Incan drinking vessels. You'll find Andean women weaving traditional textiles in the courtyard.

Cusco resonates with remnants of the ancient capital; a walking tour with the kids will take you past **Incan walls** with giant granite blocks that look like the pieces of a giant jigsaw puzzle. Have the kids count the hand-cut angles in the 12-angled stone and find the outlines of the puma stone (see "The Magic of Incan Stones: A Walking Tour" on p. 214). Observing the walls will give you a chance to impress your family with your knowledge of Andean history. Explain that the Incas built these massive walls without mortar or cement of any kind and with no knowledge of the wheel or horses, and that they constructed one of the world's greatest empires, reaching from one end of South America to another, without a written language and with runners who relayed messages to rulers.

Another good activity for artistically inclined children is to pop into **artists' studios** in the funky neighborhood of San Blas. Then walk—if you have the energy—up to the ruins of **Sacsayhuamán.** There you'll find more massive stones and gorgeous views of the city and surrounding mountains, but kids will really dig the huge rocks with slick grooves that make fantastic slides. There are also some cool tunnels cut into stones nearby, which kids might enjoy much more than their parents.

And, of course, the biggest family attraction of all lies beyond Cusco: Few are the kids who aren't fascinated by the ruins of **Machu Picchu.** The easygoing towns of the **Sacred Valley** are also great spots for families.

7 Shopping

Cusco is Peru's acknowledged center of handicraft production, especially hand-woven textiles, and its premier shopping destination. Many Cusqueño artisans still employ ancient weaving techniques, and they produce some of the finest textiles in South America. Peru's top tourist draw overflows with shops stuffed with colorful, enticing wares. From tiny one-person shops to large markets with dozens of stalls, there are few better places to shop than Cusco for excellent-value Andean handicrafts.

Items to look for (you certainly won't have to look too hard because they're everywhere you turn) include alpaca-wool sweaters, shawls, gloves, hats, scarves, blankets, ponchos (in fact, there are so many cool and cheap cold-weather items here that many people end up tossing the things they've brought for the chilly nights), and antique blankets and textiles, beautiful but pricey; woodcarvings, especially nicely carved picture frames; fine ceramics and jewelry; and Escuela Cusqueña reproduction paintings.

The barrio of **San Blas,** the streets right around the **Plaza de Armas** (particularly calles Plateros and Triunfo), and **Plaza Regocijo** are the best and most convenient haunts for shopping outings. Many merchants sell similar merchandise, so some price comparison is always helpful. If sellers think you've just arrived in Peru and don't know the real value of items, your price is guaranteed to be higher. Although bargaining is acceptable and almost expected, merchants in the center of Cusco are confident of a steady stream of buyers, and, as a result, they are often less willing to negotiate than their counterparts in markets and more out-of-the-way places in Peru. Most visitors will find prices delightfully affordable, though, and haggling beyond what you know is a fair price, when the disparity of wealth is so great, is generally viewed as bad form.

ALPACA FASHIONS

It's difficult to walk 10 feet in Cusco without running into an alpaca goods shop. Almost everyone in Cusco will try to sell you what they claim to be 100% alpaca scarves and sweaters, but many sold on the street and in tourist stalls are inferior quality (and might even be mixed with man-made materials such as fiberglass). What is described as "baby alpaca" might be anything but. To get better quality, not to mention more stylish, examples, you need to visit a store that specializes in upscale alpaca fashions; they are much more expensive but, compared to international alpaca prices, still a true bargain. The following stores are some of the best, and they all feature great-looking shawls, jackets, and sweaters: **Alpaca 3,** Calle Ruinas 472 (© **084/226-101**); **Alpaca's Best** ☜☜, Plaza Nazarenas 197–199 (© **084/245-331**); **Alpaca 111** ☜☜, Plaza Recocijo 202 (© **084/243-233**); **Alpaca Golden,** Portal de Panes 151 at Plaza de Armas and Zetas 109 at Plazoleta de Santo Domingo (no phone); **Alpaca Treasures,** Heladeros 172 (©084/438-557); and **World Alpaca,** Portal Carnes 232 (© 084/244-098). **Werner & Ana,** a Dutch-Peruvian design couple, sell stylish clothing in fine natural fabrics, including alpaca. They have a shop on Plaza San Francisco 295-A at Garcilaso (© **084/231-076**). For women only, **Montse Aucells** ☜☜, a Catalan designer resident in Cusco, has a small shop at Palacio 116 (© 084/226-330) that features by far the most fashionable and original designs I've seen in town. Many shops in Cusco feature sheep's wool or alpaca *chompas,* or jackets, with Andean designs (often lifted directly from old blankets and weavings). **Artesanías Quipu Cancha,** Plateros 321 (© **084/223-369**), stocks stylish and well-made jackets in alpaca and dozens of styles (they'll even custom-make one for you). A different take on Peruvian fashions, sure to appeal to plenty of stylish backpackers, is available at **Mundo Hemp,** Qanchipata 596, San Blas (no phone), where you'll find 100% natural hemp clothes and housewares, as well as a funky little cafe.

ANTIQUES

Most of the best antiques dealers are found in the San Blas district. **Antigüedades y Artesanías Sayre,** at Triunfo 352-B (© **084/236-981**), and **Galería de Arte Cusqueño Antigüedades,** at Plazoleta San Blas 114 (© **084/237-857**), have lots of different antiques, ranging from textiles to art and furniture. Another shop worth a peek is **El Armario,** Carmen Alto 118 (© **084/229-809**). For a selection of expensive antique Andean textiles, visit the small shop at Portal Comercio 173 on Plaza de Armas (© **084/233-484**); it appears to have no name, but the proud owner calls it **Tienda-Museo de Josefina Olivera.** You should probably take at least some of what she tells you about the origins and ages of some pieces with a grain of salt. For antique textiles, I much prefer the small stall at the end of the corridor (on the right side as you enter) within the Feria Artesanal at Plateros 334 (see below). The stalls aren't numbered, and you might have to ask the owner to pull his older, more valuable pieces from a trunk he keeps them in, but he has some of the finest quality ceremonial textiles you'll find in Cusco.

ART & HANDICRAFTS

Especially noteworthy is the **Centro de Textiles Tradicionales del Cusco** ☜☜, Av. El Sol 603 (© **084/228-117;** www.textilescusco.org), an organization dedicated to "fair trade" practices. It ensures that 70% of the sale price of the very fine textiles on display goes directly to the six communities and individual artisans it works with. On-site is an ongoing demonstration of weaving and a very good, informative textiles museum. Prices are a bit higher than what you may find in generic shops around town, though the textiles are also higher quality, and much more of your money will go to the women who work for days on individual pieces. For a general selection of *artesanía,* **Galería Latina,** San Agustín 427 (✆ **084/246-588**), has a wide range of top-end antique blankets, rugs, alpaca-wool clothing, ceramics, jewelry, and handicrafts from the Amazon jungle in a large, cozy shop near the Hotel Libertador. **Centro Artesanal Cusco,** at end of Avenida El Sol, across from the large painted waterfall fountain and Hotel Savoy, is the largest indoor market of handicrafts stalls in Cusco, and many goods are slightly cheaper here than they are closer to the plaza. Other centers with stalls and similar goods are **Feria Artesanal Tesoros del Inca,** Plateros 334 (✆ **084/233-484**); **Centro Artesanal "Conde de Gabucha,"** Zetas 109 (✆ **084/248-250**); **Centro Artesanal El Inca,** San Andrés 218; **Centro Artesanal Sambleño,** Cuesta de San Blas 548; and **Feria Artesanal Yachay Wasi,** Triunfo 374.

San Blas is swimming with art galleries, artisan workshops, and ceramics shops. You'll stumble upon many small shops dealing in reproduction Escuela Cusqueña religious paintings and many workshops where you can watch artisans in action. Several of the best ceramics outlets are also here, and a small handicrafts market usually takes over the plaza on Saturday afternoon. Check out **Artesanías Mendivil,** known internationally for its singular saint figures with elongated necks, but also with a nice selection of mirrors, carved wood frames, Cusco School reproductions, and other ceramics; it has locations at Plazoleta San Blas 619 (✆ 084/233-247), Hatunrumíyoc 486 (✆ 084/233-234), and Plazoleta San Blas 634 (✆ 084/240-527). **Artesanías Olave,** the outlets of a high-quality crafts shop that does big business with tourists, are located at Triunfo 342 (✆ 084/252-935), Plazoleta San Blas 100 (✆ 084/246-300), and Plazoleta San Blas 651 (✆ 084/231-835). **Juan Garboza** *taller* (workshop), Tandapata 676, Plazoleta San Blas (✆ 084/248-039), specializes in pre-Incan-style ceramics. **Aqlla,** located at Cuesta de San Blas 565 and marked by a sign that says ETHNIC PERUVIAN ART (✆ 084/249-018), has great silver jewelry, folk and religious art, and fine alpaca items. **Galería Sur,** Hatunrumiyoc 487-B, (✆ 084/238-371) sells fine tapestries from Ayacucho.

Several artists in the San Blas area open their studios as commercial ventures, although some of these can be fairly expensive for the opportunity to watch a painter paint. Look for flyers in cafes and restaurants in San Blas, if you're interested.

CENTRAL MARKET

Cusco's famous, frenzied **Mercado Central** near the San Pedro rail station is shopping of a much different kind—almost more of a top visitor's attraction than a shopping destination. Its array of products for sale—mostly produce, food, and household items—is dazzling. Even if you don't come to shop, this rich tapestry of modern and yet highly traditional Cusco still shouldn't be missed. If you're an adventurous type who doesn't mind eating at street stalls (which are generally pretty clean), you can get a ridiculously cheap lunch for about $1. Don't take valuables (or even your camera), though, and be on guard because the market is frequented by pickpockets targeting tourists. The market is open daily from 8am to 4pm or so.

JEWELRY

Ilaria, one of the finest jewelry stores in Peru, deals in fine silver and unique Andean-style pieces, and has several branches in Cusco: at Hotel Monasterio, Palacios 136 (✆ **084/221-192**); at Hotel Libertador, Plazoleta Santo Domingo 259 (✆ **084/223-192**); and another at Portal Carrizos 258 on the Plaza de Armas (© **084/246-253**). Many items, although not inexpensive, are a good value for handmade silver.

The contemporary jewelry designer **Carlos Chaquiras,** Triunfo 375 (© **084/ 227-470**), is an excellent craftsman; many of his pieces feature pre-Columbian designs. Another nice shop with silver items is **Platería El Tupo,** Portal de Harinas 181, Plaza de Armas (© **084/229-809**). **Chimú Art & Gifts,** Carmen Alto 187-B, San Blas (© **084/801-968**), is a funky shop featuring cool contemporary designs in silver, many based on interpretations of Chimú culture art. Rocío Pérez shows her original designs (packaged in handmade bags) at her little shop, **Jewelry Esma,** in the entryway to the Quinta Paccha Papa restaurant, at Plaza San Blas 120.

WOODWORK

Lots of shops have hand-carved woodwork and frames. However, the best spots for handmade baroque frames (perfect for your Cusco School reproduction or religious shrine) are **La Casa del Altar,** Mesa Redonda Lote A near the Plaza de Armas (© **084/ 244-712**), which makes *retablos* and altars in addition to frames; and the small *taller* (studio) where Miguel Angel León Sierra and children and grandchildren make splendid handmade cedar frames to order (the kind one sees on most art from the Escuela Cusqueña originals and imitations). The *taller* is just off Plaza de Nazarenas, at Córdoba del Tucumán 372 (© **084/236-271**).

8 Cusco After Dark

Most first-time visitors to Cusco are surprised to find that this Andean city with such a pervasive, gentle Amerindian influence and colonial atmosphere also has such a rollicking nightlife. It's not as diverse (or sophisticated) as Lima's, but the scene, tightly contained around the Plaza de Armas, is predominantly young and rowdy, a perfect diversion from the rigors of trekking and immersion in Incan and colonial history. I have heard countless young backpackers from countries across the globe exclaim, in universal MTV lingo and with pisco sour in hand, "Cusco rocks!" Some older visitors might find the late-night, spring break party atmosphere a little jarring in such a historic, stately place. But even for those with a lower-key night in mind, Cusco is especially entrancing in the early evening, as lights twinkle in the hills and the street lamps in the Plaza de Armas give a golden glow to the square.

Even though the city is inundated with foreigners during many months of the year, bars and discos aren't just gringolandia outposts. Locals (as well as Peruvians from other cities, principally Lima, and other South Americans) usually make up a pretty healthy percentage of the clientele. Clubs are in such close range of each other—in the streets just off the Plaza de Armas and in San Blas (where the city's artsy bars and cafes proliferate)—that virtually everyone seems to adopt a pub-crawl attitude, bopping from one bar or disco to the next, often reconvening with friends in the plaza before picking up a free drink ticket and free admission card from one of the many girls on the square handing them out. It's rare that you'll have to pay a cover charge in Cusco. Drinks are very cheap, but you should be careful imbibing at 11,000 feet—it quickly takes its toll.

For those who are saving their energy for the Inca Trail, there are less rowdy options, such as Andean music shows in restaurants, more sedate bars, and English-language movies virtually every night of the week. **Teatro Municipal,** Mesón de la Estrella 149 (© **084/221-847**), and **Centro Q'osqo,** Av. El Sol 684 (© **084/227-901**), occasionally schedule music concerts and dance performances. Check with the tourist information office for a schedule of events.

BARS & PUBS

In high season, bars are often filled to the rafters with gringos hoisting cheap drinks and trading information on the Inca Trail or their latest jungle or rafting adventure (or just trying to pick up Peruvians or each other). Most bars are open from 11am or noon until 1 or 2am. Many have elongated or frequent happy hours offering half-price drinks, making it absurdly cheap to tie one on. (Travelers still adjusting to Cusco's altitude, though, should take it easy—alcohol can wipe you out if your body's not ready for it.)

One of the oldest pubs in town is **Cross Keys** ⊛, Portal Confiturías 233, Plaza de Armas, second floor (no phone), owned by the English honorary consul and owner of Manu Expeditions. It's especially popular with Brits who can play darts or catch up on European soccer on satellite, and it's stuffed to the gills late at night. Pub grub is available, if you can get an order in. **Los Perros** ⊛⊛, Tecsecocha 436 (℃ 084/ 241-447), is one of the coolest bars in Cusco, a funky lounge bar owned by an Australian-Peruvian couple. "The Dogs" has comfy sofas, good food and drinks (including hot wine), and a hip soundtrack, including live jazz on Sunday and Monday nights. The bar attracts a very international crowd that takes advantage of the book exchange and magazines, and plenty of folks come back again and again for meals. **The Muse** ⊛, Tandapata 684, San Blas (℃ 084/246-332), has a similar vibe, though it's a bit scruffier. **Fallen Angel** ⊛, Plaza de Nazarenas 221 (℃ 084/258-184), bills itself as a restaurant but is so into its wildly campy, over-the-top look—complete with glass tables topping porcelain bathtubs filled with brightly colored fish—that it's hard to view it as anything but a largely gay nightclub. I ate dinner here, but I can't say I was terribly comfortable dining on a deep-red-and-black sofa with dozens of heart-shaped silk pillows. What was formerly the industrial-chic dance club Spoon has morphed into the more Peruvian sounding **Sumaq Misky** ⊛, Plateros 334. It's a restaurant and lounge-bar with English movies daily.

American-owned **Norton Rat's Tavern,** Loreto 115 (℃ 084/246-204), next door to the La Compañía church, is a rough-and-tumble bar, the type of biker-friendly place that you might find in any American Midwestern city. Nice balconies overlook the action below on the plaza. **Paddy Flaherty's,** Triunfo 124, Plaza de Armas (℃ 084/ 247-719), is an Irish pub serving Guinness on draft. It's cozy, relaxed, and often crowded, with expats catching up on "football" (soccer, of course) and rugby. **Rosie**

Tips Raw Fish: A Cure for What Ails You

If you hang out so much and so late in Cusco that you wind up with a wicked hangover—which is even more of a problem at an altitude of 3,300m (11,000 ft.)—adopt the tried-and-true Andean method of reviving yourself. For once, the solution is not coca-leaf tea—it's ceviche that seems to do the trick. Something about raw fish marinated in lime and chile makes for a nice slap in the face. When I lived in Ecuador (a country that fights with Peru not only over boundaries, but also over credit for having invented ceviche), late Sunday mornings at the *cevichería* were part of the weekly routine for pale-faced folks hiding behind sunglasses.

O'Grady's, Santa Catalina Ancha 360 near the Plaza de Armas (© **084/247-935**), is the other Irish tavern of note, considerably fancier digs in which to down your (canned) Guinness. There's live music Thursday through Saturday, and several happy hours throughout the day.

LIVE MUSIC

Live music is a nearly constant feature of the Cusco nightlife scene, and it's not all itinerant bands of altiplano musicians in colorful vests and sandals playing woodwind instruments—not by a long shot. Live music tends to begin around 11pm in most clubs, and happy hours are generally from 8 to 9 or 10pm.

You can catch traditional Peruvian bands with a beat at Ukuku's and Rosie O'Grady's (see above), but for a traditional folklore music-and-dance show with panpipes and costumes—well, ponchos, alpaca hats, and sandals, at a minimum—you'll need to check out one of the restaurants featuring nightly entertainment. In addition to **El Truco** (p. 204) and **La Retama** (p. 205), **Tunupa,** Portal Confiturías 233, second floor (© **084/252-936**), has a good traditional music-and-dance show, as well as a panoramic view of the Plaza de Armas.

By far the best place in Cusco for nightly live music is **Ukuku's** 🐸🐸, Plateros 316, second floor (© **084/227-867**). The range of acts extends from bar rock to Afro-Peruvian, and the crowd comes to get a groove on, jamming the dance floor. Often the mix is half gringo, half Peruvian. If you're looking to pick up a Peruvian *chico* or *chica,* or at least practice your Spanish, it's one of the best spots in town. Ukuku's is open till the wee hours, and there's a room with computer terminals, 24-hour Internet access, and a pizza bar, as well as daily movies in the afternoon. Get your hands on a pass for free entrance so you don't get stuck paying a cover (although often it's not even necessary to have a pass; gringos often sail right in).

Kamikase 🐸, Plaza Regocijo 274, second floor (© **084/233-865**), is the senior citizen of Cusqueño nightclubs, having been inaugurated before the tourist explosion, back in 1985. It's a cool and comfortable place, a two-level bar and a live music area with tables and funky decor. The music ranges from rock en español to reggae, and there are lots of locals—occasionally, Peruvians even outnumber gringos. (Imagine that!) There are nightly drink specials on things such as caipirinhas and mojitos. If you've imbibed one too many of those, you might want to take a breather before tackling the stairs to the street. I once had to carry a friend out (don't ask), and it was a real challenge. **Tangible Myth** 🐸, San Juan de Dios 260 (© **084/260-519**), an upstairs bar in a slightly out-of-the-way location, is a good place to go for something different; it features live jazz and Latin American rhythms, as well as DJ and jam nights. The Irish pub **Rosie O'Grady's** (see "Bars & Pubs," above) also has live music—usually Peruvian, jazz, and blues—on weekends. **Garabato Video Pub,** Espaderos 135, third floor (© **084/620-336**), is a bar/restaurant that features nightly movies on a large screen, a variety of live shows, and a dance floor and lounge. It's one of Cusco's one-stop-shopping outlets for nightlife if you want to stay in one place.

DANCE CLUBS

A couple of Cusco's cooler late-night dance clubs have come and gone in the last couple of years, but a few of the old warhorses remain very popular. A pretty young crowd, both backpackers and young Peruvians, is lured to the discos by all the free drink cards handed out on the Plaza de Armas. **Mama Africa,** Portal Harinas 191, second floor (© **084/241-979**), relocated a few years ago after its owners split up. However, it

Cafe Society

If you really just want to chill out and have a coffee, a glass of wine, or some dessert, drop into one of the city's comfortable cafes. The following are all good places for a light meal during the day, but at night they tend to take on some of that smoky Euro-cafe sheen, and travelers get all metaphysical about their treks through the Andes.

Café Ayllu, Portal de Carnes 208, Plaza de Armas (© 084/232-357), is a busy little place, drawing as many locals as gringos. It's known for its *ponche de leche* (a milky beverage, often served with a shot of pisco) and *lenguas* (a flaky pastry with manjar blanco crème in the middle). It also offers good breakfasts, sandwiches, and the mainstay, coffee. **Trotamundos,** Portal de Comercio 177, second floor (© 084/232-387), has an excellent balcony on the main square, facing the cathedral. It also has an open fireplace, which is perfect for cold evenings. Here you can enjoy good coffees and cakes, and a lively nighttime atmosphere. **La Tertulia,** Procuradores 44 (© 084/241-422), is more of a breakfast and lunch hangout, while **Café Varayoc,** Espaderos 142 (© 084/232-404), is a sophisticated place to read or get serious in the afternoon and at night. Varayoc serves excellent pastries and desserts, especially cheesecake. **Pi Centro,** Atoqsayk'uchi 559, in San Blas (no phone), is an American-owned cafe with board games, message boards, good coffee (including espresso, macchiato, and cappuccino), and sandwiches, snacks, and desserts—as well as breakfast served all day long.

Away from the center, but well located if you're making the rounds of Manu travel operators, **Manu Café** is a chic rainforest-style cafe, very swish for Cusco; it's attached to Manu Nature Tours at Av. Pardo 1046 (© 084/252-721). It serves excellent coffee (including imported roasts from around the world) and light meals, and there are racks of foreign newspapers for your perusal.

retains its sweaty charm. There's occasional live music, and DJs spin an international dance mix of Latin, reggae, rock, and techno music for a mix of locals and fleece-clad gringos. The old club is now called **Mama Amerika,** Portal Belén 115, second floor (© 084/245-550). It's just as crowded as ever, and besides serving free and cheap drinks, it also has pizza and other good munchies and a large screen showing videos.

Eko Club, Plateros 334, second floor (no phone), is one of Cusco's hottest dance clubs. The large dance floor throbs until dawn with a variety of rock, trance, and Euro-techno; for those who need a break, there's a laid-back lounge out back, good for a chair, a smoke, and a drink. **Up Town,** Suecia 302 (© 084/227-241), is Cusco's island resort disco on spring break. It offers free salsa, samba, and merengue dance classes (in English), and it's popular with locals. With two bars and a fleet of what seems like dozens of young girls enticing visitors with free drink cards, **Extrem,** Portal de Carnes 298 (© 084/240-901), changed its misspelled name from Xcess but still swarms with one of Cusco's youngest and most frenetic crowds who come for happy hour and free drinks. Those who need to rest their hips can hang by the fireplace, catch a movie, or fortify themselves at the pizzeria.

CINEMA

There aren't many traditional cinemas in central Cusco, but there are a number of places showing movies, mostly to entertain international visitors in need of a break from trekking and sightseeing. Probably the best selection of films, ranging from classic to art house to children's flicks, but mostly American, is found at **The Film Movies & Lounge,** Procuradores 389, second floor (© 084/962-5898); it's got a cute little bar, serves food and drinks, and has three screenings daily (S/2 or 60¢). Other screens showing movies on a daily basis are **Movie-Net Café,** Santa Catalina Ancha 307 (no phone), with four screenings daily; **Garabato Video Pub,** Espaderos 135, third floor (© 084/620-336); **Sumaq Misky,** Plateros 334 (no phone); **Sunset Movie Café,** Tecsecocha 2 (© 084/807-434); and **Ukuku's,** Plateros 316 (© 084/227-867).

9 Side Trips from Cusco

Many visitors "do" Machu Picchu in a single day, taking a morning train out and a late-afternoon train back to Cusco. In my book, Machu Picchu is much too important and impressive a sight to relegate it to a day trip, but that's all many people have time for. The Sacred Valley villages and famed markets (especially Pisac and Chinchero) also constitute day trips for loads of travelers. Again, though, the area is so rich and offers so much for travelers with time to do more than whiz through it that the area—including Pisac, Urubamba, Ollantaytambo, Calca, Chinchero, and Moray—is treated separately in chapter 8, along with the great Incan ruins of Machu Picchu.

A Cusco-area **ruins hike,** either on foot or on horseback, of the Incan sites within walking distance of the capital—Sacsayhuamán, Q'enko, Puca Pucara, and Tambomachay—makes for a splendid daylong (or half-day, if you make at least some use of public transportation or a taxi) excursion. For more information on the individual sites, see the earlier "Incan Ruins Near Cusco" section and the map in "What to See & Do in Cusco," earlier in this chapter.

Adventure travelers might want to concentrate on other **outdoor sports,** including additional hikes, treks, mountain-biking excursions, and white-water rafting that can be done around Cusco. See "Extreme Sacred Valley: Outdoor Adventure Sports" on p. 240 in chapter 8.

PAUCARTAMBO
110km (68 miles) NE of Cusco

Most visitors who venture to very remote Paucartambo (and there aren't many of them) do so for the annual mid-July **Fiesta de la Virgen del Carmen** ✸✸✸, one of Peru's most outrageously celebrated festivals (it lasts several days, and most attendees, be they villagers or foreigners, camp out because there is nowhere else to stay); see the "Cusco Festivals" box on p. 218 for more details. Yet the beautiful, small, and otherwise quiet mountain village might certainly be visited during the dry season

---

Tips   **Jungle Adventure**

Cusco is the gateway to the southern Amazon region. If you're interested in a jungle expedition to the Manu Biosphere Reserve or the Tambopata National Reserve, don't miss chapter 10.

And Then There Were 12: The Incan Emperors

The Incan Empire, one of the greatest the Americas has ever known, had 12 rulers over its lifetime from the late 12th century to the mid–16th century. The emperors, or chieftains, were called Incas; the legendary founder of the dynasty was Manco Cápac. The foundations of the palaces of the sixth and eighth leaders, Inca Roca and Viracocha Roca, respectively, are still visible in Cusco. Pachacútec was a huge military figure, the Inca responsible for creating a great, expansive empire. He was also an unparalleled urban planner. He made Cusco the capital of his kingdom, and, under his reign, the Incas built Qoricancha, the fortresses at Pisac and Ollantaytambo in the Sacred Valley, and mighty Machu Picchu. Huayna Cápac, who ruled in the early 16th century, was the last Inca to oversee a united empire. He divided the Incan territory, which by that time stretched north to Ecuador and south to Bolivia and Chile, between his sons, Huáscar and Atahualpa, which resulted in a disastrous civil war. Atahualpa eventually defeated his brother but was captured by Francisco Pizarro in Cajamarca and killed by the Spaniards in 1533, which led to the ultimate downfall of the Incas. The 12 Incas, in order, are as follows:

1. Manco Cápac
2. Sinchi Roca
3. Lloque Yupanqui
4. Mayta Cápac
5. Cápac Yupanqui
6. Inca Roca
7. Yahuar Huácac
8. Viracocha Inca
9. Pachacútec
10. Tupac Inca
11. Huayna Cápac
12. Atahualpa

(May–Oct), if you've got the patience to venture way off the beaten track. A few travelers stop en route to Puerto Maldonado and the Manu Biosphere Reserve.

The peaceful colonial town, once a mining colony, has cobblestone streets and a lovely Plaza de Armas with white structures and blue balconies, but not a whole lot else—that is, until it is inundated by revelers donning wildly elaborate and frequently frightening masks, and drinking as if Paucartambo were the last surviving town on the planet. The colorful processions and traditional dances are spectacular, and a general sense of abandonment of inhibitions (senses?) reigns. Mamacha Carmen, as she's known locally, is the patron saint of the mestizo population.

Outside the festival, you might be able to get a simple bed at one of two small and very basic inexpensive inns in town: the **Hostal Quinta Rosa Marina** and the **Albergue Municipal** (neither has a phone). During the festival, there's also a small office of tourist information on the south side of the plaza. More information on the celebrations is available from the main tourist office in Cusco (© **084/263-176**).

Another 45km (28 miles) beyond Paucartambo is **Tres Cruces (Three Crosses),** sacred to the nature-worshipping Incas and still legendary for its mystical sunrises in the winter months (May–July are the best). Tres Cruces occupies a mountain ridge at the edge of the Andes, before the drop-off to the jungle. From a rocky outcropping at nearly 4,000m (13,100 ft.) above sea level, hardy travelers congratulate themselves (for having gotten there, as much as for the sight they've come to witness) as they gaze into the distance out over the dense, green Amazon cloud forest. The sunrise is full of intense colors and trippy optical effects (including multiple suns). Even for those lucky enough to have experienced the sunrise at another sacred Incan spot, Machu Picchu, it is truly a hypnotic sight.

GETTING THERE   Gallinas de Rocas minibuses leave daily for Paucartambo from Cusco's Avenida Huáscar, near Garcilaso (departure times vary; the journey takes 4–6 hr.). For the Virgen del Carmen festival (July 15–17), some small agencies organize 2- and 3-day visits, with transportation, food, and camping gear (or arrangements for use of a villager's bed or floor) included. Look for posters in the days preceding the festival. To get to Tres Cruces, see whether any Cusco travel agencies are arranging trips; otherwise, you'll either have to hire a taxi from Cusco or hitchhike from Paucartambo. (Ask around in town; some villagers will be able to hook you up with a ride.) Make sure you leave in the middle of the night to arrive in time for the sunrise.

TIPON
23km (14 miles) SE of Cusco

Rarely visited by tourists, who are in more of a hurry to see the villages and Incan ruins of the Sacred Valley north of Cusco, the extensive complex of Tipón is nearly the equal of the more celebrated ruins found in Pisac, Ollantaytambo, and Chinchero. For fans of Incan stonemasonry and building technique, Tipón's well-preserved agricultural terracing is among the best created by the Incas and makes for a rewarding, if not easily accessible, visit. Peter Frost writes in *Exploring Cusco* (Nuevas Imágenes, 1999) that the terracing is so elaborately constructed that it might have been instrumental in testing complex crops rather than used for routine farming. There are also baths, a temple complex, and irrigation canals and aqueducts that further reveal the engineering prowess of the Incas. The ruins are a healthy hour's climb (or more, depending on your physical condition) up a steep, beautiful path, or by car up a dirt road. The uncluttered distant views are tremendous. The truly adventurous and fit can continue above the first set of ruins to others perched even higher (probably another 2 hr. of climbing). During the rainy season (Nov–Mar), it's virtually impossible to visit Tipón.

GETTING THERE   Combis for "Urcos" leave from Avenida Huáscar in Cusco; request that the driver drop you off near Tipón, which is between the villages of Saylla and Oropesa. The site is 4km (2½ miles) from the highway; it's open daily from 7am to 5:30pm. Admission is by the *boleto turístico.*

PIKILLACTA & RUMICOLCA
38km (24 miles) SE of Cusco

These pre-Incan and Incan ruins might go unnoticed by most, were it not for their inclusion on the Cusco tourist ticket. Although the Cusco region is synonymous with the Incas, the Huari and other cultures preceded them. **Pikillacta** is the only pre-Incan site of importance near Cusco. The Huari culture built the complex, a huge ceremonial center, between A.D. 700 and 900. The two-story adobe buildings, of rather rudimentary masonry, aren't in particularly good shape, although they are surrounded by a defensive wall. Many small turquoise idols, today exhibited in the Museo Inka in Cusco, were discovered at Pikillacta.

Less than a kilometer from Pikillacta, across the main road, is **Rumicolca,** an Incan portal—a gateway to the Valle Sagrado—constructed atop the foundations of an ancient aqueduct that dates to the Huari. The difference in construction techniques is readily apparent. The site was a travel checkpoint controlling entry to the Cusco Valley under the Incas.

GETTING THERE   Combis for "Urcos" leave from Avenida Huáscar in Cusco and drop passengers for Pikillacta near the entrance. Both sites are open daily from 7am to 5:30pm. Admission is by the *boleto turístico.*

8

Machu Picchu & the Sacred Valley of the Incas

The Urubamba Valley, better known as **El Valle Sagrado de los Incas (the Sacred Valley of the Incas)** ✦✦✦, is a relaxed and incomparably beautiful stretch of small villages and ancient ruins spread across a broad plain and rugged mountain slopes northwest of Cusco. The magnificent Incan ruins found from Pisac to Ollantaytambo and beyond—some of the finest not only in Peru, but also in all of the Americas—are testaments to the region's immense ceremonial importance. The Incas built several of the empire's greatest estates, temples, and royal palaces between the sacred centers of Cusco and Machu Picchu, positioned like great bookends at the south and north ends of the valley.

Through the valley rolls the revered Río Urubamba (called the Willcamayu by the Incas; today it is also called the Vilcanota in one section), a pivotal religious element of the Incas' cosmology. The Incas believed not only that the flow of the Urubamba was inexorably tied to the constellations and the mountain peaks, but also that the river was the earthbound counterpart of the Milky Way. With the river as its source, the fertile valley was a major center of agricultural production for the Incas, who grew native Andean crops such as white corn, coca, potatoes, and other fruits and vegetables in expansive fields and along spectacularly terraced mountain slopes. The valley continues to serve as a breadbasket for

Cusco, providing grains, peaches, avocadoes and much more.

Even though the villages of the Sacred Valley, stretching about 100km (62 miles) from Pisac to Ollantaytambo, are highlights of many tourist itineraries and are coveted by hotel developers, they remain starkly traditional. Quechua-speaking residents work the fields with primitive tools and harvest salt with methods unchanged since the days of the Incas, and market days—although now conducted to attract the tourist trade as well as intervillage commerce—remain important rituals.

Along with Cusco and Machu Picchu, the Valle Sagrado is one of the highlights of Peru—if you're visiting either of the former, the two biggest attractions in Peru, it would be a shame not to spend at least an extra day or two in the Valley. Many visitors without a lot of time on their hands whip through the valley's highlights and markets on a daylong guided bus tour, sandwiching it between Cusco and Machu Picchu on the Incan itinerary. Seeing it blitzkrieg-style is certainly doable, but it can't compare to a leisurely pace that allows you an overnight stay or two in the valley and the chance to soak up the area's immense history, relaxed character, huge sky, stunning scenery, and, in the dry season, equally gorgeous springlike weather. The valley is also about 300m (1,000 ft.) lower than Cusco, making it much more agreeable

Where to Stay in the Sacred Valley

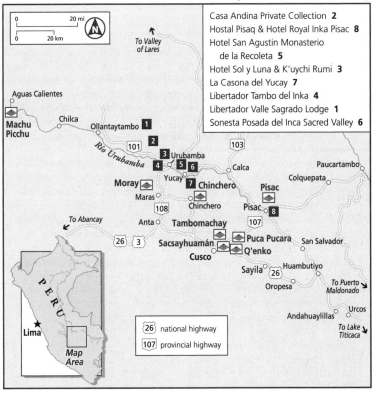

Casa Andina Private Collection **2**
Hostal Pisaq & Hotel Royal Inka Pisac **8**
Hotel San Agustin Monasterio
   de la Recoleta **5**
Hotel Sol y Luna & K'uychi Rumi **3**
La Casona del Yucay **7**
Libertador Tambo del Inka **4**
Libertador Valle Sagrado Lodge **1**
Sonesta Posada del Inca Sacred Valley **6**

26 national highway
107 provincial highway

for those potentially afflicted with altitude-related health problems. As a way to ease yourself into Peru, it may make more sense to begin in the Sacred Valley and see Machu Picchu before visiting Cusco.

More visitors are doing exactly that, spending several days in the valley, even choosing to base themselves at least initially in Pisac, Urubamba, or Ollantaytambo rather than the regional capital, Cusco. With the increased number of services (and more on the way) geared toward visitors in and around centrally located Urubamba and Ollantaytambo, this is more attractive than ever. The Sacred Valley now has some of the finest country-style hotels in Peru, especially geared toward visitors who are looking for an easy pace or all the outdoor activities

they can take advantage of (see "Extreme Sacred Valley: Outdoor Adventure Sports" on p. 240). Several highlights of the Sacred Valley, such as the ruins of Pisac and Ollantaytambo, and the market town Chinchero, are visited as part of the Cusco *boleto turístico* (see "Cusco's *Boleto Turístico*" on p. 212 in chapter 7 for complete details).

Beckoning at the end of the line, of course, is Machu Picchu. The most celebrated ruins in South America and a place that retains its mystery, allure, and spectacular beauty despite its enduring popularity, Machu Picchu is one of the most dramatic places on earth, one that holds a mystical appeal for many Peruvians and visitors. The classic route to Machu Picchu is via

> ### *Tips* Getting Around the Sacred Valley
>
> Local buses (usually small *combis* or *colectivos*) are the easiest and cheapest way to get to and around the Sacred Valley. They are often full of local color, if not much comfort. (Tall people forced to stand will not find them much fun.) Buses to towns and villages in the Sacred Valley—primarily to Pisac, Urubamba, and Chinchero—use small, makeshift terminals on Calle Puputi s/n, cdra. 2 and Av. Grau s/n, cdra. 1, in Cusco. They leave regularly throughout the day, departing when full; no advance reservations are required. Fares range between S/2 and S/4 (60¢–$1.15).
>
> Nearly every Cusco travel agency offers a good-value, 1-day Sacred Valley tour (as little as $20 per person for a full-day guided tour), and most provide English-speaking guides. The tours tend to coincide with market days (Tues, Thurs, and Sun) and generally include Pisac, Ollantaytambo, and Chinchero. It's not enough time to explore the ruins, though a quickie tour gives at least a taste of the Valley's charms. An even better way to explore the Urubamba Valley, if you have the time, is to advance town by town toward Machu Picchu or vice versa, starting out from the great citadel and returning piecemeal toward Cusco. The first Sacred Valley visit on most itineraries is Pisac. *A caveat:* Although you will travel comfortably by chartered, air-conditioned bus and will not have to worry about connections, you won't be able to manage your time at each place (indeed, you'll have precious little time in each place—only enough for a quick look around and a visit to ruins or the local market).
>
> You can also hire a taxi from Cusco to get to any of the valley towns or for a daylong tour of the Sacred Valley—expect to pay about S/60 to S/90 ($17–$26).

the Inca Trail, a marvel of sensitive development and religious appreciation for nature. Hiking the trail requires 4 days (or 2 days along the shorter, less traditional path) of pretty tough trekking across mountain passes, but the experience is unforgettable. If you don't have time or interest in walking and camping, the train to Machu Picchu nearly rivals the trail for scenic beauty, even if it doesn't provide the payoff of arriving shortly after sun-up as the mist begins to clear and rays of sunshine bathe the ruins.

1 Pisac ★★

32km (20 miles) NE of Cusco

The pretty Andean village of Pisac lies at the eastern end of the valley. Although the town is prized principally for its hugely popular Sunday artisan market, an obligatory stop on most Sacred Valley tours, Pisac deserves to be more widely recognized for its splendid Incan ruins, which rival those of Ollantaytambo and even Machu Picchu. Perched high on a cliff is the largest fortress complex built by the Incas. The commanding, distant views from atop the mountain, over a luxuriously long valley of green patchwork fields, are breathtaking.

ESSENTIALS
GETTING THERE
The bus trip from Cusco to Pisac takes 45 minutes to an hour. Colectivos drop passengers just across the river at the edge of town, a 3-block walk uphill from the main square (and market). From Pisac, buses return to Cusco and depart for other parts of the valley—Yucay, Urubamba (both a half-hour journey), and Ollantaytambo (1 hr.)—from the same spot.

Although a taxi to Pisac on your own costs about S/35 ($10), it is often possible to go by private car for as little as S/3 (85¢) per person. Private cars congregate near the bus terminal and leave when they have three or four passengers; just get in and ask the price (everyone pays the same fare).

VISITOR INFORMATION
You're best off getting information on Pisac and the Sacred Valley before leaving Cusco at the helpful **Tourist Information Office,** Mantas 117-A, a block from the Plaza de Armas (© **084/263-176**). Cusco's **South American Explorers Club** (© **084/245-484**) is also an excellent source of information, particularly on the Inca Trail and other treks, mountaineering, and white-water rafting in the valley. Inquire there about current conditions and updated transportation alternatives. Beyond that, the best sources of information are hotels.

Though you'll find an ATM machine on the main square, you should exchange much of the money you'll need in Cusco (especially if coming on Sunday to the crowded market). There's a post office on the corner of Comercio and Intihuatana.

WHAT TO SEE & DO
THE MARKET
Pisac's famed artisans' and antiques market ✦✦ draws many hundreds of shoppers on Sunday morning in high season, when it is without a doubt one of the liveliest in Peru. (There are slightly less popular markets on Tues and Thurs as well.) Hundreds of stalls crowd the central square—marked by a small church, San Pedro el Apóstolo, and massive *pisonay* trees—and spill down side streets. Sellers come from many different villages, many of them remote populations high in the Andes, and wear the dress typical of their village. Dignitaries from the local villages usually lead processions after Mass (said in Quechua), dressed in their versions of Sunday finery. The market is much like Cusco: rather touristy, though endearing and an essential experience in Peru. Even if you're not a committed shopper, it's an event.

The goods for sale at the market—largely sweaters and ponchos, tapestries and rugs, musical instruments, and carved gourds—are familiar to anyone who's spent a day in

---

Tips *Boleto Turístico* in the Valle Sagrado

The Cusco *boleto turístico* (tourist pass) is pretty much essential for visiting the Sacred Valley, in particular for the ruins of Pisac and Ollantaytambo, as well as the market and town of Chinchero. You can purchase it at any of those places if you haven't already bought it in Cusco before traveling to the Valley. See p. 212 in chapter 7 for more information.

Cusco, but prices are occasionally lower on selected goods such as ceramics. While tourists shop for colorful weavings and other souvenirs, locals are busy buying and selling produce on small streets leading off the plaza. The market begins at around 9am and lasts until midafternoon. It is so well worn on the Cusco tourist circuit that choruses of, *"¡Foto? Propinita,"* (photograph for a tip) ring out among mothers or would-be mothers with tiny children in adorable local outfits. On nonmarket days, bustling Pisac becomes a very quiet, little-visited village with few activities to engage travelers.

THE PISAC RUINS 🐾🐾

The Pisac ruins are some of the finest and largest in the entire valley. Despite the excellent condition of many of the structures, little is conclusively known about the site's actual purpose. It appears to have been part city, part ceremonial center, and part military complex. It might have been a royal estate of the Incan emperor (Pachacútec). It was certainly a religious temple, and although it was reinforced with the ramparts of a massive citadel, the Incas never retreated here to defend their empire against the Spaniards (and Pisac was, unlike Machu Picchu, not unknown to Spanish forces).

The best but most time-consuming way to see the ruins is to climb the hillside, following an extraordinary path that is itself a slice of local life. Trudging along steep mountain paths is still the way most Quechua descendants from remote villages get around these parts; many people you see at the Pisac market will have walked a couple of hours or more through the mountains to get there. To get to the ruins on foot (about 5km/3 miles, or 90 min.), you'll need to be pretty fit and/or willing to take it very slowly. Begin the ascent at the back of Pisac's main square, to the left of the church. The path bends to the right through agricultural terraces. There appear to be several competing paths; all of them lead up the mountain to the ruins. When you come to a section that rises straight up, choose the extremely steep stairs to the right. (The path to the left is overgrown and poorly defined.) If an arduous trek is more than you've bargained for, you can hire a taxi in Pisac (easier done on market days) to take you around the back way. (The paved road is some 9.5km/6 miles long.) If you arrive by car or colectivo rather than by your own power, the ruins will be laid out the opposite of the way they are described below.

From a semicircular terrace and fortified section at the top, called the **Qorihuayrachina,** the views south and west of the gorge and valley below and agricultural terraces creeping up the mountain slopes are stunning. Deeper into the nucleus, the delicately cut stones are some of the best found at any Incan site. The most important component of the complex, on a plateau on the upper section of the ruins, is the **Templo del Sol (Temple of the Sun),** one of the Incas' most impressive examples of masonry. The temple was an astronomical observatory. The **Intihuatana,** the so-called "hitching post of the sun," resembles a sundial but actually was an instrument that helped the Incas to determine the arrival of important growing seasons rather than to tell the time of day. Sadly, this section is now closed to the public, due to vandals who destroyed part of it a few years ago. Nearby (just paces to the west) is another temple,

---

Moments The Virgen del Carmen Festival

Pisac celebrates the Virgen del Carmen festival (July 16–18) with nearly as much enthusiasm as the more remote and more famous festival in Paucartambo (p. 230). It's well worth visiting Pisac during the festival if you are in the area.

thought to be the **Templo de la Luna (Temple of the Moon),** and beyond that is a ritual bathing complex, fed by water canals. Continuing north from this section, you can either ascend a staircase path uphill, which forks, or pass along the eastern (right) edge of the cliff. If you do the latter, you'll arrive at a tunnel that leads to a summit lookout at 3,400m (11,200 ft.). A series of paths leads from here to defensive ramparts **(K'alla Q'asa),** a ruins sector called **Qanchisracay,** and the area where taxis wait to take passengers back to Pisac.

In the hillside across the Quitamayo gorge, at the back side (north end) of the ruins, are hundreds of dug-out holes where *huaqueros* (grave robbers) have ransacked a cemetery that was among the largest known Incan burial sites.

The ruins are open daily from 7am to 5:30pm; admission is by Cusco's *boleto turístico* (p. 212). Note that to explore the ruins thoroughly by foot, including the climb from Pisac, you'll need at least 4 hours. Most people visit Pisac as part of a whirlwind day tour through the valley, which doesn't allow enough time either at the market or to visit the ruins. Taxis leave from the road near the bridge and charge around S/15 ($4.30) to take you up to the ruins.

WHERE TO STAY

If either of the two places below is full or beyond your budget, check out these inexpensive basic inns in town: **Hospedaje Buho,** Intihuatana 642/Camino Ruinas (© 084/203-001), on a side street near the main square, with rooms (even a few with private bathrooms) around a central patio and an *artesanía* shop; or **Kinsa Cocha Hospedaje,** Arequipa 307 (© 084/203-101), a family-run place with clean dorm rooms near the main plaza.

Hostal Pisaq ⚡ *Value* Owned by a friendly Peruvian-American couple, this small, pleasant, and perfectly central inn—a B&B, essentially—is a very good option in town. Warm and cozy, and located right on the main square in Pisac, it has murals hand-painted by the owners, a sauna, and an attractive courtyard with flowers. It also operates a small bar/restaurant with good pizza from a wood-burning oven and home-cooked meals. Rooms, full of Andean textiles, are nicely decorated for the price.

Plaza Constitución 333, Pisac. ©/fax 084/203-062. www.hotelpisaq.com. 11 units. $20 double with shared bathroom; $26 double with private bathroom. No credit cards. **Amenities:** Restaurant; bar; sauna. *In room:* No phone.

Hotel Royal Inka Pisac The most upmarket place to stay in Pisac is about a 15-minute walk from the village along the road up to the Incan ruins. The hotel, which sprawls around a pretty mustard-colored hacienda, has a surprising array of facilities and activities, including a tennis court, an indoor pool, a Jacuzzi, a sauna, massage, horseback riding, and mountain-bike rentals. Rooms are ample and comfortable; some have fireplaces. The hotel is good for those who want to spend time at Pisac's ruins and as a base for exploring the Sacred Valley—as a slightly cheaper alternative to hotels in Urubamba/Yucay (though it's a little pricey for Pisac). It caters mostly to groups, although in off season, it can get a little lonely.

Carretera Pisac Ruinas Km 1.5 s/n, Pisac. ©/fax 084/222-284. www.royalinkahotel.com/hpisac.html. 86 units. $64–$70 double. Rates include taxes and breakfast buffet. AE, DC, MC, V. **Amenities:** Restaurant; bar; indoor pool; tennis court; sauna; bike rental; room service; massage; laundry service. *In room:* TV, minibar, safe.

WHERE TO DINE

For eats in Pisac, check out **Ulrike's Café** ⚡, Plaza de Armas 828 (© 084/ 203-195), a genial and inexpensive spot for any meal, from breakfast to hearty lunches and vegetarian options. Run by a German expat, Ulrike's is a relaxed cafe on

Extreme Sacred Valley: Outdoor Adventure Sports

Peru has become a star on South America's burgeoning adventure and extreme sports travel circuit, a far cry from the days when just traveling to Peru was adventure enough. These days, many gringos in Peru have Gore-Tex boots on their feet and adrenaline rushes on their minds.

The Cusco–Sacred Valley region is one of the best in Peru—and the whole of South America—for white-water rafting, mountain biking, trekking, hang gliding, and paragliding. The most popular outdoor activity in Cusco is, of course, hiking the Inca Trail to Machu Picchu, but there are scores more trekking and other adventure opportunities. River runs are extremely popular, and justifiably so: Peru has some of the world's wildest rivers, and even for beginners, rafting is a sport that ripples with excitement. For more leisurely outdoors experiences, there are scores of good, gentle walking paths and horseback riding.

Many tour operators in Cusco organize adventure trips, some lasting a single day and others multiday camping trips focusing on one or more extreme sports. Participants range from novices to hard-core veteran adventure junkies; no experience is required for many trips, but be sure you sign up for a program appropriate for your level of interest and ability. Extreme sports being what they are, I suggest that you thoroughly check out potential agencies and speak directly to the guides, if possible. Hunting for bargains in this category is not advisable; quality equipment and good, English-speaking guides are fundamental for safety considerations. That said, booking a tour in Cusco rather than your home country may lead to a large discount. Trips booked in advance may be changed if there are not enough participants or farmed out to another, subcontracting, agency. In addition to the agencies listed below, **Viento-Sur Adventures** (© **084/201-620**; www.aventurasvientosur.com) in Urubamba offers a full range of outdoors programs, from trekking and walking to paragliding, mountain biking, and horseback riding.

Horseback Riding: Perol Chico, Carretera Urubamba-Ollantaytambo Km 77, Urubamba (© **084/201-694** or 084/624-475; www.perolchico.com), is a ranch in the Sacred Valley and one of the top horseback-riding agencies in Peru. It offers full riding vacations, with Peruvian Paso horses and stays at the ranch (in rustic cottages), as well as 1- and 2-day rides. **Viento-Sur,** Carretera Urubamba-Ollantaytambo, Urubamba (© **084/201-620**; www.aventurasvientosur.com), the adventure agency of Sol y Luna Hotel, runs a ranch and stable on the property and offers a variety of horseback-riding programs, from half-day to 14-day trips, in the Sacred Valley on Peruvian Paso horses.

Hot-Air Ballooning & Paragliding: Now that you can no longer hop a helicopter to Machu Picchu, there are other, even better ways to get aerial views of the Sacred Valley. **Globos de los Andes,** Av. de la Cultura 220, ste. 36 (© **084/232-352**; www.globosperu.com), has been on-again, off-again in the last couple years, but it's the only outfit organizing such trips. If you've got the money (ballooning isn't cheap, no matter where you do it) and you want aerial panoramas of the Sacred Valley, Incan ruins, and the majestic Andes, contact Globos to verify current flight programs. You might also check around Cusco for posters advertising tandem paraglide flights over the Sacred Valley.

Mountain Biking: Mountain biking is just really beginning to catch on in Peru, and tour operators are rapidly expanding their services and equipment. Cusco's nearby ruins and the towns, villages, and gorgeous scenery of the Sacred Valley (and the Manu jungle, for more adventurous excursions) are the best areas. **Peru Discovery,** Triunfo (Sunturwasi) 392, of. 113 (© 054/247-007; www.perudiscovery.com) is the top specialist, with a half-dozen bike trips that include hard-core excursions. **Amazonas Explorer, Apumayo Expediciones, Eric Adventures, Instinct Travel** (for contact information, see "White-Water Rafting," below), and **Manu Ecological Adventures,** Plateros 356, Cusco (© 084/261-640; www.manuadventures.com), offer 1- to 5-day organized mountain-biking excursions ranging from easy to rigorous.

Trekking: Too many highland-trekking adventures are offered to fully describe here. In addition to the groups listed in "Inca Trail Tour Agencies" (p. 270), which organize Inca Trail and other regional treks, the following companies handle a wide variety of trekking excursions: **Apu Expeditions,** Casilla Postal 24 (© 084/957-483); **Aventours,** Av. Pardo 545, of. 6 (© 084/224-050; www.aventours.com); **Enigma,** Jr. Clorinda Matto de Turner, 100 Urbanización Magisterial 1 Etapa (© 084/221-155; www.enigmaperu.com). **Manu Expeditions,** Urbanizacion Magisterio, segunda Etapa G-5 (© 084/226-671; www.manuexpeditions.com); **Mayuc,** Portal Confiturías 211 (© 084/242-824; www.mayuc.com); and U.S.-based **Andean Treks,** Av. Pardo 705 (© 800/683-8148 or 617/924-1974; www.andeantreks.com). **Peru Discovery** (see "Mountain Biking," above) also organizes excellent trekking expeditions.

White-Water Rafting: There are some terrific Andean river runs near Cusco, ranging from mild class II to moderate and world-class IV and V, including 1-day Urubamba River trips (Huambutío–Pisac and Ollantaytambo–Chillca), multiday trips to the more difficult Apurímac River, and, for hard-core rafters, the Tambopata (10 days or more) in the Amazon jungle. Recommended agencies include **Amazonas Explorer** ⟨★★⟩ (© 084/236-826 or 084/225-284; www.amazonas-explorer.com); **Apumayo Expediciones,** Garcilazo 265, Interior 3 (© 084/246-018; www.apumayo.com); **Eric Adventures,** Plateros 324 (© 866/978-4630 in US and Canada or 084/228-475; www.ericadventures.com); **Instinct Travel** (© 084/233-451; www.instinct-travel.com); **Loreto Tours,** Procuradores 50 (© 084/233-451); **Mayuc,** Portal Confiturías 211 (© 084/242-824; www.mayuc.com); and **SwissRaft Peru** ⟨★⟩, Plateros 361 (© 084/246-414; www.swissraft-peru.com).

the main square and can be counted on for a great-value lunch menu, homemade lasagna, omelets, salads, great desserts (like Ulrike's famous strudel), and coffee. **Samana Wasi,** Plaza Constitución 509 (no phone), serves good, inexpensive trout dishes straight from the river. The restaurant has a couple of basic rooms for rent as well. There's also an excellent traditional-style **bakery** on Mariscal Castilla 372 (no phone), a short walk from the plaza. It serves excellent vegetarian *empanadas* (stuffed pastries) and breads from adobe ovens—snacks that prove extremely popular on market days. **Restaurant Inti Wasi,** a restaurant about a mile beyond the city limits on the main road to Calca (© 084/203-047), serves good lunches, including fresh fish, to tourist groups on bus tours through the Sacred Valley. If you're not on an organized tour, it's still a good place for lunch, although it's a bit out of the way.

2 Urubamba & Environs ★ ★

78km (48 miles) NW of Cusco

Centrally located Urubamba is the busiest of the Sacred Valley towns, if only because it's the best equipped to handle visitors. Although the town itself doesn't have a whole lot more than a handsome main plaza and magnificent mountain scenery to offer, the surrounding region is lovely, and several of the best hotels in the region are located just south near Yucay, about 3km (1¾ miles) down the road, and north toward Ollantaytambo. Yucay is an attractive colonial village backed by a sophisticated system of agricultural terraces and irrigation canals. The area is a fine base from which to explore the Sacred Valley region.

ESSENTIALS
GETTING THERE

BY BUS   To Urubamba, a 2-hour bus ride from Cusco, you can go either via Pisac or via Chinchero (a slightly more direct route). Buses, or combis, (S/3, or 85¢) depart from Calle Puputi s/n, cdra. 2 and Av, Grau s/n, cdra. 1, in Cusco and arrive at **Terminal Terrestre** (no phone), the main bus terminal, about a kilometer (½ mile) from town on the main road to Ollantaytambo. Buses from the Urubamba terminal depart for Cusco and Chinchero (1 hr. away), as well as Ollantaytambo (30 min. away). Combis for other points in the Sacred Valley depart from the intersection of the main road at Avenida Castilla. To continue on to Yucay, just a couple of kilometers down the road, catch a mototaxi or a regular taxi in Urubamba or a colectivo along the highway (headed east, the opposite direction of the bus terminal from town).

BY TAXI   From Cusco, you can catch a cab to Urubamba for as little as S/50 ($14), although most drivers will at least try to charge S/70 ($20) or more. If you're headed directly to the Valley upon arrival in Cusco, have your hotel arrange for pickup at the airport. If it's a market day, you can easily arrange for the driver to take you to Pisac or Chinchero for a brief stopover along the way.

BY TRAIN   Travelers keen on exploring the Sacred Valley in tandem with Machu Picchu can travel from Urubamba on the **Sacred Valley Railway.** The Vistadome service goes from Urubamba to Ollantaytambo and on to Machu Picchu and back ($71.50 adults round-trip, $43 one-way). The train departs Urubamba at 6:10am and arrives at Machu Picchu at 8:20am. The return is at 4:45pm, with arrival at Urubamba at 7:15pm (trains depart Machu Picchu at other times during the day but stop at Ollantaytambo only; see "Essentials" under "Machu Picchu & the Inca Trail," later in this chapter). For reservations, call © 084/238-722 or visit www.perurail.com.

VISITOR INFORMATION

You should pick up information on the Sacred Valley before leaving Cusco, either at the helpful main **Tourist Information Office,** Mantas 117-A, a block from the Plaza de Armas (© 084/263-176); or from Cusco's **South American Explorers Club** (© 084/245-484). In Urubamba, you might be able to scare up some limited assistance at Av. Cabo Conchatupa s/n; in Yucay, try the office of Turismo Participativo, Plaza Manco II, 103 (© 084/201-099).

FAST FACTS   If you need cash, you'll find ATMs on either side of the main road to Yucay from Urubamba. For medical assistance, go to **Centro de Salud,** Av. Cabo Conchatupa s/n (© 084/201-334), or **Hospital del Instituto Peruano de Seguridad Social,** Av. 9 de Noviembre (© 084/201-032).

Urubamba is the best spot for Internet *cabinas* in the Sacred Valley region, with a good supply of machines and fast connections. **Academia Internet Urubamba,** established with the help of an American exchange student, is 2 blocks northeast of the Plaza de Armas, on the corner of Jr. Belén and Jr. Grau. There are also a couple of Internet cabinas on the main square. If you need a post office in Urubamba, you'll also find one on the Plaza de Armas.

WHAT TO SEE & DO

The main square of Urubamba, the **Plaza de Armas,** is attractively framed by a twin-towered colonial church and pisonay trees. Dozens of mototaxis, a funky form of local transportation not seen in other places in the valley (and seen in only a couple of other places in Peru), buzz around the plaza in search of passengers. Worth visiting in town is the beautiful home workshop of **Pablo Seminario** ✸, a ceramicist whose whimsical work features pre-Columbian motifs and is sold throughout Peru. Visitors either love or hate the style. The grounds of the house, located at Berriozábal 111 (© 084/201-002; www.ceramicaseminario.com), are a minizoo, with llamas, parrots, nocturnal monkeys, falcons, rabbits, and more. The workshop is open Monday through Saturday from 10am to 6pm. Seminario now has shops in the Sonesta Posada del Inca hotel in Yucay as well as Cusco. **Lanandina** (© 084/201-390; call for directions), operated by an Austrian resident of Urubamba, makes fantastic handmade wool houseshoes, bags, and hats using a centuries-old Mongolian formula.

A groovy bar in Urubamba is **Inti Killa,** Av. Grau 708 (no phone), which sounds as though it could be named for a Peruvian rap star. About a block from the main square, the bar/club has good dance beats, a large dance floor separate from the bar and a lounge area, and good pitchers of pisco sours.

Yucay is a pleasant and quiet little village with extraordinary views of the surrounding countryside. The Spaniards "bequeathed" the land to their puppet Incan chieftain, Sayri Tupac, who built a palace here. Incan foundations are found around the attractive **main plaza,** and some of the best agricultural terracing in the valley occupies the slopes of mountains around the village.

Very worthwhile side trips from Urubamba and Yucay are the ancient Incan salt pans of Maras or the Incan site at Moray; see "Beyond Urubamba," below, for additional information.

WHERE TO STAY

A cheaper alternative to the more upscale hotels reviewed below is the pleasant and good-value, if rather generic, **Posada Las 3 Marías,** Jr. Zavala 307, Urubamba

(© **084/201-006;** posada3marias@yahoo.com). It's a modern house in the center of town with gardens and seven large rooms for a relatively modest price ($30 double).

EXPENSIVE

Casa Andina Private Collection *Kids* One of this upstart Peruvian chain's select upscale offerings, this large, mountain-chalet type hotel has a beautiful setting, with gardens and large and handsomely decorated rooms with excellent views of the countryside. Rooms are large and handsomely decorated, with high ceilings and spacious bathrooms; the two-story suites with balconies are especially alluring. The hotel features a very good, though occasionally noisy, restaurant and often plays host to groups of diverse size. Activities such as river rafting, trekking, mountain biking and horseback riding are offered. Look for a large spa and outdoor pool to be added in late 2006.

5 to Paradero, Yanahuara. © **084/976-550.** Fax 01/445-4775. www.casa-andina.com. 85 units. $135 double; $194 suite. Rate includes breakfast buffet. AE, DC, MC, V. **Amenities:** Restaurant; business center; gym; room service; laundry service. *In room:* TV, minibar, safe.

Hotel San Agustín Monasterio de la Recoleta Close to Urubamba, just off the main road, is this charming and rustic hotel inhabiting parts of a 16th-century Franciscan monastery. Now that it is being sensitively renovated, it stands to become one of the finest properties in the region. It has the potential to become a mini–Hotel Monasterio (of Cusco) in the Urubamba Valley. The beautifully remodeled rooms (nos. 401–404) have outstanding views and remains of original Incan walls, and they greatly surpass the original, far simpler rooms. Services are still somewhat limited compared to other top-end hotels in the region. Climb up to the bell tower above the old chapel for great views of the valley. A nearby sister property is the similar, though somewhat less inviting, Hotel San Agustín Urubamba (© **084/201444**).

Recoleta s/n, off the main Urubamba-Ollantaytambo road. © **084/201-004.** Fax 084/201-666. www.hotelessanagustin. com.pe. 25 units. $110–$130 double. Rates include taxes and breakfast. AE, DC, MC, V. **Amenities:** Restaurant; outdoor pool; room service; laundry service. *In room:* TV.

Hotel Sol y Luna *Kids* Opened in 2000, Sol y Luna is one of the most attractive properties in the valley. Set back from the main road on the way to Ollantaytambo, amid spectacularly landscaped gardens, is this French- and Swiss-owned cluster of 28 invitingly decorated, circular bungalow-style rooms (including four family bungalows) with rustic decor, private terraces, and gorgeous mountain views. As the hotel has grown, the property has grown more crowded, and attention to details may have suffered. There have been some disturbing reports of price-gouging on services. The hotel has a rather small outdoor pool but one of the best restaurants in the area. It also operates its own adventure club, offering all sorts of outdoor activities in the region, including horseback riding, but those activities are more expensive than they are if arranged with other hotels and agencies in the region. Sol y Luna is no longer the sole luxury accommodation in the Valle, and travelers may find that they can do better at one of its newer competitors.

Carretera Urubamba-Ollantaytambo s/n, Huicho (2km/1¼ miles west of Urubamba). © **084/201-620.** Fax 084/ 201-084. www.hotelsolyluna.com. 14 units. $127 double; $182 family bungalow. Rates include breakfast buffet. AE, DC, MC, V. **Amenities:** Restaurant; pub; small pool; room service; laundry service. *In room:* TV, safe.

Libertador Tambo del Inka *Kids* This sprawling complex, recently purchased by the Libertador chain, is in the midst of being transformed into a five-star luxury property. It has nearly 12 hectares (30 acres) of beautifully landscaped gardens, a spectacular Olympic-sized pool, stupendous mountain views, river access, and spacious, bungalow-style rooms. For the time being it is a very comfortable and relaxed place to hang out in the Sacred Valley. Though it's clearly in a transitional phase, it should soon be one of the finest properties in the valley. A handful of rooms have already been updated, and they are quite sumptuous; make sure you ask for one of these rooms, as the older ones are comparatively plain. Two suites have massive Jacuzzi tubs and private gardens. There are llamas and alpacas on the grounds, as well as horses for hire.

Av. Ferrocarril s/n, Urubamba. ℂ/fax 084/201-126. 76 units. $120 double; $170 suite. Rate includes taxes and breakfast buffet. AE, DC, MC, V. **Amenities:** Restaurant; bar; indoor pool; tennis courts; 24-hr room service; laundry service. *In room:* TV, minibar, safe.

Libertador Valle Sagrado Lodge 🕮🕮 *Finds*   This intimate and thoroughly enchanting lodge, which feels more like an inn than a small hotel, is tucked away up a long dirt road from Casa Andina. It's constructed like a small colonial village with individual buildings of stucco and red-tile rooms, and gardens with fountains. Its elevated and secluded location provides fantastic mountain and valley views and makes it an excellent place to get away from it all (though you'll still be very close to Ollantaytambo and Machu Picchu). Double rooms (with either mountain or garden views) are spacious, warmly decorated, and nicely distributed among the grounds. Given its small size, it hosts individuals and very small groups only.

5 to Paradero, Yanahuara (sector Pucará). ℂ **084/251-526** for reservations or 084/812-894. Fax 084/812-895. www.vallesagradolodge.com. 16 units. $110 double. Rate includes breakfast buffet. AE, DC, MC, V. **Amenities:** Restaurant; lounge; room service; laundry service. *In room:* TV, minibar, hair dryer, safe.

MODERATE

K'uychi Rumi 🕮 *Finds*   One of the more interesting and relaxing, if least pronounceable, lodging options in the Sacred Valley, this property isn't a hotel, per se. It's a complex of a half-dozen condos: rustic two-story, two-bedroom houses, individually owned and rented when the owners aren't around (which is most of the time). The houses are connected by walkways and gardens, and all have excellent mountain views. For a couple who wants a bit of space, privacy, a kitchen, and a great fireplace, it's perfect. It's also a bargain for families or two couples who occupy the whole house. The architect who built the houses lives on-site with his wife and administers the property; their quartet of dogs is liable to be on your front porch in the morning, waiting for you to emerge. A buffet breakfast is extra ($5), and there's no restaurant on the premises (although there are several restaurants nearby, and Urubamba is just up the road), but if you're looking for a serene retreat, this might be it.

Carretera Urubamba-Ollantaytambo s/n, Urubamba. ℂ/fax **084/201-169.** www.urubamba.com. 6 units. $80–$90 double; $100–$120 family bungalow (4 people). AE, DC, MC, V. *In room:* Kitchen, fridge.

La Casona del Yucay *Value*   A lovely colonial house converted into a hotel, this low-key place is renowned for hosting a famous guest: Simón Bolívar, the great liberator of Peru, who stayed in room no. 136 in 1825. Rooms are spacious, well decorated, and set around a traditional courtyard. Room no. 141 is a coveted attic, nearly always rented but worth inquiring about nonetheless. The hotel is peaceful and understated. Gorgeous gardens lead down to the Urubamba River.

Plaza Manco II de Yucay 104, Yucay. ℂ **084/201-116.** Fax 084/201-469. 39 units. $75 double. Rate includes breakfast buffet. AE, DC, MC, V. **Amenities:** Restaurant; room service; laundry service. *In room:* TV, minibar, safe.

Sonesta Posada del Inca Sacred Valley *Kids* This handsome ranch-style hotel, recently updated, remains one of the best in the valley, even as its high-end competition has grown. Originally a monastery in the late 1600s and then a hacienda, it was converted into an atmospheric colonial-village-like complex with mountain views and relaxed comfort in 1982. The grounds feature a chapel brought in whole from a provincial town, nice gardens, a good restaurant, and a cool little museum with ancient ceramics and textiles. Room no. 115 in the old section is a nice loft space, and room no. 312 has fantastic windows and superior views. It recently added a nice spa with massages, yoga, sauna, outdoor Jacuzzi, and other treatments. There are mountain bikes for guests' use, and lots of excursion and soft-adventure programs, including rafting, mountain biking, horseback riding, and excursions to the salt pans of Maras or the Incan site at Moray, are offered.

Plaza Manco II de Yucay 123, Yucay. © **084/201-107**, or 01/222-4777 for reservations (1-800-SONESTA in US and Canada). Fax 084/201-345. www.sonesta.com. 84 units. $95 double; $118 suite. Rate includes breakfast buffet. AE, DC, MC, V. **Amenities:** Restaurant; bar; spa; lounge; bike rental; 24-hr room service; laundry service. *In room:* TV, minibar, safe.

WHERE TO DINE

Many guests dine at their hotels, and the major ones above (Casa Andina, Libertador, and Sonesta) all have very good restaurants. Perhaps better for drop-ins is the fine restaurant of Hotel Sol y Luna (p. 244). Its **Killa Wasi** is a lovely two-story space with an open fireplace and pub on the second floor. The restaurant is open to nonguests, and it serves very nicely prepared *criollo* and Nouveau Andean specialties, including *ají de gallina* and stuffed river trout, as well as fresh pastas. Call for reservations because the restaurant is often full with hotel guests.

Several restaurants are scattered about the main valley highway. A favorite of groups that storm through the Sacred Valley three times a week on market day is **Tunupa,** Km 77 Carretera Pisaq-Ollantaytambo (on the left side of the road on the way to Ollanta; © **084/963-0206**), owned by the same folks who own the restaurant of the same name in Cusco. In a massive, purpose-built hacienda with long corridors that form dining halls overlooking the Urubamba River, it's something akin to a Peruvian bierhall. It must seat at least 300 diners, and it's all buffet, all the time. Even though it can get crowded on market days at lunchtime, it's a fair value for an all-you-can-eat buffet for $14, including a pisco sour. Even better is **Alhambra**, Carretera Urubamba-Ollantaytambo s/n (near Hotel Sol y Luna; © **084/201-200**), also a hacienda-style restaurant targeting bus tours, but in a more relaxed and intimate manner. The dining rooms are smaller, and there are tables outdoors under a thatched roof, with lovely garden and mountain views. Its buffets are only on market days (Tues, Thurs, and Sat). At other times, the three-course *menú turístico* ($10) is excellent; choose main courses such as stuffed lake trout with quinoa in a nut sauce.

On the main road going toward Yucay, **Quinta Los Geranios,** Av. Cabo Conchatupa s/n (© **084/201-093**), is a pretty good open-air restaurant set around a garden. It gets hit midday with tour buses but still manages to concoct fine versions of Peruvian standards such as *rocoto relleno* (stuffed hot peppers) and a number of indigenous soups. The three-course lunch *menú* is a good value. A similar tourist-group restaurant across the street is **El Maizal,** Av. Cabo Conchatupa s/n (© **084/201-054**); it offers a buffet lunch and has both indoor and outdoor seating.

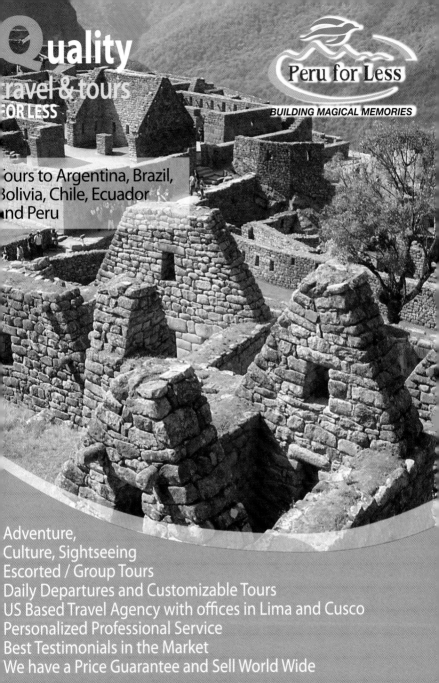

The new way to get AROUND town.

Make the most of your stay. Go Day by Day.

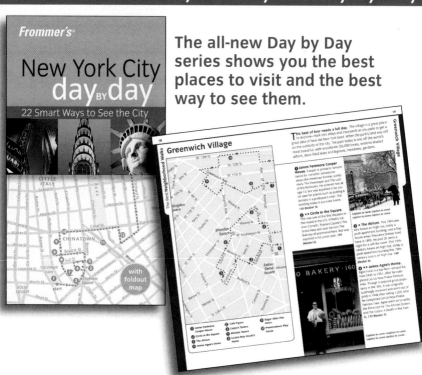

Frommer's

New York City
day BY day
22 Smart Ways to See the City

The all-new Day by Day series shows you the best places to visit and the best way to see them.

- Hundreds of color photos and maps
- One-to-three-day itineraries
- Star-rated hotel and restaurant listings
- Museums, literary haunts, and offbeat places
- And more!

Available now:
Frommer's Amsterdam Day by Day
Frommer's London Day by Day
Frommer's New York City Day by Day
Frommer's Paris Day by Day
Frommer's Rome Day by Day
Frommer's San Francisco Day by Day
Frommer's Venice Day by Day

The best trips start here.

Frommer's
A Branded Imprint of ⊗WIL
Now you know.

Tips *Chicha* **Here, Get Your Warm** *Chicha*

Throughout the valley, you'll see modest homes marked by long poles topped by red flags (or red balloons). These *chicha* flags indicate that home-brewed fermented maize beer, or *chicha*, is for sale inside. What you'll usually find is a small, barren room with a handful of locals quietly drinking huge tumblers of pale yellow liquid. Tepid *chicha*, which costs next to nothing, is definitely an acquired taste.

In Urubamba itself, **La Casa de la Abuela** ⊛, Bolívar 272 (© **084/622-975**), a charming and sprawling house a couple of blocks from the Plaza de Armas, used to be one of my favorite places to eat in the region. After a couple of years of spotty activity, due to the owner's illness, the restaurant is again operating at more or less full speed, if without the enthusiasm of past years. It specializes in pizzas from a wood-burning oven, pastas, and tasty home-cooked Peruvian dishes. The restaurant has terra-cotta walls, several dining rooms, and an inviting living room/bar area. It looks and feels like someone's house—in fact, it is the house of the friendly owner's great-grandmother. **The Muse Too,** Plaza de Armas (at the corner of Comercio and Grau; © **084/201-280**), a sister establishment of the San Blas bar The Muse in Cusco, is a low-key two-story pub/restaurant with a single corner balcony upstairs. It features pretty decent soups and sandwiches. At night, it operates more as a bar than restaurant.

BEYOND URUBAMBA
SALINERAS DE MARAS ⊛⊛
58km (36 miles) NW of Cusco

About 6km (3¾ miles) down the main road toward Ollantaytambo (northwest of Urubamba) is the amazing sight of the **Salineras de Maras,** thousands of individual ancient salt pans that form unique terraces in a hillside. The mines, small pools thickly coated with crystallized salt like dirty snow, have existed in the same spot since Incan days and are still operable. Families pass them down like deeds and continue the back-breaking and poorly remunerated tradition of salt extraction (crystallizing salt from subterranean spring water). Although I found it truly memorable and almost surreal to watch workers standing ankle-deep and mining salt from one of many hundreds of pools cascading down the hillside, I can imagine some travelers being somewhat less taken with the sight of salt pans.

GETTING THERE   To get to the salt pans, take a taxi (S/5 or $1.40) from Urubamba to a point near the village of Tarabamba (next to the restaurant Tunupa); you can either have the taxi wait for you or hail a combi on the main road for your return. From there, it's a lovely 4km (2½-mile), or 1-hour, walk under a huge sky and along a footpath next to the river. There are no signs; cross the footbridge and bend right along the far side of the river and up through the mountains toward the salt pans. As you begin the gentle climb up the mountain, stick to the right path to avoid the cliff-hugging and only inches-wide trail that forks to the left. One could also walk the 10km (6¼ miles) from the village of Maras, as most of the salt-pan workers do; allow a couple of hours.

MORAY ⓐ
9km (5½ miles) NW of Maras

Among the wilder Incan sites you'll come across are the enigmatic concentric ring terraces found in Moray. Unique in the Incan oeuvre, the site is not the ruins of a palace or fortress or typical temple, but what almost appears to be a large-scale environmental art installation. Three main sets of rings, like bowls, are set deep into the earth, forming strange sculpted terraces. The largest of the three has 15 levels. Viewed from the air, I'm pretty certain they would prompt a sense of intrigue much like the Nasca Lines, but they're just as cool to walk around while you contemplate their ancient functions (something you can't do at Nasca). Most likely, the site was an agricultural development station where masterful and relentlessly curious farmers among the Incas tested experimental crops and conditions. The depressions in the earth (caused by erosion) produced intense microclimates, with remarkable differences in temperature from top to bottom, that the Incas were evidently studying. Given the rings' peculiar forms, however, it's difficult to discount other, more spiritually inclined purposes.

GETTING THERE   Unfortunately, Moray is not easy to get to because it's removed from the main road that travels from Urubamba to Chinchero, with no public transportation of any kind, so it tends to draw only very committed travelers and Incan completists. The most convenient option is to take a taxi from either Urubamba or Chinchero; the driver will have to wait for you because there's nothing nearby, so the trip is sure to set you back at least S/175 ($50). Another option is to take a colectivo or bus that climbs up to Chinchero from Urubamba (or vice versa), getting off on the road to the village of Maras. (Make sure you ask the driver for the *desvío a Maras.*) From that point, you'll need to hike along the road about 4km (2½ miles) to Maras and then walk along an 8km (5-mile) trail to the site, for a total of at least 3 hours. Occasionally, a car or taxi will pass, but don't count on it. If you do go to Moray, it's possible to add on to your hike by walking another 7km (4⅓ miles) along a trail down to the Salineras de Maras. The only people you'll likely see along the trail are workers from the salt pans; many of them walk back and forth from Moray to work (as if their work weren't grueling enough).

CHINCHERO ⓐ
28km (17 miles) NW of Cusco

Popular among tour groups for its bustling Sunday market that begins promptly at 8am, Chinchero is spectacularly sited and much higher than the rest of the valley and even Cusco; at 3,800m (12,500 ft.) and far removed from the river, technically Chinchero doesn't belong to the Urubamba Valley. The sleepy village has gorgeous views of the snowy peak of Salcantay and the Vilcabamba and Urubamba mountain ranges in the distance. Sunset turns the fields next to the church—where child shepherds herd their flocks and grown men play soccer without goal posts—gold against the deepening blue sky.

It might once have been a great Incan city, but except on the main market day, Chinchero remains a graceful, traditional Andean Indian village. Its 15,000 inhabitants represent as many as 12 different indigenous communities. The town's main points of interest, in addition to the fine market, are the expansive main square, with a handsome colonial church made of adobe and built on Incan foundations, and some Incan ruins, mostly terraces that aren't quite as awe-inspiring today as their counterparts in Ollantaytambo and Pisac.

In the main plaza is a formidable and famous Incan wall composed of huge stones and 10 trapezoidal niches. The foundations once formed the palace of the late-15th-century Inca Tupac Yupanqui. The early-17th-century *iglesia* (church) ☞ has some very interesting, if faded, frescoes outside under the porticoes and mural paintings that cover the entire ceiling. The church is open Monday through Saturday from 9am to 5pm and Sunday from 9am to 6pm. Across the plaza is a **Museo de Sitio,** the rather spare municipal museum that holds a few Incan ceramics and instruments; it's open Tuesday through Sunday from 8am to 5pm, and admission is free.

The market comprises two marketplaces: one focusing on handicrafts and the other consisting mainly of produce. **Chinchero's market** ☞ is one of the best places in the entire valley for Andean textiles and common goods such as hats, gloves, and shawls. Even on Sunday, it feels more authentic than the one at Pisac (although some visitors might find Pisac more lively and fun). Chinchero's sellers of *artesanía*—who are more often than not also the craftspeople, unlike the mere agents you'll find in Pisac and other places—dress in traditional garb, and even the kids seem less manipulative in pleading for your attention and soles. Midweek (especially Tues and Thurs) there are usually fewer sellers who set their wares on blankets around the main square, and you'll have a better chance of bargaining then.

Through the terraces to the left of the church is a path leading toward a stream and to some finely sculpted Incan masonry, including stone steps, water canals, and huge stones with animal figures.

GETTING THERE   Colectivos leave every half-hour or so from Tullumayo in Cusco for Chinchero (a 90-min. journey). Buses also leave every 20 minutes or so from the Terminal Terrestre in Urubamba (a 50-min. trip). Entrance to Chinchero—officially to just the market and church, but, in practice, to the whole town, it seems—is by Cusco *boleto turístico.* If you try to visit the church and main square without a *boleto,* you will be asked to purchase one. Nearly everyone visits Chinchero on a half-day visit from either Cusco or Urubamba; there's not much else in the way of infrastructure to detain you, although there are a handful of inexpensive restaurants on the main road where the bus drops you off for lunch. One serving pretty good Andean specialties is **Abarrotes Bar Restaurant,** Av. Mateo Pumacahua 143 (© **084/306-052**). There are a just a couple of spots in town to spend the night (the better of the two is the small and inexpensive Hostal Los Incas), unless you want to camp in the fields just beyond the plaza where the market is held. You're much better off visiting during the day and staying elsewhere in the Sacred Valley, where there are considerably more services.

3 Ollantaytambo ☞☞☞

97km (60 miles) NW of Cusco; 21km (13 miles) W of Urubamba

A tongue twister of a town—the last settlement before Aguas Calientes and Machu Picchu—this historic and lovely little place at the northwestern end of the Sacred Valley is affectionately called Ollanta (Oh-*yahn*-tah) by locals. Plenty of outsiders who can't pronounce it fall in love with the town, too. The scenery around Ollantaytambo is some of the most stunning in the region. The snowcapped mountains that embrace the town frame a much narrower valley here than at Urubamba or Pisac, and both sides of the gorge are lined with Incan stone *andenes,* or agricultural terraces. Most extraordinary are the precipitous terraced ruins of a massive temple-fortress built by

Tips **When Not to Go**

The Incan ruins at Ollantaytambo are often overrun with tourists doing the bus tour of the Sacred Valley on Sunday afternoons, typical market day. The ruins are so special and so enjoyably serene on other days that if you can't get there early in the morning on Sunday, it's worthwhile visiting another day, if you can.

the Inca Pachacútec. Below the ruins, Ollantaytambo's old town is a splendid grid of streets dating to Incan times and lined with adobe brick walls, blooming bougainvillea, and perfect canals, still carrying rushing water down from the mountains. Though Ollanta has exploded in popularity in just the last few years, except for the couple of hours a day when tour buses deposit large groups at the foot of the fortress (where a handicrafts market habitually breaks out to welcome them) and tourists overrun the main square, the town remains pretty quiet, a traditional and thoroughly charming Valle Sagrado village.

Ollantaytambo is one of the best spots to spend the night in the Sacred Valley, especially if you want to be able to wander around the ruins alone in the early morning or late afternoon, before or after the groups overtake them.

ESSENTIALS
GETTING THERE
BY TRAIN   Ollantaytambo lies midway on the Cusco–Machu Picchu train route. All trains traveling to Aguas Calientes (Machu Picchu) from Cusco stop first at Ollantaytambo. Trains depart Cusco from **Estación San Pedro,** Calle Cascaparo s/n (© **084/221-352** or 084/221-313), and arrive in Ollantaytambo 90 minutes later. The train station in Ollantaytambo is a long 15-minute walk from the main square. The **Backpacker** shuttle ($53 adults round-trip, April-Oct only) departs Ollantaytambo at 9:05am and arrives at Machu Picchu at 11am; it makes the return at 4:20pm and arrives in Ollantaytambo at 6pm. Travelers can also hop the **Vistadome** train ($43 adults one-way; $72 round-trip), that originates in either Urubamba or Cusco and makes stops in Ollantaytambo, departing at 7:05am, on the way to Machu Picchu (where it arrives at 8:20am); for additional details, see "Getting There" in "Machu Picchu & the Inca Trail," later in this chapter.

BY BUS   There are a couple of direct buses daily to Ollantaytambo (S/3–S/4, or 85¢–$1.15) from Cusco, but it's frequently easier to catch a bus to Urubamba and change buses at the terminal there. Buses drop passengers at the Plaza de Armas in the old town, about a kilometer (½ mile) from the ruins. The train is a much more expensive option from Cusco.

From Ollantaytambo, buses for Cusco depart from Avenida Estación, the main street leading away from the rail terminal. For Urubamba, colectivos depart from the Plaza de Armas.

BY TAXI   Taxis between Ollantaytambo and Cusco generally charge about S/70 ($20) each way.

VISITOR INFORMATION
You're better off getting information on the Sacred Valley before leaving Cusco, either at the helpful main **Tourist Information Office** (© **084/263-176**) or at Cusco's

Ollantaytambo

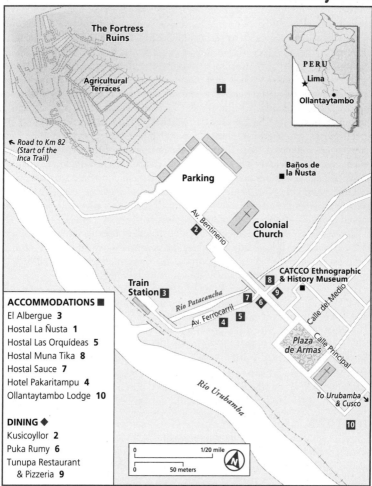

The Fortress Ruins

Agricultural Terraces

← Road to Km 82 (Start of the Inca Trail)

PERU

Lima ★

● Ollantaytambo

1

Parking

Baños de la Ñusta ■

Av. Bentinerio

2

Colonial Church

CATCCO Ethnographic & History Museum

8 ■

Train Station 3

Río Patacancha

7

6

9

Calle del Medio

5

Av. Ferrocarril

4

5

Río Urubamba

Plaza de Armas

Calle Principal

To Urubamba & Cusco →

10

ACCOMMODATIONS ■

El Albergue **3**

Hostal La Ñusta **1**

Hostal Las Orquídeas **5**

Hostal Muna Tika **8**

Hostal Sauce **7**

Hotel Pakaritampu **4**

Ollantaytambo Lodge **10**

DINING ◆

Kusicoyllor **2**

Puka Rumy **6**

Tunupa Restaurant & Pizzeria **9**

0   1/20 mile

0   50 meters

N

branch of the **South American Explorers Club** (© 084/245-484). In Ollantaytambo, try the **Museo CATCCO,** located off Calle Principal (© 084/223-627), for assistance.

Your best bet for exchanging cash in Ollantaytambo is in small shops. If you need medical assistance, go to **Centro de Salud,** Calle Principal (© 084/204-090). The **post office** is located on the Plaza de Armas.

WHAT TO SEE & DO
FORTRESS RUINS ☆☆☆

The Incan elite adopted Ollantaytambo, building irrigation systems and a crowning temple designed for worship and astronomical observation. Rising above the valley and an ancient square (Plaza Mañaraki) are dozens of rows of stunningly steep stone terraces carved into the hillside. The temple ruins, which appear both forbidding and admirably perfect, represent one of the Incan Empire's most formidable feats of architecture. The Incas were able to successfully defend the site against the Spanish in 1537, protecting the rebel Manco Inca after his retreat here from defeat at Sacsayhuamán. In all probability, the complex was more a temple than a citadel to the Incas.

The upper section—reached after you've climbed 200 steps—contains typically masterful masonry of the kind that adorned great Incan temples. A massive and supremely elegant doorjamb—site of many a photo—indicates the principal entry to the temple; next to it is the **Temple of Ten Niches.** On the next level are six huge pink granite blocks, amazingly cut, polished, and fitted together; they appear to be part of rooms never completed. This **Temple of the Sun** is one of the great stone masonry achievements of the Incas. On the stones, you can still make out faint, ancient symbolic markings in relief. Across the valley is the quarry that provided the stones for the structure; a great ramp descending from the hilltop ruins was the means by which the Incas transported the massive stones—thousands of workers essentially dragged them around the river—from several kilometers away.

A footpath wends up the hill behind an outer wall of the ruins to a clearing and a wall with niches that have led some to believe prisoners were tied up here—a theory that is unfounded. Regardless of the purpose, the views south over the Urubamba Valley and of the snowcapped peak of Verónica are outstanding.

The ruins are open daily from 7am to 5:30pm; admission is by Cusco's *boleto turístico.* To experience the ruins in peace before the tour buses arrive, plan on getting to them before 11am. Early morning is best of all, when the sun rises over mountains to the east and then quickly bathes the entire valley in light.

At the bottom of the terraces, next to the Patacancha River, are the **Baños de la Ñusta (Princess Baths),** a place of ceremonial bathing. Wedged into the mountains facing the baths are granaries built by the Incas (not prisons, as some have supposed). Locals like to point out the face of the Inca carved into the cliff high above the valley. (If you can't make it out, ask the guard at the entrance to the ruins for a little help.)

OLD TOWN 🏯🏯

Below (or south of) the ruins and across the Río Patacancha is the finest extant example of the Incas' masterful urban planning. Many original residential *canchas,* or blocks, each inhabited by several families during the 15th century, are still present; each *cancha* had a single entrance opening onto a main courtyard. The finest streets of this stone village are directly behind the main square. On my last visit to Ollanta, stonemasons were busy redoing every last old cobblestone street, so the Old Town should be in pristine shape again. Get a good glimpse of community life within a *cancha* by peeking in at **Calle del Medio** (Chautik'ikllu St.), where a couple of neighboring houses have a small shop in the courtyard and their ancestors' skulls are displayed as shrines on the walls of their living quarters. The entire village retains a solid Amerindian air to it, unperturbed by the crowds of gringos who wander through it, snapping photos of children and old women. It's a starkly traditional place, largely populated by locals in colorful native dress and women who pace up and down the streets or through fields absentmindedly spinning the ancient spools used in making hand-woven textiles.

On the edge of the old town, 2 blocks northwest of the Plaza Mayor, is an enjoyable and well-presented but not indispensable **Museo CATCCO (Centro Andino de Tecnología y Cultural de las Comunidades de Ollantaytambo),** a museum of ethnographic and historical exhibits in the Antiguo Parador Casa del Horno, Patacalle s/n (just off Calle Principal; ✆ 084/223-627). It's small but informative, with interesting exhibits on local artisanship, archaeology, culture, and costume; plan to spend up to an hour here. It's open Tuesday through Sunday from 10am to 1pm and 2 to 4pm; admission is S/5 ($1.40).

Ollantaytambo is an excellent spot in the valley for gentle or more energetic walks around the valley and into the mountains, as well as horseback riding. You can rent slow-moving horses for S/10 ($2.85) per hour from José Luis in a shop on the main square.

WHERE TO STAY

In addition to the hotels below, budget travelers gravitate toward **Hostal Las Orquídeas** (✆ 084/204-032), which has clean and simple rooms with a shared bathroom around a courtyard for $20; and **Hostal La Ñusta,** Carretera Ocobamba (✆ 084/204-032), a clean and friendly place with good views from the balcony but small and plain rooms. Rooms are $10 per person with a shared bathroom. Also worth a look if the town is getting full is **Hostal Muna Tika,** Av. Bentinero s/n (✆/fax 084/204-111; tika@latinmail.com), with pleasant, simple double rooms for $25. Seven of the 19 rooms have private bathrooms; the others are S/50 ($14) per person.

EXPENSIVE

Hotel Pakaritampu ✿ On the road from the train station to town, this new hotel is quite upscale for unassuming Ollantaytambo. With beautiful gardens, great views, and cozy touches such as a fireplace lounge and a library, it retains a lived-in country feel, even though it's only a couple of years old. Rooms are tasteful, with sturdy, comfortable furnishings, and there's a nice restaurant/bar. It's owned by one of Peru's best-known athletes, an Olympic volleyballer.

Av. Ferrocarril s/n, Ollantaytambo. ✆ 084/204-020. Fax 084/205-105. www.pakaritampu.com. 20 units. $104 double. Rate includes taxes and breakfast. AE, DC, MC, V. **Amenities:** Restaurant; bar; laundry service.

MODERATE

El Albergue ✿ *Value* This rustic and homey *hostal,* owned by a longtime American resident of Ollantaytambo, may not be the most luxurious spot in town but it's still my favorite place to stay. It has large, comfortable, and nicely—if austerely—furnished rooms with excellent beds, great gardens, a wood-fired sauna, three Labrador retrievers roaming the grounds, and a spot right next to the train to Machu Picchu.

⟨*Tips* Sacred Valley Festivals

The traditional Andean villages of the Sacred Valley are some of the finest spots in Peru to witness vibrant local festivals celebrated with music, dance, and processions. Among the highlights are Christmas, **Día de los Reyes Magos (Three Kings Day,** Jan 6), **Ollanta-Raymi** (celebrated in Ollantaytambo the week after its big brother, Cusco's Inti Raymi, during the last week of June), and Chinchero's **Virgen Natividad** (Sept 8), the most important annual fiesta in that village. The **Fiesta de las Cruces (Festival of the Crosses,** May 2–3) is celebrated across the highlands with enthusiastic dancing and the decoration of large crosses. Pisac celebrates a particularly lively version of the **Virgen del Carmen** festival held in Paucartambo (July 16).

Hiking Trails in the Sacred Valley

Energetic travelers with a fierce desire to get outdoors and exercise their legs in the Sacred Valley can do much more than the standard ruins treks and even the Inca Trail, although the latter is certainly the best known trek in Peru. Other trails are considerably less populated, so if you're looking for isolation in the Andes, give some of the following treks a try.

The entire valley is virtually tailor-made for treks, but Ollantaytambo and Yucay are particularly excellent bases for treks into the lovely, gentle hill-sides framing the Urubamba Valley. The Cusco office of the **South American Explorers** (✆ 084/245-484) is very helpful with trip and trail reports for members. For guided walking and trekking in the valley, check out **Viento-Sur** (✆ 084/201-620; www.aventurasvientosur.com).

- **Km 82 of the Inca Trail:** Whether or not you're planning to do the Inca Trail, hiking the section from Km 82 to Km 88 is a nice addition to the classic or miniroute. By staying to the north (or railroad) side of the Río Urubamba, you'll pass several good ruins sites, including Salapunku and Pinchanuyoq, finally reaching the Incan bridge at Km 88.

- **Pumamarca ruins:** You can reach the small but well-preserved Incan ruins of Pumamarca by a pretty trek along the banks of the Río Patacancha, which takes you through tiny villages. The walk from Ollantaytambo takes about 5 hours round-trip. To get there, take the road that leads north out of Ollanta along the Patacancha. After it crosses the river, it turns into a footpath and passes the village of Munaypata. Veer left toward the valley and terracing, and then turn sharply to the right (northeast), toward the agricultural terraces straight ahead.

- **Pinculluna:** The mountain looming above Ollantaytambo makes for an enjoyable couple-hour trek up, past Incan terracing. However, the trail isn't very clearly marked in sections, so it might be worthwhile to ask around town for a guide.

- **Huayoccari:** Adventurous trekkers in search of solitude should enjoy the 2-day hike (one-way) from Yucay to the small village of Huayoccari, which passes some of the valley's loveliest scenery, from the Incan terraces along the San Juan River ravine to Sakrachayoc and ancient rock paintings overlooking caves. After camping overnight, trekkers continue to the Tuqsana pass (4,000m/13,100 ft.) and descend to Yanacocha Lake before arriving at Huayoccari.

It's frequently full—Inca Trail groups come through regularly—even though it's more expensive than other budget accommodations in town. You can't miss the *hostal;* it's right next to the train terminal, and painted on the wall is the name of the proprietor in capital letters: Wendy Weeks.

Av. Estación s/n (next to the railway station platform), Ollantaytambo. ✆/fax **084/204-014**. www.rumbos peru.com/elalbergue. 6 units. $30 double with shared bathroom. Rate includes taxes and continental breakfast. No credit cards. **Amenities:** Cafe; sauna; laundry service. *In room:* No phone.

Hostal Sauce   Sandwiched between the main square of the village and the CATCCO museum, this modern and comfortable free-standing building has a smattering of very clean, nicely equipped rooms and a small restaurant. Some rooms have superb views of the ruins. The inn's name, which might strike some English speakers as a little odd, refers to the *sauce* tree out front.

Ventiderio 248, Ollantaytambo. ⓒ 084/204-044. Fax 084/204-048. www.hostalsauce.com.pe. 8 units. $79 double ($10 discount if paying cash). Rates include taxes and breakfast. V only. **Amenities:** Restaurant; fireplace bar; laundry service.

Ollantaytambo Lodge *Value*   This new, midsize property, given a makeover almost right from the start, is tucked away just two blocks south of Old Town. It's a relaxing, good-value place to stay—like a low-budget version of some of the larger and swankier country inns of the Sacred Valley. The earthy, ochre-colored rooms are clean, good size, and built around a garden. Even better, they're generally quiet, since the hotel is removed from the tourist buses that crowd the main square during the day.

Quinta Cruz Esquina s/n, Ollantaytambo. ⓒ/fax 084/272-436. www.ollantaytambolodge.com. 30 units. $35 double. Rates include taxes and breakfast. V only. **Amenities:** Restaurant/bar; room service; safe. *In room:* No phone.

WHERE TO DINE

If you're staying in Ollantaytambo and don't mind a drive, you might also consider catching a taxi to one of the fine restaurants along the main road from Urubamba to Ollantaytambo; see "Where to Dine" in "Urubamba & Environs," earlier in this chapter.

Kusicoyllor, Plaza Araccama s/n (ⓒ 084/204-103) is a cool cafe/bar right next to the entrance to the ruins, so you might expect it to be touristy and overpriced. It is, but it's still a nice, cozy place. It serves standard Peruvian and predominantly Italian dishes and offers a fixed-price $7 menú. Breakfast is especially good, making it a fine stop after an early morning tour of the ruins.

Tunupa Restaurant & Pizzeria ⓕ, on Av. Beniterio s/n (no phone), the main drag between the ruins and Old Town, is an inexpensive family-run terrace joint with a very agreeable open-air atmosphere. It serves breakfast, lunch, and dinner, from pancakes to pizza. The owner's adorable young son, Abel, often helps out as a waiter. Across the street, **Puka Rumy,** Av. Beniterio s/n, is a little bar/cafe with a couple of tables outdoors for people-watching and serves everything from eggs to *churrasco* (barbecue) and chicken, but it's especially good for a cold beer on the tiny terrace. Other cheap restaurants in Old Town, principally pizzerias, such as **Bar Ollantay** and **La Fortaleza,** ring the main square in the Old Town. **Hostal Sauce** (see above) also has a nice (though frequently empty) restaurant serving lunch and dinner.

4 Machu Picchu ⓕⓕⓕ & the Inca Trail ⓕⓕⓕ

120km (75 miles) NW of Cusco

The stunning site of Machu Picchu, the fabled "lost city of the Incas," is South America's greatest attraction. The Incas hid Machu Picchu so high in the clouds that it escaped destruction by the empire-raiding Spaniards, who never found it. It is no longer lost, of course—you can zip there by high-speed train or trek there along a 2- or 4-day trail—but Machu Picchu retains its perhaps unequaled aura of mystery and magic. No longer overgrown with brush, as it was when it was rediscovered in 1911 by the Yale archaeologist and historian Hiram Bingham with the aid of a local farmer who knew of its existence, from below it is still totally hidden from view. The majestic setting the Incas chose for it remains unchanged: The ruins are nestled in almost brooding Andes Mountains and are frequently swathed in mist. When the early morning sun rises over the peaks and methodically illuminates the ruins row by row of granite stones, Machu Picchu leaves visitors as awestruck as ever.

The great majority of visitors to Machu Picchu still visit it as a day trip from Cusco, but many people feel that a few hurried hours at the ruins during peak hours, amidst throngs of people following guided tours, simply do not suffice. That certainly is my opinion. By staying at least 1 night, either at the one upscale hotel just outside the grounds of Machu Picchu or down below in the town of Aguas Calientes (also officially called Machu Picchu Pueblo, although most Peruvians still call it by the original name), you can remain at the ruins later in the afternoon after most of the tour groups have gone home, or get there for sunrise—a dramatic, unforgettable sight. Many visitors find that a single day at the ruins does not do it justice.

The base for most visitors, Aguas Calientes is a small and humid tourist trade town with the feel of a frontier town, dominated by sellers of cheap *artesanía* and souvenirs, and weary backpackers resting up and celebrating their treks along the Inca Trail over cheap eats and cheaper beers. The Peruvian government, along with the help of PeruRail, is doings its level best to spruce up the town, lest its ramshackle look turn off visitors to Peru's greatest spectacle. It has fixed up the Plaza de Armas, built a nicely paved *malecón* riverfront area, and added new bridges over and new streets along the river, and the town does look better than at any time I can remember. It's still probably not a place you want to hang out for long, though. There are some additional good hikes in the area, but most people head back to Cusco after a day or so in town.

ESSENTIALS
GETTING THERE
If you were hoping to soar over the Andes to Machu Picchu in a helicopter, you're out of luck: All flights have been suspended indefinitely.

BY TRAIN   The 112km (70-mile) train from Cusco to Machu Picchu is a truly spectacular journey. It zigzags up Huayna Picchu and then through lush valleys hugging the Río Urubamba, with views of snowcapped Andes peaks in the distance. There are three tourist trains from Cusco to Machu Picchu, taking less than 4 hours: the **Backpacker,** the slowest and least expensive ($68 round-trip; $44 one-way); the **Vistadome,** the faster first-class service ($105 round-trip; $62 one-way); and the top-of-the-line and very pricey luxury line **Hiram Bingham** *$$*, named after the discoverer of Machu Picchu ($495 round-trip only, including 2 meals, cocktails, and a guided tour at the ruins).

The tourist trains, all of which now belong to Orient-Express/PeruRail, depart from Cusco's **Estación San Pedro** on Calle Cascaparo; it's open Monday through Friday from 5am to 3pm, and Saturday and Sunday from 5am to 12:30pm. Hiram Bingham trains depart from **Estación Poroy,** a 15-minute drive from Cusco, 6 days a week in high season (Apr–Oct) and 4 days a week in low season (Nov–Mar). Tickets for trains can also be purchased at **Estación Huanchac** on Avenida Pachacútec; it's open Monday through Friday from 8:30am to 5:30pm, and Saturday and Sunday from 8:30am to 12:30pm. The *Backpacker* departs Cusco at 6:15am and arrives in Aguas Calientes at 10:15am (returning at 3:55pm and arriving in Cusco at 8:20pm); the *Vistadome* leaves twice daily, at 6am and 7am, and arrives at 9:40am and 11am, respectively (returning at 3:30pm and 5pm and arriving in Cusco at 7:20pm and 9:25pm);

and the *Hiram Bingham* sets out at 9am and arrives at 12:30pm (returning at 6pm and arriving in Cusco at 9:25pm). *Tip:* For the best views on the way to Machu Picchu, sit on the left side of the train.

Travelers already based in the Urubamba Valley can go to Machu Picchu by the **Sacred Valley Railway.** The journey takes 2 hours and 20 minutes from Urubamba, and about 90 minutes from Ollantaytambo. *Vistadome* service originates in Urubamba (departing at 6:10am) and Ollantaytambo (departing at 7am, 10:30am, and 2:55pm); *Backpacker* service originates in Ollantaytambo (departing at 9:25am). Returning to Ollanta, Vistadome trains leave at 8:35am, noon, and 4:45pm; the Backpacker train departs Machu Picchu Pueblo at 5pm. The trip costs $71.50 in Vistadome class ($43 one-way) and $53 in Backpacker round-trip (one-way service not available).

Train schedules and fares change frequently, so check **www.perurail.com** or the tourist information office in Cusco before purchasing train tickets. It's wise to make your reservation at least a day (or more) in advance, especially in high season. For the luxury Hiram Bingham service, reservations several weeks or more in advance are recommended.

Estación Machu Picchu Pueblo, the train station in Aguas Calientes, is on the river side of the tracks, just beyond the market stalls of Avenida Imperio de los Incas. Porters from Machu Picchu Pueblo Hotel and other inns greet the trains upon arrival each morning.

BY BUS   You can't travel from Cusco to Machu Picchu by bus, but unless you walk the Inca Trail—or ascend the slope to the ruins from the town of Aguas Calientes by foot—you will have to take one of the frequent shuttle buses that leave from down by the railroad tracks. The buses wend their way up the mountain, performing exaggerated switchbacks for 15 minutes before suddenly depositing passengers at the entrance to the ruins. The cost is $12 round-trip. There's no need to reserve in advance; just purchase your ticket at the little booth in front of the lineup of buses, at the bottom of the market stalls. Buses begin running at 6:30am and come down all day, with the last one descending at dusk. Some people choose to purchase a one-way ticket ($6) up and walk down (30–45 min.) to Aguas Calientes.

BY FOOT   The celebrated **Inca Trail (Camino del Inca,** or Camino Real) is almost as famous as the ruins themselves, and the trek is rightly viewed as an attraction in itself rather than merely a means of getting to Machu Picchu under your own power. There are two principal treks: one that takes 4 days (43km/27 miles) and another shorter and less demanding route that lasts just 2 days. The trails begin outside Ollantaytambo (at Km 82 of the Cusco–Machu Picchu railroad track); you can return to Cusco or Ollantaytambo by train. See "Hiking the Inca Trail," later in this section, for more details; many new regulations have been introduced in the past couple of years.

Tips Train Schedules to Machu Picchu

Train schedules have changed with alarming frequency in the past few years, according to season and, it seems, the whims of some scheduler. It would be smart to verify hours and fares at your hotel (if you're staying in one of the better ones with good service and informed personnel), the Tourist Information Office in Cusco, or on the PeruRail website (www.perurail.com).

Endangered Machu Picchu

Machu Picchu survived the Spanish onslaught against the Incan Empire, but in the last few decades, it has suffered more threats to its architectural integrity and pristine Andean environment than it did in nearly 500 years of existence. UNESCO threatened first to add Machu Picchu to its list of endangered World Heritage Sites and not to withdraw that status unless stringent measures were taken by the Peruvian government to protect the landmark ruins.

In 2001, a film company shooting a TV ad for a Peruvian beer sneaked equipment into the site and irreparably damaged the stone Intihuatana atop the ruins (the camera crane operator was sentenced to 6 years in prison in 2005). Developers once planned to build cable cars that would run from Aguas Calientes to Machu Picchu to facilitate access. The plan, endorsed by the government, would have quadrupled the number of visitors and created an eyesore among the majestic peaks that surround the ruins. Fortunately, those ill-conceived plans were finally scuttled. Responding to the pressure from UNESCO, foreign governments, and watchdog groups, the Peruvian government also introduced measures to clean up the historic Inca Trail and restrict access to it. In a unique debt-swap initiative, the government of Finland traded 25% of Peru's outstanding debt (more than $6 million) for conservation programs.

The World Monuments Watch list of the 100 Most Endangered Sites in the World formerly included Machu Picchu, but in 2002, the site was removed from the notorious list in recognition of the government's more stringent regulations on the Inca Trail and the suspension of the cable-car plan.

For those who take the train to Aguas Calientes but still want a small dose of what it's like to walk to Machu Picchu, it's straightforward (if a little difficult) to walk up to the ruins from town up a steep path that cuts across the switchback road. It takes a little over an hour to make it up and about 45 minutes to descend. Because you'll probably want to save your energy for exploring Machu Picchu, if you are fit and want to walk at least one way, I recommend walking down from the ruins (which is still pretty strenuous on one's knees).

VISITOR INFORMATION

Aguas Calientes has an **iPerú** office, Av. Pachacútec, cdra. 1 s/n (© **084/211-104**), about one-third of the way up the main drag in town. It has photocopies of town maps and some basic hotel and Machu Picchu information.

FAST FACTS   There are no banks in Aguas Calientes. To exchange money (cash or traveler's checks), try **Gringo Bill's Hostal** at Colla Raymi 104, just off the main square. Shops and restaurants along the two main streets, Avenida Imperio de los Incas and Avenida Pachacútec, buy dollars from gringos in need at standard exchange rates.

You'll find the **police** on Avenida Imperio de los Incas, down from the railway station (© **084/211-178**).

Machu Picchu

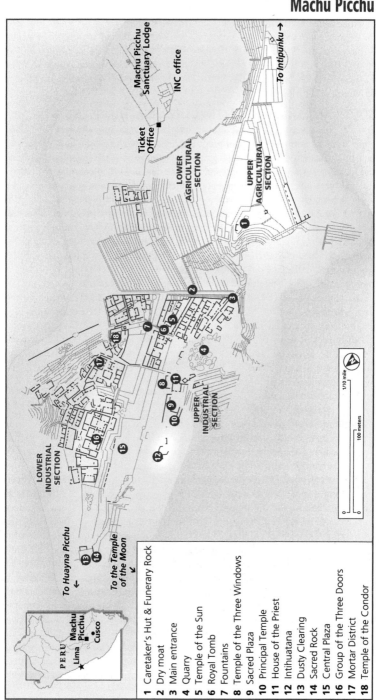

Machu Picchu Sanctuary Lodge

INC office

Ticket Office

To Intipunku →

LOWER AGRICULTURAL SECTION

UPPER AGRICULTURAL SECTION

1

2

3

7 6 5

4

18

17

8 11

9

10

UPPER INDUSTRIAL SECTION

12

15

16

LOWER INDUSTRIAL SECTION

13 14

To Huayna Picchu ↓

To the Temple of the Moon

1/10 mile

100 meters

PERU

Lima

Machu Picchu

Cusco

1 Caretaker's Hut & Funerary Rock
2 Dry moat
3 Main entrance
4 Quarry
5 Temple of the Sun
6 Royal Tomb
7 Fountains
8 Temple of the Three Windows
9 Sacred Plaza
10 Principal Temple
11 House of the Priest
12 Intihuatana
13 Dusty Clearing
14 Sacred Rock
15 Central Plaza
16 Group of the Three Doors
17 Mortar District
18 Temple of the Condor

There are Internet cabinas at the **Café Internet** (no phone) on Avenida Imperio de los Incas, a block away from the main square on the railroad tracks, and at a couple of places on the Plaza de Armas. **Gringo Bill's Hostal** (📞 **084/211-046**), on Colla Raymi 104, also has Internet access. There's a **post office** on the corner of Manco Cápac at Avenida Imperio de los Incas. The **Telefónica del Perú** office (no phone) is at Av. Imperio de los Incas 132.

SOUTH AMERICA'S TOP ATTRACTION: MACHU PICCHU ⭐⭐⭐

Since its rediscovery in 1911 and initial exploration by an American team of archaeologists from Yale during the next 4 years, the ruins of Machu Picchu have resonated far beyond the status of mere archaeological site. Reputed to be the legendary "lost city of the Incas," it is steeped in mystery and folklore. The unearthed complex, the only significant Incan site to escape the ravenous appetites of the Spanish conquistadors in the 16th century, ranks as the top attraction in Peru, arguably the greatest in South America and, for my money, one of the world's most stunning sights. Countless glossy photographs of the stone ruins, bridging the gap between two massive Andean peaks and swathed in cottony clouds, just can't do it justice. I distinctly remember seeing pictures of Machu Picchu in a textbook when I was 5 years old and dreaming that someday I would go there. When I did, for the first time in 1983, the glorious city of the Incas more than lived up to all those years of expectation. It is dreamlike.

Invisible from the Urubamba Valley below, Machu Picchu lay dormant for more than 4 centuries, nestled nearly 2,400m (8,000 ft.) above sea level under thick jungle and known only to a handful of Amerindian peasants. Never mentioned in the Spanish chronicles, it was seemingly lost in the collective memory of the Incas and their descendants. The ruins' unearthing, though, raised more questions than it answered, and experts still argue about the place Machu Picchu occupied in the Incan Empire. Was it a citadel? An agricultural site? An astronomical observatory? A ceremonial city or sacred retreat for the Incan emperor? Or some combination of all of these? Adding to the mystery, this complex city of exceedingly fine architecture and masonry was constructed, inhabited, and deliberately abandoned all in less than a century—a mere flash in the 4,000-year-history of Andean Peru. Machu Picchu was very probably abandoned even before the arrival of the Spanish, perhaps as a result of the Incas' civil war. Or perhaps it was drought that drove the Incas elsewhere.

Bingham mistook Machu Picchu for the lost city of Vilcabamba, the last refuge of the rebellious Inca Manco Cápac (see "Bingham, the 'Discoverer' of Machu Picchu" on p. 264). Machu Picchu, though, is not that lost city (which was discovered deeper in the jungle at Espíritu Pampa). Most historians believe that the Inca Pachacútec, who founded the Incan Empire and built most of the greatest and most recognizable of Incan monuments, had the complex constructed sometime in the mid-1400s, probably after the defeat of a rival group in 1438. Machu Picchu appears to have been both a ceremonial and agricultural center. Half its buildings were sacred in nature, but the latest research findings indicate that it was a royal retreat for Incan leaders rather than a sacred city, per se. Never looted by the Spaniards, many of its architectural features remain in excellent condition—even if they ultimately do little to advance our understanding of the exact nature of Machu Picchu.

One thing is certain: Machu Picchu is one of the world's great examples of landscape art. The Incas revered nature, worshipping celestial bodies and more earthly streams and stones. The spectacular setting of Machu Picchu reveals just how much they

We Call It *Choclo:* Foods of the Incas

Wondering what the Incas cultivated on all those amazing, steeply terraced fields that so elegantly grace the hillsides? Sure, they grew *papas* (potatoes) and *coca* (coca leaves), but corn was perhaps the Incas' most revered crop. Although corn was important throughout the Americas in pre-Columbian times, the Incan Empire raised it to the level of a sacred state crop. Corn was a symbol of power, and the Incas saved their very best lands for its cultivation. The *choclo* of Cusco and the Sacred Valley was considered the finest of the empire. It is still an uncommon delight: Huge, puffy, white kernels with a milky, sweet taste, it's best enjoyed in classic corn-on-the-cob style, boiled and served with a hunk of mountain cheese.

Pachamanca is a classic *sierra* dish perfected by the Incas. The word is derived from *Pachamama,* or "Mother Earth," in Quechua. A pachamanca is distinguished by its underground preparation. Several types of meat, along with potatoes, chopped *ají* (hot pepper), herbs, and cheese, are baked in a hole in the earth over hot stones. Banana leaves are placed between the layers of food. The act of cooking underground was symbolic for the Incas; they worshipped the earth, and to eat directly from it was a way of honoring Pachamama and giving thanks for her fertility. Peruvians still love to cook pachamancas in the countryside.

Quinoa, which comes from the word that means "moon" in Quechua (another central element in the Incan cosmology), was the favored grain of the Incas. The grain, which expands to four times its original volume when cooked and contains a greater quantity of protein than any other grain, remains central to the Andean diet. Most often seen in *sopa a la criolla*, it is often substituted for rice and incorporated into soups, salads, and puddings.

reveled in their environment. Steep terraces, gardens, and granite and limestone temples, staircases, and aqueducts seem to be carved directly out of the hillside. Forms echo the very shape of the surrounding mountains, and windows and instruments appear to have been constructed to track the sun during the June and December solstices. Machu Picchu lies 300m (1,000 ft.) lower than Cusco, but you'd imagine the exact opposite, so nestled are the ruins among mountaintops and clouds. The ruins are cradled at the center of a radius of Andean peaks, like the pistil at the center of a flower.

Appreciating Machu Picchu for its aesthetic qualities is no slight to its significance. The Incas obviously chose the site for the immense power of its natural beauty. They, like we, must have been in awe of the snowcapped peaks to the east; the rugged panorama of towering, forested mountains and the sacred cliff of Putukusi to the west; and the city sitting gracefully like a proud saddle between two huge *cerros,* or peaks. It remains one of the most thrilling sights in the world. At daybreak, when the sun's rays creep silently over the jagged silhouette, sometimes turning the distant snowy peaks fiery orange, and then slowly, with great drama, cast brilliant light on the ruins building by building and row by row, it's enough to move some observers to tears and others to squeals of delight.

Fun Fact **Not a Woman's World**

For years, the world thought Machu Picchu had been almost entirely populated by the Inca's chosen "Virgins of the Sun." Bingham and his associates originally reported that more than three-quarters of the human remains found at the site were female. Those findings have been disproved, however; the sexual makeup of the inhabitants of Machu Picchu was no different than anywhere else in society: pretty much 50/50.

VISITING THE RUINS

As many as 2,000 visitors a day visit the ruins during high season, from May to the end of September; more than 400,000 people visit Machu Picchu annually. You've got to arrive early or stay late for a bit of splendid Incan isolation, but Machu Picchu's huge numbers of visitors are rarely overwhelming. The place is large enough to escape most tour group bottlenecks, although people fearful of the crush should plan to arrive before 11am and/or stay past 3pm. Perhaps the worst time to visit is from July 28 to August 10, when Peruvian national holidays land untold groups of schoolchildren and families at Machu Picchu. During the rainy season (Nov–Mar), you are very likely to get rain for (usually) brief periods during the day, and Machu Picchu is usually obscured by clouds in the morning.

For information on the shuttle buses to the ruins, see "Getting There," earlier.

The ruins are open from dawn to dusk: The first visitors, usually those staying at the hotel or arriving from the Inca Trail, enter at 6am. Everyone is ushered out by 6pm. The entrance fee is S/79 ($22.50) or S/70 ($20) for students with an ISIC card. You will be given an official Institute of National Culture map of the ruins, which gives the names of the individual sections, but no detailed explanations. The numbers indicated in brackets below follow our own map, "Machu Picchu," on p. 259. English-speaking guides can be independently arranged on-site; most charge around S/70 ($20) to S/105 ($30) for a private 2-hour tour. Individuals can sometimes hook up with an established group for little more than S/7 ($2) or S/10.50 ($3) per person.

INSIDE THE RUINS

After passing through the ticket booth, you can either head left and straight up the hill, or go down to the right. The path up to the left takes you to the spot above the ruins, near the **Caretaker's Hut** and **Funerary Rock** [1], that affords the classic postcard overview of Machu Picchu. If you are here early enough for sunrise (6:30–7:30am), by all means do this first. The hut overlooks rows and rows of steep agricultural terraces (generally with a few llamas grazing nearby). In the morning, you might see exhausted groups of trekkers arriving from several days and nights on the Inca Trail. (Most arrive at the crack of dawn for their reward, a celebratory sunrise.)

From this vantage point, you can see clearly the full layout of Machu Picchu, which had clearly defined agricultural and urban zones; a long **dry moat** [2] separates the two sectors. Perhaps a population of 1,000 lived here at the high point of Machu Picchu.

Head down into the main section of the ruins, past a series of burial grounds and dwellings and the **main entrance to the city** [3]. A section of stones, likely a **quarry** [4], sits atop a clearing with occasionally great views of the snowcapped peaks (Cordillera Vilcabamba) in the distance (looking southwest).

Down a steep series of stairs is one of the most famous Incan constructions, the **Temple of the Sun** ⚘⚘⚘ [5] (also called the Torreón). The rounded, tapering tower has extraordinary stonework, the finest in Machu Picchu: Its large stones fit together seamlessly. From the ledge above the temple, you can appreciate the window perfectly aligned for the June winter solstice, when the sun's rays come streaming through at dawn and illuminate the stone at the center of the temple. The temple is cordoned off, and entry is not permitted. Below the temple, in a cave carved from the rock, is a section traditionally called the **Royal Tomb** [6], even though no human remains have been found there. Inside is a meticulously carved altar and series of niches that produce intricate morning shadows. To the north, just down the stairs that divide this section from a series of dwellings called the **Royal Sector,** is a still-functioning water canal and series of interconnected **fountains** [7]. The main fountain is distinguished by both its size and excellent stonework.

Back up the stairs to the high section of the ruins (north of the quarry) is the main ceremonial area. The **Temple of the Three Windows** ⚘⚘ [8], each trapezoid extraordinarily cut with views of the bold Andes in the distance across the Urubamba gorge, is likely to be one of your lasting images of Machu Picchu. It fronts one side of the **Sacred Plaza** [9]. To the left, if you're facing the Temple of the Three Windows, is the **Principal Temple** [10], which has masterful stonework in its three high walls. Directly opposite is the **House of the Priest** [11]. Just behind the Principal Temple is a small cell, termed the **Sacristy,** renowned for its exquisite masonry. It's a good place to examine how amazingly these many-angled stones (one to the left of the doorjamb has 32 distinct angles) were fitted together by Incan stonemasons.

Up a short flight of stairs is the **Intihuatana** ⚘ [12], popularly called the "hitching post of the sun." It looks to be a ritualistic carved rock or a sort of sundial, and its shape echoes that of the sacred peak Huayna Picchu beyond the ruins. The stone almost certainly functioned as an astronomical and agricultural calendar (useful in judging the alignment of constellations and solar events and, thus, the seasons). It does appear to be powerfully connected to mountains in all directions. The Incas built similar monuments elsewhere across the empire, but most were destroyed by the Spaniards (who surely thought them to be instruments of pagan worship). The one at Machu Picchu survived in perfect form for nearly 5 centuries until 2001, when a

---

Tips One-Stop Package Visits to Machu Picchu

Machu Picchu packages that include round-trip train fare between Cusco and Aguas Calientes, shuttle bus and admission to the ruins, a guided visit, and sometimes lunch at Machu Picchu Sanctuary Lodge for same-day visits can be purchased from travel agencies in Cusco. Package deals generally start at around $110; it's worth shopping around for the best deal. Try **Milla Turismo,** Portal Comercio 195 (Plaza de Armas; © **084/234-181;** www.millaturismo.com); **SAS Travel,** Portal Panes 167, Plaza de Armas (© **084/255-205;** www.sastravel peru.com); Chaska Tours, Plateros 325 2nd floor (© **084/240-424;** www.chaska tours.com); **Top Vacations,** Portal Confituria 265, Plaza de Armas (© **084/ 263-278**), or any of the tour agencies listed later in this section that organize Inca Trail treks. Packages that include overnight accommodations at the ruins or in Aguas Calientes can also be arranged.

Bingham, the "Discoverer" of Machu Picchu

Hiram Bingham is credited with the "scientific discovery" of Machu Picchu, but, in fact, when he stumbled upon the ruins with the aid of a local campesino, he didn't know what he'd found. Bingham, an archaeologist and historian at Yale University (and later governor of Connecticut), had come to Peru to satisfy his curiosity about a fabled lost Incan city. He led an archaeological expedition to Peru in 1911, sponsored by Yale University and the National Geographical Society. Bingham was in search of Vilcabamba the Old, the final refuge of seditious Inca Manco Cápac and his sons, who retreated there after the siege of Cusco in 1537.

From Cusco, Bingham and his team set out for the jungle through the Urubamba Valley. The group came upon a major Incan site, which they named Patallacta (Llactapata), ruins near the start of the Inca Trail. A week into the expedition, at Mandorpampa, near today's Aguas Calientes, Bingham met Melchor Arteaga, a local farmer, who told Bingham of mysterious ruins high in the mountains on the other side of the river and offered to guide the expedition to them. In the rain, the two climbed the steep mountain. Despite his grandiose claims, the ruins were not totally overgrown; a small number of campesinos were farming among them.

In *The Lost City of the Incas,* Bingham writes: "I soon found myself before the ruined walls of buildings built with some of the finest stonework of the Incas. It was difficult to see them as they were partially covered over by trees and moss, the growth of centuries; but in the dense shadow, hiding in bamboo thickets and toggled vines, could be seen here and there walls of white granite ashlars most carefully cut and exquisitely fitted together . . . I was left truly breathless."

Bingham was convinced that he'd uncovered the rebel Inca's stronghold, Vilcabamba. Yet Vilcabamba was known to have been hastily built—and Machu Picchu clearly was anything but—and most accounts had it lying much deeper in the jungle. Moreover, the Spaniards were known to have ransacked Vilcabamba, and there is no evidence whatsoever of Machu Picchu having suffered an attack. Despite these contradictions, Bingham's

camera crew sneaked in a 1,000-pound crane, which fell over and chipped off the top section of the Intihuatana.

Follow a trail down through terraces and past a small plaza to a **dusty clearing** [13] with covered stone benches on either side. Fronting the square is a massive, sculpted **Sacred Rock** [14], whose shape mimics that of Putukusi, the sacred peak that looms due east across the valley. This area likely served as a communal area for meetings and perhaps performances. Many locals (as well as visitors) believe that the Sacred Rock transmits a palpable force of energy; place your palms on it to see if you can tap into it.

To the left of the Sacred Rock, down a path, is the gateway to **Huayna Picchu** ✸✸, the huge outcrop that serves as a dramatic backdrop to Machu Picchu. Although it looks forbidding and is very steep, anyone in reasonable shape can climb it. The steep pronouncement was accepted for more than 50 years. The very name should have been a dead giveaway: Vilcabamba means "Sacred Plain" in Quechua, hardly a description one would attach to Machu Picchu, nestled high in the mountains.

In 1964, the U.S. explorer Gene Savoy discovered what are now accepted as the true ruins of Vilcabamba, at Espíritu Pampa, a several-day trek into the jungle. Strangely enough, it seems certain that Hiram Bingham had once come across a small section of Vilcabamba, but he dismissed the ruins as minor.

The Machu Picchu ruins were excavated by a Bingham team in 1915. A railway from Cusco to Aguas Calientes, begun 2 years earlier, was finally completed in 1928. The road up the hillside to the ruins, inaugurated by Bingham himself, was completed in 1948. Bingham died still believing Machu Picchu was Vilcabamba, even though he'd actually uncovered something much greater—and more mysterious.

Bingham took some 11,000 pictures of Machu Picchu on his second visit in 1912 and eventually removed more than 45,000 artifacts for study in the U.S. (with the permission of the Peruvian government under the agreement that they would be returned to Peru when there was a suitable place for their storage and continued study). Peru claims the agreement was for 18 months, but the objects have now been stored at Yale University's Peabody Museum in New Haven, Connecticut (www.peabody.yale.edu/exhibits/machupicchu.html) for more than 90 years. A U.S. traveling exhibition was organized in 2003, but that seems only to have hardened the Peruvian government's contention that the collection constitutes national patrimony and demand that many of the Bingham artifacts be returned to Peru. Peru has threatened to sue Yale, but the Ivy League school so far has agreed to return only part of the collection and to help install and maintain those pieces in a Peruvian museum. Peru's Institute of National Culture hopes to build a Machu Picchu museum in Aguas Calientes, where the entire Bingham collection would be housed, in the near future.

path up takes most visitors about an hour or more, although some (including me) have ascended the peak in less than 25 minutes. Guards at a small booth require visitors to sign in and out. (The path is open 7am–1pm, and you must return before 3pm, or they'll come looking for you.) At the top, you'll reach a platform of sorts, which is as far as many get, directly overlooking the ruins. Others who've come this far and are committed to reaching the apex continue on for a few more minutes, up through a tight tunnel carved out of the stone, to a rocky perch with 360-degree views. There's room for only a handful of hikers up there, and the views are so astounding that many are tempted to hang out for hours—so new arrivals might need to be patient to win their place on the rock. The views of Machu Picchu below and the panorama of forested mountains are quite literally breathtaking.

Ascending Huayna Picchu is highly recommended for energetic sorts of any age. (I've seen octogenarians climb the path at an enviable clip.) In wet weather, you might want to reconsider, though, because the stone steps can get very slippery and become very dangerous.

Returning back down the same path (frighteningly steep at a couple points) is a turnoff to the **Temple of the Moon,** usually visited only by Machu Picchu completists. The trail dips down into the cloud forest and then climbs again, and is usually deserted. Cleaved into the rock at a point midway down the peak and perched above the Río Urubamba, it almost surely was not a lunar observatory, however. It is a strangely forlorn and mysterious place of caverns, niches, and enigmatic portals, with some terrific stonework, including carved thrones and an altar. Despite its modern name, the temple was likely used for worship of the Huayna Picchu mountain spirit. The path takes about 1 to 1½ hours round-trip from the detour.

Passing the guard post (where you'll need to sign out), continue back into the main Machu Picchu complex and enter the lower section of the ruins, separated from the spiritually oriented upper section by a **Central Plaza** [15]. The lower section was more prosaic in function, mostly residential and industrial. Eventually, you'll come to a series of cells and quarters, called the **Group of the Three Doors** [16] and the **Mortar District** or Industrial Sector [17]. By far, the most interesting part of this lower section is the **Temple of the Condor** [18]. Said to be a carving of a giant condor, the dark rock above symbolizes the great bird's wings and the pale rock below quite clearly represents its head. You can actually crawl through the cave at the base of the rock and emerge on the other side.

For those who haven't yet had their fill of Machu Picchu, the climb up to **Intipunku (Sun Gate)** is well worth it. The path just below the Caretaker's Hut [1] leads to the final pass of the route Inca Trail hikers use to enter the ruins. The views from the gateway, with Huayna Picchu looming in the background, are spectacular. Two stone gates here correspond to the all-important winter and summer solstices; on those dates, the sun's rays illuminate the gates like a laser.

For a more detailed guide of the ruins and Machu Picchu's history, Peter Frost's *Exploring Cusco* (Nuevas Imágenes, 1999), available in Cusco bookstores, is quite excellent.

HIKING THE INCA TRAIL

At its most basic, the Inca Trail (Camino del Inca) was a footpath through the Andes leading directly to the gates of Machu Picchu. Contrary to its image as a lone, lost, remote city, Machu Picchu was not isolated in the clouds. It was the crown of an entire Incan province, as ruins all along the Inca Trail attest. Machu Picchu was an administrative center in addition to its other putative purposes. That larger purpose is comprehensible only to those who hike the ancient royal route and visit the other ruins scattered along the way to the sacred city.

More than that, though, the Incas conceived of Machu Picchu and the great trail leading to it in grand artistic and spiritual terms. Hiking the Inca Trail—the ancient royal highway—is, hands down, the most authentic and scenic way to visit Machu Picchu and get a clear grasp of the Incas' overarching architectural concept and supreme regard for nature. As impressive as Machu Picchu itself, the trail traverses a 325-sq.-km (125-sq.-mile) national park designated as the Machu Picchu Historical Sanctuary. The entire zone is replete with extraordinary natural and man-made sights: Inca ruins, exotic vegetation and animals, and dazzling mountain and cloud-forest vistas.

The Inca Trail

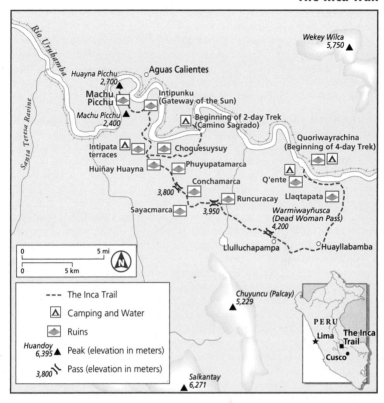

Today the Inca Trail—which, as part of the Machu Picchu Historical Sanctuary, has been designated a World Heritage natural and cultural site—is the most important and most popular hiking trail in South America, followed by many thousands of eco-tourists and modern-day pilgrims in the past 3 decades. Its popularity in recent years—more than 70,000 people a year hike the famous trail—led to concerns among environmentalists and historians that the trail was suffering potentially irreparable degradation. The National Institute of Culture (INC) and the Ministry of Industry, Tourism, Integration, and International Trade (MITINCI), reacting to pressure from groups such as UNESCO (which threatened to rescind Machu Picchu's World Heritage Site status), instituted far-reaching changes in practices in 2001 designed to limit the number of visitors and damage to Machu Picchu and the Inca Trail; see the "Inca Trail Regulations" box on p. 272.

There are two ways to walk to Machu Picchu: either along a fairly arduous 4-day/3-night path with three serious mountain passes, or as part of a more recently opened and more accessible 2-day/1-night trail. You can hire porters to haul your packs or suck it up and do it the hard way. Independent trekking on the Inca Trail without an official guide has been prohibited since 2001. You must go as part of an organized group arranged by an officially sanctioned tour agency (at last count, 29 agencies, most in Cusco, were allowed to sell Inca Trail packages). A couple or a small number of people can organize their own group if they are willing to pay higher prices for the luxury of not having to join an ad-hoc group.

Even with the new regulations, hiking the Inca Trail, beautiful and mystical as it is for most, is not a silent, solitary walk in the clouds laid out only for hard-core hikers. Although you'll either join up with others in a group or form your own, at least in high season, you will contend with groups walking the trail both in front of and behind you. Some will invariably be noisy student groups.

PREPARING FOR YOUR TREK

The classic **4-day route** is along hand-hewn stone stairs and trails through sumptuous mountain scenery and amazing cloud forest, past rushing rivers and dozens of Incan ruins. The zone is inhabited by rare orchids, 419 species of birds, and even the indigenous spectacled bear. The trek begins at Qorihuayrachina near Ollantaytambo—more easily described as Km 88 of the railway from Cusco to Aguas Calientes. The 43km (26-mile) route passes three formidable mountain passes, including the punishing "Dead Woman's Pass," to a maximum altitude of 4,200m (13,800 ft.). Most groups enter the ruins of Machu Picchu at sunrise on the fourth day, although others, whose members are less keen on rising at 3:30am to do it, trickle in throughout the morning.

The **2-day version** of the trail is being promoted by authorities as the Camino Sagrado del Inca, or "Sacred Trail," although it might also be called the Camino "Lite." It is a reasonable alternative to the classic trail if time or fitness are lacking. The path rises only to an elevation of about 2,750m (9,020 ft.) and is a relatively easy climb to Huiñay Huayna and then down to Machu Picchu. The minitrail begins only 14km (8¾ miles) away from Machu Picchu, at Km 104, and it circumvents much of the finest mountain scenery and ruins. Groups spend the night near the ruins of Huiñay Huayna before arriving at Machu Picchu for sunrise on the second day.

Either way you go, it is advisable to give yourself a couple of days in Cusco or a spot in the Sacred Valley to acclimatize to the high elevation. Cold- and wet-weather technical gear, a solid backpack, and comfortable, sturdy, broken-in hiking boots are musts (also needed: sleeping bag, flashlight, and sunblock). Above all, respect the ancient trail and its environment. Whatever you pack in, you must also pack out. You should also choose your dates carefully. The dry season (June–Sept) is the most crowded time on the trail, but it's excellent in terms of weather. Shoulder seasons can be best of all, even with the threat of a bit of rain; May is perhaps best, with good weather and low numbers of trekkers. Other months—especially December through March—are simply too wet for all but the hardest-core trail vets. The entire trail is now closed for maintenance and conservation during the month of February—which was one of the rainiest and least appealing months for trekking to Machu Picchu anyway. For the most popular months (May through September), early booking is essential.

The Peruvian government has sought to limit the number of trekkers on the Inca Trail, but also to maximize revenue from one of its foremost attractions. Thus, the cost of hiking the trail has steadily climbed—it now costs about three times what it did just 3 years ago. Standard-class 4-day treks, the most common and economical service, cost between $315 and $400 per person, including entrance fees ($60 for adults, $30 for students, free for children under 11) and return by tourist train ($46). Note that entrance fees for the Inca Trail will rise in August 2006 to $90 for adults and $45 for students, and surely result in a proportionate rise in overall costs for the trail. Independent trekkers generally join a mixed group of travelers; groups tend to be between

On the Trail of "New" Incan Cities: The Discovery Continues

Since the demise of the Incan Empire, rumors, clues, and fabulous tales of a fabled lost Incan city stuffed with gold and silver have rippled across Peru. The tales prompted searches, discoveries, and, often, reevaluations. Machu Picchu wasn't the lost city Hiram Bingham thought it was—Vilcabamba the Old was the last refuge of the Incas. The search continues, though, and incredibly, new discoveries continue to occur. First, it was Choquequirao in the 1990s. More recently, other teams have announced the discoveries of other lost Incan cities.

The discovery of **Qorihuayrachina** (also called **Cerro Victoria,** the name of the peak it rests on), 35km (22 miles) southwest of Machu Picchu in the Andes, was announced by the National Geographic Society in March 2002. Led by Peter Frost, a group of explorers uncovered the ruins of a large settlement that might have been occupied by the Incas long before they'd built a continent-spanning empire. Among the ruins are tombs and platforms, suggestive of an important burial site and sacred rites, although there are also indications that the site was an entire city. The ruins cover 6 sq. km (2⅓ sq. miles) and occupy a spectacular mountaintop location with panoramic views of the Vilcabamba range's snowcapped peaks, which were considered sacred by the Incas. Archaeologists, claiming that Qorihuayrachina is one of the most important sites found in the Vilcabamba region since it was abandoned by the Incas nearly 500 years ago, have high hopes that the ruins will help them piece together the Incan Empire from beginning to end.

Frost claimed the site was the largest of its kind found since 1964. Comprising 100 structures, including circular homes, storehouses, cemeteries, funeral towers, roadways, waterworks, farming terraces, a dam, and a pyramid, the city might have been occupied by the Incas who fled Cusco after the Spanish conquest. The ruins are secluded in cloud forest in the remote Vilcabamba region.

Just months after the discovery of Qorihuayrachina in 2002, the British Royal Geographic Society, led by Hugh Thompson and Gary Ziegler, announced the finding of a major new Incan site, **Cota Coca,** only a few kilometers away but across a deep canyon from Choquequirao (a road might have connected the two). Wholly unknown to the outside world until its discovery, Cota Coca—97km (60 miles) west of Cusco—appears to have been an administrative and storage center.

Llactapata, rediscovered by a U.S. and British team using remote (aerial) infrared technology and reported in November 2003, is the latest Incan city to surface. Just 3km (1¾ miles) from Machu Picchu, it, too, had been visited by Bingham and several explorers in the 1980s, so it's open to question how new its discovery is.

How long these discoveries might go on is anyone's guess. According to Hugh Thomson, "The physical geography of southeast Peru is so wild, with its deep canyons and dense vegetation, that it is possible that there are even more ruins waiting to be discovered. The fact that we have found two in 2 years means there could be many more out there."

12 and 16 people, with guaranteed daily departures. The cost includes a bus to Km 88 to begin the trek, an English-speaking guide, tents, mattresses, three daily meals, and porters who carry all common equipment. Tips for porters or guides are extra. Personal porters, to carry your personal items, can be hired for about $50 for the 4 days. Premium-class services generally operate smaller group sizes (a maximum of 10 trekkers), and you generally get an upgrade on the return train. Prices for premium group treks, organized for private groups, range from $450 to more than $700 per person.

Prices vary for trail packages based on services and the quality and experience of the agency. In general, you get what you pay for. Rock-bottom prices will probably get you a guide who speaks little English, food that is barely edible, camping equipment on its last legs, and a large, rowdy group. Especially important is the ability of an agency to guarantee departure even if its desired target number of travelers is not filled.

Never purchase Inca Trail (or, for that matter, any tour) packages from anyone other than officially licensed agencies, and be careful to make payments (and get official receipts) at the physical offices of the agencies. If you have questions about whether an agency is legitimate or is authorized to sell Inca Trail packages, ask for assistance at the main tourism information office in Cusco.

To guarantee a spot with an agency (which must request a trek permit for each trekker) it is imperative that you make a reservation and pay for your entrance fee at least 15 days in advance (at least 1 month or more in advance if you plan to go during peak months of May–Oct). Reservations can be made as much as a year in advance. Gone are the days when trekkers could simply show up in Cusco and organize a trek on the fly. Changing dates once you have a reservation is difficult, if not impossible. If spots remain on agency rosters, they are offered on a first-come, first-served basis.

The entrance ticket for the 2-day Camino Sagrado, purchased in Cusco, is $25 for adults and $15 for students. Basic pooled service (maximum 16 trekkers) costs about $100 per person (including the entrance fee). There are no premium-class services for the 2-day trek.

INCA TRAIL TOUR AGENCIES

Only officially sanctioned travel agencies are permitted to organize group treks along the Inca Trail. With the higher-end agencies, it is usually possible to assemble your own private group, with as few as two hikers. Budget trekkers will join an established group. In addition to cost, hikers should ask about group size (15 or fewer is best), the quality of the guides and their English-speaking abilities, the quality of food preparation, and porters and equipment. You should also make certain that the agency guarantees daily departures so that you're not stuck waiting in Cusco for a group to be assembled.

Recommended agencies that score high on those criteria include:

- **Andean Life,** Plateros 372 (© **084/221-491;** www.andeanlife.com). A relatively new, reputable midrange company offering both pooled basic and premium private treks. Good guides.
- **Big Foot Tours,** Triunfo 392, 2nd level (© **084/238-568;** fax 084/222-123; www.bigfootcusco.com). A popular budget agency.
- **Chaska Tours,** Plateros 325, 2nd floor (© **084/240-424;** www.chaskatours.com). A very capable midrange company, run by a Dutch and Peruvian team, praised for its private and group treks to Machu Picchu as well as Choquequirao.
- **Enigma,** Jr. Clorinda Matto de Turner, 100 Urbanización Magisterial 1 Etapa (© **084/221-155;** fax 084/221-153; www.enigmaperu.com). A new adventure

> ## *Tips* Howling at the Moon
>
> For a truly spectacular experience on the Inca Trail, plan your trip to depart 2 or 3 days before a full moon. Locals say the weather's best then, and having your nights illuminated by a full or near-full moon, especially for the early rise and push into Machu Picchu on the last day, is unforgettable.

travel operator with a good reputation and specialized and alternative hiking and trekking options, good for small-group and private treks.

- **Explorandes,** Av. Garcilaso 316-A (© **084/238-830;** fax 084/233-784; www.explorandes.com). One of the top high-end agencies and the most experienced in treks and mountaineering across Peru. Especially good for forming very small private groups.
- **Inca Explorers,** Suecia 339 (© **084/241-070;** fax 084/239-669; www.inca explorers.com). One of the best agencies, offering midrange, comfortable Inca Trail treks. Porters carry hikers' packs, and groups are small (including private group treks).
- **Mayuc,** Portal de Confiturías 211, Plaza de Armas (© **084/232-666;** www. mayuc.com). Especially good for pampered Inca Trail expeditions (porters carry all packs); aims to be low impact. Smaller groups.
- **Q'Ente,** Garcilaso 210 (© **084/222-535;** fax 084/222-535; www.qente.com). Receives very high marks from budget travelers. Very competitively priced, with responsible, good guides.
- **SAS Adventure Travel,** Portal de Panes 167 (Plaza de Armas; © **084/255-205;** fax 084/225-757; www.sastravelperu.com). Large, long-established agency serving budget-oriented trekkers. Very popular, responsible, and well organized.
- **United Mice,** Plateros 351 (© **084/221-139;** www.unitedmice.com). Started by one of the trail's most respected guides, this is another of the top agencies organizing affordable midrange treks.

DAY-BY-DAY: THE CLASSIC 4-DAY INCA TRAIL TREK

The following is typical of the group-organized 4-day/3-night schedule along the Inca Trail.

DAY 1   Trekkers arrive from Cusco, either by train, getting off at the midway stop, Ollantaytambo, or Km 88; or by bus, at Km 82, the preferred method of transport for many groups. (Starting at Km 82 doesn't add an appreciable distance to the trail.) After crossing the Río Urubamba (Vilcanota), the first gentle ascent of the trail looms to Incan ruins at **Llactapata** (also called **Patallacta,** where Bingham and his team first camped on the way to Machu Picchu). The path then crosses the Río Cusicacha, tracing the line of the river until it begins to climb and reaches the small village (the only one still inhabited along the trail) of **Huayllabamba**—a 2- to 3-hour climb. Most groups spend their first night at campsites here. Total distance: 10 to 11km (6¼–6¾ miles).

DAY 2   Day 2 is the hardest of the trek. The next ruins are at **Llullucharoc** (3,800m/12,460 ft.), about an hour's steep climb from Huayllabamba. **Llullucha-pampa,** an isolated village that lies in a flat meadow, is a strenuous 90-minute to 2-hour climb through cloud forest. There are extraordinary valley views from here. Next up

Inca Trail Regulations

For decades, individuals trekked the Inca Trail on their own, but hundreds of thousands of visitors—as many as 75,000 a year—left behind so much detritus that not only was the experience compromised for most future trekkers, but the very environment was also placed at risk. The entire zone has suffered grave deforestation and erosion. The Peruvian government, under pressure from international organizations, has finally instituted changes and restrictions designed to lessen the human impact on the trail and on Machu Picchu itself: In the first couple of years, regulations were poorly enforced, but in 2003, the government announced its intentions to fully and strictly enforce them.

All trekkers are now required to go accompanied by a guide and a group. In addition, prices for both the trail and the ruins were tripled to S/59.50–S/210 ($17–$60) adults, S/31.50–S/105 ($9–$30) students; the overall number of trekkers permitted on the trail was significantly reduced, to 200 per day; only professionally qualified and licensed guides are allowed to lead groups on the Inca Trail; the maximum loads porters can carry has been limited to 20 kilograms (44 lb.); tourists are no longer permitted to travel on the local train from Aguas Calientes to Machu Picchu (or vice versa); and all companies must pay porters the minimum wage (about S/105 or $30).

These changes have cut the number of trekkers on the trail in half and have made reservations essential in high season. Guarantee your space on the trail by making a reservation at least 1 week in advance of your trip (but 1 month or more in advance for high season May–Oct; reservations can be made as much as a year in advance). Travelers willing to wing it *might* still find available spots a couple of days before embarking on the trail, perhaps even at discounted rates, but waiting is a huge risk if you're really counting on doing the Inca Trail.

The key changes for travelers are that it is no longer possible to go on the trail independently and no longer dirt cheap to walk 4 days to Machu Picchu. The good news is that the trail is more organized and that hope for its preservation is greater.

is the dreaded Abra de Huarmihuañusqa, or **Dead Woman's Pass,** the highest point on the trail and infamous among veterans of the Inca Trail. (The origin of the name—or who the poor victim was—is anybody's guess.) The air is thin, and the 4,200m (13,780-ft.) pass is a killer for most: a punishing 2½-hour climb in the hot sun, which is replaced by cold winds at the top. It's not uncommon for freezing rain or even snow to meet trekkers atop the pass. After a deserved rest at the summit, the path descends sharply on complicated stone steps to **Pacamayo** (3,600m/11,810 ft.), where groups camp for the night. Total distance: 11km (6¾ miles).

DAY 3   By the third day, most of the remaining footpath is the original work of the Incas. (In previous sections, the government "restored" the stonework with a heavy hand.) En route to the next mountain pass (1 hr.), trekkers encounter the ruins of

Runcuracay. The circular structure (the name means "basket shaped") is unique among those found along the trail. From here, a steep 45-minute to 1-hour climb leads to the second pass, **Abra de Runcuracay** (3,900m/12,790 ft.), and the location of an official campsite just over the summit. There are great views of the Vilcabamba mountain range. After passing through a naturally formed tunnel, the path leads past a lake and a stunning staircase to **Sayacmarca** (3,500m/11,480 ft.), named for its nearly inaccessible setting surrounded by dizzying cliffs. Among the ruins are ritual baths and a terrace view point overlooking the Aobamba Valley, suggesting that the site was not inhabited but instead served as a resting point for travelers and as a control station.

The trail backtracks a bit on the way to **Conchamarca,** another rest stop. Here, the well-preserved Incan footpath drops into jungle thick with exotic vegetation, such as lichens, hanging moss, bromeliads, and orchids, and some of the zone's unique bird species. After passing through another Incan tunnel, the path climbs gently for 2 hours along a stone road, toward the trail's third major pass, **Phuyupatamarca** (3,800m/12,460 ft.); the final climb is considerably easier than the two that came before it. This is a spectacular section of the trail, with great views of the Urubamba Valley. Some of the region's highest snowcapped peaks (all over 5,500m/18,040 ft.), including Salcantay, are clearly visible, and the end of the trail is in sight. The tourist town of Aguas Calientes lies below, and trekkers can see the backside of Machu Picchu (the peak, not the ruins).

From the peak, trekkers reach the beautiful, restored Incan **ruins of Phuyupatamarca.** The ancient village is another one aptly named: It translates as "Town above the Clouds." The remains of six ceremonial baths are clearly visible, as are retaining-wall terraces. A stone staircase of 2,250 steps plummets into the cloud forest, taking about 90 minutes to descend. The path forks, with the footpath on the left leading to the fan-shaped **Intipata terraces.** On the right, the trail pushes on to the extraordinary ruins of **Huiñay Huayna,** which are actually about a 10-minute walk from the trail. Back at the main footpath, there's a campsite and ramshackle trekker's hostel offering hot showers, food, and drink. The grounds are a major gathering place for trekkers before the final push to Machu Picchu, and for some, they're a bit too boisterous and unkempt, an unpleasant intrusion after all the pristine beauty up to this point on the trail. Although it's closest to Machu Picchu, the Huiñay Huayna ruins, nearly the equal of Machu Picchu, were only discovered in 1941. Its name, which means "Forever Young," refers not to its relatively recent discovery, but to the perpetually flowering orchid of the same name that is found in abundance nearby. The stop was evidently an important one along the trail; on the slopes around the site are dozens of stone agricultural terraces, and 10 ritual baths, which still have running water, awaited travelers. Total distance: 15km (9⅓ miles).

DAY 4   From Huiñay Huayna, trekkers have but one goal remaining: reaching Intipunku (Sun Gate) and descending to Machu Picchu, preferably in time to witness the dramatic sunrise over the ruins. Most groups depart camp at 4am or earlier to reach the pass at Machu Picchu and arrive in time for daybreak, around 6:30am. Awaiting them first, though, is a good 60- to 90-minute trek along narrow Incan stone paths, and then a final killer: a 50-step, nearly vertical climb. The descent from Intipunku to Machu Picchu takes about 45 minutes.

Having reached the ruins, trekkers have to exit the site and deposit their backpacks at the entrance gate near the hotel. There, they also get their entrance passes to Machu Picchu stamped; the pass is good for 1 day only. Total distance: 7km (4⅓ miles).

Tips   Shunning the Masses: Alternatives to the Inca Trail

The Inca Trail was once very much off the beaten path and at the cutting edge of adventure travel. Although the Peruvian government has adopted new measures to restrict the numbers of trekkers along the trail, it has become so popular and well worn that in high season it's tough to find the solitude and quiet contemplation such a sacred path deserves. Hard-core trekkers and travelers looking for a little more privacy, authenticity, or bragging rights are seeking alternatives, and many adventure-travel companies are catering to them by offering other, less accessible trails to keep ahead of the masses. Several international operators now offer custom-designed alternatives to the traditional Inca Trail. **Adventure Life** (© 800/344-6118; www.adventurelife.com) promotes a 10-day "Cachiccata Trek: The Inca Trail Less Traveled"; **Andean Treks** (© 800/683-8148; www.andeantreks.com) suggests a 4-day "Moonstone to Sun Temple" trek, as well as others like the 6-day "Vilcanota Llama Trek"; **Mountain Travel Sobek** (© 888/687-6235; www.mtsobek.com) offers a 12-day (7 days hiking) "Other Inca Trail"; and **Wilderness Travel** (© 800/368-2794; www.wildernesstravel.com) has a 12-day (6 days hiking) "Salcantay to Machu Picchu Hidden Inca Trail" tour. Prices range from about $550 to $3,800 per person.

Or you may want to skip Machu Picchu altogether (or at least the idea of trekking there). If you're one who wants to go where few others do, talk to one of the local trek tour agencies in Cusco (such as Q'Ente or Enigma) about **Salcantay** or **Vilcabamba** treks or **Choquequirao,** a "lost" Incan city only truly unearthed in the past decade. It takes 5 days to get there over an arduous trail, but when you get back to Cusco, you can be sure that not everyone in the coffeehouse will have the same bragging rights.

AGUAS CALIENTES (MACHU PICCHU PUEBLO)

Renamed Machu Picchu Pueblo by the Peruvian government—one can only guess so as not to confuse tourists—Aguas Calientes is quite literally the end of the line, a gringo outpost of *mochileros* (backpackers) outfitted in the latest alpaca and indigenous weave fashions designed to tempt them. Hats, gloves, sweaters—they are walking (if unshaved) advertisements for Peruvian artisanship. Making it Peru's own Katmandu, the trekkers hang out for a few days after their great journey to Machu Picchu, sharing beers and tales, and scoring a final woven hat or scarf to wear as a trophy back home.

To be honest, there's not much else to do in Aguas Calientes, which might as well be called Aires Calientes, given its sweltering heat and humidity. The town has *baños termales,* or outdoor **thermal baths**—the source of the town's name—that are a 10-minute climb up Avenida Pachacútec. Many visitors find them a bit hygienically challenged, if not downright nasty, but they're popular with folks who've completed the Inca Trail and are in desperate need of muscular relaxation (not to mention a bath). The one pool with freezing mountain water can be tremendously restorative if

Aguas Calientes (Machu Picchu Pueblo)

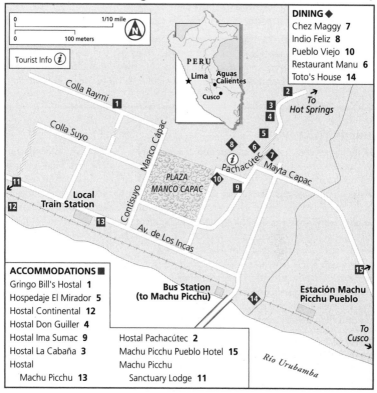

0   1/10 mile
0   100 meters

Tourist Info (i)

PERU
Lima Aguas
     Calientes
Cusco

Colla Raymi 1

Colla Suyo

Manco Capac

Contisuyo

Local
Train Station

PLAZA
MANCO CAPAC

Pachacútec

Mayta Capac

To
Hot Springs

2
3
4
5
8 6 7
10 9
11
12
13

Av. de Los Incas

DINING ◆
Chez Maggy **7**
Indio Feliz **8**
Pueblo Viejo **10**
Restaurant Manu **6**
Toto's House **14**

ACCOMMODATIONS ■
Gringo Bill's Hostal **1**
Hospedaje El Mirador **5**
Hostal Continental **12**
Hostal Don Guiller **4**
Hostal Ima Sumac **9**
Hostal La Cabaña **3**
Hostal
    Machu Picchu **13**

Hostal Pachacútec **2**
Machu Picchu Pueblo Hotel **15**
Machu Picchu
    Sanctuary Lodge **11**

**Bus Station
(to Machu Picchu)**

14

**Estación Machu
Picchu Pueblo**

15

To
Cusco

Río Urubamba

you've just finished a long day at the ruins. The springs are open from 5am to 9pm; admission is S/5 ($1.40). Just be sure to leave your valuables locked up at the hotel.

Adventurous sorts not yet exhausted from climbing might want to climb the sacred mountain **Putukusi** ☆, which commands extraordinary distant views across the river to the ruins of Machu Picchu. The trail begins on the right side of the railroad just out of town. (A signpost reads KM 111.) Veer to the right up stone steps and get ready for an athletic feat, struggling up vertical ladders until you reach a clearing and series of stone-carved switchbacks. At the top, Machu Picchu is nestled like an architectural model between its two famous peaks. The trek up takes about 75 minutes; the descent takes 45 minutes. Gazing across the valley at the ancient Incan city? Priceless. Although they've repaired the trail and fixed missing steps, it is still mostly for fit climbers.

Another good trail, particularly for bird-watchers, is the short trail to **Mandor Ravine** and a waterfall found there. From the railroad tracks, walk downstream (beyond the old train station) until you come to the ravine (about 3km/1¾ miles). A short climb takes you to the waterfall.

In the evening, most folks take to the bars for a few beers. A good spot for music and drinks is **Blues Bar Café,** Av. Pachacútec s/n (☎ 084/211-125), an airy, cabin-like two-level place next to the park on restaurant row. In the late afternoon, it's a fine place to chill and gaze out at Putukusi, the mountain across from Machu Picchu.

Tips **About Tipping**

At the end of the Inca Trail, guides, cooks, and especially porters expect—and fully deserve—to be tipped for their services. They get comparatively little of the sum hikers pay to form part of the group, and they depend on tips for most of their salary, like waitstaff in American restaurants. Tip to the extent that you are able.

WHERE TO STAY

At the upper end, hotels in and around Machu Picchu Pueblo have suddenly gotten very expensive—more costly than anything comparable in all of Peru. And it's usually only the very fortunate—those who not only plan far ahead, but who also have healthy bank accounts—who have the option of staying at the one upscale hotel next to the ruins. For the rest of us, below the ruins in Aguas Calientes, there are scores of *hostales* (inns) aimed at the grungy backpacker crowd, a couple of midrange options, and one self-styled ecolodge that's perfect for bird-watchers who want to take it easy. Sorry, there's no camping within Machu Picchu.

Although a few new hotels have popped up to take advantage of Machu Picchu's ever-expanding popularity, there are growing concerns about the environmental impact of new construction. Indeed, UNESCO, which named the whole Machu Picchu Historical Sanctuary as a World Heritage Site, has threatened to withdraw the honor if Peru doesn't address growth and environmental concerns.

VERY EXPENSIVE

Machu Picchu Sanctuary Lodge *&&*   Back in the 1970s, the Peruvian government built a temporary hotel on the top of the mountain just steps from the entry to Machu Picchu as a way to show off the ruins to international movers and shakers. As the ruins grew in popularity as a destination, the hotel was rewarded with a begrudged permanence. Today the hotel stands as the only major alteration to the ruins' isolated setting, but as hotels go, it is pretty sensitively inserted into the hill and is not visible from the ruins themselves.

Formerly a rather plain but overpriced modern hotel, the rustic inn was taken over by Orient-Express Hotels (which also manages the Hotel Monasterio in Cusco) and transformed into a luxury lodge, now with a full meal plan program for guests. Without question, it has one of the most dramatic and unique settings in the world, and, as the only hotel perched right next to the ruins, it can pretty much charge what it wants (and does). Guests need very deep pockets to stay here; despite the cost, the hotel remains in very high demand most of the year, so advance reservations are absolutely essential. Rooms are not especially large, but they now have a good deal of Peruvian character, with some lovely modern furnishings, and most have small terraces that open to lovely gardens with impressive views of the ruins and the surrounding Andes.

Although some will always decry the hotel as an unwelcome modern intrusion in this mystical and sacred place, it's here to stay. And who can blame travelers for wanting to stay as close to Machu Picchu as possible, waking up to see the sun rise over the ruins and, at night, visiting the ruins in the dark or gazing at the stars from an elevation of 2,400m (7,870 ft.)? If you can afford it as a special treat, you'd be wise to reserve 3 to 6 months in advance during high season (May–Sept). The buffet lunch ($25) is open to all ruins visitors.

Machu Picchu (next to the ruins). ℂ **084/246-419.** Fax 084/246-983. www.orient-express.com. 33 units. $715–$935 double; $1045 suite. Rates include taxes and 3 meals daily. AE, DC, MC, V. **Amenities:** Restaurant; cafeteria; snack bar; 24-hr room service; laundry service. *In room:* TV, minibar, hair dryer, safe.

EXPENSIVE

Machu Picchu Pueblo Hotel ✿✿   This upscale hotel, tucked into lush gardens near the train station, has real flavor and is easily the best place to stay if you can't get into the fancy hotel next to the ruins (or don't want to pay its exorbitant prices). It's also the best place for naturalists who want to get a glimpse of some of the extraordinary bird- and plant life in this part of the Machu Picchu Historical Sanctuary; the hotel offers orchid tours, bird-watching, and guided ecological hikes. The compound of Spanish colonial, tile-roofed *casitas* (bungalows) is surrounded by 5 hectares (12 acres) of cloud forest beside the Vilcanota River, with a tea plantation and more than 100 species of birds and 250 species of butterflies. Regular rooms are large and comfortable, and junior suites have fireplaces and small terraces. A pretty spring-water pool makes this a great place to relax while taking in the grandeur of Machu Picchu. It's especially popular with an older set, and the only strike against it is that it sits about a 10-minute, inconvenient walk along the railroad tracks from Aguas Calientes's restaurants and bars—but that's the price to pay for a superior natural setting.

Av. Imperio de los Incas (Km 10 Línea Férrea Cusco, Quillabamba). ℂ **800/442-5042** in the U.S. and Canada or 084/211-122, or 084/245-314 for reservations. Fax 084/211-124. www.inkaterra.com.pe. 86 units. $195–$270 double; $300–$390 suite. AE, DC, MC, V. **Amenities:** Restaurant; cafe; bar; outdoor pool; 24-hr room service; laundry service. *In room:* Hair dryer.

MODERATE

Gringo Bill's Hostal *(Finds*   Gringo Bill's, established by an American expat, is a backpacker's institution that has been around since the early 1980s, when Machu Picchu began to take off. I first stayed here in 1983, at a time when there were very few other options (and it, frankly, was a dump). Tucked into the hillside behind the left corner of the Plaza de Armas, the cheery and plant-filled *hostal* has become quite a bit upscale lately. But it still has a great vibe, with a cool patio, a lounge bar with a fireplace where travelers hang out watching videos, and a pretty good restaurant. The

---

Mudslides at Machu Picchu

In October 2005, an avalanche destroyed part of the train track leading from Cusco to Machu Picchu, stranding 1,400 tourists. Before that, in April 2004, two massive mudslides at the tail end of the rainy season hit Aguas Calientes, killing at least six local people and stranding as many as 1,500 tourists for the duration of Easter weekend. Seventy people were left homeless, and about 600 tourists had to be evacuated by helicopter. A portion of the railroad track that takes hundreds of thousands of tourists to the famed Incan ruins annually was damaged—though normal rail service to and from Cusco reopened 2 days later—as were a couple dozen homes near the river.

Though the heavy rains were unusual, they highlight both the dangers of traveling during the wet season as well as the precarious infrastructure of the town and its ill preparedness to handle the growth of tourism in recent years. The tragedies are likely to reignite calls in Peru to further limit the numbers of tourists permitted at Machu Picchu.

comfortable and clean rooms have good beds, and many have great views of the Upper Amazon tropical rainforest from bedroom windows and balconies. Throughout the inn are trippy cosmic murals painted by the Cusco artist Gonzalo Medina. Visitors headed to Machu Picchu or out on treks can pick up bagged lunches to go. A stay of 2 or 3 nights will earn you a 10% discount, but some backpackers still find it comparatively expensive for budget travel.

Colla Raymi 104, Plaza de Armas, Aguas Calientes. ②/fax 084/211-046, or 084/241-545 for reservations. Fax 084/211-046. www.gringobills.com. 86 units. $60–$90 double. Rates include taxes and continental breakfast. AE, MC, V. **Amenities:** Restaurant; bar; laundry facilities; TV room. *In room:* TVs in newer rooms, no phone (in older rooms).

INEXPENSIVE

Hostal Continental *(Value)*   One of the better inexpensive *hostales* along the main drag and railroad tracks, this basic hotel is very tidy (it was refurbished in 2001), and you won't lack for hot water. Rooms aren't large, but they have style, and the beds are pretty decent, to a budget backpacker's delight. It used to have great river views, but, sadly, boomtown construction has done away with them. Extras include a library.

Av. Imperio de los Incas 177, Aguas Calientes. ② 084/211-065 or 084/244-598. presidente@terra.com.pe. 12 units. $32 double with shared bathroom. Rate includes taxes and continental breakfast. No credit cards. **Amenities:** Laundry service; library. *In room:* No phone.

Hostal Machu Picchu   Across from the police station and, in true frontier fashion, right on the train tracks (a better location than it sounds—a balcony on the other side overlooks the Vilcanota River, and the hostel is perfectly positioned for barhopping), this midsize hotel is one of the better inexpensively priced options in Aguas Calientes, though that's not saying a whole lot. It has very clean, well-furnished, and airy rooms, some painted in funky colors. Its sister hotel next door, the Presidente, has 28 rooms and is pretty similar but slightly costlier.

Av. Imperio de los Incas s/n, Aguas Calientes. ② 084/211-065 or 084/244-598. Fax 084/212-034. presidente@terra.com.pe. 24 units. $40 double with shared bathroom. Rate includes taxes and continental breakfast. MC, V. **Amenities:** Cafe; bar; laundry facilities.

WHERE TO DINE IN AGUAS CALIENTES

Scores of small and friendly restaurants line the two main drags (okay, the only two real streets) in Aguas Calientes, Avenida Imperio de los Incas and Avenida Pachacútec. There's always a proliferation of cheap pizzerias/pit stops hugging the railroad tracks. If you're looking for an easy meal of wood-fired pizza, almost any spot in town can accommodate you; **El Fogón de las Mestizas** (Av. Pachacútec) and **Incawasi, Inti Killa, Pizzería Su Chosa,** and **Pachamama** (all on Av. Imperio de los Incas) are all dependable. Menú hawkers, often the children of the cook or owner, will try to lure you in with very cheap menú deals.

For lunch during visits to the ruins, you have two choices: the expensive buffet lunch at Machu Picchu Sanctuary Lodge or a sack lunch. I recommend the latter, especially because lunchtime is when lots of tourists vacate the ruins (pick one up at Gringo Bill's or assemble one from the breakfast buffet of your hotel).

MODERATE

Indio Feliz *(R R)* *(Value)* PERUVIAN/FRENCH   A restaurant named "The Happy Indian" might not sound too P.C., especially for a place that sits at the foot of a city abandoned by the Incas sometime before the Spanish invaded, but this is Aguas Calientes's best restaurant. An attractive and friendly two-level place with lots of plants, it's usually

---

Tips **More Places to Crash in Aguas Calientes**

Aguas Calientes fits the classic definition of a tourist town: It basically exists to accommodate gringos on their way up to or down from Machu Picchu. The town is little more than two main streets crammed with basic hostels, restaurants, and bars. But in the winter months (June–Aug), it gets very crowded, and finding accommodations can be a little complicated if you're the backpacker type arriving on the fly. In addition to the choices reviewed in this section, you might want to check out the following, which are all pretty decent, clean, and moderately priced (ranging from S/20, or $6, per person to $25 for a double room with a private bathroom):

- **Hostal Don Guiller,** Av. Pachacútec 136 (✆ **084/211-128**)
- **Hostal Ima Sumac,** Av. Pachacútec 173 (✆ **084/211-021**)
- **Hostal La Cabaña,** Av. Pachacútec 20 (✆ **084/211-048**)
- **Hostal Pachacútec,** Av. Pachacútec s/n (✆ **084/211-061**)
- **Hospedaje El Mirador,** Av. Pachacútec 135 (✆ **084/211-194**)

---

jam-packed with gringos, save the backpacker set. Even though its fixed-price menú is a great value, the restaurant qualifies as distinctly upscale in this ramshackle town. Nearly everyone opts for the three-course menú because ordering a la carte will get you basically the same thing at higher prices. Starters include quiche Lorraine and *sopa a la criolla* (Peruvian milk-based soup); the standout among main courses is the lemon or garlic trout. The ginger chicken is also quite nice, as are the desserts.

Lloque Yupanqui 4–12 (down an alley to the left off Av. Pachacútec). ✆ **084/211-090.** Reservations recommended in high season. Main courses S/23–S/35 ($6.55–$10); fixed-price menú S/38 ($11). MC, V. Daily noon–midnight.

Pueblo Viejo PERUVIAN   One of the more animated spots on restaurant row (right at the beginning, off the plaza), Pueblo Viejo is fairly large but simple and cozy, with live Andean music and a roaring fire. It specializes in *parrilladas,* or grilled lamb, pork and alpaca, and grilled trout, and it draws plenty of backpackers and families for the low-priced fixed menús: Choose from vegetarian, *menú de la casa,* and *menú turístico* versions. You can also get good pizza.

Av. Pachacútec 108. ✆ **084/211-193.** Reservations not accepted. Main courses S/20–S/36 ($6–$10). MC, V. Daily noon–midnight.

Toto's House *Finds* *Value* PERUVIAN/PIZZA   This large restaurant, perched between the railroad tracks and the banks of the Río Vilcanota, is a terrific addition to Aguas Calientes. It's one of the nicest in town, although the food at Indio Feliz is more sophisticated. Owned by the same people who run Pueblo Viejo, it features an open area overlooking the river with refreshing mountain views. The dining room is dominated by a barbecue pit and most days features live Andean music. The menu is extensive and varied, ranging from a mixed grill and trout to the standby of all restaurants in town, pizza. The lunch buffet ($11) is a good deal and is popular with folks waiting for the train back to Cusco.

Av. Imperio de los Incas s/n. ✆ **084/211-020.** Reservations not accepted. Main courses S/22–S/38 ($6.30–$11). MC, V. Daily noon–midnight.

INEXPENSIVE

Chez Maggy *(Value)* PERUVIAN/PIZZA   On the right side of restaurant row, as you walk toward the hot springs, this longtime favorite and branch of the legendary Chez Maggy in Cusco is a good, relaxed place for wood-fired pizzas, pisco sours, and cold beers. You can also get a whole range of Peruvian *comida típica* and Mexican dishes, but everyone I've seen here is always gorging on pizza or pasta.

Av. Pachacútec 156. © 084/211-006. Reservations not accepted. Main courses S/12–S/35 ($3.40–$10). MC, V. Daily 10am–10pm.

Restaurant Manu PERUVIAN/PIZZA   At the top end of restaurant row, toward the hot springs, Manu—named for the great Amazon reserve—is a relaxed and friendly spot with a nice terrace and gardens. With a vaguely tropical look and feel, it's just as good a place to hang out and sip pisco sours as it is to have lunch or dinner. If a group comes in, it can get pretty animated. Almost everyone seems to order pizzas baked in the wood-fired oven, but the menu also features lots of international and Peruvian items, including homemade pastas, baked trout, and grilled chicken.

Av. Pachacútec 139. © 084/211-101. Reservations not accepted. Main courses S/8–S/26 ($2.30–$7.40). MC, V. Daily 10am–10pm.

Southern Peru

Southern Peru ranks just behind Cusco and the Sacred Valley on the visitors' circuit. The mountainous desert landscapes are some of Peru's most distinctive, and the region is a beacon to outdoors enthusiasts who enjoy hiking, mountain climbing, and river running. The deep sapphire expanse of Lake Titicaca, the world's highest navigable body of water at nearly 4,000m (13,100 ft.) above sea level, is one of the world's unique sights. The volcanoes and deep canyons near Arequipa hold tremendous opportunities for trekking and viewing the elusive Andean condor, one of the world's great birds, which at one celebrated spot above Colca Canyon soars directly over the heads of spectators every morning.

As cities go, bleak and often brutally cold Puno is not one of Peru's most interesting or attractive, although its position on the banks of Lake Titicaca and the creative partying at folkloric festivals couldn't be more spectacular. Arequipa, on the other hand, is perhaps Peru's most sophisticated city, a pretty colonial town built mostly of white volcanic stone and framed by three snow-capped volcanoes. The people of Arequipa have earned a reputation for thinking themselves different or better than their compatriots to the north (and thus also earned the antagonism of many Peruvians). Indeed, the city's elegant historic center looks quite different from the rest of Peru. Within the thick walls of the Santa Catalina monastery, one of Peru's most glorious sights, you almost feel as though you were in southern Spain rather than southern Peru.

1 Puno & Lake Titicaca ⟨★⟨★⟨★

388km (241 miles) S of Cusco; 297km (185 miles) NE of Arequipa; 1,011km (628 miles) SE of Lima

Puno, founded in the late 17th century following the discovery of nearby silver mines, is a ramshackle town that draws numbers of visitors wholly disproportionate to its innate attractions. A mostly unlovely city on a high plateau, it has one thing going for it that no other place on earth can claim: Puno hugs the shores of fabled Lake Titicaca, the world's highest navigable body of water, a sterling expanse of deep blue at 3,830m (12,566 ft.) above sea level. South America's largest lake, Titicaca is also the largest lake in the world above 2,000m (6,560 ft.). The magnificent lake straddles the border of Peru and Bolivia; many Andean travelers move on from Puno to La Paz, going around or, in some cases, over Lake Titicaca.

Before leaving Puno, though, almost everyone hops aboard a boat to visit at least one of several ancient island-dwelling peoples that seem to have materialized straight out of the pages of *National Geographic*. A 2-day tour takes travelers to the Uros Floating Islands—where Indian communities consisting of just a few families construct tiny islands out of totora reeds—and two inhabited natural islands, Amantaní and Taquile.

Southern Peru

To many Peruvians, Lake Titicaca is a mystical and sacred place. Manco Cápac, the original Incan chieftain believed to be a direct descendant of the Sun, is said to have risen from the lake's waters along with his sister to found the Incan Empire. The Uros Indians might remain on their floating islands because they believe themselves to be lake people by birth, the very descendants of the royal siblings.

Puno has one other thing in its favor. Though dry and often brutally cold, the city is celebrated for its spectacular festivals, veritable explosions of *cultura popular.* The unassuming town, where the people descended from the Aymara from the south and the Quechua from the north, reigns as the capital of Peruvian folklore. Its traditional fiestas, dances, and music—and consequent street partying—are without argument among the most vibrant and uninhibited in Peru. Among those worth planning your trip around are February's Festival de la Virgen de la Candelaria (Candlemas) and **Puno Week** 🎭🎊, celebrating the birth of the city and the Incan Empire, in early November.

ESSENTIALS
GETTING THERE
BY PLANE   Puno does not have an airport; the nearest is **Aeropuerto Manco Capac** (© **051/322-905**) in Juliaca, 45km (28 miles) north of Puno. **LanPeru**

Puno

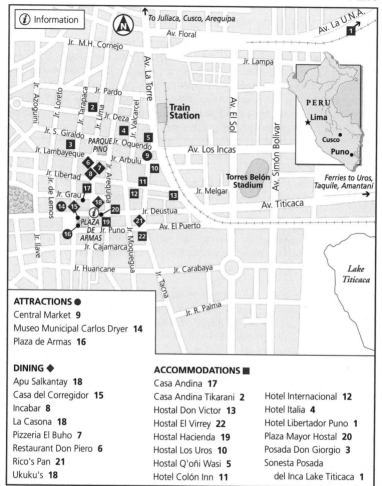

Information

↑ To Juliaca, Cusco, Arequipa

Av. La U.N.A.

Av. Floral

Jr. M.H. Cornejo

Jr. Lampa

Jr. Pardo

Av. La Torre

Train Station

Av. El Sol

PERU

Lima

Cusco

Puno

Jr. Azoguini

Jr. Loreto

Jr. Tarapaca

Jr. Lima

Jr. Deza

Av. Valcarcel

Jr. S. Giraldo

PARQUE PINO

Jr. Oquendo

Av. Los Incas

Jr. Lambayeque

Jr. Arbulu

Jr. Libertad

Av. Simón Bolívar

Ferries to Uros, Taquile, Amantaní →

Torres Belón Stadium

Jr. Melgar

Jr. de Lemos

Jr. Grau

Jr. Arequipa

Jr. Deustua

Av. Titicaca

PLAZA DE ARMAS

Jr. Puno

Jr. Moquegua

Av. El Puerto

Jr. Cajamarca

Jr. llave

Jr. Huancane

Jr. Carabaya

Jr. Tacna

Lake Titicaca

Jr. R. Palma

ATTRACTIONS ●
Central Market **9**
Museo Municipal Carlos Dryer **14**
Plaza de Armas **16**

DINING ◆
Apu Salkantay **18**
Casa del Corregidor **15**
Incabar **8**
La Casona **18**
Pizzeria El Buho **7**
Restaurant Don Piero **6**
Rico's Pan **21**
Ukuku's **18**

ACCOMMODATIONS ■
Casa Andina **17**
Casa Andina Tikarani **2**
Hostal Don Victor **13**
Hostal El Virrey **22**
Hostal Hacienda **19**
Hostal Los Uros **10**
Hostal Q'oñi Wasi **5**
Hotel Colón Inn **11**
Hotel Internacional **12**
Hotel Italia **4**
Hotel Libertador Puno **1**
Plaza Mayor Hostal **20**
Posada Don Giorgio **3**
Sonesta Posada
    del Inca Lake Titicaca **1**

(© **01/213-8300;** www.lanperu.com) and **TANS** (© **01/213-6000;** www.tansperu. com.pe) fly daily from Lima and Arequipa to Juliaca; flights range from $79 to $110, one-way. LanPeru flies from Cusco to Juliaca for similar fares. Tourist buses run from the Juliaca airport to Puno (a 1-hr. trip), depositing travelers on Jr. Tacna (S/10, or $2.85).

BY BUS   Puno has a modern, safe bus station, **Terminal Terrestre,** Jr. (© **051/364-733**), Primero de Mayo 703, Barrio Magistral. Road service to Puno from Cusco has been greatly improved in recent years, and many more tourists now travel by bus, which is faster and cheaper than the train. The terrific views during the day are pretty much the same. Most buses drop passengers at Melgar, a few short blocks from downtown.

> ### *Tips* In Juliaca, Hit the Ground Running
>
> Juliaca, site of the regional airport, is perhaps the most disgraced city in all of Peru. If you are flying into Juliaca on your way to Puno, don't linger. The town is a chaotic and ugly mess of half-finished houses, potholed dirt roads, and trash-strewn streets clogged with sales carts and *ciclotaxis.* If that weren't enough, Juliaca is also reputed to be downright dangerous. The only reason it was awarded an airport is that Puno is boxed in by mountains and local politicians had a stranglehold on Lima's purse strings.

From Cusco, executive-, imperial-, or royal-class buses make the trip in less than 7 hours (though some services, such as Inka Express, make stop-offs at Incan ruins en route, extending the trip a couple of hours, highly recommended if you have the extra time) and range in cost from S/52.50–S/87.50 ($15–$25). **Imexso** (© **084/240-801**), **Inka Express** (© **051/365-654**), and **Cruz del Sur** (© **051/622-626**) operate buses with videos and English-speaking tour guides. **Ormeño** (© **084/227-501**) has daily direct departures between Cusco and Puno (6 hr.). Regular buses are as cheap as S/12 ($3.40), but they are uncomfortable, have no restrooms or videos, and are potentially dangerous.

The trip between Puno and Arequipa by bus is no longer tortuous; the long-awaited highway between the cities, completed in 2002, has dramatically shortened travel time from 12 hours to just 5. **Cruz del Sur** (© **051/622-626**) and **Ormeño** (© **051/352-321**) make the trip for around $10.

BY TRAIN   The Titicaca Route journey from Cusco to Puno, along tracks at an altitude of 3,500m (11,500 ft.), is one of the most scenic in Peru. Though it is slower (10 hr. and prone to late arrivals) and has experienced its share of onboard thievery, it is a favorite of travelers in Peru and preferable to the bus if you've got the time and money. Keep a careful eye on your bags and, if possible, lock backpacks to the luggage rack; keep valuables close to your person. Trains from Cusco to Puno depart from **Estación Huanchaq** (© **084/238-722**), at the end of Avenida Sol. Service to Puno is Monday, Wednesday, and Saturday year-round, departing at 8am and arriving at 6pm. Andean Explorer (first class) costs $119 one-way in swank coaches and includes lunch in luxurious dining cars; tourist (backpacker) class, which is comfortable enough but offers no food or drink, costs $16.66. Only Andean Explorer tickets can be pre-reserved. The Puno train station (© **051/351-041**) is located at Av. La Torre 224.

Train service from Arequipa to Puno is available by charter only; see www.perurail.com for details.

VISITOR INFORMATION

An **iPerú tourist information office** is located at the pedestrian-only main drag of Puno, Jr. Lima 549 (© **051/365-088**, at Jr. Deustua, just off the Plaza de Armas). There you can pick up a map and get a couple of hints on sights in town. However, you're better off going to one of the travel agencies that organizes Lake Titicaca–area trips, such as **All Ways Travel** or **Edgar Adventures** (see "Organized Tours," later in this section), for information on Puno's most important attractions, all of which lie beyond the city.

FAST FACTS   You'll find banks and ATMs located along Jr. Lima (aka Pasaje Lima), as well as at Hotel Casa Andina, Jr. Independencia 185. Banks include **Banco Continental,** at Jr. Lima 400, and **Banco de Crédito,** on the corner of Jr. Lima and Jr. Grau. Money-changers can generally be found along Jr. Tacna, where most bus stations are located, and at the market near the railway and Avenida de los Incas.

For those crossing into Bolivia, the **Bolivian Consulate** is located at Jr. Arequipa 120 (© **051/351-251**). North Americans, Europeans, New Zealanders, and Australians do not need a visa to enter Bolivia, but the border is a historically problematic one (it was closed for more than a month in 2001 and again in 2005 during the widespread strikes that paralyzed parts of Bolivia), so you might need to check on the status of the crossing before traveling to Bolivia.

In a medical emergency, go to **Clínica Puno,** Jr. Ramón Castilla 178–180 (© **051/ 368-835**), or **Hospital Nacional,** Av. El Sol 1022 (© **051/369-696**). The **tourist police** are located at Jr. Deustua 538 (© **051/352-720**).

Pretty fast Internet connections are available at **Qoll@internet,** Jr. Oquendo 340 (Parque Pino), where you can make inexpensive international calls. It's open Monday through Saturday from 8am to midnight and Sunday from 3 to 9pm; rates are S/1.5 (40¢) per hour. A nice, quiet spot for surfing the Internet is behind the café at **La Casa del Corregidor,** Deustua 576 (© **051/351-921**). Other Internet *cabinas* are located along Pasaje Lima. Puno's main **Serpost post office** (© **051/351-141**) is located at Moquegua 269; it's open Monday through Saturday from 8am to 8pm. The **Telefónica del Perú** office is on the corner of Moquegua and Arequipa.

GETTING AROUND

Few visitors spend more than a day or two in Puno (unless lingering at a festival), and the little getting around that needs to be done in town is either on foot or by taxi to your hotel. The small downtown area is pretty easily managed on foot, although several of Puno's nicest hotels lie several kilometers away, on the banks of Lake Titicaca. The port is only about 10 blocks east from the Plaza de Armas in the center of town. The main pedestrian thoroughfare, Jirón Lima, connects the Plaza de Armas to Parque Pino.

Visits to Lake Titicaca and its islands, as well as the ruins on the outskirts of town, are most conveniently done by organized tour.

BY TAXI   Taxis are inexpensive and plentiful, easily hailed on the street, and best used at night and to get back and forth from the hotels on the banks of Lake Titicaca. Most trips in town cost no more than S/3 (85¢). Taxis can also be hired for round trips to nearby ruins or for half- or full days. Call **Taxi Milenium** (© **051/363-134**) or **Taxi Tour Puno** (© **051/369-900**). **Rossy Tours** (© **051/366-709**) runs inexpensive combi taxis to the airport in Juliaca (picking passengers up at their hotels) for just S/10 ($2.85) per person.

Tips Take It Easy

Puno's elevation of 3,830m (12,566 ft.) is even higher than Cusco, and unless you've already spent time in the Andes, you'll almost certainly need to rest for at least a day to acclimatize. See "Health & Safety," in chapter 2, for more information on how to address altitude sickness.

Puno & Lake Titicaca Festivals

Official travel literature rarely tires of labeling Puno the folkloric capital of Peru. Its festivals, celebrated with spectacularly vibrant pre-Columbian dances and costumes, certainly rank among the most spectacular in the country. Festivals in Puno are not just colorful; they're usually wild affairs. (Excessive imbibing seems to be as important a ritual as singing or dancing.) Locals zealously guard their ancestral traditions and cultural expressions, which are known for their unusual variety, singular choreography, and lilting altiplano music. The local cultures are responsible for registering more than 360 dances in the National Institute of Culture.

Foremost among local festivals is the **Festival de la Virgen de la Candelaria (Candlemas),** held during the first 2 weeks of February. The celebration of Puno's patron saint brings bands and more than 200 groups of dancers from villages and towns all over the region. The festival owes its origins to ancient rituals linked to agricultural cycles and harvests. Festivities blend traits associated with the dominant native local groups: the sobriety of the Quechua people and the *joie de vivre* of the Aymara. The principal Candlemas dance is the *diablada,* or devil dance. Dancers wearing spectacular costumes and grotesque masks play panpipes and make offerings to Pachamama, or Mother Earth. You'll see terrifying devil masks with twisted horns and angelic, sequined "suits of lights." Official functions are held in the stadium, while more popular exercises are on the streets of Puno. The

BY FOOT   Puno is small enough to get around almost entirely on foot, unless you're staying at one of the upscale hotels on the shores of Lake Titicaca several kilometers from the center of town.

BY BOAT   You can independently hire boats at Puno harbor to take you out on Lake Titicaca, but it's simpler to sign up for economical organized tours to the islands (see "Organized Tours," later in this section).

WHAT TO SEE & DO

Puno itself is a rather bleak and unimpressive place if you don't count its enviable geography. The main attractions in Puno are outside the city: the communities of Lake Titicaca and the ancient Sillustani ruins. What there is to see in Puno doesn't delay most visitors for more than a half-day or so. However, if you stumble upon one of Puno's famously colorful festivals, you might want to linger.

PUNO HIGHLIGHTS

The large **Catedral** (Cathedral), on the west side of the Plaza de Armas at the end of Jirón Lima, is the focal point of downtown Puno. The 18th-century baroque church is large, but no great shakes; the elaborate exterior is much more impressive than the spartan, spacious, chilly interior. Also on the main square is the 17th-century **La Casa del Corregidor,** Deustua 576 (© **051/351-921**), purportedly Puno's oldest house, with an impressive Spanish balcony; it now houses a very nice "cultural cafe" and is the best spot in town to take a breather. Nearby, the **Museo Municipal Carlos Dryer,** more informal events are a real highlight for most observers. Festival dances are divided clearly between two historical epochs: pre-Columbian dances, celebrated on Saturday, and the post-Columbian dances, which take place on Sunday. On Monday is a grand 12-hour Folkloric Parade throughout Puno. Street dancing is observed every day of the week, so even if you miss the first couple of days, you're sure to get a healthy dose of the Virgen de la Candelaria.

Puno Week, celebrated during the first week of November, remembers Manco Cápac, who, according to legend, rose from the waters of Lake Titicaca to found the Incan Empire. A major procession leads from the shores of the lake to the town stadium. Dances and music pervade the city, and things sometimes get pretty wild, with plenty of people staggering and falling down drunk by the end of the evening.

Puno is also well known for its pre-Lenten **Carnaval** celebrations (late Feb to early Mar). Not quite the same as Brazil's hedonistic party, Carnaval is celebrated with native dances, lots of drinking, and water bombs.

Other lively festivals in and around Puno and Lake Titicaca, worthy of planning your trip around, include **San Juan de Dios** (St. John; Mar 7–8); **Fiesta de las Cruces Alasitas** (May 8); **San Juan, San Pedro, and San Pablo** (St. John, St. Peter, and St. Paul; June 24–29); and **Apóstol Santiago** (St. James; July 25), which is the most enthusiastically celebrated day on Isla Taquile.

Conde de Lemos 289, is the town's principal (but small) museum. It has a decent selection of pre-Incan ceramics and textiles, as well as mummies with cranial deformations, but the collection is not very well illuminated. The museum is open Monday through Friday from 7:30am to 3:30pm; admission is S/3.5 ($1).

For a superb view of Lake Titicaca and a vantage point that makes Puno look more attractive than it really is, climb the steep hill to **Mirador Kuntur Wasi** and **Huajsapata Park,** about 10 minutes southwest of the main square. On top is a blazing white statue of Manco Cápac, the legendary first Inca and founder of the empire. Back down below, Jr. (Pasaje) Lima is a pedestrianized mall, chock full of shops, restaurants and bars, that runs from the Plaza de Armas to pretty **Parque Pino,** a relaxed square populated by locals just hanging out. Puno's seedy **central market** is 2 blocks east of here, and it spills across several streets. While unattractive, it's a realistic look at the underbelly of the Peruvian economy. Beyond the railroad tracks is a *mercado de artesanía* (artisans' market) targeting tourists with all kinds of alpaca and woven woolen goods, often much cheaper those than found in Cusco and other cities. (Try on those sweaters, though; they rarely seem to fit as well as you'd expect.)

LAKE TITICACA

South America's largest lake and the world's highest navigable body of water, Lake Titicaca has long been considered a sacred place among indigenous Andean peoples. The people who live in and around the lake consider themselves descendants of Mama Qota, or Sacred Mother, and they believe that powerful spirits live in the lake's depths.

Tips   Titicaca's Antique British Steamship

Nowadays, fleets of tourist boats set out daily for the floating and natural islands of Lake Titicaca. The oldest ship to ply the world's highest navigable waterway, the **Yavarí**, built in 1862 in Birmingham, England, today sits inactive on the shore of the lake (outside the Sonesta Posada del Inca hotel). The restored steamship, which was originally shipped as a kit to Arica, Chile (and then carried by mule over the course of 6 years to Lake Titicaca), sailed Titicaca for 100 years. It has now been converted into a small museum and bar. The ship is owned by a foundation, Asociación Yavarí. To arrange a free visit with Capt. Carlos Saavedra and his crew, call *℃* **051/369-329,** visit www.yavari.org, or stop by the ship on most afternoons.

According to Andean legend, Lake Titicaca—which straddles the modern border between Peru and Bolivia—was the birthplace of civilization. Viracocha, the creator deity, lightened a dark world by having the sun, moon, and stars rise from the lake to occupy their places in the sky.

Worthy of such mystical associations, Lake Titicaca is a dazzling sight. Its deep azure waters seemingly extend forever across the altiplano, under the monstrously wide sky at an elevation of more than 3,800m (12,460 ft.). The lake covers more than 8,500 sq. km (3,282 sq. miles); it is 176km (109 miles) long and 50km (31 miles) wide. The sun is extraordinarily intense at this altitude, scorching off 600 cubic m (21,189 cubic ft.) of water per second. Daybreak and sunset are particularly stunning to witness.

Massive Titicaca has been inhabited for thousands of years. Totora-reed boats roamed the lake as early as 2500 B.C. Titicaca's islands—both man-made and natural—are home to several communities of Quechua and Aymara Indians, groups with remarkably different traditions and ways of life. Visiting them and staying overnight on one of the islands if you can is certainly one of Peru's highlights and one of the most unique experiences in South America.

The most convenient way to visit is by an inexpensive and well-run guided tour, arranged by one of several travel agencies in Puno (see "Organized Tours," later). Although it is possible to arrange independent travel, the low cost and easy organization of group travel don't encourage it. Even if you were to go on your own, you'd inevitably fall in with groups, and your experience wouldn't differ radically. You can go on a half-day tour of the Uros Floating Islands or a full-day tour that includes Taquile Island, but the best way to experience Lake Titicaca's unique indigenous life is to stay at least 1 night on either Taquile or Amantaní, preferably in the home of a local family. Those with more time and money to burn may want to explore the singular experience of staying on private **Isla Suasi,** home to little more than a solar-powered hotel and a dozen llamas and vicuñas.

Uros Floating Islands (Las Islas Flotantes) *⋆*
5km (3 miles) N of Puno

As improbable as it sounds, the Uros Indians of Lake Titicaca live on floating "islands" made by hand from totora reeds that grow in abundance in the shallow waters of the lake. This unique practice has endured since the time of the Incas, and today there are some 45 floating islands in the Bay of Puno. The islands first came into contact with

the modern world in the mid-1960s, and their inhabitants now live mostly off tourism. To some visitors, this obvious dependency is a little unseemly.

Many visitors faced with this strange sight conclude that the impoverished islanders can't possibly still live on the 40-odd islands, that it must be a show created for their benefit. True, the islands can seem to be little more than floating souvenir stands; the communities idly await the arrival of tourist boats and then seek to sell handmade textiles and reed-crafted items while gringos walk gingerly about the spongy islands—truly an odd sensation—photographing houses and children. Yet the islands and their people are not just a tourist show. Several hundred Titicaca natives continue to live year-round on the islands, even if they venture to Puno for commercial transactions. The largest island, Huacavacani, has not only homes, but also a floating Seventh-Day Adventist church, a candidate for one of the most bizarre juxtapositions you're likely to find in Peru—or anywhere. Others have schools, a post office, public telephone, small hotel, and souvenir shops. Only a few islands are actually set up to receive tourists. The vast majority of the Uros people live in continual isolation and peace, away from curious onlookers and camera lenses.

The Uros, who fled to the middle of the lake to escape conflicts with the Collas and Incas, long ago began intermarrying with the Aymara Indians, and many have now converted to Catholicism. Fishers and birders, they live grouped by family sectors, and

---

(*Fun Fact* **Say What?**

The undeniably exotic name Titicaca might cause giggles among some school-children, but the name isn't derived from Spanish: It's a hybrid of the local native languages Aymara and Quechua. To locals, Titicaca might mean "Sacred Lake," but in fact *titi* means "cat" in Aymara, while *caca* means "the sacred rock on the island of the sun" in Quechua.

---

entire families live in one-room tentlike thatched huts constructed on the shifting reed island that floats beneath. They build modest houses and splendid gondolas with fanciful animal-head bows out of the reeds and must continually replenish the fast-rotting mats that form their fragile islands. Visitors might be surprised, to say the least, to find some huts outfitted with televisions powered by solar panels (which were donated by the Fujimori administration after a presidential visit to the islands). Incredibly, the Fujimori government also built some solar-powered aluminum houses on several islands, but few if any locals actually dwell in them, because they are very hot during the day and brutally cold at night. For a fee, locals will take visitors on short rides from one island to another in the reed boats, but you should consider it a contribution to the community: At $2 a head for a 5-minute jaunt, it's hardly the best deal in Peru, but may be worth it if you're looking for a photo op.

GETTING THERE   Inexpensive tours (normally $6 per person) that go only to the Uros Islands last about 3 hours and include hotel pickup, an English-speaking guide, and motorboat transportation to the islands. Unless you're unusually pressed for time, it's much more enjoyable and informative to visit the Uros as part of a brief stop en route to the natural islands of Amantaní or Taquile. You can go on your own by catching a *lancha* (small boat) at the port. Depending on how many people you or the skipper are able to assemble, the cost will usually be between S/10 ($2.85) and S/15 ($4.30).

Taquile Island (Isla Taquile) 𝈁𝈁
35km (22 miles) E of Puno

Life on the natural islands of Lake Titicaca is more authentic feeling and less overtly dependent on tourism than on the man-made Uros islands. Taquile is a fascinating and stunningly beautiful island about 4 hours from Puno. The island is narrow, only a kilometer (½-mile) wide, but about 6km (3¾ miles) long, and it rises to a high point of 264m (866 ft.). The island is a rugged ruddy color, which contrasts spectacularly with the blue lake and sky, and its hillsides are laced with formidable Incan stone agricultural terraces and other Incan and pre-Incan stone ruins.

The island is as serene as the distant lake views. Taquile has been inhabited for 10,000 years, and life remains starkly traditional; there isn't electricity, you won't run into vehicles, and islanders quietly go about their business. Taquile natives, of whom there are still about 3,000 or so, allow tourists to stay at private houses (in primitive but not uncomfortable conditions), and there are a number of simple restaurants serving visitors near the central plaza. Although they're friendly to outsiders, the Quechua-speaking islanders remain a famously reserved and insular community. Their dress is equally famous: Taquile textiles are some of the finest in Peru. Men wear embroidered, woven red waistbands (*fajas*) and embroidered wool stocking caps (*chullos*)—so tightly

Moments Celebration and Quiet on Taquile

If you are lucky enough to catch a festival on the island, you will be treated to a festive and stubbornly traditional pageant of color, marked by picturesque dances and women twirling in circles, revealing as many as 16 layered, multicolored skirts. (Easter, Fiesta de Santiago on July 25 and Aug 1–2, and New Year's are the best celebrations.) Any time on the island, though, offers unique experiences—especially once the day-trippers have departed and you have the island and incomparable views of the blue waters framed by stone archways virtually to yourself. Taquile then seems about as far away from modernity and "civilization" as one can travel on this planet. At the top of the island on a clear night, under a carpet of blazing stars, Taquile is more magical still.

Access to the island from the boat dock is either by a long path that wends around the island or by an amazing 533-step stone staircase that climbs to the top, passing through two stone arches with astonishing views of the lake. Independent travelers sign in and pay a nominal fee. Those who want to stay the night can arrange to be put up in a family house. If you stay, expect to rough it a bit without proper showers. Many islanders do not speak Spanish, and English is likely to be met with blank stares.

knitted that they can hold water—that indicate marital status: red for married men, red and white for bachelors. Women wear layered skirts and black shawls over their heads. Taquile textiles are much sought after for their hand-woven quality, though they are considerably more expensive than mass-produced handicrafts in other parts of Peru. Along with agriculture, textiles are the island's main source of income. A cooperative shop operates on the main plaza, and laid-back stalls are set up during festivals and the high season of tourist travel (June–Sept). Sadly, a new, hideously modern municipal building now dominates the main square, looking woefully out of place. Locals are much more resistant to haggling than are artisans in other parts of Peru. (Usually they simply refuse to bargain.) There's very little of the noise and activity that's present at most Peruvian markets. If you go with a group, you're also likely to visit one of the individual communities on the island, and perhaps have a home-cooked meal after a low-key demonstration of their quotidian customs. Buying lunch is one way to contribute money to a community, although many guests also like to tip the head of the community for opening their doors to outsiders.

GETTING THERE The only feasible way to visit Taquile is as part of an inexpensive and convenient organized tour, which also takes in the Uros Islands ($9–$12 per person). Most single-day tours of the Uros and Taquile islands depart early in the morning and stop at the islands of Uros for a half-hour en route. For most visitors, a day trip, which allows only an hour or two on the island and 8 hours of boat time, is too grueling and insufficient to appreciate the beauty and culture of Taquile Island. A 2- or 3-day visit ($15), with time to spend the night on either Taquile or Amantaní, is preferable.

Amantaní Island (Isla Amantaní) ✦✦
36km (22 miles) NE of Puno

Amantaní, a circular island located about 4½ hours from Puno (and about 2 hr. from Taquile), is home to a very different, although equally fascinating, Titicaca community. Also handsomely terraced and home to farmers, fishers, and weavers, in many ways Amantaní is even more rustic and unspoiled than Taquile. It is a beautiful but barren and rocky place, with a handful of villages composed of about 800 families and ruins clinging to the island's two peaks, Pachatata (Father Earth) and Pachamama (Mother Earth). The island presents some excellent opportunities for hikes up to these spots, with terrific views of the lake and the sparsely populated island landscape. The agricultural character of the island is perhaps even more apparent than on Taquile. Long, ancient-looking stone walls mark the fields and terraces of different communities, and cows, sheep, and alpacas graze the hillsides.

The islanders, who, for the most part, understand Spanish, are more open and approachable than natives of Taquile. The highlight of a visit to Amantaní is an overnight stay with a local family. Not only will the family prepare your simple meals, but you will also be invited to a friendly dance in the village meeting place. For the event, most families dress their guests up in local outfits—the women in layered, multicolored, embroidered skirts and blouses, and the men in wool ponchos. Although the evening is obviously staged for tourists' benefit, it is low-key and charming rather than cheesy.

Amantaní islanders also make lovely hand-woven textiles, particularly the show-stopping black shawls embroidered with seven colors. The main festival on Amantaní, Fiesta de la Santa Tierra, is on the third Thursday in January, when the population splits in two—half at the Temple of Pachamama and the other half at the Temple of Pachatata (a perfect illustration of their dualistic male/female belief system). Other good festivals are the anniversary of Amantaní (Apr 9, lasting 3 days) and Carnaval (Feb or Mar).

Amantaní is best visited on a tour that allows you to spend the night (visiting the Uros Islands en route) and travel the next day to Taquile. Tour groups place groups of four or five with local families for overnight stays. The tour price normally includes accommodations, lunch, and dinner on the first day and breakfast the following morning.

It's a good idea to bring small gifts for your family on Amantaní because they make little from stays and must alternate with other families on the island. Pens, pencils, and batteries all make good gifts.

GETTING THERE   The only feasible way to visit Amantaní is by organized tour. Almost all tours that go to Amantaní also visit the Uros and Taquile islands, stopping en route at Uros and spending the night on Amantaní before visiting Taquile the following day.

Suasi Island (Isla Suasi) ✦✦
80km (50 miles) NE of Puno

The only island in private hands on Lake Titicaca, S-shaped Isla Suasi is tiny (just 48 hectares, or 117 acres), isolated, serene, and beautiful. And it makes for a wholly unique getaway, even if it is a long way to go for isolation and relaxation. Though reachable by fast *lancha* (motorized boat) in under 3 hours, most boats take upwards of 5 or 6 to get there (and either way, you'll have to pay around $300 for the privilege

---

Fun Fact **Fun with Language & Geography**

Lake Titicaca, which covers some 3,200 square miles and is South America's largest lake, is more or less evenly shared by Peru and Bolivia. Peruvians are fond of saying it is in fact more like a 60–40 breakdown, as there are maps that label the lake with "Titi" covering the Peruvian half and "caca" designating the Bolivian half.

---

of round-trip transportation). However, once you arrive, you really have traveled far. There are no inhabitants other than the island's owner and part-time resident, the sociologist Martha Giraldo, the few employees of the solar-powered refuge she started (which has since become an upscale ecolodge, administered since 2005 by the Casa Andina hotel chain), and a dozen alpacas, six free-ranging vicuñas, and a dog named Chiju. No cars, no TV, and no electricity. If you're lucky, you'll be one of just a handful of guests to enjoy the stunning high-altitude sunsets, gorgeous panoramic views of Titicaca—which extends in all directions like a sterling, placid cobalt sea—and total peace and quiet. The **eco-friendly lodge** *✸✸✸* is luxurious but sensitively designed (rooms have great lake views), its restaurant outstanding, and the personnel friendly. Activities are pretty much limited to reading in hammocks, canoeing around the island (which is small enough that it takes just about an hour to circle), hiking and trying to spot the vicuñas, trekking up to the *cerro* (hilltop) for sunset, and stargazing at night. I can't think of a more peaceful place in all of Peru. Many guests find their sunset visits to the hilltop to be a mystical experience; the sky blazes with unimaginable streaks of violet, red, and gold; and guests have built a series of *torrecitas,* small towers of stacked, balanced stones, echoing an ancient native practice of leaving stones at high elevations (where one is presumably closer to the *apus,* or gods). You can return to Puno either by boat again or by a very scenic but extremely rough ride in a car or van (the first 38km/24 miles are murder, but then it gets worse; asphalt only arrives after 2 hr.). For additional information, including arranging transportation, see www.casa-andina.com or call ☎ **01/446-8848** or 01/962-2709. Rates are $230 double.

OTHER ATTRACTIONS NEAR PUNO
Sillustani Ruins *✸*
32km (20 miles) NE of Puno

Just beyond Puno are mysterious pre-Incan ruins called *chullpas* (funeral towers). The finest sit on the windswept altiplano on a peninsula in Lake Umayo at Sillustani. The Colla people—a warrior tribe that spoke Aymara—buried their elite in giant cylindrical tombs, some as tall as 12m (39 ft.). The stonemasonry is exquisite (many archaeologists and historians find them more complex and superior even to Incan engineering), and the structures form quite an impression on such a harsh landscape.

The Collas dominated the Titicaca region before the arrival of the Incas. After burying their dead along with foodstuffs, jewels, and other possessions, they sealed the towers. Dress warmly for your visit here.

GETTING THERE   By far the best way to visit Sillustani is by guided tour, usually in the afternoon around 2 or 2:30pm (see "Organized Tours," below). Tours are inexpensive ($5–$7) and very convenient. Going on your own generally isn't worth it because the site is a pain to reach and, once there, you've no guide to explain the significance of the ruins. If you insist, though, catch a "Juliaca" colectivo from down-town Puno and request to be let off after about 20 minutes, at the fork in the road that leads to Sillustani (DESVIO PARA SILLUSTANI). From that point, it's 15km (9⅓ miles) and a half-hour farther away, but *colectivos* aren't frequent. To return, you're best off trying to hitch a ride back to Puno. In other words: Take the guided tour.

Chucuito: Fertility Temple
18km (11 miles) S of Puno

On a small promontory on the southern shore of Lake Titicaca, Chucuito, a small Aymara town, is one of the oldest in the altiplano region. The town, capital of the province during colonial times, has a lovely main square and a colonial church, **Nuestra Señora de La Asunción** (built in 1601). Chucuito was also the primary Incan settlement in the region. Another colonial church, **Santo Domingo** is a most curious—though many would say dubious—construction, and the town's main attraction. Said to date to pre-Columbian times, Inca Uyo is composed of dozens of large, mushroom-shaped phallic stones, most a few feet high, which locals claim were erected as part of fertility rituals. The anatomically correct stones, which until a few years ago were kept in a sterile museum, leave little doubt as to what their creators were getting at. Some point up at the sun god, Inti, while others are inserted into the ground, directed at Pachamama, or Mother Earth. At the center of the ring, lording over the temple, is the king phallus. Local guides tell tales of the exact rituals during which virgins pur-portedly sat for hours atop the phalluses to increase fertility. The stones might predate the Incas, but some contend that they, or at least the manner in which they are dis-played, are fake, a hoax perpetrated by locals to rustle up tourist business. Spanish mis-sionaries did everything in their power to destroy all symbols and structures they considered pagan, and it is highly unlikely that they would have constructed two churches nearby but left this temple intact.

If you find yourself drawn to the stones at Inka Uyo, you can stay the night at **Las Cabañas de Chucuito,** a comfortable International Youth Hostel at Jr. Tarapacá 153 (𝒞/fax **051/351-276;** lodgecabanas@hotmail.com). It has bungalows with private bathrooms for $7 per person and a nice setting by the lake. Also worth a look is the **Chucuito Resort Hotel,** Carretera Panamericana Sur Km 17 (𝒞 **051/622-208;** fax 051/352-108). The hotel has good views of Lake Titicaca and nice carpeted rooms.

GETTING THERE   Acora-bound colectivos leave from Puno's Avenida El Sol. The ride to Chucuito costs S/2 (60¢) and takes 15 to 20 minutes; tell the driver you want to get off at Chucuito, which lies about halfway between Chimú and Acora.

ORGANIZED TOURS
Most travel agencies in Puno handle the conventional tours of Lake Titicaca and Sil-lustani, along with a handful of other ruins programs. Two of the best agencies are **All Ways Travel** 𝒢𝒢, Jr. Deustua 576 (in the courtyard of La Casa del Corregidor) (𝒞 **051/353-979**) and Jr. Tacna 234 (𝒞 **051/355-552;** www.titicacaperu.com), which is run by the friendly and very helpful Victor Pauca and his daughter Eliana (currently on leave in the U.S.), with good guides and progressive cultural trips in addition to the standard tours (including a library bus that takes tourists to rural com-munities to donate books and toys to children); and **Edgar Adventures,** Jr. Lima 328 (𝒞 **051/353-444;** edgaradventures@terra.com.pe), which is run by a Peruvian hus-band/wife team. Both agencies can arrange bus and air travel as well, including travel

to Bolivia. Other agencies worth checking out for travel arrangements are **Highland Travel Experts,** Independencia 273 (© **051/964-139;** hightravel@latinmail.com), and **Pirámide Tours,** Jr. Deza 129 (© **051/367-302**).

Uros Islands half-day trips cost about $6 per person. Uros Islands and Taquile Island full-day trips cost $9 to $10 per person. Uros, Taquile, and Amantaní trips, lasting 2 days and 1 night, cost $15 per person. Sillustani and Chucuito tours, usually 3 hours long, cost $5 to $7 per person.

SHOPPING

Although it has very few nice shops on the order of Lima, Cusco, or Arequipa, Puno is one of the better places to load up on inexpensive woolen and alpaca goods, including hats, gloves, scarves, shawls, and blankets. They are cheaper here than in those cities, although you might not encounter the quality found at some upscale shops. The **open-air market** just beyond the railroad tracks (between Jr. Melgar and Av. Titicaca) has a couple dozen stalls specializing in alpaca and woolen goods. There is a cluster of souvenir and clothing shops along **Jr. Lima,** the pedestrian-only main drag, as well on Jr. Grau (just off Lima). A place worth seeking out is the non-profit **Fair Trade Store (La Tienda de Comercio Justo)** ✱ in the patio of La Casa del Corregidor, Jr. Deustua 576 (© **051/365-603**). Fifty percent of the purchase price of alpaca and wool scarves, ponchos, and the like goes directly to the artisans (identified by name on the garments) in rural communities (decidedly not the case in most transactions). It's open daily but does not accept credit cards.

WHERE TO STAY

Puno has grown rapidly as a tourist destination in the past few years, and its offer of accommodations is no longer geared almost exclusively toward a budget backpacker crowd. There are a couple of good midrange options in town, but, if you don't mind relying on taxis to get back and forth, the best options are out on the banks of Lake Titicaca (about a 10-minute cab ride). Many of the cheap places in town are very basic, and several of those are dingy, noisy dives with fleeting hot water. If you're looking at the bottom end, check the place out first and ask to see a couple of rooms. Outside high season (June–Sept), most hotels and *hostales* (inns) are more than willing to bargain.

EXPENSIVE

Hotel Libertador Puno ✱ Ensconced in serenity and splendid isolation on the shore of a small island 5km (3 miles) from Puno, overlooking the expanse of Titicaca, this large, stark-white hotel, built in the late 1970s, may stick out on the banks of the lake, but it takes full advantage of its privileged—or inconvenient—location, depending on your perspective. Part of the luxury Libertador chain, the hotel has rooms that are spacious if a little bland, and about half have panoramic views of the lake. Those views, though, are spectacular. Service is excellent and the large, white-block hotel has soaring ceilings, but it doesn't have as much character as the better-value Sonesta Posada del Inca (see below), which has views that are almost as good. The hotel is linked to the mainland by a causeway, and the only way back and forth to Puno is by taxi (about $3 each way).

Isla Esteves s/n, Lake Titicaca. (© **051/367-780.** Fax 051/367-879. www.libertador.com.pe. 123 units. $190 deluxe double; $215–$240 suite. Rates include breakfast buffet. AE, DC, MC, V. **Amenities:** Restaurant; bar; fitness center; sauna; concierge; 24-hr. room service; laundry service. *In room:* A/C, TV, minibar, hair dryer, safe.

Sonesta Posada del Inca Lake Titicaca 𝕽𝕽 *Value* *Kids*   Like the Libertador, Posada del Inca is perched on the shores of Titicaca and boasts splendid views, but it fits more sensitively into its enviable surroundings. The hotel is imaginatively designed, with warm colors and Peruvian touches, including bright modern art and folk artifacts. Rooms are large and comfortable, and bathrooms are also large and nicely equipped. The restaurant and many rooms look over the lake; other rooms have views of the mountains. The relaxed lobby has a cozy fireplace. Service is friendly, and the staff can arrange visits to Titicaca's islands. Children will enjoy the mini version of a floating lake community on the grounds by the lake.

Sesquicentenario 610, Sector Huaje, Lake Titicaca. ℂ 051/364-111. Fax 051/363-672. www.sonesta.com/peru_ puno. 62 units. $100–$125 double. Rates include breakfast buffet. Children under 9 stay free in parent's room. AE, DC, MC, V. **Amenities:** Restaurant; cocktail lounge; concierge; business center; 24-hr. room service; laundry service. *In room:* A/C, TV, minibar, hair dryer, safe.

MODERATE

Casa Andina Tikarani 𝕽 *Value*   This professional Peruvian chain of popular and comfortable midsize hotels with good service and impeccable, if predictably decorated, rooms has two locations in downtown Puno; this branch, 5 blocks from the Plaza de Armas, is the larger and quieter of the two. (The other, Casa Andina Puno Plaza, on Jr. Grau 270, is just a short block from the square and one off the main pedestrian drag.) As always, the rooms are good-sized, extremely clean, and well-equipped. Those on the second floor in the interior are quietest. In April 2006, Casa Andina opened one of their signature upscale hotels, Private Collection Puno, on the banks of Lake Titicaca (ℂ 051/365-992). I visited it in when it was under construction, and it certainly looks like it will be an excellent luxury option (especially the huge suite with marvelous lake views).

Jr. Independencia 185, Puno. ℂ 051/367-803. Fax 051/365-333. www.casa-andina.com. 53 units. $70 double. Rates include breakfast buffet. AE, DC, MC, V. **Amenities:** Concierge; laundry service. *In room:* A/C, TV, minibar, hair dryer, safe.

Hostal Hacienda   Built around a pair of sunny courtyards on a busy downtown street, this cheerful midsize hotel is pleasant and does its best to impersonate a hacienda-style inn. Rooms are simple, carpeted, and nice enough. A project continually expanded over the past few years, half the hotel's rooms were newly constructed at the end of 2001. Request one of the newer accommodations because they have much-improved bathrooms (with tubs) and double beds.

Jr. Deustua 297, Puno. ℂ/fax 051/356-109. hacienda@latinmail.com. 40 units. $50 double. Rate includes taxes and continental breakfast. MC only. **Amenities:** Restaurant; cafe; bar; concierge; laundry service. *In room:* TV.

Hotel Colón Inn 𝕽 *Value*   A small and charming Belgian-owned hotel (but affiliated with Best Western) in the heart of Puno, the Colón inhabits a 19th-century republican-era building on a corner. Built around an airy, sky-lit, colonial-style lobby, it has three floors of good-size and comfortably appointed carpeted rooms with desks and marble bathrooms. The cozy top-floor pub is advertised for its panoramic views, but in reality, all you can see are the tops of concrete buildings. The two restaurants, Sol Naciente and Pizzeria Europa, are a couple of the better places in Puno for lunch or dinner.

Calle Tacna 290, Puno. ℂ/fax 051/351-432. www.titicaca-peru.com. 21 units. $53 double. Rate includes taxes and breakfast buffet. AE, DC, MC, V. **Amenities:** 2 restaurants; bar; room service; laundry service. *In room:* TV, minibar, safe.

Tips Additional *Hostales*

If you arrive in Puno during festival time and there's a crunch on affordable accommodations, try these modest hotels and budget-backpacker places:

Hostal Don Victor   Located near the railroad tracks, this *hostal* is clean and well maintained. The 12 rooms have private bathrooms, and some have pretty decent views of Lake Titicaca. Melgar 166. *©* **051/366-087**. S/50 ($14) double.

Hostal El Virrey   El Virrey has pretty clean rooms with private bathrooms, TVs, and hot water. Some rooms even have views of Titicaca. Tacna 510. *©* **051/354-495**. S/75 ($21) double.

Hostal Q'oñi Wasi   Located across from the train station, this *hostal* has simple rooms with twin beds, private bathrooms, and electric showers. It also has a decent little breakfast room. Av. La Torre 119. *©* **051/353-912**. S/25 ($7.15) double.

Posada Don Giorgio   A step up from the others listed here, this recently renovated *hostal* is quite a good midrange choice; its four carpeted rooms (all with private bathrooms) are very comfortable and attractively decorated for the price. Tarapacá 238. *©*/fax **051/363-648**. $33 double.

Hotel Italia   A modest little hotel in the midst of Puno's hubbub, the Italia is homey and well maintained, and it has an attractive small restaurant and breakfast room. The rooms are clean, decent size, and, for the most part, tastefully decorated, although many are marred by scary circular fluorescent lights. The staff is very friendly and helpful. An unusual feature for a small, moderately priced hotel: free porn on channel 39 (more a feature of local cable than of this otherwise modest hotel, I'm guessing).

Jr. Teodoro Valcarcel 122, Puno. *©*/fax **051/367-706**. www.hotelitaliaperu.com. 21 units. $44 double. Rate includes taxes and continental breakfast. MC only. **Amenities:** Restaurant; cafe/bar; concierge; laundry service. *In room:* TV.

Plaza Mayor Hostal   Prior to the arrival of the nearby Casa Andina hotels, this midsize hotel filled a gaping void in Puno—a decent option in the heart of downtown. It's since been surpassed by those, but if they're full or too expensive, this isn't a bad place to stay for a night. Just off the main square, it's perfect if you want to be close to the bars and restaurants on busy Jr. Deustua and Jr. Lima. Although it's far from a luxury hotel, it is a step up from Puno's cheap downtown hotels. Rooms are a little dank and feature standard hotel decor, with flowery bedspreads and white-marble bathrooms, but they are clean and the beds are comfortable. It's not quite as nice as the Hotel Colón, but with a better location.

Jr. Deustua 342, Puno. *©*/fax **051/369-089**. www.plazamayorhostal.com. 34 units. $56 double. Rate includes taxes and breakfast. AE, DC, MC, V. **Amenities:** Restaurant; bar; room service; laundry service. *In room:* TV, safe.

INEXPENSIVE
Hostal Los Uros   Los Uros is one of the most popular Puno *hostales* targeting backpackers, representing a decent value at the low end. The very basic rooms are clean, beds are pretty decent, the place is quiet, and if you get chilly, the staff will dole out

extra wool blankets. About half the rooms have private bathrooms; the rest have shared bathrooms. Your best bet for hot water is in the evening. Breakfast is available at the simple cafeteria.

Jr. Teodoro Valcarcel 135, Puno. ℂ 051/352-141. Fax 051/367-016. www.losuros.com. 21 units. $12 double w/ private bathroom; $10 w/shared bathroom. Rates include taxes. No credit cards. **Amenities:** Cafeteria. *In room:* No phone.

WHERE TO DINE

Chilly, drab Puno isn't a place for fine dining. It's better suited for pizzas from wood-fired ovens and simple, straightforward Peruvian cooking. On those scores, it succeeds. Besides, at this altitude, it's not a great idea to overindulge in eating or drinking. Most of Puno's more attractive restaurants, popular with gringos, are located on the pedestrian-only main drag, Jr. Lima. In addition to those listed below, check out the two restaurants at **Hotel Colón Inn** (p. 296) and, especially for a light and inexpensive lunch, the attractive cafe **Casa del Corregidor,** Jr. Deustua 576 (ℂ **051/351-921**), which serves good salads and sandwiches and has a nice, quiet courtyard.

MODERATE

Apu Salkantay PERUVIAN/INTERNATIONAL   This genial restaurant, named for a Quechua mountain god, attracts plenty of travelers for drinks next to the fire-place-stove and occasional live folkloric music. But it's also a good place for Peruvian dishes, like *cuy;* alpaca steak with quinoa; and alpaca *piqueo* with fries, onions, tomatoes, and peppers; and standard soups and basic fish (kingfish and trout). The daily *menú* includes a soft drink, bread, and main course.

Jr. Lima 425. ℂ 051/363-955. Reservations not accepted. Main courses S/17–S/25 ($4.85–$7.15); daily menú S/22 ($6.30). DC, MC, V. Daily 9am–10pm.

Incabar ✹✹ NEW PERUVIAN/INTERNATIONAL   Awfully stylish and down-right funky (as well as relatively expensive) for rough-around-the-edges Puno, this lounge bar/restaurant aims high. The menu is much more creative and flavorful than other places in town (even if dishes don't always succeed), with interesting sauces for lake fish and alpaca steak, curries and stir fries, and artful presentations. For a recent meal, I had *pescadito crocante*—lake kingfish *(pejerrey)* in quinoa grain, fried and served with apples and blackberry jam. There are also interesting pastas and big salads, as well as sandwiches and snacks served until 5pm. Incabar is also a good place to hang out, have a beer or coffee, and write postcards—the colorful back room has comfortable sofas. Breakfast is also served (S/10 or $2.85).

Jr. Lima 356. ℂ 051/368-031. Reservations recommended. Main courses S/18–S/25 ($5.15–$7.15). AE, DC, MC, V. Daily 9am–10pm.

La Casona ✹ *Value* PERUVIAN/INTERNATIONAL   Puno's most distinguished eatery calls itself a "museum-restaurant." In a town like Puno, with relatively few attractions, that's fair enough. La Casona ("big house") has traditional, rather old-style Spanish charm, with lace tablecloths. The three dining rooms are filled with antiques and large religious canvasses, but it retains a decidedly informal appeal. Its specialty is Titicaca lake fish, such as trout and kingfish *(pejerrey),* served La Casona style, which means with a kitchen-sink preparation of rice, avocado, ham, cheese, hot dog, apple salad, french fries, and mushrooms. Chicken and beef are prepared the same way. If that's a little overwhelming for you, go with the simple trout served with mashed potatoes. In the evening, make a point about asking for the *menú del día,* which is offered but not advertised; it's a great deal (essentially half-price). Service can be a little slow, but there's not much to do in Puno anyway.

Jr. Lima 517. ✆ 051/351-108. Reservations recommended. Main courses S/15–S/36 ($4.30–$10); menú S/18 ($5.15). DC, MC, V. Daily 9am–10pm.

Restaurant Don Piero PERUVIAN/INTERNATIONAL   A longtime standard of Pasaje Lima, the pedestrian boulevard at the heart of Puno, Don Piero now seems a little stale. It still cranks out the same standard Peruvian and international fare in large portions as it always has, but the nondescript, midrange place doesn't appeal much to backpackers, and more interesting competition has cropped up on the street for more discriminating palates. Outside on slow days, bow-tied waiters looking bored halfheartedly appeal to tourists to enter. The menu has barbecued chicken and a long list of Peruvian favorites such as *palta rellena* (avocado stuffed with chicken salad) and *lomo saltado* (beef strips with french fries, onions, and peppers).

Jr. Lima 348–364. ✆ 051/351-766. Reservations not accepted. Main courses S/15–S/34 ($4.30–$9.70). DC, V. Daily 11am–10pm.

Ukuku's ✸ PIZZA/PERUVIAN   In a second-story space overlooking Jr. Lima, the main drag, this large pizzeria is a relaxed spot that's good looking enough for Puno, with hardwood floors and wood tables and chairs. It focuses on pizzas from a wood-burning oven, but also offers a full menu of Peruvian specialties, such as alpaca steak cooked in red wine, ceviche, and even *chifa* (Peruvian Chinese cooking). If that's not enough, you can also get a passable plate of pasta. There's a second location at Libertad 216.

Jr. Grau 172 (at Jr. Lima). ✆ 051/367-373. Reservations not accepted. Main courses S/10–S/25 ($2.85–$7.15). MC, V. Daily 11am–10pm.

INEXPENSIVE

Pizzería El Buho *(Value* PIZZA/ITALIAN   El Buho's new location is bigger and a bit less cozy, but its wood-burning oven/chimney still kicks out some of Puno's best pizzas. It's extremely popular with both gringos and locals. The menu also lists a good number of pastas and handful of soups, but I swear I've never seen anyone have anything other than pizza.

Jr. Lima 371. ✆ 051/363-955. Reservations not accepted. Main courses S/8–S/18 ($2.30–$5.15); pizza S/8–S/25 ($2.30–$7.15). DC, V. Daily 4:30–11pm.

Rico's Pan CAFE/BAKERY   You know what to expect at a small cafe and bakery with a name like "Tasty Bread," and Rico's Pan doesn't disappoint. Drop by for inexpensive sandwiches, pastries, and cakes. It also serves very good coffees, including espresso and cappuccino, and is a good spot for breakfast or for stockpiling goodies for boat trips on Titicaca.

Lima 420, Puno. ✆ 051/354-179. Reservations not accepted. Main courses S/4–S/10 ($1.15–$2.85). No credit cards. Daily 7am–11pm.

PUNO AFTER DARK

Though the city is the country's capital of folklore, there's not a whole lot happening in Puno after dark. Outside of festivals, nightlife is pretty much confined to a single street, consisting of a handful of bars and discos strung along (or just off) the pedestrian mall, Jr. Lima. My favorite watering hole is **Kamizaraky Rock Pub** ✸, Pasaje Grau 148 (no phone). A cozy and cool hangout with a loft space, it looks like a

Traveling to Bolivia

Plenty of travelers make their way across the Andes to Puno not only to visit Lake Titicaca, but also to continue on to Bolivia, which shares a border with Peru. Several travel agencies (see "Organized Tours," earlier in this section) in Puno sell packages and bus tickets to Bolivia.

The most common and scenic route is from Puno to La Paz via **Yunguyo** and **Copacabana.** You get dropped off at the border and then pick up a colectivo or taxi shuttle across, where you go through Customs and passport control. If you're going on your own, you'll need to catch another colectivo to Copacabana, just over a half-hour away. The trip to La Paz takes 7 or 8 hours by bus. Buses also go to La Paz via **Desaguadero.** Or, you can go by a combination of overland travel and hydrofoil or catamaran, a unique but very time-consuming journey (13 hr.).

At the border, visitors get an exit stamp from Peru and a tourist visa (30 days) from Bolivia. Foreigners are commonly tapped for phony departure and entry fees; resist the officials' blatant attempts at corruption.

For more information about Bolivia, pick up a copy of *Frommer's South America.*

graffiti-filled mountain cabin and serves excellent cocktails to a young, gregarious clientele (with occasional live rock music). The jungle lodge and reggae-themed **Positive Vibrations** (no. 345; no phone) and **Apu Salkantay** (no. 425; © **051/363-955**) are among the bars worth a stop for some decent music and hot drinks to warm up. **La Hostería** (no. 501) and **Ekeko's** (no. 355; no phone) often have live bands, and the latter has a large-screen TV showing soccer or videos, and a small dance floor. **Kusillo's Pub,** Libertad 259 (© **051/351-301**), has a nightly happy hour and reggae, jazz, and blues, as well as occasional folklore shows. **Shaman,** Jr. Puno 505 (on the Plaza de Armas; no phone), is a second-floor bar that has free Internet access, pizzas, and drinks.

2 Arequipa ★★★

1,020km (634 miles) S of Lima; 521km (324 miles) S of Cusco; 297km (185 miles) SW of Puno

The southern city of Arequipa, the second largest in Peru, might be the most handsome in the country. Founded in 1540, it retains an elegant historic center constructed almost entirely of *sillar* (a porous, white volcanic stone), which gives the city its distinctive look and the nickname *la ciudad blanca,* or "the white city." Colonial churches, mansions, a splendid Plaza de Armas and the sumptuous 16th-century Santa Catalina convent gleam beneath palm trees and a brilliant sun. Ringing the city, in full view, are three delightfully named snowcapped volcanic peaks: El Misti, Chachani, and Pichu Pichu, all of which hover around 6,000m (20,000 ft.). And to be observed in a small museum is an astounding local discovery, a perfectly preserved Incan maiden sacrificed more than 500 years ago.

Arequipa has emerged as a favorite of outdoors enthusiasts who come to climb volcanoes, raft on rivers, trek through the valleys, and, above all, head out to Colca

Canyon—twice as deep as the Grand Canyon and the best place in South America to see giant condors, with their legendary wingspan, soar overhead. Suiting its reputation as an outdoor paradise, Arequipa enjoys perfect weather: more than 300 days a year of sunshine, huge blue skies, and low humidity.

The commercial capital of the south, Arequipa not only looks but also feels very different from the rest of Peru. Arequipeños have earned a reputation as aloof and distrusting of centralized power in Lima. Relatively wealthy and home to prominent intellectuals, politicians, and industrialists, Arequipa has a haughty air about it—at least to many Peruvians who hail from less distinguished places—but you'd hardly know it in the evenings, when the historic quarter is alive with bar and restaurant patrons.

As beautiful and confident as it is, Arequipa has a history of natural disaster. The latest devastating earthquake (which registered 8.1 on the Richter scale) struck the city and other points farther south in 2001. Although international reports at the time painted a picture of a city that had caved in on itself, thankfully, that wasn't the case. Poorly constructed housing in some residential districts was destroyed, but the colonial core of the city survived intact, as elegant as ever.

ESSENTIALS
GETTING THERE
BY PLANE There are daily flights to Arequipa from Lima, Juliaca, and Cusco on **LanPeru** (℃ **01/213-8200;** www.lanperu.com) and **TANS** (℃ **01/213-6000;** www. tansperu.com.pe). Flights from Lima and Cusco range from $79 to $199, one-way.

Aeropuerto Rodríquez Ballón (℃ **054/443-464** or 054/443-458), Av. Aviación s/n, Zamácola, Cerro Colorado, is about 7km (4⅓ miles) northwest of the city. From the airport to downtown hotels, transportation is by taxi ($5) or shared colectivo service (about $2 per person).

BY BUS The main **Terminal Terrestre** (℃ **054/427-798**), Av. Andrés Avelino Cáceres at Av. Arturo Ibáñez s/n, is about 4km (2½ miles) south of downtown Arequipa. Nearby is a newer station, **Nuevo Terrapuerto** (℃ **054/348-810**), Av. Arturo Ibáñez s/n. A huge number of bus companies travel in and out of Peru's second city from across the country, and you'll need to ask if your bus departs from Terminal or Terrapuerto.

From Lima (a 16-hr. ride), recommended companies include **Ormeño** (℃ 01/472-5000), **Cruz del Sur** (℃ 01/424-1005), **Civa** (℃ 01/332-5236), and **Oltursa** (℃ 01/475-8559). For service from Puno (5 hr.) and Juliaca, contact **Cruz del Sur** (℃ 051/216-625), **Civa** (℃ 051/426-563), and **Julsa** (℃ 051/331-952). **Ormeño** travels to Arequipa from Puno (Av. Titicaca 318; ℃ 051/352-321) as well as Cusco (Plaza Tupac Amaru 114; ℃ 084/228-712). Other options from Cusco (10–12 hr.) are **Civa** (℃ 084/812-813) and **Cruz del Sur** (℃ 084/233-383). From Chivay/Colca Canyon (3–4 hr.), call **Reyna** (℃ 054/426-549) or **Cristo Rey** (℃ 054/213-094).

Note: Arequipa's bus stations—and especially the buses themselves—are notorious for attracting thieves. Travelers are advised to pay very close attention to their belongings, even going so far as to lock them to luggage racks. The route between Arequipa and Puno especially has earned a bad reputation. It's best to opt for more exclusive and safer bus companies recommended above.

BY TRAIN Puno-to-Arequipa trains are now available only by private charter for groups of 40 or more, and there are no trains to or from Lima. However, the former trajectory might be reinstated at some point in the future (for updates or charters, visit www.perurail.com). The Arequipa rail station is 8 blocks south of the city center, at Av. Tacna y Arica 201 (© 054/215-640). The PeruRail ticket office is open Monday through Friday from 6:30 to 10:30am and 2 to 6pm, and Saturday and Sunday from 8am to noon and 3 to 6pm.

VISITOR INFORMATION

There's a **tourist information booth** at the Aeropuerto Rodríquez Ballón (© 054/444-564), open Monday through Friday from 9am to 4pm. The best information office in town is in **Casona de Santa Catalina,** Santa Catalina 210 (across from the convent; © 054/221-227); it's open daily from 9am to 9pm. There's also an office on the Plaza de Armas across from the cathedral at Portal de la Municipalidad 112 (© 054/211-021); it's open daily from 8am to 6pm. You can also get information and free maps from the **tourist police,** Jerusalén 315 at the corner of Ugarte (© 054/201-258).

FAST FACTS   You'll find ATMs located in the courtyards of the historic Casa Ricketts at San Francisco 108, now the offices of **Banco Continental.** Other banks in the historic center include **Banco Latino,** at San Juan de Dios 112, and **Banco de Crédito,** at General Morán 101. Money-changers can generally be found waving calculators and stacks of dollars on the Plaza de Armas and major streets leading off the main square. There are several *casas de cambio* near the Plaza de Armas and Global Net ATMs in several shops around the Plaza; one is **Arequipa Inversiones,** Jerusalén 109.

The general emergency number in Arequipa is © **105.** If you need the police, call the **Policía Nacional** (national police) at © **054/254-020,** or **Policía de Turismo** (tourist police), Jerusalén 315 at the corner of Ugarte, at © **054/201-258.** For fire emergencies, call © **116.** If you need medical attention, go to **Clínica Arequipa,** Avenida Bolognesi at Puente Grau (© 054/253-416), which has good service and English-speaking doctors. You can also try **Hospital General,** Peral s/n (© 054/231-818) and **Hospital Regional,** Av. Daniel Alcides Carrión s/n (© 054/231-818).

Arequipa has plenty of Internet cabinas. Most are open daily from 8am to 10pm, charge S/1.5 (40¢) per hour, and have Net2Phone or other programs that allow very cheap Web-based international phone calls. Two of the cheapest and fastest cabinas are **La Red,** Jerusalén 306B (© 054/286-700), and **TravelNet,** Jerusalén 218 (© 054/205-548). Another good spot is **Catedral Internet,** in the small passageway behind the cathedral. An only slightly more expensive option that's open a bit later is **Catedral Internet,** Pasaje Catedral 101 (© 054/282-074), on the pedestrian mall just behind the cathedral.

The main **post office** is located at Moral 118 (© 054/215-247); it's open Monday through Saturday from 8am to 8pm, and Sunday from 9am to 2pm. A **DHL** office is located at Santa Catalina 115 (© 054/220-045); it's open Monday through Friday from 8:30am to 7:30pm, and Saturday from 9am to noon. **Telefónica del Perú** offices are located at Alvarez Thomas 209 (© 054/281-112) and Av. Los Arces 200B, in the Cayma district (© 054/252-020). They're open Monday through Friday from 8:30am to 6pm, and Saturday from 9am to 1pm.

GETTING AROUND

Arequipa is compact, and most of its top attractions can easily be seen on foot and with an occasional taxi. The historic center is built around the stately Plaza de Armas, marked by the cathedral on the north flank and porticoed buildings on the other three

---

Tips **A Note about Safety**

Arequipa has earned a reputation as one of Peru's more unsafe cities, mostly in terms of pickpocketing, although some locals talk about tourist robberies and even "strangle muggings." I found some citizens to be quite alarmist. Several people were outspoken about what you should carry on your person (nothing of value, including a camera) and how to conduct yourself (be on guard at all times), even in the daytime, when plenty of police patrol the streets in the old quarter. I've never had a problem in Arequipa, but I do think that late at night you should be especially cautious when exiting bars and restaurants in the historic center; as always, leave your daypack and other unnecessary belongings in your hotel. Some taxi drivers in Arequipa also warn about their colleagues who set tourists up for ambushes. They suggest either calling for a cab or getting into taxis with older drivers because most of the crimes have been perpetrated by younger drivers.

---

sides. Most sites of visitor interest, including most hotels and restaurants, are found in the blocks immediately north of the plaza. A few blocks west of the main square is the Río Chili and, beyond it, the residential neighborhood Yanahuara and La Recoleta monastery. Two bridges, Puente Grau and Puente Bolognesi, lead from the center to these areas.

BY TAXI Taxis are inexpensive and plentiful, easily hailed on the street, and best used at night. Most trips in town cost no more than S/3 (85¢). To call a taxi at night, try **Taxi Seguro** (© 054/450-250), **Taxi Sur** (© 054/465-656), **Master Taxi** (© 054/220-505), or **Ideal Taxi** (© 054/288-888). An excellent private driver for trips to Colca and elsewhere is Manuel Pino Torres of **Privatour** (© 054/952-6495).

BY CAR A car isn't necessary in Arequipa unless you want to explore the countryside, especially Colca and/or Cotahuasi canyons, independently. Try **Lucava Rent-a-Car,** Aeropuerto Rodríguez Ballón (© **054/650-565**) and Centro Comercial Cayma no. 10 (© **054/663-378**); and **Avis,** Aeropuerto Rodríguez Ballón (© **054/443-576**) and Palacio Viejo 214 (© **054/282-519**).

WHAT TO SEE & DO
THE TOP ATTRACTIONS
Monasterio de Santa Catalina ✦✦✦ *Kids* Arequipa's stellar and serene Convent of Santa Catalina, founded in 1579 under the Dominican order, is the most important and impressive religious monument in Peru. Santa Catalina is not just another church complex; it is more like a small, labyrinthine village, with narrow cobblestone streets, plant-lined passageways, and pretty plazas, fountains, chapels, and cloisters. Tall, thick walls painted sunburned orange, cobalt blue, and brick red hide dozens of small cells where more than 200 sequestered nuns once lived. Built in 1579, the convent remained a mysterious world unto itself until 1972, when local authorities forced the sisters to install modern infrastructure, a requirement that led to opening the convent for tourism. Today only 30 cloistered nuns ages 18 to 90 remain, out of sight of the hundreds of tourists who arrive daily to explore the huge and curious complex.

Santa Catalina feels like a small village in Andalusia, Spain, with its predominantly *mudéjar* (Moorish-Christian) architecture, intense sunlight and shadows, silent patios, painted arches, secret niches, and streets named for Spanish cities. In all, it contains 3 cloisters, 6 streets, 80 housing units, a square, an art gallery, and a cemetery. No less an expert than the great Portuguese architect Alvaro Siza called Santa Catalina a "magnificent lesson in architecture." Although the nuns entered the convent having taken vows of poverty, they lived in relative luxury, having paid a dowry to live the monastic life amid servants (who outnumbered the nuns), well-equipped kitchens, and art collections. Today the convent has been nicely restored, although it retains a rustic, contemplative appeal; it is a feast for the senses. Visitors are advised to wait for an informative guided tour (in English and other languages, available for a tip), though it's also transfixing just to wander around, especially before the crowds arrive. Among the convent's highlights are the Orange Tree Cloister, with mural paintings over the arches; Calle Toledo, a long boulevard with a communal *lavandería* at its end, where the sisters washed their clothes in halved earthenware jugs; the 17th-century kitchen with charred walls; and the rooms belonging to Sor Ana, a 17th-century nun at the convent who was beatified by Pope John Paul II and is on her way to becoming a saint. Visitors can enter the choir room of the church, but it's difficult to get a good look at the main chapel and its marvelous painted cupola. To see the church, slip in during early morning Mass (daily at 7:30am); the cloistered nuns remain secluded behind a wooden grille. Allow a couple of hours to see the convent in all its glory.

Santa Catalina 301. ⓒ 054/229-798. www.santacatalina.org.pe. Admission S/25 ($7.15). Daily 9am–4pm.

Museo Santuarios Andinos 🌟🌟🌟 *(Kids)* Now in a new location south of the Plaza de Armas, the small Museum of Andean Sanctuaries features a collection of fascinating exhibits, including mummies and artifacts from the Incan Empire, but it is dominated by one tiny girl: Juanita, the Ice Maiden of Ampato. The victim of a ritualistic sacrifice by Incan priests high on the volcano Mount Ampato and buried in ice at 6,380m (20,932 ft.), "Juanita"—named after the leader of the expedition, Johan Rhinehard—was discovered in almost perfect condition in September 1995 after the eruption of the nearby Sabancaya Volcano melted ice on the peak. Juanita had lain buried in the snow for more than 550 years. Only Incan priests were allowed to ascend to such a high point, where the gods were believed to have lived. Juanita, who became famous worldwide through a *National Geographic* report on the find, died from a violent blow to the head; she was 13 at the time of her death. Her remarkable preservation has allowed researchers to gain great insights into Incan culture by analyzing her DNA. Today, she is kept in a glass-walled freezer chamber here, less a mummy than a frozen body, in astoundingly good condition, nearly 600 years old. It struck me as a true privilege to observe such a monumental discovery and window onto the legacy of the Incan people. Displayed nearby and in adjacent rooms are some of the superb doll offerings and burial items found alongside Juanita's corpse and those of three other sacrificial victims also found on the mountain. Guided visits, which begin with a good *National Geographic* film, are mandatory. Allow about an hour for your visit.

La Merced 110. ⓒ 054/200-345. Admission adults S/15 ($4.30), students S/5 ($1.40), free for seniors. Mon–Sat 9am–6pm; Sun 9am–3pm.

PLAZA DE ARMAS 🌟

Arequipa's grand Plaza de Armas, an elegant and symmetrical square of gardens and a central fountain lined by arcaded buildings on three sides, is the focus of urban life. Dominated by the massive, 17th-century neoclassical **Catedral** 🌟, it is perhaps the loveliest main square in Peru, even though its profile suffered considerable damage when the great earthquake of 2001 felled one of the cathedral's two towers and whittled the

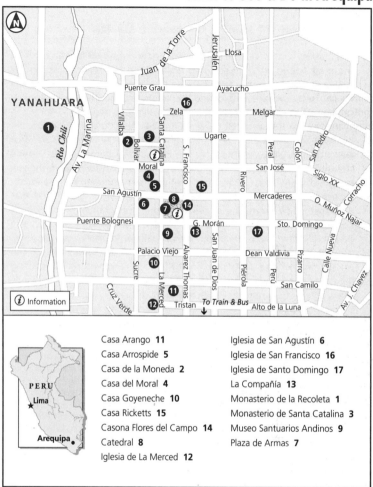

Casa Arango **11**
Casa Arrospide **5**
Casa de la Moneda **2**
Casa del Moral **4**
Casa Goyeneche **10**
Casa Ricketts **15**
Casona Flores del Campo **14**
Catedral **8**
Iglesia de La Merced **12**

Iglesia de San Agustín **6**
Iglesia de San Francisco **16**
Iglesia de Santo Domingo **17**
La Compañía **13**
Monasterio de la Recoleta **1**
Monasterio de Santa Catalina **3**
Museo Santuarios Andinos **9**
Plaza de Armas **7**

other to a delicate pedestal. The cathedral, previously devastated by fire and other earthquakes, has now been fully restored to its original grandeur and you'd never know an earthquake struck. The interior is peach and white, with carved arches and a massive pipe organ. The cathedral is open Monday to Saturday from 7 to 11:30am and 5 to 7:30pm, Sunday from 7am to 1pm and 5 to 7pm.

La Compañía ⭑, just off the plaza at the corner of Álvarez Thomas and General Morán, opposite the cathedral, is a splendid 17th-century Jesuit church with an elaborate (Plateresque) facade carved of *sillar* stone. The magnificent portal, one of the finest in Peru, shows the end date of the church's construction, 1698, more than a century after work began on it. The interior holds a handsome carved-cedar main altar, bathed in gold leaf, and two impressive chapels: the Capilla de San Ignacio, which has a remarkable painted cupola, and the Capilla Real, or Royal Chapel. Painted murals in the sacristy feature a jungle motif in brilliant colors. Next door to the church are

The Discovery of Juanita, the Ampato Maiden

The mummy of the teenage Incan maiden now christened Juanita is one of the most important archaeological finds of the last few decades in the Americas. The first frozen female found from the pre-Columbian era in the Andes, her body, packed in ice and thus not desiccated like most mummies, preserved a wealth of information about her culture and life.

Juanita was discovered at the summit of the Ampato volcano in September 1995 by the American anthropologist Dr. Johan Reinhard, the *National Geographic* explorer-in-residence. She immediately became news around the world. Reinhard, who had spent 2 decades looking for clues in the volcanoes of the western Andes near Arequipa, was working on a project co-sponsored by Arequipa's Catholic University of Santa María and was accompanied by Carlos Zárate, a locally famous mountaineer who for years has run one of the best mountain-climbing-expedition tour companies in Peru. Juanita had been remarkably preserved in ice for more than 500 years, but hot ashes from the eruption of the nearby Mount Sabancaya volcano melted the snowcap on Ampato and collapsed the summit ridge, exposing what had been hidden for centuries. Reinhard and Zárate at first saw only the feathers of a ceremonial Incan headdress. It took the two men 2 days to descend the peak with the 80-pound mummy, fighting against time to conserve her frozen body and get her back to Arequipa and the Catholic University labs.

Juanita was selected by Incan priests to be sacrificed as an appeasement to Ampato, whose dominion was water supply and harvests. The offering was almost certainly a desperate plea to stave off drought and starvation. Reinhard and his team later discovered two additional mummies, a girl and a boy, several thousand feet below the summit—probably companion sacrifices leading to the more important sacrifice of the princess on Ampato's summit.

The mummy's incredibly well-preserved corpse allows scientists to examine her skin, hair, blood, and internal organs, and even the contents of her

the stately Jesuit cloisters, of stark *sillar* construction, now housing upscale boutiques (enter on Calle Morán). Climb to the top for good views of the city's rooftops and distant volcanoes. The church is open Monday through Saturday from 9 to 11am and 3 to 6pm; admission is free.

On the east side of the plaza at Portal de Flores 136 is the **Casona Flores del Campo** (© 054/244-150), the oldest house in Arequipa. Begun in the late 1500s but not finished until 1779, today it is in deplorable condition, having suffered through earthquakes and a lack of funds that have left it barely standing, and is now closed to the public for safety considerations.

MORE ATTRACTIONS

Casa del Moral ℱ   An extraordinary mestizo baroque mansion, built in 1733 by a Spanish knight and nicely restored with period detail in 1994, Casa del Moral offers stomach. Her DNA makeup is being studied. Juanita was dressed in superior textiles from Cusco, clues to her probable nobility. Incredibly important was the fact that the ceremonial site was undisturbed, with all ritual elements in place, allowing anthropologists to essentially re-create the ceremony.

The peak of Apu Ampato was sacred to the Incas, and only priests were allowed to ascend to it. It is most extraordinary that the Incas were able to climb 6,000m (20,000-ft.) peaks without the assistance of oxygen or other modern climbing equipment. Juanita's transfer and sacrifice there, at the age of 13 or 14, was part of an elaborate ritual. Having first met with the Incan emperor in Cusco, she must have known her fate: an imminent journey to meet the mountain gods so revered by the Incas. Sacrifice was the greatest honor bestowed upon an individual. Led up the frozen summit by priests, in sandals and surely exhausted, she was probably made to fast and might have been given drugs or an intoxicating beverage before she was killed by a swift blow to her right temple. Scientists at Johns Hopkins University in Baltimore examined the mummy with a CT scan that revealed a crack in the skull, just above the right eye, and internal bleeding.

More than 100 sacred Incan ceremonial sites have been found on dozens of Andes peaks, although no mummies have been uncovered in the frozen condition of Juanita. Anthropologists believe that hundreds of Incan children might be entombed in ice graves on the highest peaks in South America from central Chile to southern Peru. The Incas believed that they could approach Inti, the sun god, by ascending the highest summits of the Andes. The mountain deities they believed to live there were considered protectors of the Incan people. Sacrifices were frequently responses to cataclysmic events: earthquakes, eclipses, and droughts.

Juanita and many of the ritualistic elements found at the ceremonial site are now exhibited at the **Museo Santuarios Andinos** (p. 304). More information about the Mount Ampato expedition can be found in the June 1996 edition of *National Geographic*.

one of the best windows onto colonial times in Arequipa. Named for an ancient mulberry tree—the *moral* found in the courtyard—the home is also distinguished by a magnificent stone portal with heraldic emblems carved in *sillar*. Handsome furnishings, carved wooden doors, and Cusco School oil paintings decorate large salons, built around a beautiful courtyard, the largest of the colonial residences in the city. Look for 17th-century maps that depict the borders and shapes of countries quite differently from their usual representations today. A second courtyard, painted cobalt blue, was used as the summer patio. Climb to the rooftop for a great view of Arequipa and the surrounding volcanoes. Visits are by guided tour (at no extra cost).

Moral 318 (at Bolívar). (C) 054/210-084. Admission S/5 ($1.40) adults, S/3 (85¢) students. Mon–Sat 9am–5pm; Sun 9am–1pm.

Monasterio de la Recoleta 👉 A 10-minute walk from the Plaza de Armas across the Río Chili, distinguished by its tall brick-red-and-white steeple, is the Recoleta convent museum. Founded in 1648 and rebuilt after earthquakes, the peaceful Franciscan convent contains impressive cloisters with *sillar* columns and lovely gardens; today just four of the original seven remain. The convent museum includes several collections. In one room is a collection of pre-Incan culture artifacts, including funeral masks, textiles, and totems; in another are mummies and a series of paintings of the 12 Incan emperors. At the rear of the convent is a small Amazonian museum, stocked with curious items collected by Franciscan missionaries in the Amazon basin. The missionaries were understandably fascinated by prehistoric-looking fish, crocodiles, piranhas, and the clothing of indigenous communities. These souvenirs pose an interesting contrast to the Dominicans' fine library containing some 20,000 volumes, including rare published texts from the 15th century. Guides (tip basis) are available for 1-hour tours in English, Spanish, and French.

Recoleta 117. 📞 054/270-966. Admission S/5 ($1.40) adults, S/3 (85¢) students, free for seniors. Mon–Sat 9am–noon and 3–5pm.

SHOPPING

Arequipa is perhaps the number one spot in Peru—better even than Cusco and Lima—to shop for top-quality baby alpaca, vicuña, and woolen goods. Although many items are more expensive than the lesser-quality goods sold in other parts of Peru, in Arequipa you'll find nicer designs and export-quality knit sweaters, shawls, blankets, and scarves. In many parts of Peru, what is sold as alpaca or baby alpaca is often a mix of alpaca and synthetics. Many of the finest pure alpaca woven items in Peru come from Arequipa. Vicuña wool, which is softer, rarer, and more expensive than alpaca, is also now found at a couple of shops, but keep in mind that a simple shawl runs about $1,600. The city also produces very nice leather goods, and there are several excellent antiques shops featuring colonial pieces and even older items (remember, though, that these antiques cannot legally be exported from Peru; see "Entry Requirements & Customs," in chapter 2, for regulations). **Casona de Santa Catalina,** Santa Catalina 210 (📞 054/281-334) and **Patio del Ekeko,** Mercaderes 141 (📞 054/215-861), are two small shopping malls near the Plaza de Armas with several good, upscale shops, including alpaca goods, handicrafts, jewelry, and food shops.

ALPACA GOODS Three general areas are particularly good for alpaca items. One is the **cloisters** next to La Compañía church, where you'll find several alpaca boutiques and outlets. Another good place is **Pasaje Catedral,** the pedestrian mall just

---

Tips **Photo Op**

One of the best views in Arequipa is from the *mirador* (lookout point) on Avenida del Ejército, in the tranquil suburb of Yanahuara just across Puente Grau. Next to a small plaza, a series of *sillar* stone arches beautifully frames the snowy peak of El Misti. Across from the mirador is the small church of Yanahuara, also built of *sillar* in the mid–18th century and featuring a splendid baroque carved facade and bell tower. A good way to visit the mirador is to combine it with lunch at Sol de Mayo (p. 316), just a few blocks south.

House Tour: Arequipa's Colonial Mansions

Arequipa possesses one of the most attractive and harmonious colonial nuclei in Peru. Several extraordinary seigniorial houses were constructed in white *sillar* stone. They are predominantly flat-roofed, single-story structures, a construction style that has helped them withstand the effects of frequent earthquakes that would have toppled less solid buildings. Most of these houses have attractive, though small, interior patios and elaborately carved facades. Best equipped for visitors is the recently restored **Casa del Moral** (p. 306), but several others are worth a look, especially if you have an interest in colonial architecture.

Just off the main square at San Francisco 108, **Casa Ricketts** (also called **Casa Tristán del Pozo**), a former seminary and today the offices of Banco Continental, is one of the finest colonial homes in Arequipa. Built in the 1730s, it has a beautiful portal, perhaps Arequipa's finest expression of colonial civil architecture, with delicate representations of the life of Jesus. Inside are two large, beautiful courtyards with gargoyle drainage pipes.

On the other side of the cathedral at the corner of Santa Catalina 101 at San Agustín, **Casa Arróspide** (also called **Casa Iriberry**), from the late 18th century, is one of the most distinguished *sillar* mansions in the city. Now the Cultural Center of San Agustín University (© **054/204-482**), its several *salas* host temporary exhibits of contemporary art and photography; you'll also find an art shop and nice little cafe with a terrace and great views over the top of the cathedral.

Other colonial houses of interest include **Casa Arango**, a squat and eclectic 17th-century home located on Consuelo at La Merced; **Casa Goyeneche**, La Merced 201, today the offices of Banco de Reserva; and **Casa de la Moneda**, Ugarte at Villaba.

About a 15-minute cab ride outside of town, in Huasacache, is the **Mansión del Fundador** (© **054/442-460**), one of the most important *sillar* mansions in Arequipa. It is said to have been constructed by the founder of Arequipa, Manuel de Carbajal, for his son. It features terrific vaulted ceilings and a large interior patio. The house is open daily from 9am to 5pm; admission is S/10 ($2.85).

behind the cathedral, and a third is **Calle Santa Catalina.** Shops with fine alpaca items include **Millma's Baby Alpaca,** Pasaje Catedral 177 (© 054/205-134); **Baby Alpaca Boutique,** Santa Catalina 208 (© 054/206-716); **Anselmo's Souvenirs,** Pasaje Catedral 119 (no phone); **Wari,** San Francisco 311 (© 054/223-301); **Alpaca Azul,** Moral 223–225 (© 054/228-331); and **Alpaca 111,** Zela 212 (© 054/223-238). Two **Incalpaca** (Grupo Inca) factory outlets are good spots to get last season's items at discounted prices: One is in town, within the courtyard of La Compañía, on General Moran and Alvarez Thomas (© 054/205-931); the other is about 10 minutes outside of town, Av. Juan Bustamante s/n, in the Tahuaycani district (© 054/251-025). The latter also has a small zoo of camelids to entertain the kids while parents shop for alpaca and hard-to-find and expensive vicuña items.

(Tips **Arequipa's Colonial Churches**

Arequipa has a wealth of colonial churches that are well worth a visit if you have the time. They include **Iglesia de San Francisco** (Zela 103), built of *sillar* and brick in the 16th century with an impressive all-silver altar and a beautiful vaulted ceiling; **Iglesia de San Agustín** (at the corner of San Agustín and Sucre), with a superbly stylized baroque facade, an excellent example of 16th- and 17th-century mestizo architecture (it was rebuilt in 1898 after earthquake damage and was restored, with an unfortunate new belltower, again in October 2005); **Iglesia de Santo Domingo** (at Santo Domingo and Piérola), with handsome 1734 cloisters; and **Iglesia de La Merced** (La Merced 303), built in 1607 and possessing a lovely carved *sillar* facade and an impressive colonial library.

ANTIQUES   Calle Santa Catalina and nearby streets have several antiques shops. I found lots of items I wished I could have taken home at the following three stores: **Curiosidades,** Zela 207 (© 054/952-986); **Alvaro Valdivia Montoya**'s two well-stocked shops at Santa Catalina 204 and Santa Catalina 406 (© 054/229-103); and **Arte Colonial,** Santa Catalina 312 (© 054/214-887).

BOOKS   A very good and friendly bookstore with art books and English-language paperbacks is **Libería El Lector,** San Francisco 221 (no phone).

HANDICRAFTS   There is a general handicrafts market *(mercado de artesanía)* with dozens of stalls in the old town jail, next door to the Plazuela de San Francisco (between Zela and Puente Grau). For handmade leather goods, stroll along Puente Bolognesi, which leads west from the Plaza de Armas, and you'll find numerous small stores with handbags, shoes, and other items.

WHERE TO STAY

Arequipa has an ample roster of hotels and *hostales* (inns) at all levels. A number of them occupy historic houses in the old quarter, within very easy walking distance of major sights, restaurants, and bars. Even budget travelers can do very well in Arequipa—it's a good place for a significant step up in comfort and style (but not price) from the usual backpacker dregs. The area north of the Plaza de Armas is nicer and less chaotic (though full of restaurants and bars) than the streets south of the square.

Note: If you hop in a taxi from the airport or bus station, insist on going to the hotel of your choice; local taxi drivers often claim that a particular hotel is closed in order to take you to one that will pay them a commission.

EXPENSIVE

Casa Arequipa ★★★ *(Value*   This outstanding inn is something that's very unusual in Peru, akin to a European boutique hotel, and it is one of the most luxurious places to stay in the country—for a bargain price. In a beautifully restored, pink 1950s mansion in the quiet Vallecito residential district, just a short walk or cab ride from the Plaza de Armas, it features elegantly designed guest rooms, with nicely chosen antiques, very comfortable beds, and the finest towels and bed linens you'll find in Peru. Photographs of the Andes, taken by the owner—who splits his time between Arequipa and Washington, D.C.—decorate rooms, and fresh flowers are placed in every room and throughout the house. The excellent bathrooms, several with tubs, are

ACCOMMODATIONS ■

Casa Andina **4**
Casa Arequipa **21**
Colonial House Inn **7**
Hostal Núñez **5**
Hotel Libertador Arequipa **3**
La Casa de Melgar Hostal **9**
La Casa de Mi Abuela Hostal **2**
La Maison d'Elise **1**
La Reyna **10**
Los Balcones de Moral
   y Santa Catalina **15**
Sonesta Posada del Inca **7**
Tambo Viejo **22**

DINING ◆

Ary Quepay **6**
El Cerrojo **17**
El Turko II **14**
El Viñedo **13**
Govinda **16**
La Tratorria del
   Monasterio **12**
La Truffa **18**
Los Leños **8**
Sol de Mayo **20**
Tradición
   Arequipeña **23**
Zig Zag **11**

of gleaming marble. The breakfast buffet and personal attention is worthy of a five-star hotel.

Av. Lima, Vallecito, Arequipa. ☏ **054/284-219.** Reservations in U.S., ☏ 202/332-1942. Fax 054/253-343. www.arequipacasa.com. 88 units. $75 double. Rates include taxes. AE, DC, MC, V. **Amenities:** Concierge; CD library. *In room:* A/C, TV, CD player.

Hotel Libertador Arequipa ⭐ *Kids*   Arequipa's swankest large hotel within reach of the historic center is in this handsome, sprawling 1940s colonial-style building. In the midst of quiet Selva Alegre, the largest park in Arequipa, the midsize hotel, recently renovated and part of a small upmarket Peruvian chain, is about a 15-minute walk from the main square. It maintains a colonial theme throughout, with soaring ceilings, historical murals, and older-style dark-wood period furnishings in expansive, elegantly appointed rooms. Accommodations, equipped with marble bathrooms, are about as large as you're likely to find. The hotel has a lovely, large outdoor pool among nice gardens and tall palm trees. Families will appreciate the outdoor recreation and game area for children.

Plaza Bolívar, Selva Alegre, Arequipa. © **054/215-110.** Fax 054/241–933. www.libertador.com.pe. 88 units. $148 deluxe double; $185 suite. Rates include taxes. AE, DC, MC, V. **Amenities:** 2 restaurants; bar; large outdoor pool; fitness center; Jacuzzi; sauna; concierge; 24-hr. room service; laundry service. *In room:* A/C, TV, minibar, safe.

La Maison d' Elise ★ *(Finds* This small gem of a hotel is hidden behind a nondescript, rather unappealing facade. Across from the park on the other side of Puente Grau, just beyond the historic center, this 14-year-old hotel is like a small Mediterranean village. Ochre and white villas are clustered around courtyards ripe with cactus and colorful flowering plants. Double rooms are very large and comfortably furnished; matrimonial suites have a lower-level sitting room. There are also apartments with private terraces. The hotel has a small pool with a rock waterfall, and a notable and nicely decorated restaurant. Deals are sometimes available. The hotel is less luxurious overall than the Libertador (see above), but it's got a quirkier charm and is much more affordable.

Av. Bolognesi 104, Yanahuara, Arequipa. © **054/256-185.** Fax 054/253-343. http://aqplink.com/hotel/maison. 88 units. $70 double; $78–$96 suite. Rates include taxes. AE, DC, MC, V. **Amenities:** 2 restaurants, bar; pool; room service; laundry service. *In room:* A/C, TV, safe.

Sonesta Posada del Inca ★ Now that it's been acquired by the Sonesta chain, things are looking up for this hotel with the most coveted location in Arequipa, right on the stately Plaza de Armas. Even if that's the best thing about this large hotel, it's still plenty. It's perfectly located to allow you to see and do everything in Arequipa with ease. The hotel has gotten a partial but not yet full makeover, so the dated casino lobby decor, an awkward step back into the 1970s, is thankfully gone. Rooms are spacious and comfortable, if not luxurious, with a retro feel to them; the desirable executive rooms on upper floors have attractive terraces under the porticoes with plaza views. There's also a nice little rooftop pool framed by flower beds and sweeping views of the cathedral and volcanoes in the distance, and the restaurant bar has seats overlooking the Plaza. Look out for Web-only specials that can be as little as half the rack rate.

Portal de Flores 116, Plaza de Armas, Arequipa. © **054/215-530.** Fax 054/234–374. www.sonesta.com. 58 units. $125 standard double; $140 deluxe double; $155 suite. Rates include taxes and buffet breakfast. AE, DC, MC, V. **Amenities:** Restaurant; bar; outdoor rooftop pool; concierge; business center; 24-hour room service; laundry service. *In room:* A/C, TV, minibar, safe.

MODERATE

Casa Andina ★ *(Value* This large downtown hotel, popular with groups and contemporary in style, with a curved and colorful facade, is on the edge of the historic quarter of town (about a 10-min. walk from the Plaza de Armas). A good value, its rooms are pretty spacious and modern, with splashes of color, bold fabrics, and rustic touches such as *sillar* volcanic stone. Although Arequipa has a couple of small inns with more local flavor, the Casa Andina is perfect for anyone who prefers the services and anonymity of a larger hotel. Although the Libertador is a small step up from the Casa Andina, it is quite a bit more expensive and a bit less conveniently located.

Jerusalén 601, Arequipa. © **054/202-070.** Fax 054/287-420. www.casa-andina.com. 94 units. $60–$70 double; $85 suite. Rates include taxes and breakfast buffet. AE, DC, MC, V. **Amenities:** Concierge; business center; laundry service. *In room:* A/C, TV, hair dryer upon request.

La Casa de Melgar Hostal 🐸🐸 A spectacular colonial house made of white *sillar* (volcanic stone), this charming small hotel is one of the nicest and most relaxed in Peru, as well as one of the best values. Just 3 blocks from the Plaza de Armas, the lovingly restored 18th-century mansion—the former residence of the bishop of Arequipa—has thick, massive walls and three interior courtyards. It echoes the rich, brick-red and royal-blue tones of the Santa Catalina Monastery and is the perfect place to stay if you're a fan of colonial architecture. The ample rooms have good beds. Some rooms—especially those on the ground floor that have high vaulted brick ceilings—exude colonial character; if the hotel isn't full, ask to see a couple. A new wing of rooms, also in a colonial building with *sillar* walls at the rear, behind a nice garden and terrace, are also lovely; some have incredibly high ceilings.

The staff here is very friendly, and breakfast is served in the neat little cafe next door in one of the courtyards. Advance reservations are a must in high season, as the inn is justifiably popular.

Melgar 108, Cercado, Arequipa. ©/fax 054/222-459, or 01/446-8343 for reservations. www.lacasademelgar.com. 30 units. $35 double. Rates include taxes and breakfast. V only. **Amenities:** Restaurant; bar; laundry service.

La Casa de Mi Abuela Hostal 🐸 One of the friendliest and best-run small hotels in Peru, "my grandmother's house" is tucked behind a security gate but welcomes everyone with open arms and an easygoing atmosphere. An organic place that has grown from a tiny B&B operation into a very popular 50-room hotel, it is still family run. Today it's a self-contained tourism complex and miniresort, with a live-music peña bar, free (but limited) Internet access, book exchange, travel agency, and beautiful, relaxing gardens with views of El Misti. Some rooms have roof terraces; others have balconies. Many rooms are plainly decorated and cramped, but the *hostal* is still a very good deal, given the level of services, facilities, and security. The *hostal* is about a 10-minute walk (6 blocks) north of the main square; it's often filled, so make advance reservations. Nice breakfasts are served in the garden (extra charge).

Jerusalén 606, Cercado, Arequipa. © 054/241-206. Fax 054/242-761. www.lacasademiabuela.com. 50 units. $33–$44 double. Rates include taxes. DC, MC, V. **Amenities:** Restaurant; bar; outdoor pool; game room; travel agency; laundry service. *In room:* TV, minibar, safe.

INEXPENSIVE

Colonial House Inn 🐸*Finds* A rambling 200-year-old house—continually owned by the same family—in the old quarter, this friendly, eclectic inn is perfect for backpackers or budget travelers in search of some local flavor. It has a great rooftop terrace; nice large rooms, all with a private bathroom; a comfortable covered patio; a library and book exchange; and good breakfasts in a little cafe area. Book in advance, as it is frequently full.

Puente Grau 114, Arequipa. ©/fax 054/223-533. casos@ec-red.com. 7 units. $18 double. Rate includes taxes. No credit cards. **Amenities:** Restaurant; laundry service.

Hostal Núñez *Value* This colonial inn is attractive and affordable—and thus popular. Friendly and family-owned, it's on a street in the old quarter loaded with travel agencies. Rooms aren't anything special, but they are ample and have hardwood floors and cable TV, and they're decorated with actual color schemes, a rarity at these prices. Public rooms are very congenial and loaded with plants. A huge rooftop terrace has excellent views of the city, and there are other unusual amenities at this level, including an on-site salon. Breakfast on the terrace is a great perk. Couples or friends sharing a room are best off: Single rooms are pretty small.

Jerusalén 528, Arequipa. ©/fax **054/218-648**. 7 units. S/60 ($17) double with private bathroom; S/30 ($8.55) with shared bath. Rate includes taxes. No credit cards. **Amenities:** Cafeteria; tour desk; salon; laundry service. *In room:* TV.

La Reyna   A popular backpacker inn in town, La Reyna is smack in the middle of the historic center, just a block from the famed Santa Catalina monastery and paces away from plenty of bars and restaurants. The *hostal*'s many rooms feed off a labyrinth of narrow staircases that climb up three floors to a roof terrace, a popular spot to hang out and write postcards and plan hiking expeditions, or to veg out and stargaze late at night. There are simple, rock-bottom dormitory rooms for zero-budget travelers and a couple of rooftop casitas that, although basic in their decoration, have private bathrooms and their own terraces with awesome views of the mountains and the monastery below—something akin to backpacker penthouse suites. (No. 20 is worth reserving, if you can.) The *hostal,* though a little haphazardly run, organizes lots of canyon treks and volcano-climbing tours, and even offers Spanish classes.

Zela 209, Arequipa. ©/fax **054/286-578**. 20 units. $10 double with shared bathroom; $12 double with bathroom; $5 per person in shared rooms. Rates include taxes. No credit cards. **Amenities:** Laundry service.

Los Balcones de Moral y Santa Catalina ★ *(Value)*   This inviting small hotel is very comfortable and decently furnished, a nice step up from budget hostels for not too much more money. In the heart of the old quarter, it's only a couple of blocks from the Plaza de Armas. Half of the house is colonial (1st floor); the other is republican, dating from the 1800s. The house is built around a colonial patio with a sunny terrace. Furnishings are modern, with wallpaper and firm beds. Eleven of the good-size rooms have hardwood floors and large balconies with nice views looking toward the back of the cathedral; the other rooms are carpeted and less desirable (though quieter). All have good, tiled bathrooms.

Moral 217, Arequipa. ©/fax **054/201-291**. losbalconeshotel@hotmail.com. 17 units. S/90 ($26) double. Rate includes taxes. MC, V. **Amenities:** Restaurant; laundry service. *In room:* TV.

Tambo Viejo *(Value)*   This budget *hostal,* occupying an old colonial family home, is a 15-minute walk south of the Plaza de Armas, but it's popular and usually full of backpackers drawn by good word of mouth about the tranquil and genial atmosphere. There are rooms with shared and private bathrooms, a big garden with sun terraces and volcano views, a cafe serving veggie breakfasts and other meals, a book exchange, a TV lounge, and hot water all day.

Av. Malecón Socabaya 107, Arequipa. © **054/288-195**. Fax 054/284-747. www.tamboviejo.com. 20 units. $18–$24 double with private bathroom; $12–$15 double with shared bathroom. Rates include American breakfast and taxes. DC, MC, V. **Amenities:** Cafe; bike rental; tour desk; laundry service.

WHERE TO DINE

Arequipa is one of the finest cities in Peru for gastronomic adventures, and at very reasonable prices. Though it has few chic, luxuriously appointed places, the historic center and zones just beyond its limits are very well stocked with excellent casual restaurants. Arequipeño cooking is famous throughout Peru, and several restaurants specialize in traditional regional specialties, a couple of them with fabulous outdoor seating and excellent views of the volcanoes. Several restaurants in the historic quarter—the two streets leading north from the Plaza de Armas, Santa Catalina, and San Francisco are the main hub of nighttime activity—specialize in traditional Arequipeño cooking, though two of the best are a short taxi ride beyond downtown.

MODERATE

Ary Quepay *Value* PERUVIAN/AREQUIPEÑO   A relaxed and friendly, family-owned restaurant with a gardenlike dining room under a bamboo roof and skylights, Ary Quepay, a longtime favorite of both locals and in-the-know visitors, specializes in authentic, traditional Peruvian cooking. It's less fancy than a couple of the better-known restaurants specializing in Arequipeño cooking, but the others are on the out-skirts of the city, and a tad bit more expensive. Starters include *choclo con queso* (corn on the cob with cheese), *palta rellena* (stuffed avocado), and *sopa a la criolla* (with beef, noodles, and eggs). Main courses are classic: *rocoto relleno* (stuffed spicy red peppers), *adobo* (pork stew with *ají*), and *escabeche de pescado* (spicy fish stew). There are a num-ber of dishes for vegetarians, and good breakfasts, juices, and milkshakes. In the evenings, there's often live folkloric music.

Jerusalén 502. ℂ **054/672-922.** Main courses S/11–S/30 ($3.15–$8.55). DC, MC, V. Daily 10am–11pm.

El Cerrojo PERUVIAN/INTERNATIONAL   Predictably, scores of restaurants ring the main square, and a couple are plain tourist traps. On one side, upstairs along a very long balcony that extends practically the length of one side of the Plaza de Armas, this restaurant is probably the best of the bunch, not least because the views of the square are brilliant. The lengthy menu offers *platos típicos* of Peruvian cooking, of course, as well as well-prepared meats (rabbit and pork chops) and fish dishes such as grilled shrimp, *corvina* (sea bass), and ceviche. But plenty of people come just for the views and simple fare such as pizza and pasta. You can count on getting serenaded by a peripatetic band of Peruvian musicians, just like you can count on getting accosted by the restaurant's advertising gals handing out free drink cards every time you pass under the arches of this side of the square.

Portal San Agustín 111. ℂ **054/201-842.** Main courses S/14–S/32 ($4–$9.15). AE, DC, MC, V. Daily noon–midnight.

El Turko II *Finds* TURKISH/MIDDLE EASTERN   Turkish and Middle Eastern specialties are a find in Peru, but this handsome little joint sits proudly on restaurant row in Arequipa, in a long space carved out of *sillar* and opening onto a relaxing court-yard, where tables are set up. It serves up vegetarian Turkish dishes such as *Tübyaz* (zucchini stuffed with tomatoes, cheese, egg, and coconut and served with Turkish rice) as well as international and Arequipeño dishes. But the reason to stop by is to get your hands on *sis kebaps* and other dishes hard to come by. Happily, this isn't one of those austere falafel joints; it's nice looking, with contemporary art, good music, and attractive lighting, making it ideal for a sunny lunch or surprisingly chic dinner.

San Francisco 315. ℂ **054/215-729.** Reservations not accepted. Main courses S/14–S/39 ($4–$11). MC, V. Daily 8am–midnight.

El Viñedo ARGENTINE/GRILLED MEAT   I can't say whether this Argentine restaurant would satisfy the purist carnivore instincts of my friends from Buenos Aires, but at least in Peru, this rustic yet refined spot on Arequipa's restaurant row is a win-ner. It does a good enough job with its *parrilladas* (mixed grills) to convince this gringo. There are also "Argentine" pizzas (topped with ingredients such as grilled chorizo and served on wood boards) and the old standby, pastas. The interior is sprawling, cozy, and candlelit, with a tango music soundtrack, a half-dozen separate dining rooms, and a garden courtyard that a waiter told me is perfect for couples. Although the ceilings are bamboo and the walls are wood-paneled, waiters wear white gloves and tuxedo shirts. A bonus for those who can eat only so much meat: a free salad bar. The wine list might not earn the restaurant's name ("the Vineyard"), but it's a decent list. Connected to the restaurant is El Jayari, a restaurant serving Peruvian dishes (and sharing the same chef and kitchen).

San Francisco 319-A. ✆ **054/205-053.** Reservations recommended on weekends. Main courses S/10–S/33 ($2.85–$9.40). AE, DC, MC, V. Daily 1pm–midnight.

La Trattoria del Monasterio ★★ ⓥalue ITALIAN   Cleaved into the outer *sillar* wall of the splendid Santa Catalina monastery, this chic but unassuming Italian eatery—a new addition to the Arequipa dining scene—is an excellent spot for lingering over an intimate dinner. It's considerably quieter than the hopping restaurant row just 1 block over on San Francisco. Spilling into three elegant, small, and whitewashed dining rooms, it specializes in Italian favorites like risottos, lasagnas, ravioli, and osso buco. For cognoscenti, it features both long and short pastas. The menu was prepared by the hot chef of the moment in Peru, Gastón Acurio of Astrid & Gastón, La Mar, and others in Lima and up and down South America. You'll also find a good selection of wines, great desserts and fine, attentive service.

Santa Catalina 309 ✆ **054/204-062.** Reservations recommended. Main courses S/18–S/28 ($5.15–$8). AE, DC, MC, V. Mon–Sat, noon–3pm and 7pm–11pm; Sunday noon–4pm.

La Truffa ⓥalue ITALIAN   A charming little restaurant tucked behind the cathedral on a pedestrian-only *pasaje* lined with alpaca boutiques and a couple of cafes, La Truffa (the truffle) is decorated like someone's cozy house, with oil paintings and local artifacts. The menu specializes in homemade pastas and good pizzas, but it's also a great place to get well-prepared fish dishes such as *delicia de corvina* (sea bass served with cheese, shrimp, and mushrooms). There are only a handful of tables in two rooms, and it's popular with gringos and locals, so don't be surprised if you have to wait. Rooftop tables are the most sought-after on a temperate evening.

Pasaje la Catedral 111. ✆ **054/242-010.** Reservations recommended. Main courses S/12–S/29 ($3.40–$8.30). DC, MC, V. Mon–Sat 11am–11pm.

Sol de Mayo ★★★ ⓥalue PERUVIAN/AREQUIPEÑO   A 5-minute taxi ride from the *centro* in Yanahuara, the city's nicest residential neighborhood, this longtime stalwart (it's been around for more than a century) is the standard-bearer for Arequipeño cooking. A favorite of upscale locals and tourists alike, it has the most delightful setting of the city's restaurants. The colonial tables are set around the edges of a breezy, picture-perfect courtyard with thick grass, geraniums, a small pool and cascading waterfall, and strolling altiplano musicians. There are also indoor dining rooms inside the brick-red and yellow *sillar* stone building, but nothing beats eating outdoors here. Peruvian specialties are Sol de Mayo's calling card: *chicharrón de chancho* (fried pork), ostrich, fresh shellfish, and a tantalizing lineup of ceviche. Starters include a yummy mixed salad of *choclo* (white corn), tomato, and avocado. Good pisco sours are a must to start off your meal. Even for budget-oriented backpackers, this is the place in Arequipa to splurge, though splurging in southern Peru means no more than $10 to $15 a head.

Jerusalén 207, Yanahuara. ✆ **054/254-148.** Reservations recommended. Main courses S/14–S/38 ($4–$11). AE, DC, MC, V. Daily 11am–10pm.

Tradición Arequipeña ★★ ⓥalue PERUVIAN/AREQUIPEÑO   It's a few kilometers outside town on a busy avenue in the district called Paucarpata, so you'll need to grab a taxi to get to this classic open-air restaurant. Elegantly set amid beautiful gardens and stunning views of snowcapped El Misti from the upper deck, it's open only for lunch (although you could also squeeze in an early dinner at 5 or 6pm). Most encouraging is how popular it is not only among tourists, but also among locals. In fact, it's the restaurant that seems most highly recommended to foreigners by Arequipeños. It serves large portions of classic Peruvian and Arequipeño dishes, such as *cuy, adobo,* and ceviche, but they're more carefully prepared here than in many other *comida típica* restaurants. A good starter is combination fried cheese and fried yuca with picante sauce and salsa verde. The prices are very affordable for such an elegant place.

Av. Dolores 111, Paucarpata. ⓒ 054/426-467. Reservations recommended on weekends. Main courses S/10–S/38 ($2.85–$11). AE, DC, MC, V. Daily noon–7pm.

Zig Zag *✿✿* SWISS/GRILLED MEAT   Perhaps the hippest restaurant in Arequipa, Zig Zag, which recently expanded into the space next door, has an awful lot going for it. Occupying a cool two-level, *sillar*-walled space with a fantastic, twisting iron staircase, it's chic enough to appeal to young people on dates and comfortable enough for families and small tourist groups. The house specialty is stone-grilled meats, including ostrich and alpaca, served either unadorned on a sizzling stone or with a variety of sauces. The owners like to educate their customers about these lean meats as a healthy alternative to other meats. Try the ostrich carpaccio in lemon or ostrich stone-grilled with Swiss-style hash browns. If you're not a carnivore, other favorites are trout and shrimp, or fondues and pastas (such as the interesting Peruvian-Italian quinoa gnocchi). The two-level restaurant plays hip music and has attentive service, and a couple of tables upstairs are perched on a ledge overlooking the attractive Plazuela San Francisco.

Zela 210. ⓒ 054/206-020. Reservations recommended. Main courses S/25–S/36 ($7.15–$10). AE, DC, MC, V. Daily 6pm–midnight.

INEXPENSIVE

Govinda *Value* VEGETARIAN   A good all-around vegetarian restaurant, Govinda—part of a chain across Peru, with the original in London—has a pleasant outdoor garden dining area and good-value menús and dishes. It serves vegetarian Italian, Asian, and Peruvian items, as well as pizzas, pastas, soups, salads, and yogurt dishes, a nice reprieve from many travelers' overdose of chicken, pork, and alpaca in Peru. The daily menús are very cheap, although the self-service buffet is not all-you-can-eat and its lineup of vegetarian dishes isn't the most creative you've ever seen. It's a good place for breakfast, with muesli, brown bread, fruit salads, and juices.

Santa Catalina 120. ⓒ 054/285-540. Reservations not accepted. Main courses S/6–S/18 ($1.70–$5.15); menú del día S/6–S/15 ($1.70–$4.30); buffet S/10.50 ($3). No credit cards. Daily 7am–9:30pm.

La Canasta SANDWICHES/BREAKFAST   A charming bakery and lunch and breakfast nook, hidden away inside the courtyard of a massive colonial mansion on a heavily trafficked street, La Canasta only has a couple of tables on the patio. You can get pizzas, *empanadas* (stuffed pastries), sandwiches, and hamburgers, as well as some of the best breakfasts you're likely to come across in Peru.

Jerusalén 115. ⓒ 054/287-138. Reservations not accepted. Main courses S/3–S/6 (75¢–$1.75). No credit cards. Mon–Sat 7am–8:30pm.

Los Leños *Value* PIZZERIA   At this charming cave of a pizza place, diners share long wooden tables and the footprints of many hundreds of travelers carry on in the graffiti that cover every square inch of stone walls up to a vaulted ceiling. It looks and feels like a college tavern. The house specialty is pizza from the wood-fired oven; among the many varieties, the Leños house pizza is a standout: cheese, sausage, bacon, ham, chicken, and mushrooms. Those who've had their fill of pizza can opt for other standards, such as lasagna and a slew of other pastas. Los Leños opens early; choose from among 20 different "American breakfasts."

Jerusalén 407. (℃ 054/289-179. Reservations not accepted. Main courses S/6–S/13 ($1.70–$3.70); menú del día S/6–S/15 ($1.70–$4.30); buffet S/10.50 ($3). No credit cards. Daily 7am–11pm.

AREQUIPA AFTER DARK

Arequipa has a pretty hopping nightlife in the old quarter, with plenty of bars, restaurants, and discos catering to both gringos and locals. On a busy night, Arequipa does its best impression of the Cusco bar scene. Just as in Cusco many bars are housed in impressive colonial digs, in Arequipa you're likely to do your drinking in a bar with vaulted *sillar* ceilings. Sunday through Wednesday is usually pretty quiet, with things heating up beginning on Thursday night. Virtually every bar in town advertises elastic happy hours, with drinks going for as little as 3 for S/10 ($2.85). Calles San Francisco and Zela are the main hot spots, while there are also a number of bars along Pasaje Catedral, the alleyway behind the cathedral, and Santa Catalina.

Las Quenas, Santa Catalina 302 (℃ 054/281-115), is a peña bar and restaurant featuring live Andean music Monday through Saturday from 9pm to midnight, and special dance performances on Friday and Saturday nights. It's a cozy little place that serves pretty good Peruvian dishes. You can also catch peña music most evenings at **El Tuturutu,** Portal San Agustín 105 (℃ 054/201-842), a restaurant on the main square and Afro-Peruvian and folkloric music at **La Troica,** Jerusalén 522 (℃ 054/225-690), a tourist-oriented restaurant in an old house.

As for pubs and bars, **Siwara,** Santa Catalina 210 (℃ 054/626-218), is a great-looking beer tavern that spills into two patios in the building of the Santuarios Andinos museum, across from the Santa Catalina monastery. **Farrens Irish Pub,** Pasaje Catedral 107 (℃ 054/238-465), very popular with visiting gringos, is a cool two-level joint with good drink specials and a rock and pop soundtrack. Another good spot for a drink is **Montreál Le Café Art,** Ugarte 210 (℃ 054/931-2796), which features live music Wednesday through Saturday and has happy hours between 5 and 11pm. **La Casa de Klaus,** Zela 207 (℃ 054/203-711), is a simple and brightly lit tavern popular with German, British, and local beer drinkers.

For a little more action, check out **Forum Rock Café,** San Francisco 317 (℃ 054/202-697), a huge place that is equal parts restaurant, bar, disco, and concert hall. It sports a rainforest theme, with jungle vegetation and "canopy walkways" everywhere. Live bands (usually rock) take the stage Thursday through Saturday. The upstairs grill has great panoramic views of the city. Just down the street, **Déjà Vu,** San Francisco 319 (℃ 054/221-904), has a good bar with a mix of locals and gringos, a lively dance floor, and English-language movies on a big screen every night at 8pm. It also has a spectacular rooftop terrace, which is a good spot for dinner or even breakfast after a long night partying. **Kibosh,** Zela 205 (℃ 054/626-218), is a chic, upscale pub with four bars, wood-oven pizza, a dance floor, and live music Wednesday through Saturday (ranging from Latin to hard rock).

SIDE TRIPS FROM AREQUIPA

Easy day trips from Arequipa include jaunts to the suburbs of **Paucarpata** and **Sabandía,** in the countryside surrounding the city. But the excursions of primary interest to visitors—for many, the main reason for a visit to Arequipa—is **Colca Canyon,** where the highlight is **Cruz del Cóndor,** a lookout point where giant South American condors soar overhead; see "Colca Valley," below, for more information. The region around Arequipa is unimaginably blessed by nature. It has soaring, active volcanoes, perfect for experienced mountaineers and trekkers; the two deepest canyons in the world, Colca and Cotahuasi; and chilly rivers that lace the canyons. The opportunities for trekking, rafting, and mountaineering expeditions through the valley are some of the finest in Peru. Out in the desert are ancient petroglyphs at **Toro Muerto.**

Tour agencies have mushroomed in Arequipa, and most offer very similar city and countryside *(campiña)* highlight trips (about $20 per person). Going with a tour operator is economical and by far the most convenient option for visitors with limited time and patience—public transportation is poor and very time-consuming in these parts. Of the many agencies that crowd the principal streets in the old quarter, only a handful of tour operators in Arequipa are well run, and visitors need to be careful when signing up for guided tours to the valley. Avoid independent guides who don't have official accreditation.

THE OUTSKIRTS (CAMPIÑA TOURS)

Paucarpata, 7km (4⅓ miles) southeast of Arequipa, is a pretty little town surrounded by Incan-terraced farmlands and El Misti volcano in the distance. About a kilometer down the road, the peaceful village of **Sabandía** is where many Arequipeños visit on weekends for country-style restaurants. For out-of-town visitors, the highlight of the village is a large stone *molino,* or water-powered mill, from the early 17th century. There are several nice colonial estates in the surrounding countryside. One of the nicest is **La Mansión del Fundador,** a handsome colonial mansion in the suburb of **Huasacache,** 10km (6¼ miles) from Arequipa. The house, once the property of the founder of Arequipa, Don García Manuel de Carbajal, is nicely outfitted with original antique paintings and furnishings. It's open daily from 9am to 5pm; admission is S/10 ($2.85).

GETTING THERE If you are one of the few who decides not to go with an organized tour, you can catch a Sabandía colectivo from San Juan de Dios or Independencia, a few blocks from the Plaza de Armas, but it's much simpler to take a taxi (S/10 or $2.85). The molino is on the same road as the **El Lago Resort** at Camino al Molino s/n, Sabandía (© **054/448-383**), a good spot for lunch.

TORO MUERTO

About 3 hours from Arequipa, near the town of Corire, is **Toro Muerto,** touted as the world's largest field of petroglyphs. Whether it is actually the world's largest number of petroglyphs in one place is hard to say; many contend that other places have more. But the site is certainly exceptionally big, unique, and fascinating: Carved on hundreds of volcanic boulders, the glyphs lie scattered in an area at least a couple kilometers long. Most historians believe that they were created by the Huari culture more than 1,000 years ago (and perhaps added to by subsequent peoples such as the Incas).

The enormous scale and the beautiful desert setting, more so than the individual drawings, are what most impress visitors to the site. The carvings comprise somewhat crude animal, human, and geometric representations. Although some estimates claim that there are 6,000 engraved stones at Toro Muerto, many more stones are not carved, so walking among the boulders in the sand and under a hot desert sun in search of the engraved stones requires considerable effort. The site draws very few tourists. Its distance from Arequipa and the difficulty getting there (and, no doubt, the competing popularity of Colca Canyon) preclude many groups from going to Toro Muerto.

GETTING THERE   General-service tour agencies in Arequipa arrange group trips to Toro Muerto; see "Getting There: By Organized Tour" under "Essentials" in the "Colca Valley" section, below. You can also hire a taxi from Arequipa at a cost of $35 to $40.

3 Colca Valley ✶✶✶

165km (103 miles) N of Arequipa

Mario Vargas Llosa, the Peruvian novelist and most famous Arequipeño, described Colca as "The Valley of Wonders." That is no literary overstatement. Colca is one of the most scenic regions in Peru, a land of imposing snowcapped volcanoes, narrow gorges, artistically terraced agricultural slopes that predate the Incas, arid desert landscapes and vegetation, and remote traditional villages, many visibly scarred by seismic tremors common in southern Peru. Some of Peru's most recognizable wildlife, including llamas, alpacas, vicuñas, and the celebrated giant Andean condors, roam the region.

The Colca River, one of the sources of the mighty Amazon, slices through the massive canyon, which remained largely unexplored until the late 1970s, when rafting expeditions descended to the bottom of the gorge. Reaching depths of 3,400m (11,150 ft.)—twice as deep as the Grand Canyon—*el Cañón del Colca* forms part of a tremendous volcanic mountain range more than 100km (62 miles) long. Colca, though, is no longer considered the world's, or even southern Peru's, deepest canyon; Cotahuasi, at the extreme northwest of the Arequipa department, has wrested away that honor. Among the region's great volcanoes, several of which are still active, are Mount Coropuna (6,425m/21,079 ft.), Peru's second-highest peak, and Mount Ampato (6,310m/20,702 ft.), where a sacrificed Incan maiden, known to the world as Juanita, was discovered frozen in 1995 (see "The Discovery of Juanita, the Ampato Maiden" on p. 306). The valley and its summits are a rapidly growing extreme-sports destination for hiking, mountain climbing, river rafting, and mountain biking.

Dispersed across the Colca Valley are 14 colonial-era villages, which date to the 16th century and are distinguished primarily by their small but often richly decorated churches. Local populations in the valley, descendants of the Collaguas and Cabanas, pre-Incan ethnic communities that have lived in the region for some 2,000 years, preserve ancient customs and distinctive traditional dress. They speak different languages and can be distinguished by their hats; Collagua women wear straw hats with colored ribbons, while the Cabanas sport elaborately embroidered and sequined felt headgear. (The men once wore distinctive dress as well but today are decidedly less colorful.) Colca villages are also celebrated for their vibrant festivals, which remain as authentic as any in Peru, throughout the year. The valley's meticulous agricultural terracing, even more extraordinary and extensive than the Incan terraces seen in the Sacred Valley near Cusco, were first cultivated more than 1,000 years ago.

Travelers are now spending more time in the Colca Valley, lapping up its extraordinary beauty, quiet traditional life, and opportunities for outdoor adventure sports, but the number-one draw remains the almost ineffable wonder of seeing majestic, giant condors with massive wingspans soar overhead at Cruz del Cóndor lookout point over Colca Canyon and head out along the river.

The best time to visit Colca is during the dry season, May through November, and the condors put on their best show from June to September. *Note:* The Colca Valley is lush and green just after the heavy rains from January to March, but most of the rest of the year it is arid and dusty. Though sunny during the day, it can also get quite cold (below freezing) at night—which is not unexpected, since Chivay is higher than Cusco.

ESSENTIALS
GETTING THERE

Colca Valley is a long half-day (3–4 hr.) trip from Arequipa along dusty roads that climb steadily, passing through the **Reserva Nacional Salinas y Aguada Blanca,** populated only by a collection of grazing alpacas and vicuñas, en route. The road poses less suffering than it did just a few years ago; the section of unpaved and bumpy travel is down to just 23km (14 miles), from 120km or 75 miles. (The entire trajectory should be completed by late 2006.) The **Mirador de los Andes,** 27km (17 miles) outside Chivay, is the highest point in the valley, a place where a small army of *apachetas,* tiny towers of piled stones, marks the spot highest to the *apus,* or gods. (Originally *apachetas* were offerings to the gods, but most if not all of these have been left behind by tourists.)

Tips **The Air up There**

The road from Arequipa to the Colca Valley climbs impressively, reaching 4,800m (15,748 ft.) at the Patapampa lookout point. The air is very thin at this altitude, and breathing is not at all easy. The main town in the valley, Chivay, sits at an altitude of nearly 3,600m (11,800 ft.), and nights can be brutally cold. Travelers who haven't yet spent time in either Cusco or Puno/Lake Titicaca should take it easy for a couple of days in Arequipa before heading out to Colca. *Soroche,* or acute altitude sickness, is common. See "Health & Safety," in chapter 2, for additional information on how to combat it.

The great majority of visitors to the Colca Valley and the canyon do so on guided tours, arranged in Arequipa. Entry to Colca is $7 per person; you'll get a *boleto turístico* that serves for admission to a half-dozen sights in the region, including churches and the Cruz del Condor.

BY ORGANIZED TOUR   Conventional travel agencies offer day trips to Cruz del Cóndor, usually leaving at 3 or 4am, with brief stops at Chivay before returning to Arequipa—it's an awful lot to pack into a single day, especially at a high altitude, and it leaves no time to enjoy what makes the region unique (though you do arrive in time to see the condors at 8 or 9am). Expect to pay about $20 per person. Two-day "pool" (grouped) tours are much more enjoyably paced and cost $30 to $75 per person, depending on hotel arrangements (they include transportation, a guide, hotel accommodations, and breakfast; other meals are extra). Other *campiña* tours offered by many agencies include the Toro Muerto petroglyphs; Mejía lagoons, a bird sanctuary; Laguna Salinas, a saltwater lagoon populated by flamingos; Aguada Blanca Nature Reserve; and the remote Valley of the Volcanoes, a lunar landscape located more than 13 hours from Arequipa. The best all-purpose agencies in Arequipa, which offer everything from city tours to general and private tours of Colca, as well as hard-core adventure, are **Giardino Tours,** Jerusalén 604-A (© 054/241-206; www.giardinotours.com); **Ideal Tours,** Urbanización San Isidro F-2, Vallecito (© 01/9-883-5617; ideal peru@terra.com.pe), **Santa Catalina Tours,** Santa Catalina 219 (© 054/216-994; santacatalina@star.com.pe); Colonial Tours, Santa Catalina 106 (© 054/286-868; colonialtours@mixmail.com); and **Illary Tours,** Santa Catalina 205 (© 054/220-844; illarytour.aqp@latinmail.com). All of these agencies are also equipped to organize private transportation and hotel packages, which range from $85 per person for one-day trips to $240 per person with accommodations at one of the top lodges in the region, such as Colca Lodge or the Parador del Colca.

BY BUS   Local buses travel from Arequipa to Cabanaconde (6 hr.), near Cruz del Cóndor, with stops in Chivay (4 hr.). Two companies that make these runs are **La Reyna,** Terminal Terrestre, Arequipa (© 054/426-549), and **Cristo Rey,** San Juan de Dios 510, Arequipa (© 054/213-094). The ride costs S/15 ($4.30). Unless you have plenty of time and patience, or a real need to be on your own, your best bet for getting to Colca is to go with an organized group.

VISITOR INFORMATION

A **Centro de Visitantes (Visitor's Center),** with maps and a small exhibit on the region, is located within Aguada Blanca National Reserve, 45km (28 miles) outside of

Arequipa. The office of the local **Tourist Police** (© **054/488-623**) can be found on the Plaza de Armas in Chivay. It's open daily in the afternoon and should be able to provide hiking information. You can also pick up information in Arequipa from the tourist information office or one of the travel agencies that organize Colca trips.

WHAT TO SEE & DO

MAIN COLCA VILLAGES: CHIVAY & CABANACONDE

The Valle del Colca is generally thought of in terms of left (south) and right (north) banks of the canyon, with villages and hotels of interest on either. Villages aren't separated by many kilometers, but the roads on both sides are rocky, dusty, and meandering, making for arduous and time-consuming driving. The left bank, which leads to Cruz del Cóndor, sees most of the tourists.

Although **Chivay,** on the left bank, is the valley's main town, it is still a largely sleepy little place that not long ago got on just fine without electricity. For many travelers on their way to Cruz del Cóndor and other spots in the valley, Chivay, which has the lion's share of restaurants and affordable hotels in the region, amounts to little more than a stopover. For those adhering to a leisurely pace, though, Chivay can be an enjoyable place to hang out; it benefits from an extraordinarily scenic natural setting. The attractive, low-key Plaza de Armas is the focus of attention in town and the site of several restaurants and *hostales.*

Most visitors hit the soothing and clean **La Calera hot springs** while in town. Though they can't compare with the thermal baths of Colca Lodge (see later in this chapter), they're enjoyable and easy to get to, just a 4km (2½-mile) walk or a colectivo ride from town, and inexpensive (S/10 or $2.85); they're open daily from 8am to 8pm.

The first village past Chivay (10km or 6¼ miles) is **Yanque,** a modest town with a baroque 18th-century church. In **Maca,** a village destroyed by a 1979 earthquake, which is on the way to Cruz del Condor, you'll find Santa Ana, a restored, brilliant white church with a surprising gilded interior. Nearby, perched overlooking the river, is the **Choquetico stone,** a pre-Incan carved-stone scale model of the mountains across the canyon, as well as a handful of Incan tombs carved out of the cliff face.

The tiny, reserved village of **Cabanaconde,** the last town in the Colca Valley, is a couple of hours from Chivay. Some independent travelers prefer to stay here because it is within (hearty) walking distance, 15km (9⅓ miles), or a 15-minute drive, from the Cruz del Cóndor lookout point, and it's well positioned for other hikes in the canyon and throughout the valley. The views of the canyon are tremendous, and short walks take you to excellent vantage points overlooking some of the most brilliant agricultural terracing in the area. The locals are descendants of the Cabanas people, and they maintain traditional dress and customs; women wear hats embroidered with flowers and wide skirts. There is a good small hotel and a couple of inexpensive *hostales* in the village (see "Where to Stay & Dine," below).

The right (north) side of Colca Canyon is less visited. **Coporaque,** just across the river from Chivay, is a sleepy village with the oldest church in the valley, the charming **Templo de Coporaque,** built in 1569 with twin bell towers. Just outside the village, and on the way to Colca Lodge, is the stunning **Mirador de Ocolle,** an amphitheater formed by agricultural terraces of varying shades of green. A new bridge from Pinchollo to **Lary** leads across a gorgeously terraced valley of pink rock and abundant cacti. Lary's primary attraction is its splendidly simple 1886 church, **Templo de la Purísima Concepción de Lari.** White with red trim, an orange and green portal, and double bell towers, it looks like a rural Mexican church or something that would decorate the top of a cake. It has recently been restored, and the interior is full of colorful murals and paintings, while the entire altar is adorned with brilliant baroque murals and painted columns. If you're not on a tour, you may have to ask at the shop next door for the key.

CRUZ DEL CONDOR 𝕽𝕽𝕽

Cruz del Cóndor, or Condor Cross, about 50km (31 miles) west of Chivay, is nothing more than a lookout point on one side of Colca Canyon that has become famous throughout Peru for its spectacular inhabitants, graceful Andean condors *(Vultur gryphus)*. At a spot 1,200m (3,937 ft.) above the canyon river, large crowds gather every morning, zoom lenses poised, to witness a stunning wildlife spectacle. Beginning around 9am, the condors—the largest birds in the world, with awesome wingspans of 3.5m (11½ ft.)—suddenly begin to appear, circling far below in the gorge and gradually gaining altitude with each pass, until they literally soar silently above the heads of awestruck admirers. Condors are such immense and heavy creatures that they cannot simply lift off from the ground; instead, they take flight from cliff perches. Each morning, from around 9 to 10am or later, condors both young and mature glide and climb theatrically before heading out along the river in search of prey. Witnessing the condors' majestic flight up close is a memorable and mesmerizing sight, capable of producing goose bumps on even the most jaded travelers. It's little wonder that the Incas believed them to be sacred creatures.

The dry months of June through September are when you're likely to see the largest group of condors in flight, and that's when they tend to circle and circle just over spectators' heads as they gain altitude, catch hold of a current, and set off down the river. On one trip to Colca, I saw at least two dozen condors take off over the canyon, and a guide I spoke with claimed he once saw 54 in a single morning. On my most recent visit, however, I saw just 3. The smallest number of condors is visible during the wet months of January through April and even October to December. The condors return late in the afternoon, but only a small group of people attend the show then. Photographing the condors in flight demands skill, patience, and a substantial zoom lens.

INDEPENDENT HIKING IN COLCA

Those looking to spend some quality hiking time in the valley and canyon can get to the region by public transportation or rental car from Arequipa and go out on their own. The largest number of inexpensive hotel accommodations is in Chivay. You can also camp throughout the canyon and valley, with the exception of Cruz del Cóndor.

The region is loaded with excellent hikes that can be done independently if you have suitable gear and camping equipment. Unless you're an experienced hiker, however, it's best to go with a guide (see "Tour Agencies for Rafting, Trekking & Mountaineering Expeditions," below).

Among the best hikes is a 2- to 3-hour, 1,300m (4265 ft.) **descent into Colca Canyon** from the Cruz del Cóndor lookout. Because of the arduous, lengthy 5- or 6-hour climb back out, most travelers who do this hike end up camping down below near the **Sangalle oasis** with palm trees and water suitable for swimming. Hikes down to the canyon floor require good physical conditioning and preparedness (plenty of water, food, sunscreen, and so on). The trails are quite difficult in sections, and the altitude complicates the trek—the drop is more than 1,000m (3,281 ft.). An even longer and more demanding hike is to the village of **Tapay,** beginning at Cabanaconde

A Typical Guided Tour of Colca Valley

Most organized tours of the region are very similar, if not identical. The road that leads out of Arequipa and into the valley, bending around the El Misti and Chachani volcanoes, is poor and unbearably dusty. It passes through the **Laguna Salinas** and **Aguada Blanca Nature Reserve,** where you'll usually have a chance to see rare vicuñas, llamas, and alpacas from the road. The altiplano landscape is barren and bleak. Most tours stop at volcano and valley lookout points along the way before heading to Chivay.

From **Chivay,** the valley's main town and the gateway to the region, many organized tours embark on short hikes above the canyon and visit the wonderfully relaxing hot springs of **La Calera** near Chivay (p. 323). Evening visits to the hot springs allow visitors to bathe in open-air pools beneath a huge, starry sky; artificial light in the valley is almost nonexistent. Charming colonial villages in the valley that are often visited by tours include Yanque, Coporaque, Maca, and Lari. Most 2-day tours head out early the following morning for **Cruz del Cóndor** to see the Andean condors begin to circle around 9am.

Organized tours generally include transportation, an English-speaking guide, hotel accommodations in Chivay or a nearby village (with breakfast), and park entrance fees to Colca and Cruz del Cóndor. Additional meals are extra.

and following a good trail from the oasis via the Río Colca (about 6 hr. each way). The path is very steep.

Less taxing hikes are possible simply walking from one village to another in the region. From **Chivay** to **Yanque** along the main road is about 7km (4⅓ miles). You can continue from Yanque to the villages of **Achoma** (another 7km or 4⅓ miles), **Maca** (12km or 7½ miles), and **Pinchollo** (10km or 6¼ miles). From there, on the way to Cabanaconde, it's about an hour to the **Colca Geyser (Hatun Infiernillo).**

EXTREME COLCA VALLEY: RAFTING, TREKKING & VOLCANO CLIMBS

The countryside around Arequipa, laced with canyons and volcanoes, is one of the best in Peru for outdoor adventure travel. Trails crisscross the Colca Valley, leading across mountain ridges, agricultural terraces, and curious rock formations, and past colonial towns and fields where llamas and vicuñas graze. The most common pursuits are river running, treks through the canyon valleys, and mountain climbing on the volcanoes just beyond the city. Many tour agencies in Arequipa offer conventional 2- and 3-day visits to Colca Canyon, as well as longer, more strenuous treks through the valley and to Cotahuasi Canyon. Some of the most interesting (but most time-consuming and difficult) expeditions combine rafting and trekking. Your best bet for organizing any of these activities is with one of the tour operators mentioned below; several in Arequipa focus solely on eco- and adventure tourism.

On Those Camelids

You'll likely have a chance to see three types of South American camelids common to the Andes: the domesticated llama and alpaca, and the considerably rarer wild vicuña. Llamas have been domesticated in the Andes for more than 5,000 years, used for meat, clothing, shelter, and fertilizer. Pre-Columbian civilizations also sacrificed llamas and alpacas as offerings to gods. Vicuñas are the smallest members of the camelid family, as well as the most prized and endangered. These camelids are native to the high plains of the Andes Mountains in Bolivia, Chile, and, primarily, Peru.

Alpacas and llamas differ in size and fiber quality. Adult alpacas are usually about a foot shorter than llamas, and the former produces 10 pounds a year or more of high-quality fiber in a single fleece. Alpaca hair is extremely fine, soft, smooth, and lightweight. It is stronger, warmer, and longer lasting than wool. "Baby alpaca" is the first clipping of the shearling, and, extraordinarily soft, it is universally prized and expensive. Llamas, on the other hand, have a less fine dual fiber fleece, and the animals are better equipped to serve as excellent beasts of burden, perfect for mountain-trekking expeditions. Both llamas and alpacas graze at elevations of 3,000m (9,800 ft.) and higher. Llamas and alpacas are intelligent and gentle animals, but they have a reputation for a nasty habit: spitting. They usually spit at each other over food, but female llamas also spit at male llamas to ward off advances.

The vicuña is a national symbol in Peru, which is home to more than half the world's vicuña population. The Incas dressed their nobility in its ultra-soft fibers, considered the finest and warmest in the world, considerably lighter even than cashmere. Vicuña fleece sells for as much as $1,500 a pound; a man's sport coat made of vicuña costs at least $5,000. Poaching nearly rendered the vicuña extinct; it was declared endangered, and trade in vicuña products was banned internationally in 1975. With the vicuña community back up to approximately 200,000 animals throughout the Andean highlands, the animal is now considered threatened rather than endangered, and control over the harvesting of vicuña coats was placed under the ownership and management of Peru's Indian communities in the 1990s. Limited vicuña trade is now allowed; only garments stamped with the "Vicuñandes" trademark or "Vicuña" and the country of origin are deemed legal.

RIVER RAFTING

The rivers and canyons around Arequipa pose some excellent river-running opportunities for both novices and experts. The best months for rafting are May through September, when water levels are low. (In the rainy season, when water levels are high, the canyon rivers can be extremely dangerous.) The most accessible rafting, suitable for first-timers, is on the **Río Chili,** just 15 minutes from downtown. It offers Class III and IV runs, and is a great way to get your feet wet during a half-day trip. Year-round runs of similarly moderate difficulty and scenic beauty can be arranged on day trips to the **Río Majes** (the Río Colca beyond the gorge). Rafting in Cotahuasi and Colca canyons is serious stuff for confident rafters; there are 3-day rafting trips to Colca (about $125) for those with moderate experience, and longer, 10- to 12-day trips to either canyon for serious white-water runners. The **Río Colca** (Class IV–V) is extremely technical, although some upriver sections are less dangerous and difficult. **Río Cotahuasi** was first explored only in 1994; it has 120km (75 miles) of Class IV and V rapids (and some Class VI). A few agencies offer annual trips that combine trekking with hard-core white-water rafting in Cotahuasi. These organized trips are expensive ($2,000 and up) and lengthy, usually 12 to 14 days total.

MOUNTAIN & VOLCANO CLIMBING

At the foot of the western Andes, Arequipa is ideally positioned for a variety of ascents—many of them not technically challenging—to volcano summits and mighty Andes peaks. Climbers in good physical condition can bag 5,000m (16,400-ft.) summits on ascents of 2 days or less. The best months for climbing are July through September, although some peaks can be climbed year-round. Climbers should be sufficiently acclimatized before making any ascents; if you've spent several days in Cusco or Puno before arriving in Arequipa (and are in good physical shape), you should be fine. Adventure travel operators in Arequipa provide logistical support, porters, and guides, but you must provide your own sleeping bag and boots. Be sure to ask plenty of questions about weather conditions, equipment, and experience before setting out with any guide.

El Misti, a nearly 6,000m (19,680-ft.) volcano, dominates the Arequipa landscape from a distance of about 20km (12 miles). The most popular climb among both locals and visitors, Misti is a demanding 2- or 3-day trek with few technical challenges. It is suitable for inexperienced climbers accompanied by professional guides. Most climbers stay the first night at the base camp Nido de Aguilas (Eagle's Nest) and reach the summit after about 7 hours of climbing on the second day. Arequipa's other major volcano, **Chachani** (6,075m/19,931 ft.), also presents an excellent and technically straightforward climb, a good opportunity for inexperienced climbers to brag about reaching a 6,000m (19,680-ft.) summit.

The Colca Valley has a number of peaks that draw serious climbers, including the **Ampato** volcano (6,288m/20,630 ft.), a 3- or 4-day climb, and the **Hualca Hualca** glacier (6,025m/19,767 ft.). **Coropuna** (6,425m/21,079 ft.), perhaps the most stunning mountain in the Cotahuasi Valley, requires a couple of days of travel from Arequipa to begin the difficult climb.

Tips **Cotahuasi Canyon**

Reputedly the deepest canyon in the world, Cotahuasi (3,354m/11,000 ft. at its deepest point) was only explored by rafting teams a few years ago. As enticing as trekking or rafting in the world's deepest canyon no doubt is to many, the effort required to get to Cotahuasi is substantial. It's a full 12 to 15 hours from Arequipa by bus, more than 400km (250 miles) on pretty difficult roads. Although some adventurers do go independently, trekking or rafting in the Cotahuasi is much better and more safely organized by a professional outfit such as Zárate Aventuras (see "Tour Agencies for Rafting, Trekking & Mountaineering Expeditions," below).

TOUR AGENCIES FOR RAFTING, TREKKING & MOUNTAINEERING EXPEDITIONS

The best general agencies in Arequipa (see "Getting There," earlier) arrange entry-level rafting and trekking itineraries. Almost all are located on just two streets in Arequipa, Jerusalén, and Santa Catalina, so it's pretty simple to browse up and down and get a feel for an agency.

Apumayo Expediciones 🐾🐾, Garcilaso 265, Cusco (© **084/246-018;** www.apumayo.com), is excellent for adventure trips in the region, including long trekking/rafting expeditions to Cotahuasi and Colca. **Cusipata Viajes y Turismo** 🐾, Jerusalén 408-A (© **054/203-966;** www.cusipata.com), is the local specialist for Chili and Colca rafting and kayaking (including courses), and its guides, led by Gianmarco Vellutino, frequently subcontract out to other agencies in Arequipa. **Ideal Tours,** Urbanización San Isidro F-2, Vallecito (© **054/244-439**), handles Chili and Majes rafting, as well as Colca and other standard tours.

Apu Expediciones, Casilla Postal 24, Cusco (© **084/957-483;** www.geocities.com/TheTropics/Cabana/4037), arranges rafting trips to Majes and Colca, among other adventure options. **Colca Trek** 🐾, Santa Catalina 204 (© **054/202-461;** www.colcatrek.com), and **Peru Trekking,** Jerusalén 302-B (© **054/223-404**), are two other Arequipa outfits that offer canyon treks of 3 to 5 days or more and a number of other adventure activities, such as horseback riding, mountain biking, rafting, and climbing.

For hard-core mountain climbing and trekking, one agency stands out: **Carlos Zárate Aventuras** 🐾🐾, Santa Catalina 204, no. 3 (© **054/202-461;** www.zaratead ventures.com), is run by Carlos Zárate, perhaps the top climbing guide in Arequipa (a title his dad held before him). He can arrange any area climb and has equipment rental and a 24-hour mountain-rescue service. Climbing expedition costs are (per person) El Misti, $50; Chachani, $70; and Colca Canyon, $75. Mountain biking and rafting trips are also arranged.

For specialized birding programs (as well as other nature tours), **Tanager Tours,** La Estrella F-9, in the J. L. Bustamante y Rivero district (© **054/426-210;** www.tanager tours.com), is the top choice in Arequipa.

WHERE TO STAY & DINE

Most agencies offering 2- and 3-day trips to Colca Canyon put passengers up at modest hotels in the village of Chivay. If you can afford to step up a notch from budget accommodations, the following rustic inns in and around the canyon—primarily between Chivay and Cabanaconde—are the most comfortable and atmospheric places to stay in Colca. Comparatively luxurious, they are by far the best choices if offered by tour operators (often at bargain rates) or if you're traveling to Colca independently.

In the center of Chivay, **Casa Andina Colca** 🐾, Huayna Cápac s/n, Chivay (© **054/531-020;** fax 054/531-098; www.casa-andina.com), is the latest entry into the Colca rustic hotel category and an indication that many people in the industry are betting on Colca's further development. It's easily the nicest place in the hub of Chivay. It recently expanded to 52 accommodations in the style that has become so popular in the region: stone walls, thatched roofs, and cozy furnishings with thick wool blankets. The new bungalow-style rooms are slightly larger and have higher ceilings. A double room costs $58. The restaurant features folk music and dance shows as well as a cool planetarium and telescope.

There are several restaurants in town, which are for the most part open for the lunch-time tourist groups that come through town. One of the most popular is **Witite,** Calle Siglo XX 328 (© **054/531-036**), which serves a general Andean menu and is named for a locally famous dance competition. **Solar Rosario,** Calle Arequipa 504 (© **054/531-133**), is a good-looking spot that offers a buffet lunch for S/17 ($4.85), and **Casablanca,** Plaza de Armas 705 (© **054/521-019**), serves a good-value menú and boasts a handful of vegetarian dishes. If you stay the night, you may want to check out a little peña action (served up with dinner) at **El Encanto del Colca,** Calle Mariscal Castilla 500 (no phone), down a little side street. Good folkloric peña music can also be found at **El Nido,** Zarumilla 216 (© **054/531-010**), around the corner from El Encanto.

El Mirador de los Collaguas ✱, Piura s/n, Yanque (©/fax **054/203-966;** www.miradordeloscollaguas.com), is a small country inn within easy walking distance of Yanque's attractive plaza. The 12 rooms, in small adobe bungalows, cost $65 per double. Some are nicely decorated loft spaces with terrific views over the river toward Colca Lodge; other rooms have no views at all. The inn features a nice restaurant, La Casa Nostra, with a wood-burning stove and good alpaca steak and trout dishes.

Parador del Colca ✱✱✱, Fundo Curiña s/n, on the outskirts of Yanque (© **01/ 242-3425;** colca@peruorientexpress.com.pe), part of the upscale Orient Express chain that owns the Hotel Monasterio in Cusco and Machu Picchu Sanctuary Lodge, is the most special inn in the valley. The Parador oozes rustic charm, elegance, and intimacy. It's the kind of place where César, the general manager, greets you at the door and addresses you by name, and where you'll find your bed turned down at night with strategically placed hot-water bottles and candles blazing. It has just seven rooms for now, though it is in the midst of a big renovation that will add 10 luxury cabanas and a new dining room (and, eventually, a spa). Perched on the lip of the canyon, the rustic ranch-style ecolodge features solar energy and electricity, a breakfast terrace with gorgeous valley views of extensive gardens, terraced fields, and the river. The rooms have loft spaces and private patios with fire pits overlooking the canyon. The small kitchen turns out wonderfully fresh dinner and excellent breakfasts using ingredients from the garden, and the lodge also offers horseback riding. The seven double rooms are just $70–$80, a bargain for this kind of country luxury, although prices for the new individual cabanas, to be finished in late 2006, are likely to be considerably higher. I hope the additions won't alter the singular spirit of the place; if it's up to César, I trust they won't.

Colca Lodge ✱✱, about 10km (6¼ miles) from Chivay (© **054/202-587;** fax 054/ 220-407; www.colca-lodge.com) is beautifully situated across the river from Yanque and has one feature no other lodge can match: its own private thermal baths, carved in stone and secluded along the banks of the river. The continually expanding lodge is a very comfortable, eco-style hotel with adobe, stone, and thatched-roof architecture, and solar power. Its level of luxury is just a small step down from the Parador del Colca (see above), the top choice in the region (although those hot springs make it a close call). The views of the valley are excellent from nearly everywhere. The hotel also has a sophisticated lodge-style restaurant serving a fairly expensive lunch and dinner. The lodge's 29 rooms cost $60 to $70 per double. If you're not a guest, you can experience the thermal pools for $10.

Giardino Tours books its Colca tour guests at one of the newer country inns in the Colca Valley, **La Casa de Mama Yacchi** ✱, Coporaque (© **054/241-206;** fax

054/242-761; www.lacasademamayacchi.com). Located just outside the village of Coporaque, it has 50 very comfortable rooms with exposed beams, great views, a fireplace lounge, and an attractive rustic restaurant featuring good local preparations. It's owned by the same folks who run La Casa de Mi Abuela Hostal in Arequipa. Rooms cost $51 per double.

There are just a few *hostales* and one hotel in quiet Cabanaconde, which will appeal to those who wish to spend a couple of days hiking in the canyon. The top spot is **Hotel Kuntur Wassi** ⓐ, La Ladera 360 (© **054/832-170;** www.kunturwassi.com). On a hill above the village, this rambling small hotel, built of adobe and stone, has nicely decorated rooms with high ceilings, faux stone bathrooms, and lots of plants lining the walkways along the property. With a good restaurant and bar overlooking town, it's a very nice place to relax after a long hike. The 25 rooms are $50 for double, $60 for a suite. Ask about special multi-night package deals. **La Posada del Conde,** San Pedro at Bolognesi (© **064/440-197;** http://espanol.geocities.com/pdelconde/Hotel.html), is the next best choice in the village: a decent, clean place and value, with private bathrooms.

10

Amazonia

Nearly two-thirds of Peru is Amazon rainforest, which thrives with some of the richest biodiversity on the planet. Covering 6,475,000 sq. km (2,500,000 sq. miles), the Amazon basin represents 54% of all remaining rainforest on the planet. This vast, largely impenetrable region, with the smallest human population in the country and few towns of any size, clearly is not the Peru of great pre-Columbian civilizations and Incan ruins. For the traveler, it stands in stunning contrast to rugged Andean peaks and arid desert coasts. The humid frontier towns of the jungle, well past stages of oil and rubber boom and now hell-bent on ecotourism, are worlds removed from the historic cities Cusco and Arequipa and the modern madness of Lima.

Many naturalists and biologists believe that Peru's Amazon rainforest holds the greatest diversity in the world. It teems with a staggering roster of wildlife: 400 species of mammals, 2,000 species of fish, 300 reptiles, 1,800 birds, and more than 50,000 plants. Recent studies have shown that a region just south of Iquitos has the highest concentration of mammals anywhere in the world.

Not surprisingly, jungle ecotourism has exploded in Peru, as it has in several other Latin American countries. Peru's jungle regions are now much more accessible than they once were—which is both a good and a bad thing, of course—and there are more lodges and eco-options than ever. (However, remote as the Amazon jungle surely seems, it is possible to find yourself at an ecolodge in as little as 12 hours after boarding a flight in the U.S.) Still, accessibility is a crucial factor in jungle trips: The more remote a lodge or camping trek is, and the more pristine and unspoiled the environment is, the more it's going to cost you to get there in terms of both time and money. Rivers define life in the jungle even more than do the forests; for both locals and visitors, almost all transport along the vast river system that stretches across the whole of eastern Peru is by dugout canoe, motorboat, or large riverboats *(lanchas)*.

The southern Amazon region, which extends to the Bolivian and Brazilian borders, is concentrated in the Madre de Dios department, the least populated area in Peru. Although it is accessible by land from Cusco, it is an exceedingly difficult route. Most travelers fly to Puerto Maldonado (the gateway to the Tambopata National Reserve) and travel overland to the Manu Biosphere Reserve, returning by small aircraft.

The northern Amazon reaches all the way to Peru's borders with Colombia and Brazil. The gateway to Peru's northern Amazon basin is Iquitos. As an example of how huge the Amazon is, Iquitos lies nearly 3,220km (2,000 miles) from the mouth of the great Río Amazonas, the second-longest river in the world. Other than an arduous journey by boat, the only way to get to Iquitos is by airplane (usually from Lima).

The best time to visit the Amazon is during the dry season, May through the end of October. During the rainy season in the southern Amazon, parts of the jungle are flooded and impassable. The northern jungle does not have a rainy season, per se, and travel there is less restricted during the winter. However, water levels can rise from 7.5m (25 ft.) to more than 15m (50 ft.) from December to May, and some jungle villages become flooded. Many naturalists find high-water months best for wildlife observation.

1 The Southern Amazon Jungle ★★★

Easily accessible from Cusco, the southern jungle boasts some of Peru's finest and least spoiled Amazon rainforest. The area has been less penetrated by man than has the northern Amazon; indeed, the southern jungle remained largely unexplored until expeditions into the remote rainforest were undertaken in the 1950s. Two of Peru's top three jungle zones—and two of the finest in South America—dominate the southeastern department of Madre de Dios. The region's two principal protected areas, the **Manu Biosphere Reserve** (which encompasses the Parque Nacional del Manu, or Manu National Park) and the **Tambopata National Reserve (Reserva Nacional de Tambopata),** are both excellent for jungle expeditions, although they differ in terms of remoteness and facilities.

Manu, one of the largest protected natural areas in the Americas and considered to be one of the most pristine jungle regions in the world, remains complicated and time-consuming to visit. Flights in and out of Boca Manu are now handled by the National Air Force rather than commercial carriers, and travel is possible only with one of eight officially sanctioned agencies. Expeditions last a minimum of 5 or 6 days (and most are a week or more), involve both significant overland and air (not to mention extensive river) travel, are expensive, and are very rustic, with the focus much more on contact with nature than creature comforts. Access is easiest from Cusco, although it involves a (spectacular) day's travel overland (or a half-hour flight), followed by a couple of days by boat.

Travelers without the time or budget to reach Manu often find Tambopata a most worthy alternative: Its wildlife and jungle vegetation are nearly the equal of Manu in some parts. Most lodges in Tambopata are considerably easier to get to and cheaper than those in Manu, although a couple require up to 8 or even 12 hours of travel by boat from Puerto Maldonado. The jungle frontier city of Puerto Maldonado, which is the capital of Madre de Dios department and just a half-hour flight from Cusco, is the jumping-off point to explore Tambopata. Travelers interested in the least time-consuming and least expensive way to see a part of the Peruvian jungle can visit one of the lodges on Madre de Dios River or Lago Sandoval, the latter an oxbow lake within a couple of hours of Puerto Maldonado.

In travel packages to both destinations, round-trip airfare from Cusco to Puerto Maldonado or Boca Manu (the gateway to the Manu Biosphere Reserve) is usually extra. Cheaper tours travel overland, stay at lesser-quality lodges (or primarily at campsites), and might travel on riverboats without canopies. Independent travel to Tambopata and two-way overland travel to either are options only for those with a lot of time and patience on their hands. Independent travelers not only find it complicated to enter many parts of the jungle, but they are also not permitted to enter the most desirable section of Manu, the Reserve Zone. Organizing a trip with one of the lodges or specialized tour operators listed below is highly recommended, in terms of

both access and convenience. Most have fixed departure dates throughout the year. Do not purchase any jungle packages from salesmen on the streets of Cusco; their agencies might not even be authorized to enter restricted zones, and last-minute "itinerary changes" are likely.

Searing heat and humidity are year-round constants in the jungle (though in the southern jungle, occasional cold fronts called *friajes* are common). Appropriate gear for steamy tropical conditions is a must. Dry season (May–Oct) is the best time for southern jungle expeditions—during the rainy season, rivers overflow and mosquitoes gobble up everything in sight. Be careful to note when a tour operator's fixed departures leave (some are every Wed, others every Sun, and so on). Most lodge visits include boat transportation and three meals daily, as well as guided visits and activities (some, such as canopy walks and distant clay-lick outings, entail additional fees).

PUERTO MALDONADO

Founded in 1902 and once a prosperous rubber town, Puerto Maldonado is a humid, scruffy, and fast-growing place, a frontier market town that has gone through several phases of boom and bust, as have most jungle outposts. After the rubber boom came the game hunters and loggers. It's the kind of place where streets just off the main square are still unpaved and full of muddy potholes. Today the town's primary industries continue to be based on exploiting the rainforest that surrounds Puerto Maldonado: gold prospecting, Brazil-nut harvesting, and ecotourism. For most travelers, Puerto Maldonado is merely a gateway to the jungle, and groups booked on Tambopata package tours often blow through town with little notice, ferried directly from the airport to waiting river boats. For some visitors, it's a stiflingly hot one-horse (and motor-scooter) town, but the frontier atmosphere, which continues to draw dreamers from across Peru, proves interesting to others, at least for a day or two before they push on into the jungle.

ESSENTIALS

GETTING THERE   The **Aeropuerto Internacional Padre Aldamiz Puerto Maldonado** (© 082/571-531) is 8km (5 miles) outside of the city. Flights arrive from Cusco and Lima on **TANS** (© 01/611-5555; www.tansperu.com.pe), and **AeroCondor** (© 01/614-6000; www.aerocondor.com.pe). Health Ministry nurses are on hand to vaccinate visitors against yellow fever *(fiebra amarilla)*. To get from the airport to town, the best bet is a *motocarro* (a motorcycle rickshaw), which costs S/5 to S/7 ($1.40–$2).

Budget travelers with bountiful patience and perseverance, and those looking for a new warrior experience and the bragging rights that go with it can travel by truck to Puerto Maldonado from Cusco. The journey takes at least 3 days in the dry season and up to 10 days in wetter conditions, and the route traverses more than 500km (310 miles) with zero comfort to speak of; it's certainly one of the worst (if not *the* worst) roads in Peru connecting two points of obvious interest. It costs about $15 and will provide you with stories for months, but you will definitely suffer for the dubious privilege. Trucks leave from Plaza Tupac Amaru in Cusco and arrive in Puerto Maldonado at the Mercado Modelo on Calle Ernesto Rivero. Take the challenge at your own risk; though the scenery is said to be astounding, the trip is not something I can recommend.

Tips Preventive Medicine for the Jungle

Yellow fever vaccinations are a wise idea before visiting the jungles of southeastern Peru. Even though the only reported outbreaks of yellow fever in the last couple of years have been in the northern Amazon around Iquitos, local authorities in Puerto Maldonado make sure that visitors who want to be protected are. At the airport arrival terminal, yellow fever shots are administered by Health Ministry nurses.

Other vaccinations worth considering (speak to your doctor or consult the World Health Organization or Centers for Disease Control websites) are those for Hepatitis A and typhoid. Malaria pills are also a good idea, especially if you're planning to venture deep into the jungle. You should carry your vaccination records with you while traveling in Peru. For more information on health issues, see p. 43.

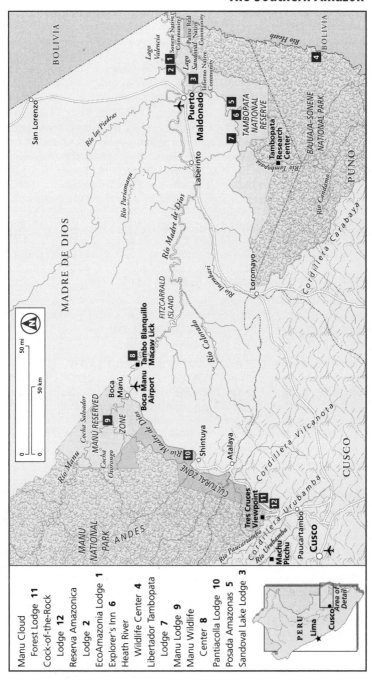

The Southern Amazon

BOLIVIA

San Lorenzo

Rio las Piedras

MADRE DE DIOS

Rio Pariamanu

Rio Manu

Cocha Salvador

MANÚ RESERVED ZONE

Boca Manu

Cocha Otorongo

Cocha

Rio Manu

MANU NATIONAL PARK

ANDES

CULTURAL ZONE

Rio Madre de Dios

Shintuya

Atalaya

Tres Cruces Viewpoint

Machu Picchu

Rio Paucartambo

Rio Urubamba

Cordillera Urubamba

Cordillera Vilcanota

Paucartambo

CUSCO

Cusco

Rio Madre de Dios

Boca Manú Airport

Tambo Blanquillo Macaw Lick

FITZCARRALD ISLAND

Rio Colorado

Rio Inambari

Rio Inambari

Toromayo

Rio Candamo

Cordillera Carabaya

PUNO

Rio Tambopata

TAMBOPATA NATIONAL RESERVE

Tambopata Research Center

Rio Heath

Palma Real Native Community

BAHUAJA-SONENE NATIONAL PARK

BOLIVIA

Laberinto

Puerto Maldonado

Lago Valencia

Lago Sandoval

Sonene Native Community

Sandoval Native Community

Inferno Native Community

50 mi

50 km

N

Lodge index

Manu Cloud Forest Lodge **11**
Cock-of-the-Rock Lodge **12**
Reserva Amazonica Lodge **2**
EcoAmazonia Lodge **1**
Explorer's Inn **6**
Heath River Wildlife Center **4**
Libertador Tambopata Lodge **7**
Manu Lodge **9**
Manu Wildlife Center **8**
Pantiacolla Lodge **10**
Posada Amazonas **5**
Sandoval Lake Lodge **3**

PERU

Lima

Cusco

Area of Detail

335

VISITOR INFORMATION   In Puerto Maldonado, there's a small booth at the airport that can give very limited information on the city and jungle lodges. Most visitors leave for the southern jungle from Cusco, so if you spend a few days there first, it's worthwhile to pick up more complete information on Puerto Maldonado and the rest of the jungle at the main **Tourist Information Office** at Mantas 117-A, a block from the Plaza de Armas (© **082/263-176**). Anyone traveling to Manu or Tambopata with an organized expedition should be able to get all the necessary information from the tour organizer.

FAST FACTS   Banks on the Plaza de Armas include **Banco de la Nación,** Jr. Carrión 233 (© **082/571-064**), and **Banco de Crédito,** Arequipa 334 (© **082/571-001**). Only Banco de Crédito changes traveler's checks. There are also *casas de cambio* along Jr. Puno. Credit cards are not widely accepted in Puerto Maldonado, so you should plan on bringing cash for incidentals if you've already booked a lodge or tour program.

For required exit stamps to travel to Bolivia via Puerto Heath (a trip of 3–4 days by boat), visit the **Peruvian Immigration Office** at 26 de Diciembre 356, a block from the Plaza de Armas. It's open Monday through Friday from 9am to 1pm.

For medical attention, go to **Hospital Santa Rosa,** Jr. Cajamarca 171, at Velarde (© **082/571-019**). The **police** can be found at Jr. Carrión 410 (© **105** or 082/571-022). The **post office** is located on Av. León Velarde 675 (© **082/571-088**). There's a **Telefónica del Perú** office at Jr. Puno 670 (© **082/571-600**).

GETTING AROUND   Quick, easy, and cheap, *motocarros* are everywhere; most rides in town cost S/2 (55¢). Ferries cross the Ríos Madre de Dios and Tambopata if you just want to cruise across the river; you'll have to negotiate the price, but expect to spend S/15 to S/20 ($4.30–$5.70) per person.

WHAT TO SEE & DO NEAR PUERTO MALDONADO

Good jungle experiences, with possibilities of some fauna sightings and attractive walks in primary and secondary forest, are within easy reach of Puerto Maldonado. However, your experience will be vastly improved if you go farther from the city, particularly for stays of 2 nights or more at one of the lodges discussed below. Still, a couple of easy and inexpensive day trips from the regional capital—vastly better than comparable close-in trips from Iquitos—can be arranged.

LAGO SANDOVAL 🐟🐟   Sandoval Lake is about 5km (3 miles), or an hour by boat, from Puerto Maldonado. Even if you don't stay at the lodge on the lake or one of those nearby along the Río Madre de Dios (see "Tambopata Lodges," below), this pretty and serene oxbow lake, ringed by palm trees, makes an excellent day trip downriver from Puerto Maldonado. It boasts a surprising diversity of wildlife, including macaws, parrots, herons, kingfishers, caimans, turtles, and even a family of giant river otters that can frequently be spied in the lake. The best way to get here is to catch a canoe or motorboat at the port. You'll then have to walk a couple kilometers along a path through the jungle, but it's a beautiful (if very hot) hour-long trek. Most jungle lodges along the Madre de Dios offer excursions to Lago Sandoval among their activities, though they usually arrive in the heat of the day, when wildlife activity is least observable (birds, monkeys, and the lake's caimans and resident river otters are much more active in the early morning and early evening hours).

Map legend:

0 — 1/5 mile
0 — 200 meters

Río Madre de Dios

Port

Jr. Billinghurst

Jr. Loreto

PLAZA DE ARMAS

Jr. Carrión

Jr. Cusco

Av. 2 de Mayo

Jr. González Prada

Jr. J. Troncoso

Jr. Tacna

Jr. Ernesto River

Jr. Moquegua

Jr. Puno

Av. Léon Velarde

Jr. Arequipa

Jr. 26 de Diciembre

← To Airport

PERU
Lima
Puerto Maldonado
Cusco

ACCOMMODATIONS ■
Don Carlos Hotel **3**
Hostal Residencial
 Cabañaquinta **2**
Wasaí Maldonado Lodge **6**

DINING ◆
El Califa **1**
Hostal Residencial
 Cabañaquinta Restaurant **2**
Pizzeria El Hornitos **4**
Pollos a la Brasa La Estrella **5**
Wasaí Maldonado Restaurant **6**

WHERE TO STAY & DINE

Most people who stay overnight in Puerto Maldonado are either resting up from a trip to the jungle or trying to arrange one. In town, there are only a couple of decent and comfortable hotels, in addition to about a dozen very basic hostels.

The best place to stay in Puerto Maldonado is **Wasaí Maldonado Lodge** ℱ, Jr. Guillermo Billinghurst (② **082/571-355;** www.wasai.com). Although it's only a block from the main square in town, this inn is built much more like a mini jungle lodge, with 6 of the 18 bungalows perched on stilts. The location is quite stunning, overlooking the Madre de Dios River. The spacious and comfortable bungalows are cabin-like paneled rooms with refrigerators, private bathrooms with hot water, air-conditioning (or fan), and TV. The small swimming pool, which looked abandoned on my last visit, overlooks the river. The lodge restaurant, the best and most upscale in town, is in a gazebo that sits above the riverbank; on the second floor is a new bar with good river views. Doubles in bungalows with river views cost $48. Ecotours and jungle expeditions with stays at the Wasaí Tambopata Lodge and Research Center, 120km (75 miles)—about 6 hours— upriver on the Río Tambopata, can be arranged (4 days/3 nights, $291).

Don Carlos Hotel, Velarde 1271 (② **082/571-029;** www.hotelesdoncarlos.com), sits above the banks of Tambopata River about 5 blocks south of the center of town

---

Fun Fact **Native Foods**

Local jungle dishes worth a try include *patarashca,* a steamed river fish wrapped in banana leaves; *timbuche,* a thick soup made with local fish; and *tacacho,* or bananas cooked over coals and served with fried pork and chopped onions. Locals also eat *motelo* (turtle soup served in its shell) and *muchangue* (turtle eggs with steamed bananas), but, given that river and sea turtles are endangered species protected by Peruvian law, it seems especially criminal for gringos to indulge this custom. *Mazato* is a local beverage of fermented yuca, bananas, and milk.

---

and is surrounded by native flora. Smaller, more rustic, and more low-key than the chain's other hotels, this inn nonetheless has a host of services and amenities, including a restaurant, laundry, 24-hour room service, an outdoor swimming pool, and air-conditioning. The 15 rooms aren't anything special, but they're a pretty good value, at $26 for a double. **Hostal Residencial Cabañaquinta,** Cusco 535 (© **082/571-045;** perutourytravel@hotmail.com), is a comfortable inn with 50 pretty decent rooms with private bathrooms, a nice garden, and one of the better restaurants in town. Double rooms cost $25.

The top restaurant in town is the one at **Wasaí Maldonado Lodge.** The hotel restaurants at **Don Carlos** and **Cabañaquinta** are also frequented by visitors to town, but there are a slew of basic eateries, *chifas,* and cafes clustered near the Plaza de Armas and lining León de Velarde, the main street. **Pizzería El Hornito,** Jr. Carrión 271/Plaza de Armas (© **082/572-082**), is a good and cozy pizza joint and pub serving wood-fired pies. It's open daily until midnight and accepts credit cards. Next door, down a long passageway, is **Bulevard Video-Pub** (no phone), which has a large screen playing music videos; you can get a pizza and beers there, but El Hornito is far more agreeable. **El Califa,** Piura 266 (© **082/571-119**), on a small side street, is a local, open-air joint that, with bright green paneling, ceiling fans, a tin roof, and verdant garden, very much looks the part of small-town tropical eatery. It serves local jungle cuisine and good Peruvian meals, including ceviche, at lunch. Grilled and rotisserie chicken, always a good bet in Peru, can be had at **Pollos a la Brasa La Estrella,** Velarde 474 (© **082/573-107**).

TAMBOPATA NATIONAL RESERVE &&
650km (404 miles) NE of Cusco; 37km (23 miles) SW of Puerto Maldonado

Upstream from Puerto Maldonado, jungle lodges in and around the **Tambopata National Reserve (Reserva Nacional de Tambopata)**—a massive tract of humid subtropical rainforest in the department of Madre de Dios—are located either along the Tambopata or Madre de Dios rivers. The National Reserve covers 275,000 hectares (nearly 680,000 acres), while the entire area, including the Bahuaja-Sonene National Park, encompasses some 1.5 million hectares (3.7 million acres) of Amazonian jungle. The Peruvian government prohibited hunting and logging in the area in 1977 and created the reserve, then called the Tambopata-Candamo Reserve Zone, in 1990. Nearly one-third the size of Costa Rica, Tambopata has more species of birds (595) and butterflies (more than 1,200) than any place of similar size on earth.

Visits to lodges here are considerably more accessible than those in Manu. Most trips involve flying a half-hour from Cusco and then boarding a boat and traveling by river for 45 minutes up to 5 hours to reach a jungle lodge. Primary lodges are those that travelers can get to the same day they arrive by plane in Puerto Maldonado. Although mankind's imprints are slightly more noticeable in the Tambopata region, the area remains one of superb environmental diversity, with a dozen different types of forest and several gorgeous oxbow lakes. Environmentalists claim that Tambopata's great diversity of wildlife is due to its location at the confluence of lowland Amazon forest with three other ecosystems. At least 13 endangered species are found here, including the jaguar, ocelot, giant armadillo, harpy eagle, and giant river otter. The farther one travels from Puerto Maldonado, the greater the chances of significant wildlife viewing.

The Tambopata macaw clay lick *(collpa de guacamayos)* within the reserve is one of the largest natural clay licks in the country and one of the wildlife highlights of Peru. Thousands of brilliantly colored macaws and parrots arrive daily at the cliffs to feed on mineral salts.

Most visitors prearrange tours to Tambopata in Cusco or in their country of origin, although one could also book a lodge visit by stopping in the local offices of travel agents and tour operators in the center of Puerto Maldonado or at the airport (though you will have less information and opportunity to compare offerings). Access to Tambopata is by boat from Puerto Maldonado. Packages begin with 2-day/1-night arrangements, but 3-day/2-night packages are preferable. Lodge stays generally allow visitors to see a large variety of trees, plants, and birds, but sightings of wild mammals, apart from monkeys and otters, are rare. Large and rare species such as jaguars and tapirs are infrequently seen, though visitors to Lago Sandoval, an oxbow lake, have the exciting opportunity to see an extended family of resident giant river otters (known in Spanish as *lobos de río*).

Lodges are located predominantly either along the Río Tambopata, which extends south of Puerto Maldonado, or the Río Madre de Dios, east of the city. The area around the Río Tambopata, with greater primary forest, is generally considered better for wildlife viewing.

EAST OF PUERTO MALDONADO: ALONG THE RÍO MADRE DE DIOS

Lodges within a couple of hours by boat from Puerto Maldonado are generally cheaper (and, of course, less time-consuming to get to) than those deeper in the Tambopata National Reserve. Because they are located in secondary jungle and are not nearly as remote, they best serve as introductory visits to the Amazon. The forest along the Madre de Dios is generally not as pristine as that found along the Tambopata

---

Tips **¿Qué Frío?**

The weather in the Madre de Dios region is usually extremely hot and sticky, as you would expect. But the southern jungle's proximity to the Andes produces periodic cold spells called *friajes,* which originate in the South Pole, from June through September. When they hit, *friajes* drop the temperature to 48°F (9°C) for a period of 2 or 3 days. It's a good idea to pack a jacket and even some gloves on the off chance that the jungle turns cold on you.

River. The following lodges are several of the best that are easily accessible from Puerto Maldonado (as little as a half-hour by boat).

- **Sandoval Lake Lodge** ⋆⋆, Calle Ricardo Palma N J1, Urb Santa Monica, Cusco (② **084/255-255;** www.inkanatura.com). This pioneering lodge, located on high bluffs overlooking lovely Sandoval Lake (see p. 336) and surrounded by palm trees and thick forest, is the best option close to Puerto Maldonado if you're more into wildlife than plush accommodations. It is one of just three in the Amazon in a nationally protected zone, and by far its greatest advantage is its unique location on one of the jungle's prettiest oxbow lakes. The journey to the lodge is part of the experience; after a 45-minute boat ride, you walk a couple kilometers (another 45 minutes) through secondary forest, then you hop in a wooden canoe and paddle along a canal and then across the lake. The rustic, spacious facility consists of a large main dining room and lounge, and two wings of rooms with private bathrooms (but open ceilings). Wildlife-viewing centers around leisurely paddled catamaran and canoe trips on the lake at prime viewing hours, early morning and again in early evening; most visitors not only see a wealth of aquatic and jungle birds, including macaws, but several species of monkeys, caimans, and the elusive, highly prized community of giant river otters (on my last trip here I witnessed the complete group of 10 playing and lounging on a log in the lake). Prices range from $215 to $295 for 3- to 4-day stays. InkaNatura's newest lodge is the remote **Heath River Wildlife Center,** situated another 3 hours downriver near the Bolivian border, within easy reach of a large macaw clay lick and owned and staffed by the indigenous Ese'Eja Sonene people; it is possible to combine a couple of nights at either lodge. Heath River prices range from $530 for 4 days to $760 for 6 days. InkaNatura, which administers the lodge, is the Peruvian partner of the American environmental organization Tropical Nature (which handles international marketing). Outside Peru, trips can be organized through **Tropical Nature Travel,** P.O. Box 5276 Gainesville, FL 32627-5276 (② **877/827-8350** toll-free in the U.S. and Canada; www.tropicalnaturetravel.com).

- **Reserva Amazónica Lodge** ⋆⋆, Plaza Las Nazarenas 211, Cusco (② **800/442-5042** in U.S. and Canada; 800/458-7506 in the U.K.; 084/245-314 in Cusco or 01/610-0400 in Lima; www.inkaterra.com). Although one of the oldest lodges in the Peruvian Amazon, this recently upgraded place—operated by the folks behind the swanky Machu Picchu Pueblo Hotel—just 15km (9⅓ miles), or 1 hour down the Madre de Dios from Puerto Maldonado, is also one of the plushest. In other words, it is *the* place for an upscale jungle experience and creature comforts. Its large main house, stylishly designed like an Indian roundhouse, features a dining room and upstairs lounge, perfect for swilling drinks after a day in the jungle. The 43 thatched-roof, African-style bungalows, attractively strewn about the riverside property, are a model of rustic chic, a fancy step up from most accommodations in the jungle. Rooms have private bathrooms and terraces with hammocks. Though there's no electricity in the rooms, the kerosene lamps left at the door add to the romance of the place. The superior cabanas and suites are particularly luxurious. Food is excellent, and the guides are very professional (they even wear matching Disney-like eco-outfits). Although the surrounding forest doesn't teem with wildlife (except for sonorous russet-backed Oropendula birds that make waking up a treat), there's a good system of trails nearby, as well as an island that is

---

Fun Fact What's an Oxbow Lake?

An oxbow lake is a natural lake formed by the normal shifting of river waters, which have fashioned a new streambed in the riverbanks. The old riverbed fills with water and forms a lake. Oxbow lakes are essentially designed to become extinct. After forming, they have life expectancies of perhaps 400 years; they expand but then become shallower as river flooding and run-off deposits sediment, sand, and leaves and then begin to dry up as grasses and trees take root. Oxbow lakes, which can be very large and superb spots for wildlife viewing, are so named because they are shaped like an old-fashioned U-shaped yoke.

---

home to a dozen or so rescued monkeys and a terrific new canopy walk. A small spa that offers massages will be expanding its services. Rates range from $245 for 2 nights in a standard cabana to $540 for 3 nights in a swanky Amazonia suite.

- **EcoAmazonia Lodge,** Calle Garcilazo 210, Of. 206, Cusco (© **084/236-159;** www.ecoamazonia.com.pe). About an hour by boat from Puerto Maldonado, this large lodge features long rows of basic bungalows and trails that lead to a canopy-viewing platform. It's a friendly and comfortable place that primarily caters to large groups, and it offers *ayahuasca* ceremonies (see "Trippin' Amazon Style" on p. 360). A 2-day, 1-night stay is $110.

TAMBOPATA LODGES
South of Puerto Maldonado: Along Río Tambopata

- **Explorer's Inn** ⭐⭐⭐, the only lodge located within the Tambopata National Reserve, is a comfortable 30-year-old lodge that hosts both ecotourists and scientists. It's a little over 3 hours upriver from Puerto Maldonado along the Tambopata River, and is excellent for viewing fauna, including otters, monkeys, and particularly jungle birds. Accommodations are in rustic, thatched-roof bungalows. The inn is excellent for fauna, particularly jungle birds. (It's probably the top spot in Tambopata for birding.) Established in 1976, the complex has seven thatched-roof bungalows and 30 rooms with private bathrooms. The lodge has a good network of nearly 32km (20 miles) of trails, including several to nearby oxbow lakes. Guides are Peruvian and international biologists (or biologists in training). Trips are arranged through **Peruvian Safaris,** Alcanfores 459, Miraflores, Lima (© **01/447-8888;** www.explorersinn.com or www.peruviansafaris.com), or Plateros 365, Cusco (© **084/235-342**). Prices range from $180 for 2 nights to $450 for a 4-night Macaw Clay Lick program.

- **Posada Amazonas** ⭐, about 2 hours up the Tambopata River from Puerto Maldonado, is owned jointly with the Infierno indigenous community and is quite good for inexpensive, introductory nature tours. It has an eagle nest site and a canopy observation tower, and two parrot clay licks are located within a kilometer of the lodge. The lodge, inaugurated in 1998, featuring 30 rustic rooms and a wall open to the forest, is operated by the award-winning **Rainforest Expeditions** ⭐⭐, Portal de Carnes 236, Cusco (© **877/905-3782** in the U.S., or 084/232-772 or 01/421-8347), and Jr. Arequipa 401, Puerto Maldonado (© **082/571-056;** www.perunature.com). This veteran ecotourism company promotes tourism with environmental education, research, and conservation, and operates two Tambopata lodges. The 13-room **Tambopata Research Center** 𝕽𝕽𝕽 is more remote (8 hr. upriver from Puerto Maldonado), located just 500 meters from the jungle's largest and most famous Macaw Clay Lick. Just one of three Peruvian lodges in a protected national nature reserve, it is the best lodge in Tambopata for in-depth tours and viewing wildlife, including several species of monkeys. It's certainly *the* place to see flocks of colorful macaws and parrots. Trips usually entail an overnight at Posada Amazonas before continuing on to the Research Center. Prices are $690 to $870 for 5- to 7-day trips.

• **Libertador Tambopata Lodge,** Nueva Baja 432, Cusco (© **084/245-695;** www. tambopatalodge.com). Operated by an upscale Peruvian hotel chain, this private reserve lodge is about 3 hours upstream from Puerto Maldonado along the Río Tambopata. The lodge, with a handsome dining room and bar, is more luxurious than most and has more of a jungle hotel feel than others; newer bungalows are constructed of cement rather than wood. The lodge has 25km (16 miles) of trails nearby, including trails to lake systems on the opposite bank of the Tambopata River, in about 100 hectares of secondary forest, and offers overnight trips to the macaw clay lick. Prices range from $211 for 3 days to $585 for 5 nights.

MANU BIOSPHERE RESERVE 𝕽𝕽𝕽
242km (150 miles) NE of Cusco

Manu, a UNESCO World Biosphere Reserve and World Heritage Site, certainly doesn't lack for distinctions and accolades. The Biosphere Reserve encompasses the least accessible and explored jungle of primary and secondary forest in Peru, and it is about as close as you're likely to come to virgin rainforest anywhere in the world. In fact, it's so remote that not only did the Spaniards, who found their way to virtually every corner of Peru except Machu Picchu, never enter the jungle, but the Incas, who created an empire that stretched from Ecuador to Chile, never conquered the region, either. The forest wasn't really penetrated until the late 1800s, when rubber barons and loggers set their sights on it. Peru declared it a national park in 1973.

Tips **Birds, Plants? Check. Monkeys and Macaws? Check. Caimans? Check. Jaguars? Good Luck!**

Peru's Amazon jungle regions have some of the greatest recorded biodiversity and species of plants and animals on earth. However, you may be disappointed if you go expecting a daily episode of *Wild Kingdom.* An expedition to the Amazon is not like a safari to the African savanna. Many mammals are extremely difficult to see in the thick jungle vegetation, and though the best tour operators employ guides skilled in ferreting them out, there are no guarantees. Even in the most virgin sections, after devoting several patient days to the exercise, you are unlikely to see a huge number of mammals, especially the rare large species such as tapirs, jaguars, and giant river otters. If you spot a single one of these prized mammals, your jungle expedition can be considered a roaring success. (Your best shot at seeing jaguars is in Manu during the months of May and June.) However, in both Manu and Tambopata you are very likely to see a wealth of jungle birds (including the region's famous and fabulous macaws), several species of monkeys, black caimans, butterflies, and insects.

> ## ⟨Tips⟩ Manu Tour Considerations
>
> The best deals are usually available by arranging your trip on-site in Cusco rather than your home country. However, doing so carries some risks. Your chosen tour operator might not have space available. Another warning worth heeding is that previous travelers have gone to Manu but had their returns delayed (by weather conditions and mechanical and other mishaps) by several days. It's wise to schedule a Manu expedition in the middle of your trip, with a few buffer days before your scheduled departure.

Only slightly smaller than the Pacaya-Samiria National Reserve (see "Into the Wild: Farther Afield from Iquitos" on p. 362), Manu—about half the size of Switzerland—is one of the largest protected areas in South America, with just less than 2 million hectares (nearly 5 million acres). Its surface area of varied habitats includes Andes highlands, cloud forests, and lowland tropical rainforests. The park encompasses an area of almost unimaginable diversity, climbing as it does from an altitude near sea level to elevations of 3,500m (11,480 ft.).

A single hectare of forest in Manu might have 10 times the number of species of trees that a hectare of temperate forest in Europe or North America has. Manu, which contains the highest bird, mammal, and plant diversity of any park on the planet, offers visitors perhaps their best opportunity for viewing wildlife that has been pushed deep into the rainforest by man's presence. It boasts nearly 1,000 species of birds, 1,200 species of butterflies, 20,000 plants, 200 species of mammals, and 13 species of primates. Species in danger of extinction include the spectacled bear, giant armadillo, and cock-of-the-rock.

Birders thrill at the prospect of glimpsing bird populations that account for 10% of the world's total, more than what's found in all of Costa Rica. Hugely prized among wildlife observers are giant river otters, parrots, and macaws at a riverbank clay lick; preening and bright red cocks-of-the-rock; and lumbering lowland tapirs gathering at a forest clay lick. Scientists estimate that perhaps 12,000 to 15,000 animal species remain to be identified. Manu is also home to dozens of native Amerindian tribes, some of which have contact with the modern world and others that remain secluded.

Going with a group tour to Manu is the only realistic way to visit the park, and only a handful of travel agencies in Cusco are authorized to organize excursions to the Manu Biosphere Reserve. The Reserve comprises three zones: **Manu National Park,** an area of dedicated conservation reserved for scientific study (the largest zone, it occupies 3.7 million hectares/9.1 million acres, or about three-fourths of the entire reserve); the **Reserve Zone,** up the River Manu northwest of Boca Manu, accessible by permit and accompanied by an authorized guide only for ecotourist activities; and the Multi-Use or **Cultural Zone,** home to traditional nomadic groups and open to all visitors. Traveling independently to the Cultural Zone is possible but extremely demanding and time-consuming—too much so for all but the hardiest ecoadventurers with plenty of time.

Most trips to Manu visit jungle trails and lakes Cocha Salvador and Cocha Otorongo. Both are uniquely endowed with wildlife, including several types of caimans and wild monkeys. Cocha Otorongo is home to a prized, endangered group of giant otters. Virtually all tours make stops at key observation piers, platforms, and towers for wildlife viewing. Many longer Manu trips include visits to a macaw clay lick.

Getting to Manu is itself an ecoadventure. Overland access to the Manu Reserve Zone from Cusco (from Puerto Maldonado is much more difficult) is a stunning (and stunningly beautiful) 2-day journey through 4,000m (13,120-ft.) mountains and cloud forest before descending into lowland rainforest. The scenery along the narrow road, full of switchbacks and great panoramic views of glaciers and the eastern Andes, is so extraordinary that many lodges and tour operators travel overland and return to Cusco by small aircraft (a 25-min. flight from Boca Manu). The trip passes through Paucartambo (see chapter 7) and travels along roads whose steep descents are thrilling—though unsettling to some travelers—on the way to high jungle. Bus or plane travel to Boca Manu is followed by up to a couple of days of river travel to lodges, campsites, and principal points of interest in the reserve. Because Manu is so isolated and access is so restricted, reserve visits are expensive and plainly beyond the scope of most budget travelers ($500–$2000 or more per person for a 5- to 8-day trip). Most visits to Manu require about a week.

MANU TOUR OPERATORS

Only eight tour companies are permitted to run organized expeditions to Manu, and the number of travelers they can take there each week is strictly limited. The best firms listed below are closely involved with conservation efforts and local development programs. The least expensive expeditions bus travelers in and out or return by small plane. Land (and river) travel is very time-consuming, but it makes for an excellent opportunity to experience the diverse terrain and types of forest that comprise Manu. Note that most companies operate with fixed departure dates only in the dry season, from May to November. The prices below do not include air transportation from Cusco.

Most of the tour operators below post detailed itineraries and information about their Manu trips on their websites.

- **InkaNatura** _&&&_, Calle Ricardo Palma N J1 Urb Santa Monica, Cusco, ((© **084/ 255-255;** www.inkanatura.com). Perhaps the most serious and sophisticated outfit operating ecotourism trips in the Peruvian Amazon, InkaNatura, associated with the Peruvian conservation group PerúVerde and the American organization Tropical Nature, organizes stays at the famed **Manu Wildlife Center.** The lodge, opened in 1996, is located near the world's largest tapir clay lick, as well as the Blanquillo macaw clay lick, and it features 48km (30 miles) of nature trails and

---

Tips **All Alone in the Forest . . . with a Few Good Friends**

As remote and huge as the Manu Reserve Zone is, don't expect to find yourself enveloped and alone in the quiet of the jungle during high season. The few lodges and tour operators with a presence in the zone are very busy during the months of June, July, and August, and travelers' contact with each other might greatly outdistance their contact with species native to the rainforest. This is the case despite the official limits of 30 travelers per agency per week. (If all 10 agencies have full loads, that's still 300 people traveling many of the same waterways and racing to arrive first at primary observation points.)

two canopy-viewing platforms. Accommodations are in 22 spacious, private bungalows with tiled bathrooms. Packages at the Manu Wildlife Center range from 4 days and 3 nights for $1035 to 5 days and 4 nights for $1,135. InkaNatura also operates several lodges in Tambopata (see earlier). Outside Peru, trips can be organized through **Tropical Nature Travel,** P.O. Box 5276 Gainesville, FL 32627-5276 (**(℃ 877/827-8350** toll-free in the U.S.; www.tropicalnature travel.com).

Other Manu lodges run by InkaNatura include **Manu Wildlife Center** ⚘⚘ (of which InkaNatura is a joint owner); and **Cock-of-the-Rock Lodge,** in the Selva Sur Nature Reserve at an elevation of 1,600m (5,250 ft.), excellent for birders.

• **Manu Ecological Adventures,** Plateros 356, Cusco (**(℃ 084/261-640;** www.manu adventures.com). This 8-year-old agency offers some of the most affordable trips, ranging from 5 days/4 nights (in and out by plane, $724) to 8 days/7 nights (overland, $550), with 2 nights in open-air lodges and the rest in campsites. A 4-day visit to the Cultural Zone is $300 (overland).

• **Manu Expeditions** ⚘⚘⚘, Urbanización Magisterio, segunda Etapa G-5, P.O. Box 606, Cusco (**(℃ 084/226-671;** www.manuexpeditions.com). One of the pioneering ecotourism operators in southern Peruvian Amazon, Manu Expeditions—run by an ornithologist who is the British Consul in Cusco—has been organizing rainforest tours for more than 2 decades. Tours include stays at the **Manu Wildlife Center,** of which the group is part owner (see above), near the famed macaw clay lick, and a safari camp facility deep at Cocha Salvador within the Manu Biosphere Reserve. The Wildlife Center is considered the best lodge in Peru for birding. The longer tours include initial stays at the **Cock-of-the-Rock Lodge** in cloud forest. First departures of each month include stays at **Casa Machiguenga Lodge.** Four-, 6-, and 9-day tours range from $980 to $1,745 per person.

• **Manu Nature Tours** ⚘⚘⚘, Av. Pardo 1046, Cusco (**(℃ 084/252-721;** www. manuperu.com). A highly professional, prize-winning outfit with 20 years' experience in Manu—it was one of the first to send expeditions to the reserve—it operates the well-known and comfortable **Manu Lodge,** situated next to a pristine oxbow lake and the only full-service lodge within Manu National Park itself (5-day, 4-night trips, $929–$1,403), and the excellent **Manu Cloud Forest Lodge,** the first of its kind in Peru, overlooking a waterfall (3-day, 2-night trips, $314–$466). The agency claims that the oxbow lake is one of the best spots anywhere in the jungle to view giant river otters. Add-on options include mountain biking, rafting, and tree canopy climbs. The office in Cusco is attached to a Patagonia outdoor gear shop and a rainforest cafe, in case you needed any reassurance of their commitment. The agency has expanded its activities to include trekking programs in the southern and central highlands, as well as more traditional tourist trips throughout Peru.

• **Pantiacolla** ⚘, Saphy 554 or Plateros 341, Cusco (**(℃ 084/238-323;** www. pantiacolla.com). An initiative of a Dutch biologist and Boca Manu-born conservationist, this agency operates the small **Pantiacolla Lodge,** with double rooms in bungalows, on bluffs overlooking the Madre de Dios River at the edge of Manu National Park. The organization also operates a community-based ecotourism project with the Yine Indians of the Manu rainforest, with a lodge that will be entirely turned over to the community in 2011. Pantiacolla is favored by ecotravelers on a

Bird Watching and Macaw Clay Licks

While Tambopata is superb for bird watching, with nearly 600 species, Manu enjoys a nearly mythic reputation among birders. And it should: It has the highest concentration of birdlife on the planet. In addition to its many thousands of species of plants, more than a dozen species of monkeys, and hundreds of mammals, the Manu Biosphere Reserve contains some 1,000 species of birds, including seven species of colorful macaws. That's more than half the bird species in all of Peru—one of the top countries in the world (along with Colombia and Indonesia) for recorded bird species within its borders. That's more species than are found in all of Costa Rica, and it's one of every nine birds in the world! The forests of the western Amazon enjoy the highest density of birds per square mile of any on Earth.

The immense variety of birds is due to the diversity of altitudinal zones, habitats, and ecosystems spread across Manu, which encompasses cloud forest and upper and lowland tropical forest. In addition, Manu shimmers with vastly different types of forests, lakes, and microclimates. From the Andes Mountains surrounding Cusco, the road to Manu plummets an amazing 4,000m (13,120 ft.) down to the dense tropical forests of the Amazon basin. For every 1,000m (3,280 ft.) of change in elevation, the indigenous bird life changes just as dramatically. The twisting road near the Cock-of-the-Rock Lodge has been called "the best road in the world" by leading bird-tour companies.

In visits of just 2 to 3 weeks in Manu, dedicated birders have recorded a staggering 500 species. Birders can expect to come into contact with quetzals, toucanets, tanagers, and the famed, blazing-red Andean cocks-of-the-rock at their numerous leks. Also of interest to birders, among many dozens more, are the blue-headed macaw, white-cheeked tody-tyrant, bamboo antshrike, and Manu antbird. On riverbanks, expect daily sightings of giant macaws and other parrots, while mixed-feeding flocks containing dozens of different types of birds—a defense against predators—soar overhead.

budget, offering camping and lodge trips ranging from $745 for 5 days to $985 and up, depending on the number of travelers, for Cultural Zone lodge tours.

Other reputable Manu tour companies and lodges, which run economical camping-based trips, especially for budget travelers, include:

- **Expediciones Vilca,** Plateros 359, Cusco (© **084/253-773;** www.cbc.org.pe/manuvilca). Vilca has been organizing Manu expeditions for a decade, with trips that split time between lodges and campsites. It has earned a sturdy reputation among budget-minded travelers.
- **Mayuc,** Portal de Confiturías 211, Plaza de Armas, Cusco (© **084/242-824;** www.mayuc.com). Mayuc is a traditional tour operator with programs across Peru, plus good budget-camping programs to Manu.
- **SAS Travel,** Portal Panes 167, Plaza de Armas, Cusco (© **084/255-205;** www.sas travelperu.com). This well-run and popular all-purpose agency offers varied programs to both Manu and Tambopata, and stays at various lodges.

For many visitors, viewing *guacamayos,* or macaws, remains the holy grail of Amazon bird-watching. One of the most rewarding birding experiences in Tambopata or Manu is the spectacle of hundreds of macaws and other birds feeding at a *collpa,* or clay lick. Many birds and mammals (such as tapirs) supplement their diets with minerals found in clay, which is loaded with minerals and salts. Early in the morning, parrots gather in trees above the river. They then descend in large numbers and feed at the clay. Gorgeously colored and noisy macaws arrive next. Visitors often view the scene from a small catamaran. **Blanquillo Macaw and Parrot Lick,** the subject of a 1994 *National Geographic* report and subsequent TV special on macaws, is the most famous *collpa* in Manu. *Collpa* viewings are during the dry season only and are best from July to September; macaws do not feed at the clay licks during the month of June, for reasons unknown.

All the Manu tour operators focus to some extent on birding, of course, but for specialists, the **Manu Wildlife Center,** jointly owned by Manu Expeditions, itself run by a well-known ornithologist, is perhaps best suited for enthusiastic birding in Manu. Also recommended by birders is **Pantiacolla Lodge,** where birders have recorded 500 birds in a month's time. **Tanager Tours** ⍟, La Estrella F-9, J. L. Bustamante y Rivero, Arequipa (© 054/426-210; www.tanagertours.com), organizes birding trips to Manu, Puerto Maldonado, and many other spots in Peru; the Dutch-owned group also has a branch in Cusco.

Birders and would-be birders should check out **Birding Peru** (www.birdingperu.org) and **Ornifolks** (www.ornifolks.org) for additional bird-watching trips to Peru. **WorldTwitch** (www.worldtwitch.com) has helpful links to birding lodges, tour operators, and organizations throughout Peru, as well as the Americas and the Caribbean.

2 Iquitos & the Northern Amazon ⍟⍟

1,860km (1,156 miles) NE of Lima

Iquitos, the gateway to the northern Amazon, is Peru's largest jungle town and the capital of its largest department, Loreto, which occupies nearly a third of the national territory and is nearly the size of Germany. You must fly to get here—unless you have a week to kill for hot and uncomfortable river travel—but the pockets of jungle down- and upriver from Iquitos are among the most accessible of the Peruvian Amazon basin. Some of the best jungle lodges in the country, some of which are approaching their fifth decade of ecotourism, are located just a few hours by boat from Iquitos. Because the region is the most trafficked and developed of the Peruvian Amazon, costs are lower for most jungle excursions than they are in the more exclusive Manu Biosphere Reserve in southeastern Peru.

The most important port city of the Amazon lies at the confluence of the Nanay and Itaya rivers. The city was founded in 1754 by Jesuit missionaries, although some

The Amazon in Danger

Could the vast Amazon rainforest disappear from the face of the Earth during our lifetimes? Some scientists now maintain that the forest itself—not to mention the many thousands of plant, animal, bird, and insect species that call it home—is in imminent danger of extinction. A mathematical model by an American researcher, presented at a 2001 Geology Society conference in Scotland, suggests that the destruction of Amazonian rainforests could be irreversible in less than 10 years, and forecasts the wholesale destruction of Brazil's rainforest in 40 or 50 years.

Peru, the origin of the great Amazon River, boasts some of the largest and most biologically diverse rainforests in the world. The country counts 84 of 103 existing ecosystems and 28 of the 32 climates on the planet among its remarkable statistics. Peru has 72 million hectares (178 million acres) of natural-growth forests—70% in the Amazon jungle region—that comprise nearly 60% of the national territory. But Peru is losing nearly 300,000 hectares (740,000 acres) of rainforest annually. In other Amazon basin countries, the picture is even bleaker. Half the world's known plant and animal species live in rainforests, but according to the World Resources Institute, more than 100 species become extinct in the world every day due to tropical deforestation. Less than 50 years ago, 15% of the earth's land surface was rainforest. Today that total has been reduced to a mere 6%.

The primary threats to Peru's tropical forests are deforestation caused by agricultural expansion, cattle ranching, logging, oil extraction and spills, mining, illegal coca farming, and colonization initiatives. In the southern Amazon's Madre de Dios department, 3 decades of gold prospecting have pushed isolated Mashco-Piros, Amahuaca, Yaminahuas, and Yora tribes to the edge of extinction. Knowledge of plants and natural medicines, traditional ways of life, and even languages are lost.

Governments in developing countries have traditionally been reluctant to adopt tough measures to halt deforestation, bowing to the need for "economic development" and offering inducements to industry and extraction practices that have ranged from rubber extraction to logging and oil drilling. Slash-and-burn clearing of land, unproductive farming, and overhunting by marginalized people living in and around the jungle have further denuded the landscape of vegetation and animals. And, 500 years ago, an estimated 10 million indigenous people inhabited the Amazon rainforest; by the 21st century, that population had dropped to less than 200,000.

Can anything be done to save the Amazon and its people, plants, and animals? Leaving the rainforests intact, with their wealth of nuts, fruits, oil-producing plants, and medicinal plants, has greater economic value than destroying them for unsustainable short-term interests. More than six times as much can be earned from sustainable harvests of fruit, cocoa, timber, and rubber from the rainforest tract than commercial logging produces. Slash-and-burn practices destroy the land's capacity to produce: A plot can be burned just twice before a farmer must abandon it and search for another, uncultivated piece of land.

For most of the 20th century, Peru gave carte blanche to oil and gas exploration by multinationals in the Amazon basin, and the government looked the other way with regard to invasive gold mining in Indian communities. However, Peru has done a slightly better job of setting aside tracts of rainforest as national park reserves and regulating industry than have some other Latin American and Asian countries. The Manu Biosphere Reserve, the Tambopata National Reserve, and the Pacaya-Samiria National Reserve are three of the largest protected rainforest areas in the world, and the government regulates entry of tour groups. INRENA, Peru's Institute for Natural Resource Management, enforces logging regulations and reseeds Peru's Amazon forests. A handful of international and Peruvian environmental and conservation groups, such as ProNaturaleza, Conservation International, and the Rainforest Action Network are active in Peru, working on reforestation and sustainable forestry projects.

What about ecotourism initiatives in the rainforest? Do visitors to lodges in primary forest and jungle trekkers add to the threats facing native communities and species, or do they in some way ensure their protection? Many conservationists have mixed feelings about promoting ecotourism in endangered habitats. Responsible tourism has the potential to educate people about the rainforest and its threats and could spur much-needed activism. The income produced by ecotourism is vital to local communities—many of whom are increasingly dependent upon tourists to buy their handicrafts or to lead on treks into the jungle—and to countries, as an incentive to protect the very things tourists come to see. A small handful of lodges in the rainforest have successfully integrated local tribes into the running of the lodges. But mankind's heavier imprints in the jungle are, of course, a potentially grave threat, pushing species and native communities ever farther from their natural habitats.

The lodges and tour operators I've recommended for travel in the Amazon all profess to practice responsible, low-impact tourism. Please do your utmost to follow suit. If you witness a tour group or lodge practicing unsafe ecotourism, by all means report it to either **INRENA** (© **01/224-3298**) or **PromPerú** (© **01/224-3279**; www.promperu.org), or to the tourist information offices in Cusco (© **084/263-176**) or Iquitos (© **065/235-621**).

For additional information on threatened species, visit the **World Conservation Union**'s website at www.iucn.org and check out its "Red Book" list. Other excellent resources are the **World Rainforest Information Portal** at www.rainforestweb.org and the **Survival International** website at www.survival-international.org.

continue to claim that it actually was not founded until nearly a century later. The city's proximity to South America's greatest rainforest and its isolation from the rest of Peru have created a unique tropical atmosphere. In the late 1860s and 1870s, pioneering merchants got rich off the booming rubber trade and built ostentatious mansions lined with glazed tiles along the river. Iquitos rivaled Manaus in Brazil for leadership of the rubber trade. The city went from boom to bust, although oil exploration, shipping, logging, and other export trade later revived and sustained the city's fortunes. Today tourism is quite evidently among Iquitos's most important industries.

Iquitos is far from the grand port of old. The modern city of nearly a half-million is composed of descendants of original ethnic groups such as the Yaguas, Boras, Kukama, and Iquitos, as well as significant populations of immigrant groups from Europe and Asia. Those great homes along the *malecón* are now faded monuments to the city's glory days, and just blocks from the main square lies the fascinating Belén district, where families live in a squalid pile of ramshackle wooden houses on the banks of the river. Some are propped up by spindly stilts, while others float, tethered to poles, when the river rises 6m (20 ft.) or more.

The Belén district looks distinctly Far Eastern, and Iquitos has more in common with steamy tropical Asian cities than the highlands of Peru. Like a South American Saigon, the air is waterlogged and the streets buzz with unrelenting waves of motorcycles and motocarros. Locals speak a languid, mellifluous Spanish unmatched in other parts of the country, and pretty prostitutes loll about the Plaza de Armas. Locals dress not in alpaca sweaters and shawls, but in flesh-baring tank tops and short skirts.

Iquitos has a relaxed, intoxicating feel that's likely to detain you for a couple of days at least. But for most visitors, the lure of the Amazon rainforest is the primary attraction. Virgin rainforest, though, is hard to find. To lay eyes on exotic wildlife, such as pink dolphins, caimans, and macaws, you have to get far away from Iquitos, at least

---

Tips Malaria & Yellow Fever in Northern Peru

According to the Centers for Disease Control and Prevention, epidemic malaria rapidly emerged in the northern Amazon in the 1990s. Peru has the second-highest number of malaria cases in South America (after Brazil), with the majority of cases from the Loreto department. From 1992 to 1997, malaria increased 50 times in Loreto, a rate more than 10 times greater than in the rest of the country. Malaria around the city of Iquitos accounts for the greatest number of cases in Loreto.

In 2001, the Peruvian Ministry of Health also reported an outbreak of yellow fever in the Loreto department in three districts, including Iquitos. Eight cases of yellow fever were confirmed, with two deaths. In 2003, the Pan American Health Organization recorded 22 cases and 13 deaths in Peru, just one of five Latin American nations grappling with an outbreak that claimed 99 lives by the end of the year.

These outbreaks should not deter most travelers from visiting the Amazon of northern Peru, but they should emphasize the need for proper vaccinations and medication before (and during) traveling to the region. See "Health & Safety," in chapter 2, for more information.

The Northern Amazon

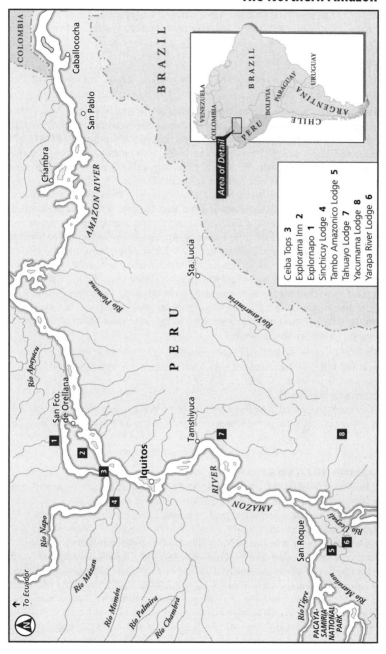

Ceiba Tops **3**
Explorama Inn **2**
Explornapo **1**
Sinchicuy Lodge **4**
Tambo Amazonico Lodge **5**
Tahuayo Lodge **7**
Yacumama Lodge **8**
Yarapa River Lodge **6**

COLOMBIA

Caballocoocha

San Pablo

Chambra

AMAZON RIVER

BRAZIL

Río Plomana

Sta. Lucia

Río Yanamimún

PERU

Río Apayacu

San Fco. de Orellana

1

2

Iquitos

3

Tamshiyuca

7

8

AMAZON RIVER

4

Río Napo

To Ecuador

Río Mazan

Río Momón

Río Palmira

Río Chambra

San Roque

5

6

Río Ucayali

Río Tigre

Río Marañón

PACAYA-SAMIRIA NATIONAL PARK

N

Area of Detail

VENEZUELA

COLOMBIA

BRAZIL

PERU

BOLIVIA

PARAGUAY

URUGUAY

CHILE

ARGENTINA

80km (50 miles) out and onto secondary waterways. Options for rainforest excursions include lodge visits, river cruises, and, for the adventurous, independent guided treks.

ESSENTIALS
GETTING THERE
Water-locked Iquitos can be reached only by airplane or boat. For most travelers, air is the only practical option.

BY PLANE Iquitos's **Aeropuerto Francisco Secada Vigneta,** Av. Abelardo Quiñones Km 6 (© **065/260-147**) was once an international airport, receiving flights from Miami, but those were suspended several years ago. **Aviandina** (© **01/242-4242** or 01/484-1177) and **TANS** (© **01/213-6000;** www.tansperu.com.pe) fly daily to Iquitos from Lima and from Pucallpa and Tarapoto, other cities in the Loreto department. Flights from Lima cost between $69 and $79.

The airport is usually chaotic when flights arrive, with dozens of representatives of tour operators, and countless touts and con men competing for your attention. Do not let anyone take your bags, and don't let anyone you don't know hop in a cab with you. Definitely wait before even discussing Amazon lodge packages. To downtown Iquitos, an automobile taxi costs about S/10 ($2.85); a motocarro costs S/7 ($2). If a taxi driver offers to take you for less, he will certainly take you directly to a hotel where he can earn commission, not where you necessarily want to go. (The difference could be a lot more than the few soles you save on the taxi fare.) City buses (S/.50 or 14¢) are available outside the gates of the airport on the main road (they travel along Ocampo/Tacna/Grau), but unless you have a very manageable backpack as your only luggage, it's not worth the hassle.

BY BOAT Arriving by boat is an option only for those with the luxury of ample time and patience. It takes about a week when the river is high (and 3–4 days in the dry season) to reach the capital city of Loretos upriver along the Amazon from Pucallpa or Yurimaguas.

To travel to Colombia or Brazil by boat, your best bet is by river cruise, although in 2002, trips to Manaus were suspended and there is no word of them being reinstated. The Iquitos port, Puerto Masusa, is about 3km (1¾ miles) north of the Plaza de Armas. See "Cruises," later in this section, for more details.

VISITOR INFORMATION
A municipal **tourism information booth** (© **065/260-251**) is at the arrivals terminal baggage claim at the airport. It maintains a chart of hotels and costs, and the staff is happy to dispense information (and frequently opinions) about the various jungle-tour and lodge operators.

One of Peru's most helpful tourism information offices is on the north side of the Plaza de Armas at Napo 232 (© **065/236-144**). The English-speaking staff has free maps and lists of all recommended hotels and tour operators (including photo albums of lodges), and will try to sort through the (often intentionally) confusing sales pitches of jungle-tour companies. The office is open Monday through Saturday from 8am to 8pm, as well as occasional Sunday mornings.

FAST FACTS ATMs and banks are located along Putumayo and Próspero, on the south side of the Plaza de Armas. Two banks that exchange traveler's checks and cash are **Banco de Crédito,** Putumayo 201 at Próspero, and **Banco Continental,** Sargento Lores 171. Money-changers can usually be found hanging around the Plaza de Armas

ATTRACTIONS ●
Barrio de Belén
  (market & port) **18**
Casa de Fierro **9**
Iglesia Matriz **10**
Lago Moronacocha &
  Santo Tomás **16**
Malecón Tarapacá **12**
Museo Amazónico **14**
Parque/Laguna
  de Quistococha **17**
Plaza de Armas **7**
Puerto Bellavista/Río Nanay **1**

ACCOMMODATIONS ■
El Dorado Plaza Hotel **6**
Hobo Hideout
  Travellers Hotel **11**
Hospedaje La Pascana **2**
Hotel Victoria Regia **15**
Real Hotel Iquitos **8**

DINING ◆
El Nuevo Mesón **3**
Fitzcarraldo **4**
Montecarlo **5**
Regal (Casa de Fierro) **9**
Restaurant Gran Maloca **13**

and along Putumayo and Próspero, but calculate the exchange beforehand and count your money carefully.

If you're looking to cross into Brazil or Colombia, the **Brazilian Consulate** is located at Sargento Lores 363 (℗ **065/232-081**), and the **Colombian Consulate** is at Callao 200 (℗ **065/231-461**). You should make contact with the embassies in Lima or even at home before traveling to Peru. For questions about border-crossing formalities for jungle travel to and from Brazil and Colombia, visit or call the **Migraciones** office at Malecón Tarapacá 382 (℗ **065/235-371**).

In an **emergency,** call ℗ 105. You can also call **Cruz Roja (Red Cross)** at ℗ 065/ 241-072 for medical emergencies, and ℗ 065/267-555 for **fire emergencies.** For medical attention, go to one of the following hospitals or clinics: **Clínica Ana Stahl,** Av. la Marina 285 (℗ 065/252-535); **EsSalud,** Av. la Marina 2054 (℗ 065/250-333);

or **Hospital Regional de Loreto,** Av. 28 de Julio s/n, Punchana (✆ 065/252-004). The **tourist police** office is located at Sargento Lores 834 (✆ 065/242-081). There's also a **Tourist Protection Service** office at Huallaga 311 (✆ 065/243-490).

Most Internet *cabinas* in Iquitos stay open late, and rates are about S/2 (60¢) per hour. One to try is **Estación Internet,** Fitzcarrald 120 (✆ **065/223-608**). Several other cabinas are located near the Plaza de Armas, particularly on Próspero and Putumayo. The small cabina (no name) next to the entrance to the Casa de Fierro is pretty dependable.

Iquitos's **post office** is located at Arica 403, on the corner of Morona (✆ 065/223-812); it's open Monday through Saturday from 8am to 7:30pm. The **Telefónica del Perú** office is at Arica 276; it's open Monday through Friday from 9am to 6pm.

GETTING AROUND

For all practical purposes, Iquitos is an island city, defined by water—not just the mighty Amazon, which borders it to the west, but also a complex network of smaller rivers and streams, and a series of lakes just outside the city. The riverfront along the Amazon is a long boulevard, Malecón Tarapacá, with a pedestrian walkway. It reaches all the way from the focal point of downtown, restaurants and bars near the Plaza de Armas, to the shabby but picturesque Belén district. Próspero is the main avenue of communication from the main square to residential zones south.

BY MOTOTAXI & TAXI   Motocarros are everywhere in Iquitos; if you don't mind the noise and wind in your face (and aren't worried about accidents), it's a great way to get around. In-town fares are S/1.50 (40¢). Regular car taxis are only slightly less ubiquitous; most trips in town cost S/2 (60¢).

BY BUS   *Combis* and *ómnibuses* (buses) travel principal routes but are much less comfortable and not much less expensive than more convenient motocarros. The fare is S/0.50 (15¢).

BY MOTORCYCLE   If you want to travel around town as Iquiteños do, rent a small *moto,* or motorcycle. Try **Visión Motos,** Nauta 309 (✆ **065/234-759**). Rates are about $40 per day or $5 per hour.

BY FOOT   Although the city is spread over several square miles, the core of downtown Iquitos is compact and easy to get around on foot, and even the waterfront Belén district is easy to walk to. Some hostels and hotels are a distance from the main square, though, requiring at least the occasional use of inexpensive motocarros.

WHAT TO SEE & DO
IN IQUITOS

Although the **Plaza de Armas** is perhaps not Peru's most distinguished, it is, as always, one of the focal points in town. It is marked by the early-20th-century neo-Gothic **Iglesia Matríz** (parish church), built in 1919. Many of the church's most attractive elements, such as the tower, were later additions. Across the square stands the **Casa de Fierro,** or Iron House, which was designed by Gustave Eiffel for the 1889 Paris Exhibition. The walls, ceiling, and balcony are plastered in rectangular sheets of iron. Said to be the first prefabricated house in the Americas, it was shipped unassembled from Europe and built on-site where it currently stands.

One block back from the plaza, facing the Amazon River, the riverfront promenade **Malecón Tarapacá** was enlarged and improved a few years back with fountains (one a giant pink dolphin), benches, and street lamps, making it the focus of Iquitos urban

---

Tips Biblioteca Amazónica

The Iquitos municipal library, Biblioteca Amazónica (Malecón Tarapacá 354, 2nd floor; © 065/242-353), is a handsome public space inhabiting an old rubber baron's mansion and overlooking the *malecón* and Río Amazonas. The reading room features lots of carved wood and colorful tiles. If a visit to the Amazon has whetted your appetite for old maps or information on the jungle, you can find it here, in the largest collection of historical documents on the Amazon basin in Peru. It's open Monday through Friday from 9am to noon.

---

life. The *malecón* is lined with several exquisite 19th-century mansions, relics from the rubber heyday, lined with Portuguese glazed tiles, or *azulejos*. The most spectacular is probably **Casa Hernández,** nos. 302–308. Other houses worth checking out along the boulevard are **Casa Fitzcarrald,** Napo 200–212, an adobe house belonging to a famed rubber baron; **Casa Cohen,** Próspero 401–437; **Casa Morey,** Brasil, on the first block off the *malecón;* and the **Logia Unión Amazónica,** Nauta 262.

The **Museo Amazónico,** Malecón Tarapacá 386 (© 065/231-072), occasionally has interesting exhibits of Amazon folklore and tribal art, and a curious collection of 76 Indian statues made of fiberglass but fashioned as if they were bronze. Reportedly, some of the mothers whose children served as models for the works freaked out when they were covered in plaster for the moulds, thinking the children would be buried alive. The museum building, which dates to the mid–19th century, is a nicely restored example of the *malecón*'s period mansions. The museum is open Monday through Friday from 8am to 1pm and 3 to 7pm, and Saturday from 9am to 1pm. Admission is S/3 (85¢).

The waterfront **Barrio de Belén** *←*, about a 15-minute walk south along the *malecón,* is Iquitos's most unusual quarter. Known for its sprawling, colorful, and odiferous open-air market, where you'll find a bounty of strange and wonderful Amazon fish, fauna, and fruits, Belén's residential district is a seedy and extremely poor but endlessly fascinating shantytown. Houses are constructed above the waters of the Amazon, and when the river is high, transportation is by canoe. Visitors are free to walk about in dry season (or, for much of the year, to take a locally arranged canoe trip) and see the houses—some on stilts, others floating during the rainy season; go in a group and during the day only. It's an atmospheric and photogenic place, akin to Calcutta—you'll see scrappy kids tumbling out of clapboard houses and playing with pet monkeys, and a few houses proudly outfitted with cable TV and other modern conveniences. Exercise some caution and restraint if walking around the area with expensive camera equipment. Most residents of the neighborhood, while perhaps puzzled at foreigners' interest in the aesthetics of their dilapidated streets, are more than approachable for photos, if you ask respectfully. The animated market, which extends over several blocks, is itself a wild place to visit, with all sorts of extraordinary exotic items for sale, including potions used by faith healers, *paiche* fish, and yummy Amazonian fruits such as *maracuyá* (passion fruit), *aguaje, cocona,* and others. Look for the stands set up with blenders, cranking out fruit juices and smoothies (*refrigerios* and *jugos*).

ATTRACTIONS NEAR IQUITOS
PUERTO BELLAVISTA & RIO NANAY   This Río Mañon port and suburb, a couple kilometers from downtown at the northern edge of Iquitos, has a pretty white-sand

beach (Playa Nanay) that locals enjoy and that is safe for swimming during summer months. It's also a good spot to hire a boat and cruise down to the confluence of the Amazon and Nanay rivers, where you can appreciate the difference in water colors (muddy brown and black), passing beaches, and a handful of local communities—among them the Boras and Yaguas—along the way. To get there, take a colectivo marked "Bellavista/Nanay," which leaves from points along Próspero.

PARQUE/LAGUNA DE QUISTOCOCHA A resort complex about 13km (8 miles) south of Iquitos, the Quistococha Lagoon and Tourist Park has a nice beach and swimming area. It's mostly a spot for local families to hang out on weekends. There are picnic grounds, paddleboats, an aquarium, a walking path around the lagoon, and a zoo with exotic jungle animals and fish, including monkeys, serpents, jaguars, and pumas. A fish hatchery is populated by giant *paiche* fish. There's a restaurant on the grounds, as well as informal food stalls set up near the entrance to the park. To get there, you can take a 20-minute ride in a motocarro (about $3) or catch a colectivo marked "Quistococha" (S/2 or 60¢) on the corner of Moore and Bermúdez.

LAGO MORONACOCHA & SANTO TOMAS Southwest of Iquitos, the lake at Moronacocha is little more than a place to relax at a couple of bars by the water, although locals head out there to swim and water-ski. Another 16km (10 miles) or so south of Moronacocha is another lake complex, Rumococha, and the small fishing village of Santo Tomás, known for its pottery artisans. It also has a lake (Lago Mapacocha) and resortlike activities, such as paddleboats and dugout canoes. To get there, board a colectivo marked AEROPUERTO on Tacna/Grau; ask to be let off at the turnoff to Santo Tomás. There are colectivos waiting at the intersection that ferry people back and forth to Santo Tomás. You can also get there by motocarro; the 20-minute ride is about $4.

SHOPPING IN IQUITOS

The most intriguing shopping option is the Belén open-air market (see above), although you'll likely find more to photograph and smell than to actually buy. For local artisans' goods, there aren't many options; try **Centro Artesanal Anaconda,** Malecón Tarapacá-Boulevard, the sparsely populated market downstairs from the *malecón,* or **Mercado Artesanal de San Juan,** the larger market with wooden outdoor stalls selling hammocks, woodcarvings, and paintings. The market's on Avenida Quiñones Km 4.5, on the way out to the airport (about 3km/1¾ miles from downtown). Unlike most markets in Peru, here many of the sellers are also the craftspeople behind the work. Some of the best crafts, including textiles and pottery, come from the Shipibo Indian tribe of the Amazon.

Art Gallery Camu-Camu, Trujillo 498 (© **065/253-120**), showcases the work of the most famous local artist, Francisco Grippa, whose colorful paintings evoke Amazonian themes, including jungle flora and fauna. Grippa's exuberant and expressive style, known in the United States and Europe, has been labeled "grippismo." He uses local materials, including a canvas made from tree bark. The gallery is open daily from 10am to 1pm and 4 to 7pm. Tour groups often visit the Grippa's home/gallery in Pevas, the oldest town in the Peruvian Amazon, about 150km (93 miles) downriver from Iquitos.

JUNGLE TOURS, LODGES & RIVER CRUISES

The mighty Amazon reaches widths of about 4km (2½ miles) beyond Iquitos, and the river basin contains 2,000 species of fish (among them everyone's favorite, piranhas);

4,000 species of birds (including 120 hummingbirds); native mammals such as anteaters, tapirs, marmosets, and pink dolphins; and 60 species of reptiles, including caimans and anacondas.

Although the town itself holds a kind of sultry fascination, ecotourism is the primary draw for visitors to Iquitos, and the giant Amazon river system just beyond the city holds a wealth of natural wonders: rustic jungle lodges, canopy walks, and opportunities for bird-watching, piranha fishing, visits to Indian villages, and wildlife spotting (as well as less-standard activities, such as shaman consultations and *ayahuasca* drug ceremonies). Your options for exploring the jungle are **lodge stays,** which include jungle activities such as treks and canoe excursions; **river cruises;** or more adventurous **camping treks** with private guides. Most people head for lodges of varying degrees of rusticity and distance from Iquitos. The jungle is immense, and most parts of it are inaccessible. Immersing yourself in anything resembling pristine jungle is both costly and time-consuming. The northern Amazon basin within reach of Iquitos has been explored and popularly exploited far longer than the more remote southern jungle areas of Manu and Tambopata.

Don't expect to spend your time in the jungle checking off a lengthy wildlife list of sightings; no matter where you go, your opportunities for viewing more than a couple of species of birds, fish, and mammals will be severely limited. You'll see lots of birds and, if you're lucky, perhaps a few monkeys, caimans, and pink dolphins. (For deeper and more adventurous treks into the jungle, see "Into the Wild: Farther Afield from Iquitos," on p. 362, and "Independent Guides," later in this section.)

For a quick and simple experience, you can stay at a lodge only an hour or two (within a 50km/31-mile radius) by boat from Iquitos, in secondary jungle. You're likely to see more fauna and have a more authentic experience in primary rainforest, but you'll have to travel much farther (beyond a radius of 80km/50 miles; up to 4 hr. by boat) and pay quite a bit more for the privilege. Generally, you must trade comforts for authenticity. Very short trips (2–3 days) are unlikely to produce much in the way of wildlife, although you can still expect enjoyable contact with the Amazonian habitat. A true foray into virgin jungle, far from the heavy footsteps of thousands of guides and visitors before you, requires at least a week of demanding camping and trekking. Hard-core eco-types might want to contract private guides to go deep into the *selva* and camp. (Ask at the tourism information office for a list of licensed, official guides; the office also has a list of blacklisted guides.)

Prices for lodges and tours vary tremendously. For conventional lodges contracted in Iquitos, lodge tours average around $40 to $50, and $100 or more per person per day for lodges located farthest from the city. Some budget lodges offer bargain rates, as little as $25 to $30 a day (although, in most cases, you get what you pay for), and independent guides might charge as little as $15 a day. Costs are directly related to distance from Iquitos; the farther they are, the more expensive they are. Costs include transportation, lodging, buffet-style meals, and guided activities (beverages cost extra).

Be careful: There are lots of look-alike lodges and tours. Lodges and ecotourism companies come and go, and everyone's competing for your dollars. Hustlers, con artists, and all manner of disreputable touts abound in Iquitos, and you need to exercise a certain amount of caution before handing over money for a promised itinerary. The local tourism office (© **065/260-251**) works hard trying to ferret out guides, tours, and lodges with bad reputations. The office has photo albums of lodges and a thick book of travelers' comments, with pages and pages of frank opinions on virtually every lodge and tour. If you're making a tour decision on the ground in Iquitos, it's a good idea to visit the office first for the most up-to-date information.

Most jungle lodges feature either individual rustic thatched-roof bungalows or main buildings with individual rooms, beds with mosquito netting, communal dining areas, hammock lounges, covered plank walkways, toilets, and either hot- or cold-water sinks and showers. A few lodges have extras such as swimming pools, lookout towers, canopy walkways, and electricity. Guests are taken on guided day- and night-time excursions, including jungle walks, piranha fishing, and canoe and motorboat trips to spot birds, caimans, and dolphins. Many lodges offer artificial, even cheesy, visits with local Indian tribes, staged for your pleasure, and some host *ayahuasca* rituals (see "Trippin' Amazon Style" on p. 360).

JUNGLE LODGES

The following are tour operators and lodges with good reputations. The list is not by any means exhaustive; there are dozens more agencies and lodges, but reports on many of them are less than stellar.

- **Explorama** ⟨⟩, Av. la Marina 340, Iquitos (© **065/252-530,** or 800/707-5275 in the U.S. and Canada; www.explorama.com). The longest-established jungle-tour company in Iquitos (now into its 5th decade) and owned by an American, Explorama operates three lodges and a campsite, ranging from 160km (100 miles) to 40km (25 miles) downriver from Iquitos. The company has one of the best reputations of the Northern Amazon lodge operators, bolstered by good guides, very good facilities and food, and a range of flexible activities. The company's first lodge, **Explorama Inn** (80km/50 miles from Iquitos), is large and attractive, with two long wings and a lovely restaurant/bar and communal area. Explorama owns the jungle's most luxurious lodge, **Ceiba Tops** (40km/25 miles from Iquitos), a jungle resort hotel with air-conditioning, a spectacular pool with a slide, and a Jacuzzi. There are trails nearby, and boats can take you out onto the river for dolphin-spotting and fishing, but Ceiba Tops is much more about relaxing in style surrounded by jungle. Near **Explornapo** (the Explorama lodge deepest in the jungle),

---

⟨Tips⟩ Eco-nomizing

Although the prices of some lodges might seem steep to backpackers accustomed to dropping $8 to $10 for a place to sleep in other parts of Peru, getting by on $40 to $50 a day or a little more is really a pretty decent bargain, considering that food, river transportation, English-speaking guides, fishing and wildlife trips and treks, and shelter are all included. That said, you can almost certainly get a better deal when signing up with a lodge or tour on the ground in Iquitos by going door-to-door to the sales offices and comparing programs and prices than you would contracting one in Lima or from your home country before stepping foot in Peru. Especially during the off season, lodges are willing to negotiate. However, you risk not getting the tour you want when you want it. For many travelers, the extra hassle and uncertainty might not be worth the dollars saved. Prices quoted on websites and through travel agents might be quite negotiable if you contact operators directly, depending on season and occupancy levels.

there's a splendid **canopy walkway** ⓡ, one of the longest in the world. At a height of 36m (118 ft.) and a rambling length of 500m (1,640 ft.), it alone is one of the highlights of a visit to this part of the Peruvian Amazon. It's possible to mix and match lodges; a popular plan for many travelers is several days at Explornapo (or, more adventurous still, the rustic Explortambos campsite) followed by a couple days of relative luxury at Ceiba Tops. Prices range from $200 for a 2-day, 1-night trip to $820 for a 5-day, 4-night trip to Explornapo. Web specials are frequently available.

- **Paseos Amazónicos,** Pevas 246, Iquitos (ⓒ **065/231-618** or 01/417-576 in Lima; www.paseosamazonicos.com). This company operates three well-run lodges, **Tambo Amazónico, Sinchicuy,** and **Yanayacu.** The farthest, Tambo Amazónico, is 180km (112 miles) upriver from Iquitos on the Yarapa River; the other two are much closer and focus on quick in-and-out tours. The Sinchicuy (30km/19 miles from Iquitos) is one of the oldest established lodges in the zone. Yanayacu lodge is 60km (37 miles) from the city. The company is honest and professionally run, and offers good and clean budget- to midrange standard tours in rustic shared lodges. The lodges are offered by several Peruvian and international travel agents and tour operators. Adventurers might be interested in the company's camping trips to the Pacaya-Samiria National Reserve, one of the best opportunities to rough it and catch glimpses of Amazonian wildlife (see "Into the Wild: Farther Afield from Iquitos" on p. 362). A 4-day, 3-night trip to Tambo Amazónico costs $385, while 2-night trips to the nearer lodges cost about $100.

- **Tahuayo Lodge** ⓡⓡⓡ, Amazonia Expeditions, 10305 Riverburn Dr., Tampa, FL 33647 (ⓒ **800/262-9669;** www.perujungle.com). One of the most outstanding Amazon ecolodges in Peru, this 9-year-old low-impact eco-property, associated with the Rainforest Conservation Fund, lies on the shores of the River Tahuayo, about 4 hours from Iquitos. *Outside* magazine has touted it as one of the top-10 travel finds in the world. It is the only lodge with access to the Tamshiyacu-Tahuayo Reserve, a splendid area for primate and other wildlife viewing (it counts 500 species of birds). Because of its remoteness, it recommends visits of at least a week; programs are individually tailored. The 15 cabins are open year-round, and the lodge offers an excellent schedule of excursions ranging from rugged (jungle survival training) to relaxed; most enticing are zip-line canopy ropes for treetop viewing. An 8-day/7-night trip is $1,295 per person.

- **Yacumama Lodge** ⓡⓡ, Sargento Lores 149, Iquitos (ⓒ **065/235-510,** or 800/854-0023 in the U.S. and Canada; www.yacumamalodge.com). Yacumama is an American-owned, first-class lodge with a handsome main house, private bungalows, solar power, and eco-sensitive flush toilets deep in the Amazon—186km (116 miles) upriver on Río Yarapa (a tributary of the Río Ucayali). It's located on an excellent 7,000-hectare (17,290-acre) forest reserve with a cool 10-story canopy tower; the treetop perspective is nearly as spectacular as the Explorama canopy walkway, although you miss the possibility of walking above the trees. In operation since 1993, Yacumama has built a solid reputation with its environmentally sound engineering, good jungle treks, and possibilities for dolphin sightings, and the company dedicates a percentage of its profits to conservation efforts. The company offers Machu Picchu/Cusco program extensions. A 4-day/3-night stay costs $750; discounts might be available in Iquitos.

- **Amazon Yarapa River Lodge** ⓡⓡ (ⓒ **800/771-3100** in the U.S. and Canada or 065/993-1172; www.yarapariverlodge.com). Associated with Cornell University

---

Fun Fact **Trippin' Amazon Style**

Several Amazon lodges offer *ayahuasca* ceremonies, which involve the privilege of taking a natural hallucinogenic potion prepared by an "authentic" Indian shaman, at $15 a shot. It's the local version of taking peyote with Don Juan, but at some joints, it teeters on the edge of spring break at the ecolodge. *Ayahuasca* is an authentic ritual and herbal drug with deep roots in local communities. A shaman boils diverse Amazonian plants and roots for up to 6 hours, and the resulting potion can indeed be very hallucinogenic. It is taken as part of a cleansing ritual, to purify the body and mind. The ceremony is not to be taken lightly, although some lodges seem to do just that, for the sake of selling a cool Amazon experience. Reports circulate about some travelers losing their minds, but it's hard to say if they should be taken seriously. At a minimum, *ayahuasca* is a cultural practice that should be respected and not abused by gringos.

(which built a tropical biology field lab for students and faculty here), this terrific conservation-minded lodge—winner of a World Travel Award as the top resort in Peru for 2005—is 177km (110 miles) upriver on the Yarapa River, an Amazon tributary, near the Reserva Nacional Pacaya-Samiria. Surrounded by pristine jungle and oxbow lakes that teem with wildlife, the beautiful lodge features full solar power, composting, and flush toilets with a waste-management system. Both lodge facilities and guides are first-rate and among the finest in the Peruvian Amazon; spacious private bungalows are almost luxurious. A 4-day/3-night trip (with private bathroom) runs $760 per person; 7 days, 6 nights, $1,190 per person. Travelers can opt for an overnight in the remote Pacaya-Samiria National Park Reserve, 4 hours away by boat.

CRUISES

Riverboat cruises down the Amazon and along its tributaries don't allow you to see much in the way of fauna or pristine jungle, although you will likely spot lots of birds and dolphins. Cruises are best for people who don't want to rough it too much and who like the romance of traveling the Amazon by boat, although varying degrees of rusticity and luxury are available. Many cruises stop off at reserves for jungle walks and visits to local villages. Some of the best cruises are those to the Pacaya-Samiria National Reserve; see "Into the Wild: Farther Afield from Iquitos," below, for details.

- **Amazon Tours & Cruises,** Requena 336 (© **800/423-2791** in the U.S. and Canada, or 065/231-611; www.amazontours.net). This American-owned company has been active in the northern Amazon for more than 4 decades. Its midlevel cruises are aboard older, air-conditioned fleets that aren't as nice or as expensive as those of Jungle Expeditions (or Junglex; see below). They offer 3- and 6-night Río Amazonas cruises, as well as river trips to Colombia (Leticia) and Manaus, Santarém, and Belém (Brazil). A 5-night cruise to Pacaya-Samiria begins at $956 (per person in double room).

- **Jungle Expeditions** ⊛, Av. Quiñones 1980 (© **065/261-583;** www.junglex.com). This company offers luxury river cruises on a fleet of six very elegant, 19th-century style boats, and cruises upriver along the Río Ucayali. Prices range from

$1,698 to $2,598 for 9-day expeditions. The company only accepts passengers through their Lima booking office (© **01/241-3232**) or International Expeditions (© **800/633-4734;** www.internationalexpeditions.com) in the United States, which offers air-inclusive packages and programs with Cusco and Machu Picchu extensions.

INDEPENDENT GUIDES

For travelers who want to get away from the lodges and groups and riverboats, more flexible independent treks into the jungle could be the way to go. You'll see more fauna, and especially flora, than will other travelers, and you'll get to visit native communities that aren't merely putting on a show for your benefit. You'll rough it in varying degrees (everything from eating cans of tuna and rice and beans cooked over an open fire, to enjoying fresh-caught fish straight from the river, to camping in makeshift sites along the way). To immerse yourself in the dense Amazonian jungle, you need an experienced, reliable wilderness guide. Scores of independent guides operate in the jungle around Iquitos and scout for tourists in the city. Their quality and professionalism varies tremendously, however, and many plainly are not to be trusted. Several guides in Iquitos have criminal records for robbing the very tourists who trusted them. The local tourism office maintains a book of disreputable, blacklisted guides.

Because you're going to be spending all your time in the jungle with the guide, depending on him to lead you, communicate with you, cook for you, and build good campsites, selecting a competent guide is of the utmost importance. Most guides are "extralegal"; only a couple of guides in Iquitos are officially licensed to operate as full-fledged independent jungle guides (possessing a license, an expensive bureaucratic requirement out of reach of most guides, isn't the only determination, however). No matter what you hear from other travelers, if you're considering hiring a guide for a solo or small-group trek into the jungle, visit the tourism information office in Iquitos before exchanging monies; ask for the office personnel's recommendations—which they're usually happy to dispense—and take a look at the review books of comments about guides. Rates depend on the number of travelers and length of trips; they can range from $35 to $40 a day per person to more than $100 per day.

In the previous edition of this book, I recommended an independent and unlicensed guide who began to ask unassuming travelers for $200 advances to pay for "his sick daughter's medical treatment." If you manage to locate a guide for an independent trip, never pay upfront before your arrival in Iquitos.

WHERE TO STAY

For many visitors, Iquitos amounts to little more than a way station on their journey to the Amazon. As a result, the city has fewer good hotels than its environs have attractive jungle lodges. Things are improving, though, and Iquitos finally got its first high-end hotel a couple years back. Midrange hotels are more expensive than similarly equipped hotels in many other parts of the country, but discounts are frequently available at most top-level and midrange hotels.

All but the cheapest *hostales* (inns) will usually arrange for a free airport transfer if you pass on your arrival information ahead of time. Even so, be careful whom you tell at the airport that you're expecting a certain hotel to pick you up; always make sure that the driver already knows your name before going anywhere with him.

Into the Wild: Farther Afield from Iquitos

The opportunities for enjoying spectacular wildlife sightings and experiencing how locals truly live in the Amazon are severely diminished in most areas where the jungle lodges are located. For primary rainforest and more authentic native villages, you have to be willing to rough it more than traditional lodges force you to. However, as jungle tourism in Peru continues to grow, several midrange and luxury cruise operators are now organizing river cruises to one of Peru's greatest jungle zones.

About 300km (190 miles) south of Iquitos, a couple days removed by boat and sandwiched between the Marañon and Ucayali rivers, is the **Pacaya-Samiria National Reserve** ⚘⚘, the largest protected area in Peru and one of the most pristine in the world. Established in 1982, it contains 2,080,000 hectares (5,139,800 acres) of thick, untouched rainforest and wetlands. Incredibly, that accounts for 1.5% of Peru's total surface area. Riddled with rivers and 85 lakes, it's huge and daunting, and should be explored only with an experienced guide. Some of the Amazon's finest and most abundant wildlife resides in the reserve, such as pink dolphins, macaws, black caimans, spider monkeys, and giant river turtles. The reserve's numbers are staggering: It is home to 539 species of birds, 101 species of mammals, 256 kinds of fish, and 22 species of orchids. Guides typically take visitors by dugout canoe from **Lagunas** (upstream from Iquitos) through the reserve. Villages on the outskirts of the reserve worth visiting are **San Martín de Timpishia** and **Puerto Miguel.** To enter the reserve, officially you need permission from **INRENA,** the Peruvian parks authority. Contact its office in Iquitos (Pevas 350; ℂ **065/231-230**) or in Lima (Los Petirrojos 355, Urbanización El Palomar; ℂ **01/224-3298**) for additional information. You'll need a minimum of 4 or 5 days to do the trip from Iquitos. Jungle Expeditions, Amazon Tours and Cruises, and Paseos Amazónicos all organize Pacaya-Samiria National Reserve river cruises and, in the case of the latter, camping trips (for contact information, see "Jungle Lodges" and "Cruises," above).

The Cocamas native community at San Martín de Tipishca, in the northern edge of the Pacaya-Samiria National Reserve, has a young American

EXPENSIVE

Hotel El Dorado Plaza ⚘   With a privileged place on the Plaza de Armas, the El Dorado Plaza has filled a gaping hole in the Iquitos hotel scene—the city never before had a bona fide high-end hotel. A modern high-rise building, with a soaring lobby, a good restaurant, and an excellent outdoor pool, this is clearly the finest hotel in town. Rooms are large and nicely outfitted, if not quite at the upper-echelon levels found in Lima or Cusco. Guests have a view of either the main square or the pool. The hotel has quickly become popular with foreigners who come to Iquitos for top-of-the-line jungle tours. The staff is very friendly and helpful. See the website for frequent deals—occasionally as much as half the rack rate.

woman working with it as an interpreter and is reaching out to travelers who want an experience of close contact with the people of an Amazon village. Reports are that the trips are extremely professional in character. Contact **Virginia Blum,** care of her office at Piura 1072 in Iquitos (© **065/251-185;** virginiablum@yahoo.com). The community charges $40 per day per person, plus the $19 permit to enter the preserve. Trips usually last 4 to 5 days and are limited to groups of 12 to 15 people (although as few as two people can arrange a trip). Other, less involved visits to local native communities, such as the Huitotos, Boras, and Yaguas, can also be arranged. Inquire about independent trips at the tourism office on the Plaza de Armas in Iquitos.

Another option for down-and-dirty exploration of Amazon culture and sights is to cruise the rivers not on (relatively) pampered boats that take tourists out to lodges, but aboard the **three-decked riverboats** that form the transportation backbone of the region, ferrying people back and forth from villages on Amazon tributaries to Iquitos and other towns. The boats are rough going, stuffed with animals and densely packed families and their household goods, and are almost entirely absent of comforts. You should take along plenty of bottled water, a hammock, and foodstuffs such as fruit and canned items. Journeys can last several days, but slinging yourself into a hammock on the top deck and floating slowly down the Huallaga or Ucayali will certainly win points among your friends when it comes to regaling them with vacation heroics. For budget travelers, it's a perfect antidote to high-priced lodges and river cruises: It's virtually impossible to spend more than $10 a day, including transportation.

For more details about how to organize trips to Pacaya-Samiria or simple river transport along the rivers, contact the helpful folks at the tourist information office on the Plaza de Armas in Iquitos for up-to-the-minute suggestions. See also "Independent Guides," below, for information on treks with independent guides.

Napo 258 (Plaza de Armas), Iquitos. © **065/222-555.** Fax 065/224-304. 65 units. $130 double. Rate includes breakfast buffet. AE, DC, MC, V. **Amenities:** Restaurant; 2 bars; coffee shop; excellent outdoor pool; fitness center; Jacuzzi; sauna; concierge; 24-hr. room service; laundry service. *In room:* A/C, TV, minibar, hair dryer, safe.

MODERATE

Hostal Ambasador Associated with Hostelling International, this small hotel is an especially good value for HI members. A centrally located, modern white block, it has well-maintained rooms with good amenities (such as a restaurant with 24-hr. room service) and private bathrooms. For most backpackers used to bargain-basement hostels, this is a definite step up—it might be a good place to crash after a few days in the wild.

Pevas 260, Iquitos. © **065/233-110.** Fax 065/231-618. postmaster@p-amazon.com.pe. 25 units. $30–$40 double; discounts for HI members. Rates include taxes. MC, V. **Amenities:** Bar/cafe; 24-hr. room service; laundry service. *In room:* A/C, TV.

Real Hotel Iquitos *(Finds)*   The former (and formerly grand) state-owned Hotel de Turistas is now a curious hotel with a unique appeal to those who shy away from perfectly run, internationally flavored chain hotels. Part of a Peruvian group with a half-dozen hotels spread across the country, this midsize entry seems larger and emptier than it is. Some of the rooms are surprisingly expansive, and a few have enviable balconies overlooking the *malecón* and the river. If you score such a room (ask to see a few first), you'll have yourself a deal (no. 312 is huge and has its own terrace). They're simply furnished, with some unique touches, such as red curtains and green walls (kind of cool in an offbeat way), although I admit that it's not the place for folks in search of great air-conditioning and top-shelf service. No other hotel can boast these river views, though—and the Amazon is why you came to Iquitos, isn't it? Interior rooms, with no view and considerably smaller, are half as expensive as the larger accommodations.

Malecón Tarapacá s/n, Iquitos. ©/fax 065/231-011. 54 units. $45 double with view; $23 double without view; $80 suite. Rates include continental breakfast. MC, V. **Amenities:** Restaurant; bar; laundry service. *In room:* A/C, TV.

Victoria Regia *(Value)*   An extremely comfortable and friendly midsize hotel, the Victoria Regia—named for the lily found throughout the Amazon—is a good choice for both independent travelers and business execs with long-term affairs to attend to in Iquitos. A modern block hotel on a busy residential street about 10 minutes from the main square, the hotel's rooms, with air-conditioning that really cranks, are built around an attractive indoor pool and are only a notch below the Hotel El Dorado Plaza in terms of comfort. The Victoria Regia is part of a small, local, family-owned chain of hotels, which includes the Hotel Acosta and the Heliconia and Zungarococha lodges.

Av. Ricardo Palma 252, Iquitos. © 01/421-9195 for reservations; ©/fax 065/231-983. www.victoriaregiahotel.com. 45 units. S/205–S/240 ($59–$69) double; S/240–S/305 ($69–$87) suite. Rates include breakfast buffet. AE, DC, MC, V. **Amenities:** Restaurant; bar; covered pool; small business center w/Internet access (for a small fee); laundry service. *In room:* A/C, TV, minibar, hair dryer, safe.

INEXPENSIVE

Hobo Hideout Travellers Hotel *(Value)*   Jimmy and Sandra recently opened this budget *hostal,* run by a small ecotour operator, Great Amazon Safari & Trading Company, that was built with jungle materials, including palm leaves and native woods. The rooms are well maintained and comfortable for the low prices. It's just 1 block from the main square, and particularly good for backpackers who don't mind sleeping in dorm rooms. Besides a kitchen, it has a common reading and TV rooms, a laundry area, and a small swimming pool. The space is replete with jungle plants and a true jungle feel, which sets it apart from the much more austere Pascana hospedaje.

Jr. Putumayo 437, Iquitos. © 065/234-099. 30 beds. $7 per person in dormitory rooms. Rate includes taxes and continental breakfast buffet. No credit cards. **Amenities:** Bar; outdoor pool. *In room:* No phone.

Hospedaje La Pascana *(Value)*   One of the better budget inns in Iquitos, the Pascana is a friendly, small place with rooms built around a long, plant-lined, and open-air courtyard. Rooms are very simple, but not uncomfortable, and they have fans rather than air-conditioning. The place is quiet and peaceful, and just a 2-minute walk from the *malecón* and the Plaza de Armas—reasons why it's often full and popular with small budget-level groups. Don't expect much hot water at this price, although you probably won't care in the sweltering heat.

Pevas 133, Iquitos. © 065/231-418. Fax 065/233-466. pascana@tsi.com.pe. 18 units. $14 double. Rate includes taxes and continental breakfast buffet. No credit cards. **Amenities:** Cafeteria.

> ### *Tips* Amazonian Delicacies
>
> Throughout South America, the Amazon region is famed for its exotic fruits. In Iquitos, check out stands around the Plaza de Armas for natural fruit juices and ice creams made from stuff hard to get at home, such as *aguaje, maracuyá,* and *cocona.*

WHERE TO DINE

Easygoing restaurants in Iquitos are a good place to sample dishes straight out of the Amazon, such as *paiche,* hearts of palm salad, and *juanes* (rice tamales made with minced chicken, pork, or fish, prepared with black olives and egg and wrapped in *bijao* leaves). Although protected species are not supposed to appear on menus, they often do. You might want to think twice before encouraging restaurateurs by ordering turtle-meat soup or alligator. If you venture into the Belén market, be prepared for even more exotic foodstuffs, such as monkey and lizard meat.

EXPENSIVE

Montecarlo *☆* INTERNATIONAL/PERUVIAN   The exterior of this restaurant, behind the cheesy, glittering gold lights of a casino, doesn't look too auspicious. Yet upstairs from the gaming tables is an elegant place that produces the most refined dining in this jungle city. It's perhaps the only restaurant in Peru where you'll sit down to a full set of silver, and wine and water glasses. The decor goes for an upscale treetop look, with ferns, wood-beamed ceilings, jungle murals, and a little Disneyesque Indian hut in the corner. Yet Montecarlo, which sits above a downstairs casino (making after-dinner plans easy for some), serves exquisitely prepared seafood and jungle specialties such as turtle stew and tropical gator (although I hate to report these items on menus). If you can't bear to bite into an endangered species, try the *pescado a la diabla,* lightly fried John Dory fish drenched in squid and shrimp, and topped with a spicy ginger and tomato sauce; hearts of palm stuffed with shrimp; or daily specials such as *cazuela de pescado y marisco* (fish and seafood casserole). There are also some appetizing steaks and pastas.

Napo 140, 2nd floor. ✆ 065/232-246. Reservations recommended. Main courses S/17–S/32 ($4.85–$9.15). AE, DC, MC, V. Daily noon–3:30pm and 6pm–midnight.

Regal (Casa de Fierro) INTERNATIONAL/PERUVIAN   In the famed Iron House on the Plaza de Armas, this British pub and hangout is also a reputable restaurant exuding a desultory colonial atmosphere. There are great views from the wrap-around iron balcony, with its slowly rotating old-style ceiling fans, overlooking the plaza. It's a good place to try local dishes such as *paiche,* served any number of ways, or the house specialty, *regal lomo fino* (beef tenderloin in port-wine sauce, served with salad, Greek rice, a peach stuffed with Russian salad, and fries). The food might not hold up to the general ambience, and it's a tad overpriced, so you might opt just to kick back with the expat Brits around the bar for a pint.

Putumayo 182, 2nd floor, Plaza de Armas. ✆ 065/222-732. Reservations recommended. Main courses S/16–S/38 ($4.55–$11). AE, DC, MC, V. Daily noon–10pm.

Restaurant Gran Maloca *☆* *Value* PERUVIAN/AMAZONIAN   One of Iquitos's most celebrated traditional restaurants, located in a grand, tile-covered (and air-conditioned!) 19th-century house, Gran Maloca serves both jungle dishes and standard upscale fare. Try Amazon-style venison (with cilantro, coconut, and yuca), tropical alligator, or less risky items such as filet mignon, tenderloin with mushroom risotto, or chicken a la Maloca (chicken breast stuffed with ham and baked in white wine). The split personality of the restaurant is present in the decor: The would-be formal trappings and pastel color scheme coexist with a large collection of colorful butterflies adorning the walls. (If you like those, wait until you get a load of the framed Amazonian bugs, tarantulas, and other creepy crawlers in the bathrooms.) Gran Maloca serves a good-value (meaning cheap), three-course daily lunch special for just S/12 ($3.40).

Sargento Lores 170. (*C*) **065/233-126.** Reservations recommended. Main courses S/18–S/35 ($5.15–$10). AE, MC, V. Daily noon–10pm.

MODERATE

El Nuevo Mesón PERUVIAN   Open to the passing parade of people, souvenir sellers, and curious locals on the *malecón,* this lively restaurant is a good place for an introduction to regional specialties and the city itself. If you come on a weekend night, you'll be entertained not only by altiplano musicians inside, but also by all kinds of locals hovering about the sidewalk tables, some gawking at your meal. (Several kids jostled for the rights to my leftovers; disadvantaged people often hang around outside restaurants hoping for part of a meal.) Service can be a little haphazard, but most dishes are pretty well prepared. Try dishes such as the regional favorite *pescado a la loretana* (fish filet with yuca, fried bananas, and palm-heart salad), and freakier fare such as alligator crisps with fried manioc or curried turtle. There are steaks, *mariscos* (shellfish), and a long list of fish, dominated by *dorado* (a kind of flaky white catfish) served in a variety of styles, such as "poor boy," with potatoes, salad, bananas, eggs, and rice.

Malecón Tarapacá 153. (*C*) **065/231-837.** Reservations recommended for groups. Main courses S/15–S/26 ($4.30–$7.40). MC, V. Daily noon–midnight.

Fitzcarraldo 👻 INTERNATIONAL   This popular joint right on the *malecón* has a diverse menu to appeal to travelers of all stripes and appetites. You can go light, choosing from a number of salads, such as *chonta* (palm-heart salad) with avocado and tomato; or regular dinners, including *pescado a la loretana* or even turtle in ginger sauce with manioc. There are also excellent pizzas, sandwiches, and hamburgers, as well as large salads. The restaurant is a convivial place in an open-air house (which

---

Tips Chifas in Iquitos

To some observers, there's something distinctly Asian-feeling about hot, humid, and motorcycle-crazed Iquitos. Waves of Chinese immigrants came as laborers to Iquitos throughout the 20th century, which is the biggest reason there are so many *chifas* (Peruvian-Chinese restaurants) in town. Eating Chinese food at the edge of the Amazon instead of exotic jungle fruits and fish might not be your first impulse in Iquitos, but *chifas* are plentiful and reasonably priced— perfect fallback dining options. Try **Wai Ming,** San Martín 464 at Plaza 28 de Julio ((*C*) **065/234-391**); **Chifa Chong,** Huallaga 165 (no phone); **Hueng Teng,** Nauta at Pucallpa (no phone); and **Chifa Can Chau,** Huallaga 173 (no phone). Others *chifas,* cheaper still, line Avenida Grau near Plaza 28 de Julio.

once belonged to a British rubber company) featuring updated colonial touches and views of the Amazon, along with good music and sidewalk tables and, unfortunately, underpowered ceiling fans.

Napo 100 (at Malecón Tarapacá). ℂ 065/243-434. Reservations recommended for groups. Main courses S/10–S/38 ($2.85–$11). MC, V. Daily noon–midnight.

INEXPENSIVE
Ari's Burger AMERICAN   A quintessential gringo hangout right on the Plaza de Armas, this brightly lit fast-food joint is open to the street on two sides—great for people-watching. It seems nearly every visitor to the city hits Ari, called "Gringolandia" by locals both for its clientele and American-style menu, at least once for a burger and fries, ice cream, or fresh-squeezed juice or a milkshake. It's open late and is very popular with folks after rounds at the bars and discos.

Próspero 127 (at the corner of Napo). No phone. Reservations not accepted. Main courses S/3–S/18 (85¢–$5.15). MC, V. Daily 8am–3am.

IQUITOS AFTER DARK
More locals than gringos usually make it to the coolest spot in Iquitos, **Café-Teatro Amauta,** Nauta 250 (ℂ **065/233-366**), a bar-cum-theater with great bohemian flavor and a romantic interior with thick, red curtains framing a small stage that opens to sidewalk tables. Calling itself "El Rincón de los Artistas," (Artists' Corner) it supports live Peruvian, Latin, and Amazon music Monday through Saturday from 10pm until 3am. Try some of the funky *aguardientes* ("fire waters") made from Amazonian herbs. Along the *malecón* are a couple of lively bars with good views of the river. **Arandú Bar,** Malecón Tarapacá 113 (ℂ **065/243-434**), is particularly hopping, a good place for sharing a pitcher of sangria and loud rock 'n' roll. You can also grab a drink at the **Yellow Rose of Texas,** Putumayo 180 (ℂ **065/241-010**), a spot owned by the (controversial and Texan) former head of the local tourist office. Locals hang out at **Noa-Noa,** Pevas 298 at Fitzcarraldo (ℂ **065/232-902**), a disco and rock bar near the Plaza de Armas. When the two-level dance floor is happening, the smoke machines crank and the sound system pumps out salsa and Latin rock.

11

Northern Peru

Northern Peru is vastly underappreciated as compared to the more popular south. In fact, most of the region—with the exception of the north-central Cordillera Blanca and Callejón de Huaylas, beacons to international mountain climbers and trekkers—is virtually unknown to most foreigners who travel to Peru. The few who make the effort to get to know the north are mainly those with a specific interest in ancient Peruvian cultures, or hikers and adventurous travelers (including surfers) looking to get out into the rugged country, beyond the reach of the majority of gringos who trod well-beaten paths in the Andes and southern Peru. If you make it to this part of Peru, you might be in for the not unwelcome treat of being one of the few.

You wouldn't know it from the paucity of foreign visitors, but the northern coastal desert of Peru holds some of the country's greatest archaeological treasures: Chan Chan, the great adobe city of the Chimú civilization; 1,500-year-old Moche temples; and the royal tomb that brought the great Lord of Sipán to the world's attention in 1987—Peru's very own King Tut. Northern beaches draw surfers to some of the best waves off South America, and nestled in the *sierra* is one of the country's most charming and beautiful mountain towns, Cajamarca, which could fairly be called Cusco of the north.

Gringos of a particularly rugged ilk and style of outdoor performance gear do make it in significant number to the Cordillera Blanca, which holds some of the most beautiful peaks in South America and some of the finest trekking on the continent. Huaraz is the primary base in the Callejón de Huaylas for excursions into the valleys and mountain ranges of the northern Andes. For years, the destination has been favored principally by sports and adventurer travelers, especially hard-core hikers, but the range of trekking destinations and activities is opening up and appealing more to other travelers who also want a taste of Peru's great outdoors.

1 Trujillo ✦

561km (349 miles) N of Lima; 200km (124 miles) S of Chiclayo; 298km (185 miles) SW of Cajamarca

Trujillo, the capital of La Libertad department, is the third-largest city in Peru and one of only two of commercial importance on the entire north coast. Yet the town, founded in 1534 by Diego Almagro on the orders of Francisco Pizarro, retains the Spanish colonial feel of a much smaller town. Locals saunter along the grandly laid-out plaza, and the downtown area is an attractive grid of streets lined with elegant, pastel colonial mansions embellished by wrought-iron window grilles.

The importance of this area greatly predates the arrival of the Spaniards, however, and Trujillo is celebrated mostly for a stunning collection of pre-Columbian sites that abound on the outskirts of the city. Looming in the desert are five major archaeological

Northern Peru

sites, including two of the richest ensembles of Moche temples and ruins of the Chimú culture in Peru. Chan Chan, a monumental adobe complex of royal palaces covering more than 52 sq. km (20 sq. miles), is the primary draw for visitors, but archaeological tours also visit the fascinating Temples of the Moon and Sun (Huacas del Sol y de la Luna), built by the Moche culture around A.D. 500. Several of these sites have been partially restored, but they still require some imagination to conjure a sense of their immensity, the busy daily activity, and the grandeur of the ceremonies once held there.

Near Trujillo is Huanchaco, a laid-back beach resort that serves as a virtual bedroom community for many visitors, particularly younger travelers with an interest in surfing. Ideally positioned for ruins visits, Huanchaco is also a lot less hectic than Trujillo and has a good roster of cheaper small hotels, budget *hostales* (inns), and seaside seafood restaurants.

ESSENTIALS
GETTING THERE

BY PLANE   Trujillo is well connected to the rest of the country, but by far the easiest way to get here is to fly. **Lan** (© **01/213-8200;** www.lan.com), **AeroCondor** (© **01/614-4000;** www.aerocondor.com.pe), and **Star Peru** (© **01/705-9000;** www.star peru.com) fly daily to Trujillo from Lima (1 hr). Flights arrive at the **Aeropuerto**

Carlos Martínez de Pinillos on Carretera Huanchaco in the Huanchaco district (℡ **044/464-013**). The airport is about 20 minutes northwest of downtown.

A taxi to downtown Trujillo costs as little as S/15 ($4.30) if you bargain, although most drivers start by charging S/20 ($5.70). Huanchaco-Trujillo buses and *colectivos* pass in the general direction of the airport, but at a distance of about a mile from the entrance, making public transportation to and from the airport impractical for anyone with luggage.

BY BUS   Like most big cities, Trujillo is serviced by several domestic bus companies from Lima and most major points along the north coast and northern highlands. Many long-distance buses travel at night only. There is no central bus station in Trujillo. Most individual company terminals are near downtown, located to the northwest by the Estadio Mansiche, to the southwest near Avenida España, or to the east near Avenida El Ejército.

The major companies making the 8-hour trip from Lima are **Ormeño** (℡ **01/472-5000**), **Cruz del Sur** (℡ **01/424-6158**), and **Oltursa** (℡ **01/225-4499**). For the 6-hour trip from Cajamarca, **Transportes Línea** (℡ **044/245-181** in Trujillo, or 076/823-956 in Cajamarca) has two classes of service, *económico* and *especial,* which is slightly faster, a bit more comfortable, and a tad more expensive than *económico* class. Transportes Línea (℡ **074/233-497**) is also the major company for the 3-hour journey from Chiclayo and the 8-hour journey from Huaraz. **ITTSA** (℡ **044/222-541**) runs from Lima, Chiclayo, and Piura. Note that night buses especially have a reputation for being unsafe. In Trujillo, **Ormeño** is located at Av. Ejército 342, **Cruz del Sur** at Amazonas 437, **Línea** at Av. América Sur 2857, and **ITTSA** at Mansiche 145.

VISITOR INFORMATION

The **iPerú** offices are located at the airport (℡ **044/464-226**) and downtown at Jr. Pizarro 412, on the Plaza Mayor (℡ **044/294-561**); the downtown office is open Monday through Friday from 9am to 1pm and 2 to 5pm. A small and friendly (although not very well equipped) tourist information office belonging to the **Cámara Regional de La Libertad** is located at Independencia 628, 1 block north of the Plaza de Armas (℡ **044/938-922**). The office is open Monday through Saturday from 9am to 6pm. It has free maps, and the staff can advise you on the easiest way to visit Chan Chan and the other major archaeological sites beyond the city.

FAST FACTS   Banks that exchange traveler's checks and cash and that have ATMs are **Banco de Crédito,** Jr. Gamarra 562 (℡ **044/242-360**); **Banco Latino,** Jr. Gamarra 572 (℡ **044/243-461**); and **Banco Continental,** Pizarro 620, in the colonial Casa de la Emancipación. **Interbanc,** located at Pizarro and Gamarra, has a Cirrus/PLUS ATM. Money-changers can usually be found hanging about the Plaza de Armas or along Gamarra.

In case of emergency, call ℡ **105.** The helpful **tourist police** are located at Independencia 630, in the Casa Ganoza Chopitea (℡ **044/291-705**). For complaints, you can also call the **Tourist Protection Service** at ℡ **044/204-146.**

If you need medical attention, you're likely to find English-speaking doctors at **Clínica Peruana-Americana,** Av. Mansiche 702 (℡ **044/231-261**). Other hospitals are **Hospital Regional Docente de Trujillo,** Av. Mansiche 795 (℡ **044/231-581**), and **Hospital Belén,** Bolívar 350 (℡ **044/245-281**). In Huanchaco, a clinic *(posta médica)* is located at Atahualpa 437 (℡ **044/461-547**).

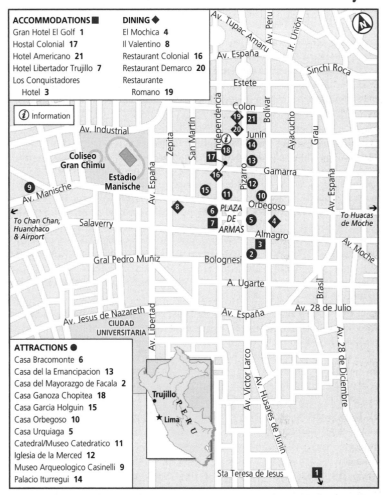

ACCOMMODATIONS ■
Gran Hotel El Golf 1
Hostal Colonial 17
Hotel Americano 21
Hotel Libertador Trujillo 7
Los Conquistadores
  Hotel 3

DINING ◆
El Mochica 4
Il Valentino 8
Restaurant Colonial 16
Restaurant Demarco 20
Restaurante
  Romano 19

ℹ Information

ATTRACTIONS ●
Casa Bracomonte 6
Casa del la Emancipacion 13
Casa del Mayorazgo de Facala 2
Casa Ganoza Chopitea 18
Casa Garcia Holguin 15
Casa Orbegoso 10
Casa Urquiaga 5
Catedral/Museo Catedratico 11
Iglesia de la Merced 12
Museo Arqueologico Casinelli 9
Palacio Iturregui 14

For Internet access, two *cabinas* to try are **Cibercafé Internet,** Manuel María Izaga 716 (℡ **044/228-729**), and **Deltanet/Telecom,** Orbegoso 641 (℡ **044/294-327**). Both charge about S/2 to S/2.50 (55¢–70¢) per hour.

Trujillo's **post office** is located at Independencia 286 (℡ **044/245-941**); it's open Monday through Saturday from 8am to 8pm and Sunday 9am to 1pm. A **DHL/ Western Union** branch is at Almagro 579 (℡ **044/203-686**). The **Telefónica del Perú** office is at Pizarro 561; it's open Monday through Saturday from 8am to 8pm. A *locutorio* (public calling place) is located at Gamarra 454.

GETTING AROUND

Downtown Trujillo is a grid of relatively short blocks ringed by Avenida España. At the heart of the *centro* is the Plaza de Armas, and the main sights are all nearby on the

Tips **Guided Tours**

Agencies offering standard city and archaeological tours include **Guía Tours,** Jr. Independencia 580 (© 044/245-170); **Chacón Tours,** Av. España 106 (© 044/255-212); **Consorcio Turístico del Norte,** Jr. Pizarro 478 (© 044/205-645); and **Trujillo Tours,** Diego de Almagro 301 (© 044/233-091). Most standard tours cost S/42 to S/53 ($12–$15) per person. Tours to El Brujo are generally S/88 to S/105 ($25–$30).

major streets leading off the square. Getting around the small centro is thus best managed on foot. However, you'll need to take either a taxi or a public bus to visit the major archaeological sites outside Trujillo, or the beachside suburb, Huanchaco.

Confusing as can be are Trujillo's street names: Nearly every street and avenue has two names and two corresponding signs, one a smaller printed version and the other a fancier painted sign. Most maps go by the smaller, printed name, which is what I give in this chapter.

Several *urbanizaciones,* or residential districts, lie just beyond Avenida España. Urbanización El Recreo, where several resort-style hotels are located, is just west of Av. 28 de Julio. Chan Chan is just 5km (3 miles) northwest of the city, on the way to the airport and Huanchaco. The Huacas de Moche are 8km (5 miles) south of town beyond the Carretera Industrial.

BY TAXI   Taxis, all uniformly painted black and yellow, are plentiful in Trujillo. Most in-town fares, inside the Avenida España ring, are about S/3 (85¢). A taxi ride to Chan Chan or Huanchaco costs about S/15 ($4.30). You can hire taxis by the hour (S/15 or $4.30) or by the day S/88 to S/125 ($25–$35) to tour archaeological sites in the environs of Trujillo. Be sure to negotiate or ask first in the tourist office to determine the going fares because price gouging is not uncommon in Trujillo. Official taxis are identified by a coat of arms of the city.

BY BUS   *Combis* and *ómnibuses* cost S/1 (30¢). Somewhat rickety buses will take you to Huanchaco for S/3 (85¢).

BY CAR   If you want to rent a vehicle to make trips to Chan Chan and other sites, or even to travel around the northern region, try **Global Car Rental,** Ecuador 122, oficina 201, Urbanización El Recreo (© **044/295-548**).

WHAT TO SEE & DO
COLONIAL TRUJILLO

Trujillo has an impressive collection of elegant colonial- and republican-era houses *(casas antiguas)* and baroque churches, as well as one of Peru's odder museums of ancient ceramics. A tour of Trujillo rightly begins with the graceful **Plaza de Armas,** where vendors hang out and families in their Sunday finery pose for pictures in front of the Libertad monument. On the square is the **Catedral,** built in the mid–17th century but rather sober and uninteresting, although it has a **Museo Catedrático** (© **044/235-083**) with silver and gold chalices and bishops' vestments. The plaza is ringed by colorful examples of fine colonial-era mansions, including the one that is now home to the Hotel Libertador. Trujillo's pastel colonial buildings are distinguished by their ornamental wrought-iron window grilles, unusual in Peru.

Casa Ganoza Chopitea ☆ Better known in Trujillo as La Casa de los Leones (House of the Lions) because of the lions crowning the main door, this 17th-century house is one of the most splendid of the colonial era. Opposite the San Francisco church, the entrance is loaded with baroque and rococo details, including river stones *(canto rodado)* on the ground. A *concha venera,* or welcoming shell, is placed above the door. Inside the house, you'll pass through the Salón de Varones (Men's Hall), with a high wooden ceiling, followed by the Salón de Damas (Women's Hall). Look for the curious air holes in the latter—they go all the way to the roof to allow fresh air to circulate.

Jr. Independencia 630. No phone. Free admission. Mon–Fri 9am–1pm and 3–5pm.

Casa Orbegoso This huge yellow-and-brown mid-18th-century house, once the property of former president Luis José de Orbegoso, stretches around the block and has its own plaza facing the San Agustín church. In the entrance are Moorish-Christian mural paintings that were buried beneath successive baroque, rococo, and finally neoclassical murals. Inside are some original furnishings and mural paintings that can still be seen around the lower sections of some rooms. The front part of the house still belongs to descendants of the original owners. Orbegoso, who fought alongside Bolívar in the War of Independence, is buried in a mausoleum in the house.

Orbegoso 553. ☎ 044/234-950. Free admission. Mon–Sat 9am–1pm and 4–7pm.

Casa Urquiaga (Casa Calonge) ☆☆ This grand colonial mansion, royal blue with white window grilles, conserves the 18th-century desk of Simón Bolívar, who lived here for 2 years after proclaiming Peru's independence in 1824. The home, with three lovely interior courtyards, is one of Trujillo's most magnificently restored and most historic. It hosted the first viceroy of Peru in 1604 and was the headquarters of the first bank in Trujillo. The dining room features spectacular French porcelain, and throughout there are beautiful chandeliers and mirrors. In a second patio is an exhibit of Moche and Nasca ceramics. Look for the gold Chavín necklaces and several Chimú ornamental pieces, also in gold. Today the mansion is owned by the Banco Central.

Jr. Pizarro 446, Plaza de Armas. No phone. Free admission; passport or other identification required. Mon–Fri 9:15am–3:15pm.

Iglesia de La Merced On a small square set back from the street and next to the Corte Superior de Justicia (itself worth a peek), La Merced, one of Trujillo's most impressive churches, dates to 1636. It is especially notable for the colorful carved figures in relief around the cupola, including alternating series of small angels and

---

Tips Trujillo's Other *Casas Coloniales*

Besides the colonial and republican houses that allow visitors, other houses worth a look from outside (and occasionally inside, if they're public buildings) are the bright yellow **Casa de la Emancipación** (now Banco Continental), Pizarro 610, where independence from Spain was proclaimed on December 29, 1820; **Casa Bracamonte,** Independencia 441; **Casa Lynch,** on the Plaza de Armas opposite the cathedral; **Casa Aranda,** Bolívar 621; **Casa del Mayorazgo de Facalá,** Pizarro 314; and **Casa García Holguín,** Independencia 527 on the Plaza de Armas.

cherubs supporting the top section—perhaps 100 in all. Inside, the church is salmon and white, with white stone arches. At the rear, apparently jammed into the organ loft, is a massive rococo pipe organ.

Jr. Pizarro 550. No phone. Free admission. Daily 8am–6pm.

Iglesia y Monasterio El Carmen 🔆   This lovely church and monastery, founded in 1724 and occupying an entire city block, has the most important collection of colonial art in Trujillo. Its Carmelite museum (Pinacoteca Carmelita) possesses 150 baroque and rococo paintings, the majority of them from the 17th and 18th centuries, as well as paintings of the Quito Art School. The final room shows the process of restoration of paintings, although explanations are in Spanish only. The church's central gilded altar is marvelous. The main *retablo* (altar) was created by Master Fernando Collado de la Cruz, a free black Peruvian. Floral murals in soft pastels line each side of the church. The monastery has two cloisters (and 10 cloistered nuns) and contains a fair portion of the convent's art collection, but it cannot be visited.

Jr. Bolívar (at Colón). ℂ 044/233-091. Admission to church and museum S/3 (85¢) adults, S/1 (30¢) children. Mon–Sat 9am–1pm.

Museo Arqueológico Casinelli 🔆 *Finds*   One of the most curious places you'll ever see fine ceramics exhibits is this private museum, about a 10-minute walk from the Plaza de Armas, housed in a dumpy space beneath a Mobil gas station. What are the odds of a gas-station and car-wash owner devoting all his money, time, and attention to assembling and displaying one of the largest private collections of ancient ceramics? Going on over 40 years of existence, with dreams of greater recognition and expansion, Señor Casinelli's superb collection of the Moche, Nasca, Chavín, Huari, and Chimú cultures (among others) holds about 4,000 pieces (although only 2,000 can be displayed "for lack of space and lack of support from the Peruvian government") and spans more than 2,500 years. There are some excellent examples of all those cultures displayed on pressboard shelves, including, behind a wall meant to protect innocent eyes, the famed erotic ceramics of the Moche. (You might have to ask the old guy to open the case, a feeling akin to asking the pharmacist for condoms.) Casinelli owns the gas station upstairs and has an architect's model of the much larger museum, along with a hotel, he'd like someday to build (but he's now in his eighties, so that dream is growing dim). Guided tours are in Spanish only.

Av. Nicolás de Piérola 607 (at intersection of Huanchaco and Carretera Panamericana). ℂ 044/246-110. Admission S/5 ($1.40). Mon–Sat 9am–12:30pm and 3–6:30pm; Sun 9:30am–12:30pm and 3:30–6:30pm.

Palacio Iturregui   This bright yellow mansion, an excellent example of neoclassical civil architecture that dates to the 19th century, is home to the Club Central, Trujillo's traditional social club. Although the club continues to be members-only, visitors can tool around for a view of an only slightly dilapidated exclusivity. The two-story mansion, with a large central courtyard, is outfitted with window grilles, thin columns, and Italian marble statues. Upstairs is a small museum containing Moche ceramics. Members in semiformal dress still drop by for lunch or dinner at the club, followed by a game of cards.

Jr. Pizarro 688. ℂ 044/234-212. Admission (guided tour) S/5 ($1.40). Mon–Sat 8–11am (before 10am, ring bell for entrance).

Tips Catch Some *Ondas*

If you want to check out some waves along Peru's north coast, check the "Spot Atlas" at **www.wannasurf.com**. If you can read Spanish, another good surfing site is **www.peruazul.com**.

HUANCHACO ⚐

Huanchaco, 12km (7½ miles) northwest of Trujillo, is a tranquil and traditional fishing village now doubling as pretty low-key resort. On summer weekends, though, it gets jumping with folks from Trujillo and vacationing Peruvians. Huanchaco is a very good alternative to Trujillo as a base for exploring the archaeological sites of the Chimú and Moche (and a day's visit to the capital city is easily accomplished from Huanchaco).

The town's fishing character is apparent in the long jetty that juts out over the water and the pointy handcrafted boats called *caballitos del mar* (or *caballitos de totora*), for which Huanchaco has become famous and which remain the photogenic vessel of choice for fishers. These small boats, made of bound totora reeds, have been used by fishermen for more than 1,000 years, since the reign of the Moche. The area around Huanchaco is one of the few places in Peru where this ancient sea-vessel tradition has not disappeared from use. When not out on the water, they're parked on the beach in groups like slender tepees.

Besides a stroll on the beach and visit to Huanchaco's pleasant *artesanía* market, there's not too much to see or do. A 16th-century colonial church clings to a cliff, but it's a long walk uphill from town. More than anything else, Huanchaco's easy pace and proximity to the sea are its main attractions. It has several agreeable resort hotels, seafood restaurants, and nice stretches of beach. The big waves here attract local surfers and a few board-carrying tourists, although the biggest and best waves are at **Puerto Chicama** (also known as **Malabrigo**), about 80km (50 miles) farther up the coast. Waves there can be ridden up to a half-mile, and it's the site of the largest left wave in the world. (Another good spot in the far north is **Cabo Blanco,** about 110km/68 miles south of Tumbes.) La Casa Suiza *hostal* (p. 382) rents out body boards.

To get there, pick up a Huanchaco bus (S/3 or 85¢) along Independencia in Trujillo; the buses go along the first part of the beach before turning on Los Ficus. You can get to Puerto Chicama by colectivos, which depart hourly from the Terminal Interurbano on Calle Santa Cruz in Trujillo; the journey takes about 90 minutes. A taxi from Trujillo is about S/14 or S/18 ($4–$5).

ARCHAEOLOGICAL SITES NEAR TRUJILLO ⚐⚐

Chan Chan ⚐⚐   One of the most important archaeological sites in Peru (although, in its present state it might not seem as "complete" to the layman observer as some of the Incan stone ruins in the highlands), Chan Chan is an enormous adobe city in the Moche valley, just 5km (3 miles) from Trujillo. The great capital of the Chimú Empire, which stretched some 966km (600 miles) along the northern coast of Peru from Lima to the Ecuadorian border, is the largest complex of its kind from pre-Columbian America. The urban Chimú was the chief state in Peru before the continental conquest of the Incan Empire. Begun around 1300, it reaches all the way from Huanchaco port to Campana Mountain, an area covering more than 25 sq. km (9¾ sq. miles) of desert floor.

First excavated in the mid-1960s, the crumbling mud city was once home to perhaps as many as 60,000 inhabitants. In all, the UNESCO Cultural Mankind Heritage Monument comprises more than a dozen citadels and a maze of living quarters, thick defensive walls, ramps, plazas, gardens, workshops, warehouses, narrow streets, a huge reservoir, a royal cemetery, and pyramidal temples. Nine palaces were the personal domains of Chimú chieftains; when one died, he was buried in an elaborate ritual in the palace and a new royal compound was built for his successor. These were almost certainly overflowing with gold and silver riches, and were later ransacked not by the Incas, but by the Spaniards and subsequent *huaqueros* (grave robbers, or treasure hunters). The fragile buildings themselves have fallen victim to erosion caused by recurring El Niño floods; in 1986, Chan Chan was listed on World Heritage Sites in Danger due to both physical erosion and acts of continued pillaging.

The Chimú kingdom began around A.D. 1000 and reached its apex in the 15th century before succumbing to the Incas in 1470 and 1471, after more than a decade of resistance. Today one can only imagine what this massive complex looked like and the sophisticated society that once inhabited it. Unfortunately, no written records or documents aid our understanding of the establishment of the city or reconstruct the daily activities that took place there. Long walls are embellished with friezes of geometric figures, stylized birds and fish, ocean motifs, and mythological creatures—although some might be considered a bit too impeccably restored. There are no doors or arches in the entire complex, and there are no stairs—only ramps.

There are four main sites at Chan Chan, all spread over a large area that requires either a lot of walking or a couple of taxi rides. The principal complex, named the **Tschudi Palace** for a 19th-century Swiss explorer, has been partially restored, and a walking tour is indicated by painted arrows. The royal palace was home to a noble population of 500 to 1,000. The first area of interest is a ceremonial courtyard decorated with aquatic-themed friezes. The original walls were 18m (59 ft.) high. Just beyond the courtyard are walls with interesting friezes of fish and seabirds. The most fascinating component of the palace is the large area known as the Sanctuary, whose walls are textured like fishing nets. Although Chan Chan contains the ruins of an additional eight royal compounds, none has been restored like Tschudi, and very little can be seen or understood from viewing them.

The **Museo de Sitio de Chan Chan,** along the road back toward Trujillo, has a small collection of ceramics from Chan Chan and some exhibits about the nature of

---

Tips Chan Chan Crime Report

Chan Chan is spread out over several kilometers, and some visitors walking alone among the component parts have reported robberies and attacks. To be safe, stick to the main paths between the major sites and avoid wandering along smaller paths in the open fields around Tschudi Palace. Chan Chan is just a couple of kilometers from the beach, but the route to the water has a very bad reputation and should be avoided; too many reports of muggings and worse have been registered over the years to risk it. There have also been crime reports in the neighborhoods around Huaca Arco Iris and Huaca Esmeralda; it's best to take a taxi there from the Museo de Sitio de Chan Chan.

Fun Fact **The Peruvian Rat Dog**

Near the Chan Chan site museum and elsewhere in northern Peru, you might spot a peculiar smooth, black-skinned creature, often with blotches. This less than blessed creature is the *biringo,* or Peruvian hairless dog. Ancient and—to my Labrador-loving tastes—ugly as all get out, these dogs were kept by several of the pre-Incan cultures of the region, and they're still around and kept as pets. These dogs are hot to the touch, and it is said that ancient nobles kept them as portable heaters. The Lambayeque and Chimú not only domesticated the animal, though; they also made it part of their diets. Eeww.

---

the city and its history. The museum is equipped with a new auditorium and models of Chan Chan; an audio and light presentation is given in English as well as Spanish. The museum is at least a 20-minute walk from Tschudi Palace.

Huaca Esmeralda and Huaca Arco Iris are two smaller pyramidal temples that are rather removed from the main palace. They are included in the Chan Chan ticket, but one must go to either the museum or Tschudi Palace first. **Huaca Esmeralda** is in the Mansiche district, midway between Chan Chan and Trujillo (several blocks behind the church, to the right). The huaca consists of a couple platforms and some friezes that have not yet been restored; although they are less impressive than others, at least visitors get a clear chance to see original reliefs.

Huaca Arco Iris (**Rainbow Temple,** also called **Huaca El Dragón**), lies in the La Esperanza suburb a couple kilometers from Trujillo, west of the Pan-American Highway. It is in much better condition than Huaca Esmeralda, having been excavated only in the 1960s, and its well-conserved rainbow-shaped friezes are fascinating. Some have interpreted the central motif to be that of a dragon. Outer walls have reliefs of snakes and peculiar lizards. The fairly large structure has several ramps, and visitors can climb to platforms at the top of the temple.

To visit all the sites, you'll need the better part of a day. Many people choose to break up the visit over 2 days. A visit can begin at either Tschudi Palace or at the Museo de Sitio, transferring between them by bus or taxi, and then going to the adjunct temple sites by taxi.

Valle de Moche. (Huaca Arco Iris: Jr. Pedro Murillo 1681, La Esperanza, Trujillo, Panamericana Norte). Admission S/10 ($2.85); ticket is good for 48 hr. and all 4 sites of the complex. Guides are available at the entrance to Tschudi Palace for S/20–S/30 ($5.70–$8.55) per group. Daily 9am–4pm. Catch the Huanchaco bus (S/3 or 85¢) on Av. España (at the corner of Independencia/Ejército) and ask to be let off at the turnoff to Chan Chan. Occasionally, there are taxis waiting here; otherwise, walk nearly a mile down a dirt road to the left, to the Tschudi Palace. For the Museo de Sitio, catch a bus returning to Trujillo. Taxis from Trujillo cost S/14–S/17.5 ($4–$5). Because transportation among the 4 sites is not always available, it might be worthwhile to contract a taxi to take you to the sites and wait for you.

El Brujo *☆* Difficult to get to and explore without a private guide, the remote Moche complex of El Brujo nonetheless makes a very worthwhile visit for those intrigued by what they've seen at Chan Chan and the huacas near Trujillo. Because it is so little explored—until recently, it was closed to the public—many visitors enjoy El Brujo even more than those other sites. (Because of ongoing excavations, some groups are reportedly still occasionally turned away.)

El Brujo lies in the Chicama Valley, about 60km (37 miles) north of Trujillo along the coast, or 1½ hours by car. A number of cultures developed in the Chicama Valley region since the pre-ceramic period, and at least one of the three temples here, **Huaca Prieta,** is about 5,000 years old. Oddly enough, it's essentially a giant, prehistoric garbage dump—not much to see for nonspecialists, but containing a wealth of non-biodegradable information for archaeologists researching the ancient people of the same name. (The Huaca Prieta civilization inhabited the area from around 3500–2200 B.C.) The main temple of interest at El Brujo is **Huaca Cao,** a leveled-off pyramid with terrific and huge multicolored friezes—some of the finest in northern Peru. They depict figures of warriors, priests, and sacrificial victims. Nearby, **Huaca Cortada** has some cool and menacing figures in high relief brandishing a knife in one hand and a recently decapitated head in the other.

Near Magdalena de Cao, Valle de Chicama. Admission S/20 ($5.70). Daily 9am–4pm. Several tour agencies in Trujillo organize excursions to El Brujo; be sure to ask about the status of the current admissions policy at the site. Private guides who frequently take individuals and small groups are Michael White and Clara Luz Bravo (© **044/243-347**). Ask at the Tourism Information Office (© **044/938-922**) about other guides.

Huacas de Moche ⚐ About 8km (5 miles) south of Trujillo in the desert Valle de Moche, this complex of Moche ruins is enigmatic from a distance. Two imposing rounded-off and weathered adobe pyramids, partially eroded, sit in a dusty open field at the foot of Cerro Blanco. Built by the Moche people around A.D. 500, they are about 7 centuries older than the ruined city of Chan Chan. The two masses constituted a religious center and an urban settlement.

The first pyramid, the **Huaca del Sol (Temple of the Sun),** is nearly 20m (66 ft.) high, although it was once bigger by perhaps two-thirds, and it was very likely the largest man-made structure in the Americas in its day. Heavy rains of the El Niño phenomenon, and the Spaniards' diversion of the nearby Moche River, precipitated the erosion. It is said to have been built by 250,000 men and 140 million adobe bricks. The pyramid once surely was composed of multiple staircases and platforms. The *huaca* (pyramid) remains unexcavated, and it looks very fragile, as though a major rainstorm could easily take it out. Signs warn visitors against climbing on the ruins (NO ESCALAR), but plenty do climb up to the top along steep trails. Additional foot traffic only furthers the erosion, though, and the views are equally good from the Huaca de la Luna across the way. Some visitors inevitably find this lumpen mass a bit of a disappointment, just a massive mound of muddy earth; if you find yourself in that camp, hurry over to the neighboring *huaca.*

Across the open field, where burial sites have been found and living quarters were once erected, is the smaller but more interesting **Huaca de la Luna (Temple of the Moon).** It is better preserved than the Temple of the Sun and has been excavated; many of the most important finds took place in the 1990s, and excavations are ongoing. The structure consists of five independent levels, with no communication among them—perhaps a result of the fact that the huaca was constructed in major phases over 600 years. Inside the adobe walls (at the top of an entrance ramp) are polychromatic friezes of large rhomboids, featuring a repeated motif of the fearsome anthropomorphic figure Ai-Apaek, known as *El Degollador* (the decapitator), and several secondary figures. The yellow, red, white, and black designs are quite remarkable; the god is said to have the hair of the sea and eyes of an owl. From the top of the Huaca de la Luna, there are excellent views of Huaca del Sol and the surrounding countryside. Near the ticket booth, where you can arrange for a guide, is a small refreshment stand and souvenir shop.

Moche Culture

Anyone who has spent time in a small museum room crammed with the famed erotic ceramics of the Moche culture might feel that we know almost too much about this ancient civilization, certainly more than plenty of people are comfortable seeing depicted on vases and other vessels. But our knowledge isn't limited to the Moche's sexual mores. The Moche, who inhabited the northern coastal desert of Peru from A.D. 100 to 700, left detailed information about their entire civilization in their finely detailed ceramics, which are some of the finest produced in pre-Columbian Peru. The Moche are, along with the contemporary Nasca people from the desert coast south of Lima, the best-documented culture of the Classical period.

The apogee of Moche society was A.D. 500–600. Although they possessed no written language, their superior painted pottery presents evidence of nearly all elements of their society, from disease and dance to architecture, transportation, agriculture, music, and religion. The Moche (also referred to as "Mochica," although the latter term is losing some currency) were a strictly hierarchical, elite-dominated society that developed into a theocracy. They also constituted one of the first true urban cultures in Peru. Religious temples or pyramids, called *huacas,* were restricted to nobles, warriors, and priests; common citizens—farmers, artisans, fishers, and slaves—lived in areas removed from the temples.

The finest selection of Moche ceramics in the country is found at the Museo Arqueológico Rafael Larco Herrera (p. 138) in Lima, the largest private collection of pre-Columbian art in the world. The founder of the museum is the author of the classic study *Los Mochicas.* The Museo de Arte Precolombino (p. 215) in Cusco also has a fine, although small, collection of Moche artifacts.

Valle de Moche. ✆ 044/291-894. Admission S/10 ($2.85); cost includes a Spanish- or English-speaking guide (tip expected). Daily 9am–4pm. Catch the yellow "Campiña de Moche" colectivo (S/1 or 30¢) on Suárez (at Av. Los Incas), several blocks northeast of the Plaza de Armas. Otherwise, you can take a taxi there for about S/18 ($5.15). In high season, you won't need to have the driver wait because there are frequent buses and taxis returning to Trujillo. If there are few people around, however, you can usually get the driver to wait an hour or so to take you back to Trujillo for around S/35 ($10) round-trip.

SHOPPING

Trujillo doesn't have much to interest potential shoppers, unless you need eyeglasses; Calle Bolívar is loaded with opticians. For a taste of what shopping means to most Trujillo natives, check out the sprawling **street mercado** that operates daily along Avenida Los Incas. It's one of the more unruly (and headache-inducing) markets in Peru, with vendors struggling to be heard over the incessant sounds of car horns. The market stretches across several blocks and spreads out into the street, selling an unending variety of vegetables, fish, and household items; there are even carts full of charcoal.

Most visitors will be better off shopping in Huanchaco. **Artesanía del Norte,** Los Olivos 504 (✆ **044/461-220**), has some of the coolest exclusive ceramics designs in

Peru. They'll ship pieces to your home if you can't limit yourself to just one. The **mercado de artesanía** fronting the beach in Huanchaco has a number of stalls and is also an excellent place for jewelry, including pieces made with the sought-after blue stone lapis lazuli.

WHERE TO STAY

Visitors have the option of staying in downtown Trujillo, which has a nice colonial feel to it but can be rather noisy and harried, or staying in the less expensive and more relaxed beachside town of Huanchaco, just 12km (7½ miles) away, where there are several laid-back resort hotels and some good budget *hostales*. Because the focus of many travelers' attentions is Chan Chan, which is located northwest of the city toward Huanchaco, staying beachside is a very practical option.

DOWNTOWN TRUJILLO
Expensive
Gran Hotel El Golf *(Kids)*   This modern resort hotel, the largest in the north of Peru, is built around a large circular swimming pool and is located close to a golf country club in one of the most upscale residential districts of Trujillo (5 min. driving from the Plaza de Armas). However, the hotel certainly doesn't have the character of the Hotel Libertador on the main square, which beats it with its location and historic building. Rooms are spacious, as are bathrooms, but I wouldn't call them luxurious. The Golf's two-story units overlook the pool and nice gardens. For those (particularly families) looking for some relaxation and space for the kids to run around in, it's not a bad bet. Additional distractions include tennis courts, a spa, children's games, and nearby beaches.

Los Cocoteros 500, Urbanización El Golf, Trujillo. © **044/282-515.** Fax 044/282-231. 120 units. $80–$95 double. Rate includes taxes and breakfast buffet. AE, V. **Amenities:** Restaurant; bar; outdoor pool; nearby golf course w/guest privileges; *frontón* and 2 tennis courts; spa; concierge; business center; 24-hr. room service; laundry service. *In room:* A/C, TV, minibar, hair dryer, safe.

Hotel Libertador Trujillo *(Kids)*   The top place to stay in Trujillo, and not a bad value given its superb location and amenities, is right on the Plaza de Armas, in a beautiful salmon-colored colonial mansion with a courtyard patio and a nice pool with palm trees and lots of vegetation. The place has a fair amount of colonial elegance and flavor. Rooms are not spectacularly luxurious, but they are certainly comfortable and well outfitted with somewhat dated furnishings. Rooms on the interior are quieter and have views of the pool. Other rooms look out onto the busy but pretty plaza, and some have small balconies that are perfect for people-watching (but be prepared for the trade-off: street noise until late). The hotel has a handsome bar, a good restaurant, and both dry and steam saunas. On Sunday, there's a big-time brunch starting at noon, with both Peruvian and international foods (S/35 or $10 for adults; half-price for children).

Jr. Independencia 48, Plaza de Armas, Trujillo. © **044/232-741,** or 01/442-995 for reservations. Fax 044/235-641. www.libertador.com.pe. 78 units. $100–$115 double; $150–$1950 suite. Rate includes taxes and breakfast buffet. AE, DC, MC, V. **Amenities:** Restaurant; bar; excellent outdoor pool; sauna; concierge; 24-hr. room service; laundry service. *In room:* A/C, TV, minibar, hair dryer, safe.

Moderate
Los Conquistadores Hotel *(Value)*   On a busy street just a couple blocks from the Plaza de Armas, this modern and very clean midsize independent hotel is a nice surprise.

With handsome public rooms set way back from the street and its hubbub, it has a very welcoming atmosphere and good service. All of the quiet rooms are large and carpeted, with pretty standard modern hotel decor and good beds decked out in flowery bedspreads. Suites are especially large, with separate sitting areas. Walk-in discounts are frequently available. In this price range, Los Conquistadores is your best bet.

Diego de Almagro 586, Trujillo. (✆) **044/203-350.** Fax 044/235-917. conquistadores@viabcp.com. 50 units. $73 double. Rate includes taxes and continental breakfast. AE, DC, MC, V. **Amenities:** Restaurant; bar; business center; room service; laundry service. *In room:* A/C, TV.

Inexpensive

Hostal Colonial ✰ *(Finds)* *(Value)*   My taxi driver turned me on to this small Belgian-owned hotel, and for once, the driver wasn't just trawling for a commission—he was right. A handsome and recently restored colonial house just a block from the Plaza de Armas, it is an excellent value. Some of the rooms, though large, are a bit plain. The rooms looking over the interior patio are best; a couple of them have balconies with chairs. If you don't mind a bit of street noise, the rooms facing the street are also good bets. Attached to the hotel is a genial little cafe that's a good, cheap place for lunch.

Jr. Independencia 618, Trujillo. (✆) **044/258-261.** Fax 044/223-410. hostcolonialtruji@latinmail.com. 24 units. S/60 ($17) double. Rate includes taxes and breakfast. No credit cards. **Amenities:** Restaurant; room service. *In room:* TV.

Hotel Americano   This formerly grand hotel is a shadow of its former self, but fans of faded splendor—better put, lovers of down-in-the-chops decadence—might find themselves at home here. The huge hotel has a few hints of its bygone elegance and grand architecture (now totally uncared for) in the lobby, such as cool reliefs—if you squint hard enough. The rooms, though, are pretty dingy. Floorboards are in bad shape, the fluorescent lighting stinks, and the place feels abandoned. It's a shame, because if it were restored and kept up, it would look like an early-20th-century North African hotel straight out of *The English Patient.* Comparatively, the Hostal Colonial or any of the *hostales* in Huanchaco are a much better value. Then again, staying at the Americano might have its own peculiar value for some travelers, inexplicably drawn to places in free-fall decline.

Jr. Pizarro 764, Trujillo. (✆) **044/241-361.** 120 units. S/35 ($10) double with bathroom and hot water; S/16 ($4.55) double without bathroom. Rate includes taxes. No credit cards. *In room:* No phone.

HUANCHACO
Moderate

Hostal Bracamonte *(Value)* *(Kids)*   A mini resort tucked behind a high gate and a couple of blocks from the beach, this relaxed *hostal* has a bit of a motel atmosphere. Rooms and bungalows are positioned around a large pool. Perfect for families, the hotel has a playground and gardens for kids to run around, as well as several terraces, a barbecue grill area, and a game room. Bungalows have room for three or four guests each. Rooms have a beachy, unadorned feel, with tile floors but comfortable beds. Overall, it's a pretty good, if not outstanding, value, and it's an especially welcome retreat for those traveling with children.

Jr. Los Olivos 503, Huanchaco. (✆) **044/461-162.** Fax 044/461-266. www.hostalbracamonte.com. 28 units. $28–$32 double; $50–$55 bungalow. Rates include taxes. AE, DC, MC, V. **Amenities:** Restaurant; cafeteria; bar; outdoor pool; game room. *In room:* A/C, TV.

Huanchaco International Hotel ✰ *(Kids)*   This Belgian-owned modern beach resort hotel, positioned right on the beach but a bit out of town, on the road to Huanchaco, is a welcoming place, especially for families. Popular with vacationing Peruvians, it has a huge pool, yellow and white bungalow accommodations dotting the property, and gardens with sea views. Breakfast is served on a terrace overlooking the beach. Rooms are large and very clean; many of the little houselike bungalows—which can house four adults—are attractively positioned up stone steps. If you're staying for a few days, ask about package deals that include area visits.

Autopista a Huanchaco Km 13.5, Playa Azul, Huanchaco. ℂ/fax **044/461-754**. www.huanchacointernational.com. 40 units. $49 double; $69–$89 bungalow. Rates include taxes and breakfast. Packages available for longer stays. AE, DC, MC, V. **Amenities:** Restaurant; bar; cafe; large outdoor pool; solarium; car-rental desk; laundry service. *In room:* TV.

Inexpensive
La Casa Suiza ⚐ *Finds*   A favorite of backpackers for more than a quarter of a century, this inn run by a Swiss-Peruvian family—still referred to as "Heidi's house" by longtime vets—is an extremely friendly place to hang out and meet up with other travelers. The large and comfortable rooms are simply adorned, but the star at this *hostal* is the great rooftop terrace, where guests line-dry their laundry and write in their journals. The terrace is topped by a tile table and glowing red Swiss lamp. There's a cable TV room, a book exchange, and Internet access (and even a laser printer). Would-be surfers are well cared for here; the *hostal* has gear (including wet suits and boards) for rent. Breakfast is prepared by Wendy, a Swiss woman who's practically an institution at this friendly joint. Most rooms are shared, although three have private bathrooms.

Los Pinos 451, Huanchaco. ℂ **044/461-285**. Fax 044/461-302. www.huanchaco.net/casasuiza. 8 units. $15 double with private bathroom; $5 per person in shared room with shared bathroom. Rates include taxes. No credit cards. **Amenities:** Breakfast room. *In room:* No phone.

WHERE TO DINE
Dining out is a pretty low-key affair in Trujillo. Even though it's Peru's third-largest city, it doesn't have many sophisticated restaurants. One hotel restaurant that's worth a visit even if you're not staying there—especially for brunch on the weekend—is the restaurant at the Hotel Libertador (see p. 380). Most visitors enjoy eating out in Huanchaco, which has one excellent luxury restaurant and a number of simple seafood places along the beach.

TRUJILLO
Moderate
El Mochica ⚐ PERUVIAN   The one restaurant that everyone in Trujillo recommends is a bit of a surprise. From the outside, it looks to be a pretty sophisticated joint: It's housed within a beautiful colonial building with an impressive carved-wood balcony. Inside, though, the dining room is a little jarring, with white plastic chairs and a large TV blaring videos in the front room but waiters dressed in black tie. A second room has a bar and a stage for live music on weekends. Despite the inauspicious surroundings, El Mochica produces very well-prepared and good-value *criollo* cooking and classic dishes such as roasted guinea pig and *parrilladas* (mixed grilled meats), in addition to fresh fish such as *corvina* (sea bass).

Bolívar 462. ℂ **044/293-441**. Reservations recommended for live music on weekends. Main courses S/8–S/28 ($2.30–$8). AE, DC, MC, V. Daily 8pm–1am.

Il Valentino ⚐ ITALIAN   Across from Trujillo's jam-packed Cine Primavera is the city's classiest-looking restaurant. An attractive, somewhat Mediterranean-style place, it has yellow walls and arched doorways, subdued lighting, and tables on two levels with tablecloths and fake flowers. The menu is dominated by pizzas and pastas of the upscale variety, plus a few steaks. It's perfectly located for dinner before or after a movie (Cine Primavera shows films in their original language), although service here can be a bit slow, so I recommend going to the movie first and having dinner afterward.

Orbegoso 224. ✆ **044/246-643**. Reservations recommended on weekends. Main courses S/15–S/30 ($4.30–$8.55). AE, DC, MC, V. Tues–Sun noon–11pm.

Restaurante Demarco _Value_ ITALIAN/INTERNATIONAL   A pleasant cafe-style restaurant, which resembles an ice cream parlor crammed with small tables and ceiling fans, Demarco has something for just about everyone and every time of day. From a good breakfast selection to sandwiches, pizza, pastas, and other Italian fare, as well as excellent cakes and ice creams, it draws a consistent crowd of locals. The extensive menu also has _criollo_ specialties such as _asado de res con puré y arroz_ (roast beef with mashed potatoes and rice), _churrasco con tacu tacu_ (grilled meats served with rice and beans), and the classic _lomo saltado_ (strips of beef with onions, tomatoes, and french fries over rice). It has a daily lunch _menú_ (inexpensive set-price meal) but is just as good for a midafternoon snack or late dessert.

Pizarro 725. ✆ **044/234-251**. Reservations not accepted. Main courses S/12–S/27 ($3.40–$7.70); menú del día S/10 ($2.85). AE, DC, MC, V. Daily 8am–midnight.

Restaurante Romano ITALIAN/INTERNATIONAL   Located on one of the city's main thoroughfares, this uncomplicated and cheery restaurant is a good, easygoing place for pizzas, rice dishes, salads, and omelets, as well as more substantial items such as steak, pork loin, and filet mignon with mushrooms. There are also homemade pastas, including ravioli, lasagna, and cannelloni. The weekday set-price menu is a very good value; it might be a tuna and vegetable salad to start, followed by baked chicken with rice and mashed potatoes, plus juice and bread. Romano is open for breakfast and has a nice selection of desserts and excellent coffees, including cappuccino and espresso. It's very popular with local regulars, especially at lunch. Waiters bring the food through the front door, which looks odd, as if they are going out to the street to fetch your meal. (The kitchen is around the other side of the restaurant.)

Pizarro 747. ✆ **044/252-251**. Reservations not accepted. Main courses S/9.50–S/21 ($2.70–$6); menú del día S/6–S/10 ($1.70–$2.85). AE, DC, MC, V. Daily 8am–midnight.

Inexpensive
Restaurant Colonial PERUVIAN   This cute and relaxed cafe, with just six tables, is attached to the Hostal Colonial (and shouldn't be confused with the recommended Club Colonial in Huanchaco). It has floor-to-ceiling wall murals of colonial Trujillo and Moche motifs from Las Huacas and other sites in the area. It offers simple Peruvian fare, but it's perfect for a great midday menú (just S/4 or $1.15), which might include a soup or _papa a la huancaína_ (boiled potato with a creamy cheese sauce) and a main course of _churrasco_ (barbecued meats) or _arroz con pollo_ (chicken and rice). The menu also has pork, Chinese-style fried rice, spaghetti, and omelets, as well as three breakfast options.

Jr. Independencia 618. ✆ **044/258-261**. Reservations not accepted. Main courses S/8–S/12 ($2.30–$3.40); menú del día S/4 ($1.15). No credit cards. Daily 8am–9pm.

HUANCHACO
Moderate
Club Colonial *Finds* *Finds* BELGIAN/FRENCH A romantic and magnificently inviting restaurant occupying a renovated 1790s mansion on a quiet square, this is the most refined place to dine in northern Peru. Enter through a small courtyard and stunning Art Nouveau stained-glass doors. The warm dining salon is straight ahead, and off to the right is a small bar with well-chosen cafe tables and chairs. The colorful decor lives up to the restaurant's name and reeks of French colonial atmosphere. Walls are bright blue, orange, red, and yellow, and the place is brimming with large mirrors, antiques, fresh flowers, and dark wood. It looks like some cool expat's house.

The menu is an interesting mix of Peruvian and Franco-Belgian items. Starters include excellent salads, ceviches, and homemade pastas. Main courses include French brochette in three sauces, cordon bleu, and pork loin with curry pineapple sauce. But for my money, the stars are the exquisitely prepared fish dishes, such as *corvina a la vasca* (Basque-style sea bass) and lobster. Desserts, such as crêpes suzettes and crêpes suchards (with ice cream and chocolate), are also outstanding. Service lags in comparison to the food and surroundings, but you're unlikely to care. After you've dined, wander out to the garden courtyard past the bar to see the 12 penguins and 2 small caimans. Club Colonial is more expensive than other restaurants in northern Peru but is definitely worth it.

Grau 272. © **044/461-015**. Reservations recommended. Main courses S/18–S/35 ($5.15–$10). AE, DC, MC, V. Daily noon–10pm.

Inexpensive
El Peñón *Value* SEAFOOD Huanchaco, a fishing village, is rightly famous for its fresh fish. And there are few better places to plunge into the local catch than this casual and comfy place, one of the first tourist-oriented restaurants in Huanchaco. It couldn't be simpler: white plastic chairs, tables with green tablecloths, and the roar of the sea. (There is also indoor seating, but the best spot is on the small terrace.) Located right across the street from the surf, the family-run restaurant is a favorite of locals, and the amiable owner seems to know everyone. Try one of the excellent ceviches, seafood omelets, or main courses such as *arroz con mariscos* (shellfish rice), *calamares* (squid), or *pulpo* (octopus).

Corner of Av. Víctor Larco and Raymondi. © **044/461-549**. Reservations recommended in high season. Main courses S/6–S/20 ($1.70–$5.70). DC, MC, V. Daily noon–10pm.

La Barca SEAFOOD A popular, homey little place with basic tables and chairs and very little fuss, "The Boat" serves up very good and reasonably priced fresh seafood dishes, as well as some *criollo* standards. I'd stick to the fish: succulent ceviche, *langostinos* (prawns), or *cangrejo* (crab). There's a daily set menú Monday through Friday, and on Saturday evening, there's a piano bar. There's a second, similar branch (© **044/ 461-052**) at Av. Víctor Larco 514, just a couple blocks away, facing the beach.

Jr. Unión 209. © **044/461-549**. Reservations recommended in high season. Main courses S/6–S/22 ($1.70–$6.30). DC, MC, V. Daily noon–10pm.

TRUJILLO AFTER DARK
Trujillo is pretty quiet except on weekends, when it springs to life. A few nightclubs and peñas are clustered in the centro, but most of the hopping discos that go all night are very local and young affairs, on the outskirts of the city. Trujillo has a surprising

roster of casinos and movie houses (including two multiplexes showing recently arrived English-language films), and those are as good as any destination for an evening out.

Las Tinajas, Pizarro 383 (ⓒ **044/296-272**), with a balcony overlooking the Plaza de Armas, is a pretty chic and popular bar with a downstairs disco, good for drinks mid-week. On weekends, it features live rock and pop; the cover is S/5 ($1.40). **El Estribo,** San Martín 810, is a lively and large open music hall with peña music and Mariah Carey wannabes occasionally performing. The cover charge is S/7 ($2). **La Canana,** San Martín 791 (ⓒ **044/232-503**), is another nearby peña with a good restaurant and live music and dancing on weekends. The cover is usually about S/10 ($2.85).

Luna Rota, at América Sur 2119 in the Santa María district at the end of Huayna Cápac (ⓒ **044/228-877**), is an all-in-one complex with a thumping disco for teenagers, a pub, and a casino for slightly more mature folks. The cover in the disco and pub is S/7 to S/10 ($2–$2.85).

Cine Primavera, Orbegoso 239, near the Plaza de Armas (ⓒ **044/241-277**), has first-run American and European films in their original languages and draws long lines of moviegoers. Among the collection of casinos along Orbegoso and Pizarro is **Casino Solid Gold,** Orbegoso 554 (ⓒ **044/207-662**). Open daily 24 hours, it has cocktail waitresses in flashy short skirts and a low-rent Vegas feel to it; its cheesy theme is "Chan Chan Lost World."

2 Chiclayo ⓡ

770km (478 miles) N of Lima; 200km (124 miles) N of Trujillo; 235km (146 miles) NW of Cajamarca

Although it's Peru's fourth-largest city, with a population of just under a half-million, Chiclayo would be just another busy commercial town, generating little notice among travelers, were it not for the city's strong associations with Peru's ancient cultures. The primary draw is Chiclayo's proximity to the archaeological sites Sipán and Túcume, two of the most important related to the Moche and Lambayeque cultures, and the spectacular Museo Tumbas Reales de Sipán, which houses one of the country's most remarkable finds of the past several decades: the tomb of the Lord of Sipán.

Chiclayo is a modern and relatively new city. Although it was founded in the mid–16th century, most of its real development dates to the late 1800s and early 1900s. (The Parque Principal, or main square, didn't come into existence until 1916.) Today Chiclayo is a sprawling, bustling place; the city itself holds little interest for most visitors. Frankly, most people come here to get out of town. The capital of the Lambayeque department, Chiclayo calls itself "La Ciudad de la Amistad"—the City of Friendship. There's no real reason for such a distinction as far as I can see, but why not? It's not Peru's prettiest, biggest, or most fascinating city, but it is an agreeable, down-to-earth place.

About 12km (7½ miles) northwest of Chiclayo, Lambayeque, site of the distinguished archaeological museums, Museo Tumbas Reales de Sipán and Museo Brüning, was once the more important of the two towns. Today that is true only from the traveler's perspective. It is a slow-moving, rather dilapidated town with a smattering of interesting colonial buildings, none of which is particularly well restored or open to visitors. Except for the draw of the Lord of Sipán, the town lives in the shadow of Chiclayo's ever-growing commercial importance.

ESSENTIALS
GETTING THERE
BY PLANE   **Star Peru** (© 01/705-9000) and **Aviandina** (© 01/447-8080) fly daily from Lima to Chiclayo; flights start at around $69. **Lan** (© 01/213-8200) flies from Trujillo; flights run from $81 to $114, though occasional promotional offers can be found for around $50. There are also flights north to and from Piura, and occasional charter flights from Cajamarca.

Flights arrive at **Aeropuerto José Quiñones González,** Av. Bolognesi s/n (© 074/233-192), just 2km (1¼ miles) east of downtown. To the center of Chiclayo, a taxi costs S/5 ($1.40).

BY BUS   Chiclayo is serviced by several domestic bus companies from Lima and most major points along the north coast and northern highlands. Many long-distance buses travel at night only. There is no central bus station in Chiclayo; most companies have their own terminals at offices on Avenida Bolognesi, 5 blocks south of the Parque Principal.

The major carriers making the 8-hour trip from Lima are **Ormeño** (© 01/472-5000), **CIVA** (© 01/428-5649), **Cruz del Sur** (© 01/424-6158; www.cruzdelsur. com), and **Oltursa** (© 01/225-4499; www.oltursa.com). **Transportes Línea** (© 044/245-181,** or 076/823-956) and **ITTSA** (© 044/222-541) make the 3-hour trip from Trujillo to Chiclayo, as do a number of colectivos and combis. Transportes Línea is also the major carrier from Huaraz (© 074/233-497) and Cajamarca (© 076/830-753).

VISITOR INFORMATION
Chiclayo has two accessible tourist information kiosks, run not by the municipal government, but by two related restaurants. One is on the Parque Principal, or the main plaza. Another is on Avenida José Balta Sur (at Manuel María Izaga), in front of the Hebrón restaurant. Both kiosks give out maps of the city and the area, and they'll give you some basic information about how to get around (and they'll put in a plug for barbecue chicken, to boot).

The official tourism information office is the **Ministry of Industry and Tourism (MITINCI),** at Sáenz Peña 838 (© 074/233-132); it's a large, bureaucratic office of little assistance to most travelers looking for general information. **Sipán Tours,** 7 de Enero 772 (© 074/229-053), is more amiable and willing to dispense information without giving you the hard sell for package tours (but if you're interested, it's one of the most reputable agencies in town offering city and archaeological tours). Another excellent agency, which has specialized in archaeology tours and independent travel in northern Peru and offers bilingual guides in several languages, is **Indiana Tours,** Colón 556 (© 074/222-991 or 1-9883-5617; www.indianatoursperu.com).

FAST FACTS   Most banks are clustered around the Parque Principal, including **Banco de Crédito,** José Balta 630, and **Interbanc,** Elías Aguirre 680. Money-changers usually hang around in front of banks.

In an **emergency,** call © 105. The helpful **tourist police** are located at Sáenz Peña 830 (© 074/236-700). For medical attention, go to **Hospital Las Mercedes,** González 635 (© 074/237-021); **Clínica Lambayeque,** Vicente de la Vega 415 (© 074/237-961); or **Clínica Santa Cecilia,** González 668 (© 074/237-154). In Lambayeque, head to **Hospital Belén de Lambayeque,** Ramón Castilla 597 (© 074/281-190).

For Internet access, try **Sic@n Internet,** Vicente de la Vega 204 (© 074/227-668), or **Efenet,** Elías Aguirre 181 (no phone). There are also Internet cabinas clustered around the Parque Principal and on Manuel María Izaga near Avenida Balta.

Chiclayo's **post office** is located at Elías Aguirre 140 (© 074/237-031), about 6 blocks from the Parque Principal. It's open Monday through Saturday from 8am to 8pm and Sunday from 8am to 2pm. The **Telefónica del Perú** office is behind the cathedral at Elías Aguirre 631 (© 074/232-225); it's open from Monday to Saturday from 8am to 6pm.

GETTING AROUND

Chiclayo is a busy and fairly congested city. The center of town is, as always, the Plaza de Armas—although, in Chiclayo, it more often goes by the name Parque Principal. About 4 blocks north of the main square is the other focal point in the city: the Mercado Modelo, a sprawling, spirited open street market with stalls spread across several blocks. The main axis in town is Avenida José Balta, which runs north to south and extends on either side of the Parque Principal (with designations Sur [south] and Norte [north]). Lambayeque is 12km (7½ miles) due west of Chiclayo; the airport and Sipán are to the east of Chiclayo.

Walking around the centro is easy enough, but you'll need public or private transportation to get to Lambayeque or the major archaeological sites.

BY TAXI   Inexpensive *mototaxis* buzz about downtown, as do regular taxis. You can hire the latter by the hour (S/21 or $6) or by the day (S/105–S/122 or $30–$35) to tour archaeological sites or to visit Lambayeque. A round-trip taxi ride to Túcume from Chiclayo costs between S/52.50 ($15) and S/70 ($20).

BY BUS   Combis and ómnibuses are most useful for getting to Lambayeque and several archaeological sites outside Chiclayo. There are several terminals around the city serving different destinations. The fare is about S/1 (30¢).

BY CAR   If you want to rent a car to make trips to Lambayeque, Sipán, Túcume, and other sites, try **Chiclayo Rent a Car** in the Gran Hotel Chiclayo at Av. Federico Villarreal 115 (© **074/237-512**). It rents four-wheel-drive vehicles.

WHAT TO SEE & DO
IN CHICLAYO

A brief look around Chiclayo should be sufficient. Start at the **Parque Principal,** the attractive and overwhelming focal point of life in the city. People camp out on park benches and slurp on ice cream cones, shoeshine boys scurry from one pair of scuffed-up loafers to the next, and pigeons flutter from treetops to sidewalks to rooftops. The white, twin-domed neoclassical **Catedral** that dominates the square dates to 1869. About 10 long blocks south of the plaza, the **Paseo de las Musas** is an attractive park area rather inexplicably outfitted with neoclassical statuary of mythological figures.

The fascinating **Mercado Modelo** ⊛, 5 blocks north of the Parque Principal, is one of Peru's most raucous open street markets. Open daily from dawn to dusk, it carries virtually everything under the sun, but it's famed for the section of small stalls crammed with the elixirs and potions of shamans and faith healers. The so-called *mercadillo de brujas* (witches' little market), near Calle Arica, is redolent with exotic spices and drying herbs, wild with visual overload: hanging shells, small altarpieces and bottles filled with hooves and claws, snakeskins, miniature desiccated crocs, claws, skunks, and fish eggs. Echoing throughout are the distinctive come-ons of vendors. The city of stalls is about as close as you'll get to India or Morocco in Peru, but it's nonetheless a primer on the country's extensive informal economy. You'll find luggage, natural Viagra substitutes, baskets, guitars, hats, calf brains, children's clothes, vats of peanut butter, stuffed animals, shops of canned goods that look like someone's pantry, machetes, and butcher knives. There are dozens of beauty salons under wooden ceilings, and shoe and electronics repair headquarters.

IN LAMBAYEQUE

The splendid, modern **Museo Tumbas Reales de Sipán** (see later in this section) is the undisputed highlight of this small, quiet, and dusty town that was once considerably more important than its bigger neighbor but which has long since been overtaken, at least in terms of commercial importance, by it. The new museum has stolen quite a bit of the thunder of the **Museo Arqueológico Brüning,** where the Lord of Sipán used to reside. A few clues to Lambayeque's former status are evident in a number of colonial houses and the baroque **Iglesia de San Pedro,** a large and impressive yellow-and-white church built in 1700 and located on the main square. It's worth a look inside for the impressive mural paintings on the ceiling of the central nave and the cupola. Columns are painted to look like real marble, which I suppose they do if you squint hard enough. The rest of the church is done up in pastel hues of green, blue, and yellow.

On the corner of Dos de Mayo and San Martín is Lambayeque's other building of import, **Casa de la Logia** (also known as **Casa Montjoy**). Erected in the 16th century, it claims the longest balcony in Peru, a pretty wooden wraparound structure 67m (220 ft.) long. The house can be viewed only from the exterior.

Lambayeque really springs to life only on market day, Sunday. Otherwise, there's little to detain visitors. If you're looking for a bite to eat after visiting the Brüning Museum, check out Dos de Mayo, where there are several *cevicherías* and other restaurants.

Museo Arqueológico Brüning ⚔ Until its Sipán treasures were removed and transferred to the new Tumbes Reales Museum 2 blocks away (see below), this was the preeminent museum in northern Peru. Without its star attraction, the museum, founded in 1966, no longer draws crowds, but it still retains some important archaeological finds, such as Sicán masks from Batán Grande, excellent Moche ceramics, and an assortment of artifacts found at Tucumé. The collection includes some 1,500 items from the Lambayeque, Moche, Chavín, Vicus, and Incan civilizations. Some pieces date back 10,000 years.

Av. Huamachuco (Block 7), Lambayeque. © **074/282-110**. Admission S/10 ($2.85), students S/3 (85¢). Guides available for S/10 ($2.85). Daily 9am–5:30pm. Colectivos to Lambayeque depart Chiclayo from the corner of Av. Angamos and Vicente de la Vega, and pass right in front of the Brüning Museum about a half-hour later. The main plaza is a couple blocks from the museum (across the street).

Museo Tumbas Reales de Sipán ⚔⚔⚔ This stunningly modern museum certainly stands out in northern Peru, land of dusty archaeological pyramids and colonial towns. Its daring architecture of bold angles, glass and orange concrete makes a statement by echoing the ancient Moche pyramids of the region, but the principal attraction is within. It holds one of Peru's most spectacular exhibits, the tomb of the **Lord of Sipán,** discovered in 1987, which ranks as one of the most important archaeological discoveries in Peru of the past 50 years. Unearthed at the Huaca Rajada at Sipán, the multilevel royal funeral tomb of El Señor de Sipán, a Moche royal figure buried more than 1,700 years ago, was remarkable for its undisturbed, methodical layers and wealth of ceremonial ornaments and treasures that provided key clues to Moche culture. Buried along with the king, who was presumed to be a sort of living deity, were companions joining him on his journey to the afterlife: a Moche warrior, a priest, three female concubines, a dog, two llamas, a child, 212 food and beverage vessels, and a guard with a copper shield, gold helmet, and amputated feet—symbolic of his everlasting protection over the king's tomb.

The space dedicated to the Lord of Sipán is one of the most impressive and unforgettable sights under a roof in Peru—a revelation for visitors who've visited several of the archaeological sites in northern Peru and been disappointed to find little more than difficult-to-decipher colossal piles of clay. In this marvelously designed three-level museum, the spectacular Sipán finds articulate the grandeur and achievements of pre-Incan cultures and help us comprehend their religious beliefs, social structure, and sophistication. On display from the main funerary chamber—amazingly, never looted—are headdresses, garments, and breastplates of gold, silver, and precious stones that tell an intricate story of power and rank. Several pieces, such as the royal necklace of 20 peanuts, half gold and half silver, are stunning. Other tombs uncovered and re-created here are those of the priest, the mythical "Bird-Man" and top-ranking religious official, and the Viejo Señor de Sipán (or Old Lord of Sipán), a Moche spiritual dignitary whose death preceded that of the newer lord's and whose remains were found buried farther below.

The Tumbes Reales Museum is one of the best organized and best designed in Peru, an eminently worthy resting place for this monumental discovery. You'll need at least a couple of hours to explore it fully.

Juan Pablo Vizcardo y Guzman s/n, Lambayeque. © 074/283-977. Admission S/7 ($2), seniors S/2.50 (70¢), students S/1 (85¢). Guides available for S/15 ($4.30). Tues–Sun 9am–5pm. Colectivos to Lambayeque depart Chiclayo from the corner of Av. Angamos and Vicente de la Vega, and pass right in front of the Tumbes Reales Museum about a half-hour later.

IN FERREÑAFE

Museo Nacional Sicán 🐴🐴   Although not quite as celebrated as the Museo Tumbes Reales, this handsome, modern and excellent museum, inaugurated in 2001, is very much worth a visit to round out an understanding of the region's ancient civilizations. Like its better-known sibling, it too is pyramid-shaped and a study in cement and glass, but it focuses on the Sicán culture (also called Lambayeque) that succeeded the Moche and thrived until the 14th century. The Sicán (which means "Temple of the Moon"), who were the first to discover bronze in northern Peru, buried their dead in unique vertical rooms and surrounded them with large collections of valuable metals. Those graves provided looters throughout Peru with a wealth of sought-after gold objects. Sicán masks with *ojos alados,* or "winged eyes," are very prized among institutions and collectors, and some excellent examples are on view here. The museum is located in Ferreñafe, 20km (12 miles) north of Chiclayo, along the road that leads to Batán Grande (see below).

Av. Batán Grande (Block 9), Carretera a Pítipo, Ferreñafe. © 074/286-469. Admission S/7.50 ($2.15), seniors and students S/3 (85¢). Guides available for S/10 ($2.85). Tues–Sun 9am–5pm. Colectivos to Ferreñafe depart Chiclayo from the Terminal de Epsel, Av. Oriente at Nicolás de Piérola.

ARCHAEOLOGICAL SITES NEAR CHICLAYO

Batán Grande   The Batán Grande archaeological complex is a set of ruins from the Sicán culture that comprises some 50 adobe pyramids. Here archaeologists discovered a network of tombs from the middle Sicán period (A.D. 900–1000). Some of the finest pre-Columbian artifacts in Peruvian museums were found here, including a nearly 7-pound gold Tumi (ceremonial knife) figure and an estimated 90% of all gold pieces from the Lambayeque civilization. Set amid a large nature reserve of mesquite forest (El Bosque Seco de Pómac), there's an on-site interpretation center for visitors, but the pyramids are not as established on the tourist circuit as are those at Túcume.

Located 57km (35 miles) SE of Chiclayo, and 5km (3 miles) NE of Túcume. © 074/201-470. Admission S/7 ($2) adults, S/2.50 (70¢) students. Guides available for S/10 ($2.85). Daily 7am–4pm. Colectivos leave from the Terminal de Epsel at the corner of Av. Oriente and Nicolás de Piérola in Chiclayo, a somewhat unsavory area. It's more convenient to visit Batán Grande by organized tour; contact Sipán Tours at © 074/229-053.

Templo de Sipán   The site where the Lord of Sipán was discovered in 1987, this Moche burial ground 35km (22 miles) from Chiclayo was overlooked by archaeologists for decades. Grave robbers, who'd beaten scientists to countless other valuable sites in Peru, had just begun to loot the ones here, tipping off Peruvian archaeologist Dr. Walter Alva to the presence of the tomb in time to save it. The Sipán sarcophagus held greater riches than any other found to date in Peru and, today, is recognized as one of the most outstanding of the Americas. The twin adobe pyramids, connected by a platform, held five royal tombs. The most elaborate was that of El Señor de Sipán; deeper still was the tomb of an older spiritual leader, now referred to as El Viejo Señor. The remains of both are exhibited at the Museo Tumbes Reales in Lambayeque. Near the original site, Huaca Rajada ("Cracked Pyramid") is a small site museum with photos of the excavations and some replicas of tombs. Although it's interesting to see where the tombs were found, and the views from the top of the large pyramid across from the Sipán excavation site are excellent, Templo de Sipán is no substitute for the splendor of jewels and ornaments now housed at the Museo Tumbes Reales.

Complejo Arqueológico de Huaca Rajada, Sipán. ⓒ **074/800-048**. Admission S/5 ($1.40). Guides available for S/7 ($2). Daily 8am–6pm. Colectivos leave from the Terminal de Epsel at the corner of Av. Oriente and Nicolás de Piérola in Chiclayo, a somewhat unsavory area, and take about 45 min.

Túcume 🐸🐸 Located 33km (20 miles) north of Chiclayo, this magnificent, massive complex of 26 adobe pyramids (not for nothing do locals call it "El Valle de las Pirámides") was constructed by the Sicán civilization around A.D. 1000 and developed over a period of nearly 500 years. The site was settled and enlarged by the Chimú culture in the 14th century and, finally, occupied by the Incas. Túcume was the most important elite urban center of the region and is considered the last great capital of the Lambayeque culture.

You can wander freely around the maze of courtyards and pyramids, and even scale several of them, which are still being excavated and together present an enigmatic desert ensemble. Walking around sites such as these is almost more evocative of what a contemporary archaeologist's life is like than of the lives of those ancient cultures that lived there. The Túcume complex's stunning size, more than a mile long in each direction (a total of 32 hectares/79 acres), is more impressive than any individual structure. The pyramid toward the back of the complex, known as **Huaca Larga,** is reputed to be the largest adobe brick structure in South America. It measures (even after erosion) 700m (2,297 ft.) long, 280m (919 ft.) wide, and 30m (98 ft.) high. A massive platform with several patios and courtyards connected by ramps and corridors, the huaca has walls covered in red, white, and black murals. Archaeologists have uncovered evidence of the three major stages of construction in Huaca Larga, from the original Lambayeque to Chimú, whose "Temple of the Mythical Bird" dates to 1375, and finally an Incan structure built on top of the Chimú building at the end of the 15th century. Inside the Incan room was a burial tomb, where 22 bodies were discovered, including a local ruler and warrior, interred along with two other males and 19 females.

An interestingly conceived site museum exhibits photographs of the excavations and discusses the involvement of a Norwegian explorer, the late Dr. Thor Heyerdahl, who sought to connect ancient Peruvian culture to that of Polynesia. (He sailed a balsawood craft called the *Kon Tiki* from Peru to the Polynesian islands.) Heyerdahl was the director of the 1989 to 1994 Túcume Project, which carried out excavations at the site. Also on-site are a handicrafts-and-ceramics workshop and a snack shop. You'll often find women cooking out in the open on the grounds.

Complejo Arqueológico, Caserío La Raya, Campo. ⓒ **074/422-027**, or 074/800-052 site museum. Admission S/7 ($2) adults, S/2.50 (70¢) students. Guides available for S/10 ($2.85). Daily 8am–4:30pm. Colectivos leave from Av. Angamos between Naturaleza and Pardo in Chiclayo (a 45-min. ride), although they leave travelers a good mile or so from the site. Look for a taxi or *mototaxi,* or walk along the road. A good idea is to visit the Museo Arqueológico Brüning in the morning and head out to Túcume in the afternoon. Buses leave for Túcume from very near the museum in Lambayeque; the ticket office can indicate exactly where. Tell the driver you'll be getting off at Túcume.

The Sicán Civilization

The Sicán culture (often designated the Lambayeque civilization, referring to the region where it grew to prominence) developed on the north coast of Peru in the 7th century following the collapse of the Moche civilization. A sophisticated culture whose economic mainstay was agriculture, the Sicán specialized in irrigation engineering. The society reached its apogee between A.D. 900 and 1100, and established religious and administrative headquarters at Batán Grande in the Pómac forest, near the Leche River. The site there is known as the "Temple of the Moon" in the ancient local dialect, Muchik. Around 1100, the Sicán abandoned Batán Grande, which they appear to have set fire to, and moved their capital across the valley to El Purgatorio, a hill in the midst of what are now the Túcume ruins. There they built a splendid urban center, the most important in the region, but the civilization was eventually conquered by the Chimú in 1375.

Zaña   Ruins of an entirely different sort, this 16th-century ghost town was once an important and wealthy colonial outpost, loaded with churches and monasteries. On the fast track toward becoming the Peruvian capital, it underwent a turbulent period of slave rebellion and pirate attacks. Wealthy families fled to Lambayeque city, and Zaña was soon afterward wiped out by a massive flood in 1720. The overflowing Río Zaña caused such structural damage that the population abandoned the city. Today it's a curious sight of ornate columns, church arches, and the remains of the once-grand Gothic Convento de San Agustín (as well as three other convents). A small, inhabited village (also called Zaña) is nearby.

46km (29 miles) SE of Chiclayo. Colectivos leave from the Terminal de Epsel on the corner of Av. Oriente and Nicolás de Piérola in Chiclayo, a somewhat unsavory area. Numerous tour agencies also include Zaña in organized outings, probably the most efficient way of visiting the town; try Sipán Tours at © 074/229-053.

NEARBY BEACHES: PIMENTEL & SANTA ROSA

Pimentel is a beach resort 14km (8¾ miles) west of Chiclayo, with a nice enough beach that's very popular in summer and a small fishing community that still employs the *caballitos de mar* (totora-reed boats) seen in Huanchaco, near Trujillo. Just 6km (3¾ miles) south of Pimentel is **Santa Rosa,** a more attractive beach and fishing village with totora-reed and gaily painted wooden fishing boats. It has a handful of good seafood restaurants. Both beaches are low-key and a good antidote to touring archaeological sites.

Buses and colectivos run from Vicente Vega and Angamos in Chiclayo to Pimentel. In summer, they continue along a "circuito de playas" to Santa Rosa, Puerto Etén, and Monsefú, none of which is spectacular.

WHERE TO STAY

Chiclayo is hardly brimming with good, interesting hotel options. The best among the bunch are merely functional. Travelers used to a high level of comfort and style won't find much to their liking in Chiclayo, and the paucity of good hotels extends down to the budget level.

EXPENSIVE

Gran Hotel Chiclayo   Several blocks removed from the heart of downtown, Chiclayo's largest and most luxurious hotel is a modern, massive concrete block with mainstream corporate style. Rooms are large and well equipped, if without much personality. This hotel has all the amenities and services that business travelers demand, as well as a nice round pool for leisure visitors. The El Caballito disco and the happening "Karaoke Solid Gold" casino draw plenty of locals throughout the week.

Av. Federico Villarreal 115, Chiclayo. ℂ **074/234-911.** Fax 074/223-961. www.granhotelchiclayo.com.pe. 129 units. $80 double; $93–$155 suite. Rates include taxes, breakfast buffet, and airport transfer. AE, DC, MC, V. **Amenities:** Restaurant; bar; outdoor pool; concierge; car-rental desk; business center; 24-hr. room service; laundry service. *In room:* A/C, TV, minibar, hair dryer, safe.

MODERATE

Costa del Sol 🌴 *Value*   A mini high-rise building on Chiclayo's most important and busiest street, this midsize hotel offers a good mix of amenities and easygoing charm. The remodeled, newly sedate rooms are spacious and comfortable, and bathrooms are also of a good size. Unexpected features are the cute rooftop pool and the Jacuzzi with a dry sauna. All in all, it's a good value with enough personality to set it apart from the more expensive and more standard Gran Hotel Chiclayo.

Av. José Balta 399, Chiclayo. ℂ **074/227-272.** Fax 074/209-342. www.costadelsolperu.com. 40 units. $65 double; $85–$90 suite. Rates include taxes and continental breakfast buffet. AE, DC, MC, V. **Amenities:** Restaurant; bar; outdoor pool; Jacuzzi; sauna; concierge; small business center; 24-hr. room service; laundry service. *In room:* A/C, TV, minibar.

Las Musas Hotel & Casino *Value*   Formerly the Hotel María Alejandra, now revamped as a casino and hotel, Las Musas is pleasant and one of Chiclayo's better values. I certainly like it better than the more-expensive Garza. Its modern exterior doesn't do much for me, but it has good services, a casino, and a nice view of the city from a fairly calm residential area. The rooms aren't luxurious but they are quite nicely decorated in subdued colors, and all have nice, large bathtubs—which is a real luxury.

Los Faiques 101 (facing Paseo de las Musas), Urbanización Santa Victoria, Chiclayo. ℂ **074/273-445.** Fax 074/273-450. tours@perutravelnet.com. 42 units. $53 double; $83 suite. Rates include taxes and continental breakfast. AE, DC, MC, V. **Amenities:** Restaurant; bar; car-rental desk; 24-hr. room service; laundry service. *In room:* A/C, TV, minibar.

INEXPENSIVE

Hostal Royal   This large, rambling old colonial hotel, with a formerly grand, winding central staircase, sits right on the Parque Principal. The place is a bit run-down, although some travelers will find it full of local character. Rooms are large and spartan, with hardwood floors. Beds are a bit soft, though, and bathrooms are tucked behind cheapo partitions, which makes privacy a problem. The best rooms, although surely not the quietest, are those with balconies overlooking the plaza.

San José 787, Chiclayo. ℂ **074/233-421.** Fax 074/228-171. 30 units. S/32 ($9.15) double. Rate includes taxes. No credit cards. *In room:* No phone.

WHERE TO DINE

Jhon *Finds* SEAFOOD/CEVICHE   A tiny neighborhood place with just 10 tables, this informal *cevichería* specializes in fish, shellfish, and, of course, several types of ceviche. Among the latter, try the *conchas negras* (black scallops) or *mixto a la Jhon* (with octopus, white fish, shrimp, and conchas). A more substantial entree is one of the *arroces* (rice dishes) with fish or shellfish. There are also several preparations of fish,

The Ruins of Kuélap

Everyone—at least everyone on his or her way to Peru—has heard of Machu Picchu. Very few have heard of **Kuélap** 🎘🎘, thought of by some as the true adventurer's alternative to the once lost but today easily accessible Incan city. Tucked in highland cloud forest on top of an Andean mountain ridge at an altitude of 3,000m (9,840 ft.), Kuélap is a stupendous and titanic set of ruins that predates the Incas. More than 800 years old, Kuélap is one of the (least known) wonders of Peru.

Located northeast of Cajamarca, near the small town of Chachapoyas (itself something of a poor man's Cusco, given the assortment of ruins littered about it), and discovered in the mid–19th century, the site is said to have employed more stone during its 200-year construction than even the Great Pyramids of Egypt. An impossibly scenic but wearying 18- to 24-hour bus ride from Cajamarca, or a less exciting 9- to 10-hour journey from Chiclayo, Kuélap hardly has the name recognition of other ruins in Peru. Ripe for discovery by a wider swath of visitors to Peru, Kuélap is still primarily a destination for independent travelers with a sense of adventure.

such as *mero* (grouper) and a nice *picante de camarones* (spicy shrimp). Note that Jhon, which is a local favorite, is open only for lunch or a very early dinner.

Colón 276 (at Tacna). ✆ 074/208-593. Reservations not accepted. Main courses S/7–S/16 ($2–$4.55). No credit cards. Daily 10am–6pm.

La Parra 🎘 *Kids* GRILLED MEATS   Enter past a busy, open grill—an indication of the meat-dominated menu you'll find inside. This comfortable, relaxed restaurant is very popular with families. It's nice, if a tad nondescript, with a vaulted wood ceiling, wood paneling, stucco walls, and hardwood floors—and odd incongruous touches such as a framed portrait of Jesus and a deer head. Everyone chows down on grilled meats, served with fries and a salad, not just because it's the house specialty, but also because it's the only thing La Parra serves. *Lomo fino* (sirloin), shish kabob, sausage, and chicken are among the excellent choices from the grill. A great family option is the parrillada for four. Next door is a good chifa by the same owner.

Manuel María Izaga 752. ✆ 074/227-471. Reservations recommended on weekends. Main courses S/7.50–S/21 ($2.15–$6). AE, DC, MC, V. Daily noon–11pm.

Pueblo Viejo 🎘🎘 *Value* PERUVIAN   Chiclayo's most chic and best restaurant, this relaxed and attractive two-story place serves traditional Chiclayano cooking and *comida criolla,* but only for lunch. The menu is interesting and creative, derived from old recipes from the surrounding area. Especially good are the fish and shellfish dishes, such as *tiradito de la casa* (sliced fish with lemon, chiles, corn, and onions), ceviche, and *tollito a la panca* (dogfish with *chicha,* cilantro, and corn, served in a clay pot). Other options are fish soup, tender goat, and dried roasted beef. A tasty appetizer is the *humitas de la abuela,* a white-corn tamale stuffed with pork. The nicest area is upstairs under the colored skylights, with lots of plants and wooden walkways, which give it the feel of a well-equipped tree house. (Okay, that might be a stretch, but it's head and shoulders above the norm of plain Peruvian eateries in the north.)

Manuel María Izaga 900 (at Calzoncillo). ✆ **074/228-863**. Reservations recommended on weekends. Main courses S/10–S/25 ($2.85–$7.15). No credit cards. Daily noon–5pm.

As discussed in "The Ruins of Kuélap," above, the Incan ruins of Kuélap consist of nearly 400 buildings, most of them round, and surrounded by a 30m-high (98-ft.) defensive wall. Kuélap was home to 2,000 people from A.D. 1100 to 1300, but little is known about its builders and inhabitants. They were most likely the Chachapoyans or Sachupoyans, both groups that were later brought into the Incan fold that unified the highlands. Unlike other ruins in Peru, most of what exists at Kuélap is original, although some reconstruction has been initiated. The ruins are open daily from 8:30am to 5pm; admission is S/10 ($2.85). Getting to Kuélap independently remains a laborious endeavor, involving buses to Chachapoyas and/or Tingo, plus a long and very difficult 5- to 6-hour hike. Organized visits from Cajamarca might not suit modern-day Hiram Binghams, but they are by far the most convenient way to get to what remains a very remote outpost. Group trips usually cost $200 per person and last 5 days round-trip. If you've got the time and money to spare, and a sense of adventure, check with **Cumbe Mayo and Inca Baths Tours** (see "Getting Around" in "Cajamarca," below) or **Chachapoyas Tours,** Jr. Grau 534, Chachapoyas (✆ **041/478-078** or 866/396-9582 in the U.S.; www.kuelapperu.com), which specializes in tours of Kuélap (from comfortable to rugged) leaving from Chachapoyas. There's a small Institute of National Culture albergue with dorm-style sleeping arrangements available.

3 Cajamarca ★★

855km (531 miles) NE of Lima; 298km (185 miles) NE of Trujillo; 235km (146 miles) SE of Chiclayo

Delightful and historic Cajamarca, the jewel of Peru's northern highlands, deserves to be better appreciated. Those who know the city often call it "the Cusco of the north," and comparisons to that tourist magnet farther south are not illegitimate. This stately and traditional mountain town possesses some of the same attributes as Cusco, but it is refreshingly free of many of the hassles associated with the gringo capital of South America. Although it's surrounded by the Andes at an altitude of nearly 2,700m (8,900 ft.) above sea level, Cajamarca is a down-to-earth and unassuming place that doesn't get caught up in its colonial beauty and Andean grace. Townspeople, nearly all of them decked out in marvelously distinctive *sombreros de paja* (straw hats), merely go about their business.

Cajamarca is the largest town in a fertile agricultural region that is virtually unsurpassed in Peru for its luxurious, verdant countryside. The climate is pleasantly springlike, with clear blue skies, most of the year. The city's Carnaval celebrations in February are among the most raucous in Peru. Cajamarca is ringed by archaeological sites and handsome hacienda estates, which make getting out to the country a must. Cajamarca's rural roots and agriculture-based economy have been given a jolt with the discovery of one of Latin America's largest gold mines, Yanacocha, which has quickly become the region's largest employer and brought an influx of foreign executives and their families. (The mine is jointly operated by Peruvian and U.S. firms.)

ESSENTIALS
GETTING THERE
BY PLANE   There are daily 2-hour flights from Lima and 1-hour flights from Trujillo aboard **AeroCondor** (✆ **01/614-6000;** www.aerocondor.com.pe) and flights from Lima on **LC Busre** (✆ **01/619-1300;** www.lcbusre.com.pe). Flights range from $79 to $99.

The **Armando Revoredo Aeropuerto de Cajamarca** (© **076/822-523**), recently expanded, is just 3km (1¾ miles) east of the Plaza de Armas. To downtown Cajamarca, a taxi costs S/5 ($1.40).

BY BUS   **Cruz del Sur** (© **01/472-5000**) and **Expreso Cia** (© **01/428-5218**) make the 12-hour trip from Lima to Cajamarca. **Transportes Línea** (© **076/823-956** or 044/245-181) travels from Lima, Trujillo (6 hr.), and Chiclayo (5–6 hr.). The bus companies have their own terminals, which are located mostly on Avenida Atahualpa and Avenida Zavala, about 3km (1¾ miles) from the center of town.

VISITOR INFORMATION

There's a branch of the **Regional Tourism Office** within the massive Conjunto Monumental de Belén complex at Jr. Belén 600 (© **076/822-903**). It's open Monday through Friday from 8:30am to 1pm and 2:30 to 6:30pm. The office has a handful of photocopied materials and some brochures for sale, including a self-published tourist information guide. There's another small **Oficina de Información Turística,** associated with the university, at Batán 289 (© **076/821-546**), which is very helpful and friendly and gives out free city maps. It's open Monday through Friday from 8:30am to 1pm.

Caxamarca: A Brief History

The Cajamarca Valley was the epicenter of a pre-Incan culture called Caxamarca, which reached its apex between A.D. 500 and 1000. Cajamarca was part of a small northern highlands kingdom called Cuismango, which was influenced by two great cultures, Chavín and Huari. The Incas, led by Cápac Yupanqui, conquered Cajamarca around 1465, annexing the territory and solidifying the empire's hold on the northern Andes. Cajamarca soon became an important administrative, political, and religious center and a major link in the transcontinental Andes highway; the Incas constructed great palaces and temples in the city.

Francisco Pizarro and a small band of troops, numbering around 160, reached the Cajamarca Valley in November 1532. November 16 shook the very foundations of the Incan Empire and changed Spanish-American and Peruvian history. Pizarro's men ambushed Atahualpa, the last Incan emperor, and held him prisoner. Incan troops, numbering more than 50,000 but already in the midst of civil war, offered no resistance. Atahualpa proposed a huge ransom to win his release, but the Spaniards killed him anyway, 7 months after a staged trial condemning him for attempting to arrange his rescue. The end of the Incan Empire was near, as the Spanish moved south toward Cusco. Cajamarca became a colonial city in 1802. Besides a few stone foundations, only Atahualpa's Cuarto de Rescate (Ransom Room) remains of the grand Incan masonry that once distinguished Cajamarca. But the city's post-Incan colonial roots are very much evident in Spanish-style architecture throughout Cajamarca.

Cajamarca

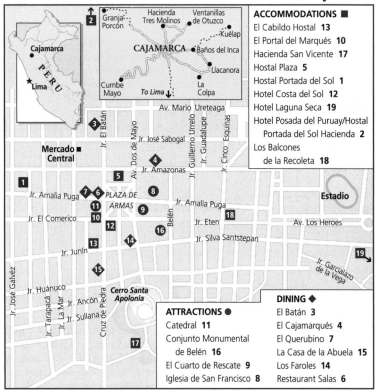

ACCOMMODATIONS ■
El Cabildo Hostal **13**
El Portal del Marqués **10**
Hacienda San Vicente **17**
Hostal Plaza **5**
Hostal Portada del Sol **1**
Hotel Costa del Sol **12**
Hotel Laguna Seca **19**
Hotel Posada del Puruay/Hostal
 Portada del Sol Hacienda **2**
Los Balcones
 de la Recoleta **18**

ATTRACTIONS ●
Catedral **11**
Conjunto Monumental
 de Belén **16**
El Cuarto de Rescate **9**
Iglesia de San Francisco **8**

DINING ◆
El Batán **3**
El Cajamarqués **4**
El Querubino **7**
La Casa de la Abuela **15**
Los Faroles **14**
Restaurant Salas **6**

FAST FACTS   Two banks are **Interbank,** 2 de Mayo on the Plaza de Armas (✆ **076/ 822-4600**), and **Banco de Crédito,** Jr. del Comercio 679 (✆ **076/822-742**). Neither of these banks exchanges traveler's checks. There are generally money-changers on the Plaza de Armas and Jirón del Batán; there are also several small *casas de cambio* in the same area.

In an **emergency,** call ✆ **105.** The **police** are located at Amalia Puga 807 (✆ **076/ 822-941**). For medical attention, go to **Hospital Regional (Base Cajamarca),** Mario Urteaga 500 (✆ **076/822-414**); **Clínica San Francisco,** Av. Grau (✆ **076/822-050**); or **Clínica Limatambo,** Puno s/n (✆ **076/824-241**).

For Internet access, try **Efenet,** Jr. Dos de Mayo, **CyberNet,** Comercio 924, or **Atajo,** Jr. del Comercio 716 (✆ **076/822-245**). Atajo is open until 1am and offers cheap international Internet calls.

Cajamarca's **post office** is located at Amalia Puga 778 (✆ **076/824-065**); it's open Monday through Saturday from 8am to 8pm. There's a **DHL/Western Union** office at Dos de Mayo 323 (✆ **076/825-674**), within the Cajamarca Tours office. The **Telefónica del Perú** office is at Dos de Mayo 460 on the Plaza de Armas (✆ **076/ 821-008**); it's open Monday to Saturday from 8am to 6pm.

⌜Moments⌝ Carnaval in Cajamarca

Cajamarca is a very traditional Andean highland city, but it lets loose once a year during Carnaval. Its pre-Lenten festivities are said to be the wildest in Peru. Full of music and dance, it also takes on aspects of a high-school locker room. Paint, water, and even bodily fluids (!) are flung around with abandon, so wear a raincoat. If you want to experience (subject yourself to?) Cajamarca's Carnaval, plan ahead. It's very popular with Peruvians, and hotels sell out. Another festive time in Cajamarca, formerly Peru's grandest Incan celebration, is Corpus Christi (May or June), which includes lots of processions, music, bullfights, and horse shows.

GETTING AROUND

The major sights of interest in Cajamarca are all around the Plaza de Armas or within easy walking distance of it. Except for the Inca Baths, you're unlikely to require transportation unless you're staying at one of the country hotels on the outskirts of town, which are serviced by taxi and, to a lesser extent, colectivo.

BY TAXI Taxis are easy to come by in the center of Cajamarca. They circulate around the Plaza de Armas and the streets leading off it. Most in-town fares are about S/3 (85¢). To call a cab, try **Taxi Seguro** (© 076/825-103) or **Taxis Unidos** (© 076/828-888).

BY ORGANIZED TOUR Reliable tour agencies include **Inca Baths Tours,** Jr. Amalia Puga 653 (© 076/821-828); **Cumbe Mayo Tours,** Jr. Amalia Puga 635 (© 076/822-938); **Cajamarca Travel,** Jr. Dos de Mayo 570 (© 076/828-642); and **Cajamarca Tours,** Jr. Dos de Mayo 323 (© 076/825-674). These companies offer city tours and inexpensive, pooled half- and full-day tours to sights in the countryside around Cajamarca (including Cumbe Mayo, Otuzco, Colpa, and Inca Baths). Most standard tours cost S/12 to S/15 ($3.40–$4.30). Several agencies also offer long-distance tours to the famed but remote Kuélap ruins for around $200. All agencies advertise English-speaking guides, but fluency is a relative term. The best bets are Inca Baths Tours and Cumbe Mayo Tours.

WHAT TO SEE & DO
IN CAJAMARCA

Colonial Cajamarca has several sights of interest, although the town's principal appeal might lie in its relaxed and proudly traditional air, as yet undisturbed by a tourist onslaught. Many of Cajamarca's premier tourist attractions are just outside the city in the beautiful pastoral countryside, within easy reach for day trips. Most are best visited by convenient organized tour (see "Getting Around," above).

Plaza de Armas ⌖

The heart of city life, Cajamarca's expansive and utterly graceful Plaza de Armas is one of the loveliest in Peru. In the days of the Incas, it was also the focal point of town, but it was a triangular courtyard rather than a square, per se. The plaza was taken in dramatic fashion by Pizarro's small band of invading troops in 1532, and the Incan Emperor Atahualpa was killed there after a mock trial. The fountain at the center of the square dates back more than 300 years, and the plaza is marked by handsome topiaries and low trees. Two grand churches front the square, and it can be difficult to determine which one is the cathedral. On one side is the **Catedral** (Cathedral), built in the 17th and 18th centuries. Its baroque facade is ornately carved from volcanic stone. The gloomy interior features a bold, amazingly carved main altar and a pulpit of carved wood and gold leaf. If the cathedral looks a bit squat and unfinished, it's because its belfry was never completed, a drastic measure to avoid payment of a Spanish tax on finished ecclesiastical buildings. As seen in colonial churches in Cusco, the cathedral is built upon original Incan stonework.

The grander of the two churches, though, is directly across the plaza. The **Iglesia de San Francisco** ⊛, which once formed part of the San Francisco Convent, is entirely wrought from volcanic rock. Built in the first half of the 18th century, the parish church did not add the two bell towers until 1951. Covering every inch of the facade is terrific stone sculpting. Inside is a **Museo de Arte Religioso Colonial,** Jr. Dos de Mayo 435 (© **076/822-994**); it's open Monday through Saturday from 3 to 6pm and admission is S/3 (85¢). The collection of colonial art includes interesting icons and paintings. Beneath the museum are the church's catacombs, good for an eerie visit. Next door to the church is the small and beautiful Santuario de la Virgen de Dolores, or the chapel of **La Dolorosa,** named for the patron saint of Cajamarca. The 18th-century facade is one of the greatest examples of stone carving in the city.

More Attractions
Conjunto Monumental de Belén ⊛⊛   On block 6 of Belén is the city's most important and historic architectural complex, almost entirely constructed of volcanic stone. Dating to the 18th century, it includes a church and colonial women's and men's hospitals, now housing ancient medical and archaeological exhibits. The entire complex is run by the National Institute of Culture. On a small and pretty square, the **Iglesia Belén** might be the most extraordinary work of colonial architecture in Cajamarca. The church, which replaced a primitive adobe-and-wood church on the spot, was begun in 1699 and completed a half-century later. Its decorative baroque stone facade is one of the finest in Peru. The interior is replete with delightful and large, carved polychromatic figures of angels and warriors. The fantastic, richly decorative cupola was painted by highland natives.

The **Hospital de Hombres (Men's Hospital)** is located on a lovely courtyard marked by a fountain. The hospital, run by Franciscans, began receiving patients in 1630. So that they could focus on prayer, the patients' beds faced the altar and the Virgen de la Piedad. Across the street is the **Hospital de Mujeres (Women's Hospital);** on the facade, note the woman with child above the portal and, on either side of it, female figures with four breasts, symbols of the valley's super-potent fertility. Today the building houses perhaps the most interesting component of the Belén complex, a **Museo de Arqueología y Etnografía,** well laid out and exhibiting textiles and ceramics dating from as far back as 1500 B.C., replicas of Moche vessels, and local artisanship, dress (including Carnaval costumes), and silver *milagros* (prayer fetishes).

Jr. Belén s/n (at Junín). © **076/922-601.** Admission is by boleto S/4 ($1.15), which also admits visitors to El Cuarto de Rescate (see below). Mon and Wed–Fri 9am–1pm and 3–6pm; Sat–Sun 9am–1pm.

Tips **Get Out of Town on Tuesday**

Most of Cajamarca's top sights are closed on Tuesday. If you're in town that day, it would be wise to schedule a visit to the Inca Baths or another out-of-town excursion, such as Cumbe Mayo or Otuzco.

Cajamarca's Colonial Mansions & Churches

In the center of Cajamarca are several notable large houses that feature carved stone porticoes, slanted roofs, long wooden balconies, and the type of pretty garden courtyards favored by Spanish colonialists. Visitors with an interest in 17th- and 18th-century colonial and republican architecture should check out the following *casonas* and churches, in addition to those discussed elsewhere in greater detail:

- **Casa Toribio Casanova,** Jr. José Gálvez 938.
- **Casa Santiesteban,** Junín 1123.
- The **house** at Cruz de Piedra 613. Now the property of the municipal government, the house has another excellent carved portico. Also on Cruz de Piedra is a stone cross, which supposedly marks the spot where Simón Bolívar, the Great Libertador, swore to avenge the death of Atahualpa.
- **La Recoleta,** a church about 6 blocks south of the Plaza de Armas, at the end of Amalia Puga.
- **Palacio de los Condes de Uceda** (now the Banco de Crédito), Apurímac 717. A splendid yellowish-orange, well-restored noble house with a carved stone portico.
- **Palacio del Obispo,** next to the Catedral.
- **San Pedro,** a church at the corner of Gálvez and Junín.

El Cuarto de Rescate   Across the street from La Dolorosa Chapel is the most famous building in Cajamarca. When Atahualpa was taken prisoner by Pizarro and his band of men in 1532, the Incan emperor was held in a cell, which he promised to fill with gold and silver many times over if the Spaniards would spare his life. The "Ransom Room" is a small, rectangular stone room, set in the back of a colonial courtyard, once part of Atahualpa's palace. It is made of unadorned Incan masonry—the last intact example of Incan architecture in the city—and is barren except for a red line drawn across one wall, supposedly the very line Atahualpa drew to demonstrate to the Spanish how high his men would fill the cell with treasures. No one knows for sure whether this was simply Atahualpa's prison cell or if it was indeed a ransom room. What we do know is that the Incan chief was later executed by Pizarro's men, presumably on a stone right here, even before the Incas had surrendered all of the promised riches. The Cuarto de Rescate represents a crucial moment in Peruvian history, a clash in cultures with ramifications for the entire continent, but it might take some imagination to conjure the drama of the moment. The large painting at the entrance near the ticket booth, of Atahualpa being burned at the stake by the Spanish, is not entirely accurate; after accepting baptism, Atahualpa was merely strangled to death.

Amalia Puga 750 (½ block from Plaza de Armas). ⓒ **076/922-601.** Admission by boleto (S/4 or $1.15 adults; S/3 or 85¢ students), which admits visitors to the component parts of the Conjunto Monumental de Belén (see above). Mon and Wed–Fri 9am–1pm and 3–6pm; Sat–Sun 9am–1pm.

ON THE OUTSKIRTS OF CAJAMARCA

Baños del Inca *(Kids)*   Just beyond Cajamarca lies the Inca Baths complex of gardens and pools with Cajamarca's famed thermal waters. In use since the time of the Incas (supposedly, Atahualpa had to be roused from his beloved bath when Pizarro and his troops entered the city), the baths are a wonderful respite of clean air and hot waters, ideal for relaxing after days of travel in the highlands. Set in a serene valley, at an elevation of nearly 2,650m (8,700 ft.) with wonderful mountain views, the park's thermal waters are said to be medicinal and effective for treating bronchial and rheumatic conditions. The waters, which reach temperatures of 165°F (74°C; but you can control the temperature with spigots in private pools), come from two different sources, Los Perolitos and El Tragadero. The open pools with rising steam make clear the scalding nature of the waters. The modern complex is extremely popular with locals and visitors alike. You can either opt for a private, indoor bath, in which you wait for a room to be vacated and cleaned and the deep pool filled with fresh sulfurous spring waters, or the sauna or outdoor pool. Take a bathing suit and towel with you. Bath products are for sale at the entrance.

6km (3¾ miles) from Cajamarca. (€) **076/821-563**. Outdoor pool has assigned entrance times. Admission to the tourist complex (individual bathing cabins) S/4 ($1.15); to the communal baths S/3 (85¢). Daily 5am–7pm. Colectivos labeled BAÑOS DEL INCA leave from Calle Amazonas and take about 15 min.; virtually everyone gets off at the same stop, across the street from the complex. A taxi costs about S/5–S/8 ($1.40–$2.30).

Cerro Santa Apolonia   A steep but lovely climb up the stairs at the southeast end of the Dos de Mayo leads to Santa Apolonia hill. On the way to the top is a small white chapel, the Virgen de Fátima, built in 1854. Often locked, the interior can still be glimpsed through the doorway. Up more paths, through terraced gardens where there are also a handful of caged animals, is a mirador with splendid panoramic views of Cajamarca laid out at your feet. Rocks at the top, carved with petroglyphs, are believed to date to the Chavín civilization (1000–500 B.C.). Nearby, to the right of the white cross (if you're looking down at Cajamarca), sits a stone altar that has earned the popular name "the Inca's Throne." At this altar, carved like a chair, the Incan chief reportedly sat and gazed down on his city and troops. There's also a small tunnel that, according to legend, went all the way from Cajamarca to Cusco.

Reached by stairs at the end of Dos de Mayo. Park admission S/1 (30¢). Daily 8am–6pm.

ATTRACTIONS BEYOND CAJAMARCA 🏃🏃

The countryside (campiña) around Cajamarca is extraordinary: a luxuriant expanse of rolling hills, eucalyptus trees, and meadows. If you're not staying at one of the country-style hacienda hotels outside of Cajamarca, a visit to the country is highly recommended to see this gorgeous, fertile region.

Among the standard organized campiña visits are excursions to several rural haciendas, including the very worthwhile **Granja Porcón** ((€) **076/971-082**), a huge cooperative farm and agrotourism experiment supported by the Peruvian government and the European Union. It's about 30km (19 miles) north of Cajamarca. The community runs entirely on hydroelectric power, and hilltop forests have been planted at an altitude of 3,700m (12,139 ft.) to provide paper and wood products without harming the area's natural forests. There is a small *albergue* lodging and a restaurant on the premises ((€) **076/825-631**). In **Lower Porcón,** the Festival of the Crosses (on Palm Sunday at the beginning of Easter week) is a famous expression of local folklore. Huge wood and cane crosses, adorned with images of Jesus and saints, flowers, and palm fronds, are carried in devout processions.

Other area cooperatives have not been well maintained and are less worthy of a visit. They include **La Colpa** (no phone), a cattle ranch and manor house in a beautiful setting; **Llacanora** (no phone), a small mountain village with ancient cave paintings and hikes to a pretty waterfall; and **Tres Molinos** (no phone), an agricultural center and gardens, where dairy products are sold.

The best way to visit one or more of the archaeological sites beyond Cajamarca is to sign on with one of the tour operators in town. Several of the sites are not accessible by public transportation; going with a guide in a small private colectivo is economical and convenient. Most agencies charge S/15 to S/20 ($4.30–$5.70) for standard day trips. Many combine visits (for example, to the Inca Baths, Colpa, and Llacanora; or to Otuzco and Tres Molinos).

Cumbe Mayo 𝒢𝒢 A stunning natural spot of huge and fascinating rock formations set amid rolling green hills at an elevation of 3,400m (11,150 ft.), Cumbe Mayo has been called a stone forest. Equally remarkable, if not more so, is the evidence of human intervention here, first discovered in 1937: caves etched with petroglyphs and a pre-Incan **aqueduct** that is a marvel of hydraulic engineering. The remarkable open canal, carved out of volcanic stone in perfect, polished lines, served to collect and redirect water from various sources on its way to the Pacific Ocean. At points, the canal narrows and introduces right angles to slow the flow of water and lessen the effects of erosion. In all, the aqueduct stretches more than 9km (5½ miles). Created, incredibly, around 1000 B.C., it is perhaps the oldest known man-made structure in South America.

Elsewhere in the park, there's a cliff referred to as the **sanctuary,** which looks like a human head with a grotto (and more enigmatic petroglyphs) carved out inside. Stairs carved in stone lead to sacrificial altars (llamas, not humans) and platforms, signs of the ceremonial importance of the zone. As guides lead groups through the "stone forest," they point out figures that can be seen in the stones, such as a group of monks as well as phalluses, breasts, a dog climbing a hill, a tortoise, a pirate's head, and mushrooms. Some are clear, amusing likenesses; others are like trying to identify someone else's images in cloud formations.

20km (12 miles) SW of Cajamarca. Daily 8am–5pm. To get there, take an organized tour (S/15 or $4.30). It is also possible to take a colectivo that leaves from behind Cerro de Santo Apolonia; it leaves passengers a short walking distance from the entrance to Cumbe Mayo.

Kunturwasi Three to four hours away from Cajamarca, in the province of San Pablo, these ceremonial stone ruins date to 1100 B.C. Besides a series of courtyards, plazas, and platforms, many marked with large petroglyphs, burial sites were discovered here. The gold treasures from the tombs are now exhibited in a small museum in the nearby town of San Pablo.

110km (68 miles) from Cajamarca. Tours to Kunturwasi cost about S/50 ($14) per person and last a full day. Daily 8am–5pm.

Ventanillas de Otuzco 𝒢 A large necropolis whose gravesites are small square window niches carved out of a hillside, Otuzco was created by the Caxamarca culture, probably around 500 B.C. The niches were funereal tombs for elites. Many held just one body; others housed several corpses. Another 20km (12 miles) beyond Otuzco are the even more impressive (and better preserved) burial niches of **Ventanillas de Comboyo.** More extensive than Otuzco, they are holed out of a sheer volcanic cliff.

7km (4½ miles) NW of Cajamarca. Admission S/3 (85¢). Daily 8am–5pm. To get there, take an organized tour (S/15 or $4.30), which combines visits with stops at a hacienda. You can also hop on a colectivo along Batán, a few blocks from the Plaza de Armas.

SHOPPING

Relaxed and traditional, untouristy Cajamarca isn't brimming with chic shops and merchants hawking *artesanía* to visitors. Yet its colorful central market is an enjoyable place to absorb the flavor of an authentic Andean town market and pick up a regional specialty: Cajamarca has excellent handicrafts, including ceramics and Cajarmarquiña mirrors with decorative glass frames. The **Mercado Central** on Amazonas, which sprawls among several streets, is a great place to score one of those amazing, finely woven tall straw hats that virtually all natives wear. Those *sombreros de paja* are famous throughout Peru, but some are so finely made that you might be shocked at the prices. I'm told that some campesinos spend up to $400 for their hat, which is their most prideful article of clothing. As you'll see, the hats beg all sorts of individual style; forming and wearing the hat according to one's taste is part of the fashion. I own two, and they're certainly conversation pieces back home—perfect for gardening—though finding ones to fit large, non-Andean heads can be trying. Ask the seller to show you how to roll up the hat for easy packing. Other items of interest include saddlebags *(alforjas)*, decorative glass-and-silkscreen mirrors, and dairy products.

WHERE TO STAY

Like the mini-Cusco it appears to be, Cajamarca has a very nice selection of affordable small hotels, many of them in converted colonial mansions, all quite close to the main square. The finest and most relaxing hotel, however—one of the nicest in Peru—is in the countryside on the outskirts of town.

EXPENSIVE

Hotel Laguna Seca ⟨★⟩ ⟨*Kids*⟩   A luxurious country-style hotel renowned for its proximity to the Baños del Inca, this spa resort hotel is where to stay if you're looking for things you don't typically find in Peru: aerobics, massages, and in-room thermal baths. It also features thermal pools (two for adults, one for children), Turkish baths, and a host of outdoor activities (including horseback riding). Rooms are large and nicely equipped, but not nearly as luxurious as those at the similarly priced Hotel Posada del Puruay (see below).

Av. Manco Cápac 1098, Baños del Inca, Cajamarca. ⟨*C*⟩ **076/894-600,** or 01/336-7869 for reservations. Fax 044/894-646. www.lagunaseca.com.pe. 40 units. $103–$116 double; $134–$150 suite. Rates include taxes and breakfast buffet. AE, DC, MC, V. **Amenities:** Restaurant; cafeteria; bar; 3 thermal-water pools; aerobics and massage room; spa; Jacuzzi; concierge; travel agency; room service; laundry service. *In room:* A/C, TV/VCR, minibar, hair dryer.

Hotel Posada del Puruay ⟨★★★⟩ ⟨*Value*⟩ ⟨*Kids*⟩   An extraordinary country hotel housed in an impeccably restored, elegant 1830 salmon-colored hacienda, this is one of the most refined and relaxing hotels in Peru. Set amid more than 202,350 hectares (500,000 acres) of land, with eucalyptus forest, beautifully landscaped gardens, and views of the verdant, mountainous countryside, the hotel feels light-years removed from any city, yet it's only 7km (4½ miles) from downtown Cajamarca. The lovely house, built around a pretty courtyard, has rooms with names such as La Mansión and La Prisión. The first couldn't be truer: Rooms are gigantic and extremely well equipped, with large, luxurious bathrooms. The second room name, though, is very misleading: If this is prison, I want to be thrown in the slammer. The restaurant and public rooms are decorated with well-chosen antiques. Outdoors, horses beckon, as does the trail up the hill to a small structure with stupendous panoramic views. The charming and loquacious owner, Nora, and her husband and daughter live on the premises and couldn't be more gracious. The terrific restaurant and vast video-rental library make this a perfect spot to kick back for several days in the northern highlands.

Carretera Porcón-Hualgayoc Km 4.5, Cajamarca. ✆ **076/828-318**, or 01/336-7869 for reservations. Fax 076/827-928. www.posadapuruay.com.pe. 16 units. $90 double; $110–$130 suite. Rates include taxes and breakfast buffet. AE, DC, MC, V. **Amenities:** Restaurant; bar; concierge; room service; laundry service. *In room:* A/C, TV/VCR, minibar, hair dryer.

MODERATE

El Portal del Marqués 🖈 *Value*
An attractively furnished colonial casona located a block and a half from the main square, this comfortable and friendly midrange hotel is an excellent option. The carpeted rooms, placed around the brightly painted central courtyard and interior garden, are good-size and feature very clean bathrooms. Public rooms are inviting and warm, with wood-beam ceilings, stone portals, original paintings, local ceramics, and cozy armchairs and sofas. D'Marco, the good-looking bar and renovated restaurant on the premises, is one of the better spots for dinner in town, and it features a happy hour every afternoon from 6 to 8pm.

Jr. del Comercio 644, Cajamarca. ✆/fax **076/828-464**, or ✆ 01/9880-5440 for reservations. www.portaldel marques.com. 20 units. $40 double; $65 family suite. Rates include taxes and continental breakfast. V only. **Amenities:** Restaurant; bar; 24-hr. room service; laundry service, Wi-Fi access. *In room:* TV, DVD player.

Hacienda San Vicente 🖈🖈 *Finds*
Hands down the funkiest hotel you'll find in Peru, this cool old hacienda is perched on a hill up above Cajamarca. It proclaims itself a *"refugio ecológico";* it could just as easily be called a "refugio funkadelico." The seven unique rooms overflow with an oddball, rustic sense of style; some are like caves carved out of the rock. The whole place slides down the hill with cool niches, tight stone stairways, funky spaces, and great views from the gardens. Rooms have wood-beam ceilings and skylights for views of the moon and stars. Room C has a round bed under the skylight. Others have headboards carved right into the stone walls. There is also a group room, where guests stay dorm-style in bunk beds—perfect for trekking groups. For families, there's an apartment. On-site is a Gaudí-esque little chapel.

Jr. Revolución (above Cerro Santa Apolonia), Cajamarca. ✆ **076/822-644**. Fax 076/821-432. hacienda-san-vicente@yahoo.com. 7 units. $75 double; $10 per person group room. Rates include taxes, continental breakfast, and airport pickup. Weekend deals available. MC, V. **Amenities:** Restaurant; bar; courtesy car to Cajamarca; room service; laundry service. *In room:* TV, minibar.

Hotel Costa del Sol 🖈🖈 *Value*
An excellent new hotel in a handsome colonial building on the Plaza de Armas, and part of a small Peruvian chain with several properties in northern Peru, this is the best place to stay if you want to be right in town. It has very comfortable, good-sized, and nicely decorated rooms, as well as the most complete menu of amenities and services in Cajamarca, including a pool and casino. Given all it offers, it's an excellent value.

Jr. del Comercio 773, Cajamarca. ✆/fax **076/822-472**. www.costadelsolperu.com/cajamarca.html. 71 units. $76 double; $106–$160 suite. Rates include taxes and continental breakfast. V only. **Amenities:** Restaurant; bar; business center; outdoor pool; exercise room and sauna; 24-hr. room service; laundry service, Internet access. *In room:* AC, TV, minibar, hairdryer.

INEXPENSIVE

El Cabildo Hostal *Kids*
One block from the Plaza de Armas, this charming small hotel has the swankest colonial courtyard in town: It's sunny, with a central fountain, arches, and balconies on all four sides—a perfect spot to relax. Rooms have a cozy, comfortable vibe, and the beds have carved-wood headboards. Four of the rooms are

loft-style, which is perfect for families. Furnishings aren't plush, and the brown-carpet-and-orange-bedspread look could probably do with an update, but given the friendly services and pedigree of the building, it's not a bad deal.

Jr. Junín, Cajamarca. ②/fax **076/827-025**. cabildoh@latinmail.com. 22 units. S/90–S/95 ($26–$27) double. Rates include taxes and continental breakfast. DC, MC, V. **Amenities:** Restaurant; bar; small gym; spa; massage; room service; laundry service. *In room:* TV, minibar.

Hostal Plaza   This large and rambling old colonial wooden house, a favorite of backpackers, is loaded with character, even if the rooms are dormlike and completely unadorned. It's not uncomfortable, though, and it certainly has a great location—right on the Plaza de Armas—for the cheap price. The hotel is spread across two interconnected wings that are built around a pair of courtyards. Hot water comes and goes. The rickety wooden floors and varied levels have their own kind of charm for travelers looking for a bargain but who need little in the way of creature comforts.

Plaza de Armas, Cajamarca. ② **076/822-058**. 22 units. S/25 ($7.15) per person with private bathroom; S/15 ($4.30) with shared bathroom. Rates include taxes. No credit cards. *In room:* No phone.

Hostal Portada del Sol ⟨⟩ ⟨Value⟩   A cozy family inn occupying a beautiful colonial house about 5 minutes from the Plaza de Armas, this is one of the best affordable hotels in town. Rooms have wood-beam ceilings, older-style furnishings, and small bathrooms. Some rooms have upstairs loft areas. The small, covered central courtyard has a marble fountain and is set up with tables beneath the wooden balcony on three sides. El Sol Grill, a charming restaurant with a wood-burning stove, is on the premises, and service is personal and accommodating. The hotel owns the handsome hacienda hotel of the same name in the countryside outside Cajamarca (see below).

Jr. Pisagua 731, Cajamarca. ②/fax **076/823-395**, or 01/225-4306 for reservations. http://barrioperu.terra.com.pe/portada delsol/paginas/pdsol.htm. 20 units. $27 double. **Amenities:** Restaurant; bar. *In room:* TV.

Hostal Portada del Sol Hacienda ⟨⟩ ⟨Value⟩ ⟨Kids⟩   A great-value country hacienda, only 6km (3¾ miles) from the Plaza de Armas in Cajamarca, this pretty house with beautiful gardens and comfortable, nicely decorated but simple rooms is an excellent option for a relaxed stay. Owned by the same people who run a similarly named inn in town (see above), this cozy Spanish-style hacienda doesn't have the funky character of San Vicente or the classy luxury of Puruay, but it's a great middle-of-the-road choice. Almost unheard of at this price, the hotel has tennis courts, football fields, games for children, horseback riding, and trails for walking.

Camino al Cumbe Mayo Km 6, Cajamarca. ② **076/823-395**, or 01/225-4306 for reservations. http://barrioperu.terra. com.pe/portadadelsol/paginas/pdsolhac.htm. 15 units. $27 double. **Amenities:** Restaurant; bar; tennis courts. *In room:* TV.

Los Balcones de la Recoleta ⟨Value⟩   Yet another charming 19th-century house in Cajamarca, this small inn, a 5-minute walk from the Plaza de Armas, is named for its handsome balconies, which drip with vines. The central courtyard is similarly overflowing with plants and flowers. Rooms live up to the colonial character of the place, with hardwood floors and thick ceiling beams; they're nice for the price. The restaurant is recommended for Spanish specialties and the good-value lunch menu.

Jr. Amalia Puga 1050, Cajamarca. ②/fax **076/823-003**. 12 units. S/100 ($29) double. Rate includes taxes and continental breakfast. DC, MC, V. **Amenities:** Restaurant; bar. *In room:* TV, minibar.

WHERE TO DINE

Cajamarca's dining scene pretty fairly matches its roster of hotels: a laid-back selection of excellent-value restaurants, all within easy walking distance of the Plaza de Armas.

El Batán ★ (Value) PERUVIAN   A sophisticated restaurant—more contemporary than El Cajamarqués (see below), with perhaps the most elevated reputation in town—El Batán uses the tag line "buffet de arte." In fact, the place is part art gallery upstairs. Elegant but relaxed, inhabiting a handsome 18th-century colonial house entered through the courtyard, it offers a series of relatively expensive fixed-price menús, but there's also a bargain hunter's *menú ejecutivo* for just S/12 ($3.40). You can mix and match appetizers with main courses. You might have a stuffed avocado to start, followed by chicken in mushroom sauce. The menu is meat-heavy, as seems typical in Cajamarca. Meat eaters will appreciate dishes such as stuffed tenderloin with peppercorns or filet mignon in whiskey sauce. On weekends, there's peña music. Dine in either the covered courtyard or the relaxed, art-filled interior.

Jr. del Batán 369. ✆ **076/826-025.** Reservations recommended. Main courses S/12–S/25 ($3.40–$7.15); menús del día S/29 ($8.30) and S/32 ($9.15); menú ejecutivo S/12 ($3.40). AE, DC, MC, V. Daily noon–midnight.

El Cajamarqués ★ (Value) PERUVIAN/INTERNATIONAL   A large, elegant restaurant with Cusqueña School paintings (okay, copies) on the walls, a long carved-wood mirror, and a medieval-looking iron chandelier, this is one of Cajamarca's most elegant and traditional restaurants. It has high, wood-beamed ceilings and white walls, much like an old-style Spanish restaurant. It's surprisingly affordable, though, with very economical menús offered midday. The *carta,* which includes standard Peruvian and international dishes including *lomo saltado,* filet mignon, and beef stroganoff, is heavy on meats. (In fact, there's no fish on it.) The restaurant has a pretty decent wine list. The garden has a small zoo of exotic birds.

Amazonas 770. ✆ **076/822-128.** Reservations recommended. Main courses S/12–S/22 ($3.40–$6.30); menús del día S/6 ($1.70) and S/9 ($2.55). AE, DC, MC, V. Daily noon–midnight.

El Querubino ★★ (Value) PERUVIAN   An elegant new place a half-block off the Plaza de Armas, El Querubino has quickly become one of Cajamarca's trendsetters. With mustard-yellow walls, decorative tiles, and a live music duo playing altiplano tunes, it's bright, cheery, friendly, and intimate, and just a few paces from the cathedral. The restaurant qualifies as upscale for low-key Cajamarca, but it's quite popular with locals. House specialties include *mollejas al ajillo* (sweetbreads in garlic) and mustard chicken. Other options among meat dishes are also nice: beef stroganoff, filet mignon, and pork chops. There's a daily list of bargain specials such as lemon chicken written on a board at the entrance. Finally, a Cajamarca restaurant with fish on the menu! (Okay, it's only sole, but it's a start.) The wine list is a bit more extensive than at most local restaurants.

Jr. Amalia Puga 589. ✆ **076/830-900.** Reservations recommended. Main courses S/12–S/25 ($3.40–$7.15). Specials from S/10 ($2.85). AE, DC, MC, V. Daily 9am–midnight.

La Casa de la Abuela INTERNATIONAL/DESSERT   This cute, country-kitchen-style place has wood beams, a preponderance of baskets with dried flowers, and little tables with blue-and-white-checked tablecloths and blue candles. In short, it's very unusual for Peru—one of the few small restaurants with a conscious and consistent design or look. The first thing to draw your attention will be the wide selection of desserts, including ice cream, cheesecakes, and several other colorful and delectable cakes, in the case at the entrance. But "Grandma's House" also serves a variety of items for breakfast, lunch, and dinner, such as sandwiches and hamburgers, pizzas, pastas, and a gourmet selection of meats. Plenty of people pop in just for dessert and coffee.

Jr. Cruz de Piedra 671. © **076/681-027.** Reservations recommended on weekends. Main courses S/9–S/22 ($2.55–$6.30). MC only. Daily 8am–midnight.

Los Faroles ⋒ PERUVIAN   In the Hostal Cajamarca, this Spanish colonial–looking restaurant is a perfect fit for the inn. Set at the back of the handsome center courtyard of a historic house, it features a traditional *criollo* menu, with items such as *palta rellena* (stuffed avocado) and *ají de gallina* (chile cream chicken), that's well prepared. Service is attentive and friendly. Other menu items include a mixed grill, rabbit in wine sauce, grilled trout, and chicken in orange sauce, as well as a selection of pastas. Breakfast features local specialties, such as *chicharrón de puerco* (pork), as well as normal Western fare such as omelets. The midday set menú is a bargain at S/12 ($3.40).

Jr. Dos de Mayo 311. © **076/922-532.** Reservations recommended. Main courses S/8–S/21 ($2.30–$6); menú del día S/12 ($3.40). DC, V. Daily 8am–11pm.

Restaurant Salas ⟨Value⟩ PERUVIAN   From the lines at the entrance, you expect this traditional restaurant to be good—it's packed with locals daily (even though some veterans carp that it's not as good as it used to be). Occupying the same spot on the Plaza de Armas since 1947, Salas is a huge eating hall with high ceilings and white-coated waiters scurrying about. Perhaps it's so popular because of the monstrous portions. There's a daily typed list of *platos especiales* (specials), *platos del día* (daily specials), and a set menu with no choices for about $2. *Humitas* (sweet corn tamales) are excellent. Most of the menu focuses on typical Peruvian dishes and things such as churrasco and asado (roasted and barbecued meats).

Amalia Puga 637. © **076/822-867.** Reservations not accepted. Main courses S/6–S/22 ($1.70–$6.30). V only. Daily 9am–10pm.

CAJAMARCA AFTER DARK

For the most part, Cajamarca is a pretty quiet town, although it has at least two spots that make an evening out worthwhile.

Peña Usha Usha ⋒, at Amalia Puga 142 (no phone), about 4 blocks from the Plaza de Armas, is a funky little peña bar with kerosene lamps, a smattering of tables and benches, a small altar, and graffiti everywhere. It's very atmospheric and intimate, and Jamie Valera Bazán has been singing songs here, either alone or with a couple friends, for years. The bar, which serves simple mixed drinks only, opens at 9pm and doesn't close its doors sometimes until 6am. The cover charge is S/5 ($1.40). A cool boho hangout and coffee house is **Casa Luna** ⋒, Dos de Mayo 334 (© **076/333-072**); it's the place in town if you've got a hankering for open mic night and poetry readings.

The classiest and most upscale disco in town is **Los Frailones,** Av. Perú 701 (© **076/825-113;** at Cruz de la Piedra, at the base of Santa Apolonia hill). The cover charge is S/15 ($4.28) for men and S/10 ($2.85) for women. Another notable nightclub is **Up & Down,** at Tarapacá 782 (© **076/827-876**); the cover varies.

4 Huaraz & the Cordillera Blanca ⋒⋒

Rugged Peru is synonymous with the bold peaks of the Andes, and those mountains, particularly the spectacular Cordillera Blanca range 400km (250 miles) northeast of Lima, are a magnet for thousands of mountaineers and adventure-sports travelers every year. The string of dramatic snowcapped 5,000m (16,400-ft.) peaks east of the

Fun Fact **"La" Huascarán?**

The Cordillera Blanca's El Huascarán, the namesake of the mountainous National Park in Peru's central Andes, might seem to be a macho mountain: At 6,768m (22,205 ft.), it's the highest peak in Peru, the fourth highest in the Americas, and the highest tropical-zone mountain in the world. But its north peak was first climbed in 1908 by a woman, the 58-year-old American Annie Smith Peck (who 3 years later climbed Peru's Mt. Coropuna, where she proudly displayed a women's suffrage banner that read "Votes for Women").

Callejón de Huaylas Valley, accessible from the main tourist hub of Huaraz (reached by bus in 7–8 hr. from Lima), is the premier spot in Peru—and perhaps the best in all of South America—for climbing and trekking. Nearly three dozen peaks soar to more than 6,000m (19,680 ft.); Huascarán, topping out at 6,768m (22,205 ft.), is Peru's highest mountain and the highest tropical mountain in the world. Nearly the entire chain is contained within the protected Huascarán National Park, a UNESCO Biosphere Reserve and World Heritage Trust site.

Not surprisingly, the region appeals above all to experienced, veteran mountaineers and adventurers. A burgeoning lineup of other adventure sports, from white-water rafting and mountain biking to hang gliding and rock climbing, have lifted off in popularity in recent years. Above all, those kinds of adventure travelers, equipped and prepared for the rigors and thrill of roughing it outdoors, get the most out of the region.

The extraordinary mountain scenery of the region, however, also appeals to those with limited time and abilities, or only passing interest in testing their physical mettle in Peru. The valley, some 20km (12 miles) wide and 180km (112 miles) long, is also a superb destination for those who are more interested in day walks and village markets. For those who would say all play and no culture makes for a dull adventure, visitors can marry interests in adventure sports and antiquity at the marvelous ruins of Chavín de Huántar, built about 1,500 years ago, a hearty journey about 4 hours from Huaraz. Still, I'm compelled to warn you that unless you have a firm interest in the outdoors, getting to the Cordillera Blanca—the only option is by road—could be more than you bargained for. Other outdoors areas in Peru (such as the Sacred Valley between Cusco and Machu Picchu, and the Colca Canyon beyond Arequipa) are easier to get to for most light adventurers.

The best months for climbing are the dry season, between May and October; of those, July and August are perhaps best. (Note that the traditional dry season has shifted a bit in recent years, with rains often lasting until the end of May but not beginning until late November.) Mountain biking and trekking can be practiced other months as well, but the adventurous should be duly prepared for rain.

The small and bustling city of Huaraz has few attractions besides its spectacular setting, but it serves as the base for most adventure-tour operators. With its roster of restaurants, bars, and small hotels, it's where most travelers gather to get acclimated to the altitude and get organized for their forays into the mountains. Besides Huaraz, several other small towns and villages at the base of Cordillera mountains serve as starting points for trekking and climbing expeditions, but none is so well equipped as the capital of the Ancash department. Many expeditions to the scenic Llanganuco

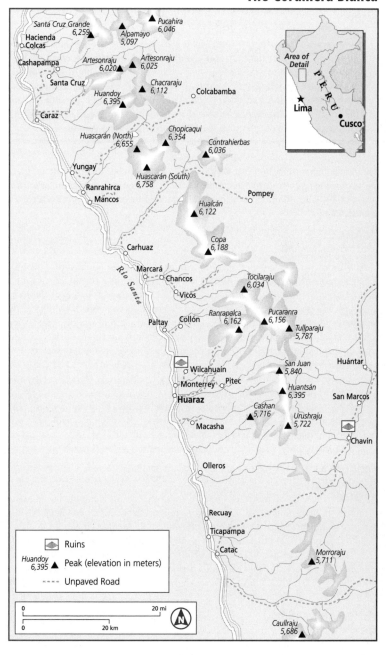

The Cordillera Blanca

Santá Cruz Grande
6,259

Hacienda
Colcas

Cashapampa

Santa Cruz

Pucahira
6,046

Alpamayo
5,097

Artesonraju
6,020

Artesonraju
6,025

Chacraraju
6,112

Colcabamba

Huandoy
6,395

Caraz

Yungay

Ranrahirca

Mancos

Huascarán (North)
6,655

Chopicaqui
6,354

Contrahierbas
6,036

Huascarán (South)
6,758

Pompey

Hualcán
6,122

Copa
6,188

Carhuaz

Marcará

Chancos

Vicos

Tocilaraju
6,034

Paltay

Collón

Ranrapalca
6,162

Pucaranra
6,156

Tullparaju
5,787

Wilcahuaín

Monterrey

Pitec

San Juan
5,840

Huántar

Huantsán
6,395

San Marcos

Huaraz

Cashan
5,716

Macasha

Urushraju
5,722

Chavín

Olleros

Recuay

Ticapampa

Catac

Morroraju
5,711

Caullraju
5,686

Río Santa

Area of
Detail

P E R Ú

Lima

Cusco

Legend

Ruins

Huandoy
6,395 ▲ Peak (elevation in meters)

- - - - Unpaved Road

0 —————————— 20 mi

0 —————————— 20 km

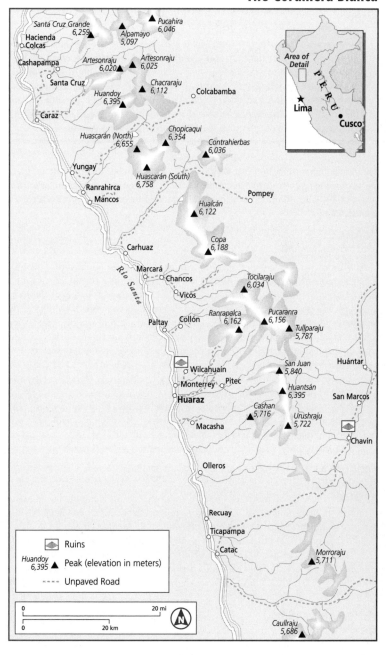

Tips **Acute Mountain Sickness**

The usual warnings about altitude in the Peruvian Andes especially apply in Huaraz and the Cordillera Blanca. Headaches and nausea are common ailments. Take several days to adequately acclimatize to the high elevation of more than 3,000m (9,840 ft.), or up to a week if you're planning to attempt a serious ascent. In the early going, don't overextend yourself physically, and drink plenty of *mate de coca* (coca-leaf tea). If symptoms persist, see a doctor. Acute mountain sickness, known locally as *soroche,* is serious business.

---

lakes in the Huascarán National Park begin at Yungay, while Caraz, a pleasant small mountain town known for its agreeable climate and flowers, serves as a quieter alternative to Huaraz and offers similar services required for ascents and other adventure activities.

HUARAZ

420km (261 miles) N of Lima

Huaraz is the primary base destination for most visitors keen on exploring the Callejón de Huaylas Valley that runs 200km (125 miles) right down the middle of Peru. At an altitude of 3,100m (10,170 ft.), Huaraz enjoys a spectacular setting at the foot of the Cordillera Blanca: The town is ringed by 20 snowcapped peaks, each higher than 6,000m (19,680 ft.), that rise in splendor just beyond reach of the city. Huaraz itself is a far cry from the postcard perfection of a picturesque alpine village, however. Unseemly and unattractive, it is a little rough around the edges—and the center. It has a major earthquake to blame for its ragged look, a product of rapid and cheap concrete construction. The massive 1970 earthquake leveled nearly the entire city, eradicating half its population in the process.

Today Huaraz hums—albeit messily—with the business of mountain and adventure tourism. A wide range of facilities has sprung up to support outdoor travel; dozens of tour operators and travel agencies, restaurants and bars, and hotels and inns can be found in town, most clustered along the main drag, Av. Luzuriaga.

ESSENTIALS
Getting There
BY BUS   Traveling by bus from Lima or from other points along the north coast or the northern Andes is the only way to get to Huaraz. Most of the individual bus company terminals are located along Avenida Raymondi or Avenida Fitzcarrald. For the 7- to 8-hour journey from Lima, major companies offering daily service are **CIVA** (© 01/332-5236), **Cruz del Sur** (© 01/424-6158), and **Móvil Tours** (© 043/422-555 in Huaraz). Others include **Empresa de Transportes** (© 01/428-6621) and **Transportes Rodríguez** (© 01/428-0506 or 043/421-353). Móvil Tours and **Transportes Línea** (© 043/245-181 or 043/261-482) are the principal carriers to and from Trujillo (8 hr.).

Visitor Information
The **iPerú** tourist office is located at Av. Luzuriaga 734 (Pasaje Atusparía, office 1), across from the Plaza de Armas (© **043/428-812**); it's open Monday to Friday 8am to 1pm and 4pm to 7pm. General tourist information is also available during the same hours from the **tourist police** office between City Hall and the Post Office on

Huaraz

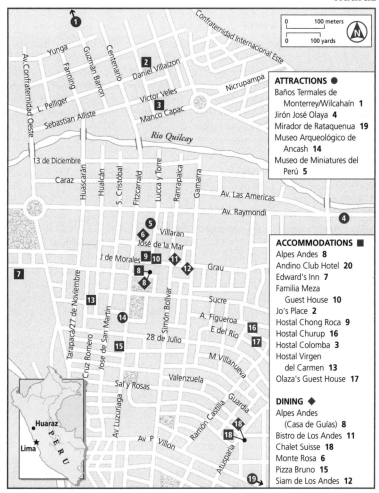

ATTRACTIONS ●

Baños Termales de
  Monterrey/Wilcahaín **1**
Jirón José Olaya **4**
Mirador de Rataquenua **19**
Museo Arqueológico de
  Ancash **14**
Museo de Miniatures del
  Perú **5**

ACCOMMODATIONS ■

Alpes Andes **8**
Andino Club Hotel **20**
Edward's Inn **7**
Familia Meza
  Guest House **10**
Jo's Place **2**
Hostal Chong Roca **9**
Hostal Churup **16**
Hostal Colomba **3**
Hostal Virgen
  del Carmen **13**
Olaza's Guest House **17**

DINING ◆

Alpes Andes
  (Casa de Guías) **8**
Bistro de Los Andes **11**
Chalet Suisse **18**
Monte Rosa **6**
Pizza Bruno **15**
Siam de Los Andes **12**

Avenida Luzuriaga (© **043/421-341**). For mountaineering and trekking information,
though, you're best off consulting the **Casa de Guías,** Parque Ginebra 28 (© **043/
421-811**). The office is open Monday through Friday from 9am to 6pm, and Saturday from 9am to 1pm. The friendly folks there have up-to-date information on trails,
maps, lists of certified guides, and message board postings for those looking to form
trekking and climbing groups. Mostly, though, they're there to set you up with a
guide. Basic information on visiting the Huascarán National Park can be obtained
from the **Parque Nacional Huascarán** office, in the Ministerio de Agricultura building on Avenida Raymondi (© **043/422-086**).

FAST FACTS   Most banks are found around the Plaza de Armas and along Avenida
Luzuriaga. Among those that exchange traveler's checks and cash and have ATMs are
Banco de Crédito, Av. Luzuriaga 669 at the corner of Sucre (© **043/421-170**);

Tips Safe Bus Travel

Night bus trips departing Huaraz for Trujillo, Chiclayo, and other cities in northern Peru have earned bad reputations for theft. Some travelers have reported
armed thieves boarding long-distance buses and forcibly relieving passengers
of their valuables. Perhaps for this reason, the better "executive-level" services
don't stop between Lima and their final destination. Be very careful with your
belongings on board, even if it means threading your arms through the straps
of your carry-on, if you plan to sleep.

Interbank, Sucre 913 (© 044/423-015); and **Banco Wiese,** Sucre 766 (no phone).
Money-changers can usually be found hanging around outside banks around the Plaza
de Armas.

In an **emergency,** call © 105. For climbing accidents and assistance, including evacu-
ations, contact **Unidad de Salvamento de Alta Montaña (High Altitude Rescue),** Av.
Arias Grazziani s/n, Yungay, at © 043/493-333 or 043/493-327; or **Casa de Guías,** Parque Ginebra 28 (© 043/421-811). If you need the police, the **tourist police** have an
office just off the Plaza de Armas (© 043/421-341); see "Visitor Information," above.
You can also contact the **national police,** Larrea y Loredo 720 (© 043/421-461). For
medical attention, go to **Hospital de Apoyo Víctor Ramos Guardia,** Av. Luzuriaga s/n
(© 043/421-290), or **Hospital Regional de Huaraz,** Av. Luzuriaga s/n (© 043/
421-321).

There are a number of Internet cabinas dotting the downtown area. Try **Avance,**
Av. Luzuriaga 672, 2nd floor (© 043/426-736), which has special deals for repeat visits and is open late.

The Huaraz **post office** is located at Av. Luzuriaga 702, across the street from the
Plaza de Armas (© 043/421-030); it's open daily from 8am to 7pm. The **Telefónica
del Perú** office is at Bolívar and Sucre, just east of the Plaza de Armas; it's open Monday to Saturday from 8am to 6pm.

Getting Around

The main axis in town is Av. Luzuriaga, which is overrun with tourist agencies, outdoor outfitters, and nearly every strolling traveler who hits Huaraz. The easiest way to
get around town is by taking an inexpensive taxi—the ones incessantly honking at
every pedestrian hoping for a fare—or a colectivo. Myriad bus companies serve the
Cordillera Blanca region, including Chavín, Caraz, and Yungay.

BY TAXI   Taxis cruise Av. Luzuriaga in search of travelers day and night. Rides in
town cost S/2 (60¢).

BY BUS   Combis service towns in the Callejón de Huaylas around Huaraz: Chavín
(4 hr.), Caraz (90 min.), and Yungay (90 min.). Most depart from the Quillcay Bridge
on Alameda Fitzcarrald; others leave from Calle Caraz, a half-block east of Fitzcarrald.
Fares are inexpensive, usually S/3 to S/10 (85¢–$2.85).

WHAT TO SEE & DO AROUND HUARAZ

The emphasis on seeing and doing in Huaraz is definitely on the latter—most visitors
are in town as long as it takes them to get acclimatized and organize an excursion into
the mountains and valleys nearby or participate in some sort of adventure-sports activity. The town itself was hastily reconstructed after the devastating 1970 earthquake. A

single street, **Jr. José Olaya** (to the right of Raymondi), gives a hint of what Huaraz looked like before it came crumbling down.

The **Museo Arqueológico de Ancash** is an interesting and well-organized small museum crammed with exhibits presenting the long history (more than 12,000 years) of the region through mummies, trepanned crania, and a terrific collection of monoliths from the Recuay and Huari cultures. There are textiles, ceramics, and other pieces from the Chavín, Huaraz, Moche, and Chimú cultures, as well as scale models of various ruins sites in the area. The museum, located at Av. Luzuriaga 762 (© **043/421-551**), is open Monday through Saturday from 9am to 5pm, and Sunday from 9am to 2pm. Admission is S/5 ($1.40); the ticket is also good for same-day entrance to the ruins at Wilcahuaín (see below).

Another diversion might be the **Museo de Miniaturas del Perú (Miniatures Museum),** in the Gran Hotel Huascarán. It houses dolls in traditional Peruvian dress and scale models of the ruins at Chavín de Huántar, pre-earthquake Huaraz, and the city of Yungay. The museum is in the gardens of the Gran Hotel Huascarán, Jr. Lúcar y Torre 46 (© **043/421-466**). It's open Monday through Friday from 8am to 1pm and 3 to 6pm. Admission is S/3 (85¢).

But because Huaraz is almost wholly about its stunning location and getting out-doors, visitors are usually more interested in the **Mirador de Rataquenua** ⊛, a look-out spot on a 3,650m (12,000-ft.) mountain pass with great panoramic views; it's just less than an hour's walk southeast of downtown. The direct trail is pretty steep; there's also a less demanding dirt road with plenty of switchbacks. Go with a group during the day because the area has experienced a spate of crime in recent years and become quite dangerous; locals warn that under no circumstances should a lone traveler walk there. To get there, head south on Luzuriaga to Villón and follow the road at the end, just beyond the cemetery.

Located about 8km (5 miles) north of Huaraz, the **Monumento Arqueológico de Wilcahuaín** is a set of ruins from the Huari culture, which lived in the region around A.D. 1000. Two sites named for their relative size, Grande and Chico, were burial grounds and storage centers. The major temple was built around 1100. The ruins don't have established opening and closing hours, but it's certainly wisest to go during daylight. Admission is S/5 ($1.40) for adults and S/2 (60¢) for students. To get there, take any combi marked "Wilcahuaín" from the Río Quillcay bridge. The trip takes about a half-hour and costs S/2 (60¢). After visiting Chico, walk down to Grande and catch a return combi to Huaraz.

A relaxing spot to visit, perhaps after you've indulged in some trekking or other adventure sports, are the thermal baths **Baños Termales de Monterrey** (© **043/427-690**). A

(*Tips* Tour Operators & Travel Agencies

Guides and travel agencies are extremely useful, if not downright indispensable, for most adventure sports in the remote and often dangerous mountains. Like Cusco and Iquitos, Huaraz is chock-full of agencies and tour operators. Unfortunately, some of them are less than reliable; others are far worse. See "Trekking & Climbing in the Cordillera Blanca," later in this chapter, for a discussion of guides and agencies. It's best to check with fellow tourists (or, before arriving in Huaraz, with the South American Explorers clubs in either Lima or Cusco) to get recent reports about services.

series of small wells and two large pools have mineral-rich waters that make the water look dark brown and rather unappealing, but your body might not be as picky as your eyes. The upper pool is the nicer of the two. The baths are open daily from 7am to 6pm, and they're usually very crowded on weekends and holidays. Admission is S/4 ($1.15). The baths are about 6km (3¾ miles) north of Huaraz along the road to Caraz; a colectivo from Av. Luzuriaga drops passengers at the entrance.

SHOPPING

Huaraz is recognized as an *artesanía* center, and all of the usual Andean handicrafts are available at markets targeting gringos. However, the city has none of the upscale, tourist-friendly shops found in Cusco and Lima. Some of the best items are custom-

---

Festival Calendar

Huaraz and the villages in the Callejón de Huaylas celebrate their Andean roots in traditional festivals that are among Peru's most spirited. If your visit coincides with a regional festival, you'll see a profusion of folk dances, costumed dances (some with extraordinary masks), and the stirring local music that accompanies them, played on exotic instruments such as *roncadoras, quenas,* and *zampoñas.* Carnaval, the Fiesta de Mayo, the Semana del Andinismo, the Patron Saint Festival, the Fiesta de las Luces, and Virgen de las Mercedes are among the most festive, but be warned that accommodations are at a premium, and prices skyrocket at these times.

Here's the complete list of regional festivals:

* **January 18 to 21:** La Virgen de Chiquinquirá (Caraz)
* **February or March:** Carnaval Huaracino (Huaraz)
* **March or April:** Semana Santa and the steps of the pilgrimage (Huaraz and Callejón de Huaylas)
* **May 2 to 10:** Fiesta de Mayo, celebrated with traditional dances, ski races, and a lantern procession (Huaraz)
* **June:** Semana del Andinismo, a celebration of outdoor adventure (Huaraz and Callejón de Huaylas)
* **June 22 to 24:** San Juan Bautista, Day of the Indian (Pomabamba and the entire Sierra Andina)
* **July 6 to 9:** La Virgen Santa Isabel (Callejón de Huaylas)
* **July 20 to 30:** Independence Celebration (Huaraz and Caraz)
* **July 28 to 29:** Fiestas Patrias
* **August 1 to 6:** Patron Saint Festival (Coyllur and Huaraz)
* **August 13 to 16:** Virgen de la Asunción (Huata and Chacas)
* **August 29 to 30:** Fiesta Patrona (Chiquián and Santa Rosa)
* **September 14:** Fiesta de las Luces (Huaraz)
* **September 14 to 27:** Señor de Burgos (Recuay)
* **September 23 to 27:** Virgen de las Mercedes (Carhuaz)
* **October 5 to 7:** Virgen del Rosario (Huari)
* **October 12:** Virgen del Pilar (Ticapampa)
* **October 28:** Fiesta Cívica (Yungay)

made and hand-tooled leather goods, wool sweaters, ponchos, and blankets. There are open-air handicrafts markets, open daily along the covered walkway (Pasaje Cáceres) off Av. Luzuriaga and along the streets Juan de la Cruz Romero, Av. Raymondi, and Av. Tarapacá. A **mercado callejero** (street market) is open Monday and Thursday on Avenida Bolognesi and Confraternidad Oeste.

PeruKraft, on Jr. 28 de Julio, stocks good-quality alpaca sweaters; **Andes Souvenirs,** Parque Ginebra next to the Casa de Guías, has handicrafts, textiles, and silver jewelry. A company called **Andean Expressions** specializes in great-quality T-shirts with cool Andean designs; its products are found in several shops in town or its factory site, at Jr. Julio Arguedas 1246.

But unless you're going on a trekking excursion with all your provisions included, shopping for foodstuffs might be more important. At the **main market** on Cruz Romero, just south of Raymondi, you can find most everything you'll need to sustain yourself for a mountain climb or a trek, including canned foods, nuts, and fresh fruits and vegetables. **Ortiz,** Av. Luzuriaga 401, is a good and well-stocked supermarket. Cheese and *manjar blanco* (a sweet) are good local items to take along on an expedition.

WHERE TO STAY

The high season in Huaraz and the Cordillera Blanca is June through the end of September. During Easter Week and other holidays (such as the Fiestas Patrias at the end of July), hotel prices can double. The Semana del Andinismo, held annually in June, brings mountain climbers from around the world; then and throughout the dry season, climbing groups and student groups (the latter especially in Oct–Nov) often take over less inexpensive *hostales*. Locals with inexpensive accommodations in their homes as well as touts acting (sometimes independently) on behalf of inns often meet incoming buses; take what the hawkers tell you (about location, comfort, and so on) with a grain of salt. Although Huaraz is loaded with budget accommodations aimed at independent trekkers, only a few are nice enough to recommend without reservation.

Expensive

Andino Club Hotel 🏵🏵   The top choice in town, this Swiss-owned, upscale alpine lodge is the favorite of well-equipped climbers and business folks in town to visit the nearby mines. A modern, raked construction about a 10-minute uphill walk southeast of the Plaza de Armas in the Pedregal district, it boasts a great deal of comfort and amenities for scruffy Huaraz. With a friendly vibe and a very good Swiss restaurant (see the Chalet Suisse review on p. 418), it's a fine place to prepare for or recover from rugged adventure travel. In high season, it's wise to book well in advance because it's popular with trekking and climbing groups. Accommodations are modern, spacious, and comfy, with big, thick, striped Andean wool blankets. Some rooms have fireplaces. The best (but most expensive) rooms are on the second floor and have excellent panoramic views of the snowcapped Cordillera Blanca and Huascarán peaks from private balconies. There's climbing equipment rental, horseback riding, and free Internet access for guests.

Pedro Cochachín 357, Huaraz. ⓒ **043/421-662,** or ⓒ/fax 01/241-5927 for reservations. www.hotelandino.com. 41 units. $106–$147 double; $219–$632 suites. Rates include taxes. AE, DC, MC, V. **Amenities:** Restaurant; small business center; travel agency; laundry service; Internet access in business center. *In room:* TV, hair dryer, safe.

Moderate

Edward's Inn 🄥🄰🄻🅄🄴   One of Huaraz's most popular and longest-running inns, Edward's is an easygoing place that packs in the trekkers during high season. Rooms are large and have good mountain views, although some detractors find the inn overpriced, given its fairly basic facilities. (The hot water, fueled by solar power, can be spotty.) The inn's also a bit removed from the action in town (about a 15-min. walk from the Plaza de Armas). Still, it's a good place to meet and hang out with fellow gringo trekkers and climbers. The eponymous owner, an experienced trekker and mountaineer, rents gear, speaks good English, and can provide good climbing and trekking information. He can also arrange tours, treks, and climbing trips. The rooftop patio is a good gathering spot.

Av. Bolognesi 121 (near the stadium), Huaraz. ℂ/fax **043/422-692**. www.huaraz.com/edwards/index.html. 14 units. $30 double with private bathroom; $20 double with shared bathroom; $10 per person dormitory. Rates include taxes. DC, V. **Amenities:** Cafe; laundry service. *In room:* TV, no phone.

Hostal Colomba 🏛🏛 *Value* An excellent-value midrange choice, this family-run *hostal* occupies the nicely landscaped grounds of a lovely old hacienda, which includes a small chapel. The hotel features bungalows scattered about a large and pretty plant-filled garden. Friendly and safe, it's located in a tranquil residential area across the river, about 15 to 20 minutes by foot to the main square. The pleasant bungalow rooms, though a bit old-fashioned, are spacious, and all have private bathrooms. This peaceful inn is a good place to unwind after a taxing trip to the mountains.

Jr. Francisco de Zela 278, Huaraz. ℂ/fax **043/421-501**. www.huarazhotel.com. 20 units. S/150 ($43) double. Rate includes taxes. DC, MC, V. **Amenities:** Dining room/cafe; room service; laundry service. *In room:* TV.

Inexpensive

Hostal Churup 🏛 *Value* One of the friendliest family-run inns in Huaraz, this low-key budget place plays happy host to lots of young gringo trekkers. Located in a quiet residential area just a short 5-block walk from the Plaza de Armas, Hostal Churup has good, clean rooms with private bathrooms for two to four people, and small dormitory rooms with shared bathrooms. The owners, the Quirós Romero family, are eager to share not only their knowledge of the area and trekking expeditions, but also their home (around the corner on Jr. Pedro Campos), where a filling and inexpensive breakfast is served with family members each morning. The lovely backyard is a good place to sit, read, and relax; the two double rooms there are the most private in the house. There's also a cool, brightly colored lounge, and guests can use the kitchen. It's a good idea to reserve in advance from June to September.

Jr. Amadeo Figueroa 1257 (near Iglesia Soledad), Huaraz. ℂ **043/422-584**. www.churup.com. 12 units. $26–30 double with private bathroom; $6–$7 per person in dorm room with shared bathroom. MC, V. **Amenities:** Laundry service. *In room:* No phone.

Olaza's Guest House 🏛 *Value* Newly expanded and spotless, this small and friendly inn, owned by one of the Olaza brothers who have their hands in everything from mountain biking to T-shirts, is one of the best values in town. Set back from the street in the Soledad district (a 10-min. walk from Av. Luzuriaga), it is quiet and safe, as well as very comfortable for the price. Rooms are simply equipped but large and have thick wool blankets and 24-hour hot water (often a rare commodity at the budget level). Bathrooms are impeccable. On the top floor is a terrace with good mountain views.

Julio Arguedas 1242 (La Soledad), Huaraz. ℂ **043/422-529**. www.andeanexplorer.com/olaza/index.htm. 9 units. $20 double. Rate includes breakfast. No credit cards. **Amenities:** Laundry facilities. *In room:* No phone.

WHERE TO DINE

Huaraz has plenty of pretty good, informal restaurants serving the band of Gore-Tex gringos that come to town. The main drag, Avenida Luzuriaga, is thick with restaurants

Tips   More Budget Accommodations

Huaraz can fill up with trekking groups and plenty of independent travelers between June and September. Many of the budget inns hawked by people who meet arriving buses are neither clean nor especially comfortable, though. If you arrive without a reservation and are looking for a solid, safe, and inexpensive inn, try one of the following:

Alpes Andes *Value*   Huaraz's official youth hostel is modern, well run, clean, and safe. Part of the informative Casa de Guías, the hostel functions as a prime meeting place for trekkers and mountaineers looking to form groups. There are kitchen and laundry facilities. Parque Ginebra 28-G. (C) 043/421-811. casa_de_guias@hotmail.com. $7.50 per person.

Familia Meza Guest House *Value*   This friendly, low-key place is run by Julio Olaza, whose Mountain Bike Adventures runs the best mountain-biking tours in the area. The hotel has a great rooftop terrace, a book exchange, kitchen and laundry facilities, and simple, clean rooms. It's a good value. Jr. Lucar y Torre 530. (C) 043/426-367. $5 per person.

Hostal Chong Roca   This plain *hostal* has large and decent rooms that have either a full private bathroom or a toilet and sink. It's okay in a pinch. Morales 687. (C) 043/421-154. S/30 ($8.55) per person.

Hostal Virgen del Carmen   This comfortable *hostal* is run by a warm older couple who have converted their attractive house into an inn with very nice bedrooms. Cruz Romero 622. (C) 043/421-729. S/25 ($7.15) double.

Jo's Place   This relaxed and friendly inn has a cool garden terrace, excellent mountain views, and very well-maintained rooms. It's on the north side of the Río Quillcay, a 10- to 15-minute walk from the center of town. The place is pretty popular with a steady stream of backpackers. Jr. Daniel Villayzán 276. (C) 043/425-505. $15 double.

offering fixed-price menus and other cheap eats. The Andean cuisine of the Cordillera includes hearty items such as Huaracino *picante de cuy* (spicy roasted guinea pig), *jacachasqui* (spicy guinea pig soup), *charqui* (dried pork), and *trucha* (fried river trout). For the less adventurous, there are several *chifas* and pizzerias in town where you can get a filling, inexpensive meal.

Alpes Andes PIZZA/INTERNATIONAL   The food here might appear to take a back seat to the planning of mountain-climbing expeditions—as many mountain guides as eager tourists come through the doors—but this relaxing and informal cafe next door to the Casa de Guías goes about its business of fortifying trekkers and adventurers for their trips to the Cordillera. Start with a breakfast of granola and yogurt, or chow down on the international trekkers' favorites: pizza and pasta (gotta load up on the carbs, you know). Morales 753. (C) 043/421-811. Reservations not accepted. Main courses S/6–S/18 ($1.70–$5.15). No credit cards. Daily 7am–11pm.

Bistro de Los Andes ✦ INTERNATIONAL/PERUVIAN   This welcoming restaurant has long been one of the most popular places in town. It offers an interesting mix of French and Peruvian items for lunch and dinner. The varied menu includes vegetarian dishes, pastas, and nicely done dishes such as *trucha a la almendra* (trout baked with almonds).

Jr. Julio de Morales 823. ⓒ **043/426-249.** Reservations not accepted. Main courses S/10–S/27 ($2.85–$7.70). DC, V. Daily 5–11pm.

Chalet Suisse ⓡ SWISS/FONDUE   This upscale restaurant has a pretty simple chalet decor, but the food is some of the city's best. The restaurant is primarily occupied by those staying in the attached Hotel Andino, so if you're not a guest, it's best to ring for a reservation. Dishes are generally hearty. The Swiss fondues, while not cheap, are delicious, as are steaks (such as the Argentine *bife angosto* and *asado al vino tinto*) and chipped beef in creamed mushroom sauce. The attractive dining room is the perfect subdued spot to celebrate your big climb (if you're too weary to hit the pubs).

Pedro Cochachín 357. ⓒ **043/421-949.** Reservations recommended. Main courses S/26–S/35 ($7.40–$10). AE, DC, MC, V. Daily noon–2pm and 7–10pm.

Monte Rosa ⓡ *Value* PERUVIAN/INTERNATIONAL   Probably Huaraz's best-looking restaurant, this two-level place with an inviting bar has an extensive menu that's all over the board but universally pretty good. Choose from traditional *criollo* cooking, *chifa,* or pizzas; there are steaks, fondues, and pastas, too. Service is friendly, and between regular dining hours, it's a fine place to linger over a book and a beer.

Jr. José de la Mar 661. ⓒ **043/421-447.** Reservations not accepted. Main courses S/10–S/35 ($2.85–$10). MC, V. Tues–Sun noon–3pm and 6:30–10:30pm.

Pizza Bruno ⓡ *Value* PIZZA/INTERNATIONAL   With a French chef but a largely Italian menu, this upscale but relaxed restaurant—with a family-run Mediterranean decor and large-format photos of Paris—might appear a little confused, but it's one of the best dining options in town. The pizzas are of the authentic thin-crust type, and the pastas are excellent. If you're in the mood for experimenting, try one of the chef's specialties, which include *"plato del diablo"* (devil's plate, or sirloin flambéed with whiskey) and trout meunière. The French touch is delivered in the desserts, which include a tarte tatin and profiteroles. Breakfast is also offered.

Morales 753. ⓒ **043/421-811.** Reservations recommended. Main courses S/13–S/32 ($3.70–$9.15). AE, MC, V. Daily 6am–11pm.

Huaraz's Cafe Culture

A number of cafes around town are inviting spots for inexpensive meals. Check out **Café Andino,** on Av. Lucar y Torre 530 (ⓒ **043/421-203**), a popular hangout with good coffee (including cappuccinos and lattes) and breakfasts. It has a library book exchange with titles in several languages, board games, and a nice selection of tunes. Also worth a stop is **El Parque** (no phone), Figueroa 1025, an informal but clean and cute cafe with filling breakfasts and very cheap lunches as well as mixed drinks. **Café California** ⓡ, Av. 28 de Julio 562 (ⓒ **043/428-354**), Café Andino's old haunt and a favorite of gringos, has fresh-roasted coffee, a sitting lounge, and a book exchange. Finally, the pub upstairs at the climbing agency **Monttrek,** Av. Luzuriaga 646 (ⓒ **043/421-121**), has tasty pizza, a roaring fireplace, and strong pisco sours.

Siam de Los Andes ⟲ THAI It's certainly unusual to alight upon a Thai restaurant in Huaraz, but hungry trekkers looking for a taste of something different are really glad when they do. It's far from the cheapest restaurant in Huaraz, but the food is authentic and very well prepared. The stir-fries and curries are especially delicious. The amiable chef/owner Naresuan likes to greet diners, and, besides cooking, he knows a thing or two about trekking in the area.

Gamarra 419 (at the corner of Julián de Morales). Ⓒ **043/428-006.** Reservations not accepted. Main courses S/12–S/30 ($3.40–$8.55). DC, V. Daily 5–10pm.

HUARAZ AFTER DARK

It's not hard to find a nightspot in Huaraz. With all the gringos gearing up for or celebrating the completion of trekking expeditions, the place hops in high season.

El Tambo, José de la Mar 776, about 3 blocks from Av. Luzuriaga (Ⓒ **043/423-417**), is the most happening disco in town. There's plenty of drinking, dancing, and smoking until the wee hours, and the music careens between international Top 40 and more home-grown Latin sounds. There's usually a pretty good mix of locals and gringos. The cover charge ranges from S/10 to S/20 ($2.85–$5.70). **Makondo's** (no phone), a cool nightclub with food and dancing, is across from El Tambo on José de la Mar.

Bars worth dropping in on include the intimate **Las Kenas,** Jr. Gabino Uribe 620 (Ⓒ **043/428-383**), which features live and recorded (often Andean) music and good pisco sours, and **Monttrek Pub,** Av. Luzuriaga 646 (Ⓒ **043/421-121**). Next door to Las Kenas (upstairs) is a slightly rowdier bar, **X-Treme** (Ⓒ **043/682-115**), a place to drink and listen to classic rock. **La Cueva del Oso,** Av. Luzuriaga 674 (no phone), is a lively peña with good music and dancing.

SIDE TRIPS FROM HUARAZ

Most folks who make it to Huaraz are understandably eager to get out into the countryside and up into the mountains. The point of a visit to Huaraz is really to explore some of the most stunning scenery on the planet; the entire valley is characterized by spectacular snowcapped mountains, stunning alpine lakes, and tranquil meadows. For information on trekking, climbing, and other adventure sports, see "Trekking & Climbing in the Cordillera Blanca," below. Less rigorous excursions by organized tour are also possible; the most popular are the spectacular Lagunas de Llanganuco and the ancient ruins at Chavín de Huántar. The small towns of the Callejón de Huaylas, the valley that splits the middle between the mountain ranges of the Cordillera Blanca and the Cordillera Negra north of Huaraz, make good bases for hikes and are worthwhile visits in themselves.

Chavín de Huántar ⟲⟲

110km (68 miles) E of Huaraz

East of the Cordillera Blanca, Chavín de Huántar, the nearly 3,000-year-old ruins of the Chavín culture, is some 4 long hours by a largely unpaved and twisting mountain road (which is very slowly being improved) from Huaraz. The ruins, a UNESCO World Heritage Site and the best-preserved ruins of the culture, consist of a U-shaped fortress-temple with excellent stonework constructed over several centuries. The Chavín, who thrived in the region from about 1200 to 300 B.C. and whose influence was felt from Ecuador all the way to southern Peru, were the most ancient of the major cultures known to exist in Peru, and certainly one of its most sophisticated. The Chavín are considered perhaps the most influential people to have existed in the Andes until the arrival of the dynasty-building Incas (who came along a mere 2,000 years later).

However, don't expect a stunning set of Machu Picchu–like ruins. The site's archaeological importance isn't nearly as transparently aesthetic. The temple comprises more than a dozen underground galleries or chambers; only a few are open to the public. Some appear as labyrinthine tunnels today because they were interred by a landslide in the 1940s. The main structure on the premises is a large pyramid, called the **Castillo,** built over well-constructed canals where water once flowed. A ways away is a large, sunken central plaza, a ceremonial gathering place. The highlight of the ruins is the **Lanzón** ✸✸✸, a remarkable cultist carving in white granite and shaped like a prism or dagger. The monolith is found in an underground passage behind the original temple, which is much smaller than the several-times-enlarged Castillo. The huge 4.5m (15-ft.) carving depicts three figures worshipped by the Chavín culture: the serpent, the bird, and the feline, the principal deity. The Lanzón remains in its original location, at an underground crossroads, even though other important artifacts, including the famous Tello Obelisk and Raymondi Stela, were removed and are now housed at Museo de la Nación in Lima. A guide and a flashlight are needed to get the most out of the site. Once visitors could walk completely around and inspect the prized Lanzón; today, however, it can be viewed only from the side and a distance, down a cramped corridor.

The **Monumento Arqueológico Chavín de Huántar** (✆ 044/754-042), which includes a small museum, is open daily from 8am to 4pm. The most convenient and fastest way to visit Chavín is by organized tour from Huaraz (Chavín Tours or Pablo Tours); most cost about S/25 ($7.15) per person (plus the S/10 or $2.85 entrance fee to the ruins). Virtually every agency offers the same program, a long day trip leaving Huaraz around 9am and returning around 8pm.

Nearby, the village of Chavín de Huántar is a traditional settlement. Although very few tourists stay overnight, the Lanzón has been known to exert a mystical hold on some visitors. There are a couple of decent inns, in case you want to stay (such as the **Hotel La Casona,** ✆ 044/754-020, on the Plaza de Armas), perhaps to make a second day's visit to the ruins.

Lagunas de Llanganuco
82km (51 miles) N of Huaraz

These two brilliant turquoise alpine lakes, at nearly 4,000m (13,120 ft.) above sea level, compose a dazzling vista at the base of the Cordillera Blanca's highest snowcapped summits. The views of Chopicalqui (6,354m/20,841 ft.), Huandoy (6,395m/20,976 ft.), and hulking Huascarán (6,768m/22,199 ft.) are simply mesmerizing. If possible, wait for a clear morning to go; the sun shining on the lakes makes them shimmer and their colors change. The glacier-fed lakes within the Huascarán National Park (entry fee S/5 or $1.40) are a popular day trip from Huaraz, and many tour companies in Huaraz offer Llanganuco as an organized tour for about S/25 ($7.15) per person. Those up for more of an adventure can also organize a day trek to the lagunas (those with more time on their hands might opt for the 4- to 5-day Llanganuco–Santa Cruz trek, one of the most beautiful and popular treks on the continent; see "Trekking & Climbing in the Cordillera Blanca," below). If you're traveling independently, the lakes are easiest to get to from Yungay, which is 26km (16 miles) away; it's simple to catch a combi or truck up to the lakes from the Plaza de Armas in Yungay (about S/18 or $5.15 round-trip), but note that the ride can take up to 90 minutes.

Glaciar Pastoruri
70km (43 miles) S of Huaraz

The Cordillera Blanca is tightly packed with towering peaks that should be ascended only by skilled and properly outfitted climbers. If you're not in that camp, this relatively flat glacier, another popular day trip from Huaraz, might be a draw. Provided that you've already become acclimatized to the altitude of the area, the 45-minute trek up the glacier (5,240m/17,187 ft.) isn't difficult and can be done without special equipment, although horses and mules are frequently available to help those having a hard time trudging through the snow. Although Peruvians often ski and snowboard on the glacier, veteran skiers will be disappointed. Bring sufficient cold-weather gear because it can be very frigid.

As an organized outing, the trip to Pastoruri is usually combined with a visit to the valley of **Pachacoto,** 57km (35 miles) south of Huaraz, an opportunity to see the Callejón de Huaylas's famous **Puya Raimondi** plants. The bizarre, spiky plants, like towering alien cacti, are the largest members of the bromeliad family (a relative of the pineapple). The species is thought to be one of the most ancient in the world, and it is found only in a few isolated, high-altitude parts of the Andes. The plant, which can reach a height of 12m (39 ft.), is like a tragic protagonist: It flowers but once in its life, and although it might live to be 100 years old, it dies immediately after flowering. Flowering is usually in May, when tour groups make pilgrimages to witness the brief, beautiful sight, like a stage set against the snowy mountains. Organized Pastoruri/Puya Raymondi visits are also about S/25 ($7.15) per person.

Carhuaz
31km (19 miles) N of Huaraz

This quiet, rather plain Andean town stands in stark contrast to the tourism hustle of Huaraz. It's becoming better known as a base in its own right for mountain-adventure travel, but it doesn't have even a fraction of the tourism infrastructure found in Huaraz. Still, it has a couple of nice *hostales* and restaurants for people looking for a more serene atmosphere. Carhuaz is locally renowned for its Virgen de las Mercedes festival, which takes place for 10 days in mid-September and is perhaps the most raucous festival in the valley.

There aren't many actual sights in town, other than the bustling Sunday market, but a few places just outside Carhuaz are worth a look. Near the small town of Mancos (a half-hour from Carhuaz by combi) is the ancient cave Cueva de Guitarreros, which some anthropologists believe to be 12,000 years old. The cave, which contains primitive rock paintings, is a nice 30-minute walk from Mancos south across the river. There are good views of Huascarán. Near Marcará, about 6.5km (4 miles) south of Carhuaz, are the Baños Termales de Chancos (hot springs).

To get to Carhuaz, take a combi from Huaraz; the trip takes about an hour and costs S/4 ($1.15). If you want to spend the night in Carhuaz, perhaps your best bet is one of the family-run guesthouses, or *casas de alojamiento.* Try **Las Bromelias,** Jr. Brasil 208 (© 043/394-033), $10 double, or, better still, **La Casa de Pocha,** (© 043/363-058), an eco-ranch outside of town, boasting a peaceful organic farm and adobe guesthouse with excellent views and opportunities for horseback riding and hiking in the forest. It runs $30 per person for a double room including meals.

Yungay

54km (33 miles) N of Huaraz

This small town is permanently marked by tragedy: It was completely buried in just a matter of minutes in a 1970 landslide, which was precipitated by the massive earthquake (7.8 on the Richter scale) that loosened tons of granite and ice from the north peak of Huascarán. The hurtling mass killed at least 20,000 people, nearly the town's entire population. Only a few children and those who, ironically, scrambled to the higher grounds of the local cemetery, survived. The rubble, called Campo Santo, is now a macabre tourist attraction. The only reminders of the life that once existed there are four palm trees that graced the Plaza de Armas and rosebushes and monuments honoring the dead. A new settlement was established about a half-mile away. Predictably, the rebuilt town isn't too easy on the eyes, save its alpine location; it's mostly a functional transportation hub for those looking to approach the stunning lakes of Llanganuco (see above). In town, there's a small museum, the **Museo de Arqueología e Historia Natural de Yungay,** Avenida Las Palmeras, Ranrahirca (© 043/682-322), which exhibits regional flora and fauna, ceramics, textiles, and other historical relics.

Combis leave from the Quillcay Bridge on Alameda Fitzcarrald Huaraz for Yungay. The trip, which takes about 1½ hours, costs S/3 (85¢).

Caraz

68km (42 miles) N of Huaraz

Caraz is the farthest of the valley towns north of Huaraz that are accessible by public transportation. More attractive than some of the other towns that have suffered great natural disaster, and located at an elevation about 1,000m (3,280 ft.) lower than Huaraz, Caraz makes a good base for trekking and climbing in the Cordillera Blanca. The town has a pleasant Plaza de Armas and a growing amount of infrastructure to serve trekkers and mountaineers, including one of the area's top outdoor-adventure agencies. Many people end up (and rest up) in Caraz after trekking the popular Llanganuco–Santa Cruz route, although nearly as many embark from here to remote treks into the northern Cordillera Blanca.

Caraz has a couple small museums: a **Museo de Arqueología,** Esquina 1 de Mayo y Manuel Cáceres (© 043/791-029), which has some deformed skulls and artifacts uncovered at the Cueva de Guitarreros, and the **Museo Amauta de Arte Ancashino,** Av. Noe Bazán Peralta s/n, which contains some ethnographic exhibits representing villages of the Callejón de Huaylas. Nearby are some pre-Chavín ruins, **Tunshucaiko,** about a half-mile from the center of town across the Río Llullán.

Although many people make their way to Caraz to begin some hard-core mountain excursions, several worthwhile and easier excursions make excellent day trips. Gorgeous **Laguna Parón** is a bold, bright blue lake that sits at an elevation of more than 4,000m (13,120 ft.) and is surrounded by a dozen snowcapped peaks, 30km (19 miles) east of town. Colectivos run from Santa Rosa in Caraz to Parón (90 min.). The **Cañón del Pato** is a fantastic, sheer canyon formed by the Río Santa, dividing the Cordilleras Blanca and Negra. Although it is more than 1,000m (3,280 ft.) deep, it is only 15m (49 ft.) wide. The road that knifes through the canyon, from Caraz to Huallanca, is one of the most thrilling in the country; it penetrates more than three dozen tunnels. By colectivo, it's about 2 hours to Huallanca, the far end of the canyon, from Caraz.

Caraz is a 2-hour combi ride from Huaraz. If you want to stay overnight in Caraz, try one of the following nice and inexpensive inns that are popular with trekkers and backpackers: **Hostal Perla de los Andes,** Daniel Villar 179 (Plaza de Armas;

ⓒ **043/392-007;** www.huaraz.com/perladelosandes; $16 double); the youth hostel **Albergue Los Piños,** Parque San Martín 103 (ⓒ **043/391-130;** $20 double); or **Caraz Dulzura,** Sáenz Peña 212 (ⓒ **043/391-523;** www.huaraz.com/carazdulzura; $15 double). In town is **Pony Expeditions,** one of the best trekking and mountaineering agencies in the valley, with equipment rental and good guides (see "Recommended Tour Companies," below), and **Apu Expeditions,** Villar 215 (ⓒ **043/392-159**). **Café de Rat,** Jr. Sucre 1286, on the Plaza de Armas above Pony Expeditions, is the place for mountaineers to hang out and fortify themselves with pizzas, pastas, crepes, and good vegetarian meals. (It also has Internet access, maps, and guidebooks.)

TREKKING & CLIMBING IN THE CORDILLERA BLANCA ✸✸✸

The Cordillera Blanca, the highest tropical mountain chain in the world, is one of South America's most impressive ranges. Its glorious and imposing mountain peaks proclaim their beauty and power over a 180km (112-mile) stretch through the heart of Peru. Most visitors to the Cordillera Blanca mountain range want to view the stunning scenery of snowcapped peaks, glaciers, lakes, and rivers from up close and on high. They have one thing in mind: strapping on high-tech gear and embarking on trekking or climbing expeditions.

This section of Peru has become one of the world's mountaineering meccas. Fifty summits soar between 4,800 and 6,662m (15,748–21,857 ft.) high, and nearly the entire range forms part of the protected Parque Nacional Huascarán. Although the most challenging peaks are beacons to some of the most tested mountaineers in the world, there are plenty of trekking and climbing activities for those who haven't quite perfected their ascent techniques. And although some of the peaks are plenty daunting, access to the trailheads is fairly simple, reached by public transportation in just a few hours from Huaraz.

The 340,000-hectare (839,800-acre) Parque Nacional Huascarán was created in 1975 to protect the region's great natural resources. Within the park are the towns Recuay, Huaraz, Carhuaz, Yungay, Huaylas, Bolognesi, Huari, Asunción, Piscobamba, and Pomabamba, several of which serve as bases for explorers. The park counts 32 peaks higher than 6,000m (19,680 ft.) and includes Huascarán, Peru's highest summit, and Alpamayo, whose legendary fourth face is considered by many mountaineers as the most beautiful in the world, as well as 269 lakes and 41 rivers among its spectacular roster of natural blessings.

Most of the top climbs in the Cordillera Blanca are best done with the assistance of local guides and experts. Several climbs are not only arduous, but also extremely dangerous. Unless you're a certified member of the hard-core ilk, it's best to contract a guide or organized tour in Huaraz. There, you'll find a whole complement of services, including licensed guides, porters, climbing-gear rentals, and rescue teams. However,

---

⎛Fun Fact⎞ Top of the Peaks

Among the highest and best known of Peru's daunting pinnacles—trophies prized by climbers the world over—are Mount Huascarán, 6,768m (22,205 ft.); the Huandoy massif's three summits, all more than 6,000m (19,680 ft.) high; Chopicalqui, 6,354m (20,846 ft.); Chacraraju, 6,112m (20,052 ft.); Alpamayo, 5,957m (19,544 ft.); and Copa, 6,118m (20,072 ft.).

> ### ⎛Tips⎞ A Gear Checklist
>
> Appropriate technical gear is required for nearly all treks and climbs in the Cordillera Blanca. If you're going with an organized group, you can rent anything you need that's not provided. Independent trekkers and climbers can also rent almost anything they need in Huaraz. Some equipment is invariably dated and in less than optimal condition, so experienced mountain climbers pursuing technical climbs will surely want to bring all their own equipment. At a minimum, you'll need cold-weather and water-repellent clothing; good backpacking or climbing boots; a tent, a sleeping bag, a camping stove, and cookware; a filter and/or water-purification tablets; a compass; and topographical maps of trails.

---

plenty of independent and self-reliant trekkers simply hire an *arriero* (muleteer) and set off without a proper guide.

In recent years, there has been a fair amount of grousing about the deteriorating state of the Parque Nacional Huascarán, from both trekkers and agencies; many complain that it is not being kept up as it should, with the most popular trails littered with refuse and bribes supplanting group payment of entry fees. If one of Peru's national treasures is being neglected, it will surely have a great impact not only on the local environment, but also on the local economy. So many individuals and communities depend upon the income produced by largely foreign adventure travelers who come to enjoy the remote beauty of the Peruvian Andes.

The fee to enter Huascarán National Park is S/5 ($1.40) for a single-day visit and S/65 ($19) for visits of 2 days or more (valid up to 1 month). The entrance ticket to Huascarán National Park can be purchased at the Llanganuco and other entrances. You should keep a copy of your passport ready when entering and leaving the park.

RECOMMENDED TOUR COMPANIES

In Peru, it's important to pick tour operators carefully to avoid being ripped off. When you're embarking on alpine adventures, especially mountain and ice climbing, it's even more essential: The risks are extreme, so it's paramount to go with an experienced, professional outfit. Accidents happen, and every year climbers are injured or killed climbing in the Andes. A good guide from a respected agency knows the routes, the weather, and the risks, and can usually steer you away from the latter. In the event of an emergency, he or she will know how to get injured parties evacuated. Huaraz is littered with freelance guides and somewhat shady agencies offering very cheap fees, but if you're serious about adventure sports, you don't want to skimp when it comes to the people to whom you're entrusting your safety and well-being. Locals suggest that you demand a *factura* (receipt) with an R.U.C. authorization number from any prospective agency or guide.

The following are all recommended agencies and guides with many years of experience and good reputations in the Huaraz/Cordillera Blanca region. Even so, ask around first. Talk to people who've recently returned from treks and climbing expeditions. Contact the **South American Explorers** either in Lima, at Av. Piura 135, Miraflores (ⓒ **01/445-3306;** www.samexplo.org); or Cusco, at Choquechaca 188, no. 4 (ⓒ **084/245-484;** cuscoclub@saexplorers.org). Also speak to the **Casa de Guías de Huaraz,** Parque Ginebra 28 (ⓒ **043/421-811**), an excellent source of current information (although understand that its mission is primarily to hook you up with one of its guides). Don't overlook your guide's ability to speak English, which could be critical if your understanding of Spanish is poor. Even if the agency says that the guide speaks good English, don't automatically take its word for it.

Virtually every agency in town runs the basic and most popular no- or little-difficulty programs to Lagunas de Llanganuco, Glaciar Pastoruri, and Chavín de Huántar (see "Side Trips from Huaraz," earlier in this chapter) for less than $10 per person. Agencies often pool travelers when they can round up enough on their own.

General Tours

- **Chavín Tours,** Av. Luzuriaga 502, Huaraz (© **043/421-578** or 01/447-0024; www.chavintours.com.pe). A good company offering standard tours, including trips to Chavín de Huántar, Pastoruri Glacier, and Llanganuco lakes.
- **Pablo Tours,** Av. Luzuriaga 501, Huaraz (© **043/421-145**). A standard tour company, similar to Chavín Tours but offering a few more options. Also organizes good group treks.

Mountain Trekking & Climbing

- **Explorandes** ⟨⟨⟨, Av. Centenario 489, Huaraz (© **043/421-960** or 01/445-0532; www.explorandes.com). This environmentally sensitive and serious agency is one of the big-name and longest-established adventure-tour operators in Peru, with fixed-departure treks in the Cordillera Blanca. It's expensive, but it's one of the best and most dependable. Explorandes offers both hard-core adventure and soft adventure programs, and will custom-tailor a trip for small groups. Programs range from llama trekking to Chavín to 12-day treks in the Cordillera Huayhuash.
- **JM Expeditions,** Av. Luzuriaga 465, office no. 4, Huaraz (© **043/428-017** or 01/426-0599; www.jmexpeditions.com). Good mountain-climbing equipment and roster of guides.
- **Monttrek** ⟨⟨⟨, Av. Luzuriaga 646, second floor, Huaraz (© **043/421-121**). One of the climbing and trekking pioneers in Huaraz, now going on 20 years in the area, this serious agency organizes hard-core ascents and expeditions, including ice and rock climbing. The company also offers programs for budget-conscious trekkers, as well as camping- and climbing-equipment rental, guides, mountain- and ice-climbing classes, and horseback riding, mountain biking, river rafting, and hang gliding. New programs include Overland Andino (aka World War II Jeep) and excursions to Cañon del Pato and Lagunas Llanganuco. With its nice upstairs pub restaurant (which has an interior climbing wall), Monttrek is a good spot to put together a group of like-minded adventurers. Serious climbers will want to speak to the owner, Pocho, and check out his technical drawings of nearly every peak in the region.
- **Pony Expeditions** ⟨⟨, Jr. Sucre 1266, Plaza de Armas, Caraz (© **043/391-642;** www.ponyexpeditions.com). This professional outfitter is run by a respected guide, Alberto Cafferata, with lots of different treks and climbs available. It offers an extensive program of trekking and climbing itineraries, mountain biking, and rock and ice climbing.
- **Pyramid Adventures,** Luzuriaga 530, Huaraz (© **043/421-864**). One of the better climbing agencies, run by a family of brothers, with good service and knowledge.

Guides & Equipment Rental

- **Galaxia Mountain Shop,** Leoniza y Lescano 603 (© **043/422-792**), and **MountClimb,** Cáceres 421 (© **043/426-060**). Both have a full range of mountain-climbing gear, including boots, sleeping bags, and crampons, for rent ($20–$30 per day for full complement of equipment).

- **Montañero Aventura y Turismo,** Parque Ginebra 30B, Huaraz (© **043/726-386,** or 043/422-603). Climbing equipment, guides, mountain bikes, and standard tours.
- **Mountain Bike Adventures** ☆☆, Jr. Lúcar y Torre 530, Huaraz (© **043/424-259;** www.chakinaniperu.com). The top company for single-track riding in the Cordilleras Blanca and Negra, run by Julio Olaza. He has Trek front-suspension bikes for rent (including helmets) and offers several 4- to 7-day itineraries, as well as 1-day bike trips. The company also runs a small and enjoyable guesthouse.

TREKKING

The Cordillera Blanca is blessed with some of the greatest trails and most spectacular scenery in South America, and it draws trekkers from the across the world. Across gorgeous valleys and mountain passes nearly 5,000m (16,400 ft.) high, past stunning lakes, waterfalls, and rivers, the region truly earns the cliché so often accorded it: It's a mountaineer and trekker's paradise. The scenery is enlivened by fantastic indigenous flora and fauna, including 800 varieties of blossoming flowers (the Puya Raimondi and ancient queñual and cacti forests among them), as well as Andean condors, vicuñas, pumas, Andean deer, and 100 species of birds. There are terrific campsites throughout the valley and excellent guides, porters, and mules to round out your expedition.

There are some three dozen well-established treks in the Cordillera Blanca (and many dozens more that draw few tourists). Of the many treks possible from Huaraz, the classic **Llanganuco–Santa Cruz** route, one of the most beautiful on the continent, is understandably the most popular. The route across the Santa Cruz gorge begins in the village of Cashapampa and makes its way to the emerald-green lakes at the Llanganuco ravine. The 45km (28-mile) trek usually takes 4 or 5 days. Other popular circuits include **Alpamayo,** a beautiful trek among snowcapped summits that takes about 12 days; **Cedros Gorge,** which takes in mountains in the northern sector of the Huascarán Park (4 days); and **Llanganuco** and **Portachuelo,** a less demanding trek through the Quillcayhuanca ravine (1–2 days).

Other well-known routes are:

- **Cojup Valley** (Huaraz to Laguna Palcacucha), 20km (12 miles), 2 days (moderate)
- **Laguna Churup,** 25km (16 miles), 1 to 2 days (difficult)

Tips The Cost of Trekking & Climbing

All multiday excursions (up to 1 month) into the Huascarán National Park carry entrance fees of S/65 ($19). If you're going with a tour operator, ask whether this fee is included in your package cost. Single-day entry costs S/5 ($1.40).

Licensed climbing and trekking guides charge between $50 and $90 per day. *Arrieros,* local porters with mules who'll lead you on trails, charge $12 per day, plus food. (*Arrieros* can be arranged at trailheads or at the Casa de Guías in Huaraz.) Organized treks with one of the firms listed earlier are generally around $25 to $30 per day, per person. A certified guide to lead technical mountain climbs can cost upwards of $70. Serious climbers should also factor in the cost of insurance (obtained at home) that protects against the prohibitive cost of rescue operations.

- **Olleros to Chavín,** a pre-Columbian trail that ends at Chavín de Huántar, 40km (25 miles), 3 days (moderate)
- **Quebrada Quillcayhuanca to Cayesh,** 25km (16 miles), 2 to 3 days (easy to moderate)

The Casa de Guías in Huaraz has detailed information about these and other treks, and South American Explorers produces a good map of various treks in the region. Another good resource is *Peru & Bolivia: Backpacking and Trekking* (Bradt Publications, 2002), by Hilary Bradt, with descriptions of a number of treks in the Cordillera Blanca.

Even more accessible hikes in this daunting region should be undertaken only by individuals in good physical shape; tackling a mountain pass at nearly 5,000m (16,400 ft.) with gear and food is not easy for those unaccustomed to high altitudes.

Llanganuco–Santa Cruz Trek 🍀🍀🍀

Touted as one of the top five treks in the world by several international outdoor-oriented magazines, the 4- to 5-day Llanganuco–Santa Cruz trail is one of the most scenic in Peru. It takes in extraordinary mountain scenery of snowcapped peaks, brilliant turquoise lakes, glacier-fed rivers, sparkling waterfalls, and serene meadows. The 62km (38-mile) trail ranges from 2,900 to 4,750m (9,512–15,580 ft.) in altitude but is rated moderate to difficult, meaning that the hike can be undertaken by anyone in good physical shape who has allowed for time to acclimatize in Huaraz. In peak season, though, the trail's popularity is its enemy. It gets quite crowded, and trash is a problem. There are established campsites and pit toilets along the route.

Trekkers can walk the trail in either direction, starting at Cashapampa (2 hr. by bus from Caraz) or Vaquería (2½ hr. by bus from Carhuaz). Many independent travelers prefer to start the trail at Vaquería because the daily bus from Huaraz allows time to

---

Cordillera Huayhuash: The New "It" Range

As the treks in the Cordillera Blanca have become more popular in recent years, intrepid trekkers who are determined to find yet more solitude and untrampled scenery are now setting out on extended trekking circuits of the **Cordillera Huayhuash** 🍀🍀🍀, which is even more pristine and remote. Although it extends only 30km (19 miles) from north to south, it, too, has phenomenal mountain vistas and sparkling lagunas—perhaps more spectacular still than the Cordillera Blanca—but only a few very isolated and primitive mountain communities.

The range, which was made a natural preserve in 2002, comprises seven peaks more than 6,000m (19,680 ft.) high and seven additional peaks higher than 5,500m (18,040 ft.). The landscape is more wide open than that of the Cordillera Blanca, which is characterized by deep canyons. The major trekking and climbing agencies in Huaraz and Caraz offer Huayhuash treks, which usually begin in the town of Chiquián at 3,400m (11,150 ft.), 110km (68 miles) south of Huaraz. Trekking in the range is difficult, with as many as eight passes higher than 4,500m (14,760 ft.), and two main circuits are popular: One is 80km (50 miles) round-trip; the other, which covers the entire range, is as much as 165km (102 miles) and takes from 12 to 14 days.

Packin' Up the Llama

Pack-laden mules on the trail are common, but what could be cooler and more authentic in Peru than trekking with a llama? An organization called **Llama 2000,** an initiative undertaken by campesino farmers from the Callejón de Huaylas and the Mountain Association of the Olleros-Chavín area, has proposed exactly that. The **Llama-Trek Expedition in Olleros-Chavín** is a roots-based ecotourism initiative, supported by PromPerú and the European Union, that begins in the small alpine town of Olleros (30km/19 miles south of Huaraz). The 4-day trek provides great views of the snowcapped peaks Shaqsha (5,703m/18,711 ft.), Cashan (5,686m/18,655 ft.), and Tuctupunta (5,343m/17,530 ft.), and offers the opportunity to share the customs and traditions of local peasant communities. The route ends at the archaeological site Chavín de Huántar. For more information on llama trekking in the Cordillera, contact **Llama 2000** in Lima at ✆ **01/224-3408. Peru Llama Trek** (✆ **043/421-266;** www.perullamatrek.com) also organizes Olleros-Chavín llama treks.

make it to the campsite on the first day and get a good jump on the high pass the following day.

All-inclusive treks from Santa Cruz to Llanganuco in a "pooled" service start at about $175 per person.

MOUNTAIN CLIMBING

Climbing in the Cordillera Blanca ranges from highly technical, multipitch ascents to rigorous but nontechnical climbs. The optimal climbing season is May through September. Huaraz serves as the principal hub for contracting qualified guides and tour operators and renting gear, but some similar infrastructure, on a smaller scale, can also be found in Caraz. The **Casa de Guías** in Huaraz (✆ **043/421-811**) is one of your best preclimb resources, with a list of registered guides.

For experienced climbers up to the challenge, the Cordillera Blanca is nirvana. The range includes 50 permanently snowcapped mountain peaks of more than 5,610m (18,400 ft.), amazingly packed into an area just 177km (110 miles) long and 19km (12 miles) wide. Tested mountaineers can hope to bag several 6,000m (19,680-ft.) summits in just a 2- or 3-week trip. Less experienced climbers can choose among several easier and more popular climbs. For anyone, though, acclimatization is paramount. Allow between 3 days and 1 week before attempting any serious ascent.

The snowy peaks of **Ishinca** (5,534m/18,156 ft.) and **Pisco** (5,752m/18,871 ft.)—essentially 3-day climbs—require appropriate gear, conditioning, and guides, but can be undertaken by inexperienced climbers. Peru's most beautiful mountain, **Alpamayo** (5,957m/19,544 ft.) is an appropriate climb for those with some experience. **Huascarán** (6,768m/22,205 ft.), the highest mountain in the Peruvian Andes and the tallest tropical mountain in the world, takes between 6 and 9 days and poses a very challenging climb, suitable only for those with technical knowledge and extensive experience.

OTHER ADVENTURE SPORTS

HANG GLIDING   Yungay's hill Pan de Azúcar is the most common spot for hang gliding. For more information, contact **Monttrek** (© **043/421-124**).

ICE CLIMBING   The Cordillera Blanca is a great spot to give this serious sport a try. The best mountains for ice climbing are Pisco, Ishinca, Huascarán, Alpamayo, Chopicalqui, and Artesonraju. Contact **Pony Expeditions** (© **043/391-642**; www. ponyexpeditions.com) or **Monttrek** (© **043/421-124**) for more information.

MOUNTAIN BIKING   The Callejón de Huaylas is one of Peru's top destinations for mountain bikers, with hundreds of mountain and valley horse trails cutting across fields, bridges, and creeks, and past traditional Andean villages. Dedicated cyclists can also look forward to the thrill of climbing to 5,000m (16,400 ft.) through mountain passes.

In Huaraz, you can rent mountain bikes for an hour, a day, or a week. During the annual Semana del Andinismo in June, there's a mountain-bike competition. Two of Peru's best mountain-bike agencies operate in the area: **Mountain Bike Adventures** in Huaraz (© **043/424259**; www.chakinaniperu.com) and **Pony Expeditions** in Caraz (© **043/391-642**; www.ponyexpeditions.com). Both have equipment rental and excellent biking itineraries.

RIVER RAFTING   Near Carhuaz, the Río Santa, which runs the length of the Callejón de Huaylas from Laguna Conococha, is where rafting in the area is practiced. Sections differ in degree of difficulty from easy (Classes II and III) to technical (Class V). The section that's most often rafted is between Jangas and Caraz. The season is May through September, when water levels are low. **Monttrek** (© **043/421-124**) and a handful of other tour operators in Huaraz offer rafting.

ROCK CLIMBING   Several agencies in Huaraz offer full-day rock-climbing tours in Caraz and Yungay, ranging from easy to moderate. Monterrey's Rocódromo and Uquia are the most popular spots. For more information, contact **Monttrek** (© **043/421-124**); the agency even has an interior climbing wall at its headquarters in Huaraz.

Appendix A:
Peru in Depth

When Francisco Pizarro, the Spanish conquistador, and his fortune-hunting cronies descended on Peru in 1528, they discovered not only vast riches, but also a highly sophisticated culture. The Spaniards soon overpowered the awed and politically weakened Incannn Empire, but they didn't find the Incas' greatest secret: the imperial city of Machu Picchu, hidden high in the Andes. Machu Picchu, finally revealed to the world in 1911 by a Yale historian, is acclaimed as the pinnacle achievement of the continent's pre-Columbian societies, yet it is only one of the exhilarating discoveries that await you in Peru.

The Incas left behind numerous examples of their exquisite stone architecture and eye for unparalleled natural settings, but a long line of equally advanced cultures preceded the relatively short-lived Incannn Empire. Over several thousand years, civilizations up and down the south Pacific coast and deep in the highlands developed ingenious irrigation systems, created sophisticated pottery and weaving techniques, and built great pyramids, temples, fortresses, and cities of adobe. Early peoples constructed mysterious cylindrical towers and the even more enigmatic Nasca Lines, giant drawings of animals and symbols somehow etched into the desert plains for eternity. Peru's fascinating history is in evidence everywhere: in open graves with bits and pieces of ancient textiles; in mortarless Incannn stones that serve as foundations for colonial churches; and in traditional dress, foods, and festivals, as well as Andean customs and beliefs that reveal a country and a people very much rooted in its past.

Peru has a habit of turning virtually every visitor into an amateur archaeologist. Ruins fire the imagination, and outstanding museum collections tell an intricate tale of complex cultures through ceramics, spectacular textiles, and remarkably preserved mummies. You can see the Lord of Sipán in all the glory of the jewels and rituals that accompanied his burial, and the frozen corpse of Juanita the Ice Maiden, an Inca princess sacrificed on a mountain ridge more than 500 years ago. And yet—Cusco and Machu Picchu's immense popularity notwithstanding—with so many temples and burial sites still being unearthed, and ruins almost continually discovered in remote jungle regions, Peru has the rare feeling of a country in the 21st century that hasn't been exhaustively explored or overrun with tourists.

Peru's recent history of suffering—2 decades of political mayhem and corruption, surprise attacks from homegrown Maoist "Shining Path" terrorists, cocaine trafficking, and violent street crime—is well documented. Throughout the 1980s and early '90s, Peruvians fled the capital and the countryside, fearful of attack; understandably, few travelers were brave enough to plan vacations in Peru. With the 2001 election of Alejandro Toledo, the nation's first president of native Indian origin, many Peruvians became hopeful that the country had finally turned a corner and that the 21st century would bring stability, progress, and prosperity. However, Toledo's presidency has been beset by economic strife and widening income disparity (despite encouraging overall growth), widespread strikes, and—perhaps most troubling—continued corruption and unease. Rumors of a Shining Path reprise have not been totally borne out, though at least two major attacks, including a bombing near the U.S. embassy in Lima, have been attributed to the group. Toledo's ineffectiveness left many Peruvians disillusioned but, hopful that the new president Alan Garcia in June 2006 will end the cycle of disappointment. For visitors, though Peru remains desperately poor, on the whole the country is vastly safer and more welcoming than it was for most of the 1980s and '90s. Too many unfortunate years of corrupt politicians, lawlessness, and economic disarray succeeded in clouding but never eclipsing the beauty and complexity of this fascinating Andean nation.

1 A Look at the Past

First inhabited as many as 20,000 years ago, Peru was the cradle of several of the most ancient and sophisticated pre-Columbian civilizations in the Americas. The Chavín, Paracas, Nasca, Huari, Moche, and Incas, among others, form a long line of complicated, occasionally overlapping, and frequently warring cultures stretching back to 2000 B.C. Before the Incas, two other civilizations, the Chavín and the Huari-Tiahuanaco, achieved pan-Andean empires. Most of what is known about pre-Columbian cultures is based on the unearthing of temples and tombs because none possessed a written language. Further complicating matters is the fact that, as one culture succeeded a previous one, it imposed its values and social structure on the vanquished but also assimilated features useful to it, making distinction among some early cultures exceedingly difficult.

Early societies were located mainly in the coastal areas and highlands. Many fell victim to warfare, cyclical floods, extended drought, and earthquakes. Evidence of pivotal pre-Columbian cultures—including ruined temples; spectacular collections of ceramics, masks, and jewelry; and tombs found with well-preserved mummies—is everywhere in Peru, and some sites are only now being excavated and combed for clues.

The first inhabitants are thought by most historians to have crossed the Bering Strait in Asia during the last ice age, worked their way across the Americas, and settled the region around 20,000 B.C. (although this migratory pattern has been disputed by some scholars). They were nomadic hunter-gatherers who lived along the central and northern coasts. The Pikimachay cave, which dates to 12,000 B.C., is the oldest site in Peru. The earliest human remains, discovered near Huánaco in highland Peru, are from around 7000 B.C. Early Peruvians were responsible for cave paintings at Toquepala (Tacna, 7000 B.C.) and houses in Chillca (Lima, 5000 B.C.). Experts say that recent analysis of findings at the coastal site Caral, in the Supe Valley, demonstrates the existence of the earliest complex civilization in the Americas. The city was inhabited as many as 4,700 years ago, 1,000 years earlier than once believed.

PRE-INCANN CULTURES

Over the course of nearly 15 centuries, pre-Incann cultures settled principally along the Peruvian coast and highlands. Around 6000 B.C., the Chinchero people along the southern desert coast mummified their dead, long before the ancient Egyptians had thought of it. By the 1st century B.C., during what is known as the Formative, or Initial, period, Andean society had designed sophisticated irrigation canals and produced the first textiles and decorative ceramics. Another important advance was the specialization of labor, aided in large part by the development of a hierarchical society.

The earliest known Peruvian civilization was the **Chavín culture** (1200–400 B.C.), a theocracy that worshipped a feline, jaguarlike god and settled in present-day Huántar, Ancash (central Peru).

Over 8 centuries, the Chavín, who never developed into a military or mercantilistic empire, unified groups of peoples across Peru. The most spectacular remnant of this culture, known for its advances in stone carving, pottery, weaving, and metallurgy, is the Chavín de Huántar temple, 40km (25 miles) east of Huaraz. The ceremonial center, a place of pilgrimage, contained wondrous examples of religious carving, such as the Tello Obelisk and the Raimondi Stella. The temple demonstrates evidence of sophisticated engineering and division of labor.

A subsequent society, the **Paracas** culture (700 B.C.–A.D. 200), took hold along the southern coast. It is renowned today for its superior textile weaving, considered perhaps the finest example of pre-Columbian textiles in the Americas. The Paracas peoples were sophisticated enough to dare to practice trepanation, a form of brain surgery that consisted of drilling holes in the skull to cure various ailments and correct cranial deformation.

The Classical period (A.D. 200–1100) was one of significant social and technological development. Likely descendants of the Paracas, the Moche and Nasca cultures are among the best studied in pre-Columbian Peru. The **Moche** (or **Mochica**) civilization (A.D. 200–700), one of the first true urban societies, dominated the valleys of the north coast near Trujillo and conquered a number of smaller groups in building their widespread empire. The Moche were a highly organized hierarchical civilization that created extraordinary adobe platform complexes, such as the Temples of the Sun and Moon near Trujillo (the former was the largest man-made structure of its day in the Americas), and the burial site of Sipán, near Chiclayo, where the remains and riches of the famous Lord of Sipán, a religious and military authority, were unearthed in remarkably preserved royal tombs. Moche pottery, produced from molds, contains vital clues to

their way of life, down to very explicit sexual representations. Its frank depictions of phalluses, labia, and nontraditional bedroom practices might strike some visitors as pre-Columbian pornography.

The **Nasca** culture (A.D. 300–800) established itself along the coastal desert south of Lima. Nasca engineers created outstanding underground aqueducts, which permitted agriculture in one of the most arid regions on earth, and its artisans introduced polychrome techniques in pottery. But the civilization is internationally known for the enigmatic **Nasca Lines,** geometric and animal symbols etched indelibly into the desert, elements of an agricultural and astronomical calendar that are so vast that they can only really be appreciated from the window of an airplane.

The **Huari** (also spelled **Wari**) culture (A.D. 600–1100), an urban society that was the first in Peru to pursue explicitly expansionist goals through military conquest, settled the south-central *sierra* near Ayacucho. Along with the **Tiahuanaco** people, with whom they shared a central god figure, they came to dominate all the Andes, with an empire spreading all the way to Chile and Bolivia. Both cultures achieved superior agricultural technology, in the form of canal irrigation and terraces.

Separate regional cultures, the best known of which is the **Chimú** culture (A.D. 700), developed and thrived over the next 4 centuries. The Chimú, adroit metallurgists and architects, built the citadel of Chan Chan, a compound of royal palaces and the largest adobe city in the world, near the northern coastal city Trujillo. The Chimú were the dominant culture in Peru before the arrival and expansion of the Incas, and they initially represented a great northern and coastal rivalry to the Incas. Other cultures that thrived during the same period were the **Chachapoyas,** who constructed the impressive Kuélap fortress in the northern highlands, the **Ica** (or **Chincha**) south of Lima, and the *altiplano* (high plains) groups that built the finely crafted *chullpa* towers near Puno and Lake Titicaca. The Sicán (or Lambayeque) culture, which built great temple sites and buried its dead with extraordinary riches, fell to the Chimú near the end of the 14th century. The Chimú themselves were, in turn, conquered by the Incas.

THE INCANN EMPIRE

Though Peru is likely to be forever synonymous with the Incas, who built the spectacular city of Machu Picchu high in the Andes and countless other great palaces and temples, the society was merely the last in a long line of pre-Columbian cultures. The Incan Empire (1200–1532) was relatively short lived, but it remains the best documented of all Peruvian civilizations. Though the height of its power lasted for little more than a century, the Incan Empire extended throughout the Andes, all the way from present-day Colombia down to Chile—a stretch of more than 5,635km (3,500 miles). At its apex, the Incan Empire's reach was longer than even that of the Romans.

The Incas were a naturalistic and ritualistic people who worshipped the sun god Inti and the earth goddess Pachamama, as well as the moon, thunder, lightning, and the rainbow, all regarded as deities. The Incan emperors were believed to be direct descendants of the sun god. The bold Andes Mountains were at least as important in their system of beliefs: The dwelling places of respected spirits, the 7,000m (22,960-ft.) peaks were the sites of human sacrifices. The Incas founded Cusco, the sacred city and capital of the Incan Empire (which they called Tahuantinsuyo, or Land of Four Quarters). The ruling sovereign was properly called the Inca, but today the term also refers to the people and the empire.

The Incas' Andean dominance was achieved through formidable organization and a highly developed economic system. The Incas rapidly expanded their empire first through political alliances and absorption, and then by swift military conquest. Though the Incas imposed their social structure and way of life, they also assimilated useful skills and practices, even granting administrative positions to defeated nobles of the Chimú and other cultures. The Incas thus succeeded in achieving political and religious unification across most of their domain.

The Incas recorded an astounding level of achievement. They never developed a system of writing, but they kept extraordinary records with an accounting system of knots on strings, called *quipus*. They laid a vast network of roadways, nearly 32,200km (20,000 miles) total across the difficult territory of the Andes, connecting cities, farming communities, and religious sites. A network of runners, called *chasquis*, operated on the roads, relaying messages and even transporting foodstuffs from the coast to the Andes. *Tambos*, or way stations, dotted the highways, serving as inspection points and shelters for relay runners. The Inca Trail was a sacred highway, connecting the settlements in the Urubamba Valley to the ceremonial center, Machu Picchu.

The Incas' agricultural techniques were exceedingly skilled and efficient, with advanced irrigation systems and soil conservation. The Incas were also extraordinary architects and unparalleled stonemasons. Incan ruins reveal splendid landscaping and graceful construction of perfectly cut stones and terraces on inaccessible sites with extraordinary views of valleys and mountains.

A rigid hierarchy and division of labor ruled Incan society. At the top, just below the Incan sovereign (who was also the chief military and religious figure and considered a descendant of the sun), was

Incann Architecture & Stonemasonry

Much of Peru's greatest architecture, it has to be said, lies in ruins. However, the civilizations that predated the arrival of the Spanish conquistadors were incredibly sophisticated engineers, stonemasons, and architects. The Moche, Sicán, and other cultures built great temples, including some that were the largest man-made structures in the Americas. But it was the Incas, the best-documented pre-Columbian culture in South America and the one that would ultimately succumb to the Spaniards, who left an astounding legacy of innovative building.

Evidence abounds in Peru of superior Incann building techniques. Chief among their architectural prowess is the massive system of roads that criss-crossed the entire empire. Nearly 32,200km (20,000 miles), of which the Inca Trail from the Sacred Valley to Machu Picchu is undoubtedly the most famous stretch, extended from Chile and Bolivia, through the mountainous Andean terrain, and all the way to Quito.

The Incas might not have invented the system of building with huge, mortarless stones or of constructing agricultural terraces on steeply inclined mountainsides, but it is fair to say they perfected it. They also mastered the art of craftily inserting structures—whether citadels, ceremonial temples, or palaces—into the nature they so revered. Machu Picchu is perhaps the finest example of this remarkable environmentally sensitive architecture, but it is by no means the only one. Great agricultural terracing can be seen at Ollantaytambo, Moray, and Pisac.

Two of the finest examples of the Incas' ability to construct walls from perfectly integrated, massive stones are the zigzagged defensive walls at Sacsayhuamán and the exquisitely tapered, curved exterior at Qoricancha in

the ruling elite: nobles and priests. Tens of thousands of manual laborers provided the massive manpower necessary to construct temples and palaces throughout the empire. The Inca kept chosen maidens, or Virgins of the Sun *(acllas),* who serviced him and Incan nobles.

Extraordinarily tight community organization was replicated across the empire. At the heart of the structure was the Inca's clan, the *panaca,* composed of relatives and descendants. Spanish conquistadors chronicled a dynasty that extended to 12 rulers, from **Manco Cápac,** the empire's founder in 1200 who was said to have risen out of Lake Titicaca, to **Atahualpa,** whose murder in Cajamarca by Spanish conquerors spelled the end of the great power.

The Inca **Pachacútec** ruled from 1438 to 1463, and he is considered the great builder of Incan civilization. Under his rule, Cusco was rebuilt, and some of the most brilliant examples of Incan architecture were erected, including Cusco's Qoricancha (Temple of the Sun), the Ollantaytambo and Sacsayhuamán fortresses, and, of course, the famed religious city of Machu Picchu. Pachacútec also initiated the empire's expansion. It was Pachacútec's successor, **Tupac Yupanqui** (1463–93), however, who achieved dominance from Ecuador to Chile. A great

Cusco. Visitors who run their hands along the smooth, seamless edges are amazed to discover that such immense and perfectly carved stones, many with beveled edges and some as large as highway tollbooths, simply *fit* together. Some stones were "female" receptors, others "males" with protruding parts: They fit together like a jigsaw puzzle. Incan workers moved these incredible blocks with no machinery, of course, and carved them with only rudimentary tools (none made of iron). As stonemasons, the Incas were peerless. Their architectural achievements, at once formidable and delicate, are mind-boggling.

How did they do it? Well, no one is sure, which is why all kinds of fantastical theories—including the use of magic herbs or the sun to dissolve the stones or even extraterrestrials to raise them—have long circulated to explain the apparently inexplicable. In his book *Exploring Cusco,* Peter Frost (Nuevas Imágenes) presents interesting theories (complete with sketches) of how the Incas might have lifted and moved such extraordinary stones. He suggests that the Incas' massive and extremely well-organized work force used inclined planes, levers, and wedges to patiently manipulate stone, dragging enormous blocks of granite over long distances and up ramps. Frost delves into technical discussions of horizontal or load-bearing joints, but much of the Incas' technique was ingeniously low-tech. Extensive teams of men used smaller stones to exhaustively pound and smooth the surfaces of the huge building blocks. In addition to Frost's guide, more information is available from **Rutahsa Adventures** (www.rutahsa.com/incaarch.html) and from Susan A. Niles's *The Shape of Inca History: Narrative & Architecture in an Andean Empire* (University of Iowa Press, 1999).

conqueror, he defeated his Chimú rivals in northern Peru.

After the death of the Inca **Huayna Cápac** in 1525, civil war ensued, brought on by the empire splitting between his two sons, Atahualpa and Huáscar. The Spaniards, arriving in northern Peru in 1532, found a severely weakened empire— a pivotal reason the Incas so swiftly succumbed to a small band of invading Spaniards. Another key was the Spaniards' superior military technology. Against cannons and cavalry, the Incas' slings, battle-axes, and cotton-padded armor stood little chance. But their defeat remains puzzling to most visitors to Peru, not to mention many scholars.

SPANISH CONQUEST & COLONIALISM

Columbus and his cohorts landed in the Americas in 1492, and by the 1520s, the Spanish conquistadors had reached South America. Francisco Pizarro led an expedition along Peru's coast in 1528. Impressed with the riches of the Incan Empire, he returned to Spain and succeeded in raising money and recruiting men for a return expedition. In 1532, Pizarro made his return to Peru overland from Ecuador. After founding the first Spanish city in Peru, San Miguel de Piura, near the Ecuadorian border, he advanced upon the northern highland city of Cajamarca, an Incan stronghold.

There, a small number of Spanish troops—about 180 men and 30 horses—cunningly captured the Incan emperor Atahualpa. The emperor promised to pay a king's ransom of gold and silver for his release, offering to fill his cell several times over, but the Spaniards, having received warning of an advancing Incan army, executed the emperor in 1533. It was a catastrophic blow to an already weakened empire.

Pizarro and his men massacred the Incan army, estimated at between 5,000 and 6,000 warriors. The Spaniards installed a puppet Inca, Tupac Huallpa, the brother of Huáscar, who had died while Atahualpa was being held. They then marched on Cusco, capturing the capital city on November 15, 1533, and emptying the Sun Temple of its golden treasures. After the death of Tupac Huallpa en route, a new puppet was appointed, Manco Inca.

Pizarro founded the coastal city of Lima 2 years later, which became the capital of the new colony, the Viceroyalty of Peru. The Spanish crown appointed Spanish-born viceroys the rulers of Peru, but Spaniards battled amongst themselves for control of Peru's riches, and the remaining Incas continued to battle the conquistadors. A great siege was laid to Cusco in 1536, with Manco Inca and his brothers directing the rebellion from Sacsayhuamán. Pizarro was assassinated in 1541, and the indigenous insurrection ended with the beheading of Manco Inca, who had escaped to Vilcabamba, deep in the jungle, in 1544. Inca Tupac Amaru led a rebellion in 1572 but also failed and was killed.

Over the next 2 centuries, Lima gained in power and prestige at the expense of the old Incan capital and became the foremost colonial city of the Andean nations. The Peruvian viceroyalty stretched all the way from Panama to Tierra del Fuego. Cusco focused on cultural pursuits and became the epicenter of the Cusco School of painting (Escuela Cusqueña), which incorporated indigenous elements into Spanish styles, in the 16th and 17th centuries.

INDEPENDENT PERU

By the 19th century, grumbling over high taxes and burdensome Spanish controls grew in Peru, as it did in most colonies in the Americas. After liberating Chile and Argentina, José de San Martín set his sights north on Lima in 1821 and declared it an independent nation the same year. Simón Bolívar, the other hero of independence on the continent, came from the other direction. His successful campaigns in Venezuela and Colombia led him south to Ecuador and finally Peru. Peru won its independence from Spain after crucial battles in late 1824. Though Peru mounted its first civilian government, defeat by Chile in the War of the Pacific (1879–83) left Peru in a dire economic position.

Several military regimes ensued, and Peru finally returned to civilian rule in 1895. Land-owning elites dominated this new "Aristocratic Republic." In 1911, the Yale historian Hiram Bingham happened upon the ruins of the imperial city Machu Picchu—a discovery that would begin to unravel the greatness of the Incas and forever associate Peru with the last of its pre-Columbian civilizations.

Peru launched war with Ecuador over a border dispute—just one of several long-running border conflicts—in 1941. Though the 1942 Treaty of Rio de Janeiro granted the area north of the River Marañon to Peru, Ecuador would continue to claim the territory until the end of the 20th century.

2 Modern Peru

Peru's recent political history has been a turbulent mix of military dictatorships, coups d'état, and several disastrous civilian governments, engendering a near-continual cycle of instability. Particularly in the 1980s and 1990s, Peru became notorious for government corruption at the highest levels—leading to the exile of two recent presidents—and widespread domestic terrorism fears.

Peru shook off the mantle of 2 decades of dictatorship in 1945 after a free election (the first in many decades) of José Luis Bustamante y Rivero. Bustamante served for just 3 years. General Manuel A. Odría led a coup and installed a military regime in 1948. In 1963, Peru returned to civilian rule, with Fernando Belaúnde Terry as president. The armed forces overthrew Belaúnde in 1968, but the new military regime (contrary to other right-leaning dictatorships in Latin America) expanded the role of the state, nationalized a number of industries, and instituted agrarian reform. The land-reform initiatives failed miserably. Re-elected in 1980, Belaúnde and his successor, Alan García (1985–90), faced, and were largely unsuccessful in dealing with, hyperinflation, nationwide strikes, and two homegrown guerrilla movements—the Maoist Sendero Luminoso (Shining Path) and the Tupac Amaru Revolutionary Movement (MRTA)—that destabilized Peru with violent terror campaigns throughout the late 1980s and early '90s. Meanwhile, Peru's role on the production end of the international cocaine trade grew exponentially.

García, who made a point of refusing to pay Peru's external debt (which prompted both the IMF and World Bank to cut off support), fled into exile after being charged with embezzling millions. With the economy in ruins and the government in chaos, Alberto Fujimori, the son of Japanese immigrants, defeated the Peruvian novelist Mario Vargas Llosa and became president in 1990. Fujimori campaigned on promises to fix the ailing economy and root out terrorist guerrillas, and in 1992, his government succeeded in arresting key members of both the MRTA and the Shining Path (catapulting the president to unprecedented popularity). Fujimori suddenly became authoritarian, however, shutting down Congress in 1992, suspending the constitution, and decreeing an emergency government that he effectively ruled as dictator. His austerity measures got Peru on the right track economically, though, with reforms leading to widespread privatizations, growth of 7%, and a drop in inflation from more than 10,000% annually to about 20%, so many Peruvians were reluctantly accepting of Fujimori's distaste for democracy.

Fujimori pushed to get the constitution amended so that he could run for successive terms, and he was re-elected in 1995, soundly defeating former United Nations Secretary General Javier Pérez de Cuellar. That same year, Peru briefly entered into armed conflict with Ecuador over the decades-old border dispute, though in 1999 Ecuador finally accepted the Rio de Janeiro treaty and the borders as established in 1942.

Most international observers denounced the announced 2000 presidential election results after Fujimori's controversial run-off with Alejandro Toledo, a newcomer from a poor Indian family. Public outcry forced Fujimori to call new elections, but he escaped into exile in Japan and resigned the presidency in late 2000 after a corruption scandal involving his shadowy intelligence chief, Vladimiro Montesinos. Videotape of Montesinos bribing a congressman and subsequent investigations (including a daily barrage of secret videotapes broadcast on national television) revealed a government so thoroughly corrupt that it was itself involved in the narcotics trade that it was ostensibly stamping out. Fujimori, currently living in Peru and fighting against extradition, was discovered to have funneled at least $12 million to private offshore accounts. Montesinos escaped to Venezuela, where he was harbored by the government until he was found and returned to Peru for imprisonment. Fujimori is also accused of ordering the murder of 25 suspected Shining Path guerrillas by death squad.

Toledo, who most observers believe would have won the 2000 election, ran again in 2001 and, amazingly, entered into a run-off with Alan García, who—though disgraced only a few years earlier—had dared to return from exile to run for the presidency. Toledo, a former shoeshine boy who went on to teach at Harvard and become a World Bank economist, won the election and became Peru's first president of the 21st century in July 2001, formally accepting the post at Machu Picchu. Also in 2001, the U.S. State Department Human Rights Report named Peru among the success stories of the year, praising the country for meeting international standards for free elections and addressing past abuses and corruption under the Fujimori administration.

Now at the end of Toledo's presidency, his once hopeful program *Perú Posible* has not remotely achieved the results Peruvians were hoping for. Instead, there is renewed crisis across Peru. Toledo's campaign promises have gone unfulfilled, government corruption and nepotism are still epidemic, and farmers and teachers on strike paralyzed Peru and prompted Toledo to declare a state of emergency. The president has been embroiled in personal scandal, revealing cocaine use in the late 1990s and an illegitimate teenage

daughter from whom he is estranged. In 2003 alone, Toledo twice overhauled his cabinet and fired two prime ministers, including the first woman named to that post. There are fears that peasant uprisings in neighboring Bolivia, triggered in part by U.S. military efforts to eradicate coca growing, could easily spread to Peru. Bolivia's resounding election of the leftist Evo Morales, who has promised to nationalize energy concerns and legalize coca farming, speaks to a growing influence of disenfranchised Amerindian populations in Andean countries, and many observers wonder what this projects for Peru's uncertain political future. For the last years of Toledo's presidency, his approval rating has hovered just above single digits; as a number of opposition politicians called for his resignation, Toledo limped to the end of his term in 2006.

PERU TODAY

Peru, the third largest country in South America (after Brazil and Argentina), is vastly undervalued as a travel destination. It receives, in its best year, only a million or so visitors. But with spectacular Andes mountains and highland culture, a section of Amazon rainforest second only to Brazil, one of the richest arrays of wildlife in the world, and some of the Americas' greatest ruins of pre-Columbian cultures, Peru deserves to be experienced by so many more people.

Most know it only as the land of the Incas, symbolized by the mysteries of Machu Picchu, the famous lost city tucked high in the Andes. Yet Peru is littered with archaeological discoveries of many civilizations, from one end to another, highland to coast. Just over a decade ago, a *National Geographic* team discovered Juanita the Ice Maiden, an Incan princess sacrificed on Mount Ampato more than 500 years ago. (Her frozen corpse is now exhibited in

Arequipa.) Archaeologists have recently unearthed more than 2,000 extraordinarily well-preserved mummies from one of Peru's largest Incan burial sites, which was found under a shantytown on the outskirts of Lima. Other sites continue to be excavated; many visitors will be shocked to find bits of ancient textiles fluttering around recently opened burial tombs that may be 1,500 years old. Researchers are now calling Caral, a site in central Peru north of Lima, the oldest city in the Americas. It is believed to date to 2600 B.C., part of a sophisticated society contemporaneous with the Egyptian pyramids.

Peru is rich in artifacts and culture, but it remains very poor and is still a society thoroughly dominated by elites. More than half the population lives at or below the poverty line. The horrendous violence of the late 1980s and early '90s has now almost completely abated, and there are no areas where visitors should not feel welcome. Though the country is beset with economic difficulties, it appears to be entering a more hopeful period. The election of Alejandro Toledo in 2001 followed a disastrous period of sustained political crisis of corruption and scandal. Toledo hoped to turn Peru around by attracting new foreign investment, tripling tourism receipts, and creating a million new jobs. The economy has grown at a rate of 3% to 4% a year, but much of that growth has been stimulated by foreign investment in the mining sector, from which very few Peruvians benefit. Toledo's administration, beset by instability, abuse of power, poor management, lack of credibility, and continuing scandal, has failed to deliver on any of its grand campaign promises.

Indeed, the government is so widely perceived as a failure that few Peruvians and international observers expect Toledo's presidency to survive to the end of his 5-year term in 2006.

The current reality is a sad one for Peru. Toledo labeled himself an "Indian rebel with a cause," alluding to his intent to recognize and support the nation's native Andean populations, or *cholos*. When he was elected, Toledo offered an encouraging symbol of hope to both Peruvians and the international community: The story of a shoeshine boy and son of peasants who goes on to Harvard and Stanford and ultimately wrestles the top office from a corrupt leader is the very embodiment of the dream of social mobility. Whether any other impoverished Peruvians will be as fortunate as their now-discredited president remains as unlikely as ever, and the country's democracy also remains fragile, especially given the instabilities of the past couple years in neighboring Andean countries like Ecuador and Bolivia.

Former president Alberto Fujimori, who fled the country to live in exile in Japan, was arrested in Chile in November 2005 attempting to return to Peru in a surprise bid to run for president. Peruvian authorities have requested his extradition, adding further intrigue to an uncertain situation.

"Peru's most recent presidential election was in April 2006, with runoff results in June 2006 annoucing the victor as former president Alan Garcia. He'll be sworn in on July 18, 2006, roughly 16 years after his first presidency—one marked by renewed guerilla violence and enonomic setbacks—ended."

3 Peruvian People & Culture

SOCIETY
POPULATION

Peruvians are predominantly *mestizo* (of mixed Spanish and indigenous heritage) and Andean Indian, but the population is a true melting pot of ethnic groups. Significant minority groups of Afro-Peruvians (descendants of African slaves, living mainly in the coastal area south of Lima), immigrant Japanese and Chinese

Terrorism in Peru

The unprecedented waves of violence that rocked Peru in the late 1980s and early 1990s were a result not of cocaine drug trafficking but the terrorist activities of two small but highly effective homegrown insurgency groups and the militaristic response by the government to root them out. **Sendero Luminoso (Shining Path)** and **MRTA** (Tupac Amaru Revolutionary Movement) waged a two-decade guerrilla war against the Peruvian state, killing more than 30,000 people and creating a climate of fear across the country.

The best known and largest of the two principal insurgency networks was Sendero Luminoso, a Maoist terrorist group formed in the late 1960s by a university professor, Abimael Guzmán. Sendero's aim was to restructure Peru along the lines of a peasant revolutionary regime and institute an merindian socialist system. Sendero Luminoso tried to create a rural-based insurgency, appropriating key elements of Indian heritage rather than political ideology to win support. However, rural *campesinos* were the most numerous victims of their violent campaign.

During its heyday, Sendero Luminoso was considered one of the most violent terrorist organizations in the world. Although based in the rural area around Ayacucho, by the late 1980s, Shining Path had become very active in urban areas, bombing institutions—from courthouses to diplomatic missions (including the U.S. embassy)—and carrying out selective assassinations. At its height, Sendero Luminoso was thought to have about 2,000 armed militants and a significant base of support, particularly in rural areas

The government's efforts to identify and destroy the Shining Path were often just as ruthless as those of the terrorists. As many as half of the terrorism-related deaths are estimated by human rights organizations to have come at the hands of the police and special forces. Alberto Fujimori ran for the presidency in 1990 in part on a campaign to eradicate the terrorist network. As president, he won a provision for emergency rule, which resulted in the capture of what the government claimed was 2,500 Sendero Luminoso terrorists. The capture of Guzmán (aka Comrade Gonzalo), the brains and spiritual heart of the operation, in September 1992 struck a mortal blow to Sendero Luminoso.

The Marxist-Leninist **Movimiento Revolucionario Tupac Amaru,** known by its Spanish-language acronym MRTA, was the smaller of the two terrorist organizations active in Peru. It formed in 1984, taking the name of an Indian who led a rebellion against Spanish colonizers in the 18th century. It hoped to establish a Marxist regime and rid Peru of imperialist influences. In 1987, it launched a campaign of armed struggle against the government of Alan García. For most of its existence, the MRTA was much less violent and less organized than the Sendero Luminoso. It orchestrated a few dozen killings, bombings, and kidnappings.

Before a majority of the organization's militants was imprisoned, the MRTA was estimated to have between 300 and 600 members and to have operated principally in the northern Amazon region. In December 1996, an

MRTA group seized the residence of the Japanese ambassador in Lima during a diplomatic reception, capturing 490 hostages. The group released many but held 72 hostages—including the brother of President Fujimori, Peru's foreign minister, supreme court judges, members of congress, and the ambassadors of Japan and Bolivia—for 4 months, until April 1997, when Fujimori ordered a violent raid on the embassy compound by Peruvian special forces. The dramatic raid freed the remaining hostages (although one died of heart failure) and killed all 14 MRTA militants, including the group's leader.

The other episode that catapulted the MRTA into the international spotlight was the arrest of a 26-year-old U.S. citizen, Lori Berenson. A freelance journalist, Berenson was accused by the government of being a sympathizer and collaborator of the MRTA and charged with helping to organize a plan to take over congress. Berenson and her supporters claimed she was unaware that she was sharing a Lima house with MRTA militants and the bounty of guns and explosives they had hidden there. Convicted of treason in 1996 by a special military court of hooded judges and sentenced to life in prison, Berenson's term was later reduced to 20 years. Many organizations in the United States, who view Berenson not as a terrorist but as a human rights activist, continue to try to win her release, citing a wealth of nonstandard practices in her arrest and subsequent trials. For more information on Berenson (from her supporters' perspective), see www.freelori.org.

Although the large-scale terrorist activities of Sendero Luminoso and MRTA were effectively stamped out in the early 1990s, in recent years there have been growing concerns about a possible resurgence of those groups (especially after a car bomb outside the U.S. embassy in Lima in 2002 killed 10 people and 71 hostages were taken near a remote southern pipeline in 2003). In December 2005, President Toledo declared a state of emergency in six central Amazon provinces after Shining Path guerrillas killed eight policemen in the remote Huanaco region again raising the specter of renewed violence across Peru.

While it remains a situation worth watching, to date the most populous (and traveled) regions of Peru have not been affected, and neither group is currently active in any of the areas covered in this book. Sendero Luminoso now largely follows the allure of narcotics trafficking rather than Maoist ideology, and the group's public battle has shifted from the streets to the courts, with supporters mounting political and legal challenges to the imprisonment of convicted group members and activists. A Peruvian court ruled in 2003 that large sections of the country's anti-terrorist statutes were unconstitutional, prompting fears that lawyers for the groups would immediately seek the release of some 1,200 "political" prisoners. President Toledo assured Peruvians that terrorist ringleaders would never be released from prison.

populations among the largest in South America, and smaller groups of European immigrants, including Italians and Germans, are among Peru's 28 million people. In the early days of the colony, Peruvian-born offspring of Spaniards were called *criollos,* though that term today refers mainly to coastal residents and Peruvian cuisine.

After Bolivia and Guatemala, Peru has the largest population by percentage of Amerindians in Latin America. Perhaps half the country lives in the *sierra,* or highlands, and most of these people, commonly called *campesinos* (peasants), live in either small villages or rural areas. Descendants of Peru's many Andean indigenous groups in remote rural areas continue to speak the native languages Quechua (made an official language in 1975) and Aymara or other Amerindian tongues, and for the most part, they adhere to traditional regional dress. However, massive peasant migration to cities from rural highland villages has contributed to a dramatic weakening of indigenous traditions and culture across Peru. The new government of Alejandro Toledo, himself a proud *cholo,* or person of direct Andean Indian roots, has committed itself to a valorization and preservation of native language and traditions.

Nearly two-thirds of Peru is jungle, and the vast Amazon basin that pertains to Peru holds a phenomenal wealth of flora and fauna but a dwindling human presence. Indigenous Amazonian tribes have been greatly reduced by centuries of disease, deforestation, and assimilation. There were once some six million people, 2,000 tribes and/or ethnic groups, and innumerable languages in the Amazon basin; today the indigenous population is less than two million. Still, many traditions and languages have yet to be extinguished, especially deep in the jungle—though most visitors are unlikely to come into contact with groups of unadulterated, non-Spanish-speaking native peoples.

RELIGION

Peruvians are a predominantly Roman Catholic people (more than 90% claim to be Catholic), although Protestant evangelical churches have been winning converts, a fact that is worrisome to the Catholic Church. Animistic religious practices (worship of deities representing nature) inherited from the Incas and others have been incorporated into the daily lives of many Peruvians and can be seen in festivals and small individual rituals such as offerings of food and beverage to Pachamama, or Mother Earth.

ARTS & CULTURE
MUSIC & DANCE

Music and dance are fundamental to the very fabric of Peru, a fact to which the country's innumerable colorful festivals will attest. Music and dance forms, like dress, vary greatly by region. Amerindian—altiplano and andina (highland)—music, played on wind instruments such as bamboo panpipes, *quena* flutes, bright-sounding and guitarlike *charangos,* and other instruments, is known the world over. It seems that wherever one goes, a Peruvian (or, in some cases, Bolivian or Ecuadorian) band is playing panpipes in public places. I've stumbled upon Peruvian musicians from Krakow to Bali. The classic Andean highland tune *El Cóndor Pasa,* adapted by Simon & Garfunkel in the 1970s, is world famous. For many visitors, altiplano and highland versions of *música folklórica* are the very rhythm of Peru, but the country also beats to the sounds of *música criolla* (creole music based on a mix of European and African forms), bouncy-sounding *huayno* rhythms played by *orquestas típicas,* and Afro-Peruvian music, adapted from music brought by African slaves.

There is evidence of music in Peru dating back 10,000 years, and each region has its own distinct sounds and dance. Musical historians have identified more than 1,000 genres of music in Peru.

Traditional instruments include *pututos* (trumpets made from seashells) and many other wind instruments crafted from cane, bone, horns, and precious metals, as well as a wide range of percussion instruments. Exposure to Western cultures has introduced new instruments such as the harp, violin, and guitar to Peruvian music. But Peruvian music can still be identified by its distinctive instruments, and there are many besides the basics of highland music.

The *cajón* is a classic percussion instrument, typical in *música criolla* and *música negra*, as well as *marinera*. A simple wooden box with a sound hole in the back, the cajón is played by a musician who sits on top and pounds the front like a bongo. The cajón has recently been introduced into flamenco music by none other than the legendary flamenco guitarist Paco de Lucía. Another classic Peruvian instrument is the **quena,** an Andean flute that dates to the pre-Columbian era. The best-known wind instrument in Peru, it's usually made out of bamboo, and it typically has five or six holes. Lengths vary to create different pitches. Another popular wind instrument is the **zampoña,** which belongs to the panpipe family and varies greatly in size. The zampoña is never absent at festivals in southern Peru, particularly Puno. String instruments are now fundamental in almost all *música folklórica*. The **charango,** very popular in the southern Andes, is like a small, high-pitched guitar with 5 or 10 strings. Its resonance box is often crafted from an armadillo or *kirkincho* shell, although increasingly it's made of wood.

Music on the coast is very different from traditional Andean sounds. *Chicha* is a relatively new addition to the list of musical genres. A hybrid of sorts of the *huayno* (see below) and Colombian *cumbia,* chicha is an extremely popular urban dance, especially among the working class. It has spread rapidly across Peru and throughout Latin America. *Música criolla* mixes African and Spanish rhythms, with a taste of everything from the foxtrot to the tango, while **Afro-Peruvian** music, especially popular on the coast around Lima, is contemporary black popular music. It originated with African slaves in Peru but was long dormant before being revived in the 1950s and '60s. The music is soulful and powerful, with intoxicating dance rhythms. Nicomedes Santa Cruz, Susana Baca, and Peru Negro are among the style's greatest exponents. Baca, in particular, has made a big ripple in the so-called world-music scene in North America and Europe.

Dances associated with Afro-Peruvian music include lively and sensual **festejo** dances, in which participants respond to striking of the cajón, one of the Afro-Peruvian music's essential instruments. The *alcatraz* is an extremely erotic dance. Females enter the dance floor with tissue on their posteriors. The men, meanwhile, dance with lit candles. The not-so-subtle goal on the dance floor is for the man to light the woman's fire (and thus become her partner).

Peruvian tourism authorities produce a guide to festivities, music, and folk art, and it features a diagram of native dances in Peru. Especially up and down the coast, and in the central corridor of the Andes, the map is a bewildering maze of numbers indicating the indigenous dances practiced in given regions. Two dances, though, have become synonymous with Peru, the huayno and marinera.

The **huayno** is the essential dance in the Andes, with pre-Columbian origins fused with Western influences. Couples dancing the huayno perform sharp turns, hops, and tap-like *zapateos* to keep time. Huayno music is played on quena, charango, harp, and violin. The **marinera,** a sleek, sexy, and complex dance of highly coordinated choreography, is derivative of other folkloric dances in Peru, dating back to the 19th century. There are regional variations of the dance, which differs most from the south coast to the northern highlands. Dancers keep time with a handkerchief in one hand. Marinera music in Lima is performed by guitar and cajón, while a marching band is de rigueur in the north. Marinera festivals are held across Peru, but the most celebrated one is in Trujillo in January.

One of the most attention-getting dances in Peru, though, is that performed by **scissors dancers.** Their *danza de las tijeras* is an exercise in athleticism and balance. Dancers perform gymnastic leaps and daring stunts to the sounds of harp and violin. The main instrument played to accompany the dance is the pair of scissors, made up of two independent sheets of metal around 25 centimeters long. The best places to see scissors dancers are Ayacucho, Arequipa, and Lima.

FESTIVALS

Peruvian festivals are some of the most vibrant in the Americas and a highlight of virtually any visit. Though Peruvian festivals have serious foundations—the honoring of patron saints, fertility rituals, prayer, and celebration for harvests—festivals in Peru are colorful escapes for many Peruvians, especially in rural areas where life can be extremely difficult and poverty is widespread. Many festivals are solemn processions, but others are marked by intricate handmade costumes (sometimes involving as many as 16 different skirt layers), elaborate masks, and abundant food and alcoholic drinks (usually *chicha,* beer made from fermented maize), all of which fuel the revelry. A classic feature of many Andean festivals is the appearance of white-stocking-masked jesters called *ukukus* (bears). Symbolic guardians of *apu* mountain spirits, *ukukus* maintain order during religious ceremonies, but they are also playful mischief-makers.

Any of the major festivals would be well worth planning your trip around, but perhaps none as much as **Inti Raymi.** The Festival of the Sun, the single most important feast of the Incas, is still celebrated on the winter solstice (the solar new year, June 24). The festival, once celebrated across the entire Incan Empire, was suppressed by the Catholic Church after the Spanish conquest. Inti Raymi was revived in the mid–20th century as an expression and valuation of native Indian culture in Peru by a group of intellectuals and artists in Cusco. Today the religious ceremony has taken on colorful, theatrical (and, some would say, touristy) proportions at the site of the Incan ruins of Sacsayhuamán. At the end of the ceremony, two llamas are sacrificed to predict the coming year.

Puno in southern Peru is reputed to be the epicenter of folkloric festivals. Its two most spectacular festivals are **Virgen de la Candelaria,** held during the first two weeks in February, and **Puno Week,** held in November.

See the "Peru Calendar of Events" in chapter 2 for details of some of Peru's most important and exciting festivals.

PERUVIAN TEXTILES

Woven textiles have to be considered among the great traditional arts of Peru. Peru has one of the most ancient and richest weaving traditions in the world; for more than 5,000 years, Peruvian artisans have used fine natural fibers for hand weaving, and the wool produced by alpacas, llamas, and vicuñas is some of the finest in the world, rarer even than cashmere. The most ancient textiles that have been found in Peru come from the Huaca Prieta temple in Chicama and are more than 4,000 years old. In pre-Columbian times, hand-woven textiles, which required extraordinary patience and skill, were prized and extremely valuable; distinctive textiles were indicators of social status and power. They were traded as commodities. Paracas, Huari, and Incan weavings are among the most sophisticated and artful ever produced in Peru.

The Paracas designs were stunningly intricate, with detailed animals, human figures, and deities against dark backgrounds. Huari weaving features abstract figures and bold graphics. The Incas favored more minimalist designs, without embroidery. The finest Incan textiles were typically part of ritualistic ceremonies—many were burned as offerings to spirits.

Whereas pre-Columbian civilizations in Peru had no written language, textiles were loaded with symbolic images that serve as indelible clues to the cultures and beliefs of textile artists. Worship of nature and spiritual clues are frequently represented by motifs in textiles. Many of the finest textiles unearthed were sacred and elaborately embroidered blankets that enveloped mummies in burial sites. Found in tombs in the arid coastal desert, one of the world's driest climates, the textiles are remarkably preserved in many cases.

Contemporary Peruvian artisans continue the traditions, sophisticated designs, and techniques of intricate weaving inherited from pre-Columbian civilizations, often employing the very same instruments used hundreds of years ago and still favoring natural dyes. The drop spindle (weaving done with a stick and spinning wooden wheel), for example, is still used in many regions, and it's not uncommon to see women and young girls spinning the wheel as they tend to animals in the fields. Excellent-quality woven items, the best of which are much more than mere souvenirs, include typical Andean *chullo* wool or alpaca hats with earflaps, ponchos, scarves, sweaters, and blankets.

4 Etiquette & Customs

APPROPRIATE ATTIRE Many travelers to Peru are dressed head-to-toe in adventure or outdoor gear (parkas, fleece wear, hiking boots, and cargo pants). This is perfectly acceptable attire for all but the fanciest restaurants, where "neat casual" would be a better solution. In churches and monasteries, err on the side of discretion (low-rise pants, midriff shirts, peekaboo thongs, and anything else that reveals a lot of skin is not usually acceptable).

AVOIDING OFFENSE In Peru, you should be tactful when discussing local politics, though open discussion of the corruption of past presidents Fujimori and García and terrorism in Peru is perfectly acceptable and unlikely to engender heated debate. Discussion of drugs (and coca-plant cultivation) and religion should be handled with great tact. Visitors should understand that chewing coca leaves (or drinking coca tea) is not drug use but a longstanding cultural tradition in the Andes.

In a country in which nearly half the population is Amerindian, expressing respect for native peoples is important. Try to refer to them not as *indios,* which is a derogatory term, but as *indígenas.* Many Peruvians refer to foreigners as *gringos* (or *gringas*) or the generic "mister," pronounced "*mee*-ster." Neither is intended or should be received as an insult.

On the streets of Cusco and other towns across Peru, shoeshine boys and little girls selling cigarettes or postcards can be very persistent and persuasive. Others just ask directly for money (using the euphemism *propinita,* or little tip). The best way to give money to those who are obviously in need of it is to reward them for their work. I get my scruffy shoes shined on a daily basis in Peru, and I buy postcards I probably don't need. If you don't wish to be hassled, a polite but firm "*No, gracias*" is usually sufficient, but it's important to treat even these street kids with respect.

Queries about one's marital status and children are considered polite; indeed, women traveling alone or with other women should expect such questions.

Coca Leaves

Coca leaves have been cultivated for thousands of years in Peru—their use by pre-Columbian civilizations dates back 4,000 years. The Incas held the coca plant sacred, restricting its use to nobles and priests. Evidence of coca cultivation and societal uses can be found in the ceramics of the Nasca and instruments of the Moche. Although coca leaves have long had important ritualistic uses in Andean society, they have also been widely masticated to lessen the effects of hunger and high altitude. Amerindian laborers who performed backbreaking tasks in post-Conquest Peru usually did so with coca leaves to spur them on (even though the Spaniards pounced on coca as a pagan element of anti-Christian worship and mysticism).

Campesinos in the Andes widely continue to chew coca leaves, mixed with saliva and lime or *quinoa* (a grain) to form a wad called a *llipta* and to produce a dulling sensation in the mouth. Travelers routinely drink *mate de coca,* or coca-leaf tea, to help them deal with the effects of altitude. Coca is as pivotal a component of Andean Peru as tea is in India or Great Britain.

Coca-leaf consumption is not illegal in Peru, though some might expect it to be because coca is the raw material from which cocaine is derived. However, coca leaf contains just 1% of cocaine among its 14 alkaloids. Chemical processing of the leaves turns it into a hard paste (semirefined cocaine). The refined product cocaine, which *is* illegal in Peru, is a very different animal, producing much different effects on the brain and body.

As the use of cocaine as a narcotic grew in the 1960s and demand in the United States skyrocketed during the '70s and '80s, cultivation of coca grew in Peru, principally on remote slopes of the eastern Andes. For poor farmers, coca was a welcome, revenue-producing crop. Easy to tend and producing as many as a half dozen harvests a year, coca was simply the raw material that others—in those days, Colombian drug lords—refined into cocaine and sold in rapidly growing markets in North America and Europe. Coca as an antidote to widespread rural poverty in rural Peru was not lost on either *campesinos* or the Peruvian government.

The U.S. Drug Enforcement Agency, in its celebrated but ineffectual war on drugs, focused its attempts to eradicate coca-growing fields in Peru (which had become the world's largest provider of cocaine raw materials),

However, discussion of how much one earns is a generally touchy subject, especially in a poor country such as Peru. Although Peruvians might be curious and ask you directly how much you make, or how much your apartment or house or car or even clothes cost, I suggest that you deflect the question. At a minimum, explain how much higher the cost of living is in your home country, and how you're not as wealthy as you might seem. Ostentatious display of one's relative wealth is unseemly, even though Peru will be blissfully inexpensive to many budget travelers.

DINING & SHOPPING   Dinner is served later than in some countries, but not as late as in Spain. Nightclubs in large cities often don't get going until after midnight, and many stay open until usually by strong-arming governments into cooperation. Many Peruvians viewed these efforts to destroy the fields of farmers who were growing a legal crop as a blatantly one-sided approach to the problem because it did little to solve the problem of demand for cocaine. Such efforts show emphatic disregard for the traditional, religious, and ritualistic role of coca leaves in Peruvian society, which long predates the recent demand for cocaine in Western society. In neighboring Bolivia, the war on coca was at the heart of peasant revolts that unnerved politicians across the Andes.

And the campaign is fraught with other problems. The United States believed it had an ally in former Peruvian president Alberto Fujimori—himself no stranger to strong-arm tactics—but it now appears that his government was itself secretly dealing in narco-trafficking, even as it reported its success in eradicating coca-producing fields in the Andes. Fujimori and his cohorts notwithstanding, Peru has never fielded a sophisticated network of drug lords and narco-traffickers, at least not to the extent that Colombia and Mexico have; like Bolivia, it has been much more restricted to a rudimentary role as provider of raw coca leaves. Still, coca was bringing in about $5 billion in annual revenues in Peru in the late 1980s.

Coca continues to serve ritualistic and medicinal purposes in Peru. Every August, villagers make offerings (called *pagos* or *pagapus*) to the Earth Mother Pachamama, thanking her for blessing their crops, and the spirits *(apus)* believed to dwell on mountaintops. Coca remains a sacred plant, one that mediates between the inner, spiritual world and the exterior world inhabited by man. It is a potent symbol of community spirit and respect. Coca leaves are chewed, dispensed from ritualistic pouches during festivals and ceremonies, and spread on blankets to predict the future. Even Pope John Paul II, on a visit to Bolivia, drank coca tea and acknowledged the deeply held respect for it by local peoples. It's one of the best short-term remedies to combat altitude sickness, so drink it liberally, but don't try to take coca leaves back home. Even the leaves are illegal in most North American and European countries, and if you're caught, you'll be treated almost as though you were smuggling cocaine—no matter how much you struggle to explain the difference.

dawn. Many shops in large and small towns close at midday, from 1 to 3pm or 2 to 4pm.

If you invite a Peruvian to have a drink or to dine with you, it is expected that you will pay (the Spanish verb *invitar* literally connotes this as an invitation). Do not suggest that a Peruvian acquaintance join you in what will certainly be an expensive restaurant or cafe for him or her, and then pony up only half the tab.

Bargaining is considered acceptable in markets and with taxi drivers, and even hotels, but only up to a point—don't overdo it.

GESTURES   Peruvians are more formal in social relations than most North

---

> **Tips   Watch Your Language**
>
> The term *cholo* is often used to describe Peruvians of color and obvious Amerindian descent, usually those who have migrated from the highlands to the city. It is frequently employed as a derogatory and racist term by the Limeño population of European descent, but President Alejandro Toledo has claimed the term for himself and all *mestizos* (those of mixed race) of Peru, in an attempt to demonstrate pride in their common culture and to take the sting out of the term. Afro-Peruvians are more commonly called *morenos(as)* or *negros(as)*. Using any of these terms can potentially be a complicated and charged matter for foreigners, especially those who have little experience in the country or fluency in the language. At any rate, it's best for *gringos* (foreigners; almost always *not* a derogatory term) simply to steer clear of such linguistic territory. It's better to refrain from making distinctions among races and colors than to risk offending someone.

Americans and Europeans. Peruvians shake hands frequently and tirelessly, and although kissing on the cheek is a common greeting for acquaintances, it is not practiced among strangers (as it is in Spain, for example). Amerindian populations are more conservative and even shy. They don't kiss to greet one another, nor do they shake hands as frequently as other Peruvians; if they do, it is a light brush of the hand rather than a firm grip. Many Indians from small villages are reluctant to look a stranger in the eye.

Using your index finger to motion a person to approach you, as practiced in the United States and other places, is considered rude. A more polite way to beckon someone is to place the palm down and gently sweep your fingers toward you.

GREETINGS   When entering a shop or home, always use an appropriate oral greeting (*Buenos días,* or good day; *Buenas tardes,* or good afternoon; *Buenas noches,* or good night). Similarly, upon leaving, it is polite to say goodbye (*Adios* or *Hasta luego*), even to shop owners with whom you've had minimal contact. Peruvians often shake hands upon leaving as well as greeting.

PHOTOGRAPHY   With their vibrant dress and expressive faces and festivals, Peruvians across the country make wonderful subjects for photographs. In some heavily touristed areas, such as the Sunday market in Pisac outside of Cusco, locals have learned to offer photo ops for a price at every turn. Some foreigners hand out money and candy indiscriminately, while others grapple with the unseemliness of paying for every photo. Asking for a tip in return for being the subject of a photograph is common in many parts of Peru; in fact, some locals patrol the streets with llamas and kids in tow to pose for photographs as their main source of income. Often it's more comfortable to photograph people you have made an effort to talk to, rather than responding to those who explicitly beg to be your subject. I usually give a small tip (50 centavos to S/1) if it appears that my camera has been an intrusion or nuisance, or especially if I've snapped several shots.

It's not common except in very touristed places (such as the Pisac market), but some young mothers carrying adorable children in knapsacks and with flowers in their hair (and outstretched hands requesting a *propinita,* or tip) aren't actually mothers (or at least, not the mothers of the children they're carrying around); to tug at your tourist heartstrings and pockets, they have essentially "rented" the babies from real moms in remote villages. I don't think it's an especially good idea to reward this practice. If a very young woman has several children in tow, all dolled up for pictures and making the rounds all afternoon, she is very likely one of these rent-a-moms.

Photographing military, police, or airport installations is strictly forbidden.

Many churches, convents, and museums also do not allow photography or video.

PUNCTUALITY   Punctuality is not one of the trademarks of Peru or Latin America in general. Peruvians are customarily a half-hour late to most personal appointments, and it is not considered very bad form to leave someone hanging in a cafe for up to an hour. It is expected, so if you have a meeting scheduled, unless a strict *hora inglesa* (English hour) is specified, be prepared to wait.

Appendix B:
Useful Terms & Phrases

Peruvian Spanish is, for the most part, straightforward and fairly free of the quirks and national slang that force visitors to page through their dictionaries in desperation. But if you know Spanish, some of the terms you will hear people saying are *chibolo* for *muchacho* (boy); *churro* and *papasito* for *guapo* (good-looking); *jato* instead of *casa* (house); *chapar* (literally "to grab or get"), slangier than but with the same meaning as *besar* (to kiss); *¡que paja está!* (it's great); *mi pata* to connote a dude or chick from your posse; and *papi* (or *papito*) and *mami* (or *mamita*), affectionate terms for "mother" and "father" that are also used as endearments between relatives and lovers (which can get a little confusing to the untrained outsider). The inherited Amerindian respect for nature is evident; words such as *Pachamama* (Mother Earth) tend to make it into conversation remarkably frequently.

Spanish is but one official language of Peru, though. **Quechua** (the language of the Incan Empire) was recently given official status and is still widely spoken, especially in the highlands, and there's a movement afoot to include **Aymara** as a national language. (Aymara is spoken principally in the southern highlands area around Lake Titicaca.) A couple dozen other native tongues are still spoken. A predominantly oral language (the Incas had no written texts), Quechua is full of glottal and magical, curious sounds. As it is written today, it is mystifyingly vowel-heavy and apostrophe-laden, full of q's, k's, and y's; try to wrap your tongue around *munayniykimanta* (excuse me) or *hayk' atan kubrawanki llamaykikunanmanta* (how much is it to hire a llama?). Very few people seem to agree on spellings of Quechua, as alluded to in chapter 6. Colorful phrases often mix and match Spanish and Amerindian languages: *hacer la tutumeme* is the same as *ir a dormir,* or "to go to sleep." In addition to these primary languages, there are dozens of Indian tongues and dialects in the Amazon region, many of which are in danger of extinction.

1 Basic Spanish Vocabulary

English	Spanish	Pronunciation
Good day	**Buenos días**	*Bweh*-nohs *dee*-ahs
Hi/hello	**Hola**	*Oh*-lah
Pleasure to meet you	**Mucho gusto/ Un placer**	*Moo*-choh *goos*-toh/Oon plah-*sehr*
How are you?	**¿Cómo está?**	*Koh*-moh es-*tah*
Very well	**Muy bien**	Mwee byehn
Thank you	**Gracias**	*Grah*-syahs
How's it going?	**¿Qué tal?**	Keh tahl
You're welcome	**De nada**	Deh *nah*-dah
Goodbye	**Adiós**	Ah-*dyohs*

Please	**Por favor**	Pohr fah-*bohr*
Yes	**Sí**	See
No	**No**	Noh
Excuse me (to get by someone)	**Perdóneme/ Con permiso**	Pehr-*doh*-neh-meh/ Kohn pehr-*mee*-soh
Excuse me (to begin a question)	**Disculpe**	Dees-*kool*-peh
Give me	**Déme**	*Deh*-meh
What time is it?	**¿Qué hora es?**	Keh *ohr*-ah ehs?
Where is . . . ?	**¿Dónde está . . . ?**	*Dohn*-deh eh-*stah*
the station	**la estación**	lah eh-stah-*syohn*
(bus/train)	**estación de ómnibus/tren**	eh-stah-*syohn* deh *ohm*-nee-boos/trehn
a hotel	**un hotel**	oon oh-*tel*
a gas station	**una estación de servicio**	*oo*-nah eh-stah-*syohn* deh sehr-*bee*-syoh
a restaurant	**un restaurante**	oon res-tow-*rahn*-teh
the toilet	**el baño** (or **servicios**)	el *bah*-nyoh (sehr-*bee*-syohs)
a good doctor	**un buen médico**	oon bwehn *meh*-dee-coh
the road to . . .	**el camino a/hacia . . .**	el cah-*mee*-noh ah/*ah*-syah
To the right	**A la derecha**	Ah lah deh-*reh*-chah
To the left	**A la izquierda**	Ah lah ee-*skyehr*-dah
Straight ahead	**Derecho**	Deh-*reh*-choh
Is it far?	**¿Está lejos?**	Eh-*stah leh*-hohs
It is close?	**¿Está cerca?**	Eh-*stah sehr*-kah
Open	**Abierto**	Ah-*byehr*-toh
Closed	**Cerrado**	Seh-*rah*-doh
North	**Norte**	*Nohr*-teh
South	**Sur**	Soor
East	**Este**	*Eh*-steh
West	**Oeste**	Oh-*eh*-steh
Expensive	**Caro**	*Cah*-roh
Cheap	**Barato**	Bah-*rah*-toh
I would like	**Quisiera**	Kee-*syeh*-rah
I want	**Quiero**	*Kyeh*-roh
to eat	**comer**	koh-*mehr*
a room	**una habitación**	*oo*-nah ah-bee-tah-*syohn*
Do you have . . . ?	**¿Tiene usted . . . ?**	Tyeh-neh oo-*stehd*
a book	**un libro**	oon *lee*-broh
a dictionary	**un diccionario**	oon deek-syoh-*na*-ryoh
change	**cambio**	kahm-byoh

How much is it?	**¿Cuánto cuesta?**	*Kwahn*-toh *kwes*-tah
When?	**¿Cuándo?**	*Kwahn*-doh
What?	**¿Qué?**	Keh
There is (Is/Are there . . . ?)	**(¿)Hay (. . . ?)**	eye
What is there?	**¿Qué hay?**	Keh eye
Yesterday	**Ayer**	Ah-*yehr*
Today	**Hoy**	Oy
Tomorrow	**Mañana**	Mah-*nyah*-nah
Good	**Bueno**	*Bweh*-noh
Bad	**Malo**	*Mah*-loh
Better (best)	**(Lo) Mejor**	(Loh) Meh-*hohr*
More	**Más**	Mahs
Less	**Menos**	*Meh*-nohs
No smoking	**Se prohibe fumar**	Seh proh-*ee*-beh foo-*mahr*
Postcard	**Tarjeta postal**	Tahr-*heh*-tah pohs-*tahl*
Insect repellent	**Repelente contra insectos**	Reh-peh-*lehn*-teh *cohn*-trah een-*sehk*-tohs
Now	**Ahora**	Ah-*ohr*-ah
Right now	**Ahora mismo (ahorita)**	Ah-*ohr*-ah *mees*-moh (ah-ohr-*ee*-tah)
Later	**Más tarde**	Mahs *tahr*-deh
Never	**Nunca**	*Noon*-kah
Guide	**Guía**	*Ghee*-ah
It's hot!	**¡Qué calor!**	Keh kah-*lohr*
Rain	**Lluvia**	*Yoo*-byah
It's cold!	**¡Qué frío!**	Keh *free*-oh
It's windy!	**¡Cuánto viento!**	*Kwahn*-toh *byehn*-toh
Money-changer	**Cambista**	Kahm-*bee*-stah
Bank	**Banco**	*Bahn*-koh
Money	**Dinero**	Dee-*neh*-roh
Small (correct) change	**Sencillo**	Sehn-*see*-yoh
Credit card	**Tarjeta de crédito**	Tahr-*heh*-tah deh *creh*-dee-toh
ATM	**Cajero automático**	Kah-*heh*-roh ow-toh-*mah*-tee-koh
Tourist information office	**Oficina de información turística**	Oh-fee-*see*-nah deh een-for-mah-*syohn* too-*ree*-stee-kah

NUMBERS

1	**uno** (*oo*-noh)	16	**dieciséis** (dyeh-see-*sayss*)
2	**dos** (dohs)	17	**diecisiete** (dyeh-see-*syeh*-teh)
3	**tres** (trehs)	18	**dieciocho** (dyeh-*syoh*-choh)
4	**cuatro** (*kwah*-troh)	19	**diecinueve** (dyeh-see-*nweh*-beh)
5	**cinco** (*seen*-koh)	20	**veinte** (*bayn*-teh)
6	**seis** (sayss)	30	**treinta** (*trayn*-tah)
7	**siete** (*syeh*-teh)	40	**cuarenta** (kwah-*ren*-tah)
8	**ocho** (*oh*-choh)	50	**cincuenta** (seen-*kwen*-tah)
9	**nueve** (*nweh*-beh)	60	**sesenta** (seh-*sehn*-tah)
10	**diez** (dyehs)	70	**setenta** (seh-*tehn*-tah)
11	**once** (*ohn*-seh)	80	**ochenta** (oh-*chen*-tah)
12	**doce** (*doh*-seh)	90	**noventa** (noh-*ben*-tah)
13	**trece** (*treh*-seh)	100	**cien** (syehn)
14	**catorce** (kah-*tohr*-seh)	200	**doscientos** (*do-syehn*-tohs)
15	**quince** (*keen*-seh)	500	**quinientos** (kee-*nyehn*-tohs)
		1,000	**mil** (meel)

2 Spanish Menu Glossary

GENERAL TERMS

Beef/steak **Lomo**

Bread **Pan**

Dessert **Postre**

Eggs **Huevos**

Fish **Pescado**

Fruit **Fruta**

Pork **Cerdo/puerco**

French fries **Papas fritas**

Rice **Arroz**

Salad **Ensalada**

Seafood **Mariscos**

Soup **Sopa (chupe)**

Vegetables **Verduras**

MEAT

Adobo Meat dish in a spicy chile sauce

Ají de gallina Spicy/creamy chicken

Alpaca Alpaca steak

Anticuchos Shish kebab

Cabrito Goat

Carne de res Beef

Chicharrones Fried pork skins

Conejo Rabbit

Cordero Lamb

Empanada Pastry turnover filled with meat, vegetables, fruit, manjar blanco, or sometimes nothing at all

Estofado Stew

Lomo asado Roast beef

Lomo saltado Strips of beef with fried potatoes, onions, and tomatoes over rice

Parrillada Grilled meats

Pato Duck

Pollo a la brasa Spit-roasted chicken

Venado Venison

SEAFOOD

Corvina Sea bass

Langosta Lobster

Langostinos Prawns

Lenguado Sole

Mero Mediterranean grouper

Paiche Large Amazon fish

Tollo Spotted dogfish

BEVERAGES

Beer **Cerveza**

Mixed fruit juice **Refresco**

Juice **Jugo**

Milk **Leche**

Soft drink **Gaseosa**

Water **Agua**
  carbonated **con gas**
  still **sin gas**

Wine **Vino**

Cocktail **Cóctel**

PREPARATION

Fixed-price menu **El menú**

Spicy **Picante**

Hot (temperature) **Caliente**

Cold (temperature) **Frío**

Raw **Crudo**

Cooked **Cocido**

Fried **Frito**

Vegetarian **Vegetariano**

PERUVIAN FAVORITES

Chaufa Chinese fried rice

Chicha Fermented maize beer

Chicha morada Blue-corn non-alcoholic refreshment

Chifa Peruvian-Chinese food

Choclo Maize (large-kernel corn)

Ceviche Marinated fish dish

Cuy Guinea pig

Flan crème Caramel custard

Manjar blanco Sweetened condensed milk

Pachamanca Roast meat and potatoes, prepared underground

Palta Avocado

Palta rellena (or palta a la Reina) Stuffed avocado (with chicken or tuna salad)

Panqueque Crepe

Papa a la huancaína Boiled potatoes in a creamy and spicy cheese sauce

Papa rellena Stuffed and fried potato

Quinua Andean grain (quinoa)

Rocoto relleno Stuffed hot pepper

Sopa a la criolla Creole soup (noodles or grain, often quinoa, vegetables, and meat)

Tamal Ground corn cooked and stuffed with chicken or pork, wrapped in banana leaves or corn husks, and then steamed

3 Quechua & Quechua-Derived Terms

Quechua ("*Ketch*-u-wa") was the language of the Incan Empire, and it remains widely spoken in Peru and throughout Andean nations 5 centuries after the Spaniards did so much to impose their own culture, language, and religion upon the region. It is the most widely spoken Amerindian language. Called *Runasimi* (literally, "language of the people") by Quechua speakers, the language is spoken by more than 10 million people in the highlands of South America. As much as one-third of Peru's 28 million people speak Quechua. Quechua speakers call themselves Runa—simply translated, "the people."

Quechua is an agglutinative language, meaning that words are constructed from a root word and combined with a large number of suffixes and infixes, which are added to words to change meaning and add subtlety. Linguists consider Quechua unusually poetic and expressive. Quechua is not a monolithic language, though. More than two dozen dialects are currently spoken in Peru. The one of greatest reach, not surprisingly, is the one still spoken in Cusco. Though continually threatened by Spanish, Quechua remains a vital language in the Andes.

In recent decades, however, many Andean migrants to urban areas have tried to distance themselves from their Amerindian roots, fearful that they would be marginalized by the Spanish-speaking majority in cities—many of whom regard Quechua and other native languages as the domain of the poor and uneducated. (Parents often refuse to speak Quechua with their children.) The 2001 presidential election of Alejandro Toledo, himself of Amerindian descent, might lead to a new valuation of Quechua (and Aymara). Toledo has said that he hopes to spur new interest and pride in native culture in schools and among all Peruvians; a telling demonstration of that desire is that the Quechua language was spoken at his inaugural ceremonies at Machu Picchu. (Even Toledo's Belgian-born wife addressed the crowd in Quechua.)

Quechua has made its influence felt on Spanish, of course. Peruvian Spanish has hundreds of Quechua words, ranging from names of plants and animals (*papa,* potato; *cuy,* guinea pig) to food (*choclo,* corn on the cob; *pachamanca,* a type of earth oven) and clothing (*chompa,* sweater; *chullu,* knitted cap). Quechua has also made its way into English. Words commonly used in English that are derived from Quechua include coca, condor, guano, gaucho, lima (as in the bean), llama, and puma.

COMMON TERMS

Altiplano   Plateau/high plains

Apu   Sacred summit/mountain spirit

Campesino   Rural worker/peasant

Chacra   Plot of land

Huayno   Andean musical style

Inca   Incan ruler/emperor

Inti   Sun

Intiwatana   "Hitching post of the sun" (stone pillar at Incan ceremonial sites)

Mestizo   Person of mixed European and Amerindian lineage

Pucara   Fortress

Runasimi   Quechua language

Soroche   Altitude sickness (hypoxia)

Tambo   In-transit checkpoint on Incan highway

Tawantinsuyu   Incan Empire

Tumi   Andean knife

Viracocha   Incan deity (creator god)

TRY A LITTLE QUECHUA

English	Quechua	Pronunciation
Yes	**Riki**	*Ree*-kee
No	**Mana**	*Mah*-nah
Madam	**Mama**	*Mah*-mah
Sir	**Tayta**	*Tahy*-tah
Thank you	**Añay**	Ah-*nyahy*

Index

THE NEW TRAVELOCITY GUARANTEE

EVERYTHING YOU BOOK WILL BE RIGHT, OR WE'LL WORK WITH OUR TRAVEL PARTNERS TO MAKE IT RIGHT, RIGHT AWAY.

*To drive home the point,
we're going to use the word "right" in every single sentence.*

Let's get right to it. Right to the meat! Only Travelocity guarantees everything about your booking will be right, or we'll work with our travel partners to make it right, right away. Right on!

Here's a picture taken smack dab right in the middle of Antigua, where the guarantee also covers you.

The guarantee covers all but one of the items pictured to the right.

Now, you may be thinking, "Yeah, right, I'm so sure." That's OK; you have the right to remain skeptical. That is until we mention help is always right around the corner. Call us right off the bat, knowing that our customer service reps are there for you 24/7. Righting wrongs. Left and right.

For example, what if the ocean view you booked actually looks out at a downright ugly parking lot? You'd be right to call – we're there for you. And no one in their right mind would be pleased to learn the rental car place has closed and left them stranded. Call Travelocity and we'll help get you back on the right track.

Now if you're guessing there are some things we can't control, like the weather, well you're right. But we can help you with most things – to get all the details in righting,* visit **travelocity.com/guarantee**.

*Sorry, spelling things right is one of the few things not covered under the guarantee.

I'd give my right arm for a guarantee like this, although I'm glad I don't have to.

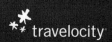

travelocity
You'll never roam alone.